CANADA

A Political & Social History

CANADA

A Political & Social History

FOURTH EDITION

EDGAR McINNIS

Formerly
Professor of History
York University

With a final chapter by
Michiel Horn

Professor of History
Glendon College
York University

HOLT, RINEHART AND WINSTON OF CANADA, LIMITED, TORONTO

Canadian Cataloguing in Publication Data

McInnis, Edgar, 1899–
    Canada: a political and social history

Bibliography: p. 727
Includes index.
ISBN 0-03-923177-1

1. Canada - History.   I. Horn, Michiel, 1939–
II. Title.

FC164.M34 1982   971   C82-094392-4
F1034.2.M34 1982

Printed in Canada

1 2 3 4 5 86 85 84 83 82

To Charles Herbert Best

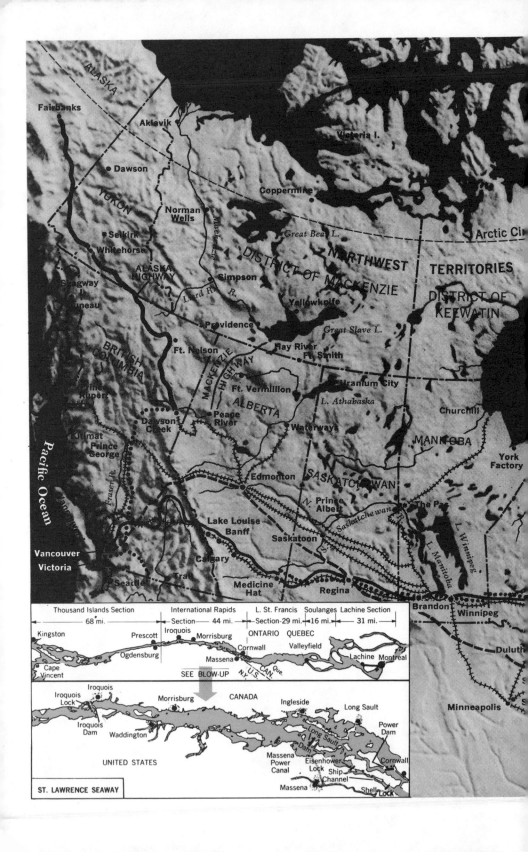

Fairbanks

ALASKA

Aklavik

YUKON

Dawson

Coppermine

Victoria I.

Norman Wells

Mackenzie

Great Bear L.

Arctic Ci

DISTRICT OF MACKENZIE

NORTHWEST

TERRITORIES

DISTRICT OF KEEWATIN

Selkirk

Whitehorse

ALASKA HIGHWAY

Simpson

Liard R.

R.

Yellowknife

Skagway

Juneau

Providence

Great Slave L.

BRITISH COLUMBIA

Ft. Nelson

Hay River

Ft. Smith

Prince Rupert

MACKENZIE HIGHWAY

Ft. Vermillion

Uranium City

ALBERTA

L. Athabaska

Churchill

Kitimat

Prince George

Dawson Creek

Peace River

Waterways

Fraser Rk.

MANITOBA

York Factory

Thompson Rk.

Edmonton

SASKATCHEWAN

N. Prince Albert

The Pas

L. Winnipeg

Vancouver

Victoria

Lake Louise Banff

Saskatoon

Saskatchewan R.

S.

L. Manitoba

Pacific Ocean

Calgary

Seattle

Trail

Medicine Hat

Regina

Brandon

Winnipeg

Duluth

SEE BLOW-UP

Thousand Islands Section
68 mi.

International Rapids
Section — 44 mi. —

L. St. Francis
Section-29 mi.

Soulanges
16 mi.

Lachine Section
31 mi.

Kingston

Prescott

Iroquois

Morrisburg

ONTARIO QUEBEC

Ogdensburg

Cornwall

Valleyfield

Lachine Montreal

Cape Vincent

Massena

CAN.
U.S.
N.Y.
Que.

Iroquois

Iroquois Lock

Morrisburg

CANADA

Ingleside

Long Sault

Iroquois Dam

Waddington

Long Sault Dam

Power Dam

UNITED STATES

Massena Power Canal

Eisenhower Lock

Cornwall

Massena

Ship Channel

Shell Lock

Minneapolis

ST. LAWRENCE SEAWAY

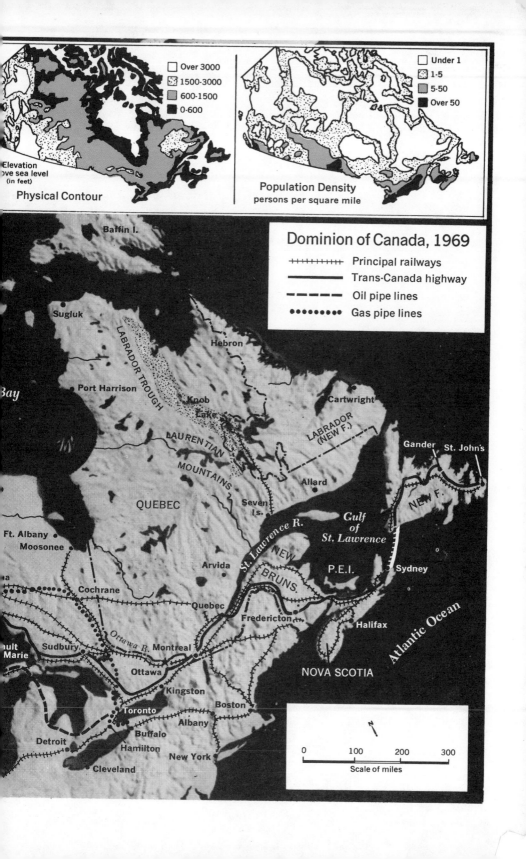

Physical Contour

Elevation
above sea level
(in feet)

- Over 3000
- 1500-3000
- 600-1500
- 0-600

Population Density
persons per square mile

- Under 1
- 1-5
- 5-50
- Over 50

Dominion of Canada, 1969

- ┼┼┼┼┼┼┼ Principal railways
- ───── Trans-Canada highway
- ── ── ── Oil pipe lines
- ●●●●●●● Gas pipe lines

Baffin I.

Sugluk

Hebron

LABRADOR TROUGH

Port Harrison

Bay

Knob Lake

Cartwright

LAURENTIAN

LABRADOR (NEW F.)

Gander

St. John's

MOUNTAINS

Allard

NEW F.

QUEBEC

Seven
Is.

Ft. Albany

Moosonee

St. Lawrence R.

Gulf
of
St. Lawrence

Arvida

NEW

P.E.I.

Sydney

Cochrane

BRUNS.

Quebec

Fredericton

Halifax

Atlantic Ocean

Sudbury

Ottawa R. Montreal

ault
Marie

Ottawa

NOVA SCOTIA

Kingston

Boston

Toronto

Albany

Detroit

Buffalo

N

Hamilton

New York

0   100   200   300

Cleveland

Scale of miles

PREFACE

The history of Canada is a study in political survival. The task of creating a distinctive society has been achieved in the face of numerous and conflicting stresses, both internal and external. Interacting factors of economics and politics and geography, of traditions and aspirations, of national unity and sectional diversity, form the complex pattern that has shaped the present Dominion. Throughout the whole story runs the constant effort to reconcile the divergent strains inherent in Canada's position and structure and to harmonize the varied and often clashing forces within a united and independent community.

This process has given a unique character to the Canadian achievement. Its essential drama does not lie in armed struggles in which the nation's destiny is at stake, or in political conflicts in which irreconcilable and contending forces press their quarrel to a decisive issue. It lies rather in the slow and tenacious advance from one step to another along the road to nationhood, the patient evolution of successive compromises in politics and government, the determined conquest of the physical obstacles to national economic development. In their very nature, few of Canada's crucial problems could be solved by violent methods or intransigent decisions. Patience and compromise were virtues born of necessity, for the alternative would not be the triumph of one or other contending group but disruption or extinction or both.

The recurrent nature of Canada's basic problems emphasizes both the urgent need for moderation and the striking degree to which this quality has been applied in Canadian affairs. Time and again, Canada has faced the gravest kind of dilemma in her relations with the two great English-speaking nations with whom her destiny is so inextricably bound up. Time and again, economic difficulties or racial antagonisms have threatened her internal structure with deadlock or collapse. Yet on each occasion Canadians have turned from extreme courses to seek a middle ground on which cooperation was possible, and outside of which lay disaster. If the difficulties have never been completely removed, they have never become completely irreconcilable. It is this sound sense of the possible that has enabled Canada hitherto to surmount each successive crisis; and each one has uniformly been followed by a new period of progress in Canadian independence and Canadian unity, and by a fresh growth in economic strength and political stature.

This book seeks to present the narrative of Canada's rise to nationhood and its evolution in the century following Confederation in terms of the basic determinants. I have taken advantage of the preparation of a new edition to amplify or modify a substantial number of passages in the earlier text in the light of recent research, and to emphasize or clarify a number of points that may help to sharpen the perspective. This applies particularly to certain aspects of the structure and development of French Canada and their bearing on French-English relations—a theme whose understanding is so essential as a background to current issues. The more significant among such issues are surveyed in a final chapter which carries the story to the federal election of June 1968.

Among those whose contributions have been especially helpful in the preparation of this edition, I would particularly thank Peter B. Waite for his suggestions based on his research for the forthcoming volume in the Centennial series covering the period 1874-1896. I extend my appreciation to the numerous individuals in public bodies and government departments who were so helpful in providing the illustrations. The staff of the Public Archives has, as always, been prompt and cooperative in responding to requests. My very special gratitude is due to Nick Balla and Ron Dick of the National Film Board, who made available a generous selection of prints from the Board's extensive archives, thus providing resources which under present circumstances I could hardly have hoped to duplicate by my own efforts.

Toronto   July, 1968   Edgar McInnis

Preface to the Fourth Edition

Edgar McInnis was a marvelous man. His gruff voice and reserved manner did not bother those who had learned to appreciate his intelligence and wit. His speech was slow-paced and deliberate, punctuated with puffs on his pipe, but it was always to the point and touched with a wry sense of humor. He had few close friends but many admirers.

His death in 1973 was a shock, particularly to those of us in the History Department of Glendon College, York University, with whom he spent time after his retirement in 1968. For several years he kept an office in the college and spoke willingly with any student or member of faculty who knocked on his door. He was the model of an academic elder statesman. In his retirement he had the title of University Orator. I can think of no person better qualified to act in such a capacity.

One clause in his will directed that the remaining royalties from his books be paid into the Principal's Trust Account for Glendon College. When the third edition of *Canada: A Political and Social History* went out of print, therefore, the matter was of concern both to the publishers and to the college. McInnis's work had held up well and the publishers were convinced that there would be a continuing demand for the book if it could be revised or updated. They approached me, among others, with a proposal to write a chapter on the years since 1968 that could be added to the existing text, and David McQueen, principal of Glendon College from 1975 to 1980, urged me to consider it seriously. As associate principal from 1978 to 1981, I shared his concern for the financial health of the trust account, but I think I would nevertheless have refused had I not known Edgar McInnis. I had done some research for him in 1966; he was chairman of the department that offered me a full-time appointment from 1968; and my research on the League for Social Reconstruction had given me the opportunity for some enjoyable conversations with him about his associates in the League and the group's early years. That I was in the mid-1970s chairman of what was once his department served as another sentimental link. I accepted the assignment.

In carrying it out I have tried to observe McInnis's own approach to the history of Canada. There is more economic and political history here, and less social history as currently practised, than might have been the case had I not been adding a chapter to a book that is still very much McInnis's. The format I have used is also very similar to his.

Anyone who writes about the very recent Canadian past is bound to owe a great deal to Jack Saywell and his associates on the *Canadian Annual Review*. I gladly acknowledge my debt to them. I want to thank David Wolfe, who gave me a copy of the paper he read to the Canadian Political Science Association in May 1981, "The demise of the Keynesian era in Canada: dilemmas of federal economic policy, 1975–1980." I found it very useful, not least for its many tables of data. Gail Brandt and David McQueen undertook to read and criticize what I wrote, the former for its historical and the latter for its economic accuracy. I am grateful to them both.

Ian Radforth revised the original bibliography, though the responsibility for the final selection—as for chapter 23—rests on my shoulders. Lack of space prevented the inclusion of many valuable works. The same reason, and the awareness that this book will be used primarily in English Canada, led me to exclude books by French Canadian scholars unless they had been translated into English.

In his preface to the third edition, McInnis wrote of the "sound sense of the possible" that had enabled Canada "to surmount each successive crisis" in domestic as well as external affairs. At the time of writing, Canada is in crisis once more. The patriation of the British North America Act without the consent of Quebec has lent new strength to the separatist movement in that province. Some western Canadians warn that "if Quebec goes, the West will go"; a few threaten that the West may secede first. The Canadian economy, with regional exceptions, is more troubled than at any time since the Depression of the 1930s. Our relations with the United States seem to be approaching an equivalently low point.

In 1968 Edgar McInnis was optimistic about the future of Canada. I hope that in the long run his optimism was justified, but I know the immediate future will be filled with domestic and international uncertainty. At such times a work of history serves, if not as a guide to the future, then at least as a way of making the past lucid. I believe that Edgar McInnis's *Canada* will continue to serve that very important purpose.

Toronto, January 1982   Michiel Horn

CONTENTS

Chapter 1

The Setting

The Face of the Land

Among the determining factors that have shaped the Canadian nation of today, the most basic is the location of Canada's southern border. The dividing line that splits the American continent into two halves is the product of a complex variety of developments, geographical and historical and political. So strong are the forces involved that it is hard to imagine any major change in the frontier that would have left Canada in existence as an independent entity. Yet the fact remains that such a change, if it had been possible, would have had the most profound effect on Canadian development. A shifting of the boundary a hundred miles to either north or south would have altered the whole racial composition and economic structure of the Dominion, with political consequences both internal and external whose extent can hardly be estimated.

The initial importance of the existing boundary is that it has determined the quantity of arable land available for settlement. It has left within the borders of the Dominion large amounts of cultivable soil, which made possible the expansion of population from coast to coast. Yet the resulting extent and distribution of such land have imposed important limitations on the progress of agrarian development, with significant effects on the other activities affecting the growth and prosperity of the nation. The present geographical structure has both curtailed and retarded agricultural settlement. It has made more burdensome the exploitation of other natural resources. And it has created serious sectional problems, both economic and political, which the persistent efforts of a full century have only partially overcome.

The habitable area of Canada is divided from east to west into four main sections. These are separated from each other by formidable geographic barriers. They are further confined by a vast northern region whose climate and geology are largely unfavorable to agricultural expansion. Thus even the available area of settlement is not continuous but is divided into a number of separate pockets by the structure of the land itself.

The eastern section of the Dominion consists of the four Atlantic Provinces, comprising Newfoundland and the three Maritime Provinces of Nova Scotia, New Brunswick and Prince Edward Island. In the physical structure of the continent that area is an extension of New England, but, whereas the provinces cover about the same area as the New England states, they contain only one-eighth as many people and an even lower proportion of wealth. There have been disgruntled natives of the Maritimes who attributed the contrast to political causes and believed that it could be overcome by a union with their southern neighbors. While changes in trade routes and tariff systems might make some difference, it is doubtful whether they could wholly offset certain geographical disadvantages, which the Maritime Provinces share with the northern portion of New England itself.

For this Acadian region, though generally low in altitude, is nonetheless mountainous in much of its basic structure. It was the result of a subsidence in which the coastal plain that exists farther south disappeared beneath the ocean to form the continental shelf, leaving only the higher land above the surface. The result was a deeply indented coast with numerous excellent harbors, which have one of the world's greatest fishing grounds almost at their gates. There is fertile land in many of the river valleys and along the Gulf of St. Lawrence, where the red soil of Prince Edward Island and the New Brunswick coast provides excellent farming country. But much of the peninsula of Nova Scotia and the interior of New Brunswick is rocky and unsuitable for cultivation, as is the greater part of the island of Newfoundland; and while forest wealth has provided some compensation, and minerals have recently assumed new and heightened importance in New Brunswick as well as in Newfoundland-Labrador, the fact remains that large areas of these provinces are still untouched by settlement.

The forests of New Brunswick are themselves a wilderness barrier between the eastern coast and the valley of the St. Lawrence. Added to them is the further obstacle of the Appalachian highlands. The mountains which enclose the coastal plain of the eastern United States extend across the border into Quebec and continue to the Gaspé Peninsula, where the Shickshock ridges rise to 4000 feet. The Appalachian barrier is no more insuperable here than it is farther south, but it does contribute to the regional division that separates the Maritime Provinces so definitely from central Canada.

It was in the St. Lawrence Valley that the foundations of Canada were laid, and this region remains the core around which the Canadian nation has been built. The lower St. Lawrence is rugged and relatively inhospitable, but beginning at Quebec the valley gradually broadens into a fertile plain

Physiographic Regions

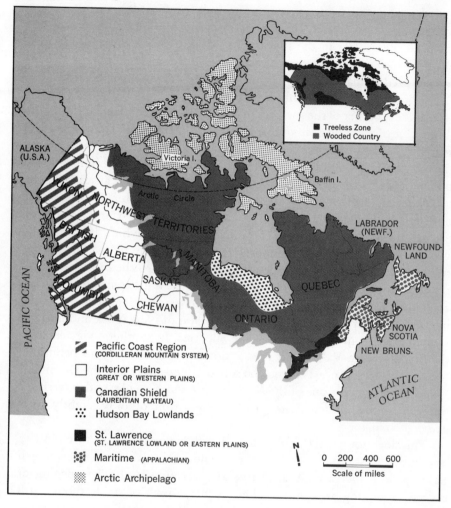

on both sides of the river, and beyond Montreal it embraces the valley of the lower Ottawa as well. Between Brockville and Kingston it is interrupted by a rocky projection known to geologists as the "Frontenac axis." Southwest of a line drawn from about Kingston to the lower end of Georgian Bay lies the Ontario peninsula, with its fertile soil left by the recession of the prehistoric lakes, Algonquin and Iroquois, whose remnants are the Great Lakes of today. The whole area has an extent of some 35,000 square miles and is the most thickly populated portion of the Dominion.

3

It is a region of widely varied activities. The land supports mixed farming and dairying and fruit growing. The bulk of Canada's manufacturing industry is concentrated in this section. Much of its commercial and financial life centers in the two leading cities of Montreal and Toronto. With its background of three centuries of development, central Canada holds a predominance in the national life that is as yet unchallenged.

Yet this region, which holds 60 percent of the population of Canada, is only a tiny corner of the vast area of the Dominion. This fact is profoundly illustrative of the rigid bounds that geography has imposed on the Canadian structure. The confines of central Canada are determined on the south by the international boundary, on the east by the Appalachian highlands, and on the north by the immense and forbidding mass of the Canadian Shield.

The Canadian Shield is the dominant physiographic feature of the northern half of the continent. A vast region of pre-Cambrian rocks, eroded by the glacial action of millions of years, which has left only vestiges of its once mountainous terrain, it extends in the shape of a tremendous U around both sides of Hudson Bay. On the east it embraces the regions of Ungava and Labrador. On the west it extends from 500 to 2000 miles to the edge of the Great Plains. Its extremities thrust across the international border to the Adirondack region of New York and into the United States south and west of Lake Superior. Its southern edge encloses the St. Lawrence Valley and presses down upon the Ontario peninsula. It covers an area of nearly 2,000,000 square miles—over half the Dominion —and its existence is one of the chief reasons why Canada, with a territory the size of the United States, had a population of only slightly over 20,000,000 in 1967.

This does not mean that the Shield is uninhabitable. In the forested area that covers its southern portion there are numerous lakes and rivers which have made it increasingly attractive as a vacation land. The opening of successive mining areas has resulted in the growth of stable though still relatively small communities around the chief centers of activity. But the nature of the Shield has made it an uncompromising barrier to the spread of agrarian settlement. At best the forest belt holds only small and isolated pockets of arable soil. Farther north the timber dwindles to scrub, which yields to muskeg underlaid by perpetual frost. Whatever its other advantages—and it contains riches that have still hardly been touched—the Shield offers little or no attraction to the farming pioneer.

Thus it has presented a colossal barrier to the spread of settlement westward from Ontario and Quebec to the prairies of western Canada. Between these two regions lies a wilderness that stretches for nearly 1000 miles along the northern shores of Lake Huron and Lake Superior and beyond the Lake of the Woods. It offered neither land that was attractive for settlement nor routes that gave easy access to the fertile plains beyond. The Canadian Pacific Railway was pushed through during the 1880s to provide communications across this barrier. But it was only in 1943, after a decade of effort, that a barely passable highway was completed north of Lake Superior, and not until 1949 that the program for a Trans-Canada Highway based on federal-provincial cooperation actually got under way.

Between the western rim of the Shield and the Cordillera region that fringes the Pacific coast lies the northern portion of the great continental plain, stretching from the international boundary clear to the Arctic Ocean. At its southern base is the largest area of cultivable land in Canada—a prairie triangle extending from eastern Manitoba to the foothills of the Rockies and projecting northward in Alberta for nearly 400 miles. Not all this region is arable, nor does it contain all the arable land of the interior plain. There is a dry belt in southwestern Saskatchewan and southeastern Alberta where the American desert reaches across the boundary. Beyond the wooded section that marks the northern limit of the main prairie region there is the fertile valley of the Peace River, and beyond that the Mackenzie Valley sweeps northward to the Arctic. But difficulty of access and the climatic conditions of the higher latitudes have retarded the development of these regions and even a full knowledge of their potentialities. It is the prairie region that has given to Canada an agricultural west into which settlement could flow once the barrier of the Shield had been overcome.

West of the prairies lies a mountainous region some 400 miles broad, which extends to the Pacific Ocean. At the eastern edge of this Cordillera system stands the rampart of the Rockies, raising a barrier between the interior plains and the coastal region of British Columbia. Beyond lies a series of ranges—Selkirk, Coast, Cascade—extending to the sea itself, and even beyond this are mountainous islands fringing the coastline. In this region there is no coastal plain, but settlement flowed into the broad southern valleys with their fertile soil and temperate climate to create the fourth distinct populated section of the Dominion—a section whose natural outlook is not eastward toward the rest of Canada, but westward toward the Pacific and southward toward the Pacific coast of the United States.

This southward attraction is felt in varying degrees by all four sections of the Dominion. Broadly speaking—and like all generalizations this must be qualified in detail—the folds of the continent run north and south. That does not mean the absence of sectional divisions along other lines. The divergence between south and north in the United States is witness to the contrary. Historically there has been a feeling of distinctness between the communities occupying the present area of Canada and those of the United States. But it is a fact that the Appalachian highlands, the Laurentian Shield, and the Rocky Mountains present barriers far more definite than any that exist along the international border. The people of the Maritime Provinces have long had intimate ties with New England. The St. Lawrence Valley leads much less easily to the Canadian prairies than southward beyond the Great Lakes to the Mississippi. The prairies themselves are part of a great continental formation, and the watershed between the Missouri and the Saskatchewan—which roughly coincides with the present boundary—is a very modest type of sectional demarcation. The 49th parallel means little or nothing physically between the Rockies and the Pacific coast. The difficulties of communications that have had to be overcome were connected with movement from east to west, and those difficulties have been a major element in Canada's geographical heritage.

Two other areas may be mentioned to complete the geographic picture. North of the Arctic regions of the continental mainland lies the Arctic Archipelago, which includes the islands at the mouth of Hudson Bay. At the southern end of the bay there is an extensive area of lowland between the coast and the edge of the Canadian Shield. It is possible that both these regions may grow in importance during the next few decades. Quite apart from the resources of the Arctic area, its location gives it a potentially strategic position in the prospective development of air traffic between the continents. The greater part of the Hudson Bay lowland is covered with muskeg and has little subsoil wealth. But within what is properly the area of the Canadian Shield it has deposited a clay belt, which offers some agricultural possibilities and into which settlement has been gradually penetrating during the past generation. Neither of these regions, however, has hitherto exercised any important influence on Canadian development or played any serious part in the history of the Dominion.

The Natural Resources

These physiographic conditions explain why Canada is a land of vast unpeopled spaces, with three-quarters of its population living within 200 miles of its southern border in irregularly spaced areas separated by long distances from each other. The great central plain of the continent lies mostly south of the boundary, projecting northward only the two arable pockets of the Ontario peninsula and the prairie triangle in the west. Neither the Appalachian nor the Cordillera region offers extensive possibilities of agriculture. Opposite the Middle Western states that spread from Indiana to Minnesota there is in Canada the wilderness of the Shield. The line that divides the continent politically has left to the northern half rich but limited fringes of the agrarian resources of North America.

Until recently it seemed that Canada was also gravely lacking in certain key industrial resources. Coal was to be found at the coastal extremities in Nova Scotia and British Columbia and the Arctic Archipelago and in the interior in the province of Alberta, but the industrial region of central Canada remained largely dependent on coal from the Pennsylvania field south of the border. Oil seemed to be confined to restricted deposits in Alberta and the Mackenzie Valley and to a few shallow pockets in southern Ontario. Since World War II this picture has been transformed by the discovery of vast oil fields underlying the prairies and the opening up of iron deposits on a major scale north of Lake Superior and in the Ungava peninsula. The foundations for industrial development, so long restricted by the lack of such primary resources, have received new accessions of strength as a result.

In other mineral resources the richness of the Dominion has been clearly though very partially revealed. The Cordilleras and the Canadian Shield are known to contain large quantities of both precious and base metals. Canada stands first among the nations in nickel production, zinc, and asbestos, and second as a producer of gold. Yet only a beginning has been made in uncovering the full extent of her mineral wealth or in prospecting the vast areas in which it still lies concealed.

The Canadian Shield is the greatest of these areas. Development so far has done little more than touch its fringes on the south and southwest, yet this has been enough to show that the Shield, so formidable in one aspect as a barrier, is at the same time a treasure house. From the Sudbury area north of Georgian Bay comes the bulk of the world's supply of nickel. Along the whole stretch of the Shield south of Hudson Bay gold has been found in large quantities. The Cobalt field is the centre of extensive deposits of silver. Radium-yielding pitchblende and vital sources of uranium have been discovered in such areas as Blind River and Great Bear Lake. Copper has been found all the way from Lake Huron to the Arctic coast, and the extent of such distribution suggests that other minerals discovered in the Shield— and they include other base metals such as lead and zinc and molybdenite— may also be scattered widely throughout the area.

The Cordillera area is less extensive than the Shield but fully as richly endowed. Nearly all the principal minerals of the Shield—nickel is the chief exception—have also been discovered between the Rockies and the Pacific coast. Gold brought the first fame to British Columbia and the Yukon, but silver and copper, lead and zinc and iron have been found in one or both of these districts. Like the Shield, the Cordillera region has extensive forests and abundant sources of water power for industrial purposes; unlike the Shield, it has coal deposits near at hand and fertile areas where agriculture flourishes. There are serious limitations of climate and topography in much of this section, but there are also evident possibilities of future development.

It is obvious, however, that resources of this type do not lend themselves to exploitation by individual pioneers. The Shield and the Cordilleras yield their wealth stubbornly and reluctantly. It takes organized efforts backed by substantial funds to get a mine into profitable operation. In many cases the full task of opening a new region is beyond the resources of private capital. Government help in various forms, from prospecting to railway building, has played a significant part in developing the mining areas of Canada. Government policies in such matters as taxation and subsidies and the national currency have been of the utmost importance. A working harmony between large-scale enterprise and the federal and provincial governments has been almost a historical necessity in the development of the Canadian economy.

This has applied to some extent even in the case of more accessible natural resources. The settlement and early development of the various sections of Canada were naturally characterized by the exploitation of those sources of wealth which lay nearest to hand, and more particularly by the development of successive staples based on such resources. Fishing became a mainstay of the economy of the Maritime Provinces and later developed into a major activity along the Pacific coast. The immense forest belt that stretched across the whole of Canada yielded its first wealth in the form of furs, and later timber and pulpwood. The clearing of the St. Lawrence Valley and the Ontario peninsula led to the rise of a wheat staple, and with the settlement of the prairies this was expanded on a scale that made Canada one of the great wheat-producing nations of the world. It was only after these successive foundations had been laid that Canada turned in earnest to the development of her mineral wealth.

Through all these stages government policy was of the most vital importance. In the earliest days of New France the fur trade was drastically affected by arbitrary alternations between monopoly and freedom of trade.

In the past generation the wheat situation has become a matter of public policy and has forced the government into measures of regulation and assistance. On more than one occasion the fortunes of Canada have been profoundly influenced by decisions over which the Canadian government itself had little or no control. It could take steps to encourage production but could not always assure for Canadian staples the external markets that were essential to them. The decisions of the British government with respect to the timber preference or the corn laws, and the American tariff policy as it affected fish or lumber have at times been factors of major importance to the Canadian economy.

Of all the aspects of government economic policy, none—not even the tariff—has been of greater importance than transportation. The development of transport and communications has profoundly affected the growth of all modern nations, but to none has it been more basic and essential than to Canada. Preoccupation with this topic is a persistent theme throughout the whole of her history. In the absence of railways, indeed, the present Dominion might never have come into existence. They have been necessary to bind the widely separated sections together both politically and economically. They have made possible the development of otherwise inaccessible mineral wealth, aided in recent years by the still wider scope offered by air transport. They have had to traverse long stretches of territory, which were unproductive of revenue or which only slowly provided a limited amount of traffic as their resources were opened up. Physiographic conditions have imposed on the Canadian economy an overhead in the shape of a transportation system that is out of all proportion to the existing population and the present national wealth.

The creation of this system was largely the result of government policy and public financial support. In the great days of the fur trade the North West Company built up an organization that spanned the continent from Montreal to the Pacific; but the company collapsed under the burden, and no successor ever emulated its achievement unaided. Even when the actual work was entrusted to private enterprise, as in the case of the Canadian Pacific Railway, it was government generosity with public land and public funds that made it possible. In most other cases the work was undertaken either by the government directly or by government-supported companies, which were a continual drain upon the treasury until their chronic financial agonies were mercifully ended by bankruptcy. Canada's canal and railway structure is the joint product of government policy and business enterprise, just as the accumulated debt that it has bequeathed to the Canadian public is a monument to the joint mismanagement of business and government in the past.

The vital importance of transportation has been further accentuated by its bearing not only on internal development but on external trade. While one road to prosperity lay in the opening of new territories, another —and at certain periods a far more promising one—lay in the commercial possibilities that appeared inherent in Canadian geography. With the St. Lawrence and the Great Lakes offering a water route connecting Europe and the North Atlantic with the great region of the American Middle West, there have been times when Canada's position seemed more important than her products. The beginnings of both the canal and the railway eras were stimulated, not by a desire to develop Canada's own resources, but by the hope of transforming her into the dominant middleman between Europe and the North American continent. Modern development of air transport for a time roused hopes that Canada's strategic position on the Great Circle routes might prove to be one of her great natural assets. With no prospect of economic self-sufficiency in spite of her vast and still unascertained resources, Canada has always looked beyond her own borders for the commercial possibilities that would round out her economic life.

That economy from the very beginning has been presented with the need for a progressive adaptation of both internal and external changes, and the process is by no means complete. Neither the ultimate bounds nor the essential balance of Canada's final economic structure can yet be laid down with certainty. The picture has undergone a very considerable change since the nineteenth century. Certain major limitations have been revealed; other avenues of expansion have opened up. At one time it was believed that the development of Canada was destined to follow much the same lines as that of the United States. Such a prospect has now been considerably modified. The nature and the balance of Canada's principal resources call for an evolution along more individual lines; and it is in a successful adaptation to the special advantages which are emerging with increasing knowledge, rather than in an emulation for which her assets are imperfectly suited, that the most promising future for the Dominion now appears to lie.

The Aborigines

The Europeans who came to the shores of North America regarded it as a vacant continent, which lay completely open to settlement from the Old World. In the final analysis this assumption was justified. It is true that the continent was already inhabited by tribes who claimed the land as their own. But in the whole of Canada there were probably no more than 220,000 Indians, and in neither numbers nor culture nor political organization were they strong enough to hold their vast hunting grounds against the pressure of land-hungry Europeans.

The aborigines made no major contribution to the culture that developed in the settled communities of Canada. They did contribute certain conveniences, such as the canoe and the snowshoe, and certain products, such as maize, which were useful to the early settlers. But in all essentials the new communities remained European in their outlook and habits and general standards of life. On the other hand, while contact with the Europeans had revolutionary effects on the Indian economy, it did little to influence them culturally or to alter their basic way of living. Even when the advance of settlement pushed them out of their accustomed hunting grounds, the Indians failed to adapt themselves to the new situation and resisted absorption into the new society. They remained a primitive remnant clinging to their tribal organization long after it had become obsolete.

Nonetheless, the Indian was of salient importance in the early development of Canada. While he was culturally alien to the newcomers, he was economically important to them and soon economically dependent upon them. In the United States, where agricultural settlement was the primary aim, the Indian was not only useless but an active menace whose speedy extermination would be an unqualified boon. The menace arose in New France as well and nearly resulted in the destruction of the colony. But while some Indians were the implacable enemies of the French, there were others whose friendship and cooperation were absolutely essential so long as the fur trade remained the mainstay of New France. The destruction of the Algonkin and other friendly tribes, or even the extinction of the Iroquois menace, which prevented the friendly tribes from transferring their allegiance to Albany as a trading center, would have been almost fatal to the colony's existence.

There were three features of Indian society that contributed to this community of interest based on mutual economic needs. In the first place, the Indians of Canada were almost totally ignorant of the art of agriculture. The Iroquois to the south had made some progress, which was shared by their kinsmen and enemies the Hurons. But Iroquois agriculture was limited by a number of factors, including the primitive nature of the available implements. At the beginning of the seventeenth century the Indians of North America had not advanced beyond the stone age. The inefficiency of stone axes meant that the clearing of land for cultivation was a laborious process, accomplished largely by charring the trees by fire. Pointed sticks or hoes with blades of shell were the only implements of cultivation. Crops were limited to maize and beans, squashes and pumpkins and sunflowers. They provided a partial food supply, but in the absence of any domesticated animal except the dog it was necessary to find other sources of both food and clothing. Outside the Ontario peninsula and the St. Lawrence Valley there was practically no Indian agriculture in Canada, and the tribes lived a nomadic life, dependent on the products of forest and stream and sea for their whole livelihood.

Partly as a result of those conditions the Indians of Canada were almost totally devoid of effective political organization. Their nomadic nature and the extent of the territory over which they roamed prevented any real coherence even among groups that shared the same language and customs. There were recognized tribal divisions based on these characteristics, but the tribe as such was rarely a political unit. The nearest approach to this was the band—a group of kindred families that claimed a definite hunting ground and acted together in the chase or in war. Usually there was at least a nominal chief, but the extent of his authority depended almost entirely on his personality. He might gain a real ascendancy by oratorical talents or by his skill as a hunter or warrior, but he had no effective way of controlling his followers if they chose to reject his guidance and follow their own course of action. Various bands might join together in some enterprise, deciding on their course in a general council or through a conference of their leaders and perhaps even selecting one of these leaders as chief. But that was a still more tenuous arrangement, and there was rarely any supreme authority for the whole tribe as such. The Indian was a rampant individualist, and that quality was one of his weaknesses in the face of European encroachments.

The Iroquois, however, had evolved a more advanced organization, which had some faint parallels among other northern tribes. In the latter part of the sixteenth century five Iroquois tribes—the Mohawk, Oneida, Onondaga, Cayuga, and Seneca—formed a league for common action in external affairs. A sixth nation, the Tuscarora, joined about 1722. The affairs of the league were directed by a council of about fifty chiefs, or sachems, who dealt with disputes between the tribes, conducted negotiations, and decided on peace or war. A similar type of confederacy was adopted by such Iroquoian tribes of Ontario as the Huron, and a faint approach toward it might be discerned among the Blackfeet of the plains. But while such organization gave to the Iroquois a degree of coherence that few of their neighbors could match, it was more impressive in theory than in practice. The actual authority of the sachems was highly questionable. Their appointment, limited by certain hereditary qualifications, rested with the matriarchs of the various tribes, and it was only by accident that they possessed qualities of leadership that would give their decisions real weight. Warlike and ambitious leaders often ignored their decisions, and the individual tribes, which claimed autonomy in domestic affairs, often exercised it also in matters of peace or war. It was difficult to unite the Five Nations in a concerted military effort, and almost impossible to arrange a peace that all of them would recognize as binding. When a band or a tribe was determined to go on the warpath, it paid little attention to the decisions of the official council.

Above all the Indian was a hunter. Even the agricultural tribes were largely dependent on hunting for food and clothing, although their crops represented a partial guaranty against starvation when game was scarce. The majority of the Canadian tribes were entirely dependent on hunting and fishing for their very livelihood. Except for this fact the story of the fur trade could never have been written. The European traders, whether in New France or on Hudson Bay, depended almost entirely on the Indian as a primary producer, and the Indian eagerly lent himself to an activity which demanded no fundamental change in his traditional way of life and which promised richer returns than he had ever before enjoyed.

The coming of the Europeans revolutionized Indian standards of living. It transported the aborigines suddenly from the stone age to the iron age. Steel hatchets and knives and needles replaced tools of shell or bone or stone. Unbreakable copper and iron pots took the place of fragile utensils of pottery or birchbark. Woolen clothes and blankets offered greater comfort than the skins in which the savages had hitherto clad themselves. The musket was an incomparable advance over the bow and arrow as a weapon in the chase and in war. The white man brought other gifts which were not so welcome. Brandy and rum were by no means blessings to the Indians. New diseases such as smallpox and typhus spread epidemics that decimated whole tribes. The Indian was exposed to new and deadly hazards; but, if he managed to survive them, his standard of life was generally—though by no means universally—higher than it had been in his primitive state.

On the other hand, his self-sufficiency was utterly destroyed. The new articles became necessities, which the Indian could not manufacture and which he could secure only by trade. But the furs that the traders sought were the products of the hunt in which the Indian was an expert and on which his whole way of life was based, and firearms and steel traps increased the efficiency with which he could pursue it. What the new situation meant was that instead of hunting wholly for subsistence the Indian now hunted partly for barter. The small fur-bearing animals, particularly the beaver, suddenly assumed a new importance, and trapping became a far more intensive activity than it had been when animals were sought primarily for food.

Thus the Indian became imbued with the profit motive and was free to pursue it with almost untrammeled individual initiative. The results from any long-range point of view were often deplorable. The reckless depletion of natural resources that has marked the development of North America was first exhibited by the fur trade. The desire for quick returns led to intensive trapping, which rapidly exhausted whole areas. In their search for new fur regions the eastern tribes pushed into the less ravaged hunting grounds of their neighbors, and the competition for sources of supply was accentuated by the struggle for control of trade routes. The accompanying depletion of food-producing areas increased the intensity of the conflicts. Indian wars for economic causes became fiercer and more widespread, and the French whose coming had contributed to this development were nearly destroyed by the outcome.

The distribution of the tribes at the beginning of the seventeenth century had much to do with the lines along which the early conflict developed. The French soon came into contact with a number of different tribes, but it so happened that at this time one dominant linguistic group stretched across Canada from the Atlantic almost to the Rockies. This was the Algonquian family, whose racial affinities and linguistic similarities tremendously facilitated both trade and exploration. The Micmacs and Malecites of this group occupied the region of Acadia. The Montagnais dwelt along the lower St. Lawrence. Westward along the Ottawa were various tribes to which the name Algonkin was specifically applied by the French. The Chippewa, or Ojibwa, the strongest of all these groups, stretched along the northern shores of Lake Huron and Lake Superior. Farther west were the Cree, and on the western prairies the Blackfoot tribes also spoke a dialect of the Algonquian tongue.

North of the prairies and west of Hudson Bay was another great linguistic group, the Athabaskan. On the Pacific coast were a number of other tribes, including the Salish of the mainland and the Haida of the Queen Charlotte Islands, which were quite distinct from the Indians of the interior. In certain respects they were also culturally superior, and their plank houses were the most permanent type of dwelling to be found among the Indians of Canada. But their social structure, which was based on three classes—nobles, commoners, and slaves—already showed signs of decadence, and their talent for political organization was fully as limited as that of the eastern tribes.

The west coast groups, although they were of real importance in the later days of the fur trade, played no major part in the early history of Canada. Much more significant were the tribes of Iroquoian stock, which occupied the Ontario peninsula. Of these the most important were the Huron, who inhabited the region between Lake Simcoe and Georgian Bay. Like the other Iroquois they had developed a basis of agriculture, and this together with their trading activities enabled them to maintain a relatively settled existence. Their traditional and ultimately fatal feud with their kindred of the Five Nations made them allies of the Algonkin and brought them into friendly relations with the French. To the southwest lay the Tobacco nation, a tribe that seems to have found in tobacco a staple that was in universal demand among the more migratory tribes; and because of their usefulness as providers of this commodity they were comparatively immune from the conflicts of their neighbors until the Iroquois scourge swept over the whole region and engulfed this people in its course. Sharing their aloofness and their ultimate fate was the Neutral nation along the north shore of Lake Erie—a group that, hemmed in by powerful and mutually hostile tribes, maintained its existence by a policy of friendship with all of them until it too was overwhelmed by the Iroquois advance.

The Iroquois of the Five Nations were thus a major factor to be reckoned with from the very earliest days of New France. In the sixteenth century their power had extended north of the St. Lawrence, but by 1600 they had been pushed back south of the river and the Great Lakes. Their territory extended from the country of the Mohawk around Lake Champlain and the Richelieu to that of the Seneca toward the western end of Lake Ontario, covering most of northern New York State. But they ranged far afield into the interior of the continent in their hunting and their wars, and wherever they went they were the terror of the tribes that they encountered.

Their strength came not only from their remarkable fierceness as warriors, but also from the fact that they were partly agricultural in their habits. Even so they led only a half-settled existence. They still had to hunt for food to supplement their limited crops. Their famous "long houses," which held as many as twenty families, were more permanent structures than the tepees of the purely migratory tribes, but even they were only frames covered with bark. Exhaustion of the soil and indifference to sanitation made it necessary to move the villages every ten years or so and to clear new ground for the crops. Yet these villages gave the Iroquois stable bases from which they could operate in both hunting and warfare, and they were often protected by palisades against attack. Since their location was known it was easier to plan an attack against them than against more mobile encampments. They could be overcome by surprise or by superior force, and the destruction of their crops was a form of attack to which they were particularly vulnerable. But few of their Indian adversaries were capable of carrying out such enterprises on any large scale, and even the French were not strong enough to attempt more than raids during the first half century of the colony. The warlike nature of the Iroquois, the comparative permanence of their territorial bases, and the strength which they gained from even a loose political federation enabled this people, numbering some 16,000, to conduct successful aggressions against tribes that were far superior numerically and to threaten at one stage to drive the French themselves from the continent of North America.

An Indian of Eastern Canada.
A line engraving from Père du Creux,
Historiae Canadansis, *1664.*

(Granger Collection)

(National Museum of Canada)

Hurons Planting Corn.

A Plains Indian.
In the costume of the dog dance.

Chapter 2

The Beginnings

From Cabot to Cartier

When Columbus set out to reach the Orient, and to his lifelong disappointment discovered America, he opened new but uncertain horizons to the maritime nations of Europe. The Norsemen who had reached the New World five hundred years earlier achieved no practical result by their discovery, largely because Europe was in no condition to profit from it. At the end of the fifteenth century the improved methods of navigation and the development of a relatively stable society, the accumulated capital that made it possible to finance overseas ventures, and the emergence of a market for the luxury products of the East provided the means and incentives for expansion, and the lure of gold and other treasures attracted not only private adventurers but also the monarchs who were finding their finances straitened in the light of their obligations and their ambitions. Yet for a considerable period there were only spasmodic and tentative efforts by France and England to emulate Spain's achievement. Internal conditions hampered an energetic pursuit of overseas enterprises, and the possible rewards were still too uncertain for any but gamblers or enthusiasts to undertake the risks involved.

During most of the sixteenth century there were two main objects of exploration, which were pursued more or less simultaneously. The dominant one was still the search for a sea route to Asia that would be shorter and more direct than those around Africa or South America. Magellan's voyage of 1519 finally removed all doubt that America was a continent and revealed the tremendous expanse of the Pacific between it and the outlying islands of Asia. But a dwindling hope remained that a passage might exist through the land mass or that a short and practicable route might be discovered across its still unascertained breadth. There also lingered the possibility that even if this failed there might be cities and treasure and mines of gold and silver in lands hitherto undiscovered, and that the European state that managed to seize them would gain a source of wealth comparable to that of Spain and offering compensation for the failure to reach the silks and spices of the East.

The very nature of these hopes explains why Canada, and indeed North America as a whole, received so little attention during the century after Columbus. It is true that after Magellan had shown the extent of South America, any hope for a shorter passage could only lie in the north. But early though cursory voyages in that direction indicated that here too was a land mass that offered no opening, at least in the temperate latitudes; and although fables persisted of wealthy cities in the interior, it was soon clear that there was no such loot in Florida or Labrador or the intervening regions as the Spaniards found in Mexico and Peru. Spain became absorbed in the exploitation of her Caribbean possessions and felt little temptation to strike north. Her rivals were not yet ready to challenge her in the Indies, and their first tentative essays in other quarters quickly discouraged any idea that North America was a comparable source of wealth.

England was the first to be disillusioned. John Cabot, Genoese by birth and Venetian by citizenship, was one of the many contemporaries of Columbus who shared the idea that the shortest route to the East would be found by sailing west. The success of Columbus helped him to get a hearing in England, where he had settled around 1480. Henry VII with typical frugality gave permission for an enterprise that might result in profit but avoided risking any funds that might involve him in loss. It was the merchants of Bristol who backed Cabot in his venture. They had already sent several expeditions to search for new islands in the Atlantic. Now there rose before them the far more exciting prospect that their port, which looked out toward the western seas, might be the gateway to the riches of the Orient. They raised the funds to equip a single ship with a crew of eighteen, and on May 2, 1497, Cabot set out from Bristol for Asia.

It is not quite certain what he actually reached, but his landfall seems to have been either Newfoundland or Cape Breton, and he explored the coast for some distance to the south. He himself, like Columbus five years previously, was convinced that he had reached an outlying part of Asia. The king was sufficiently impressed to loosen his purse strings with a gift of £10 and a £20 annuity. Cabot's backers were encouraged to provide him with five ships loaded with trade goods for another voyage in the following year. What happened on this voyage is even more obscure. Some of the ships may have reached America, but if they did they found no profitable trade and so substantial a loss put a damper on Bristol's enthusiasm for new efforts.

A few years later, however, John Cabot's son Sebastian turned to the idea of a northwest passage and succeeded in fitting out an expedition in 1509. He spent the rest of his life in claiming that he had discovered the passage and in trying to set on foot a new venture; and the more substantial the American barrier began to appear, the more convinced he was that he had found a way through it. He may actually have sailed through Hudson Strait and glimpsed the waters of the Bay; but he failed to convince any sponsor that he had found a way to Asia, and it was not for another half century that the search for a northwest passage was taken up in earnest.

During that period English interest lapsed except for a few isolated voyages, which contributed nothing of significance. The path to the Grand Banks was taken by countless fishermen, and men were familiar with the existence of Newfoundland and Labrador. But it was France that embarked on a more serious effort to find out what lay between these regions and the lands of New Spain, and her efforts led to the real discovery of Canada.

The inspiration came from Francis I. This ambitious monarch, whose expansionist activities led him into conflict with Spain in Europe, was also prepared to challenge her commercial supremacy and ultimately her colonial monopoly. His first project was to renew the search for a passage to Asia. In 1523 he sent out Verrazano, who explored the coast from either Delaware or Chesapeake Bay for a considerable distance northward. But not only did he fail to discover a passage, he did not even find the chief rivers leading into the interior. Though he entered New York harbor he remained in ignorance of the Hudson River, and he had no inkling of the existence of the St. Lawrence. To compensate for this he cherished the illusion that he had glimpsed the Pacific across a narrow isthmus (this may have been Chesapeake Bay), but this was largely discredited the very next year when Spain in her turn sent Estevan Gómez to investigate the coast from Florida to Nova Scotia. The outline of the region was gradually being traced, but any penetration beyond the coastal fringe had to wait for another decade.

Its instrument was Jacques Cartier, navigator of St. Malo. Francis I had gained little satisfaction from Verrazano's voyage, but he had not yet abandoned hope of finding a passage, and he was still envious of the treasure that Spain was drawing from the New World. Cartier in fact was commissioned "to discover certain islands and countries where it is said that he should find great quantities of gold and other valuable things," but it appears that the search for a strait was also in Cartier's mind and probably in that of his royal patron as well.

The area that he deliberately chose for investigation was the Gulf of St. Lawrence. Although the existence of a large body of water west of Newfoundland was known, it was as yet completely unexplored. Sailing directly from France to Newfoundland and through the straits of Belle Isle, Cartier was in waters already familiar to thousands of fishermen. But when in the last week of May he passed through the straits into the Gulf, he entered an area that was entirely new to the Western world.

The first glimpses of its shores were not encouraging. The southern coast of Labrador was so unpromising that Cartier felt it must be the land God gave to Cain. The western shore of Newfoundland was equally unattractive. However, striking across the Gulf, Cartier came to the Magdalen Islands, and at once his spirits rose. Two acres of this, he wrote, were worth the whole of Newfoundland; and Prince Edward Island, which he next sighted, was "the best-tempered region one can possibly see." Coasting north, he came to an entrance that to his delight seemed to lead to open sea; but on July 10 his hopes were dashed when he found himself at the head of a bay, to which he gave the name Chaleur because of the intense summer heat. Turning back, he rounded the Gaspé Peninsula, on which he set up a cross with the royal arms to mark the claim of France to the whole country. He continued westward through the channel that runs on the north side of the island of Anticosti and saw the river broaden again beyond it. The date was now August 1, and adverse currents were slowing down his progress and rousing concern over the approach of autumn storms on the Atlantic. He held a council, and the result was a decision to turn back to France.

Cartier had found neither gold nor a passage, but he still brought back encouraging reports. Even if Francis I was not interested in the fertile and temperate lands that Cartier described so glowingly, there were other tales to stir his enthusiasm. In the region of Gaspé, Cartier encountered several bands of Indians whose avidity for European products led them to strip themselves of the very furs they wore. The significance of the episode escaped Cartier, for furs had not yet reached their real importance in the markets of Europe; but from these Indians he managed to gather an impression of what lay in the interior. It was clear from their description as well as from physical indications that the St. Lawrence was a river and not a strait leading to the Pacific. On the other hand, their stories raised hopes of riches farther to the west. They told of settlements to be found in that direction—the kingdoms of Saguenay and Canada and Hochelaga— and imagination could still picture these as empires rivaling Mexico, or even as outposts of Cathay. In addition, Cartier was convinced that the Indians offered a fruitful field for missionary effort. Taking back with him two sons of a chief to be trained as interpreters, Cartier hastened to lay these various possibilities before the king.

Francis I was sufficiently impressed to send him back with three ships in the following year. This time Cartier spent several weeks searching along the northern shore of the Gulf to make sure that no passage existed; then in the latter part of August he resumed his progress up the St. Lawrence beyond Anticosti. Under the guidance of the Indians he reached the native village of Stadacona, which occupied the site of the present city of Quebec.

The Indians made him welcome—so welcome that he had some difficulty in pursuing his explorations further. They were quite prepared to describe the wonders of Hochelaga but loath to compromise their privileged position as middlemen by allowing the French to make direct contact with other Indians farther to the west. They offered bribes. They talked of fearful snow and ice. They even conjured up devils complete with horns to terrorize the French. But when all this failed they allowed Cartier to depart. On September 9 he began his voyage up river with a bark and two longboats, and on October 2 he came to Hochelaga.

Hochelaga, where the city of Montreal now stands, proved to be only another Indian village. Cartier had already passed the grim mouth of the Saguenay and discovered at Stadacona that Kanata was merely a generic name for town. Now the third of his imagined Indian kingdoms turned out to be a palisaded Iroquois settlement of 50 huts. More than that, it lay at the foot of the Lachine Rapids, which ended any hope of further progress by ship. Cartier learned, too, that there were three more rapids beyond, that the river stretched a full three months' journey, and that hidden by the Laurentians was another river—the Ottawa—coming from the west. The prospect of a passage to Asia had receded far over the horizon.

Yet Cartier refused to be discouraged. Quite apart from the magnificent prospect that opened before him from the summit of Mount Royal, the legend of kingdoms in the interior was not completely dead. Though the mouth of the Saguenay showed little promise, the kingdom of that name might still lie farther west. At Hochelaga the Indians gave renewed testimony that seemed to bear out the possibility and confirmed the reports of copper in the interior. Seizing the silver chain of a whistle that Cartier wore and touching a copper-gilt dagger handle, they indicated that such substances came from a region up the Ottawa. At Stadacona, to which Cartier returned, the Indians continued to embellish the tales to which the French were so flatteringly attentive an audience. The myth remained as a lure to further efforts.

Cartier spent the winter at Stadacona. It was a precarious time, during which all except three of his crew were stricken with scurvy and 25 out of 110 perished before an infusion, apparently of white cedar, was discovered to be a remedy. The greed of the Indians for their possessions made it distinctly possible that the weakened French would be overwhelmed by a native attack. But spring came in 1536 without a hostile outbreak, and Cartier and his surviving comrades were able to depart for France. This time they took with them the Indian chief Donnacona so that the king might hear from an authentic source concerning the wonders of Saguenay.

The Indian reputation for taciturnity has been more than a little exaggerated. Cartier had found the savages only too ready to talk, and Donnacona in France developed a loquacity heightened by a lively imagination. His descriptions of Saguenay expanded in detail as he was introduced to products such as spices and oranges, which he promptly added to the treasures to be found in his own lands. Between them, he and Cartier kept the king's interest alive. For the next five years the absorption of France in war and diplomacy prevented any further exploration, and by that time Donnacona was dead; but his evidence had done its work, and in 1541 a new expedition was set on foot.

This time the initial purpose was colonization. The avowed intention of France to plant a settlement in the New World aroused acute alarm in Spain, always nervous about the establishment of a hostile base from which an attack might be launched against the Indies or the treasure fleets. There were negotiations with Portugal for a naval attack to destroy the expedition, but the Portuguese king felt that "the French could not have gone to any place where they could do less damage to His Majesty or to himself." There were diplomatic protests to France and an appeal to the papal bull which had divided the New World between Spain and Portugal; but Francis I denied the Pope's authority in temporal matters and challenged Spain to produce Adam's will and show how he had partitioned the world. In the end the expedition sailed unhindered in May 1541. Cartier had five ships, and Roberval, lieutenant-general and military head of the proposed colony, was to follow with another three after he had satisfied his desire for action by a little privateering in the English Channel.

The colony was intended to be a base for more extended conquests. Saguenay, with its mines of gold and silver and "abundance of cloves, nutmeg and pepper," might or might not be an outlying part of Asia, but it was obviously a desirable possession. The expedition was provisioned for two years; and though its personnel was largely recruited from the prisons of France, it contained 300 soldiers and its supplies included small boats that could be fitted with light artillery and transported overland. Cartier with his first contingent set up his base at Cap Rouge some distance above Quebec and wintered there in waiting for Roberval to join him next year.

By spring, however, his enthusiasm for the whole venture had disappeared. With the opening of navigation in 1542 he abandoned Cap Rouge and set sail for France. The difficulties of the winter and the constant threat of Indian attack were no doubt at the root of his decision. In addition, the members of the expedition seemed to have convinced themselves that the pyrites and crystals that they discovered in the region were gold and jewels and wanted to hasten back to France with these treasures. At any rate, when Cartier encountered Roberval at St. John's in Newfoundland and was ordered to turn back, he disobeyed and slipped away in the night to resume his voyage to France. Roberval went on to Cap Rouge and remained there during the following winter. He may have investigated the Saguenay and the Ottawa; but whatever his experiences, they left him discouraged in his turn. In 1543 he too returned to France, and the first short-lived effort to plant a French colony in Canada was at an end.

In spite of this outcome Cartier's work was of signal importance. He had penetrated the first—and in some respects the greatest—of the four great waterways that give access to the interior of the continent. Pinada had located the mouth of the Mississippi in 1519, but that river was never effectively used as a point of entry, and it was not until the following century that Hudson discovered the river and the bay that bear his name. The path of French penetration was now marked out, and France through Cartier had established clear title to the Gulf and the valley of the St. Lawrence—a title that might conceivably be expanded to embrace the bulk of North America.

Efforts in this direction, however, were feeble and ineffectual during the remainder of the century. The Huguenots who conducted them sought more temperate climes, first in Brazil and then in Florida. The latter settlement was promptly wiped out by the Spaniards with a ferocious zeal in the extermination of heretics. It may be noted that English attempts to plant colonies in Newfoundland and Virginia met with equally little success during this period. At the end of the sixteenth century there was not a single European settlement within the bounds of North America. It was not until changed conditions provided new incentives that the attempt was renewed. French contact with Canada was never actually lost, for Cartier had opened the way to the extension of fisheries into the Gulf and to the trade contacts with the Indians, which were to develop such importance. But Canada was officially ignored by the French government, and it was only with the rise of the fur trade to a position of first importance that a new era set in, an era which saw the real founding of Canada with the coming of Champlain.

The Coming of Champlain

During the latter half of the sixteenth century the fur trade grew from a casual activity on the part of fishermen in the Gulf to a substantial industry in which important groups in France were keenly interested. Fashion gave it a stimulus by decreeing the lavish use of fur for trimmings as well as for cloaks. The discovery that the soft hairs of the beaver were unexcelled for the making of fine felt brought the vogue of the beaver hat, and with that development America became a major and essential source of supply. Competition increased for the trade of the St. Lawrence region, and enterprising French merchants began to aim at a monopoly of this lucrative activity.

This linked up with a change in political conditions in France itself. For half a century the country had been distracted by foreign and civil wars, and a weak and unstable government had no resources to spare for overseas enterprises. With the triumph of Henri IV and the end of the wars of religion, however, attention was again directed toward New France. The king became interested in the idea of resuming the exploration and settlement of Canada and converting the Indians to Christianity. The eagerness of certain merchants to secure a privileged position offered a way by which these objectives might be achieved without cost to the royal treasury. Colonization and missionary effort could be thrown on private interests in return for control of the fur trade. In spite of the opposition of his chief minister, Sully, to all schemes of colonization, Henri IV proved amenable to persuasion. In 1602, under royal permission, Aymar de Chastes formed a company composed of the principal merchants of Rouen, and it was De Chastes who enlisted Champlain as a member of the expedition that was sent to explore the ground for the new venture.

Samuel de Champlain, the son of a mariner of Brouage, began his active career as a soldier in the Catholic forces during the wars of religion. His tastes lay in the direction of navigation and exploration, however, and after the cessation of hostilities he had the good fortune to secure a place in the Spanish fleet that sailed to the New World in 1599. The sight of these new lands confirmed his desire to penetrate further into the unknown. His faculties of judgment and observation were proved by the report of his experiences that he wrote on his return. His talents sufficiently impressed Henri IV to secure for Champlain a pension and the post of royal geographer. Now a wider opportunity opened up, which was to give his true genius full play.

Champlain was the stuff of which empire builders are made. A

Frenchman and a Catholic, he was inspired by a patriotism that desired to increase the greatness of France and a religious zeal for the spread of the Catholic faith. He was also possessed of an ardent curiosity, which took little account of the hazards and hardships of exploration when its reward was an increase in knowledge. To the instincts of a geographer he added those of a naturalist and anthropologist. His keen sense of observation was always evident, whether in noting the habits of different Indian tribes, in observing the signs that marked the abrupt passing of the Canadian seasons from winter to summer, or in estimating accurately the relation between Indian descriptions of lands he was never to see and the country that he had already traversed. To these gifts as an explorer he joined the talents of a colonizer and an administrator. His daring and his patience, the initiative that led him to plunge into the interior with only the sketchiest preparation, and the tenacity with which he pursued his efforts to establish New France when all his hopes seemed to lie in ruins mark him as one of those rare personalities whose greatness of stature is the result of a complete and rounded humanity.

In 1603, in an expedition under the command of De Chastes's associate Pontgravé, Champlain made his first voyage to the St. Lawrence. This was no longer the unfrequented region of Cartier's day. Whaling and fur trading had attracted Frenchmen and Basques to the mouth of the Saguenay, where the Indian village of Tadoussac became a base for both activities. Here Champlain made his first contacts with the Montagnais tribe—contacts that were later to be renewed and extended with profoundly important results. He investigated the lower stretches of the Saguenay and the St. Maurice and journeyed with Pontgravé up the St. Lawrence as far as Lachine. Much of this was a reconnaissance of ground that others had covered before him; but Champlain supplemented his own observations by inquiries among the Indians and thus extended his knowledge far beyond his travels. He gained an accurate impression of the traverse by way of the Saguenay to Hudson Bay and of the route by the Richelieu and Lake Champlain to the Hudson. He was not so clear about the relation between the various Great Lakes; and there was also the impression gathered from Indian descriptions that Lake Huron was salt. Perhaps, thought Champlain guardedly, it might even be the South Sea, and the St. Lawrence and the Great Lakes would in that case be a water route across America to the Pacific. This possibility, coupled with his enthusiasm for everything he had seen during his trip, was decisive for the future of Champlain and of Canada. Henceforth he devoted his life to the single-minded purpose of establishing France in North America.

It was, however, another five years before his efforts became firmly centered on the St. Lawrence. De Chastes was dead when Champlain returned to France, and the monopoly of the fur trade was now transferred for ten years to the Sieur de Monts on condition that he undertake to plant a colony. The region that De Monts chose for this effort was not Quebec but Acadia. An earlier effort in this direction had been made by the Marquis de la Roche in 1598. It consisted of dumping fifty convicts on Sable Island, where they waged a losing struggle for five years before a French ship arrived to rescue eleven survivors. It was hardly a model effort, and De Monts felt no reason to be discouraged by its outcome. He himself had visited the St. Lawrence in 1600 with an earlier monopolist, Pierre de Chauvin, who had tried to set up a permanent post at Tadoussac. He failed to share the enthusiasm of Champlain for that region, which he felt was too inclement for settlement. He hoped that Acadia with its more southerly latitude would be more favorable to the success of the colony. Champlain was enlisted in the enterprise, all the more willingly because he had recently heard tales not only of mineral wealth in that region, but also of a river leading to the interior, which might offer a shorter route than the St. Lawrence to "the great lake where the water is salt." In 1604, in an expedition composed of four ships and in company with Pontgravé and De Monts and the latter's associate Poutrincourt, Champlain set out for Acadia.

The venture was a disappointment from every point of view. The location first chosen by De Monts was an island at the mouth of the St. Croix River at the entrance to the Bay of Fundy. There was no water on the island, its sandy soil was unsuited for agriculture, and the erection of houses and a storehouse used up almost all the timber and left almost none for firewood. To the sufferings from cold that the colonists experienced during the winter were added the ravages of scurvy, which carried off thirty-five out of seventy-nine persons and nearly killed half the remainder. Champlain's exploration of the New England coast disappointed the hope that a more attractive location might be found in that area. In 1605 it was decided to make a new start at Port Royal, and this met with more success. The winter was mild and the toll of scurvy less severe. Crops were successful during the following year, and the winter of 1606 was again mild. The colonists benefited from friendly relations with the local Indians under the aged chief Membertou, who claimed to have known Cartier. They enlivened their existence by hunting and by the burlesque pageantry of the *Ordre du bon temps,* which Champlain founded to keep the company amused. By 1607 the colony had taken root as the first permanent French settlement in North America.

From the point of view of de Monts, however, the effort was a failure. Though signs of copper and other minerals were found along the Bay of Fundy they gave little promise of wealth. The climate of New England seemed as severe as that of the St. Lawrence, and Champlain failed to discover the hoped-for river to the interior. Neither the St. John nor the Kennebec answered his needs, and circumstances prevented him from exploring beyond Cape Cod and reaching either the Connecticut or the Hudson. As a result, it was soon apparent that Acadia was an unpromising area for the fur trade, in which De Monts was chiefly interested. Situated as it was between the two major routes of the St. Lawrence and the Hudson, its geographical disadvantages isolated it from the main course of this traffic and indeed from that of later commerce between the American continent and Europe. The final blow came in 1607, when powerful opponents in France secured the cancellation of De Monts's monopoly. He abandoned his efforts, handed over the infant colony to Poutrincourt, and left the Acadia that he had founded to struggle on under new auspices.

But Champlain was not ready to give up hope for a more solid establishment of French power in America. Under his urging De Monts secured the renewal of his monopoly for one year and turned his attention back to the St. Lawrence. Here was the real center of the fur trade and a region that could be more effectively secured against interlopers than the long Atlantic coastline. Champlain clung to his faith in its suitability for colonization and in his hope that it might yet offer a route across the continent to the Pacific. In the spring of 1608 he sailed with two vessels to begin the long struggle that issued in the permanent founding of New France.

With an unerring strategic instinct he chose Quebec as his main base. Tadoussac was still the chief center of the fur trade, though Champlain had already recognized the greater possibilities of both Three Rivers and Montreal. But the heights of Cape Diamond, commanding the narrows above the island of Orleans, offered a natural citadel to guard the great highway into the interior; and from Quebec he could still keep open the communications with France that were so vital to the survival of the colony. Here on the river bank, on the site of the present Lower Town, he erected the habitation that was the first step in his great effort "to lay the foundations of a permanent edifice, as well for the glory of God as for the renown of the French."

The construction of these quarters, and the problems of the winter with its inevitable epidemic of scurvy, prevented Champlain from traveling far afield. With the spring of 1609, however, there came not only an opportunity for new exploration, but the necessity for a decision with respect to relations with the Indians that was to be critical for the whole future of New France.

By the beginning of the seventeenth century the situation had changed since Cartier's day. Stadacona and Hochelaga had both disappeared. The Iroquois had been driven south of the St. Lawrence, and a bitter struggle was being waged for control of the St. Lawrence and the fur trade. The Montagnais, who dwelt north of the lower St. Lawrence, saw in the French allies who had a common interest in defeating the Iroquois. In 1603 they confronted Champlain with a demand for military help, and this was renewed in 1608. On both occasions Champlain promised his support. In the spring of 1609, with the war parties gathering for an expedition into Iroquois territory, the time had come to fulfill that promise.

It was a fateful decision, but one which was almost inescapable. If the French had been willing to confine themselves to a trading post at Tadoussac or Quebec, dealing with such Indians as chose to bring their furs there, neutrality might have been maintained. But the scope of Champlain's projects necessitated a closer relationship with the natives. He needed security for his projected settlement. He was dependent on the Indians for the fur trade, whose revenue was to support the colony. Their help was necessary to make possible the exploration of the interior on which his heart was set. He hoped that they would willingly accept missionaries from France. From all these points of view an established friendship had to be created, and this could only be achieved by casting in the lot of the French with the surrounding tribes in war as well as in peace.

In its immediate purpose the expedition of 1609 could be reckoned a success. The encounter with an Iroquois band at the southern end of Lake Champlain was decided in short order by the firearms of the French, to the gratification of their native allies. Champlain on his part had the satisfaction of following the Richelieu and discovering the lake that bears his name and of gaining a more precise knowledge of the route toward Lake George and the headwaters of the Hudson. But these results were achieved at the price of the enmity of the most powerful and warlike tribes in northeastern America. Less than three months after this skirmish, Henry Hudson sailed into the river that bears his name. His discovery brought the Dutch traders to Albany, and from the Dutch the Iroquois secured the firearms that would once again place them on a par with their enemies to the north. That event enabled them not only to maintain their position but to conduct increasingly successful aggressions against the Algonkin and the Huron as well as against the French. The colony survived by the barest of margins, and even then it was faced with an Indian barrier that jeopardized the security of its southern flank for most of the rest of the century.

Champlain took part in another war party in 1610, but this added nothing new. It was another three years before he could reap the fruits of his military enterprise by extending his explorations into the regions controlled by his Indian allies. The one-year monopoly of De Monts ended in 1609, and, in the chaotic period that followed, Champlain was engaged in the dual task of maintaining control of the fur trade against a flood of competitors and trying to get the monopoly renewed. In 1612 he was successful in the latter aim, and next year he resumed the work of exploration, which business difficulties had interrupted.

He had two immediate incentives in addition to his natural desires. During the years when he was unable himself to go into the interior he had encouraged a number of adventurous younger members of his expedition who wished to investigate the country and to learn the Indian language. One of these, Nicholas Vignau, appeared in Paris while Champlain was there in 1612 and spun a circumstantial tale of having been to the northern sea and finding relics of Hudson's lost party. His account fired Champlain anew with a desire to investigate for himself. Another motive presented itself on his arrival in Canada in 1613. The Indians, disgusted with the conditions in the fur trade during his absence, had not come down as usual to Lachine. To renew contact with them and to find out the truth of Vignau's story, Champlain with four French companions and a single Indian as guide decided to take two canoes and attempt the risky trip up the unfamiliar Ottawa.

Their task was lightened after a week of travel when they met a party of Algonkin coming down the river to trade and persuaded one of them to join them as second canoeman. Another week, however, demolished Vignau's truthfulness. Near Allumette Island they came upon an Algonkin settlement; and when the chief, with whom Vignau had lived, heard of his tale he denounced it as false. Vignau confessed his deception, and it was with difficulty that Champlain saved his life. To this disappointment was added the unwillingness of the Indians to aid Champlain in further explorations, which might open direct trade contacts between the French and the tribes farther on. Champlain felt obliged to turn back, but he had made himself familiar with the first stage of a journey that he was to accomplish two years later.

The occasion was once more a war party. The struggle with the Iroquois was growing fiercer, and Algonkin and Huron desire for Champlain's help overcame their reluctance to lead him into the interior. In July 1615, Champlain was at last able to follow what became a classic route of the fur trade—up the Ottawa and Mattawa to Lake Nipissing and down the French River to Georgian Bay. Thence by way of the Severn he reached the appointed rendezvous on Lake Simcoe and traveled with the war party by the lakes and rivers leading to the Bay of Quinte and along the shores of Lake Ontario. Their goal was an Iroquois stronghold near the outlet of Lake Oneida in New York State. As a military adventure it was not a success. Another party that was to join the attack failed to arrive in time, and Champlain was unable to marshal the Indians for a disciplined assault. He was wounded in the knee, and in the end the attackers beat a discouraged retreat to Lake Simcoe. However, it marked a new stage forward in the exploration of Canada. Though the Indians, in fear of Iroquois attacks, refused to take Champlain by way of the St. Lawrence, which would have been his shortest route back to Quebec, and thus compelled him to winter with them, he had gained a new clarity of knowledge about the relation between the St. Lawrence and the Great Lakes, and the information that he gathered during the winter, though it did not enable him to complete an accurate picture, was of value as a basis for future investigations.

His return to Quebec in 1616 marked the end of Champlain's career as an explorer. Other matters were to occupy him until his death nineteen years later. He had found that Lake Huron was not salt after all, and the Indians had refused to guide him to the northern sea. His knowledge even of the Great Lakes was still limited, for he was ignorant of the existence of Lake Erie and confused about the relations of Lake Huron, Lake Michigan, and Lake Superior, though it was clear that any passage to Cathay must be far longer than he had once hoped. Yet he had set on foot a work which was to be steadily continued even during his lifetime and to be considerably extended in the years immediately following his death. Even while he was wintering with the various tribes of the Ontario peninsula, the young Etienne Brulé—who had been with the war party that failed to keep the appointment at Lake Oneida—was discovering the route by the Holland River from Lake Simcoe to Lake Ontario and wandering eastward along the Susquehanna to its outlet in Chesapeake Bay. Several years later he voyaged along the northern shore of Lake Huron and gained a clearer knowledge of the existence and the extent of Lake Superior. Another of Champlain's aides, Jean Nicolet, traveled west under his inspiration to Green Bay and up the Fox River and provided a new link in the route that would ultimately lead to the headwaters of the Mississippi. Missionaries, who also owed much to Champlain, aided the work of exploration.

Jean de Brébeuf and his companion Pierre Chaumonot filled in an important link in the Great Lakes system when they reached Lake Erie in 1640. Father Isaac Jogues visited Sault Ste. Marie in 1641 and further clarified the geography of Lake Superior. Thus the pathways of the continent were gradually revealed by Champlain's aides and successors, even while he was kept from the work for which he was so supremely equipped by his task of planting French power on a firm footing on the banks of the St. Lawrence.

The Establishment of New France

In 1607, the year before Quebec was founded, England gained her first foothold on the North American continent with the settlement of Jamestown. In 1609 the discovery of the Hudson River opened the way for the Dutch. In 1610 Hudson's last and fatal voyage gave England the claim to Hudson Bay on which she acted sixty years later. Thus at the beginning of the seventeenth century Europe suddenly began to expand into North America, and before the end of the century the French colony on the St. Lawrence found itself subjected to the pressure of English rivalry from the north as well as from the south.

During most of Champlain's life, indeed, it was a question whether France would be able to maintain any foothold at all. Champlain was determined to establish a permanent colony, but his success depended on his securing effective backing in France itself, and this was hard to find. Apart from a few enthusiasts for missionary enterprise there was little popular interest in Canada. After the death of Henri IV in 1610 the government was ineffective and indifferent until the direction of affairs fell into the strong hands of Richelieu. The mercantile groups, on whom Champlain was dependent throughout, were more interested in dividends than in empire building, and Champlain found himself at cross-purposes with them during the greater part of his career.

The establishment of a colony involved considerable initial expense. With the government unwilling to bear the cost, funds had to come from private investors lured by the hope of profit from the fur trade. Even this would not offer the certainty and the margin of profit that would justify long-range colonial projects unless it was enjoyed as a monopoly. But the grant of a monopoly was opposed by many elements in the government as well as by indignant traders who found themselves excluded. Champlain had to devote much of his energies to overcoming this opposition in France and to securing for his backers the privileged position that was essential to all his plans.

He soon found that it was vital to have a powerful friend at court in order to assure a favorable attitude on the part of the king. His efforts to renew the monopoly after its cancellation in 1609 led him to put his case in the hands of Charles de Bourbon, Comte de Soissons, a cousin of Henri IV, who in 1612 secured a new charter giving him a monopoly of trade and appointing him Lieutenant General of New France. On the sudden death of Soissons in the same year, Champlain turned to the Prince de Condé, whose patronage cost the company that was formed under him an annual salary of 3000 livres. Condé's services were highly problematical. He was arrested for conspiracy and removed as viceroy, then released and restored to office, after which he sold the viceroyalty to the Duke of Montmorency, from whom it passed in 1625 to the Duke of Ventadour. These noble sponsors were ephemeral and expensive and their direct contributions were infinitesimal, but it is possible that their connection with the colony prevented its complete abandonment during these critical years.

The mercantile aspect of the endeavor was scarcely more stable. The original company dissolved after its monopoly was canceled. The grant to Soissons, while leaving trade free in the lower St. Lawrence, renewed the monopoly for the region above Quebec. Under Condé this privilege was sublet to an association of merchants, chiefly from Rouen and St. Malo, who were to enjoy it for eleven years and to undertake the defense and settlement of Canada. Their complete failure to fulfill these obligations led to their supersession in 1620 by a new organization, in which Guillaume and Emery de Caen were the leading figures. This was no more successful as a colonizing agency, and in 1627 it was replaced by the Company of New France composed of the Hundred Associates, whom Richelieu selected as his instruments for the creation of a French empire overseas.

The earlier companies were no great successes as trading ventures and utter failures as agents of colonization. Occasionally they got as far as planning to send out settlers, but their efforts stopped there. All their incentives were adverse to any serious attempts at permanent settlement. They had no idea of using the land as a basis of revenue, and indeed the experience of such English groups as the Virginia Company soon showed how dubious this was. They had no faith in the investment value of an agricultural base that would diminish the need to import supplies for the fur-trading establishments. They concentrated on the short-run profits from the trade and refused to sink their funds in the costly and uncertain project of transporting and maintaining settlers. For one thing, they felt that the more people there were in Canada, the harder it would be for the company to enforce its monopoly. Even as it was they had to make certain tacit concessions to competitors who dared to defy their legal claims. They had a rooted belief that any settlers they might send out would automatically prefer to plunge into the fur trade rather than to clear and cultivate the soil; and the larger the colony grew, the greater would be the threat to the company's source of revenue. The result was considerable friction between Champlain and his employers. By 1619 the Rouen company grew so weary of his importunities that they proposed that he should henceforth confine his activities solely to exploration and cease troubling them for colonists. The dissolution of this company was followed by the confirmation and extension of Champlain's powers as sole authority in Canada representing the lieutenant general, but even that did little to solve the problems that he continued to encounter in France.

For nearly twenty years Champlain waged an unsuccessful struggle to get effective support for his plans. A few individuals were inspired by contact with him to try their fortunes in Canada. The first permanent settler was Louis Hébert, a retired apothecary from Paris, who came out in 1617 with his family to begin life anew in the wilderness. A number of company servants decided to stay on, including Abraham Martin, who was later granted the famous plains outside Quebec on which the fate of New France was to be decided. But in 1627 the number of permanent residents, according to Champlain, was still only sixty-five souls.

Even this tiny settlement was shortly stricken with a blow that was nearly fatal. Hostilities broke out between England and France; and, taking advantage of them, the adventurer David Kirke and his two brothers set out on a semibuccaneering expedition against the French settlements in the New World. Their three ships appeared in the St. Lawrence in 1628 in time to intercept a convoy carrying supplies and settlers which the Hundred Associates in the first flush of their enthusiasm had dispatched to Canada. The whole expedition was captured by the English ships, which had taken Tadoussac and blockaded the river below it. The event deprived Quebec not only of expected reinforcements, but also of the annual supplies upon which its very existence depended.

Meanwhile Kirke—signing himself "your affectionate servant"—had sent a letter to Champlain compassionately describing the plight to which Quebec was automatically reduced by the blockade and pointing out that its fall was inevitable. "I would desire for your sake," he wrote, "that it should be by courtesy rather than by force, to avoid the blood which might be spilt on both sides." Though Champlain was fully conscious of his desperate position, he decided not to give in without at least a show of resistance. His refusal to surrender saved Quebec for the moment. Loaded with spoils and prisoners from the captured convoy, Kirke decided to return to England rather than to press an enterprise that might involve risk as well as delay.

He could apparently afford to postpone the attack until next year. The loss of provisions reduced Quebec almost to starvation throughout the winter. Fish, roots, and acorns kept the inhabitants alive, but by May 1629, provisions were nearly exhausted. Only aid from France could save the colony. But the ships which the Company sent were wrecked or intercepted; and when in July three ships under Louis and Thomas Kirke appeared before Quebec, Champlain recognized that resistance by his tiny and half-starved company would mean only useless bloodshed. He surrendered to his determined though still courteous adversaries; he and all other officials were carried off to be transported to France; and only some thirty French remained at Quebec to keep its existence alive.

Yet this remnant was of the utmost importance. The Kirkes, as it turned out, had made a serious mistake in not attacking in 1628. By the time they actually captured Quebec, England and France had been at peace for nearly three months. Champlain no sooner learned of this situation than he set on foot an agitation for the resoration of the colony to France. The government, which left to itself might have been indifferent, took up the case and brought diplomatic pressure on England. There was a delay of nearly three years before the matter was settled, for Charles I found Quebec a useful bargaining counter to secure the remainder of the dowry which had been promised with his French bride and which had not been paid in full. But in 1632 the negotiations issued in the treaty of St. Germain-en-Laye. Canada was restored to France, and Champlain—now almost at the end of his life—returned to rebuild around the handful of settlers who remained the work which had been all but shattered.

He now had behind him the company of the Hundred Associates. In contrast to Sully, Richelieu believed that France could increase her strength by commercial and colonial expansion and that the work could be accomplished through chartered companies such as the English and the Dutch had employed with considerable success. Thus while he dissolved the Caen company because of its ineffectiveness, the Company of New France which he set up in its place was framed along very similar lines. The chief differences were a much broader composition, which included a high proportion of financiers and officials, and a more precise stipulation of the duties of the company. The earlier companies, the government charged, had sent no more than eighteen settlers in fifteen years. The new company was to bring out 200 to 300 during the first year and a total of 4000 within fifteen years. It was to provide priests, undertake defense, and maintain the colonists for three years after their arrival. In return it was granted full ownership of the continent from Florida to the Arctic Circle, together with a monopoly of commerce for fifteen years and of the fur trade in perpetuity.

Unhappily the company suffered from much the same defects as its predecessors. The loss of the first expedition at the hands of the Kirkes and the failure of the second venture in 1629 were blows from which the company never recovered. Successful lawsuits by the Caens threw new burdens on the depleted treasury. Three years of English occupation deprived the company of revenue from the fur trade during its disastrous beginnings. Funds were henceforth lacking for the extensive program to which the Associates were committed. They sought to devolve the work on private individuals who would be granted estates on condition that they bring out settlers. But this had a limited success, for many of the grants went to speculators, including the governor of the company, Jean de Lauzon, who secured hundreds of square miles for himself and his son with no intention of spending money on immigrants. In 1645, following a disastrous slump in the fur trade, the Associates handed over their monopoly to a group of Canadian inhabitants on condition that these assume the debts of the company and pay an annual tribute. This was practically the abandonment of the whole enterprise by the Associates, and by this time the interest of the government had also waned. Richelieu's attention had been absorbed by the European situation created by the Thirty Years' War. His successor, Cardinal Mazarin, showed no interest in the colony. New France was left to develop as best it could through the spontaneous efforts of interested individuals.

These were unhappily few. Canada held little lure for men of position and capital. There had been no agricultural revolution such as that which displaced the English yeomen and moved many of them to make a new start in America. The French peasant clung tenaciously to his holding in the land he knew and loved and felt little desire to embark on the hard and uncertain life of a pioneer. The urban artisan was equally reluctant to exchange the cities of France for the forests of Canada. Even religious persecution, so powerful a force in the founding of the Thirteen Colonies, brought little advantage to Canada. Richelieu had deliberately barred the admission of Huguenots in his charter to the Hundred Associates. He had no intention of seeing repeated in the New World the dissention and turbulence which had just issued in the Huguenot revolt at La Rochelle. Huguenots, it is true, had played a prominent part in the first stages of the colony. De Monts was a Protestant, and so were the Caens. But their primary interests were commercial, and they had done nothing to bring out Frenchmen of their own faith as settlers. With the ending of religious toleration by the revocation of the Edict of Nantes in 1685, a more active persecution set in which resulted in a wave of Protestant emigration. But by that time the doors of Canada were firmly closed to heretics, and it is doubtful whether any large numbers would have gone there even if the restrictions had been removed.

Thus the colony grew only slowly in the generation after its recovery from the English. Champlain had effected its re-establishment almost single-handed. He personally brought out a considerable number of colonists during the next three years. But his death in 1635 left the situation precarious, and in 1640 there were still only about 200 inhabitants in New France. Robert Giffard, who was granted the seigniory of Beauport in 1634, brought out several parties during the next few years. A trickle of laborers and colonists added to their numbers, but it was a slow process, and the most striking event during its course was the impulse that led to the founding of Montreal.

The settlers in Champlain's time were clustered around the military and administrative center of Quebec. Champlain, however, had marked out both Three Rivers and Montreal as highly desirable sites. Three Rivers lay at the mouth of the St. Maurice, which tapped a wider fur trade area than Tadoussac and the Saguenay. A fort there would be an advance post against the Iroquois and would encourage the Indians from Lake Huron and the Upper Ottawa to come by the St. Maurice route and avoid the Mohawk, who so often lay in wait at the mouth of the Richelieu. In 1634, the year before his death, Champlain established the post at Three Rivers, which laid the foundation for settlement and which for many years was the real center of the fur trade in the colony.

Meanwhile Montreal had developed into a trading center of growing importance. It was more exposed than either Three Rivers or Quebec, for the Iroquois could approach it by either the Richelieu or the upper St. Lawrence, and at times they descended the Ottawa as well. But its very position almost at the junction of these three routes made it a natural meeting place for Indians and French, and Champlain had early seen its possibilities as a base for settlement and trade.

It was not commercial but religious motives, however, that led to the actual founding of the town. While interest lapsed on the part of both government and company, various religious bodies in France continued to look hopefully to Canada as a field for missionary enterprise. They were stimulated by the annual *Relations*, in which the Jesuits described the progress and attractions of the colony and recounted their missionary efforts among the Indians. Pious laymen, inspired by the idea of founding a mission on the island of Montreal, formed a society that secured a grant of the necessary lands and raised funds by subscription. The project attracted in Maisonneuve a soldier who was fired with a zeal for carrying the gospel to the heathen and in Jeanne Mance a devoted and capable woman to organize and direct the hospital. In 1641 a party of fifty-four—soldiers, laborers, nurses—set out for the new land. Next spring they began their work, and on May 17, 1642, the first steps were taken in the founding of Montreal.

From the beginning Montreal was a frontier—a frontier of commerce and religion, of defense and national expansion. It has never wholly lost that character. Almost from the day it began it was exposed to the hazards that such a position entailed. Its strategic situation at the point of contact between Huron and Algonkin and Iroquois subjected it to the consequences of a clash between these tribes and placed it in the forefront of the struggle when the Iroquois extended their attacks from the allies of the French to New France itself.

The founding of Montreal took place just at the time when the chronic Indian warfare was assuming a new intensity. The temporary advantage that Champlain's support had given the Algonkin and Huron against the Iroquois was soon redressed. When the Dutch set up a trading post at Albany, they became the natural allies of the Iroquois, upon whom they depended for furs; and from the Dutch the Iroquois were soon acquiring firearms, which gave them superiority over the Huron and the Algonkin.

They had also an incentive for pressing the struggle more vigorously. The competition of French and Dutch for the fur trade sharpened the rivalries of their respective allies. The Indians became middlemen battling for control of the St. Lawrence trade route. The Huron in the region around Georgian Bay were in a particularly good strategic position to dominate the trade between the French and the tribes farther to the west. If they could be eliminated, the Iroquois might be in a position to monopolize the traffic and divert it to Albany to their own profit.

From the end of 1640 the raids of the Iroquois grew steadily more persistent. By 1648 the attack rose to full fury against the Huron and the surrounding tribes. In that year the large Huron village at which the Jesuits had established the mission of St. Joseph was completely wiped out. Early next spring a party of 1000 Iroquois, who had spent the winter moving deliberately through the forests, hunting as they went, fell upon the settlements of St. Ignace and St. Louis with devastating ferocity. The Huron were shattered by these blows. The chief settlement which remained —that of Ste. Marie—was abandoned as unsafe. The Indian fury fell upon the neighbouring Tobacco and Neutral Indians, who were massacred or dispersed. A few Huron sought a brief refuge near Quebec. The remainder of the broken tribes were scattered far to the north and west, and the Iroquois stood triumphantly astride both the St. Lawrence and the Ottawa.

Meanwhile the scourge had fallen on the French as well. Until 1641 the settlements had been largely immune from Iroquois attacks, but their elimination would seal the ascendancy of both the Iroquois and the Dutch, and the beginning of French expansion gave an added motive for prompt action. In particular, the founding of Montreal was a forward step that was a direct challenge to the Iroquois. With their newly acquired firearms they felt strong enough to launch harassing attacks against the French, lurking in the surrounding woods and presenting a constant danger to any of the inhabitants who ventured outside the stockade. There were occasional raids on Three Rivers and even in the immediate vicinity of Quebec itself; but it was Montreal that was in the most constant danger during the two decades that followed its establishment.

By 1650 the colony of New France was in a virtual state of siege. The organization of the Five Nations enabled them to take almost permanent occupation of the chief vantage points and to keep up a constant pressure as one war party succeeded another with only brief intermissions. Even a comparatively small number of warriors could use such methods with deadly effects. The French could count on little or no help from Algonkin and Huron. Appeals to France for soldiers brought only a meager response. The defense fell on the inhabitants, who could work in their fields only with constant vigilance and with a musket always at hand, and even then were seldom safe at any distance from the stockade. With the fur trade practically cut off and farming a perilous occupation, the prospects of the colony were precarious in the extreme.

There was a brief respite in 1653. The Iroquois in their pride had extended their attacks to other tribes, including the Erie and the Andastes, and their losses made them more willing to arrange a truce with the French. But peace with the tribes was always precarious, for the impulse of any individual band might lead to a new outbreak. In 1656 a party of

Mohawk swooped down upon the Huron who had taken refuge on the Island of Orleans and defiantly paraded the captives in their canoes under the very walls of Quebec. By 1658 the uneasy peace had been succeeded once more by open war, and the Iroquois closed with fresh determination on the colony. A mass assault on Montreal in 1660 may have been frustrated by the outcome of a haphazard clash when Dollard des Ormeaux with sixteen companions set out to intercept an Iroquois band and seize their cargo of furs. Joined by a band of some forty Algonkin, their first attempt at an ambush brought down on them an assault by 200 Iroquois warriors, soon reinforced by another 550. Though deserted by their own Indian allies, their stand to the death at the Long Sault on the Ottawa is credited in legend with discouraging the Iroquois from an attack on the more substantial defenses of Montreal itself. The incessant war of attrition continued, however, and the colony was almost at its last gasp when it was rescued by the new and vigorous policy inaugurated by Jean Baptiste Colbert and Louis XIV.

Samuel De Champlain.
There are no known authentic contemporary portraits of Champlain. This one, attributed to the French artist Moncornet, apparently made its first appearance in 1854.

(*Redrawn from Champlain's Map, 1632*)

Champlain's Map, 1632.

Chapter 3

The Old Regime

The Royal Government

By 1660 the plight of New France was beyond the possibility of remedy by the colony itself. It was too weak in numbers and resources to deal decisively with the Iroquois menace. Its economic life was strangled by the interruption of the fur trade. The slow advance of settlement and cultivation left it still dependent on France for the very necessities of life. To these external perils were added internal dissensions. The small colony was rent by quarrels between various groups of clergy, between the bishop and the governor, between the inhabitants and the authorities. From all quarters came desperate pleas to the royal government in Paris for speedy action to restore harmony and save New France from extinction.

The appeal found France itself on the verge of entering a new and brilliant era in its national development. The death of Richelieu in 1642 and of Louis XIII in the following year had been followed by a period of conflict, internal as well as external. An infant king and a woman regent seemed to offer a chance for the nobility to recover the power they had lost under Richelieu. The result was the outbreak known as the Fronde; and the struggle against the rebels temporarily weakened the Bourbon monarchy in its rivalry with the Hapsburg power in Europe. But Richelieu's successor Mazarin ultimately mastered these difficulties. The rebellion was put down in 1653. The peace of 1648, which extended French territory toward the Rhine, was followed by a new conflict with Spain, but this was brought to an end in 1659 by a treaty that gave France further gains in the direction of the Pyrenees. The authority of the monarchy had been restored and the national position of France had been strengthened. When Louis XIV took over the personal direction of affairs on the death of Mazarin in 1661, a solid foundation had been laid for his exercise of absolute power and for the attainment of French ascendancy in Europe.

The achievement of these ends was largely made possible by the work of Colbert. Though Louis XIV was determined not be be ruled by a single

44

minister such as Richelieu or Mazarin, it was Colbert as minister of finances who inaugurated the policies and provided the resources on which the strength of the monarchy rested. He was determined to make France strong and prosperous and if possible self-sufficient. He encouraged the growth of commerce and industry by tariffs and subsidies and direct government enterprise. He resumed Richelieu's policy of replacing the local power of the nobility by that of the intendants, who were the agents of the central power. He stimulated the fine craftsmanship that made France the center of arts and fashions and the royal patronage of writers and artists that lifted her to the cultural leadership of Europe. The growing wealth of the nation strengthened her military power, and Colbert sought to place that wealth and power upon still broader foundations by a policy of expansion overseas.

Thus the needs of New France and the ambitions of the motherland for the moment coincided. Colbert wholeheartedly adopted the prevalent views of economic nationalism. While foreign competition should be excluded, external trade was a source of wealth to be developed by every possible means; and colonies would provide bases for such trade as well as sources of products to supplement the economy of metropolitan France. Commerce and colonies had enabled the Dutch and the English to rise to greatness and wealth as rivals and successors of Spain in the imperial field. By the same methods France might draw from overseas the strength and the riches that would confirm her ascendancy in Europe. Both the East and the West Indies offered promising fields for expansion; but while these attracted the attention of Colbert, his energies were also directed toward the struggling colony of New France, whose position was now so precarious.

It was clear that a completely new policy was needed to retrieve the fortunes of Canada. The record of the Hundred Associates was one of failure from every point of view. The company itself was completely discouraged, for the Iroquois had ruined the fur trade and the church was threatening to undermine its chance of recovery by agitating for the prohibition of the sale of brandy to the Indians. In the face of these declining fortunes it was now confronted with the prospect that it might be called upon to fulfill the obligations of settlement and defense that it had so long neglected. It was easily persuaded to forestall suppression by a voluntary surrender of its charter in February 1663. The slate was wiped clean and full authority over Canada was taken back into royal hands.

Even in the face of past experience, Colbert retained his faith in chartered companies as instruments of imperialism. He attributed the earlier failures not to inherent defects in commercial monopolies—for the Dutch and the

English had utilized them with conspicuous success—but to the weakness of the companies as actually established. In 1664 he gave a monopoly of French interests in the Americas and on the west coast of Africa to the Company of the West Indies, whose charter gave it full control over commerce, the ownership of land in Canada, and in theory complete rights of government. But there were ambiguities from the outset in both the purpose and the structure of the new company. It did relatively little to carry out the work of colonization with which it was charged, and from the beginning the king kept the government of the colony in his own hands. The company was as complete a failure as its predecessors, and after a decade of futility it was suppressed in 1674. From then on, full responsibility for the affairs of the colony rested formally as well as actually with the royal government.

While this false start was being made toward solving the problem of new settlement, the more pressing and urgent problem remained of saving the existing settlers from extinction at the hands of the Iroquois. Here the action of the king, though none too prompt, was vigorous and direct. The Marquis de Tracy, appointed lieutenant general over all the French possessions in North and South America, spent the year 1664 in restoring French power in the Caribbean. In 1665 he arrived in Canada, and at his disposal was placed the Carignan-Salières regiment, which had just distinguished itself against the Turks. This veteran force of over 1000 officers and men far exceeded anything previously sent to the defense of Canada. It set to work at once to block the Richelieu route by erecting forts at Sorel, Chambly, and the outlet from Lake Champlain. The fact that the Iroquois at this time were under pressure from other tribes on both their eastern and western flanks gave the reinforced French an added advantage.

A winter expedition into the Mohawk country, unwisely urged by Governor de Courcelle, accomplished nothing; but in 1666 Tracy set out with a full expedition, including 600 Canadian militia. The march carried them 100 miles beyond Lake George to the principal villages of the Mohawk. Little resistance was encountered. The savages fled at the approach of the troops; their villages and crops were ravaged and burned; and the chastened tribe sent peace envoys to Quebec, where a treaty was signed in 1667 to bring the war to an end. The Iroquois were not yet broken —indeed, it was not until the beginning of the next century that a general peace was concluded—but for the moment the cloud of Indian warfare was lifted, and New France had a breathing space in which to develop under the new royal direction.

Meanwhile a framework of government had been created that was to last with few changes until the downfall of New France. The new plans to create a substantial settled colony called for more elaborate and comprehensive machinery than had been felt necessary when the colony was little more than the base for a trading company; and the model was naturally found in the institutions that the French monarchy was in process of perfecting as the instruments of a centralized despotism.

In the early days the government of New France was simple in the extreme. In France the king conferred the title of lieutenant general on an aristocratic patron and monopolist, who promptly delegated his authority to Champlain as governor on the spot. Under the Hundred Associates the lieutenant general disappeared, and the governor was appointed by the king on the nomination of the company. Champlain continued as governor until his death and was succeeded by Montmagny. Under the latter, difficulties arose. The *Compagnie des Habitants,* which took over the fur trade in 1645, was a small clique whose activities created jealousy and resentment in the colony. Complaints reached Paris and moved the king to issue a decree that was in a sense the first real Canadian constitution. In 1647 a Council of Quebec was established, consisting of the governor, the Superior of the Jesuits (until a bishop was appointed to the colony), and the governor of Montreal. The most notable feature was the provision that syndics from Quebec, Three Rivers, and Montreal, elected by popular vote, should have the right to attend the council and present their views. The next year, as the result of a counterattack by the disgruntled merchant clique upon the arbitrary power of the council, its composition was reorganized. The term of the governor was restricted to three years. Besides the governor and the head of the Jesuits, the retiring governor was to be a member of the council; and two to three others were to be chosen by these appointed members acting jointly with the syndics of the three towns. This tentative approach to a representative system was considerably extended in 1657. By a new decree the council was reorganized to the exclusion of the retiring governor and the Superior of the Jesuits.[1] In their place appeared an appointed representative of the Company of New France and four elected councilors, two from Quebec and one each from Three Rivers and Montreal. Representative government, which had disappeared in France under the later Bourbons, seemed to be emerging in Canada.

---

[1] The omission of the leading ecclesiastic was temporary. François Xavier de Laval-Montmorency was added to the council on his appointment as bishop; and in 1661 the governor virtually compelled the reluctant Jesuits to send a delegate to the council sessions.

The resumption of control by the crown brought an abrupt check to this development. Neither Colbert nor Louis XIV had any intention of sharing the royal power with popular assemblies at home or overseas. Every suggestion of popular representation was henceforth excluded from the government of Canada. When Comte de Frontenac, apparently carried away by his new dignity as governor, signaled his arrival in Canada in 1672 by calling an assembly of seigniors, clergy, and habitants on the model of the old Estates-General in France, he was sharply rebuked for his temerity. "Since," wrote Colbert, "our kings have long regarded it as for the good of their service not to call together the Estates-General of the kingdom . . . you on your part should very rarely, indeed never, give this corporate form to the inhabitants of the said country." Colbert added the further advice that even the elected syndics should be gradually suppressed; and when this office disappeared, the last vestige of representative institutions was eliminated from New France.

The suppression of the elective element, however, by no means implied the exclusion of popular influence. Protests or demands by the inhabitants were often effective in deciding the attitude of the authorities, and from time to time found means for collective expression. It was not unusual for *ad hoc* assemblies to be called to consider matters of public concern. The Brandy Parliament of 1678 was a notable example, but there were also gatherings to discuss such topics as price control and parish meetings to deal with local problems, and in 1717 royal authorization was granted for regular meetings of merchant assemblies in Quebec and Montreal. Representation as a formal element in the structure of government may have been rejected, but contact and consultation were far from absent in the relations between officials and populace.

Basically however the form of government established in 1663 stemmed directly from the absolute authority of the king and depended on his will. It vested control of the colony in a Sovereign Council composed of the governor, the bishop, and five appointed councilors, in addition to a secretary and an attorney general. The intendant, by an odd omission, was not mentioned in the original decree; but when Jean Talon arrived in 1665 he took his place at once in the council, and by 1675, the intendant had replaced the governor as the presiding official. The number of councilors was increased to seven, and in 1703 it was further increased to twelve. At first the councilors were named by the bishop and the governor, but later the appointment of all members was vested in the king.

The council combined in a single institution the functions of a legislature, an administrative body, and a supreme court for the colony.

Its legislative power, it is true, was confined to local affairs. The decree that created the new government was followed by another, which provided the colony with a body of law, the Custom of Paris, which was to be applied to the exclusion of any other local system of law that might be in force in France. The supreme right of making new laws resided with the king, whose decrees were to be registered by the council and thus brought formally into operation. But the council itself had the power to pass local regulations affecting such important matters as finance and trade and police; and in its administrative capacity it sometimes refrained from effectively enforcing royal ordinances that its members felt to be unsuited to the needs of the colony or adverse to their own interests. The council was also a court of appeal in civil and criminal cases, though the royal council in Paris was the court of final resort; and in judicial matters the Parlement of Paris was to be the model for the Canadian body.

Curiously enough, in the year after the council was established the West India Company was given by its charter the right to set up councils and to nominate governors as well as other officials. Though these rights were never exercised, their concession indicates a duality of approach and a confusion of purpose at the outset of this new era. It was not until the suppression of the company in 1674 that the contradiction was to some extent resolved, and the direction of the solution was also suggested by the later change of name from Sovereign Council to Superior Council. Just as the company had been granted in theory rights that were ignored in practice, so the council had been vested with powers far wider than it ever exercised in reality. Nominally it had very extensive authority, both legislative and judicial. But the supreme legislative power resided in Paris, and in practice all matters of policy were decided there, while the issuing of local regulations fell more and more into the hands of the intendant, who was the direct agent of the royal government in seeing that its will was carried out. The council was reduced to a minor role in legislation, and even its judicial power was whittled down by the activities of the intendant.

The triple rule of governor, bishop, and intendant was a further cause of friction. In addition to his spiritual authority, the bishop had a share in civil government as a leading member of the council. The dividing line between civil and spiritual matters, never easy to establish, became still more uncertain when the bishop was in a position to take an active part in the framing of policies affecting the moral welfare of the colony. When a self-willed governor like Frontenac was yoked with a determined prelate like Laval, conflicts concerning their respective spheres of authority were bound to arise. Their strife was embittered by questions of rank and precedence and by rivalry for control of the council, and their violent dissensions over such questions as the liquor trade with the Indians were productive of deep and prolonged divisions within the colony.

The intendant was frequently at odds with both the bishop and governor. Quarrels easily arose when either official suspected the other of encroaching on his own sphere of authority; and questions of policy from time to time found the bishop embroiled with the intendant as well as with the governor, who in his turn might well detest both his colleagues. As the eighteenth century advanced, this situation tended to abate somewhat, though even then there were plentiful complaints to Paris, accompanied by appeals by each official for redress against the wrongs inflicted upon him by the others, and the home government was periodically obliged to interfere to settle the disputes.

Unfortunately the intervention of the government in Paris was by no means confined to the smoothing out of local difficulties. Just as the monarchy was engaged in breaking down localism in France and creating a centralized despotism, so it sought to keep direct control over affairs within the colony. It was not only matters of general policy that were decided in Paris. The whole life of the colony was to be regulated by detailed instructions drawn up by the king and his ministers. It was to be a paternalistic rule by an all-wise as well as an all-powerful central government over a submissive population. All initiative was to come from above, none from the population itself. Local officials such as the intendant might suggest measures that seemed desirable, but the suggestions had to receive the approval of the king, and the detailed instructions to governors and intendants showed how narrow a scope these royal agents were expected to have in decision or in action.

This was the atmosphere in which the habits and outlook of French Canada were molded for a whole century before the conquest. In contrast to the vigorous and somewhat turbulent society that was being formed in the English colonies to the south, New France was a community built around the solid pillars of order and authority. Such a structure had many potential advantages. The policies of the central government in France could be implemented through direct and effective channels. The authorities in Canada had under their direction a coherent community whose fullest resources could at a word of command be brought into action to effect a given purpose, but the impulse for such action must come from the home government. For its effective functioning the system depended upon a sustained initiative on the part of the king and his ministers. When this was withdrawn, the colony could rely only on its own spontaneity of effort and enterprise, and these were not qualities which were encouraged by the restrictive nature of an authoritarian regime.

Yet these generalizations must not be pressed too far. The submissiveness of the habitant to both church and state had very definite limits. His pioneer life inevitably encouraged a certain independence of spirit; and while he acquiesced in the general authority of the government or the clergy or the seigniors, he showed himself ready on occasions to resist with a stubborn tenacity specific attempts to extend that authority beyond reasonable bounds. For the less acquiescent the fur trade offered an outlet for individual initiative and an escape from the restraints of an ordered and regulated community. And though the servants of the Crown were narrowly restricted by their dependence on instructions or sanctions from Paris, a strong personality could do much to shape the course of events within those limits when he had authority on the spot and when distance hampered royal supervision and control. In particular, the first decade of the new system brought forward three remarkable men in Laval, Talon, and Frontenac, and their combined achievements laid the real foundations for the subsequent development of New France.

The First Intendant

Of all the royal officials in the colony the intendant was incomparably the most important. The governor and the bishop might claim superior rank and enjoy greater prestige, but neither of them—not even the bishop, with his extensive spiritual authority—exercised so broad and continuous an influence over the daily life of the population. The intendant was the supreme agent for implementing in Canada the will of the government in Paris and the chief source of information about the needs of the colony for the guidance of the king and his ministers. Upon his ability to persuade the home authorities to adopt a wise and constructive policy and his talent in carrying out the spirit as well as the letter of his instructions with the most beneficial effects, the welfare of the colony very largely depended.

The intendant was in fact the very embodiment of a centralized paternalism. His powers ranged over almost every aspect of ordinary civil life. His functions included justice, police, and finance in the widest sense. He had the oversight not merely of taxation and expenditure, but of the whole economic life of the colony. The granting of land, the fostering of immigration, and the direction of schemes of settlement fell within the scope of his authority. Upon him largely depended the stimulus to local industries and the working out of plans for increased trade. While the governor controlled the military forces, it was the intendant who was charged with the problems of supply and administration. At one moment he might be engaged in an attempt to enforce a reasonable price ceiling against the recalcitrance and evasions of disgruntled merchants; at another he might be trying to solve the chronic shortage of specie currency by issuing treasury notes or by such unique devices as the "card money"— playing cards cut in four and signed by him—which the intendant Jacques de Meulles invented in 1685 when he lacked money to pay the troops and which ultimately became a regular part of the currency of New France in spite of the home government's shock at this unorthodox and inflationary device. As chief administrator the intendant was charged with carrying out the decrees of the king and the orders of the Superior Council. His local agents were the captains of militia, who not only served the governor in the organization of military affairs within the colony, but were even more important as the officials on whom the central administration depended to see that its decisions were carried out effectively. In his judicial capacity the intendant could take cognizance of both criminal offenses and civil disputes, and his judgments—particularly in matters affecting the relations between seignior and habitant—frequently offered a quick and simple alternative to resort to more formal courts. There were few things which were outside his control and many which depended on his sanction and even his direct intervention.

Such wide powers in the hands of an ambitious and energetic man almost inevitably led him into conflict with his leading colleagues. In carrying out his duties it was easy to intrude on the spheres that the governor or bishop regarded as his own, and this was productive of repeated conflicts. Talon's all-embracing activity roused jealousy and irritation on the part of Governor de Courcelle, who felt reduced to a secondary role once his share in the suppression of the Iroquois was over. Frontenac ruled for three years without an intendant, enjoying an extensive authority which suited his imperious nature. The arrival of Duchesneau as intendant in 1675 was anything but welcome, and the quarrels of the two men became so chronic and embittered that both were recalled in 1682. Their successors at times agreed no better. The bishop also on various occasions found his claims to spiritual jurisdiction in sharp conflict with the intendant's assertion of his civil authority, and on such issues as the brandy trade the two were often directly opposed. Harmony was none too common among the high officials, and its lack was a hindrance to efficiency in government.

The first active intendant in New France was Jean Talon. There had been an earlier appointment in 1663, but the incumbent never entered upon the duties of his post. It was the appointment of Talon in 1665 that effectively established the new office and brought to Canada a man who was the very embodiment of the new spirit which at the outset animated the personal government of Louis XIV.

The selection of Talon was itself a sign of the revived interest of Paris in the development of Canada. Like Colbert he had been trained in administration under Mazarin, and at the time of his new appointment he had behind him ten successful years as intendant of Hainault. But no one could have been less like a routine bureaucrat. In Talon's portrait, with its lively eye and firm-set jaw, there can be seen those qualities of vigor and imagination which are so evident in his career. From the first he grasped the tremendous possibilities that lay before France in America and urged upon the home government the adoption of bold imperial policies on a scale adequate to such opportunities. Colbert preferred to remain within bounds that the colony might reasonably be expected to maintain with its own resources, rather than to aspire to a vast domain which New France would lack the strength to hold. But within the straitened limits thus imposed by the decision of his superiors, Talon strove zealously to create in Canada a flourishing and expanding community; and when after seven years he returned permanently to France, he left behind a colony whose foundations were at last firmly established and whose future growth was a monument to his achievement.

The first essential was an active policy of immigration and settlement. This at once brought Talon up against the West India Company, and a first glance was enough to convince him that its existence was utterly incompatible with the purposes he had at heart. Colbert clung to the belief that commercial monopoly could be made an effective instrument of colonization. Talon was convinced that the company would concentrate on the profits of trade to the neglect of settlement and that its trade monopoly would actually be an obstacle to the growth of population. If these privileges were maintained, he asserted, there would be fewer people in Canada in ten years' time than there were at present. In one of his first dispatches after his arrival, he exposed the ambiguity of purpose that was implicit in the establishment of the company. "If the king's motive," he wrote, "was to augment the company's profits so that it may have more means to sustain its first expenses, increase the number of ships and build up a large trade useful to the state, without aiming at the extension of settlement in this country and the multiplication of its colonists, it is to my mind more useful for the king to leave the company in unreserved possession. But if he looks on this country as virgin soil for the creation of a great kingdom and the foundation of a monarchy or at least a strong and considerable state, I cannot persuade myself that he will succeed in his design by leaving in hands other than his own the overlordship, the ownership of the lands, the nomination to livings, even the commerce which is the soul of the settlement which he envisages."

Colbert, however, was not convinced. Failing to get the company suppressed, Talon fell back on a determined effort to reduce its powers and prerogatives. Already its rights of government had been practically abolished. In 1666 Talon succeeded in taking from it the right of making grants of land, although it retained legal proprietorship. In 1669 his persistent attack on the company's trade monopoly ended with a decree that granted freedom of trade to the colonists. The company retained the right to one-quarter of the beaver skins, one-tenth of the moose hides, and the monopoly of the Tadoussac trade, which had been granted it three years before in return for allowing the habitants to engage in the fur trade. But it had heavy obligations, and in its reduced state it remained a nuisance in the colony without being of profit to its shareholders. It gradually sank into bankruptcy, and in 1674 its charter was canceled. By that date Talon's work in Canada had ended, and the royal interest in the development of the colony had waned in the face of more immediate objectives in Europe.

When the granting of land was taken from the company, the task of settling the land was in effect assumed by the government. This was an urgent need if the colony was to be solidly established, and it called for positive efforts on the part of the government. There had indeed been a continuous influx, which raised the number of settlers from 240 in 1641 to perhaps 2500 in 1663. Private individuals and religious organizations had brought out occasional parties. A group of 200 arrived in 1659, half of them recruited by the Sulpicians for Montreal, and smaller contingents came out during the next few years. But immigration on a more substantial scale was necessary if the colony was to become secure and relatively self-sustaining, and this could only be accomplished by the active intervention of the government itself.

In 1661 the king made a beginning by promising to send out 300 settlers annually for the next ten years. This would be a far greater influx than the colony had ever previously enjoyed. But it was still extremely modest compared to the possibilities of Canada and the potential resources of France, and Talon set himself energetically to the task of increasing the figure. He had little direct success in stimulating the government to greater efforts. To his enthusiastic project of creating a strong and considerable state on the banks of the St. Lawrence, Colbert replied drily that the king had no intention of depopulating France for the sake of peopling Canada. Talon might well feel that the phrase was exaggerated. The proposed annual contingents could have been doubled or trebled without sapping the strength of France to any noticeable extent; but suitable pioneers were likely to be also suitable soldiers, and even at the height of its interest in the colonies this consideration lay heavy and restraining upon the French government.

Talon therefore was reduced to an effort to prevent any slackening of the government's slender efforts, and to finding supplementary sources of colonists whenever the opportunity offered. One such source presented itself in the soldiers who were sent to Canada. Talon seized upon the presence of the Carignan regiment as a chance to combine settlement and defense, pointing to the Roman military colonies as a precedent for his scheme. In spite of the opposition of the governor, who wanted the regiment kept as a purely military garrison, and of the colonel, who wanted to take his whole command back with him to France, the approval of the ministry and the desire of many of the soldiers to remain in Canada combined to favor Talon's plans. A number of seigniories were granted to officers, particularly along the Richelieu, where effective settlement would help to bar the traditional invasion route of the Mohawks, and more than 400 soldiers took up lands as settlers. In subsequent years the contingents of regular troops sent to garrison the colony provided further recruits, for many of the soldiers married and remained as settlers. Captains of merchant vessels sailing to New France were ordered to take with them a number of *engagés* proportional to the size of the ship, though with very limited results. These sources, with the additional numbers brought out by the company, the church, or private interests helped to swell the officially subsidized contingents, which provided the bulk of the immigration.

Although there was some demand for workmen and artisans, the chief desire was for able-bodied men who would clear the land and settle down to farming. The bulk of the immigration was recruited from western France, and particularly from Normandy. The settlers were recruited by offers of free passage and the assurance of land on comparatively easy terms, either after a three-year indenture, or immediately in uncleared sections with provision for their support until the first crop. A certain casualness of selection in the early years brought a strong protest from Talon, who secured a stipulation that the men should not be under sixteen or over forty and that the girls should be strong and healthy. The need to provide wives for the colonists was particularly acute when the Carignan soldiers decided to settle on the land, and the problem of finding suitable girls for a rude pioneer existence gave much concern. The orphanages offered one obvious source; but the *filles du roi* who came from these charitable institutions were not always physically fitted for the rude life and cold climate of New France, and Talon recommended that the girls should be sought in the country villages of Normandy. To make sure that their character was as acceptable as their physique, a certificate was generally asked from the local priest or magistrate, and in some cases their selection was also entrusted to the clergy. Even these precautions were not infallible. Occasional arrivals were of doubtful quality, and occasional scandals within the colony showed that past virtue was not always a guaranty against future frailty. But clerical supervision at the points of both departure and arrival was a safeguard against the introduction of women of known bad character, and clerical censoriousness may well have exaggerated the lapses of those who actually entered.

Between 1659 and 1673, Canada received some 4000 immigrants. That was the extent of the impetus given to its growth by direct efforts from France under Louis XIV. By 1672 the interest in the colony had become subordinated to other concerns. The pressure of European affairs, which had distracted both Sully and Richelieu after their first brief enthusiasm, now absorbed the attention of Louis XIV. The war with Holland launched him on that ambitious effort at territorial expansion which was to make France the paramount military power and to bring such misery upon her people. The government, with its need for strength at home, was unwilling to spare even the annual handful of colonists that it had previously sent. A few might still be recruited for particular seigniories or brought out as artisans for new industries in which the government was interested. The practice of transporting petty offenders was adopted for a time, and Canada received 761 poachers and smugglers and similar characters between 1723 and 1749. With the end of sponsored emigration there was no spontaneous movement within France which could keep the tide of population flowing toward the New World. While Britain with her expanding maritime activities continued to look overseas and to develop an increasing interest in her American colonies, a France absorbed in the struggle for European ascendancy had few resources to spare for Canada. While the royal government kept a control that was as insistent as the policy behind it was uncertain, the growth of the colony henceforth depended not on immigration but on the natural increase of the population.

This, however, was no small force. Already under Talon it had been recognized that it was a practical alternative, which had the added advantage of being cheaper than a subsidized policy of settlement. A consistent policy of encouraging early marriages and large families was part of the royal paternalism. In 1669 a comprehensive system of rewards and punishments was established by royal decree. Girls were to be married by the time they were sixteen and boys by the time they reached the age of twenty. Those who obeyed this injunction were to be rewarded by a royal gift of twenty livres each. In the case of those who hung back their parents were to be held responsible and to be subject to a fine in default of good reasons for such delay. In the case of recent arrivals other measures were adopted by Talon. As far as genuine settlers were concerned there was little difficulty. Their eagerness was such that the girls sent from France were provided with husbands almost as soon as they were off the ship, and each received from the intendant a gift of fifty livres in provisions with which to start the new life. But among the indentured servants as well as among the youths native to the colony there were those who were more attracted to the freedom and the risks of the fur trade than to the arduous life of pioneer farming. By imposing upon them the responsibilities of marriage, a check might be placed on this form of desertion, which hampered the growth of settlement; a police regulation therefore provided that a man whose indenture had expired and who failed to marry within fifteen days after the arrival of the next shipload of girls would be deprived of the right to engage in the fur trade. If there were some who still preferred to take to the woods rather than accept the yoke of domesticity, they did so in defiance of the law and at the risk of punishment.

The edict of 1669 also undertook to encourage large families. The need for this was not pressing, for the authorities noted with satisfaction that most marriages were commendably fruitful. It could therefore be taken for granted that a family of less than ten children merited no special distinction. To any couple possessing ten living children who were neither priests nor nuns an annual pension of 300 livres was granted, and for twelve children the grant was 400 livres. In addition, fathers of large families were to be preferred for local honors and appointments. Such tangible marks of official approval were sufficient to establish as a permanent characteristic the traditionally high birth rate of French Canada.

In 1666 the first official census of New France placed the population at 3215 souls. In 1673 it had risen to 6705—a figure that was probably an underestimate. By that year sponsored immigration was at an end, and henceforth the growth was by natural increase; yet in 1698 the population was 15,255; and by the time of the conquest in 1763 it was over 60,000.

Compared to the 1,500,000 in the English colonies to the south, this was a small figure, but it represented very substantial fruits from the modest seed that had been sown under Colbert and Talon.

The influx of population during Talon's rule was naturally accompanied by an extension of the area of settlement. When he came to the colony, half the meager population was grouped in the immediate vicinity of Quebec. That town, the center of administration and defense, with its direct contacts with France and its comparative remoteness from the Iroquois, offered more attractions to the average settler than either Three Rivers or Montreal. These two places were little more than fortified posts, with a few clearings in their immediate vicinity, and the colony as a whole consisted of three widely separated islands of settlement in the vast wilderness that bordered the St. Lawrence.

The need for such concentration in the face of the Iroquois peril had been inescapable. The possibility of renewed attacks gave added motive to the authorities for favoring the grouping of new settlers in villages with farms surrounding them such as are to be found in France. This was Talon's original plan, and he himself acquired a tract of land and laid out three villages on the approximate site of the present Charlesbourg near Quebec. But conditions in the new land were adverse to the general application of such a plan. The rivers, and above all the St. Lawrence, were too important to the settler. They were his only roads, and he used them both winter and summer. He needed direct access to them for transport, as well as for the fishing that provided him with an important part of his food supply. Granted that each habitant had a reasonably extensive holding, it was impossible to group them in a central community that would give all of them access to the river and still leave their fields within easy distance.

Once the danger from the Iroquois declined, therefore, settlement began to spread out along the St. Lawrence, and particularly along the north bank. Until Talon's time the south shore was almost empty of inhabitants. The establishment of soldier settlers along the Richelieu opened a new area, and settlement gradually spread opposite Three Rivers and Montreal as well as from the vicinity of Levis. But it was the expansion from the three original centers on the north bank of the St. Lawrence that was the chief development. The pushing of a road through this area, and its completion between Quebec and Montreal in 1734, stimulated the process and confirmed the direction of development. By the time of the conquest, Canada was like a long straggling village, with the St. Lawrence as its main street and with only a few areas of settlement such as that along the Richelieu striking off from this thin ribbon of settlement.

With a solid and prosperous agricultural colony as a base, Talon hoped to build in Canada an economic structure that would flourish both industrially and commercially. Like his expansive plans in other directions, this was checked by the parsimony of the government in Paris. Colbert was willing to send out a certain number of artisans to aid in the establishment of local industries but royal subsidies to the colony were not sufficiently large to provide the capital that was necessary if manufacturing was to be undertaken on any substantial scale. In 1666 he pleaded the burden of the war with England as a barrier and advised Talon: "The way to establish manufactures lies rather in the industry and efforts of the inhabitants than in any help that the king can give."

Thus obliged to rely on the local resources of the colony, Talon strove energetically to make the most of them. By the use of such raw materials as the colony itself produced, he sought to emancipate Canada from its dependence on French manufactures and to develop products for export that would stimulate commercial prosperity. The introduction of domestic animals meant that wool and hides were available. The growing of flax and hemp was encouraged. In addition to these agricultural materials, Talon set on foot a search for mineral resources, investigating reports of copper around Lake Superior and coal on Cape Breton Island. Above all, there were the forests, which could be exploited for potash and tar as well as for lumber and which offered not only spars and masts for the king's ships but an admirable opportunity to develop a shipbuilding industry in Canada itself.

Few of these hopes were realized. A few local activities such as tanning and weaving developed to meet domestic needs, particularly when war led to the interruption of supplies from France and threw the colonists back on their own products. Talon started a brewery, which was highly approved by the home government, since it cut down the expensive importation of wine and brandy from France and gave promise of reducing the drunkeness attendant on the use of more ardent liquors. His construction of a shipyard laid the foundation for an active though still modest enterprise during the next century. But industrial expansion in general was hampered by lack of capital and the problem of an adequate labor supply.

These, in fact, were the twin problems that New France never succeeded in solving. Apart from a few entrepreneurs who essayed to establish local industries, often with disappointing results, little private capital migrated from France, and only a limited amount was accumulated locally. The bulk of the profits from the fur trade ended up in France. Few local merchants accumulated even a modest fortune. The meager savings that the habitant tucked into the woolen sock in good years were soon dissipated in hard times and contributed nothing to the funds available for investment. Moreover, the range of opportunity was restricted not only by circumstances but also by government policy. The royal government was ready to assist shipbuilding and ironworks, and even to take over such enterprises. It professed, beginning with Colbert, a desire that the colony become self-sufficient. Yet there was also the feeling that the colony should provide a market for French manufactures in exchange for raw materials, and an adverse attitude toward the possible rise of local competition. Thus hatmaking, which was initially encouraged, was prohibited when the export of hats to France was proposed; weaving of linen was discouraged; the making of moccasins could be allowed, but not the making of French shoes. The dilemma is implicit in a dispatch from Paris in 1706: "Since the settlers have been compelled by necessity to manufacture cloth, let us hope that they will also find means to satisfy their other needs. As a rule, however, it is not fitting that manufactures be established in the colony, as they would be prejudicial to those of France."

Even when there was a readiness to tolerate the production of articles for local consumption—soap, glass, tiles—the shortage of skilled artisans was an impediment. The urban worker established in his trade in France was rarely anxious to venture his destiny in a raw frontier community. The arrivals who professed competence in a skilled occupation frequently had only the slenderest acquaintance with the craft. When they were adequately trained, the absence of competition enabled them to demand such high wages and easy working conditions that costs of production in the colony far outran the level in France, with adverse effects on export prospects as well as local living costs.

Efforts to build up local industry on an agricultural base also had limited success. Lumbering could to some extent be fitted in with farming, and sawmills were common by the eighteenth century. But many settlers were more interested in clearing their land quickly by burning the trees than in turning their timber into an asset; and lumber for export was often bad in quality as a result of careless handling, which in turn resulted from a lack of adequately skilled workmen. The same conditions hampered the development of the iron industry. Lack of capital prevented the working of the bog iron deposits near St. Maurice until about 1737, and bad management coupled with high labor costs prevented the commercial success of the industry. Few farmers had the time or the incentive to undertake the cultivation of hemp or the manufacture of tar or potash when these competed with the demands of ordinary farming. There was a brief boom in ginseng about the middle of the eighteenth century, but inexperience and the desire for quick profits resulted in inadequate preparation of the root for market and completely discredited the Canadian product.

In consequence no new staple, either natural or manufactured, was successfully developed for export, and this in turn prevented the commercial expansion of the colony. Direct trade with France offered few outlets for any products except lumber, and Canadian lumber had only a limited success in competing with supplies from the Baltic. Talon hoped to build up trade with the West Indies in both lumber and fish. There seemed to be a possibility of a triangular trade between Canada, the West Indies, and France similar to that which the English colonies were developing and which in the next century gave such powerful impetus to colonial shipbuilding as well as to commerce. But although such a trade did develop, its proportions were never large. The trip from the St. Lawrence was long, and the river was blocked by ice for half the year. New England was nearer and had more supplies to spare, and the fact that the trade was illegal did not seriously worry the French planters.

Thus while Canada gradually developed as an agricultural community, its commercial life remained bound up with the older staple, which from the first had dominated the colony. It was the fur trade that was the heart of the economy of New France. It was upon this lucrative traffic that the colony depended to balance its imports of needed French manufactures. If it failed, neither the farms nor the forests could sustain a decent level of prosperity. But while the fur trade was the chief source of wealth, it was also a burden that hampered the growth of the colony. It drew many of the energetic youths away from the settled life of the community. It absorbed much of the energy of the colony in an effort at ever-widening expansion under the pressure of English competition from north and south. It led ultimately to a French attempt to dominate the whole of North America and to the struggle for the continent that ended in the downfall of New France.

A Neglected Outpost

While these positive efforts were being made to establish a strong and flourishing colony on the St. Lawrence, an older foothold of French settlement remained an object of almost complete indifference to the government at home. Acadia was the stepchild of French colonial policy.

The great highways of expansion from Europe to the New World passed it by, and its intrinsic value seemed too limited to make it of much concern to either France or England. It lay between the areas in which the chief colonies were taking root, buffeted by the imperial rivalries that were beginning to develop in America, but not yet a prize for which either rival was seriously prepared to contend.

The canceling of De Monts's monopoly in 1607, and his subsequent decision to shift his efforts to the St. Lawrence, did not mean the complete abandonment of the foundation that had been laid at Port Royal. De Monts's associate Poutrincourt was determined to pursue the effort to found a colony in Acadia. He secured a grant of the area for himself, and in 1610 he returned with a party of settlers to resume occupation. His task was not an easy one. He remained dependent on France not only for supplies, but for financial aid. The government was reluctant to help, and when private assistance was secured from Madame de Guercheville, the piety and zeal of that lady brought also an insistence on the establishment of a Jesuit mission. Before long her ideas expanded to the scheme of a colony under Jesuit auspices. She bought out the claim of De Monts, secured a royal grant for Acadia, and in 1613 sent out an expedition under Jesuit auspices, which established the new settlement of St. Sauveur on the island of Mount Desert.

The establishment was short-lived. Already the Jesuits had become engaged in a bitter quarrel with Poutrincourt's son Biencourt, who was in command at Port Royal. Now their new venture brought a prompt reaction from the English who had established themselves in Virginia only six years previously. Remote though the coast of Maine might seem, they had no intention of allowing the intrusion of French Catholic enterprise into lands claimed by the English crown. Sir Thomas Dale, acting governor of the colony, at once sent Samuel Argall to deal with the matter. Only a few weeks after the founding of St. Sauveur it was wiped out by Argall's attack, and its settlers were set adrift or carried off as prisoners. Argall returned to Virginia; in the autumn he sailed once more, this time against Port Royal. It is indicative of the friction between the settlers and the Jesuits that the former accused the Jesuit Father Biard of prompting the new attack. Port Royal, from which the colonists happened to be absent at the moment, was completely devastated. Biencourt and some of the colonists remained in Acadia, living with the natives and trading with furs; but for practical purposes the French colony seemed to have been extinguished.

Into this void there stepped an enterprising Scotsman, Sir William Alexander. In 1621 he persuaded the English king, with little regard for foreign claimants, to grant him the lands between Gaspé and St. Croix under the name of Nova Scotia. During the next two years Alexander made sincere efforts to establish a colony. But he obtained little result, and his ingenious effort to stimulate other patrons to take out settlers in return for titles as baronets of Nova Scotia (for which they would also pay 3000 marks to the canny Alexander) helped him to recoup his own losses but did nothing to populate the colony. There was a brief settlement at Port Royal in 1627, which was aided by the Kirkes as part of their effort to expel France from America. But it took no real root, and it disappeared after the treaty of 1632 returned Acadia as well as Quebec to France.

For a brief moment it seemed that the interest of France in Acadia had at last been awakened. A vigorous soldier, Isaac de Razilly, was sent out as lieutenant general. His energetic efforts resulted in the sending out of some 200 colonists, the re-establishment of Port Royal, and the occupation of several harbors, including La Hève and Penobscot. But Razilly's death in 1636 removed the driving force behind the effort; his posts on the Atlantic coast remained mere fishing and trading depots; and the tiny colony was plunged into a miniature civil war by the rival claims of his successors.

These were Charles de la Tour and Charles d'Aulnay-Charnisay. La Tour was a remarkable character. He had been the friend and companion of Biencourt and claimed to be his heir to Acadia as well. In 1631 he secured the post of lieutenant general. He was an energetic fur trader who was thoroughly at home in the woods and among the Indians, yet his unique personality and his ready adaptability made him equally acceptable to more civilized circles in Boston and London and Paris. From his fort at the mouth of the St. John he sought to control the whole of the fur trade of Acadia. D'Aulnay, a grim and tenacious man, had similar ambitions, and he backed them by his claim to be the heir of Razilly and by efforts at court to secure the governorship of Acadia.

The rivalry broke out in armed conflict. The king sought to settle it in 1638 by dividing Acadia between them, giving the northern shore of the Bay of Fundy to D'Aulnay and the southern shore to La Tour. But since this left the residence of each man entirely surrounded by the territory of the other, it was not a happy inspiration. D'Aulnay continued his intrigues at court. La Tour appealed to Boston for help. Both struggled for control of the region from Canso to the Penobscot—the latter the point of a triangular struggle that involved the Plymouth colonists as well—and occasionally intruded on the domain of a third party, Nicholas Denys, who had been granted the Gulf coast from Canso to Gaspé. In 1645 the conflict reached a climax. Armed with an order that revoked La Tour's authority and commanded his arrest, D'Aulnay in La Tour's absence attacked his fort on the St. John. La Tour's wife conducted the defense with spirit and determination, but eventually the fort was captured, the garrison was remorselessly hanged by D'Aulnay's orders, and Marie de la Tour herself died three weeks later. Yet in the end it was La Tour who triumphed. D'Aulnay met his death in 1650. La Tour was able to re-establish himself in the royal favor and to secure the governorship of Acadia, and in 1653 he solved the question of D'Aulnay's heritage by marrying his widow and settling down at the age of sixty to produce a new family of five children.

But while the local feud was thus ended, external vicissitudes continued. The outbreak of war between England and Holland inspired a project for the capture of the Dutch post of Manhattan. In 1654 preparations were actively under way in Boston for the enterprise; but just as they reached completion, word arrived that peace had been concluded. The New Englanders, having girded themselves for war, found the idea of laying their weapons aside unused too much to endure. If Manhattan could not be attacked, a raid on Acadia—"to spend a lytle tyme upon ye coast in lookeinge after ye ffrench"—was an appealing alternative. Four ships promptly set off; Port Royal and the posts on the St. John and the Penobscot were easily overcome; La Tour was carried off a prisoner, and Acadia was once more in English hands.

La Tour with characteristic address promptly adjusted himself to this turn of fortune. He now claimed his rights as a British subject and backed his contention with substantial evidence. In 1628 his father had been captured by the Kirkes and taken to England. There he ingratiated himself so successfully with the leading authorities that in 1630 he was sent back to Acadia under royal auspices, with baronetcies of Nova Scotia for himself and his son and extensive grants from Sir William Alexander. It is true that on his father's arrival Charles de la Tour virtuously—and prudently—refused to abandon his allegiance to France; but the title stood, and La Tour soon convinced Oliver Cromwell of its validity. He was granted anew the whole region bordering the Bay of Fundy for 100 leagues inland, and promptly cashed in by selling part of his rights to Thomas Temple and William Crowne and retiring from the scene. The ownership of Acadia was becoming more complicated than ever, for new claimants appeared in England, and a creditor of D'Aulnay named Le Borgne had meanwhile been active in asserting his rights and had seized possession of Port Royal a short time before its capture by the English. But in 1667 Acadia was once more restored to France, and its actual transfer—delayed by Temple's efforts to get the English government to reconsider—took place in 1670.

This was the period when New France was being reinvigorated by Colbert and Talon, and it was natural to hope that Acadia would at last benefit from the royal paternalism. Talon's vigorous imagination at once evolved large and constructive schemes for the redeemed province. The limitations of the St. Lawrence as a commercial route had now become apparent. Talon had cast his eyes toward the Hudson as an outlet to an ice-free port and had urged the government to acquire Manhattan from the Dutch. This scheme was forestalled by the English conquest of the Dutch colony; but the return of Acadia seemed to offer a practical alternative. The French were re-established on the Penobscot, and Talon advocated the development of a route between that point and the St. Lawrence, which would connect Acadia with New France. Acadia itself, he felt, could with a little encouragement develop a substantial trade with both the West Indies and Quebec, and he pressed for measures to strengthen the defenses and develop the resources of this long-neglected outpost.

Nothing came of these efforts. By 1672 the French government, preoccupied with the situation in Europe, had largely thrown New France on its own resources and had nothing to spare for Acadia. The new governor brought out sixty settlers in 1671 to bring the population of Acadia to about 500, but that was the extent of aid from France. The colony was left to develop as best it could, still exposed to periodic attacks from without and dependent on its own energy and resources for its growth and even for its survival.

Yet during the next generation this stubborn handful of settlers took root and flourished in spite of vicissitudes and neglect. The population rose to 1100 in 1698 and to 1773 in 1714. It spread out from Port Royal up the Annapolis valley, along the south shore of the Bay of Fundy, and in the region around the Basin of Minas. There were a few fishing settlements on the Atlantic side of the peninsula and a few trading posts west of the St. John, but these never became real centers of settlement. Nor did settlement expand to any extent into the interior. The task of clearing the forested uplands held little attraction for the Acadian. It was the fertile marshlands inundated by the high Fundy tides that offered the best returns for the least effort. Dikes transformed them into farms and pastures; and the frequent complaints of observers about the laziness of the Acadians were an indirect tribute to the ease with which the inhabitants drew their subsistence from the soil.

There was little attempt to create a more varied and more active economy. The fur trade was on a far smaller scale than that of the St. Lawrence region, though it could still lure adventurous spirits away from the farms. The combination of fishing, farming, and shipbuilding that Nova Scotia developed at a later period was hardly apparent during the French regime. Fishing was carried on in the Bay of Fundy and small boats were built for that purpose, but the wider opportunities of the Atlantic cod fishery were left largely to New Englanders. Partly for this reason, Talon's vision of Acadia as a center of trade with the West Indies failed to develop for lack of an adequate staple, and there was little exchange between the St. Lawrence and the Bay of Fundy. The chief trade connection was with Boston, from which manufactured goods came in exchange for agricultural products. Content with a modest standard of living, and stubbornly refusing to be prodded into more ambitious efforts, the Acadians clung to their comfortable settlements with little attention to the outside world. But they were in occupation of a strategic position with which other parts of the world became increasingly concerned; and the inoffensiveness of the Acadians did not save them from becoming pawns in the international rivalries that developed at the end of the seventeenth century and in which the colony was shortly to be engulfed.

(Public Archives of Canada)

Jean–Baptiste Colbert.

A View of the Intendants Palace. — Vûe du Palais de l'Intendant.

Drawn on the Spot by Rich.ᵈ Short. — Engraved by William Elliott

Publish'd according to Act of Parliament Apr.t 5 1761 by Thos.s Short.

Chapter 4

The Structure of New France

The Seigniorial System

The direct effort by the royal government to create a populous settlement on the St. Lawrence was both brief and uncharacteristic. Throughout almost the whole period of French rule there were persistent attempts to devolve the responsibility for colonization on private individuals. At the same time the need for a definite system of land tenure, which arose immediately from the decision to plant a settled colony, naturally led to the introduction of the forms that existed in France. The result of these twin factors was the establishment of the seigniorial system in Canada.

In one aspect the adoption of the seigniorial system represented an effort to encourage colonization by private enterprise. The forms of feudalism were to be used to stimulate the profit motive, strengthened by the added incentive of social prestige. Accompanying this, however, was the desire to use the system as an agency of discipline and authority. The central control of the royal government was to be supplemented by the creation of a small privileged class of landholders under whom the bulk of the population would form a submissive tenantry.

Colonization and feudalism were thus linked from the beginning. The charter issued to the Marquis de la Roche in 1598 gave him authority to parcel out seigniories to gentlemen and persons of merit "on the condition that they shall aid in the support and defense of the territories." Similar powers were given to later monopolists. The precise obligations with respect to colonization that were undertaken by the Company of New France gave fresh importance to their right to issue seigniorial grants. After its first direct efforts met disaster at the hands of David and Thomas Kirke in 1628, the Company lost its enthusiasm for the expensive and risky work of transporting colonists. It fell back on an effort to induce private individuals to take over the labor and cost of such ventures in return for seigniories. When the royal government took over the colony it continued the seigniorial system; and although at one stage the idea was entertained of abandoning it in favor of direct tenancies under the Crown,[1] it remained in fact the basis of the land system throughout the Old Regime.

As an agency for promoting settlement, feudalism was a complete failure. Only three grants of seigniories were made before 1627. One of these was to the Jesuit Order; and, of the two lay seigniories that were granted, one was revoked shortly afterwards. The Company of New France granted sixty seigniories, but the possessors showed more interest in getting titles to extensive lands than in clearing and settling them. By 1663 the contrast between these vast holdings and the sparse and struggling population of the colony was so glaring that a royal decree provided for the confiscation of all estates that were not cleared within the next six months. This, however, brought little improvement, and the grants made by the royal government in its turn were no more effective as incentives to vigorous efforts toward colonization on the part of the recipients.

In fact the incentive was out of proportion to the burdens involved. Enterprising gentlemen in Paris were quite ready to engross large tracts of land for speculative purposes—witness Jean de Lauzon, who accumulated the whole right bank of the St. Lawrence from the region of Montreal to that of Quebec and furnished it with a total of thirteen settlers. But the prospect of seigniorial dignity and estates was not a lure that tempted men of substance to abandon their loved and familiar France and start a new career in the wilderness. The nobility, apart from a few adventurous or impecunious members, preferred the society of the Court with its varied opportunities for pleasure or advancement. Well-to-do merchants were content with the scope for their talents which they found at home and preferred the amenities of urban France to the rude pioneering life of a remote continent. A few officers attracted to the new land, a few petty bourgeois or aspiring tradesmen, might be tempted to try their fortunes in New France. Such men, however, lacked the capital necessary for vigorous and successful efforts at colonization. Many of them lacked the urge as well and were more interested in plunging into the fur trade than in clearing and developing their virgin estates. It was an exceptional seignior who was willing to devote money and energy to improving his lands, let alone to the

---

[1]"Since it has become apparent that the great number of seigniories has been only too prejudicial to the settlement of Canada, it was resolved some years ago not to grant any more; His Majesty has already explained this to Sieurs Vaudreuil and Bégon in his despatch of June 15, 1716, and his intention has by no means changed. In future he means to grant concessions only *en roture*." Dispatch to the Marquis de Vaudreuil, May 23, 1719. W. B. Munro, *Documents Relating to the Seigniorial Tenure in Canada*, p. 160.

far more expensive and uncertain task of seeking out and transporting settlers from France, who might promptly desert their farms to become *coureurs de bois*. During the period when the government undertook the work of bringing out settlers, the seigniors willingly cooperated in finding places for them. But when the brief activity of the royal government came to an end, so did any substantial immigration. Clerical orders such as the Jesuits and Sulpicians were more active than private individuals in improving their lands and increasing the numbers of settlers on them, but even their success was only moderately impressive in relation to the extent of their holdings.

Periodically, indeed, the government felt that the system offered positive obstacles to settlement and tried to prod both seigniors and tenants into fulfilling their obligations. Such efforts met with limited success. The order of 1663 for the confiscation of uncleared lands remained a dead letter. So did the modified decree of 1679 providing for an annual withdrawal of one-twentieth of every land grant found to be uncleared. Landlords waited for the gradual expansion of settlement to reach their holdings, and tenants often preferred the excitement of the fur trade to the labor of clearing their farms. At the other end of the scale, seigniors with lands in areas that were filling up naturally tried to exact the highest possible returns from prospective tenants and to keep their own expenditures to a minimum. Sometimes they neglected to give proper title deeds at the outset and then sought to impose higher terms on tenants who had cleared their farms. To check these irregularities the king in 1711 issued the Arrêts of Marly, whose purpose was to bring uniformity into the operation of the seigniorial system. Seigniors were forbidden to refuse grants to willing settlers or to charge any bonus for such grants. If they remained obstinate the settler might apply to the government, which would place him on the desired lands on the terms current in the district and would collect his dues for the benefit of the treasury. Added to this risk of partial confiscation were renewed threats of complete forfeiture if a seigniory remained uncleared; and the tenant was equally liable to lose his holding if he failed to improve it. In actual fact these threats were not serious in operation, but the decrees gave new force to the obligations assumed by both seigniors and tenants when they entered into possession of their lands.

The obligations of the tenant toward the seignior, though based in form on those which existed in France, were very different in substance. Many of the feudal rights that created the deepest grievances among the French peasantry were by their very nature inapplicable to Canadian conditions. The right of a lord to hunt over a tenant's land or to keep pigeons that fed on his crops was meaningless in a pioneer country. The obligation to bake bread in the seigniorial oven was impossible to enforce in these scattered settlements, where roads were almost nonexistent. All the same it was frequently included in the terms of grant, but many seigniors would have been seriously perturbed if they had been called upon to provide adequate oven accommodation, and the inclusion was perhaps dictated by a vague hope that the tenant might later be induced to pay a small sum for exemption from this provision. Of all the *banalités* of this type which existed in France, only the duty of the tenant to have his grain ground in the lord's mill was general in Canada. Even this was more to the advantage of the tenant than of the seignior during this period, for the toll rarely offset the expense, and the government often had to bring pressure to get the seignior to build a mill for the benefit of his tenants as well as to prevent him from charging exorbitant rates.

The chief dues were summed up under the heads of *corvée, cens et rentes,* and *lods et ventes.* The *corvée* was the obligation on the part of the tenant to work for a certain number of days on the seignior's land. Like the other obligations, its extent depended on the terms of the grant, and even then it must not exceed the limits set by the Custom of Paris. In fact it was hardly ever required before the eighteenth century, and even after that the demands were light. In general it amounted to from three to six days a year, and exemption could be secured by a small money payment. There was in addition the royal *corvée* requiring work on roads and fortifications, but that also was too light to be felt as a serious grievance.

The *cens et rentes* formed the main body of dues that the tenant paid to the seignior and on which the latter depended for revenue from his estate. The *cens* was an annual money payment; the *rentes* might be fixed in either money or produce. The first was little more than nominal. The second was usually fixed low at first to attract settlers, and custom as well as the provisions of the Arrêts of Marly combined to keep the rate extremely moderate. Governor James Murray estimated in 1766 that the average habitant paid a quitrent of about a dollar for a hundred acres. Annually at Michaelmas the tenants assembled at the manor house to pay their dues, "each bringing with him a capon or two, oats by the bushel, or other products of his lands." It was a gala occasion, on which the seignior was expected to be generous in his hospitality, and he might be lucky to have any balance of profit left after his feasting tenantry departed.

The *lods et ventes* were payable to the seignior when the tenant disposed of his holding by sale or gift or when it passed to other hands except by direct inheritance. Nominally it amounted to one-twelfth of the purchase price, but of this the seignior normally remitted one-third. It was only toward the end of the period that this became of importance, for the prevalence of large families generally assured a direct heir—indeed, the problem was one of too many heirs and excessive subdivision. It was the increase of population and the growth of the chief towns that brought greater activity in the transfer of real estate and helped to swell the revenues of the seigniors whose holdings were favorably located.

In fact, although the seigniorial system incorporated certain of the forms of feudalism, the essence of the feudal relationship was almost totally absent. The existence of two distinct social classes was assumed, but their respective rights and duties were determined by the royal government and exercised under its constant supervision. The seignior had a definite social position, which carried with it tangible marks of prestige. He was entitled to formal homage as well as to habitual respect from his tenants. He had his special pew in the most honorable place in church and precedence at religious festivals. He had judicial powers that were comprehensive in theory, though in practice they were confined to the settlement of minor local disputes. But he was not a member of a privileged aristocracy as was the noble in France. Many seigniors did receive patents of nobility—a type of reward to leading citizens that was designed to stimulate the energy of their fellows—but more often the status of the seignior bore closer resemblance to that of the English squire. The noble in France had privileges and rights that he could assert even against the Crown. The Canadian seignior did not even have an unconditional and prescriptive right to his lands, for the Crown might step in to dictate the terms that he must give his tenants and even to confiscate his seigniory if he failed to act as an efficient agent for colonization. Nor was the seignior as a rule a person of fortune. Wealth was rare in the colony and was usually acquired by merchants or fur traders rather than by landholders. Many of the impecunious gentry sought to better their lot through government posts or an army career or by engaging in the fur trade. The situation improved somewhat as the colony developed; but Govenor Murray described the gentry as generally poor, even though on reflection he considered that they were able to support their dignity.

Thus while a sharp social distinction existed between seignior and habitant, the economic gulf was often very small. The Canadian settler had a standard of life that for all its modesty was far above that of the French peasant. The seigniorial dues sat lightly upon him. His lands were virgin soil which, once cleared, produced an abundance that tempted him at times to slovenly methods of farming such as earned the disapproval of outside observers. The forest and the rivers were at his doors to provide an abundance of game and fish. He had a comfort and an independence that many impoverished gentlemen of France might envy. If he accepted the seignior as his social superior, he was ready to resist undue economic exploitation, and he could always escape to the fur trade or to lands on another seigniory. Observers felt that he took life lightly and gave little thought to the morrow. If he was deeply religious and generally law-abiding, he was also sensitive and inclined to be quarrelsome—in the words of one official, "naturally indocile." His argumentative temper and a concern with petty interests made litigation one of his favorite recreations —a form of diversion that gained wide scope from the vagueness of many land grants, and which was possibly encouraged by the otherwise happy simplicity of judical procedure.

In justice, as in administration, the intendant played a central role. While seigniorial courts, where they existed, could deal with petty suits or misdemeanors, the intendant had the power of summary decision in civil suits involving less than 100 livres. Other cases, civil as well as criminal, went to courts of first instance in the three towns, though the intendant might serve as arbitrator in civil cases at the request of the parties. The Council, presided over by the intendant, served as a court of appeal, and in serious matters as a court of first instance. The effectiveness of the system may have been due in no small measure to the exclusion of lawyers from the colony. Notaries carried out the necessary work of drawing legal documents, but a royal decree in 1667 declared that it was not to the colony's advantage to admit barristers. As the Baron de Lahontan observed with typical liveliness, if justice was sold in Canada, at least it was sold more cheaply than in France. "In Canada we do not pass through the clutches of advocates, the talons of attorneys, and the claws of clerks. Our Themis is prompt, and she does not bristle with fees, costs and charges."

A factor of significance in the structure of the colony was the military establishment. The withdrawal of the Carignan-Salières regiment was followed by the dispatch of several companies of *Troupes de la Marine*, and by 1668 New France had a garrison of some 1500. The numbers fluctuated —Vaudreuil complained in 1716 that he had only 628 regulars available— but on the eve of the Seven Years' War this had risen to around 2700. The economic effect was far from negligible. Provisions for the garrison, work on the fortifications, hard cash provided to pay the troops, all contributed to internal commerce in the colony to the advantage of merchants and habitants.

The regular force was supplemented by the local militia. A royal order of 1669 called for the raising in each parish of a company in which every able-bodied man between the ages of sixteen and sixty was liable for service. The companies were commanded by a captain of militia whose functions soon extended far beyond his military duties. In the words of Helen Manning,[2] he was "a mayor, fire-chief, road boss and chief of police rolled into one." He became the official chiefly responsible for attending to local needs and for implementing the directives of the central administration, and in practical matters he often exercised an authority more important than that of the seignior. The choice for such an appointment normally fell on men who exercised influence and commanded confidence in their own communities, and who consequently formed an invaluable link between the administration and the mass of the population.

It was a rude, yet in some respects a lively society that grew up on the banks of the St. Lawrence. The circumstances surrounding the fur trade accentuated certain frontier aspects, including a tendency to bursts of riotous living after a successful venture into the woods. Behind the fur trade stood a small but substantial class of urban merchants, who were also responsible for the normal commercial life of the colony, and who with the officials formed a leading society in the three principal towns, which in 1754 contained one-quarter of the population. Quebec as the capital was particularly distinguished by an active social life. The love of gaiety and social gatherings was occasionally deplored by authorities, both clerical and lay. One curious reflection of this was the concern of the government over the growing number of horses in the colony, which allowed their owners too many facilities for paying social visits, and which some officials feared would bring a decline in their adeptness in traveling by snowshoe.[3] But the faults on the whole were venial, and the sober virtues underneath —bravery, piety, frugality—did much to balance these defects.

To these people the seignorial system was no burden. It provided a social and economic framework that was both familiar and acceptable. If it did not actually stimulate colonization, it did provide an organized system within which settlement could expand. Such occasional obstacles as it presented were probably less serious than those which arose out of the large-scale land speculation that was one outgrowth of the English system of free enterprise in the colonies to the south. And as an element in an authoritarian structure of government the seigniorial system proved its

---

[2]Helen Manning, *The Revolt of French Canada, 1800-1835,* Toronto, 1962, p. 21.

[3]The first horse in the colony was a gift to Governor Montmagny in 1647. It was only in 1665 that a dozen horses arrived for the use of the habitants. By 1698 the number had grown to 684, and eight years later there were 1872 horses in New France.

worth, giving to the small community of New France a coherence and a responsiveness to central direction that enabled it to sustain for half a century a growing rivalry with the neighboring English colonies in spite of their overwhelming numerical superiority. If the work of settlement in New France could have proceeded as a single-minded activity, unhampered by the constant distraction of the fur trade, the contribution of the system to the outcome might have been far more striking than it actually appeared.

The Church in the Colony

The royal government, the seigniorial system, the Catholic church—on these three pillars rested the social and political structure of the settled colony of New France. Of the three, the church was by no means the least important. Its influence pervaded the whole of colonial life. Its head occupied a leading and at times a dominant position in the government of the colony. It occupied a major place in the seigniorial system, with something like two-sevenths of the granted lands held by various religious bodies. It was these bodies that maintained the hospitals and provided the only educational facilities that existed within the colony. The clergy took a direct and active part in the political and economic life of the colony and linked both these aspects intimately with the spiritual life, over which they exercised a unique and unchallenged control.

From the outset a dual motive animated Catholic enterprise in New France. Missionary zeal was fired by the prospect of converting the Indians to Christianity, and this vision was accompanied by a desire to plant a French Catholic colony as a solid base for the establishment of the faith in the New World. In the latter aim the religious and nationalist elements were so intertwined as to be virtually inseparable. Each was the handmaid of the other; and in New France, despite exceptions, there was almost as little place for the Catholic foreigner as there was for the French heretic.

Champlain himself was the embodiment of this attitude. He ardently desired the extension of the Catholic faith as well as the expansion of French power. In 1615, after persistent efforts, he secured the dispatch of four Récollets to Canada. This order, a branch of the Franciscans, gradually realized that the immense task of evangelizing a continent was beyond their unaided resources. They appealed for help to the powerful and wealthy Society of Jesus, whose missionary activities already embraced four continents and extended from Paraguay to Japan. The Jesuits had already become interested in North America through their first and unpropitious efforts in Acadia. In 1625, three Jesuit priests with two assistants arrived at Quebec. It was the beginning of one of the most remarkable passages in the history of the continent.

The work of the Jesuits, like that of the Hundred Associates, was interrupted by the English capture of Quebec before it had fairly begun. With the restoration of the colony to France, however, the Jesuits found themselves in a new and stronger position. The Récollets, to their disappointment, were forbidden to return to Quebec. It was not until 1669 that the influence of Talon enabled them to resume their missionary activities. Meanwhile the Jesuits were placed in sole charge of the spiritual affairs of the colony. For a quarter of a century, until the coming of the Sulpicians to Montreal in 1657, the Jesuits enjoyed a virtual monopoly, only slightly modified by an underlying rivalry on the part of the Montreal community; and their ascendancy extended over political and social life to an extent that made the colony a veritable theocracy.

Their rule undoubtedly contributed much to the advancement of New France. Precarious as its fortunes were before 1663, they might have failed altogether had it not been for the measure of interest which the Jesuits kept alive in influential circles. Their chief instrument to this end was the annual publication of their *Relations* from 1632 to 1673. These reports to their superiors in France enjoyed a remarkable popularity and aroused very wide interest. Naturally the achievements of the Jesuits themselves formed the main theme and lost nothing in the telling. But these accounts were propaganda for Canada as well as for the Society of Jesus. The authors consciously sought to attract support and secure colonists for the new land. They painted its attractions in glowing colors. They stressed the mundane as well as the spiritual advantages awaiting the enterprising settler. They presented it as a terrestrial paradise where eternal salvation as well as daily bread could be won with ease. "To live in New France," wrote one in a burst of enthusiasm, "is truly to live in the bosom of God."

Within the colony, however, the ascendancy of the Jesuits was far from producing harmony or tranquility. It was the fate of the order, in Canada as elsewhere, to attract a bitter hostility from many and diverse quarters. Its power and influence aroused much jealousy. The vigor and tenacity of its methods gave rise to resentment against what seemed its unlimited desire to subordinate all other elements in society to its authority. Its high aims and rigid discipline held natural attractions for fanatics who were the sort of members most likely to volunteer for service in a land that offered many openings for aspiring martyrs. But fanatics are neither comfortable colleagues nor tolerant rulers. The Jesuits were soon involved in friction with almost all the other groups in the colony. The other clergy resented their dictatorial attitude. Merchants objected to their interference with the fur trade. Reasonably devout inhabitants showed some impatience at their continuous and narrow supervision over all social and intellectual matters. Civil authorities were affronted by Jesuit attempts to dictate various policies on the ground that these were matters affecting faith and morals. Not all the blame was on one side by any means; but it can be understood how the Jesuit efforts to eliminate all taint of sin from the community should appear to others, and particularly to those who were jealous of their own liberty or authority, as nothing less than an insatiable craving for absolute power.

There were also practical disadvantages on the purely spiritual side. The paramount interest of the Jesuits in missionary activity made them reluctant to divert their energies to parish work within the colony. Yet the growth of settlement brought a demand for parish priests who would reside in the community and minister regularly to its needs. Also arising from the spread of settlement was the desire for a bishop who would exercise unquestioned authority over the various bodies of clergy; and this introduced still another element to complicate the relations between the Jesuits and their clerical rivals.

The church in France had long claimed a national status that implied considerable independence from the direct control of the Papacy. Its Gallican liberties were an affront to the champions of the Pope's supreme authority. Among these ultramontanes the Jesuits were the most stalwart, and they were determined if possible to prevent the incoporation of Canada within the organization of the Gallican church and to place it directly under papal jurisdiction.

The practical issue was raised in 1647, when the Archbishop of Rouen put forward the claim that New France, to which so many of his parishioners had gone, was in effect an extension of his own diocese and subject to his authority. A direct clash was avoided when he had the tact to appoint as his vicar-general the Superior of the Jesuits in New France. But another decade brought matters to a head. The growing rivalry between Quebec and Montreal found expression in pressure from the latter community for the appointment of a Sulpician, Abbé de Queylus, as bishop. The Jesuits at once took counteraction. They put forward as their candidate François de Montmorency-Laval, and through their influence at court they secured royal approval.

Laval was a man after the Jesuits' own heart. His deep devotion was accompanied by a strong and tenacious will and a determination to uphold the fullest claims of his office against any opponent, clerical or lay. His career in consequence was far from tranquil. His insistence at the outset that all the clergy should formally acknowledge his authority gave rise to some passing difficulties. It was not long before he was embroiled with Governor d'Argenson over questions of precedence in which both parties felt that the respective dignities of church and state were involved. The strong-minded prelate and the self-willed Frontenac clashed even more sharply on this issue. Talon, a Gallican who disliked the Jesuits and who felt that the bishop interfered unduly in civil affairs, also had a number of clashes with him. Above all, Laval waged relentless war against the brandy trade, and on this issue he ranged against him not only the civil authorities, but a considerable part of the population.

Yet Laval's active career from 1659 to 1684 was a determining period for the church in New France. When he retired, he left behind him an organization that was firmly established and whose temper and outlook had set its mark on the whole community. His retirement virtually marked the end of the theocracy, already under strong challenge from the new royal government. His successor, Jean Baptiste Saint-Vallier, was equally aggressive but far less judicious. He denounced everything and quarreled with everybody and stirred up such dissension that when he felt impelled to go to France to defend this conduct, the authorities hesitated for three years before allowing him to return to Quebec. In the course of the eighteenth century the relations between the civil and ecclesiastical powers became more tempered, and the bishops tacitly acquiesced in an interpretation of their spiritual authority that avoided serious clashes between church and state.

One of the tasks to which Laval early set himself was the provision of a native clergy to minister to the needs of the colony. It was profoundly characteristic of his approach that he should combine this with arrangements deliberately calculated to exclude any lay interference and to maintain the authority of the bishop at its maximum. The boundaries of the parishes, of which comparatively few had as yet been constituted, tended naturally to coincide with those of the seigniories. When a seignior built a church on his estate he was likely to claim the right to appoint the curé, as was the custom in France. This was one reason why the ecclesiastical authorities preferred to serve the parishes by traveling missionaries rather than by resident priests, and Laval was determined that the curés should be wholly subject to his appointment and control.

In consequence, the seminary that he founded in 1663 was intended to serve a double purpose. The first was the training of Canadians for the priesthood. The second was the creation of a close-knit and disciplined community to which its members would be bound all their lives. They would be sent out as parish priests, but they would be appointed and recalled at will, and everything they possessed would belong to the community. It was a grave blow to Laval when Saint-Vallier decided that the growing number of the clergy made this integration unworkable and separated the parish from the seminary. But Saint-Vallier and his successors continued to insist on the removability of curés, and the lack of an adequate number of priests to serve all the individual parishes justified the continuance of a system of itinerant clergy.

Closely connected with the parish system was the question of finances. Regular tithes were instituted by royal order in 1663, and the rate was fixed at one-thirteenth of everything produced by human toil. Immediately there was a violent outburst of opposition. The habitant loved his church, but not to that high degree. Ultimately the rate was reduced to one-twenty-sixth and applied only to grain. The clergy insisted that the resulting income was quite inadequate for their work and that few parishes provided enough revenue to support a *curé*. It was supplemented by a royal subsidy and by successive grants of land to add to the resources of the church. By 1700 something like half the settlers in the colony lived on these lands and contributed seigniorial dues as well as tithes to the ecclesiastical revenues.

In New France, education as well as religion was the province of the church—indeed, the connection between the two was fundamental in Catholic eyes. Besides Laval's seminary, Quebec had a Jesuit college, which was founded in 1635. The Récollets had a seminary at Three Rivers and the Sulpicians had theirs at Montreal. Laval set up a lesser seminary for the training of young boys and founded a trade school for farming and handicraft. A school for boys was created in Montreal by the Brothers Hospitalers in 1694. The Ursulines at Quebec and Three Rivers and the Congregation of Notre Dame at Montreal, in addition to their charitable labors and care of the sick, devoted themselves to the task "of educating little girls in the fear of the Lord and the practice of Christian virtues," inspired by two remarkable women—Mother Marie de l'Incarnation of the Ursulines and Marguerite Bourgeoys of the Congregation.

Outside the chief towns facilities for education were meager. Some members of the orders undertook the work in the districts to which they were assigned. A few lay teachers were engaged, with dubious success.

The era of universal primary education was still far in the future, and New France was probably not notably backward compared to other countries in the seventeenth century. If observers commented on the ignorance of the average habitant, the cause did not lie solely in the absence of schools. More serious was the censorship that the church exercised over secular thought and reading and the complete absence of any popular press. In New France there was none of the vigorous intellectual life and active public discussion that were so rife in the English colonies. In this respect the church was a powerful instrument of discipline and authority, to the detriment of intellectual freedom and initiative.

In perspective it can be seen that the Jesuits left an enduring stamp upon the colony. If it did not become the terrestrial paradise of which they had dreamed, it was nonetheless a community in which Catholicism was deeply rooted as an integral part of the life of the individual. The parish church was a center around which the life of each settlement revolved. The clergy exercised a guidance and control that extended to lay as well as spiritual matters. There was little serious questioning of the dogma and authority of the church. New France was only lightly touched by the skepticism and speculative philosophy of eighteenth-century France. If there developed an undercurrent of anticlericalism that has continued through subsequent periods, it was essentially a protest, not against religion, but against the extremes to which clerical domination was occasionally pressed, and it was still compatible with a profound devotion to the Catholic faith. There are few countries where the Catholic Church has stood through the intellectual turbulence of three centuries with so little serious challenge as in French Canada.

The Catholic Missions

The story of the early French missions is one less of achievement than of unparalleled devotion and fortitude. The actual record of converts among the Indians is not impressive. Too great a gulf separated the evangelists from their audience. The Indian language with its paucity of abstract terms was the outward expression of a mentality whose grasp was limited to the direct and concrete facts of experience. Indian logic was baffled by the subtleties of European philosophy. The complexities of the Creed left the savage bewildered and contemptuous. He could accept the idea of a Supreme Being but not the moral concepts that are basic to the Christian conception of God. The heaven of the missionaries failed to attract him; their hell failed to appall. Their ethics had little meaning to a primitive and tribal civilization in which gluttony was a social obligation and polygamy an economic asset. Religion to the Indian was bound up with superstition and magic, and as magicians the missionaries were a disappointment. They sadly acknowledged that even their rare converts were prone to backslide at the first opportunity. It was not in the number of souls won, but in the opportunity that their work afforded to testify by their lives to their faith, even to the final crown of martyrdom, that the Jesuit missionaries found their justification.

The Jesuits felt that Indians and settlers should be kept apart until the conversion of the savages had been achieved. They feared, and with good reason, that contact with the French would corrupt the Indians with new vices and place before their eyes examples that were little calculated to testify to the virtues of Christianity. The French government, on the other hand, desired to strengthen and populate the colony by the absorption of the aborigines. Dispatches flowed from Paris instructing the authorities to encourage the Indians to adopt a settled life within the colony, to have their children educated as Frenchmen, and to promote intermarriage with the object of fusing the two peoples into a single race.

The effort at absorption failed completely. A few mission settlements eventually attracted some 1500 Indians but did nothing to change their traditional habits or to turn them into industrious farmers. They clung to their accustomed pursuits as hunters and warriors who left manual labor to women. The idea of catching the Indians young had no more success. Indian parents were reluctant to surrender their children to be brought up in French schools. The few who did enter almost invariably reverted to savage life. "Of a hundred passing through our hands," lamented Marie de l'Incarnation, "scarcely one have we civilized. They may appear docile but when we least expect it they are over our enclosure and off to the forest life." The girls proved more tractable than the boys, but they showed no enthusiasm for domestic life on the French model, and not even the offer of a royal dowry could persuade them to marry Frenchmen and settle down in the colony. There were plenty of unions between French youths and Indian maidens, but the setting was the primitive and roving life of the wilderness, and their offspring remained with the mother and the tribe.

The missionaries who tried to carry the gospel to the Indians in their own habitat encountered other obstacles. Most of the tribes had no fixed habitations, and the missionary who wished for more than a passing contact had to attach himself to a band and follow its wanderings. As a rule he was anything but an honored or even a welcome guest. He was obliged to keep pace with these expert and hardy travelers through the unfamiliar wilderness, taking his full share of the strenuous labors with paddle and pack. He shared their rude and often repulsive life around the campfires or in crowded communal shelters filled with smoke and filth and the stench of unwashed humanity. His life was frequently in danger from the hazards of the journey or the capricious wrath of his savage companions, and his attempts to instruct them in the Christian faith were almost uniformly without result.

The difficulty of making any impression on the migratory tribes was vividly illustrated by the experience of the Jesuit leader Father Paul Le Jeune. He arrived in Canada in 1632, and in the autumn of the following year he attached himself to a band of Montagnais and set out with them on their wanderings. He could scarcely have plunged into a life more different from the one he had so recently known in civilized France. The Indians were wholly dependent on hunting for their food from day to day. All during the winter they were on the move through the snow-filled forests from the St. Lawrence to northern Maine. The Jesuit had to keep up with their march, traveling on unfamiliar snowshoes and carrying a pack of unaccustomed weight. When they halted it was in scanty and improvised shelters, and food was often lacking for two or three days at a time. At one stage Le Jeune was reduced to eating the eelskin with which he had patched his garments. Existence centered on the dominating physical problem of keeping alive, and Le Jeune could rouse little interest in theology among his companions. His strange costume and appearance made him the butt of crude wit; his efforts to combat the superstitions of the savages roused the active hostility of the sorcerer who was a member of the band. By the time he returned to Quebec in the spring, Le Jeune had reached the conviction that such experiences could bear little fruit. He had accomplished his desire to learn the Algonkin tongue, but this type of nomadic life offered only a barren field for missionary effort. It was only under more settled conditions that it could succeed; and, until the Indians could be persuaded to take up fixed abodes around French posts, the best hope lay with the tribes that led a more stable existence.

Of these the easiest of access were the Hurons, who were allies of the French and who had relatively established villages in the region south of Georgian bay. They had shown a reluctance to allow Europeans to enter their country, but in spite of this the Récollet Le Caron was able to pay them a visit in 1615 and the Jesuit, Jean de Brébeuf, spent some time among them in 1626. Little came of these first approaches, and the English capture of Quebec interrupted the work for a time. In 1634, however, the Hurons were persuaded to allow Brébeuf and two companions to return to their country, and a real beginning was made in the mission to Huronia.

The work progressed slowly. Life even in these semipermanent settlements was still primitive. The savages showed a continued reluctance to accept the strange habits and standard and beliefs that the Jesuits urged upon them, and whose acceptance was apt to mark the convert as a social outcast. Conversion was so uncertain a business, indeed, that the priests for a long time restricted baptism chiefly to children and only extended it to adults who were on the point of death and would have no opportunities for backsliding. The medicine men were quick to blame the presence and activities of the newcomers for any natural calamities, and their lives were frequently in danger. Efforts to extend the mission to the Neutral and Tobacco nations met with even greater perils and more definite rebuffs. It gradually took firmer root in the Huron country; but for a decade the number of converts grew only slowly, and it was not until the Iroquois menace closed upon them that the Huron in desperation turned to the magic of the black robes for temporal rather than spiritual salvation.

It had been intended at first to plant permanent missions in each of the principal Huron villages. This plan was modified as the dangers involved in it became apparent. It was decided instead to create a permanent center from which the missionaries would go out in pairs to the surrounding settlements and where they might retire for safety in time of need. Here too the converts could be gathered to preserve them from corrupting influences and to teach them a settled and civilized mode of life. Ste. Marie, a short distance southeast of the present town of Midland, was chosen as the site, and here a permanent group of buildings was set up in 1639 as the center of a growing Christian community.

The dawning hope of ultimate success in winning the Huron nation to the true faith was ruined by the Iroquois war. The determination of the Iroquois to wipe out their commercial rivals involved the Jesuit missions in the resulting catastrophe. During the first years of hostilities the issue was uncertain, and enemy ravages fell chiefly on the fringes of the Huron country. In 1648, however, there was a deeper thrust. Trade necessities compelled the warriors from St. Joseph, the southernmost of the mission centers, to go to the French settlements, leaving the village virtually defenseless. In their absence the Iroquois fell upon St. Joseph, killing or capturing the remaining inhabitants. The priest who served the community, Father Anthony Daniel, was among the victims; the church as well as the other structures in the village was burned, and only desolation remained. Within a few months there fell a still more crushing blow. In the course of the winter a thousand Iroquois warriors made their way toward the Huron country. In March they fell on the settlements of St. Ignace and St. Louis, capturing and devastating them; and among the captives were Brébeuf and his companion Father Gabriel Lalemant, whose torture and martyrdom brought the tragedy of the Huron mission to a climax.

The position of the main establishment at Ste. Marie was reduced to hopelessness by these events. A desperate counterattack by the Huron beat the Iroquois back almost from its walls; and although the Iroquois recovered and drove the Huron in flight, they felt impelled to retreat to their own lands. But there was no hope that this would be anything more than a temporary respite. The Huron, broken and panic-stricken, were ready to abandon their country. The mission was left defenseless, and in the summer of 1649 the Jesuits withdrew from St. Marie. An attempt to re-establish it on St. Joseph's Island in Georgian Bay was a failure. By 1650 it was given up, and the priests with a few hundred converts set out for the shelter of Quebec. The rest of the Huron who survived were scattered across the continent, and the mission to Huronia was at an end.

There were no other regions that offered comparable opportunities. The Iroquois had also semipermanent settlements, but their hostility was implacable. A priest named Father Isaac Jogues, who was captured and tortured in 1642, felt that his sufferings might serve to open up this field. He escaped with maimed hands and scarred body, only to return with unflinching courage to found the Mission of the Martyrs and to meet his death in 1646. During the next forty years there were repeated efforts to carry Christianity to the Iroquois, but though a certain number of converts were won over, the impact on these pagan tribes was slender at best.

Yet the disaster that wiped out the hopeful experiment in Huronia was only one episode in the story of steadily expanding missionary activity. While it was under way, other fields had not been neglected. The priests continued their efforts among the Montagnais and extended them to such eastern tribes as the Micmac and Abenaki. The influence of the Jesuits spread steadily westward as they sought to keep contact with their disciples among the dispersed Huron. They established a mission at Sault Ste. Marie and extended their labors around Lake Superior. Récollets and Sulpicians vied with them in opening new fields among the western tribes, and the work steadily expanded in the region of the Great Lakes and into the valley of the Mississippi. Priests followed the path of the fur trade and joined the explorers who were extending the French penetration of the continent.

Their zeal for their faith was accompanied by an almost equal zeal for their country. Father Le Jeune had urged the establishment of forts in the interior, not merely to facilitate the work of the missionaries, but to forestall the English and extend the power and glory of France. His successors were equally ardent in their patriotism; and in the expansion of New France that was under way by the latter part of the seventeenth century, religion and commerce and French imperialism continued to march side by side.

This meant continued contact with the Indians. The ability of the French in Canada to establish harmonious personal relations with the Indians, in contrast to the chronic hostility that marked the history of the present United States, has been variously attributed to the Latin temperament and to the flexibility of Roman Catholicism as contrasted with American Puritanism. Yet there were Scottish Puritans in the posts on Hudson Bay, where amiable and even intimate relations were far from uncommon. The real operative factors were the pressure for land in the Thirteen Colonies in contrast to the paramount importance of the fur trade in New France; and where in the one case the Indian was an obstacle to be eliminated, in the other he was an essential asset if the fur trade was to prosper or even survive.

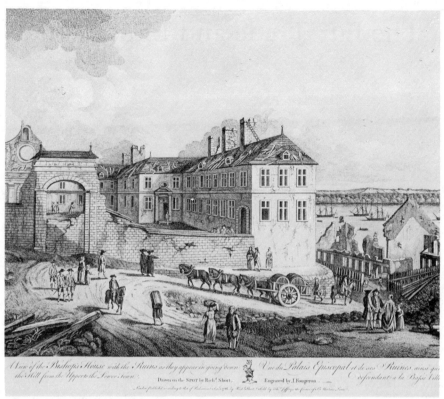

The Bishop's House at Quebec.
A drawing by Richard Short.

Habitants Paying Tithes.

Chapter 5

The Fur Trade and Expansion

The Growth of the Fur Trade

The fur trade in Canada began as a side line. Fishing vessels that touched the coast found it useful to take along a few trinkets or tools to barter with the natives and to carry back a few furs to be sold in France. But the sudden vogue for fur dictated by fashion at the end of the sixteenth century changed all that. In particular, the discovery that beaver fur was ideal for felt hats gave rise to a tremendous demand and made beaver the staple of the fur trade in North America.

This, however, was a precarious economic foundation on which to build a colony. Fashions changed, and demand varied with the changes. The supply also fluctuated, and its ups and downs did not always coincide with those of the market. Yet New France depended on the prosperity of the trade not only for its official revenues, but also for the exportable surplus with which to balance its imports of manufactured goods from Europe. The exhaustion of accessible areas or the closing of the fur trade routes by the Iroquois wars, no less than a decline in the price of furs in Europe, could threaten the colony with disaster. In the eighteenth century the trade was valued at about 1,500,000 livres a year, and about half this came from beaver skins. But the annual variations ranged all the way from 212,000 livres in 1726 to nearly 4,000,000 in 1754—a state of affairs that was hardly conducive to economic stability.

Among the Algonkin the habit of wearing beaver robes in winter was one of the best ways of producing prime pelts. The skins were first scraped on the underside, which loosened the long, coarse guard hairs. Then they were trimmed and made into garments, which were worn next to the skin. This gradually detached the guard hairs, leaving the smooth rich fur—the fat beaver or *castor gras*. But as the Indians acquired European textiles they wore fewer fur robes and preferred to trade the fresh skins (*castor sec*) for supplies. At one time, when the shortage of labor in the colony brought a suggestion that Negroes should be imported, the argument that they could not stand the climate was countered by the proposal that they be clothed in beaver robes whose quality they would improve by a winter's wear. But the demand for prime beaver also diminished as the hatmakers began to use larger proportions of dry beaver and as hats themselves became smaller in size. The fur trade had to contend with constant uncertainties at both ends of the scale.

The trade was at first carried on at the main posts along the St. Lawrence. The first of these was Tadoussac at the mouth of the Saguenay. It was soon evident, however, that the area tapped by the Saguenay was comparatively limited. Three Rivers at the mouth of the St. Maurice offered greater possibilities, but this too became secondary to Montreal. The Ottawa was the great route that led to the vast fur areas of the west, and from the early meeting with the Indians who came to trade at the Lachine rapids there developed a growing activity, which was to make Montreal for nearly two centuries the leading fur-trade center of the continent.

In the early days the traders waited for the Indians to bring their furs to the posts. This had the obvious advantage of making the Indian bear the overhead of transportation. But there were disadvantages as well. The Huron and Ottawa soon became middlemen, who stood between the French purchasers and the tribes of the upper Great Lakes who had furs to trade. From the days when Champlain sent his young men into the interior there were constant efforts by the French to break through this barrier and to establish direct contact with the original source of supply.

Two developments hastened this process. One was the exhaustion of the fur-producing areas in the region of the St. Lawrence. Second and even more important was the interruption of the Ottawa route during the struggle with the Iroquois and the dispersal of the Huron and Ottawa as a result of Iroquois attacks. For a time the colony was threatened with ruin. Not a single fur reached Montreal from the Upper Country in 1652. Next year however a few canoes got through, and in 1654 a fuller resumption of trade brought important consequences. The scattered Huron and Ottawa had made contact with western tribes, such as the Cree and Sioux, who had not hitherto been introduced to European products. These uninitiated savages were pathetically grateful for a chance to exchange large quantities of furs for worn-out knives and needles and pots. New vistas of trade opened up before the eyes of the despairing colonists. In 1654 two Frenchmen were permitted to return with the Indians to the

Upper Country to develop these opportunities. It was the first step in a process that soon resulted in the French taking over the Ottawa route and a further shift of the principal trading centers to Michilimackinac and Green Bay and Sault Ste. Marie.

This in turn altered the character of the trade in relation to the colony. When the Indians brought their furs to the St. Lawrence and when the fur-bearing areas were near at hand, the individual colonist could engage in the fur trade with little difficulty and even as a side line to other activities. Now, however, the overhead was apt to be too great for him. Distance and the resulting problem of transportation—those two factors so fundamental to the whole history of Canadian economic development—imposed the need for substantial financial backing beyond the resources of the average settler. The fur trade was passing into the realm of big business, and its organization and control fell into the hands of substantial merchants in Quebec and Montreal, whose French connections assured them markets and credit and who could finance relatively large-scale expeditions.

At the same time the conflict between fur trade and settlement became more acute than ever. It was no longer so profitable for the restless habitant to go off to the woods for a few weeks during the winter and return to spend an industrious summer on his farm. Many in fact had already shown a preference for life in the forest as a permanent career. The freedom and the dangers of the fur trade no less than its financial rewards lured them to become *coureurs de bois*. With the shift of the trading centers to the west the need for such men increased, and the occupation now demanded their full energies. Some of the Indians planted settlements near the posts, going out to hunt during the winter and returning to trade their furs in spring or summer. But the trade depended more and more on the Frenchmen who sought out more distant tribes in their villages. These men set out with the brigades that carried goods from Montreal to such posts as Michilimackinac. Thence they scattered south and west of the Great Lakes to trade with Indians who would not make long journeys to the posts. With the furs they gathered they returned to Montreal to share the profits with the merchant who had financed the expedition and who usually secured the lion's share of the returns. Such an expedition meant that the *coureur* was absent for at least a year and often for two or three. By drawing off increasing numbers of young and energetic men, the fur trade thus hampered the development of agriculture and the growth of the settled colony.

This situation placed the colonial authorities in a chronic dilemma. On the one hand they wanted to reduce the drain on settlement to the minimum. The plaints of the seigniors over desertions by their tenants and the consequent loss of seigniorial revenues added to the government's concern over the slow progress of agriculture. On the other hand the collapse of the fur trade would threaten the ruin of the colony. Even under the best of conditions the retention of the trade involved a constant struggle against the ever-present pressure of English competition. If the number of *coureurs* were reduced or their vigor and initiative discouraged, the adverse results would be felt almost immediately in New France. Between these two evils the government wavered in a compromising policy, which in theory imposed strict curbs on the settler to force him to remain on the land and in practice placed few effective obstacles in his way if he was determined to take to the woods.

The attitude of the Church was less ambiguous. The clergy as well as other landlords had solid reasons for wanting to hold the settlers on their farms. Furs paid neither tithes nor seigniorial dues, and the revenues of the Church suffered from every settler who deserted his holding, particularly if it was on lands belonging to the Church. But this was a secondary consideration compared to the moral aspect. The *coureur* was apt to be a spiritual as well as a financial loss. He escaped from the constant and diligent supervision that the Church was able to exercise over the souls of more settled parishioners. He easily and even enthusiastically adopted the pagan code and habits of his savage companions. He was apt to plunge with equal enthusiasm into dissipation and riot when he returned to civilization. To make matters worse, while he himself succumbed to the vices of the Indians, he was prone at the same time to introduce to them the vices of Europeans. The missionaries had difficulty enough in weaning the natives from their own brand of sin. Their acquisition of a second set of iniquities made the task almost impossible. The Church made strenuous efforts to keep French and Indians apart until the Indians had been won to Catholicism. "What hope can we have of bringing the Indians to Christ," they lamented, "when all the sinners of the colony are permitted to come here and give Christianity the lie by an open exhibition of bad morals!"

By the time the royal government took over the colony in 1663 the whole problem was serious. The fact that definite efforts were now made to increase the colony by officially sponsored immigration raised in acute form the question of the relation of colonization to the fur trade. The simultaneous and growing demands of the fur trade for increased French personnel added to the difficulties. Through the twenty years of peace that followed Tracy's chastisement of the Iroquois the problem gave rise to incessant agitation, and the complexities that it presented were of paramount concern all through the governorship of Frontenac.

The Regime of Frontenac

Louis de Buade, Comte de Frontenac, was appointed governor of New France in 1672. Behind him lay a long military career, which he had begun in 1635 at the age of fifteen. His qualities as a soldier were ultimately to prove of the highest importance to France in a new period of crisis. His qualifications as a civil administrator, in contrast, were by no means obvious. His love of lavish display coupled with his complete lack of judgment in the handling of his personal finances had already involved him in monetary difficulties, which his appointment was perhaps meant to ease. His imperious nature and his insistence on all the dignities due to his office involved him in violent quarrels over infinitely petty matters. The situation was not eased by his fiery temper and the outbursts of rage that he visited on those who displeased him. His first period of office was largely concerned with matters of internal policy, and his handling of these problems was not generally marked by either wisdom or restraint.

When Frontenac arrived in New France, Talon was just retiring and Laval was temporarily absent. There was thus neither bishop nor intendant to challenge the governor's supremacy. This did not prevent him from being embroiled almost at once with other dignitaries. The colony was soon rent by a controversy over Frontenac's forcible attempt to discipline the governor of Montreal for breaches of the fur-trade regulations. One of the leading Sulpicians became involved in the tangle to the extent of preaching a heated sermon against Frontenac. Laval's return in 1675 was followed by clashes between bishop and governor over precedence and policy. In the same year Jacques Duchesneau was appointed intendant, and he soon found himself at odds with Frontenac over their respective spheres of authority. But the most deep-rooted controversies were those arising out of the means by which the fur trade was carried on.

One aspect was that presented by the *coureurs de bois*. The habitants were now free to engage in the fur trade, but it was the government's intention that their activities should be carried on within the colony. They might barter with the Indians who brought their furs to Montreal or Three Rivers; but regulations issued in 1669 and strengthened in 1673 imposed stern penalties on any who went into the woods for more than twenty-four hours without official permission. The effort at a rigid restriction of licenses broke down completely. A modification in 1679, which allowed the habitant to engage in hunting between the middle of January and the middle of April, offered little remedy. The *coureurs* were ranging beyond Lake Superior, and the merchants who had a stake in the extension of the fur trade were their accomplices in violating the law. Frontenac himself was not above seeking a remedy for his chronic financial difficulties through the sale of licenses. There was the further consideration that the effective enforcement of the regulations, under which offenders might be whipped or sent to the galleys, would result in the *coureurs* taking their furs to Albany rather than risk a return to New France. In 1681 a new ordinance offered an amnesty and provided for the annual issuance of licenses to twenty-five canoes with three men each.

Leniency proved no more effective than severity. Frontenac, quite apart from his personal interest in the fur trade, recognized its prosperity as vital to the colony and the *coureurs* as essential to its effective prosecution. He proceeded to issue special permits in addition to the prescribed licenses, defeating the whole spirit of the regulations. In 1696 the home government attempted a new and drastic policy. All licenses were now suppressed. Private trade was to be completely prohibited, and the fur trade was to be confined to a restricted number of government posts. This merely meant that the officers in charge of these posts, who had already found the fur trade a comfortable source of graft, became more active than ever. The *coureurs* still found incentives, and the smuggling of furs to Albany became even harder to control. The policy, if maintained, could only have resulted in French abandonment of the west. The licensing system was restored in 1715; and although efforts at restriction continued through the subsequent period, they remained ineffective. Discipline and authority broke down in New France when it came to dealing with the *coureurs de bois*.

An even graver problem was the brandy trade. In their competition with the English, brandy as an article of trade gave the French one of the few advantages they enjoyed. But while the Indians eagerly bartered their furs for this commodity, it was recognized on all sides—even by many of the Indians—that its effect upon them was deplorable. Yet efforts to restrict or prohibit its use ran into the same difficulties as attempts to restrain the *coureurs de bois*. Both were felt to be necessary to the conduct of the fur trade and consequently to the prosperity of the colony, and commercial motives clashed with moral considerations in one of the most deep-rooted issues in the history of New France.

The clergy were forthright in their condemnation of the traffic. Laval used all his influence to check it, even to the point of issuing in 1660 a decree of excommunication against any who sold brandy to the Indians. Governor d'Argenson was affronted by this action as an intrusion on the domain of the civil power, and his successor Piérre de Bois, Baron d'Avaugour took advantage of a plea for mercy which the Jesuits put forward on behalf of a woman convicted of selling brandy to announce that he would refuse to enforce the regulations against anyone. Talon reflected even more strongly the growing pressure of the commercial interests against restriction. In 1668 he succeeded in getting the existing regulations revoked; and, although the taking of liquor to the Indians was again made an offense in 1669, the trade actually continued with little interference from the authorities.

The controversy reached a climax under Frontenac. The clergy continued to denounce the traffic and to threaten spiritual penalties. The merchants argued that if the Indians could not get brandy from the French they would trade their furs for rum to the English. Thus New France would lose their fur trade without benefiting the morals of the Indians—indeed, their state would be made even worse because they would lose their contact with Catholicism and be thrown into the arms of the heretics.

Frontenac made no secret of his strong sympathy with the merchants. His outspoken attitude added further tension to his already strained relations with the Church. The clergy accused him of being motivated by his personal interests. Frontenac retorted furiously that the Jesuit missions were merely a cloak for their interest in the fur trade. "To speak frankly," he wrote to Colbert, "their minds are set as much on the conversion of beaver as of souls. Most of their missions are pure mockeries." The controversy developed to a point where Colbert authorized Frontenac to take the unusual step of appealing to public opinion. In October 1678, twenty of the leading merchants and seigniors met with the council and governor to discuss the brandy trade. No clergy were summoned to the "Brandy Parliament," and it is not too surprising that the vote was in favor of continuing the sale of brandy to the Indians. Laval hastened to France and laid his case before the government, but Colbert put trade interests first. A decree of 1679 prohibited the carrying of liquor to the Indian settlements and made some efforts to restrict its sale within the colony; and even this limited prohibition remained largely a dead letter in the face of the pressing interest of the fur traders and the general support that they enjoyed among the mass of the colonists.

The extension of commerce upon which the civil authorities looked with increasing favor had far-reaching implications. The new centers of trade, as they became established, felt the need for protection. They also became centers of defense and points from which French imperial control could be extended still farther into the interior. At certain of them the government itself took over the conduct of the fur trade; at others it leased the trade to a private monopolist. In either case the *coureurs* remained essential agents, and the effectiveness of the trade contacts was dependent upon good relations between the French and the surrounding tribes.

This situation meant that the problems of relations with the Iroquois was always in the background. They had been at peace with the French since 1667, but they were allies of the English in the fur trade and implacable rivals of the tribes who traded with the French. The French traders on their part looked upon the Iroquois with somewhat mixed feelings. They desired to remain at peace with the Five Nations and to keep them in check, but not to eliminate them or to abate their enmity to the other Indian tribes. "Those who allege that the destruction of the Iroquois would promote the interest of the colonies of New France," wrote Baron de Lahontan, "are strangers to the true interest of that country; for if that were once accomplished, the savages who are now the French allies would turn their greatest enemies, as being then rid of their other fears. They would not fail to call in the English, by reason that their commodities are at once cheaper and more esteemed than ours; and by that means the whole commerce of that wide country would be wrested from our hands." The Church similarly felt that by making it easier for the Indians to resort to the English the difficulty of missionary work would be increased. The priests preferred to guard the pagan innocence of the savages until they had been converted to Catholicism rather than see them exposed to heresy, and joined with the traders in viewing the Iroquois threat as a useful weapon for keeping the other tribes dependent on Catholic France.

Frontenac had a lively interest in the extension both of the fur trade and of French control and in maintaining peace between the Iroquois and the French colony. These purposes were behind his decision to set up a fort at Cataraqui, where Lake Ontario flows into the St. Lawrence River. It would form a defense outpost guarding one of the approaches to Montreal and a post of trade for the surrounding area. At the same time he used the founding of Fort Frontenac in 1673 to impress the Iroquois anew with the strength of the French. He summoned their envoys to council at Cataraqui, and amid lavish pageantry and prolonged oratory, in which his dramatic personality shone at its best, he strove to bring home to them the disasters that would result from any new outbreak of war.

The Iroquois, still at war with the Andastes to the west, were sufficiently impressed to restrain any tendency they may have had toward active hostility. Nonetheless, their restiveness continued to grow through the decade that followed. They still sought to monopolize control of the fur trade between the Europeans and the other Indian tribes. They had eliminated their earlier competitors, the Huron, but other tribes farther west had taken their place as commercial allies of the French. By 1680 the Iroquois were determined to wipe out these new rivals. A war party invaded the country of the Illinois, and the French were once more confronted with the need to support their Indian allies.

The new danger arose just as Frontenac's first term of office was drawing to a close. His persistent quarrels with his colleagues and the disturbances that resulted within the colony had at last exhausted the patience of the home government. "The bishop, the ecclesiastics, the Jesuit fathers, the Supreme Council and, in a word, everybody complains of you," the king informed him. Frontenac was recalled in 1682, just at a time when his virtues would have been of positive service to New France. His successors proved incompetent to avert the rising external menace. Le Fèbvre de la Barre was weak and avaricious. He was incapable of impressing the Iroquois with his authority, and his eagerness to draw personal profits from the fur trade prevented a strong and consistent policy. He made overtures to New York, where he hoped to find in Governor Thomas Dongan—an Irishman and a Catholic—an ally against the Iroquois. But Dongan was firmly determined to keep a check on the power of New France and to attach the Iroquois more firmly than ever to the English crown. In 1684, at a council at Albany, an alliance was sealed between English and Iroquois. A situation was developing where Indian wars would now draw the rival European patrons into hostilities.

Events moved rapidly toward that end. La Barre in 1684 gathered an expedition that was meant to overawe the Iroquois. But instead of pressing an attack, he called the savages to council, only to find his menaces treated with contempt by the Iroquois, who had quickly realized that his show of force was mere bluff. He was ignominiously recalled in 1685 and the Marquis de Denonville was sent out in his stead. Denonville was a soldier and a more energetic man. He launched an expedition against the Senecas in 1687, which destroyed their villages; but he failed to crush the remaining tribes of the confederacy, and this attack, together with the seizure of a group of Iroquois who had been invited to Fort Frontenac, incited a spirit of revenge. In 1689 the Iroquois struck at the village of Lachine, destroying the settlement with a horrible massacre of its inhabitants. It was a state of open warfare, which once more brought the Indian menace to the doors of the French settlers. Denonville's attempts to establish posts at Detroit and Niagara had to be abandoned. As a crowning ignominy, Fort Frontenac was blown up as untenable. Once more New France seemed threatened with extinction at the hands of the Iroquois.

This was the situation that confronted Frontenac on his return in 1689. By this time it was realized that it was not only the Iroquois with which New France had to deal. Behind them stood the English, and until the English had been driven from the continent, New France could not hope for security. The outbreak of war in Europe made it possible to contemplate a decisive blow at English power in America by the capture of New York, and plans had already been laid for a French naval attack to be coordinated with a military expedition from Canada by way of the Hudson.

This scheme never came to pass. French naval power was inadequate for such an enterprise, and New France had not by itself the strength to conquer the English colonies. What resulted was a series of savage raids against the frontier settlements of New York and New England. They were inaugurated in 1690 by a triple blow against Schenectady, Salmon Falls, and Portland. In the years that followed an irregular frontier conflict continued. Bands led by men such as François Hertel—one of those seigniors who preferred to hunt and fight with the Indians rather than to develop his estates or cultivate his garden—ravaged the villages of New England. The Abenaki Indians, spurred on by zealous French priests such as Father Thury, joined in the effort to exterminate the heretics. The English colonies responded to the challenge with reprisals against both Acadia and New France. New York and New England in their turn planned a joint sea and land attack by way of the Hudson and the St. Lawrence. But like the French scheme, this in its turn failed through lack of resources. A force under Schuyler conducted an ineffective raid on Laprairie near Montreal in 1690. A naval expedition under Sir William Phips captured Port Royal and presented itself before Quebec; but Frontenac responded to a demand for surrender by asserting that his cannon would give his answer, and a spirited defense resulted in the failure of the subsequent attack. English and French in America had yet to come to grips in a really decisive way.

The French were more successful in their struggle against the Iroquois. Frontenac strengthened the garrisons of the posts, restored Fort Frontenac, and struck telling blows against the Iroquois in their own country—blows which reached a climax in the expedition that he led in person against the Onondaga in 1696. It was an almost bloodless enterprise, for the Indians fled at his approach; but their villages and food stocks were destroyed, and the threat of famine was added to the ravages of prolonged warfare to turn the thoughts of the Iroquois toward peace. Death came to Frontenac in 1698, before the struggle had reached a final decision. But the Iroquois had suffered heavy losses, and the Treaty of Ryswick in 1697 gave a brief breathing space in the struggle between England and France. Weakened and thrown back on the defensive, the Iroquois at length made peace in 1701. It was the end of the Iroquois menace as such. There would be new conflicts on a larger scale, but the protagonists henceforth would be the two European nations who were moving toward a struggle for the control of North America.

The Expansion of New France

Throughout the seventeenth century the hostility of the Iroquois acted as a barrier to French expansion toward the south. They stood across the route by way of Lake Champlain and the Hudson River and made the lower Great Lakes a dangerous route to travel. It was not until 1669, when an Indian guided Louis Joliet back from the Sault by way of Lake Erie, that this final link in the Great Lakes system became definitely known to Europeans. The perils that lay in that region, and the early knowledge of the Ottawa route, combined to direct the French westward; and even then it was only gradually that they extended their first-hand knowledge beyond the shores of Lake Michigan and Lake Superior.

Yet the conditions of the fur trade made it necessary for the French to push ever deeper into the interior. They were perpetually conscious of their inability to compete with the English on even terms. English manufactured goods were both better and cheaper than those which came from France, particularly the woolen cloth and metal tools and utensils that played such a vital part in barter with the Indians. Rum from the West Indies had a great advantage over brandy in price if not in quality. It was only by reaching out to new areas to which English traders or their agents had not yet penetrated that the French could keep in advance of their rivals.

Competition from Albany affected chiefly the trade that originated south of the Great Lakes. So long as the Iroquois could be kept from diverting this to the English, the French at Green Bay and Michilimackinac and the Sault had a good chance to hold their own. But their margin was never secure, and they could be sure of maintaining it only by a continued extension of their contacts to new tribes in the west. Moreover, the best beaver came from the rich forest belt of the Canadian Shield through the medium of Indian middlemen, and this part of the trade was endangered when to competition from Albany there was added a further menace from the English establishment on Hudson Bay.

It was ironical that this enterprise was the outcome of French initiative. The English had a claim to this region as a result of Hudson's discovery but showed no interest until its potential wealth in furs was brought to their notice by the Sieur de Groseilliers and Pierre Esprit Radisson. These two adventurers were brothers-in-law who during the 1650s had penetrated the region north of Lake Superior. It was a critical period for the fur trade in New France. Groseilliers may have been one of the Frenchmen who went to the Upper Country with the Huron in 1654 and returned two years later with a rich cargo of furs, to be hailed as saviors of the colony. He and Radisson brought back a still more valuable cargo in 1660 and were welcomed as heroes. But their success also roused the rapacity of the governor, D'Argenson, who refused them a license next year unless they would take along two of his servants and share half their profits with him. Defiantly they set off without a license; and on their return in 1663 they were forced to surrender some three-fifths of the proceeds of two years' trading in fines and in dues to the Company of New France. Furious at such injustice, and failing to get redress in France, they turned to the English, and their overtures led them shortly to the court of Charles II.

Charles was an impecunious monarch surrounded by hungry courtiers. He was always glad of an opportunity to satisfy them by concessions that cost him nothing. Many of them were adventurers untroubled by scruples and ready to gamble on the chance of lucrative returns. The two Frenchmen won their interest with tangible evidence of the wealth of the fur areas around Hudson Bay. A tentative expedition under their guidance brought back a handsome cargo in 1669. The success was decisive. A company was formed; the king's cousin, Prince Rupert, was placed at its head; and in 1670 a royal charter was issued giving to "The Governor and Company of Adventurers of England trading into Hudson's Bay" the monopoly of trade in that area and full ownership of all lands that were reached through Hudson Strait. During the next few years steps were taken to set up posts at the mouths of the chief rivers leading into the Bay, as permanent footholds to which the Indians might become habituated to resort for trade.

It was a profitable venture for the original backers. The initial £10,500 of stock increased in value to £104,000 during the next fifty years, and during that period there were annual dividends as high as 150 per cent. But this prosperity was by no means uninterrupted. New France was immediately alarmed. The northern Indians were urged to "abandon the plan of carrying on commerce with the Europeans who are trading toward the North sea, among whom prayer is not offered to God; and resume your old route toward Lake St. John, where you will always find some black robe to instruct and baptize." In 1671 Talon sent an expedition under St. Simon and Father Charles Albanel to open a route from the Saguenay to James Bay and establish a French claim to the region. This route proved too difficult to be developed, and a later one by Lake Temiskaming was not much more successful. Nonetheless there were persistent efforts to expel the English during the next 40 years. Radisson and Groseilliers, discontented with their new patrons, helped the French against them in 1682, only to shift their allegiance again two years later. A French *Compagnie du Nord* was formed in 1682, and its agents waged spasmodic war against the English posts in the bay. The English were reduced to the single post of Fort Nelson by 1688. They lost even this in 1691, and during the next six years it changed hands four times. But the persistence and tenacity of the English triumphed over the dash and daring of the French. English sea power once more proved to be a deciding factor; and with the Treaty of Utrecht in 1713 the French at last acknowledged defeat and the Hudson's Bay Company was left in full possession.

If the English could not be expelled from the continent, the alternative was to confine them within the narrowest possible limits. To the powerful motive that the fur trade provided for such an effort there was added the persistent hope that an easy passage to the Pacific might yet be discovered beyond the Great Lakes. Talon held high hopes of such discovery, and for a short time his optimism was shared by the government in France. "After the increase of the colony of Canada," ran one clause in Frontenac's instructions, "nothing is of greater importance for that country and for the service of His Majesty than the discovery of a passage to the South Sea."

In consequence, Talon's later period of office was marked by a vigorous effort to consolidate and extend the area of French power. His desire to guard the approaches to the St. Lawrence by garrison posts on Lake Ontario was partly realized by the founding of Fort Frontenac. His investigation of the report of copper deposits around Lake Superior was expanded to the imperial project of annexing the whole west. He sent St. Lusson to Sault Ste. Marie, and there in 1671, in a ceremony that was attended by representatives of the surrounding tribes and in which the Jesuits took a prominent part, the sovereignty of France was proclaimed over the interior of the continent.

At the same time Talon was making preparations for an expedition to reach the Mississippi. For a considerable time the French had been familiar with Indian accounts of the great river. They had not yet fully identified it with the river whose mouth the Spaniards had reached along the Gulf of Mexico. The vagueness of Indian descriptions allowed the French to cherish the hope that this might be the long-sought waterway to the Pacific. In any case it was of the utmost importance to secure its control for France and to keep the English away from its approaches.

Almost Talon's last act was to join with Frontenac in commissioning Louis Joliet to undertake the expedition. At the urging of the Jesuits, Father Jacques Marquette was allowed to go along. Both these men were familiar with the west, and French activities along the western shore of Lake Michigan had already brought them within striking distance of the Mississippi system. From the familiar starting point of Green Bay they set out in 1673 along the Fox and the Wisconsin and so reached the upper Mississippi. All through June they traveled down the river, their disappointment growing as its course continued south instead of tending toward the west. By the time they reached the mouth of the Arkansas they were fully satisfied that the river flowed into the Gulf of Mexico. They turned back, and on the return journey Joliet was guided to the Illinois River and discovered the Chicago portage, which offered the shortest way to the Mississippi from Lake Michigan.

The French government was slow to take any positive action to exploit this discovery. Talon had now been recalled, and the government at home had turned its attention toward European affairs and had no funds to spare for imperial ventures. Colbert refused to supply the funds to establish posts throughout the interior and had already expressed his opposition to any scheme that would lead to a wide dispersal of colonists before the main settlement on the St. Lawrence had been built up. Though Frontenac shared Talon's expansionist views, he was unable to secure the resources necessary for carrying them out. The task of advancing French power fell largely on private enthusiasts, and of these one of the most important was Robert Cavelier, Sieur de La Salle.

The career of La Salle is in many ways typical of both the strength and the weakness of French imperialism in North America. It shows the diversion of energy and initiative from settlement to trade and expansion, the grandiose ambitions that were out of all proportion to the available means, the failure through lack of a solid base and adequate resources to establish a firm grip on the whole of a continent. La Salle, during a period of friendship with the Sulpicians, had secured the grant of the seigniory of Lachine near Montreal. Frontenac added the seigniory that gave La Salle control of the fur trade at Fort Frontenac. But La Salle was not interested in developing his estates or even in settling down to a business-like career as a fur trader. His mind soared to schemes embracing the whole continent, politically as well as commercially, and his restless temperament drove him to prolonged ventures in exploration, which did little to advance his success in practical affairs.

Among his ventures was a scheme for reducing the transportation costs of the fur trade by using vessels on the Great Lakes to carry goods to and from the western posts. The idea was sound enough at bottom, but its outcome was symbolic of La Salle's whole career. His ship, *Le Griffon*, which he built on Lake Erie, made its first voyage to Green Bay in 1679 and was loaded with furs for the return journey. But its Danish pilot was only too well justified in his premonition that La Salle "had brought him thither to make him perish in a nasty lake and lose the glory he had acquired by his long and happy navigations on the ocean." The ship and its cargo disappeared and were never heard of again. Next spring La Salle heard that his supplies from Europe had also been lost at sea. These were ruinous blows

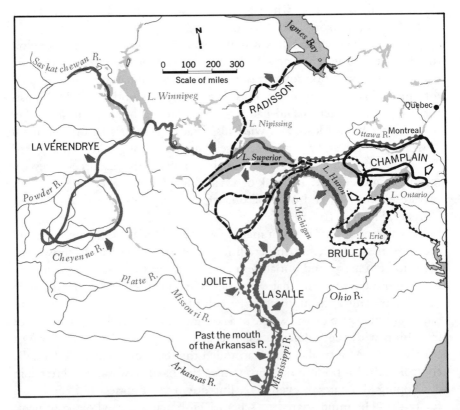

Early Explorations, 1608-1748

to his finances and to his ability to carry out the other schemes in which he was engaged.

La Salle had been closely associated with Talon and Frontenac and was an enthusiastic supporter of their expansionist ideas. Talon would have sent him toward the Mississippi in place of Joliet, but La Salle at that time had not returned from a somewhat mysterious exploration to the south of Lake Erie, which may have led him to the Ohio. He was, however, convinced that the Mississippi could be made a base for French control of the interior by the establishment of a series of forts and that these could be supported by the profits from the fur trade. In 1678 he secured a five-year concession as a basis for his effort to realize his designs.

It was not until 1682 that La Salle's personal and financial difficulties allowed him to set out on the voyage that carried him down the Mississippi to its mouth. His achievement added little that was new to the discoveries of Joliet, but it did mark the beginning of a process of consolidation that proceeded slowly during the next generation. The government in France did little to forward or support the work. La Salle's effort to found a colony at the mouth of the Mississippi went awry from the start and ended with his murder at the hands of his mutinous companions in 1687. But Bienville and D'Iberville—the roving and adventurous brothers Le Moyne, whose exploits against the English ranged from the coast of Maine to Hudson Bay—were encouraged to take up the project and planted the first settlement in Louisiana in 1699. With the founding of New Orleans in 1718 the colony was firmly established, and French power was planted on the second of the two great rivers that together bisect the continent. With outposts at Niagara and Detroit, and with a series of posts at such points as St. Louis, and Kaskaskia, and Vincennes, the French by the early part of the eighteenth century were in occupation of a strategic line through the heart of North America. France was virtually committed to an imperialist struggle for the control of the continent.

Meanwhile the penetration of the northwest was proceeding still more slowly. In spite of the desire to reach the tribes of that region and to prevent the diversion of high-quality furs to Hudson Bay, the lack of easy water routes north of Lake Superior proved a deterrent to extensive exploration. Du Lhut, one of the most enterprising of the traders, was notably active in the country beyond Lake Superior, and it was he who found the way to Lake Nipigon in 1684. Five years later Jacques de Noyon pushed on through Rainy Lake to Lake of the Woods. But much of French energy was by this time devoted to the effort to drive the English from Hudson Bay or to activities in the Mississippi region, and it was only after the eighteenth century was well advanced that a more serious effort was made to gain control of the northwest.

Again the idea of a route to the Pacific played its part in reviving interest in exploration. The Mississippi had proved a disappointment, but Indian tales gave to the Missouri and the Saskatchewan, to Lake Winnipeg and Great Salt Lake, the qualities that optimists could identify with their vision of easy access to the Western Sea. By 1717 the government in France showed a revived interest in the search, and it was this interest which La Vérendrye sought to capitalize in his plan for imperial expansion toward the west.

His project had much in common with the earlier schemes of La Salle, though it pointed in a different direction. He believed that by planting a series of posts the French could establish control of the west, forestalling the English and securing the fur trade of that whole region. He applied for a monopoly of the trade for five years, holding out the bait that this would enable him to push on his exploration. Unfortunately the result was to compromise him by a series of misunderstandings and cross-purposes. The court took the view that he was undertaking the search for the Western Sea at his own expense; and whenever he delayed to gather furs, the authorities became suspicious and hostile. On the other hand, the merchants who financed his enterprise wanted him to spend his time in trading and not waste it in exploration. He was constantly trying to find a compromise that would satisfy these different masters and still serve his own interests, and he was none too successful in the attempt.

His real achievement was in breaking through the Shield and establishing a route across the watershed to the plains and the great fur area west of Hudson Bay. Between 1731 and 1734 he established Fort St. Pierre on Rainy Lake, Fort St. Charles on Lake of the Woods, and Fort Maurepas near the mouth of the Red River, while his sons explored the region around Lake Winnipeg. By this time fresh difficulty had arisen. Comte de Maurepas, the French Minister of Marine, was growing increasingly impatient at La Vérendrye's concentration on organizing the fur trade in the new region to which he had penetrated and was not mollified by the hollow compliment of having his name given to a trading post in the midst of the wilderness. La Vérendrye had passed along fresh descriptions by the Indians of a great river toward the west and of a tribe whose dwellings were like French houses and whose domesticity was proved by the fact that they kept cats. Maurepas insisted that the work of exploration must be energetically pursued and threatened to recall La Vérendrye unless he pushed ahead.

In 1738 therefore a new effort was made. La Vérendrye reached the present site of Portage la Prairie and there built Fort la Reine. This post commanded "the road by which the Assiniboines go to the English" and the southern route which led to the Missouri; and from that strategic point La Vérendrye journeyed southward in search of the fabled tribe. This turned out to be the Mandan, who dwelt on the upper Missouri and who differed little from other Indians. The Missouri certainly was not a river flowing to the Western Sea; and though further exploration carried La Vérendrye's sons as far as the Black Hills, if not actually within sight of the Rockies, this southern region was a disappointment from the point of view of either the fur trade or a route to the Pacific.

Farther north the progress was more important. The discovery of the Saskatchewan brought the French to one of the great water routes of the west. Exploring it to the forks, they reached a main rendezvous of the Indians bringing furs to trade at Hudson Bay. In preparation for taking command of this strategic region, La Vérendrye planted Fort Dauphin on Lake Winnipegosis (or, as later research has suggested, Lake Manitoba) and Fort Bourbon on the Saskatchewan near its mouth; and in 1748 the French moved farther up the river with another fort at The Pas. But the work of completing the exploration and establishing full control of this great region was to wait for others. Government impatience had led to the cancellation of La Vérendrye's monopoly in 1744. He secured its renewal after four years' effort; but death came to him in 1749 while he was still preparing for a new effort to reach the Pacific by way of the Saskatchewan, and his sons who might have continued the effort were refused permission by the authorities.

Nonetheless, La Vérendrye had presented the French with significant gains. Though the way to the west was difficult and expensive, it placed them astride the chief supply routes of their rivals on Hudson Bay. The English in the north were being outflanked. French control of the Mississippi was a first step in setting bounds to the expansion of the English colonies in the south, and from this line the French were preparing to turn eastward to occupy the lands between the great river and the Appalachians and confine the English to the narrow coastal plain. The two communities were moving toward a clash of expansionist ambitions, which would lead to an irreconcilable conflict in which the mastery of the continent was at stake.

Canadian Voyageur on
Snowshoes.

(Granger Collection)

Louis de Buade, Comte
de Frontenac.
*The Statue by P. Hèbert in
Quebec.*

(Public Archives of Canada)

Expedition against the Iroquois.

The Hudson's Bay Company. *(Public Archives of Canada)*
The first sale of furs at Garroway's coffee house, London, 1671.

Marquette and Joliet Discover the Mississippi. *(New York Public Library)*

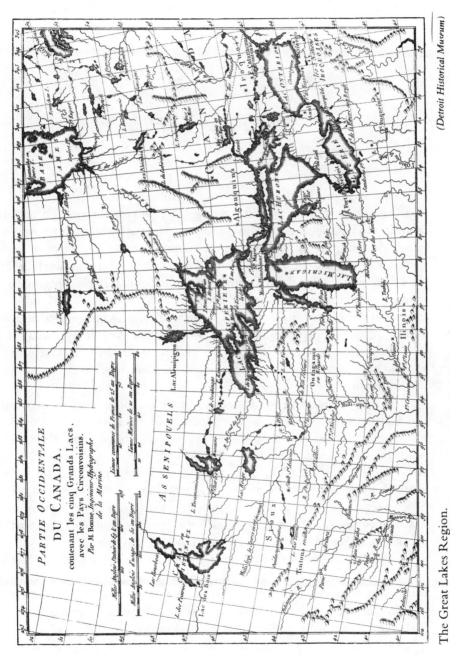

The Great Lakes Region.
Map showing the knowledge of the area at the end of the French regime.

Chapter 6

The Struggle for the Continent

The Roots of Conflict

The history of the American continent has been marked by a constant pull between the forces of unity and those of sectionalism. The heritage of European origin and culture common to the whole population, Indians apart, carried with it a legacy of racial and religious feuds rooted in the traditions of the Old World. Basic geographic conditions, which in some ways have operated powerfully on the side of unity, have also involved certain factors making for division and diversity. Community of race and language and traditions did not prevent the rise in the United States of two distinct cultural and economic regions whose antagonism issued in the Civil War. Divisions within Canada have been less acute but equally constant and have resulted in a persistent sectionalism, which is one of the major themes in Canadian national development.

The oldest and most permanent example of continental sectionalism is the division between Canada and the United States. Even this was not wholly inevitable. There was a brief period in the eighteenth century when prospects seemed bright for the ultimate political unity of all North America. But the existence of divergence and even antagonism is a far more characteristic state of affairs. The first European settlers found the St. Lawrence and the Great Lakes forming a dividing line between hostile Indian groups, and these rivalries were perpetuated by the settled communities that developed north and south of that line.

While the two communities differed in race and religion, neither factor would necessarily have led to an irreconcilable conflict. In the early days there were frequent amicable exchanges between New France and New England in spite of their underlying distrust. Between 1647 and 1651 in particular there were serious and formal efforts at close and friendly relations. But when New England took the initiative with a proposal for a trade agreement, the French insisted on a military alliance for the purpose of wiping out the Iroquois—an enterprise toward which New England felt no attraction whatever. Moreover, the very real possibility of a mutually beneficial commerce between the French and English settlements was frustrated by the authorities at home. France, reluctant to encourage even trade between New France and the West Indies when this seemed likely to cut into the profits of French merchants or manufacturers, became even more adamant against any trade with the English colonies which would curtail the market for French goods. The attitude of English officials was almost equally unfavorable. A certain amount of trade still went on, but illicit smuggling was an inadequate substitute for legal intercourse.

Practical motives, in the outcome, were not strong enough to bring the two communities together or to overcome growing divergences of interest; and when the latter prevailed, the differences in social structure and outlook added their emotional effects to sharpen the resulting sense of mutual hostility. Even then there might not have been all-out hostilities in America, in spite of occasional frontier clashes, if peace could have been maintained in Europe. Along with the emergence of grounds for conflict which were initially independent of European interests, the outbreak of war between the mother countries presented to both sides the occasion to attack their enemies in America. And when both France and England reached the conclusion that their rivalry for ascendancy in the power balance was bound up with the competition for empire and that the decisive area of this competition lay in North America, local antagonisms were absorbed into the wider issues that led to the struggle for the continent.

The economic rivalry that lay at the root of the situation in America stemmed, above all, from the fur trade. It was vital to New France to control the trade in the Upper Country, to maintain secure communications, to exclude English interference. This, in turn meant establishing firm relations with the other tribes and preventing them from falling under English influence; for even if English traders could be shut out from the west, the prospect that English blandishments might lure the Indians away from the French posts was a constant cause of apprehension. The strategy called not only for outflanking the English on the Atlantic seaboard and on Hudson Bay, but also in the process outflanking the Iroquois and the Sioux, the tribes most hostile to the French and most jealous of their economic advance.

For final security it was not enough to establish a precarious area of economic influence. What was called for was territorial possession of the interior of the continent and the total exclusion of the English, if necessary by force of arms. This had been ardently advocated by the early expansionists in New France. The home government, at first unsympathetic, began moving in this direction at the beginning of the eighteenth century. A French Prince had succeeded to the throne of Spain, precipitating the War of the Spanish Succession. Apprehensions were aroused that England might attack not only New France but also New Spain in an effort to seize the mineral wealth of Mexico. It was more than ever desirable to confine the English foothold to the area east of the Alleghenies. In particular, the consolidation of a settlement at the mouth of the Mississippi and the establishment of a chain of posts along the river would link Louisiana and Canada and set up a stronger barrier to any English advance into the interior. With the adoption of this policy, France was at last committed to imperial expansion in America.

The English meanwhile were slow to challenge the growth of French territorial claims. There was real concern in certain of the colonies, but little serious dispute over the title to the Mississippi or the Saskatchewan. Neither the mother country nor the colonies showed any haste to engage in war over such issues. The first warlike activities were largely defensive in their motives. Raids on the frontier settlements showed that New France was developing a serious threat of aggression and prompted New England and New York to turn their thoughts toward eliminating the source of the danger. The outbreak of war in Europe in 1689 gave added occasion for attack. Between that date and the Treaty of Utrecht in 1713 there were projects for the conquest of New France that got no farther than successful attacks on Acadia. During the following generation an uneasy truce punctuated by border raids subsisted between the colonies. But this period was the prelude to a new development, which would result in French control of the continent being challenged not by English commerce but by English settlement. When that happened, two diverse and incompatible societies were brought face to face, and their rival ambitions soon locked them in a decisive conflict.

Unequal Rivals

In an all-out test of strength, New France had little chance against the English colonies. Her vast imperial ambitions in the west were pursued with such scanty means that they could not possibly prevail against a really serious challenge. By the middle of the eighteenth century she had laid claims to immense territories, which it was quite impossible for her to occupy effectively. The growth of population from 2500 in 1663 to over 60,000 a century later, while remarkable in view of the lack of immigration throughout most of that period, offered absolutely no prospect of the spread of settlement to the great spaces of the west. New France indeed desired and intended to hold those spaces with a minimum of settlement at a few strategic posts, preserving the area for the forests and the fur trade. But to maintain the interior of the continent as an untouched wilderness against the pressure of English land hunger could be done in the last resort only by the use of armed force on a scale that was beyond the resources of New France.

For just as the colony was too small to occupy the Mississippi Valley by forestalling English settlement, so it was too weak to act as an effective military base for garrisoning and defending that region against English intrusion. It was hopelessly outweighed in population and wealth and resources. Against this primitive agricultural community of some 60,000 the Thirteen Colonies had a sturdy and diversified society with a population of around 1,500,000. Their fishing and shipping, their extensive maritime commerce and embryo manufacturing industries, their accumulated wealth from farm and plantation and the sea, were the foundations for an active and many-sided economic life that New France found it impossible to emulate. On the basis of statistics the English colonies were crushingly superior in the essentials, not only of peacetime prosperity, but also of the sinews of war.

Estimates of this kind, however, the Canadians either ignored or disdained. They counted on other and less tangible assets, and not least upon a racial superiority of which they were profoundly convinced. It was the result of a stubborn pride sustained to some extent by willful ignorance, but it was nonetheless tenacious for that. A French visitor, writing around 1720, gave it characteristic expression: "There reigns in New England an opulence from which it seems they do not know how to profit; and in New France a poverty concealed by an apparently unstudied appearance of comfort. . . . The Anglo-Americans have no desire for war, because they have much to lose; they do not try to win over the savages, because they believe they have no need. The youthful French, for opposite reasons, have a detestation of peace, and get on well with the aborigines, easily winning their esteem in war and their friendship at all times." Upon such factors—an extensive friendship with the Indians, the warlike talents of the French, the slowness and reluctance of the English to take up arms—the Canadians based their belief that a handful of people in the St. Lawrence Valley could attain the mastery of North America.

Up to a point these calculations had a measure of justification. When the final test came, the decisive factor was not the disparity in wealth and population between the two regions (though that still had its significance), but the relative weight of effort that the two mother countries put into the struggle for America, and, ultimately, the supremacy of British sea power. No doubt in due course the expansion of English settlement would have brought about a contest for the interior in which the superior resources of the English colonies would have been of crucial importance. But while such a clash was an emerging prospect by the middle of the eighteenth century, it had not yet reached the point of irreconcilible confrontation. The English colonies remained a prey to chronic disunity, not least in their unwillingness to combine their full resources in order to strike at New France. The failure of the Albany congress in 1754 showed a widespread indifference on the part of the middle and southern colonies toward the menace on the frontier. Colonies such as Pennsylvania were reluctant to take measures to protect their own outlying settlements, let alone to help their neighbors. All of them disliked the burden and the cost that war would impose and showed a deep reluctance to embark on serious and sustained military efforts.

So long as this situation held, New France could pursue an aggressive policy with some hope of success. Fundamentally, however, that success depended on the willingness of the English to abdicate rather than fight. If they became convinced that their vital interests were threatened and must be defended by force, then a new situation would arise. In such a case the very qualities that the French held in scorn would prove to be overwhelming assets. The pursuit of economic gain, the reluctance to divert the energies of the community from the arts of peace to frontier raids or adventurous roving in the wilderness, were reflected in the solid and prosperous foundations that had been laid by the seaboard colonies. Though they felt the strain of war, they had some surplus of both wealth and man power with which to bear the strain, as against a New France that had no margin in either respect.

The limitations of the Canadian economy, indeed, rendered the colony particularly vulnerable in time of war. Even the establishment of a growing agricultural settlement had not resulted in a self-sufficient community. In good times it could manage to feed itself, but there was little margin to spare to meet a crop failure or to develop a dependable export trade. Farming in general was primitive and unenterprising—the less happy side of that vaunted indifference to material wealth which was held to be one of the virtues of the habitant. Even the pioneering spirit of an earlier stage had largely evaporated, and colonists whose inefficient methods exhausted the lands already cleared were reluctant to carve new ones from the wilderness. Energy and initiative found in the fur trade a more attractive outlet than the arduous labor of clearing a farm. Those who stayed on the land preferred to take their share of the homestead; and the linear division of farms among the heirs to give each a river frontage resulted in ribbon farms whose narrowness made for further inefficiency. The government tried to check excessive subdivision by forbidding the building of a house on any farm with a frontage of less than 288 feet. But instead of forcing settlers to seek new lands, this order often resulted in several families crowding on a single homestead, with anything but benefit to the land or to themselves.

The result was a farming population living close to the subsistence level. Wheat remained the chief crop, and the poor quality of the grain made it vulnerable to frost and plague. Possibly because the forest and the river provided added sources of food supply, there was little care in the raising of cattle or sheep, and poor harvests meant a shortage of feed and the slaughtering of livestock. Fluctuations and uncertainty in the crops hampered the development of an exportable surplus, and the scarcity of accessible markets meant that there was only a weak incentive to serious efforts in that direction. France provided little outlet. The West Indies were distant, and Canada was unable to meet the competition of the English colonies. Some trade developed with Louisbourg, particularly after a good crop year in 1740; but the English capture of that citadel in 1745 struck a blow from which the trade never recovered even after Louisbourg was returned to France.

There was neither wealth nor stability to be drawn from agriculture under such conditions. In bad times the colony was actually dependent on imports of food from France; in all times, good or bad, it relied on the mother country for nearly all the other necessities of life. The one staple export of any importance was furs, and it was the fur trade that had to bear the task of establishing a balance of trade. It is not surprising, given the fluctuations and uncertainty in the fur trade as well as in agriculture, that it proved inadequate to the task, particularly in view of its own substantial need for trade goods from France. Only in 1741 was there a balance on the side of the colony; in all other years there were deficits to be bridged somehow by the government at home.

As a result, war struck at the very roots of the colony, particularly if the enemy was superior at sea. War involved both the Indians and the *coureurs de bois* and diverted their energies from gathering furs. At the other end, it impeded access to markets in France and to the necessary supplies from that country. It reacted disastrously on the finances of the country and led to that spiral of paper money and inflation and bankruptcies with which New France became sadly familiar. It drew heavily on the man power of the colony with serious effects on the production of food. Even in the best of times all available men were needed on the farms. To the constant drain of the fur trade was added the burden of transportation as the main posts moved farther west. No surplus man power existed; and when the militia had to be called up, the crops were likely to suffer. With complete mobilization the colony by 1750 could raise between 7000 and 10,000 men, but at the price of deserted farms and the prospect of starvation the next winter. Montcalm acknowledged that it was impossible to keep 3000 militia under arms for a full campaign without disastrous effects on seeding and harvest. If a real struggle were joined with the English colonies, New France could prevail only if France lent powerful aid, and even then only if England, by choice or necessity, remained aloof.

In actual fact neither France nor England showed much eagerness to plunge into a conflict in America. Through the eighteenth century opinion in France grew more and more skeptical of the value of Canada and hostile to the expenditures that its retention imposed on an already distressed treasury. Voltaire's contempt for "a few acres of snow" and his avowed delight at the prospect of getting rid of them expressed a widespread sentiment. The government on its part desired to retain a foothold in America, but at minimum effort and cost. It lent no aid of any importance to the expansionist efforts of New France and only a meager amount to its defense. This comparative indifference aided the growing sense of divergence between France and Canada. Even more than the Americans to the south, the Canadians of the eighteenth century were conscious of their separate identity as a community. There was virtually no immigration after 1675. The population by 1750 represented several generations of native-born and had developed an outlook and interests that were not shared by the motherland. Montcalm's officers complained indignantly that they were treated like members of a foreign and even a hostile race. Canadians clamored for more support for their ambitions from a tepid mother country and were vocal in their resentment at her reluctance to devote French resources to purely Canadian objectives.

England was also somewhat reserved toward the demands of her colonies for military aid, especially when these demands became connected with territorial claims in the interior. The colonies were already showing a perturbing spirit of independence. Their growth in population and extent would only make them harder to control. A certain feeling developed that, while the existence of French naval bases on the Atlantic was undesirable, the presence of the French on the St. Lawrence served a real purpose in keeping the colonies in restraint. Britain was slow to oppose French expansion and even slower to decide on the conquest of New France. When that decision was taken it was not for the sake of the American colonies but from the broader imperial point of view and with the aim of crushing the chief maritime and commercial rival of Britain and her empire.

The Outposts of New France

So long as the colonies were left to pursue their feuds with their own resources, there was little prospect of a decisive outcome. New France was too weak to expel the English. The English colonies were too disunited or indifferent to conquer New France. The struggle was reduced to one of outposts, in which the ravaging of border settlements by small raiding forces was the most characteristic form of campaign.

This type of warfare was more favorable to the French than to the English. There were always Indians ready to form a war party and French adventurers and *coureurs* ready to join them. Up to the beginning of the eighteenth century the Iroquois struck sporadically but savagely at the French settlements; but comparatively few English had the inclination or the skill to engage in the sort of raids in which the French were so expert. When the colonies were roused to action, their tendency was to strike not at the few outlying settlements of New France, but at the heart of that colony and the seat of French power.

New England, whose frontier bore the brunt of the raids and massacres, was more energetic than the other colonies in attempts at retaliation. But New England was not well placed for an overland attack on the St. Lawrence. Quebec was more accessible by sea, and it was to a sea expedition that the thoughts of maritime New England naturally turned.

Any such enterprise involed not only New France, but Acadia as well. New France was the center of French policy and the author of French aggression; but Acadia was a bastion that must be reduced to clear the flank of an expedition up the St. Lawrence. If Acadia had stood alone it might not so soon have become an object of attack. Its settlers were few and inoffensive. They numbered less than 1,000 in 1685 and were more concerned with tilling their farms and avoiding trouble than with expansionist designs. Even so, French possession of Acadia was by no means a matter of indifference to New England. It was a base from which France might seek to control the fisheries of the north Atlantic and to develop a competing trade with the West Indies. Port Royal was a haven from which privateers operated in time of war to prey on New England shipping. French efforts to extend control to the Penobscot conflicted with the territorial claims of Massachusetts and led to armed clashes on the border. When Quebec drew on the Indian tribes of Acadia for frontier raids, and when French missionaries in Acadia encouraged the warlike temper of the savages, the desirability of removing the French from Acadia became clear.

The outbreak of war between France and England in 1689 (King William's War) was followed by savage raids, which roused New England to action. In spite of their inability to secure aid from England, the colonies determined on an effort to eliminate the French menace. In the spring of 1690 an expedition set out under Sir William Phips with the intention of capturing Port Royal and then attacking Quebec. Port Royal, with half-prepared defenses, and a garrison of 70 men, surrendered without resistance. But the defense of Quebec was inspired by the presence and energy of Frontenac, and the ill-planned operations Phips launched met with an ignominious repulse. Plans for a fresh effort in 1692 fell through for lack of help from England, and, when help became available next year, Phips chose to regard it as too little and too late. Quebec remained without further molestation, and even Port Royal, on which the English hold was precarious, was returned to France by the Treaty of Ryswick in 1697.

The next few years were a period of uneasy truce in America as well as in Europe. It was broken in 1702 by the War of the Spanish Succession (Queen Anne's War), which brought renewed raids from New France and fresh pleas for English help to the threatened colonies. Their efforts to help themselves resulted in little more than pillaging raids against Acadia in 1704 and 1707; and it was not until the summer of 1710 that six warships and a regiment of marines—the remnants of a force originally allocated for an attack on Quebec—arrived unexpectedly in Boston. By the time New England had rallied to take advantage of the opportunity and raised four regiments, the season was too late for an attack on Quebec, and once again Acadia became the immediate objective of the enemies of New France.

As usual, Port Royal was in little state to resist the force that bore down upon it. The fort was ill prepared, ill garrisoned, and ill supplied. The governor, Subercase, had half a dozen guns and less than 300 men at his disposal, and even this meager garrison was only kept from deserting by the seizure of all the canoes in which they could get away. It is a testimony to the qualities of Subercase as a commander and his bravery as a soldier that he held out for a week under overwhelming bombardment before he agreed to surrender with full honors of war. Port Royal, renamed Annapolis Royal, was this time permanently in English hands.

Its capture was the chief event of the war in America. In Newfoundland, where the small settlement established by the French at Placentia on the south shore provided a base for the attack and capture of the English center of St. John's, the French could count a minor success. Impressive English plans for an attack on Quebec in 1711 ended ignominiously. Part of the fleet ran aground in the St. Lawrence, and a projected attack by way of Lake Champlain was abandoned on news of the disaster. Yet the outcome of the war was a serious blow to New France. Although the Treaty of Utrecht in 1713 left that colony untouched, it resulted in French surrender of Acadia and acknowledgment of the English title to Newfoundland and Hudson Bay. The lines of demarcation were more sharply drawn, and in a way this consolidated England's control of the seacoasts and her foothold on the flanks of Canada.

The treaty seriously impaired the strategic position of New France. The cession of Hudson Bay restricted access to the northern fur area. The acknowledgment of English suzerainty over the Iroquois implied a renunciation of the approaches to the Ohio. Access to the Mississippi and the Saskatchewan was still open, but the corridor had been considerably narrowed. Even access to the St. Lawrence was potentially jeopardized by the surrender of Newfoundland. No doubt the enthusiasm of David Kirke was exaggerated when he claimed that "Newfoundland is the key to the Gulf of Canada which if the English were in possession . . . they might give the law to all foreign kings." England never managed to use it to such an effective degree, and the economic loss to France was mitigated by the concession that the French might take and dry fish along the stretch from Cape Bonavista on the east coast around the northern tip of the island and down most of the western coast to Point Riche—the establishment of the French Shore that was to be a recurrent source of controversy and resentment until the early twentieth century. In sum, however, the treaty was a serious check to French aspirations in America, and inspired efforts to consolidate against further loss and to reverse the setback wherever an opportunity might offer.

The cession of Acadia meant the loss to France of a strategic position, which she had long neglected. The event momentarily jolted her from her former indifference and brought an effort to redress the situation. She was not completely dislodged from the Atlantic seaboard. The treaty left her in possession of Cape Breton, as well as of Ile St. Jean (Prince Edward Island) in the Gulf; and she tried to interpret its terms in a way that would also reduce her losses on the mainland. The provision that Acadia was to be ceded conformable to its ancient limits was made the occasion for a dispute over boundaries that a commission proved unable to settle. France insisted that only the peninsula of Nova Scotia had been surrendered, and in the succeeding period she was able to maintain effective control of what is now New Brunswick. Meanwhile she undertook to construct a new naval base to offset the loss of Port Royal. The founding of Louisbourg on the eastern tip of Cape Breton in 1720 made it clear that France was determined not only to maintain her foothold on the Atlantic, but to use it at the first opportunity to recover Acadia.

In the event, Louisbourg was symbolic of the weakness that marked the whole course of French policy toward America. It represented an ambitious design that was never backed by vigorous and sustained efforts. Louisbourg was to become the Gibraltar of America. Plans for its fortifications were drawn in accordance with the principles of the great military engineer, Vauban. But construction was carried on slowly, and the contractors found numerous opportunities to increase their profits by substituting inferior materials. Of the projected 148 guns to be mounted on the fortifications, no more than ninety were ever put in place. The garrison was composed of half a dozen companies of 100 men each, housed in damp quarters amid dismal surroundings that did nothing to improve their already dubious quality. With bad construction, inadequate armament, mutinous men and inefficient officers, Louisbourg—the pistol pointed at New England—was a weapon with a damp charge.

In addition, the hope of building an active community around the port was only partly realized. The shortage of fertile land frustrated the effort to attract settlers from Acadia. Fishing in the rich waters adjacent to the site provided the main activity, supplemented by the growth of a fairly active commerce that was favored by Louisbourg's situation. There was a modest trade with New France and a somewhat more substantial interchange with France and the West Indies and to some extent with New England. But apart from fish, Louisbourg itself had no staple on which to rely, and the lack of any agricultural settlement worth mentioning frequently left the garrison as well as the fishermen dependent on supplies from the neighboring English colonies of Acadia and New England. The lack of a solid base on which to rest this potential pivot of French power was ultimately to prove fatal to its retention.

Nonetheless, New England viewed with alarm the rise of a stronghold that might command the fisheries and the trade routes and a port that might develop a rival trade with the West Indies. A fresh outbreak of hostilities gave solid ground to their apprehension. The War of the Austrian Succession (King George's War) found England and France embroiled with each other by 1744. Louisbourg heard the news before Annapolis and promptly sent a force to destroy the English fishing establishments at Canso and to threaten Annapolis. New Englanders had visions of privateers swarming like wasps out of Louisbourg against their shipping, and under the vigorous leadership of Governor William Shirley they determined to destroy the menace.

The result was an Anglo-American amphibious expedition in 1745. New England raised a force of 4000 men under the leadership of William Pepperell. Britain provided a naval squadron under Commodore Warren. With confidence in the Lord and lively hopes of loot, the provincial militia set off to storm the most modern fortifications on the American continent. Their hopes were to be disappointed, but their confidence was not wholly misplaced, although French shortcomings were almost as important for the outcome as American valor. The fleet protected the landings and intercepted the French ships that carried aid to Louisbourg. The militia drew their siege lines about the fortress, manhandling cannon through swamps and over cliffs and opening a sustained bombardment from three sides. Within the walls of Louisbourg lay a garrison of 2000, composed of mutinous regulars and inexperienced militia, and an equal number of civilians had sought refuge there. Upon this motley collection there rained a growing intensity of shellfire, which wrecked all but a single house in Louisbourg and battered its inhabitants into submission. There never was an actual assault on the walls. Six weeks of bombardment and blockade depleted the supplies within the fortress and moved the civilians to petition the governor to surrender. On June 27 negotiations were opened, and two days later Louisbourg capitulated.

The conquest proved to be temporary. The French, it is true, failed in their efforts to regain Louisbourg by force of arms. An expedition that set out in 1746 was dogged by misfortune from the start. Plague and indiscipline and tempests, the death of one commander and the prompt suicide of his successor, sapped its effectiveness by the time it reached the shores of Nova Scotia. It was too weak to attack Louisbourg or even to assail Annapolis, and it turned back to France without striking a blow. A project for a simultaneous expedition from New France was abandoned when the English colonies began massing their forces for an attack on

Canada. But this enterprise in its turn was checked by the refusal of aid from London and the French threat to Louisbourg and the coasts. The antagonists never came decisively to grips, and the taking of Louisbourg remained the chief episode of the war in America.

In the broader imperial sphere the struggle was equally indecisive. France had suffered defeats, but not on such a scale as to force her to unconditional surrender. When peace negotiations were undertaken, part of the price she demanded was the return of Louisbourg; and in 1748, by the Treaty of Aix-la-Chapelle, the fortress was handed back to France.

The treaty, however, was little more than a truce, and both sides girded themselves for a renewal of the struggle. France embarked on efforts to put Louisbourg in a more effective state of defense. Britain, after a generation of inertia, awoke to the need of taking positive steps to consolidate her position in Nova Scotia. On Chebucto Bay the town of Halifax was founded in 1749 with the intention of establishing a naval base that would be stronger and more effective than Annapolis as a counterpoise to Louisbourg. A serious effort to colonize Nova Scotia with Protestant settlers brought immigration from Britain and Germany to supplement the trickle of New Englanders flowing into the colony in search of fresh lands. This colonization was a deliberate effort to overbalance the original French Catholic population; and the problem presented by that population now became a matter of serious concern to both British and colonial authorities.

The Expulsion of the Acadians

The Treaty of Utrecht had provided that such Acadians as desired might emigrate within a year, taking their movable property. Those who remained became British subjects with guaranties of security for their property and of the free exercise of their religion. The first impulse of France was to seek the removal of the population to build up a colony around Louisbourg and to settle Ile St. Jean. The Acadians at first expressed their willingness to emigrate, but an inspection of the available lands induced sober second thoughts. They developed a reluctance to abandon their fertile diked farms for the rugged shores of Cape Breton or even to undertake the work of clearing the rich soil of Ile St. Jean. A few did move to these islands, but the bulk of the population stayed in Acadia. Their decision was helped by the action of both French and English. The former failed to provide the necessary ships to remove the Acadians and even began to feel that their remaining in Nova Scotia might aid in the recovery of that province. The English authorities became alarmed at the prospect of wholesale depopulation and refused to do anything to facilitate the removal. In the outcome the bulk of the Acadians remained where they were.

This brought up the question of their loyalty to their new rulers. Few Acadians were actively hostile, but they had a natural desire to reduce to a minimum the effects that their change of allegiance would have on their own lives. The problem came to a head when the British authorities demanded an oath of allegiance to the king. The Acadians were prepared to pledge loyalty, but they wanted an assurance that it would not commit them to military service against France. The authorities refused to allow any exceptions. The Acadians refused to take the oath unless they were permitted to remain neutral. It was a deadlock that successive efforts during the forty years after the conquest failed to solve.

So long as the question was one of formalities, the British had little motive for risking trouble by pressing it to a decision. Left to themselves, the Acadians were peaceful and contented. There was a steady extension of settlement as their numbers grew from less than 1000 in 1714 to some 10,000 by 1750. Their farms were fertile and prosperous. Their produce found a market not only in the English garrison and to some extent in New England, but also in Louisbourg in spite of adverse regulations on both the French and the English sides. The authorities left them undisturbed in their religion and virtually immune from taxation. The seigniorial system existed in theory, but all seigniorial rights were taken over by the Crown and the dues were little more than nominal. Britain hardly drew £50 a year from the colony, and her expenditures on garrisons and public works provided welcome sources of income for the inhabitants.

This idyllic situation was ruined by the progress of the conflict between England and France. With the recovery of Louisbourg, French policy became more active and aggressive in its efforts to undermine the English position in Nova Scotia. France would no longer allow the Acadians to be neutral. They were too valuable as spearheads of the attack on the English colony. Appeals were made to the Acadians on grounds not only of race but of religion. A particularly zealous priest, Joseph Louise Le Loutre, became the chief agent in rousing the alarm of the Acadians at the prospect that their faith might be threatened and in urging them to refuse the oath and to move north of the isthmus of Chignecto to the area under French control. He also used his influence to stir the Indians to active hostility.

British parties were ambushed, new settlements such as Dartmouth became scenes of raids and massacres, and even Acadians whose French patriotism seemed tepid became victims of Indian attacks designed to warn the other inhabitants of the fate that might be theirs if they tamely submitted to English rule.

This situation gave cause for alarm not only to the authorities in Nova Scotia, but also to New England. The return of Louisbourg had revived the menace that New England had sought to eliminate. The attitude of the Acadians added greatly to the danger. Governor Shirley of Massachusetts, vigorous and self-confident and energetic, was particularly insistent that the problem must be solved by the elimination of French power from America and that the first step was the firm establishment of British control in Nova Scotia, "the key to British interests and dominion in America." He advocated substantial settlement from New England, the removal of priests and recalcitrants, and a deliberate effort to turn the Acadians into loyal Protestant subjects. His views were shared by the Council of Nova Scotia, three of whose five members were New Englanders; and as the situation moved toward a crisis, Governor Charles Lawrence of Nova Scotia became convinced that only drastic measures would avail.

A series of events helped to precipitate action. The growing threat from the French was exemplified by the appearance of a French force on the narrow isthmus of Chignecto. When in 1750 a British force was sent to expel the intruders, the French with the active assistance of Le Loutre persuaded the Acadians in the village of Beaubassin to abandon their homes and remove with their livestock into French-controlled territory. The British arrived to find the village in flames and the French barring their further advance. When they set up a defense post at Fort Lawrence, the French replied by constructing a stronger fort, which with gay provocativeness they named Beauséjour. For the next five years the two parties faced each other while their governments wrangled about the boundary and tension continued to grow.

In 1755 the quarrel in America broke into open conflict. Though France and England were at peace, the determination to prevent French encroachments led to Braddock's expedition and to associated operations, one of which was an attack on Beauséjour. The fort fell after a siege of two weeks, and among the garrison were found 300 Acadians serving in arms. The statement of the commander that they had joined under compulsion did not lessen the fact that compulsion could force the Acadians from their desired neutrality and into arms against Britain. On top of this came the accounts of Braddock's defeat and news that Louisbourg had recently been reinforced. A decisive struggle was imminent, and neither New England nor the authorities of Nova Scotia felt like facing it with a disloyal Acadian population in their rear.

Governor Lawrence now determined on a final effort to enforce the unqualified oath. He had no desire to embark on wholesale deportations, to which the government in London was decidedly averse; but he believed that the threat would serve his purpose and that at most it would be necessary to deport some recalcitrants as proof that he was in earnest. But it was difficult to convince the Acadians. Their stubborn and tenacious mentality had become a byword, and the fact that they had successfully resisted repeated demands for the oath in the past forty years encouraged them to believe that their continued refusal would meet with no serious consequences.

In July 1755, deputies from the Acadian villages were summoned to Halifax and ordered to take the oath. Their refusal brought matters to a head. The council and governor unanimously decided on a general deportation. This was far more drastic than an effort to change the obdurate minds of the Acadians by stern examples. They were in fact given no chance to repent but were treated as recusants whose presence was an active danger and who must be removed in the interests of British security.

In August the authorities struck. Military detachments were sent to the isthmus and to Minas Basin to round up the inhabitants. At Grand Pré in the latter district the men were ordered to assemble in the church, locked up under guard, and the younger portion of them placed aboard ships that were waiting in the harbor. It was intended that the women and children should be taken later when further ships arrived and that as far as possible families should be kept together and hardship reduced to the minimum. But the ships were delayed, and the commander became increasingly apprehensive over the task of holding prisoner 400 able-bodied men, who far outnumbered his available force. It was not until after five weeks that transports arrived, enabling him to make some effort to send off the whole population, but the haste and confusion prevented a general reunion of families. On the isthmus, where the difficulty of rounding up the population had been greater than at Grand Pré, some shiploads of men were sent off without waiting for the women and children. Shipwrecks and changes of destination and the success of some deportees in escaping added to the dispersion. Having no desire to strengthen New France, the authorities decided to distribute the Acadians among the English colonies. But these had not been informed and were in many cases reluctant to have a foreign and resentful influx suddenly thrust upon them. While some

Acadians were given reasonable care, many were left to shift as best they could and frequently made their way to French territory. Meanwhile the process of rounding up and deporting settlers from other localities continued and was extended after 1758 to Cape Breton and Ile St. Jean. In all, somewhere between 6000 and 10,000 Acadians were deported over a period of eight years; and though part of that number eventually returned to their burned and ravaged homesteads, the remainder were scattered far and wide.

It was an act that exceeded any deliberate intention of the British government and which left a tragic legend as part of Canada's racial heritage. Yet while the methods may have been needlessly brutal, the step itself was the outgrowth of the situation. Not Britain, but France by ruthless and aggressive policy, which used the Acadians with complete disregard of the risk that it drew upon them, was the real author of the expulsion. Possibly Nova Scotia would have been safe without it, but the authorities can be excused for their reluctance to take such a chance in the face of the war that was already looming and the certainty that the most extreme efforts would be made to stir up the Acadians to armed revolt. Even the promise of exemption from military service, which would probably have resulted in the taking of the oath by most Acadians, might well have seemed like a dangerously significant concession under the circumstances. On the other hand, the actual loss would have been insignificant, for the authorities can hardly have contemplated the raising of an Acadian militia for use against Louisbourg. But that was something on which the Acadians would have been well advised to count without a formal promise, in view of the consideration with which they had been treated since the conquest. British patience, after long 'endurance, broke abruptly; but France in a similar situation would almost certainly not have temporized for forty years.

The Downfall of New France

While Acadia was the center of this sporadic struggle, New France for half a century was spared from direct attack. Projects for expeditions from the English colonies, which created periodic alarm, seldom got beyond the preparatory stage. Apart from the Iroquois raids in the closing decade of the seventeenth century, the nearest thing to an invasion was the futile expedition of Phips in 1690. But by 1750 both sides felt that their vital interests were at stake as their expansion brought a direct clash of ambitions, which could only be decided by force.

The crisis was precipitated when France embarked on positive steps to occupy the Ohio Valley and to exclude the English from that region. One motive was the extent to which English fur traders had succeeded in establishing themselves throughout the area. Added to this was the more serious prospect of the spread of English settlement beyond the Alleghenies. Already land-hungry pioneers were beginning to find their way through the gaps in the mountains. A number of shrewd and farsighted men had grasped the prospect opened up by the imminent westward movement of the frontier and the opportunities that it offered for land speculation on a truly heroic scale. In 1748 this group formed the Ohio Company and secured a Crown grant of half a million acres of western lands. The purpose and even the name of this enterprise represented a challenge to the claims and interests of New France. The issue was squarely posed between French fur trade and English settlement. Two divergent and incompatible societies were grasping at the interior of the continent, one seeking to preserve the forests for the Indians and the beaver, the other to deliver them to the ax of the pioneer.

The French as usual moved more promptly to make their claims effective. In 1749 an expedition under Céloron de Blainville moved down the Ohio, burying lead plates and setting up the arms of France as symbols of the French claim to the region, ordering English traders from the Indian villages, and exhorting the tribes to deal only with the French. This preliminary gesture was followed up by the more effective step of building a series of forts from Lake Erie down the French River to the Ohio, and with these guarding the approaches the French began to move down the river toward the forks.

The outcries provoked in the English colonies by this advance rose loudest in Virginia. Pennsylvania showed little interest even though she had some claim to the lands occupied by the French. Other colonies looked on with indifference. New York answered an appeal for aid by expressing doubts whether the French were intruding on British soil. Clearly the leaders of that colony were not interested in the Ohio Company. But Governor Robert Dinwiddie of Virginia was one of its active members, and a number of leading Virginians were heavily involved. Dinwiddie was roused to protest against this threat to future profits, and it was he who sent George Washington to Fort le Boeuf in 1753 with a message demanding that the French withdraw. When this was met by a firm refusal, Dinwiddie decided on stronger action. He had some trouble in raising volunteers, for the average Virginian saw little reason to risk his skin for the Ohio Company; but in 1754 George Washington with some 300 men set out to expel the French.

His failure was complete. The French drove an advance party from the forks of the Ohio, where they proceeded to build Fort Duquesne. A party under Jumonville was sent to meet Washington with a demand that he retire. Before the message could be presented, a clash between this detachment and part of Washington's force resulted in the death of Jumonville and in angry French charges of murder. Washington, halted at Great Meadows, where he named his hasty defenses Fort Necessity, was attacked and obliged to surrender. The first English effort to establish control on the Ohio had been decisively repulsed.

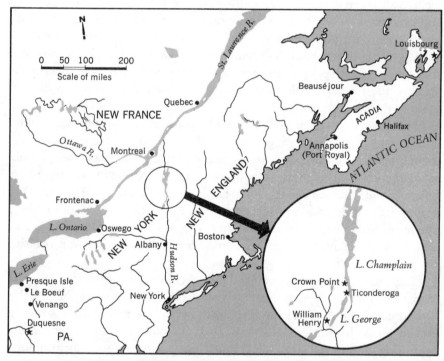

Principal Area of War, 1755-1763

Yet this frontier clash was the spark that touched off the final conflict for North America. Though Britain and France were at peace in Europe, they were now drawn into hostilities in the New World. For almost the first time, both mother countries prepared to lend substantial support to their embattled colonies. In 1755 France sent a force of 3000 men under General Ludwig August Dieskau; and although the expedition was intercepted and attacked by a British naval force in spite of the lack of an official state of war, the bulk of the ships escaped and reached Quebec in safety. In the same year Britain despatched two regiments under General Edward Braddock to Virginia to aid the colonies in their efforts to repel the French. Although the failure of the Albany congress in the previous year showed that disunity was still rampant, alarm at French designs was growing and the colonies were slowly moving toward the gathering of their resources for the decisive test.

Their first task was to crush the outposts that were the advance line of French penetration. The Great Lakes and the St. Lawrence were guarded at strategic points by such forts as Michilimackinac, Detroit, Niagara, and Frontenac. Fort Duquesne had pushed the protective buffer southward to the Ohio. Crown Point guarded the approaches by way of Lake Champlain and the Richelieu. Beauséjour and Louisbourg stood sentinels on the eastern flank. A military conference in Virginia, where the energetic Shirley found a chance to assume the role of a military genius, decided on an effort to break this outer line. While Braddock was to lead an attack on Fort Duquesne, Shirley was to attack Niagara; an expedition under Sir William Johnson was to strike at Crown Point and open the way to Canada, and a fourth force was to dislodge the French from Beauséjour.

Only the last of these enterprises was successful. Shirley never reached Niagara. Johnson, checked before he reached Crown Point, had to content himself with in turn checking the French who had advanced to meet him and with the wounding and capture of their commander Dieskau. But all these episodes were overshadowed by Braddock's defeat, which filled the French with exultation and jolted the English into a realization that far more serious efforts would have to be put forth if victory was to be won.

In 1756 the outbreak of the Seven Years' War in Europe brought a formal state of war between Britain and France. Even before it was declared, France had taken fresh steps to strengthen the defenses of Canada. Two regiments of regulars were sent out and with them came the Marquis de Montcalm to succeed Dieskau as commander of the French forces in North America.

Montcalm found a situation that demanded all the talents of skill and energy, which he so abundantly possessed, and others of patience and diplomacy, in which he was somewhat deficient. Canadian self-confidence had been raised to new heights by recent successes. It found an embodiment in the governor, the Marquis de Vaudreuil. The son of a former governor, he had been born in Canada and thoroughly identified himself with the colony and its people. His attitude found expression in unceasing attempts to vaunt the Canadian militia over the regular troops from France and in an equally persistent jealousy of Montcalm's military authority. New France had the advantage of a centralized system of government in mobilizing her resources for war, but friction such as marked the relations between the governor and the commander in chief, and the consequent efforts of the former to secure the chief credit for himself and the Canadian militia, gravely modified the efficiency of military operations and proved a constant handicap to Montcalm's plans and efforts.

The civil administration was a further source of difficulties. Most of the intendants of New France had been able and reasonably honest; but François Bigot, the last of the line, threw lasting discredit on the office by his record of unabashed corruption. He was capable and energetic, but the greater part of his energy was devoted to building up his own fortune and those of his accomplices. Though the governor did not share in the corruption, he ignored and even protected it, and the chief functionaries were active in sharing the spoils. With Bigot at their head, the members of this official ring conspired to loot the treasury on a grand scale. All the economic resources, including supplies for the army, were under their control. False returns of the militia regiments for which they drew funds, fraudulent sales of supplies, which increased their cost to the government fourfold, requisitions of food from the inhabitants at minimum prices and its sale to the army at a profit of several hundred per cent, and false returns from contractors and false claims of presents to the Indians were merely some of the devices used by the grafters to fill their own pockets at the expense of both the treasury and the people.

This state of affairs created a spirit of resentment and discontent that was bound to affect the war effort. There were other factors that had a direct and hampering effect on military activities. As always, war resulted in a serious dislocation of the Canadian economy. The militia was needed to take part in the campaigns; yet the men were also needed on the farms, particularly when the added presence of troops from France placed a fresh strain on an uncertain food supply. The manpower problem presented a constant dilemma. As early as 1755 the export of food had to be embargoed. Rationing followed, including the rationing of horse meat, to which the population was reduced by 1757. If the members of the militia were taken from their farms before seeding and kept over the harvest, the colony would be threatened with famine.

Yet without the militia Montcalm would be quite incapable of conducting a campaign of any magnitude. New France was accustomed to warfare consisting of a few swift raids against enemy outposts. But with the enemy massing against her in ever-growing numbers, such methods were now obsolete. This was war on the European model, with campaigns designed to achieve a major strategic decision. A force of some 3000 French regulars and a rather smaller number of Canadian regular troops was inadequate for operations of this kind. It was only when the militia was available that Montcalm could take the field in force. Even then their quality was dubious, and Montcalm had to use them in ways that would make them an asset rather than an encumbrance. The Indians were an even greater problem, with their insistence on being treated as allies and their tendency to leave when they felt like it. In addition, Montcalm was constantly haunted by the fear that they would get out of hand in victory as well as in defeat. Yet both militia and Indians were essential to him in this warfare in the wilderness. Conditioned by these factors, his offensive activities were reduced to swift blows against limited objectives. He was confined to an essentially defensive strategy, in which the most he could hope was to keep the enemy off balance and prevent a crushing attack by striking first at his slower moving adversaries.

The brilliance of his success in this type of strategy gave to the defense of New France an entirely misleading appearance of strength. In 1756 the English planned their main blow against Ticonderoga, the new fort that the French had built on Lake Champlain and which they called Fort Carillon. Slowness of preparation and the inefficient leadership of Lord Loudon prevented it from being launched and equally frustrated any effective measures at Oswego at the eastern end of Lake Ontario. Montcalm on his part, with his inferiority in strength, wished to abandon the western posts and concentrate his forces for the immediate defense of the colony. But the posts were sources of profit to Bigot and his gang, and Vaudreuil had conceived a plan for an attack on Oswego to which he clung with avidity. Montcalm adapted himself to the situation. He entered into Vaudreuil's plan, descended in overwhelming force on Oswego, forced the garrison to surrender, and destroyed the fort, which he did not feel strong enough to hold. It was the sole important engagement of the year, and it gave a new and valuable security to the flank of New France along the upper St. Lawrence.

Next year brought an even more spectacular stroke. Loudon now decided to make Louisbourg his objective and shifted his main force to Halifax. But adverse winds delayed the junction with the fleet, which must support the landing, and the massing of a superior French naval force at

Louisbourg completed the frustration of the scheme. Meanwhile the weakening of the frontier gave Montcalm his chance. Gathering at Ticonderoga a force of nearly 8000 in addition to Indians, he struck at Fort William Henry at the foot of Lake George. The garrison, outnumbered and with no help forthcoming from nearby Fort Edward, surrendered after six days of bombardment. The victory was marred by the sort of tragedy about which Montcalm had been apprehensive. The Indians got out of hand, and the unfortunate prisoners were assailed and a number killed in spite of the promise of safe-conduct, which Montcalm proved unable to enforce.

By 1758 the period of unqualified French triumphs was drawing to a close. Pitt was now in power in England, and under his direction the army was being reorganized and new and able commanders were being discovered. The navy was also feeling the effects of the new spirit that he infused, and British sea power now came into play to gain command of the sea lanes and to seal the doom of New France. For the first time there was a prime minister who recognized in the destruction of French maritime power the main objective of the war; for the first time there was a decision on the part of Britain not merely to repel New France but to crush her completely.

The campaign of 1758 was planned on a massive scale, with overwhelming forces directed against the three main points of Duquesne, Ticonderoga, and Louisbourg. In the face of these threats, Montcalm chose to concentrate his forces for the defense of the most vital point— Ticonderoga, which guarded the center and the direct approach to Canada. With a force of slightly over 3000 regulars and militia he made a stand at Ticonderoga and inflicted a disastrous repulse on Sir Ralph Abercromby, with three times his numbers. But this brilliant victory failed to offset the disasters on the flanks. Abercromby had reluctantly allowed Colonel John Bradstreet to detach a force for an attack on Fort Frontenac. The expedition was a complete success. Frontenac was taken and destroyed, cutting a link in the line of communications with Fort Duquesne, which the French decided to abandon. Far to the east, Louisbourg fell to an amphibious assault, with the fleet covering the landing and preventing any relief by an effective blockade and the army under Jeffrey, Baron Amherst, with James Wolfe as a brilliant if impetuous second, reducing the fortress after a siege of seven weeks. The bastion guarding the entrance to the St. Lawrence had fallen, and the way was cleared for a direct assault on Quebec.

Montcalm recognized that the outlook was virtually hopeless. The colony was in dire straits, with soldiers and civilians alike on short rations.

France had given it up for lost. Only seventy-five reinforcements had reached Montcalm in 1758, and any new forces would aggravate the problem of food. Montcalm indeed sent an emissary to France to plead for aid, but the response was that the king could not spare forces proportionate to those available to the English and that an effort would only inspire England to send still more troops to America. Already Britain and her colonies had set on foot a force of some 50,000, almost equal to the whole population of Canada. Writing to the minister of war, Montcalm stated flatly that, without some unexpected stroke of luck, Canada would be lost in the next campaign.

Again the English planned a triple campaign, which would converge by way of the upper and lower St. Lawrence and Lake Champlain. In the west the attack on Niagara succeeded with little trouble, but the force involved proved too weak to turn and threaten Montreal. In the center Montcalm gave up the effort to hold the advance post of Ticonderoga. He left there a covering force, which destroyed the fort on the approach of Amherst's superior force and retreated up Lake Champlain. Their instructions were to fight a tenacious rearguard action that would bar the English from the Richelieu, and aided by Amherst's deliberate movements they succeeded in their purpose. As a result, Montreal was saved from attack that year, and Montcalm was able to concentrate the bulk of his forces against Wolfe at Quebec.

For the defense of that vital point he had gathered some 10,000 men, to which could be added perhaps another 4500 consisting of the town garrison together with Indians and other auxiliaries. A French convoy that slipped through in the spring brought a few reinforcements and some badly needed supplies; but once the British force appeared in the St. Lawrence, no further help could be expected from France. British sea power once again asserted itself as a decisive factor, transporting the expedition to Quebec, gaining command of the river above as well as below the citadel, and establishing a complete blockade, which isolated New France for the duration of the campaign.

It was one thing to appear before Quebec; it was quite another to take it. Wolfe, in command of some 9000 men, landed in June on the Island of Orleans and seized Levis opposite Quebec, from which position his guns opened a devastating bombardment against the town. But he found no vulnerable point against which he could launch an assault. Above Quebec a mobile force under Louis Antoine de Bougainville patrolled the river bank, alert to repel an attempted landing. Below the town the French were strongly entrenched in the Beauport lines guarding the rising ground across the St. Charles, with their eastern flank protected by the gorge of the Montmorency. A direct assault on Quebec was too formidable to attempt. Wolfe found it impossible to effect a crossing of the Montmorency and take the French from the rear. An assault on the Beauport lines on the last day of July met with a bloody repulse. "The enemy," complained Wolfe, "has shut himself up in inaccessible entrenchments so that I can't get at him without spilling a torrent of blood."

Such resolutely defensive tactics represented Montcalm's best chance of saving the colony for another year. By the beginning of September it almost seemed that he would succeed. The fleet could not stay much longer without being shut up for the winter. Its withdrawal would mean that the army must abandon the siege and retire from Canada. Wolfe, ill and feverish, saw success slipping from his grasp. In his desperation he contemplated another effort against the Beauport lines. His brigadiers saved him from possible disaster by favoring an alternative plan of attacking above Quebec somewhere between Cap Rouge and Pointe-aux-Trembles. This was almost equally risky, and it was Wolfe himself who found the solution. About two miles above Quebec was a cove, the Anse au Foulon, from which a path led to the Plains of Abraham outside the city. It was guarded by a weak detachment under an incapable officer, and a surprise assault offered the best chance of breaking the deadlock the continuance of which would spell defeat.

It was an operation that called for the most perfect precision of timing. To keep Montcalm's force divided and scattered, Bougainville was drawn away by feints toward Pointe-aux-Trembles, and the force at Beauport under Vaudreuil was pinned down by a naval demonstration that seemed to threaten an assault in that quarter. Then on September 12, in the darkness of a moonless night, the attack was launched. A shock detachment crossed silently in small boats. The fact that the French were expecting a convoy of supplies from Montreal helped the party to deceive a sentry, whose challenge was answered in convincing French. The guard at the top of the path was routed by the first force ashore. The vital position was seized and held, and by daylight Wolfe had got his whole force ashore and was marshaling them on the Plains of Abraham.

"There they are," exclaimed Montcalm, "where they have no right to be!" His defensive position had been pierced, and he must now come directly to grips with the enemy. He had a choice between taking the offensive and attacking Wolfe before he could entrench and consolidate, or waiting behind the walls of Quebec until he could unite his forces with those of Bougainville and Vaudreuil and strike with his full strength. He may have feared that the latter course would mean a siege, which Quebec, with its weak defenses on the landward side and its supplies almost exhausted, had little hope of standing for long. His temperament, strained by months on the defensive, impelled him to immediate action. He decided to attack.

Wolfe asked nothing better. In numbers Montcalm's force was about equal to his own 4500 and superior to his immediate strength on the field of battle. But Wolfe's regiments were regulars, while half of Montcalm's force was composed of militia. Wolfe's confidence was shown by his action in drawing up his men in a thin, two-deep line in order to gain length. He trusted in their steadiness to stand the shock of the six-deep French assault. The weight of that assault was hampered by the tactics of the Canadian militia, who opened fire at comparatively long range and then threw themselves on the ground to reload, somewhat disorganizing the advance of the regulars. The British held their fire until the French were within forty yards. Then they loosed a shattering volley, followed by a second, and the whole line charged forward. The militia broke and fled. The regulars were unable to stand against the tide that swept down upon them. Montcalm, trying to rally his forces, was mortally wounded. Wolfe in the moment of victory was also mortally stricken, but his work was done. Fifteen minutes had sufficed to decide the battle and to send the French reeling back within the walls of Quebec.

The battle of the Plains of Abraham is rightly regarded as one of the decisive events in the history of North America, but the decision was not immediately clinched. The abandonment of the Beauport lines and the surrender of Quebec on September 18 eased the situation of the British, for Levis was at that moment approaching with a relief force from Montreal and might have caught them between two fires. But their position in Quebec throughout the winter was far from happy. The ruined town offered none too adequate shelter, and it was hard to find supplies in a countryside that the British themselves had devastated in order to keep supplies from Montcalm. Early the next year, as soon as the river was navigable, Levis moved again against the British garrison, which had been seriously weakened by frostbite and disease. Murray, the commander, decided to fight in the open rather than behind inadequate walls, but his rash tactics resulted in a costly defeat at St. Foy. Levis was not at the moment strong enough to follow up with a prompt assault on the town, but Quebec's position was precarious in the extreme. If a naval expedition from France could get through, as Levis hoped, Wolfe's victory might be canceled out. But the ships which appeared at Quebec on May 9 were British ships, and their arrival sealed the doom of Canada. British forces from Quebec and Lake Champlain and Oswego now converged on Montreal, and there on September 8 Vaudreuil signed the capitulation that surrendered the whole of Canada.

The surrender was ratified by the Treaty of Paris in 1763. In the interval some doubts had been raised about the final disposition of Canada. The unflattering fact emerged that neither side wanted the colony for its own sake. There was strong pressure in England for taking the sugar island of Guadeloupe instead, and considerable argument that by taking Canada from France there was danger that England would facilitate the independence of her other American colonies. In France there was equally strong pressure on the government to get rid of a colony that had proved such a drain on the financial and military resources of the mother country. In the end the decisive factor was the desire to strike a final blow at French imperial power. By the treaty, France abandoned all her possessions on the mainland of North America. Canada was ceded to Britain. Spain was given Louisiana, and Britain gained possession of the Floridas. From Hudson Bay to the Gulf of Mexico, the whole eastern half of the continent came under English control.

The Defence of Quebec, 1690.
The defenders repel the British expedition under Phips.

William Shirley.
Governor of Massachusetts and a vigorous advocate of the conquest of Acadia.

Halifax Harbor.
A drawing by Richard Short.

Expulsion of the Acadians.
A romanticized illustration by Frank Dicksee for an early edition of Evangeline.

Braddock's Defeat.

Marquis de Montcalm.

The Attack on Louisbourg.

The Battle of the Plains of Abraham. *(Public Archives of Canada)*

The Landing at Anse au Foulon. *(McCord Museum, McGill University)*

The Plan of Quebec.

PLAN OF QUEBEC, Reduc'd from an Actual Survey 1763.

References.
A. Residence of the Governor-
General.
B. Fort St. Louis.
C. The Bishops Palace
D. Seminary
E. Jesuits College
F. Recollets
G. Ursuline Convent
H. Hotel de Dieu
I. The Palace

High Water Mark.

St. Charles River.

(Courtesy of The New York Historical Society, New York City)

Chapter 7

The First Years of British Rule

The Aftermath of Conquest

The acquisition of Canada injected a new and complicating factor into an already complicated imperial situation. The war had emphasized the growing need for a more positive and clear-cut policy toward the empire on the part of the British government. The need was accentuated by the fact that provision now had to be made for the new conquests; and Britain's efforts to solve the problems thus confronting her ended in the disruption of her empire in America.

The outcome of the war placed Britain in possession of four new colonies. In addition to Canada she acquired Grenada and East and West Florida. The problems presented by West Indian sugar islands, the almost unsettled region of the Floridas, and Canada, with its compact French population and far-reaching trade connections, were obviously very diverse. They were also quite different from those presented by the English colonies on the Atlantic seaboard. Yet the initial approach was not merely to treat the new possessions all alike, but to assimilate them to the older empire by establishing a uniform system on the model of the existing royal colonies.

In certain respects Nova Scotia offered a precedent for such a policy. That conquest, to which New England had so largely contributed, had been followed by a proposal to annex the territory to Massachusetts. Britain, however, preferred not to strengthen that commonwealth, whose independent tendencies were even then suspect. But while Nova Scotia was made a separate province, it was intended that it should ultimately be a self-governing one on the model of Virginia. The governor's instructions in 1719 indicated that an assembly was contemplated as soon as conditions warranted. In the meantime the colony was ruled by a governor and council, but this was looked on as temporary until the increase in population should warrant the calling of a representative body.

The interim was prolonged by the slow progress of settlement. It was not until 1749 that systematic efforts were made to promote immigration, and for some years the results were decidedly mixed. Discharged soldiers and distressed artisans from England proved to be of limited value as pioneers. The same applied to the Protestants who were recruited in France and the Rhineland, though a group of Germans established a small but lasting settlement at Lunenburg. The most suitable and efficient settlers were New Englanders, whose influx speeded up when the lands of the exiled Acadians became available and the capture of Louisbourg removed the French menace. Even so the inflow at first lagged behind expectations. New Englanders were little disposed to live under a government in which they had no voice. Those within the province clamored for an assembly. Those who might have come were deterred by the absence of self-government. The authorities in London favored concessions, but Governor Charles Lawrence fought against them and delayed the carrying out of his instructions. In the end, however, he received positive orders that he could no longer evade, and in 1758, at the height of the Seven Years' War, the first assembly of Nova Scotia came into being.

The results seemed to justify the policy of the home government. A real immigration from New England began in 1760. Settlers occupied the Acadian lands around the Bay of Fundy. Fishermen founded villages on the south coast convenient to the fishing grounds. A number of expelled Acadians filtered back. Scottish Highlanders displaced by the enclosure movement sought lands on Cape Breton and Prince Edward Island as well as on the mainland. The fact that France had finally been expelled from the whole region and that the settlers could live in relative security, the approaching exhaustion of available lands in New England, the barriers and uncertainties that hampered movement beyond the Alleghenies, all contributed to a northward expansion of population. After 1768 it ebbed as the tide set in toward the Ohio valley. But meanwhile self-government had been followed by an encouraging growth of settlement, and it might well seem that a similar policy might succeed equally well elsewhere.

In actual fact, however, Nova Scotia was of limited value as a precedent for Canada. The latter colony had a French population far more numerous than the handful of Acadians that Britain inherited after the Treaty of Utrecht. There would be no wholesale deportations that would make already cleared farms available to English settlers. The opening of the Ohio Valley to settlement, which acted as a check on emigration from New England to Nova Scotia, would prove still more adverse to any early movement from the English colonies to Canada. Yet it was upon the assumption that Canada would shortly be settled by an English Protestant population that British authorities drew up the first plans for the government of the new colony.

It was only after the conclusion of peace that these plans began to emerge. In the interval, authority was vested nominally in the commander in chief and practically in the military governors of Quebec, Three Rivers, and Montreal. Though there were local differences in the problems of these three communities and the consequent actions of the governors, the general approach was almost identical; and probably no conquered country ever enjoyed such propitious beginnings under its new rulers as did Canada during the five years after the fall of Quebec.

This was due in part to the moderation and restraint with which the governors exercised their powers and in part to the circumstances in which they found themselves. Until 1763 there was no certainty that Canada would remain permanently in British possession. There was in consequence no reason for the governors to inaugurate drastic and permanent changes. Their chief concern was to avoid any disturbances that might make their task more difficult, and they had every motive to avoid interference with the accustomed ways of life of the civilian population.

In addition their powers of action were restricted by the terms of surrender, which were binding until the conclusion of peace. The capitulations of Quebec in 1759 were followed next year by the more comprehensive capitulations of Montreal, which applied to the whole colony. Vaudreuil in negotiating the surrender of Canada tried to secure the maximum guaranties for its inhabitants. He asked that the old laws and taxes should continue unchanged and that the Canadians should be exempted from bearing arms against France. He tried to secure the legal continuation of the tithe and even the right of the French king to name the bishop of Quebec. Amherst rejected these demands; but he conceded the free exercise of the Catholic religion and promised security of property for the inhabitants. He also agreed to allow the various orders of nuns to continue unmolested, though he refused to extend this promise to such male orders as the Jesuits and Sulpicians. With these qualifications, some of which might still be modified by royal generosity, the terms of surrender left the basic social structure of Canada largely intact.

The succeeding period of military rule was marked by a deliberate and successful effort to carry on the affairs of the colony with as little dislocation as possible. The seigniorial system was left untouched. The tithe was not enforced, but no serious effort was made to interfere with its continued collection by the priests. Although judicial power rested with the military courts, they drew on the precedents of the old regime for their decisions and on the old personnel for assistance in their work. The militia captains in particular were used as local magistrates. The military courts made use of French clerks and French attorneys. The governors themselves assumed much of the authority formerly vested in the intendants, hearing appeals and issuing ordinances and regulating prices in very much the manner to which the Canadians were accustomed.

The war and its aftermath brought a number of special problems. Economic life had been severely dislocated by the burden of hostilities and the severance of normal contacts with France. The distress of the local merchants was aggravated by the fact that Bigot had flooded the country with a mass of paper money the value of which was highly dubious. France ultimately agreed to its partial redemption, and in the meantime the British made an effort to establish a specie currency, leaving custom and the courts between them to work out its relation to the discredited paper, which became generally stable at a discount of 85 per cent. The consequences of royal bankruptcy were thus added to the burdens and ravages of war, which had fallen with greatest severity on the district of Quebec. The town itself lay half in ruins. Many of the surrounding farms had been devastated by the invaders, and almost all had suffered from the absence of the men on military service. Even seed for the next harvest was lacking. It was the task of the governors to restore agriculture, to regulate the supplies of necessities and establish maximum prices, to stabilize the currency in the interests of internal commercial life; and to a very large extent they achieved these ends during the first year of military rule.

The process of readjustment was made easier by the relative complacence with which the Canadians accepted the conquest. Some of the Canadian nobles took advantage of the terms that allowed them to emigrate to France within eighteen months; but the exodus was not large, and the bulk of the population was chiefly concerned with a speedy and permanent return to the ways of peace.

There were inevitable social dislocations. The return to France of royal administrators, particularly the leading officials, meant the departure of an important group from among the social elite. Military officers naturally left with their regiments, and these included a certain number of native Canadians. Many of the leading merchants had been agents for French firms, or itinerants operating privately, and their exodus seriously depleted the colony's bourgeoisie. Most of the wholesale and a considerable part of the retail trade had been in their hands; the residue was left to small merchants, operating in a colony whose total population at its peak scarcely matched that of present-day Sherbrooke or Three Rivers. But it was the groups which had no indigenous roots in the colony that were superseded by English officials and merchants and military personnel. The habitants and small traders, the bulk of the seigniors and the clergy, remained on their native soil. The community lost important leading elements, but the community itself was basically unchanged. Resting on the twin pillars of the church and the seigniorial system, it remained a compact and integrated society as it faced the task of survival under a new and alien rule.

The general temper at the outset was one of acquiescence in the fortunes of war, and in some cases even gratification at the outcome. "Cease your compassion for us," wrote a local merchant to a French correspondent, "out lot is less unfortunate than it was previously."

In contrast to the earlier situation in Acadia, there was now no nearby French base from which the Canadians could be provoked into resistance to the conquerors. Rather there was a resentful feeling that France had abandoned the colony to its fate, accompanied by a growing recognition that the fate was far from onerous. The presence of British troops laid on the civilians certain obligations such as the billeting of soldiers and the supplying of provisions and firewood; but the troops also brought in a welcome amount of hard cash, and the inhabitants were paid in solid coin for supplies and services. They were subject to certain restrictions such as the curfew, but in general the economic and civil regulations imposed by the governors were scarcely more stringent than under the old regime. The newcomers provided a market for local products, which stimulated the revival of economic life. They made no effort to interfere with religion or laws or language. They exercised their powers with a paternalism that was well calculated to heal the wounds of war, which laid a promising foundation for future harmony between French settlers and British rulers.

The framing of a more permanent system rested in the first instance with the Board of Trade, the advisory body of the British government in colonial matters. It had to consider the measures most suitable for the immediate situation, the long-term policy with respect to Canada and the best means of implementing it, and the relation of the Canadian arrangements to the wider imperial policy affecting the whole of British North America. The report of the board on June 8, 1763, revealed a measure of confusion, which foreshadowed the unfortunate tangle of purposes and provisions that was to follow. In particular, the western problem bulked large and was accentuated by Pontiac's revolt, which broke out in May; and British policy toward the west had a direct and significant bearing on decisions with respect to Canada.

The basis of that policy was a desire to end the Indian menace. Behind this lurked a certain reluctance to facilitate the expansion of settlement into the interior; but the immediate reason for restricting settlement was the need to reassure the Indians about their lands. Until treaties for the surrender of these lands could be negotiated, settlers were to be excluded from them and the west was to be preserved as Indian territory. There was a suggestion that the region should be annexed to Canada as the colony from which effective jurisdiction could most conveniently be exercised. But the board feared that this might give the impression, particularly among the Indians, that the French claim to that region had been valid, and it objected both to the special advantages that annexation would confer upon Canada in respect to the fur trade and to possible friction between the governor and the commander of the garrisons in the west. The decision was therefore in favor of a separate area under direct imperial authority and a consequent restriction of Canada's southern boundary.

The decision to prohibit settlement in the west, at least temporarily, was justified by the claim that plenty of land was now available in Canada and the Floridas as well as in Nova Scotia. The board, it is true, expressed some doubt whether any large British population could be expected in Canada for a considerable period. It therefore suggested boundaries that would largely restrict the colony to the existing limits of French settlement on the east, leaving the present area of New Brunswick under the government of Nova Scotia and annexing the north shore of the Gulf with its fisheries to Newfoundland. The report pointed out that such restriction would make it possible to treat Canada as a separate problem and to leave the French in possession of their existing rights and usages. Yet along with this recognition of Canada as a separate problem went the assertion that British and Protestant settlement should be increased as rapidly as possible and that a regular form of government suited to this purpose should be established.

The tendency to treat Canada on a distinct basis was abandoned almost at once. Pontiac's revolt, which gave new urgency to the need to reassure the Indians, resulted in the Proclamation of 1763 forbidding settlement west of a line along the heads of the rivers falling into the Atlantic. In the same document the government lumped together its decisions respecting the boundaries of the new colonies and the system of government to be established there. It invited settlers to move into these territories, promising them the full enjoyment of the laws of England and representative assemblies such as existed in the older colonies. These provisions applied to Canada as well as to the Floridas and Grenada. It was created the province of Quebec, with boundaries that confined it to the lower St. Lawrence Valley.

Its southern boundary ran from Lake Nipissing to the St. Lawrence in the vicinity of the present city of Cornwall, and thence along the 45th parallel to the highlands that were assumed to separate it from the seaboard colonies. This confined area, remote from the other English settlements, was ill designed to attract an influx of pioneers. Yet the proclamation tacitly assumed such an influx by providing for the establishment of English law and by promising an assembly as soon as circumstances allowed.

Therein lay the seeds of future trouble. It did not arise at once, for the French had little political instinct or experience. They would accept any form of government that did not bring with it the general uprooting of the customs and institutions with which they were familiar. Even the introduction of English law only gave rise to dissension when its practical inconvenience became apparent through experience. And those dissensions themselves were not in the first instance a quarrel between races. Racial questions were at their roots; but the first protagonists were not the French and English sections of the population, but two groups among the conquerors—the British merchants, who clamored for the immediate fulfillment of the promises held out by the proclamation, and the British governors and officials, who made a determined effort to protect the French from the changes that such promises implied.

Merchants and Habitants

The first British merchants came to Canada with the invading army. They were the contractors and purveyors, who found a profitable occupation in supplying the needs of the troops, and the enterprising adventurers who seized on the commercial opportunities presented by the dislocation resulting from war and conquest. Amherst issued a public invitation to traders "to repair hither with all kinds of commodities and provisions" so that the distress of the colony might be relieved and its economic life restored. These incentives drew a number of merchants from the older colonies. Some of them were American born; others had come from the British Isles by way of the American colonies in the wake of the army.

The influx was not large. The substantial merchants, as distinct from small shopkeepers, probably numbered less than 100 during the decade after the conquest. But their importance was out of all proportion to their numbers. The existing commercial life of the colony had been stricken at its roots. The French merchants had lost the connection with Europe on which they relied for their supply of goods. The conquest transferred Canada's commercial dependence from Paris to London, and it was the British merchants with their connections in England who were the essential instruments of trade and prosperity. They stepped right into the key positions in the economic life of the province of Quebec, and that fact made them of salient importance in political affairs as well.

Their arrival introduced a new element, which was both invigorating and disturbing. They came to make money. They wanted to make as much as they could as quickly as possible without too many scruples about the means. But little though they realized or cared, they were the heralds of forces that were of the most profound consequence for the future development of Canada. Into a feudal Catholic community they brought the modern spirit of economic individualism and capitalist enterprise. Something of that spirit was already evident in the fur trade under the French, but the broader activities of the newcomers gave it a crude and lusty manifestation that heightened its significance. Implicit in the resulting situation was the divergence between two incompatible views of society— the ordered and largely stable community such as the Church and Crown had tried to create in New France, and the competitive and progressive type, which had already emerged in the English colonies.

As the practical results of this divergence became evident, a broadening gulf would open between the two races. The growing strength of the mercantile element would give rise to new problems affecting the relations between government and business. Their expanding needs and ambitions would accentuate the problems presented by the physical geography of Canada and would call for new political as well as new economic departures to overcome them. To questions of internal policy would be added others concerned with external relations, and Canada's economic development would become more and more entangled with similar developments in both Britain and the United States.

At the outset there was little direct friction between French and English. The two races were too important to each other. The English, with their contacts in London, controlled the bulk of export and import trade and took over much of the wholesale business. In the city of Quebec they became interested in the Gulf fisheries. In Montreal they established connections with the fur trade. They supplied the imported goods upon which the colony depended and provided a market for a large part of its produce. In turn they depended on the French for the products in which they dealt as exporters. The two races discovered a harmony of economic interests that gave brief promise of a mutually profitable partnership.

The French indeed had much cause to feel that their fortunes had been improved by the change of masters. Initially the British army during the period of occupation provided a market for local products. By the time it was disbanded or withdrawn, other opportunities had opened up. Quebec was now within the British mercantile system, which offered wider markets than the old French empire. The energy of the British merchants was stimulating even when the sharpness of their competition was occasionally confusing and upsetting to the habitant. By instruction and example the farming methods of the habitant were improved, and production was stimulated by the opening of markets in Britain and the West Indies. Bounties were offered on deals and planks and staves. Wheat and timber, two of the future staples of Canada, began to emerge in importance; and other embryo activities, from the manufacture of potash to domestic weaving of linen and woolens, gave promise of further development.

All such activities, however, were of minor importance compared to the fur trade. After the conquest as before it, the fur trade dominated the Canadian economy. But the conflict between fur trade and agriculture, which dominated the old regime, was now largely resolved. As population and settlement expanded in spite of all distractions, even the French authorities became less acutely concerned over the preference of able-bodied young men for the life of the *coureur* or *voyageur*. The conquest brought to completion a transition that was already in progress. British merchants were chiefly interested in the possibilities of Quebec as a commercial state. If they made no attempt to wean the habitant from agriculture—indeed, they rather encouraged him to increase his efficiency as a farmer—neither did they feel it essential to keep him on the land. And as commercial life fell more and more into English hands, the distinctive French society became the settled feudal community along the banks of the St. Lawrence.

This distinction between English commerce and French agriculture emerged only slowly. At the outset the fur trade continued to depend largely on French personnel for its very existence. The Indians were suspicious of the English and resentful of their claims to replace the political authority of France. It was the French trader who knew the paths to the west and whose talent for dealing with the tribes was a paramount asset in maintaining the fur trade. It was the Canadian *voyageur* whose hardihood and skill made possible an efficient system of transportation to the Upper Country. It was the French merchant on whose knowledge of how the trade was organized, and what supplies and personnel were necessary, the new arrivals at first depended. The English had the connections needed for credit and goods and markets. The French had the experience and technique necessary for the actual conduct of the fur trade. The two races at once came together in an active cooperation, which continued the close commercial connection between the St. Lawrence Valley and the vast interior of the continent.

One result was that the English merchant who became involved in the fur trade developed almost at once a specifically Canadian outlook and interest. The rivalry of Montreal with Albany and Hudson Bay was entirely independent of race. It was rooted in economics and geography, and the British conquest of Canada did little to abate it. Such change as resulted was in fact to the advantage of Montreal. The Canadian fur trade had hitherto been hampered by the superiority of English trade goods over those from France. Now English goods were available; and in combination with French aptitude and low-cost French labor, this fact restored the ascendancy of Montreal traders in the west. There was some competition from French traders who pushed north from New Orleans. But the efforts of Albany and Philadelphia to compete were less and less successful, and many merchants from those places were gradually drawn to Montreal as the strategic center of the western fur trade. Even the Hudson's Bay Company felt the impact of the new vigor and efficiency; and while the low cost of transportation to Hudson Bay would tell in the end, the incursions of Montreal traders into the Saskatchewan region, where the French had already pioneered, were in this period a serious threat to the company's profits and position.

Such were the factors that made for harmony between English and French immediately after the conquest. It was in the political field that an incipient conflict emerged. Even this was not joined immediately. But as commerce became a paramount English field and interest and as the French outlook narrowed to that of an agricultural state, the economic bonds were weakened, and the resulting divergence of views on social matters was sure to be reflected eventually in diverse views over the political future of the colony.

The situation first arose as the aftermath of the Proclamation of 1763. The merchants viewed that document with mixed feelings. The refusal of the Board of Trade to annex the west to Canada was partly motivated by the desire to deny to Montreal an advantage over such centers as Albany and Philadelphia. To Montreal it seemed that the new and narrow boundaries were a deliberate disruption of the natural connection between the St.

Lawrence and the west. Once engaged in the fur trade, the English merchants, like the French before them, felt the vital need for control of the Ohio and Mississippi valleys.

Their resentment was increased by restrictions that delayed and hampered the revival of the fur trade. It was intended that trade in the west should be equally open to all colonies under a license system. But Pontiac's revolt meant that traders were in fact excluded until 1765; and when a license system was set up in that year, the traders found that they had to give bond for double the value of the goods they took into the interior. This was a serious and for some an insuperable obstacle. Moreover, the first regulations laid it down that trade was to be carried on only at the posts. This was the system to which the Albany traders were accustomed, and it was relatively easy in the Ohio Valley. But Michilimackinac was a center for trade with the Indians over a radius of several hundred miles. Unless the traders went to the villages, the Indians would turn to Spanish and French interlopers from New Orleans. The restrictions proved impossible to maintain in practice. They were gradually relaxed, and full freedom was restored in 1768. With this development, the Quebec boundary lost much of its commercial importance, and Montreal resumed its former ascendancy in the west.

On the political side, however, the merchants viewed the proclamation with gratification. The promise of English law and a representative assembly seemed to give them an assurance of an effective voice in the government of the colony and adequate protection for their interests. It was not so much the principle of self-government that interested them as its practical effects. So long as the actual government supported their desires and favored their interests, they were ready to devote their energies to making money without any urgent desire for direct political influence. But if the governor and council embarked on policies adverse to the unchecked expansion of commerce, the mercantile community would clamor for the fulfillment of promises that would place political power in their hands.

This was in fact what happened. The new civil government adopted the attitude that the promises of the proclamation were inapplicable to the existing situation. In particular the governor felt that their application would do serious injustice to the French, and he made himself their champion even though they showed every sign of willingness to accept the changes that the proclamation envisaged. The "new subjects" were to be protected against the overthrow of their familiar laws and customs. The "old subjects" were to be denied the rights which they claimed as their

British heritage and which they had been assured they would not lose by resorting to the new colony. Out of this situation arose a violent quarrel between the local British government and the British mercantile community; and behind this clash lay still graver implications, in which racial divisions were inherent.

The Merchants and Murray

On August 10, 1764, military government in the province of Quebec gave way to civil rule. General James Murray, who had become commander at Quebec after the death of Wolfe and who was governor of that district during the military regime, was now appointed governor-general of the whole colony. The system he had to apply was defined by the proclamation, supplemented by his commission and instructions, and together these documents formed the first constitution of Canada under British rule.

There were many features of the old system that remained untouched by the new provisions. Seigniorial land tenure was not for the present affected. English settlers were still few in numbers. Some discharged soldiers remained in the province as farmers or innkeepers. A few merchants bought up seigniories, but their attitude toward feudal tenure was rather favorable than otherwise. Freedom of worship also remained undisturbed. There were still hopes of strengthening the Protestant element in the colony and even of eventually winning over the French; but this was manifested for the present in a desire to avoid strengthening the Catholic Church rather than in any active interference with it.

In this connection one acute problem had already arisen. Murray was instructed that the article in the treaty which granted the Catholics freedom of worship "as far as the laws of Great Britain permit" involved the exclusion of any foreign ecclesiastical jurisdiction. The restriction threatened to create a delicate situation. The bishop of Quebec had died in the spring of 1760, and it was hard to see how a successor could be appointed without acknowledging the authority of Rome. In the end, however, the British government recognized the need for a bishop, both to satisfy Canadian desires and to provide some regular and responsible authority over the Church in Quebec. In 1765 the British authorities acquiesced in the papal consecration of Jean Olivier Briand, a candidate whose moderate and conciliatory temper made him acceptable to London and whose appointment solved a potentially serious problem.

In matters of law and government the changes were more drastic, at least on paper. Though London later denied any intention of sweeping away the whole French system of law, that seemed to be the effect of the clause in the proclamation that promised settlers the benefit of the laws of England. The English provisions that excluded Catholics from public office were explicitly extended to Canada by Murray's commission. The province was to be ruled by a governor and council until an assembly could be set up; but the temporary nature of this system was shown by the stipulation "that nothing be passed or done, that shall any ways tend to affect the life, limb or liberty of the subject, or to the imposition of duties or taxes." Full legislative power, as well as the power to tax, was to await the calling of the assembly, and under present regulations this body would have to be composed entirely of Protestants.

From the start Murray felt it necessary to modify these provisions very extensively, and even then they were hard to apply. The small number of Protestants in the colony made it difficult to find an adequate number of competent persons to work the new system. Murray selected eight members for his council, but an assembly seemed to him quite out of the question. The judiciary presented a serious problem. An ordinance of September 17, 1764, entrusted police cases and minor civil suits to justices of the peace, created a court of common pleas for civil cases above £10, and set up a Court of King's Bench to hear both civil and criminal cases as well as to handle appeals. It was far from easy to staff this hierarchic system, which in theory was to apply English law and in practice was in many instances conducted in the English language.

The use that Murray had hitherto made of French personnel, including the captains of militia, was no longer possible. They had to be replaced by English appointees, and there were few qualified men available. Many of those who were chosen knew no English law, let alone French; yet some French law simply had to be applied if chaos was to be avoided. Murray decreed that all suits begun before October 1, 1764, were to be decided by French law. Other cases were to be determined "agreeable to equity, having regard nevertheless to the laws of England, as far as the circumstances and present situation of things would permit."

This was a wide loophole, which hardly increased the certainty of the legal system and which was of highly dubious legality. Other modifications, admitting the French to juries and allowing them to practice before the courts, received belated sanction when the law officers in England decided that the disabilities of Catholics in England did not after all extend to Canada. Murray, however, was concerned with the practical rather than the legal aspect. To exclude the French from juries, he wrote, "would constitute 200 Protestants perpetual judges over the lives and property of not only 80,000 of the new subjects, but likewise of all the military in the province."

This last phrase was a revealing comment on the relations that had now developed between the governor, the army, and the English minority. Already a feud had sprung up between soldiers and civilians. The merchants were lively and turbulent and undisciplined. They regarded themselves as men of consequence whose lawful activities were restricted by petty and domineering regulations on the part of the governor and his military associates. They resented all restraints, from the order that everyone abroad on the streets at night must carry a lantern to the restrictions on trade at the western posts. Personal quarrels flared between merchants and soldiers. Merchants found it hard to collect their just debts. Officers occasionally undertook to evict civilians from lodgings desired by the military. An attack by disguised soldiers on a merchant named Thomas Walker cost the latter an ear and created a crisis that shook the whole colony. The merchants gave loud expression to their detestation of military rule, and they looked on Murray's conduct of civil government as a mere continuation of that odious despotism.

Murray returned the dislike of the merchants in full measure. He looked with suspicion on their American origins and the principles of independence that seemed to imbue them. He came to regard them as "a set of licentious fanatics," whose settled aim was the destruction of the French as well as the undermining of his own authority. The more he detested the merchants, the more affection he conceived for the French. At first his admiration for the habitant had been distinctly restrained. But as he contrasted the obedient feudal nature of French society with the constant challenge to authority presented by the English merchants, he grew in his attachment to the conquered race. Canadians, he wrote, were "perhaps the bravest and best race upon the globe, a race, who could they be indulged with a few privileges which the laws of England deny to Roman Catholics at home, would soon get the better of every national antipathy to their conquerors and become the most faithful and useful set of men in this American empire."

This judgment as to the possibility of attaching the French to their new masters had much to recommend it. There would have to be modifications, not only in the matter of religious disabilities, but in other aspects of the legal system. Eighteenth-century English law had its virtues, but clarity and simplicity were not among them. Litigation had been one of the favorite recreations of the habitant. Now he found that a lawsuit involved delays and uncertainties, which diminished his enjoyment and caused him serious inconvenience and expense. The French were also becoming concerned over the prospect of an assembly from which they would be excluded. But if these features were modified, there was a good chance that the population would accept the general application of English laws and institutions.

Unhappily the quarrel between the governor and the merchants prevented a patient and reasonable attempt to work out a compromise. Murray felt that the merchants were apostles of anarchy. They looked on him as a despot who was deliberately denying their rights and opposing their interests. They attacked the judicial system he had created, not only because of its concessions to the French, but because it worked in a vexatious way that hampered their commercial transactions and also because it included no provisions for the writ of *habeas corpus*. They used their control of the Grand Jury to voice their grievances. They demanded the immediate calling of an assembly for whose candidates the French might be allowed to vote, but of which only Protestants were to be members. They carried their complaints to the home government with a petition for the replacement of Murray by a governor "acquainted with other maxims of government than military only." Their growing clamor convinced the government that a change was needed; and in 1765 Murray was recalled.

His successor was Sir Guy Carleton, whose name dominated the succeeding and critical phase of Canadian development. Like Murray, Carleton was a soldier with the temper and outlook of an autocrat. But he had political talents that were at once more subtle and more profound than those of his predecessor, and a readiness as well as an ability to pursue extremely devious paths with patience and tenacity in order to achieve his ends. He possessed vigor and imagination and a profound devotion to his concept of duty. But his judgment was tragically at fault on certain vital matters, and his constructive work was largely stultified by his own miscalculations in combination with incalculable events.

Carleton's first acts were indicative of his character and methods. He came to Canada with a preconceived hostility to Murray and his supporters, and he set out at once to eliminate this group from the government. He called together only part of the council, excluding Murray's closest associates, and he used this selected group to pass measures that reversed previous actions taken by the full council. When the excluded councilors protested, Carleton treated them as agitators whose design was to stir up opposition to the government. When they joined in a public petition criticizing the handling of the case of Thomas Walker, which had been enmeshed in a tangle of legal complications, Carleton seized on their action as "an open attempt to disturb the peace and interrupt the free course of justice." He dismissed the offenders from the council and thus sealed his own supremacy in the government.

His success was followed by a brief period of tranquillity in the public life of the colony. The French raised no difficulties. The merchants were gratified by the recall of Murray and the gradual removal of trade restrictions. They used their strength on the juries to block the collection of the old customs duties, and the government lacked the power to impose new ones. Montreal rejoiced in a system of free imports, which gave it a fresh advantage in the western fur trade, to which it had full access after 1768. Protests against Murray's judicial system brought modifications that contented the merchants for the moment. With a government on which they felt they could count for sympathy and support, the merchants were less impatient at the delay in calling the assembly and felt less urge to acquire direct political power.

The Quebec Act

The lull that descended after the early days of Carleton's administration proved to be deceptive. A change was in preparation, and one of the determining factors was the change in Carleton's own viewpoint. He started out by reversing Murray's attitude and throwing his influence on the side of the merchants. But he had scarcely been a year in the colony before he was converted to Murray's basic point of view, with its unrestrained admiration for the French and its unchecked enthusiasm for feudalism as a system. A major contribution to this change of outlook was Carleton's growing preoccupation with the strategic importance of Canada as a military base. Its full security called for loyalty and political tranquillity on the part of the population. The dangers implicit in the growing spirit of resistance that was evident in the older American colonies, and still more the possibility of a renewed war with France, convinced him that Canada was likely to become "the principal scene where the fate of America may be determined." It was thus imperative to strengthen the defenses of Canada and to rally the loyalty of the Canadians, and for the latter purpose it was absolutely essential to satisfy the French.

The issue was raised when the British government recognized that the situation in Quebec was confused and unsatisfactory and that steps must be taken to regulate it. In 1769 the Board of Trade surveyed the whole matter in a report that called for the liberal fulfillment of the promises of 1763. By this time the scheme for a uniform imperial system accompanied by direct imperial administration of the west had virtually collapsed, but the board still stood firm for the extension of English institutions to Quebec. The report, however, repudiated the idea of reducing the French to a position of subordination and condemned their exclusion from office on the grounds of religion. New as well as old subjects were to share the full benefits of English law and government. The board advocated the immediate calling of an assembly, to which French as well as English should be admitted, and a policy of equality and self-government, which it believed would at once satisfy the merchants and remove the apprehensions of the French.

Against this project Carleton protested with all the vigor at his command. "The better sort of Canadians," he wrote, "fear nothing more than popular assemblies, which, they conceive, tend only to render the people refractory and insolent. . . . A popular assembly, which preserves its full vigor, and in a country where all men appear nearly on a level, must give a strong bias to republican principles." He pointed to the basic flaw in the scheme of 1763—the assumption that Canada would shortly receive a substantial influx of English settlers. "The Europeans who migrate," he asserted, "will never prefer the long inhospitable winters of Canada, to the more cheerful climate and more fruitful soil of His Majesty's southern provinces . . . so that, barring catastrophe shocking to think of, this country must, to the end of time, be peopled by the Canadian race." It was thus upon the French that the value of Canada as a military base must largely depend. He believed that they could provide about 18,000 men well able to carry arms. He also believed that their active loyalty depended largely on attaching their leaders, and especially the seigniors, to the British government. If the seigniors and the clergy could be satisfied, Carleton was convinced that Canada would be secure. But this called for a recognition and even a strengthening of the chief features of the old regime and a complete abandonment of the idea of introducing English laws and English representative government.

Carleton's views fell on sympathetic ears. By 1770 the British government was moving toward a reversal of the Proclamation of 1763. The report of the Board of Trade was carefully suppressed. New demands for an assembly by the merchants, who were becoming uneasy over the change they sensed in Carleton's attitude, were countered by petitions from

French leaders for a restoration of their old laws and privileges. The merchants called attention to the promises that had induced them to risk their persons and property in the new colony and practically accused the Crown of a breach of faith. They expressed a willingness to accept a continuance of the French law of property. If they could not get an assembly, they would reluctantly agree to an enlarged council, which might contain a minority of French members. The attorney general, Francis Masères, presented the case of the merchants to the British government with vigor and cogency. But all these efforts were in vain. The government was convinced by Carleton; and in 1774—the year of crisis following the Boston Tea Party, the year of the Intolerable Acts, which precipitated the final stage of the quarrel leading to revolution—the Quebec Act was passed by the British parliament.

The act was a final abandonment of the effort at a uniform system of colonial government based on English institutions. Canada was accepted as a special problem to be dealt with in a special and separate way. That was a return to authoritarian government. All intention of calling an assembly was now given up. Authority was placed in the hands of the governor and an appointed council of from seventeen to twenty-three members, to which the French were to be admitted without restriction. English criminal law was retained, but French civil law, as embodied in the Custom of Paris, was now established. The seigniorial system of tenure was specifically guaranteed. Not only was freedom of Catholic worship reaffirmed; the right of the Church to collect tithes from all Catholics was at last conceded. There were still possibilities of modifications and adjustments such as might mollify the merchants. In particular, the right of the council to legislate by majority vote opened the way for the introduction of English commercial law and the adoption of *habeas corpus*. But Carleton had no desire to take advantage of these opportunities. He was convinced that the Canadians could best be ruled by a feudal authoritarian system; and the Quebec Act, with its extension of privileges to the church and the seigniors, represented the triumph of his aims.

The new act effected a change in boundaries as well as in government. The collapse of the earlier schemes for the west led to the revival of the idea of annexing that area to a single colony. Quebec was the natural choice, and the need to establish an effective centralized authority over the vast western region provided an added motive for the type of government embodied in the Quebec Act. The extension of the boundaries to take in the Ohio Valley would in other circumstances have gratified the merchants as a fulfillment of their long-expressed desires. Coupled as it was with a

Old Province of Quebec, 1763-1791

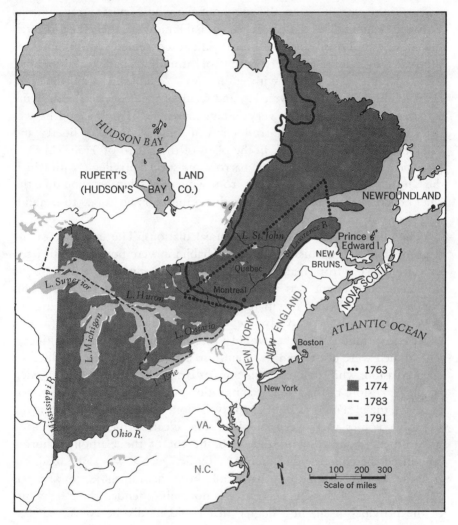

RUPERT'S LAND (HUDSON'S BAY CO.)

HUDSON BAY

NEWFOUNDLAND

L. St. John

St. Lawrence R.

Quebec

Prince Edward I.

NEW BRUNS.

Montreal

L. Superior

L. Huron

L. Ontario

L. Michigan

L. Erie

NEW YORK

NEW ENGLAND

NOVA SCOTIA

ATLANTIC OCEAN

Boston

Mississippi R.

New York

VA.

Ohio R.

N.C.

···	1763
■	1774
--	1783
—	1791

N

0 100 200 300

Scale of miles

repudiation of the promises of self-government and English law, the territorial change failed to compensate for the blow that the act struck on the political side.

The Quebec Act has been praised, and with considerable justification, as a measure of unprecedented generosity toward a conquered people. Yet it was generosity in the interest of reaction. Grasping and self-interested as the merchants may have been, their purposes nonetheless forced them to stand as the champions of political liberalism against Carleton's desire for a strict authoritarian system. Throughout the whole controversy, with its growing element of racial divergence, the habitant was largely the forgotten man. Carleton hoped to make him loyal and contented, but his aim was motivated by a desire for effective control through the habitant's superiors. The old regime, he wrote with enthusiasm, "established subordination, from the highest to the lowest . . . and secured obedience to the supreme seat of government from a very distant province." For this end he was determined to prevent the introduction of those elements of liberty and equality which were implicit in the plans of the Board of Trade. In their place he secured a system built on narrow and special privilege, with which the Church would be satisfied but from which the seigniors would be the chief beneficiaries; and on this oligarchic foundation he hoped to establish a firm system of autocratic rule.

This view was based on grave miscalculations. The influence of the seigniors and the submissiveness of the habitant were both overestimated by Carleton. Far from being gratified by the recognition of the seignior's position, the habitant was in many cases left sullen and resentful. This outcome in turn helped to vitiate the ultimate purpose that the change of government was meant to advance. Canada was not after all transformed into the key military base that would assure control of the whole continent. The French were not rallied to an enthusiastic defense against rebellion or even invasion, while colonial suspicions of British designs were heightened by the provisions of the act. The annexation of the west to Quebec seemed to revive the idea of a "wall of circumvallation," which would confine the English colonies to the coastal plain. The creation of an authoritarian government, coupled with the establishment of the Catholic Church, convinced the colonists that French Catholic Quebec was to be used as a base for a military despotism that would keep them in subjection. Francis Masères wrote of the Quebec Act: "It not only offended the inhabitants of the province itself, in a degree that could hardly be conceived, but alarmed all the English provinces in America, and contributed more, perhaps, than any other measure whatsoever, to drive them into rebellion against their sovereign." That was an exaggerated view, but so is the traditional statement that the Quebec Act saved Canada for Britain. There are strong indications that, on the contrary, it nearly led to the loss of Canada, and it certainly made its contribution to the loss of America.

(*Public Archives of Canada*)

Entrance to St. John's Harbor, Newfoundland.
From the log book of HMS Pegasus, 1786.

General James Murray.

Sir Guy Carleton, Lord Dorchester.

Chapter 8

"Catastrophe
Shocking to Think of"

The Disruption of the Empire

The conflict of policies and interests that ultimately issued in the Quebec Act was only one phase of the broader imperial controversy that marked the decade after 1763. The expulsion of France from America had brought to a head the problem of the relations between the mother country and the colonies. To questions of trade and government there was now added the question of western settlement with its controversial bearing on the mercantile theory of empire. This in turn accentuated the problem of imperial defense, which had been brought to the forefront by the struggle with France, and gave rise to the issue of imperial taxation, which became the immediate focus of colonial resistance.

The grievances rapidly spread until they embraced almost every aspect of the imperial relationship. Speculators and settlers objected to the restrictions imposed by the Proclamation Line. Merchants and shipowners and rum distillers cried out that they would be ruined by the enforcement of the Navigation Acts. Resistance to imperial taxation, first roused by the imposition of direct taxes under the Stamp Act, was extended to the indirect taxes levied under the Townshend duties. Once the taxing authority of the imperial parliament was called into question, it was no great step to questioning its authority to legislate. Colonial claims to self-government expanded steadily as colonial nationalism grew in self-consciousness, until they reached a virtual repudiation of all imperial authority except for a nominal allegiance to the Crown.

The Quebec Act was one more spark dropped into an explosive situation. Its provisions were at least partly motivated by British alarm over the spirit of resistance in the older colonies. Its effect was to strengthen that spirit. The annexation of the West to Quebec seemed to confirm the intention of Britain to prevent the westward expansion of settlement. The abandonment of the principle of colonial self-government and the concessions to the Catholic Church seemed designed to revive the menace from French Canada as a check upon colonial liberties. The coincidence of the Quebec Act with the punitive provisions of the Intolerable Acts heightened the alarm in the colonies and strengthened the determination to resist imperial interference. The growing tension culminated in the armed clash at Lexington and Concord, which fired the train leading to revolution.

From this movement two mainland colonies stood aloof. The revolution failed to draw either Nova Scotia or Quebec into its orbit. When the test came, the forces of geographic and economic sectionalism proved stronger than the ties of race or kinship. The settlers who had migrated from New England to Nova Scotia and the merchants who had gone from the older colonies to Quebec inherited many of the rivalries that had previously set the French in those areas at odds with the English to the south. The two provinces felt little concern over the grievances that moved the Thirteen Colonies to revolution. They had grievances of their own, which inclined some of their inhabitants to sympathize with the revolt; but these did not really constitute common ground, and they were offset by the divergences of interest between the two northern colonies and the other English communities. There were also wide divergences between Nova Scotia and Quebec; but though their motives were different, they led to the same result when it came to a choice between loyalty and rebellion.

Certain general considerations, moreover, helped to determine the action of both colonies. On the negative side, they were little moved by the issues that had stirred their neighbors to resistance. The threat to exclude settlement from the West was of no concern to Nova Scotia, where settlers and land speculators had vacant territory closer at hand, while it was a positive benefit to those among the Canadian merchants whose interest was in the Western fur trade. There was no serious resentment in either colony against the Navigation Acts. On the contrary, the commercial interests had a real stake in preserving the system of imperial protection. As for the issue of imperial taxation, neither the Stamp Act nor the Townshend duties imposed a serious enough burden to make the colonists feel that their interests were threatened or their liberties in danger.

For these colonies the burdens of imperial rule were in fact outweighed by its benefits. Their pioneer state made them economically dependent on the mother country to a far greater degree than was the case in the older colonies, with their greater wealth and stability. The commercial connection with Britain was important to Nova Scotia and vital to the Quebec mercantile community. British financial grants and expenditures on supplies and public works played a considerable part in the local economy. British garrisons, whose presence was so much resented in other colonies, were customers who brought welcome supplies of hard cash to Nova Scotia and Quebec. The results of this economic dependence were reflected in the political sphere. Nova Scotia, in contrast to Quebec, had attained representative government, but neither colony was so advanced politically that it could regard itself as possessing all the attributes of an independent state. Above all, the growing sense of nationalism that the crisis stimulated to self-consciousness in the older colonies was absent in the two newer ones. The elements of nationalism were present in French Canada, but they hardly formed a bond between that region and the Thirteen Colonies. To the Americans, in the stage of development they had now reached, the price of loyalty seemed excessive. To most Nova Scotians and to important elements in Quebec, the price of rebellion seemed ruinous.

Nova Scotia indeed would have found it hard to rebel successfully even if it had wanted to. Its population of some 17,000 was scattered around the coast in isolated communities, which could not easily consolidate their strength or concert their actions against the constituted authorities. Halifax was a garrison center and a naval base that overshadowed the rest of the province; and John Adams scornfully described the inhabitants as "a set of fugitives and vagabonds who are also kept in fear by a fleet and an army."

But in fact few Nova Scotians had any desire to join the Revolution. The bulk of the settlers had come from New England, but their sympathy with their kinfolk stopped short of armed aid. Most of their trade was with New England, but such interference with normal commerce as resulted from the Revolution was offset by increased wartime demands for provisions. In contrast to the violence of political agitation in Massachusetts, political affairs in Nova Scotia were conducted with a moderation the extremely practical roots of which lay in a wide sharing of public favors. A shrewd oligarchy in Halifax maintained its ascendancy by a judicious distribution of spoils and patronage. The hand of the home government lay lightly and benevolently on the province. There was little interference with the general conduct of affairs by the legislature. The financial grant was reasonably generous, and the royal officials were reasonably lenient. The customs officers winked at enough smuggling to satisfy the outlying ports, and the people paid enough duties to content the treasury. There were occasional disputes over the handling of finances or the tariff on rum, but they were seldom pressed to extremes. In spite of the efforts of a radical-minded editor, only short-lived agitation could be roused against the Stamp Act or the Townshend duties, and the mutterings over the Tea

Act never issued in action. The chief crisis during the period was created by Governor Francis Legge, who embarked on an effort to break up the existing spoils system. He pursued this laudable object with more zeal than discretion, and the rising opposition in the province occupied public attention there during the height of the controversy that precipitated the American Revolution. The home government decided in 1776 that whatever might be said in Legge's favor, the discontent he had roused necessitated his recall; and this willingness to relieve the province of an unpopular official helped to confirm the general view of the imperial authorities as benevolent protectors of the populace against local oppression —a view that was distinctly in contrast to the attitude prevalent in New England at that date.

But if Nova Scotia had no desire to get involved in the Revolution, neither had it any desire to become engaged against it. Like the Acadians before them, the Yankee settlers became actively convinced of the blessings of neutrality and determined to enjoy them without interference. The government failed completely in its effort to raise recruits for the army. When fear of an American invasion led to the calling up of part of the militia and the levying of a defense tax, the measures roused widespread opposition. "We were almost all of us born in New England," protested the inhabitants of Yarmouth, "we have fathers, brothers and sisters in that country." The government wisely decided not to press the matter, particularly when it became clear that no serious attack threatened the province. Thus saved from the dilemma of having to choose between their loyalty and their affections, the Nova Scotians settled down to enjoy the fruits of neutrality in the form of increased trade with the British forces, supplemented by a considerable illicit commerce with the rebel colonies. Only a handful of the inhabitants came out openly on the side of the Revolution in the Cumberland rising of 1776, and their enterprise was short-lived.

In Quebec the situation was both more complex and more critical. There were acute divisions of opinion on issues that had no existence in Nova Scotia. Boundaries and the system of law and the form of government had been subjects of heated controversy, which was by no means ended by the Quebec Act, and behind these matters lay the comprehensive question of the political and social basis on which the colony was to be established. It was a local problem, which did not in itself involve the broader imperial issues that convulsed the older colonies, but it gave rise to a serious possibility that dissatisfied and indignant elements might throw in their lot with the Revolution.

Involved in this situation were racial factors that had no parallel in Nova Scotia. Yet while racial divisions were emerging, the cleavage over the revolution actually cut across racial lines. The English merchants were generally affronted by the Quebec Act, and their first impulse was to join with their brethren to the south in resistance to imperial authority. Their sympathy found tangible expression in the autumn of 1774 in a gift of funds from Montreal and 1000 bushels of wheat from Quebec for the relief of distress in Boston. Montreal merchants took the lead in forming a local committee and persuading Quebec to follow suit; and while their immediate purpose was to petition for the repeal of the Quebec Act, they could readily be turned into committees of correspondence to concert action with the other colonies.

There were, however, barriers to such a development. Disaffection was one thing; overt action was quite another. The bulk of the English merchants remained acutely conscious of their economic dependence on the mother country. This was particularly true of those who were connected with the fur trade; but other traders joined in a reluctance to risk their fortunes by adopting nonimportation agreements at the behest of the Continental Congress. An ardent minority helped to spread American propaganda and sought to draw the colony into support of the Revolution. But most of the merchants were aware that the severance of the British connection would cut off their markets and credits and supplies and leave them helpless before American competition, and these considerations effectively deterred them from giving any practical help to the American cause.

The French were less affected by these economic motives. For them, as for the merchants, the starting point was the Quebec Act. Their leaders were fully conscious of the benefits that this measure conferred upon them. To the degree that they welcomed its authoritarian system of government as a barrier to popular rule, their attachment was strengthened by American efforts to spread the doctrines of political liberty. But the French were far from unanimous in this attitude. A serious rift appeared between the more substantial elements, including the urban merchants as well as the seigniors, and the mass of the population. The habitant failed to share the satisfaction of his betters with the Quebec Act. "An act passed for the express purpose of gratifying the Canadians," wrote Chief Justice Livius in August 1775, "and which was supposed to comprehend all that they either wished or wanted is become the first object of their discontent and dislike."

This development exposed the hollowness of Carleton's illusions, upon which his whole policy was based. He had looked on the habitant as a passive and docile being, who was entirely submissive to the clergy and the seignior. But the habitant was a very different person from the French peasant. His relation to the seignior in New France had been much nearer that of tenant and landlord than that of subject and overlord. The feudal bonds had been more impressive in form than in substance. The habitant had much of the independent spirit of the pioneer, which did not readily yield submission to the gentry. He was far from gratified by the confirmation of seigniorial rights under the Quebec Act. He was outraged by the discovery that this included rights and claims that had never been effectively exercised or had lapsed during the years since 1763. What he felt was not gratitude toward Britain for restoring the old institutions, but a sullen resentment at the imposition of new burdens for the benefit of a small privileged group. He had little affection for the seignior, who asserted his new rights with enthusiasm, and no confidence in him as a military leader. Carleton's vision of the nobility rallying their loyal tenants for the defense of the province was dissipated as soon as the attempt was made in May 1775. "Though the gentlemen testified great zeal," he reported sadly, "neither their entreaties or their example could prevail upon the people."

Even more startling was the revelation of the limits of the influence of the Church. The concessions of the Quebec Act assured the loyalty of the clergy. Their attitude was strengthened by Bishop Briand's missive in May 1775, condemning the revolt of the Americans against their lawful sovereign and their attempt to draw the province into the same course. "Your oaths, your religion lay upon you the unavoidable duty of defending your country and your king with all the strength you possess," he told the people; and he warned them that a violation of this duty would entail the refusal of the sacraments.

This stand assured the support of most of the parish priests to the government. It had less effect on the attitude of their parishioners. There may have been some resentment over the legal re-establishment of the tithe. There was certainly a resistance by the habitant to this effort by the Church to instruct him in his civil duties. Not for the first or the last time, the habitant felt that the Church was exceeding its authority and insisted on following his own judgment.

Briand noted disconsolately that his *mandement* had provoked "mean and pitiable comment, quite contrary to the spirit of religion." A later circular approving the revival of the militia evoked a storm of protest. Priests who strove to recall their flocks to their civic duties were openly defied. In a revealing expression of the underlying racial divisions, a *curé* with the sound French name of Maisonbasse was accused by his parishioners:

"You are an Englishman, and you want to force us to submit and become English too." Within a few months the discouraged bishop was confessing that a few troops would have a more persuasive effect than the word of God in impelling the populace to lend active support to the government.

What the mass of the French Canadians really wanted was to keep out of the struggle. They were thoroughly sick of war and its attendant burdens. They were largely indifferent to the issues of the conflict. They had little cause to love the American colonists, with whom they had been at odds for the past century. But they had grievances against the existing British regime, which were increased by Carleton's wartime measures—the attempt to call up the militia, the declaration of martial law, the requisition of forced labor for military purposes. A handful of French Canadians joined the Americans. Another small minority, chiefly in the towns, gave active aid to the government. But the bulk of the population fell back on an attitude of determined neutrality, ready to acquiesce in the victory of whichever side proved the stronger but stubbornly refusing to take an active part on either side.

In consequence the hope that the Quebec Act would make Canada a secure military base by rallying the support of the French was completely shattered. Carleton had stated that they could provide a force of 18,000. But the attempt to call up the militia, though it met with some response in Quebec and Montreal, completely failed in the countryside. "The Canadian peasantry," Carleton was obliged to confess, "not only deserted their duty but numbers of them have taken up arms against the Crown." Only a few hundred did in fact join the Americans. The danger was less that they would aid the rebellion than that their defection would allow it to succeed and would deliver Quebec into the hands of the revolution. Carleton summed up his disillusionment in his final judgment: "I think there is nothing to fear from them while we are in a state of prosperity, and nothing to hope for while in distress."

The American Invasion of Canada

There was no serious effort to coerce Nova Scotia into joining the Revolution. When an attack on that province was suggested, George Washington opposed it on the pious ground that aggression and conquest were contrary to the principles on which the Revolution was based. A more practical reason was his inability to spare the resources necessary for such an enterprise. Men and supplies were more urgently needed for the struggle within the revolted colonies themselves. Even more important, the lack of naval power made it almost hopeless to attack the main British naval base in the North Atlantic with any prospect of success.

As a result, Nova Scotia remained undisturbed except for minor incursions. The most enthusiastic was led by Jonathan Eddy, a settler from New England who hoped to provoke a rising among his fellow settlers in Cumberland County. In 1776, after an effort to raise recruits in New England, he launched an invasion with a force of seventy-two men. Another hundred or so joined him from Cumberland County, and with this force he laid siege to Fort Cumberland, which guarded the isthmus connecting the peninsula of Nova Scotia with the mainland. Both the siege and the defense were conducted with more sound than fury, and after three weeks the comic-opera episode was ended by the arrival of a small relieving force. This was the nearest thing to invasion or rebellion experienced by the province. There were a few raids across the border and some privateering off the coast, but no serious threat to the security of the British hold on Nova Scotia.

The province of Quebec was a different matter. The leaders of the Revolution were acutely suspicious of British designs to use Canada as a military base and extremely conscious of the danger from that quarter. From Canada an effort might be launched to seize the line of the Hudson and cut the colonies in two. This was a threat that the Revolution must try to forestall, by persuasion if possible, but if necessary by force of arms.

The attempt at persuasion had indeed begun even before the outbreak of armed resistance. The passage of the Quebec Act was the signal for an appeal by Congress to the French Canadians, accompanied by simultaneous overtures to the disgruntled English merchants.

The results were disappointing. Among the merchants there was a group, led by the energetic and indignant Thomas Walker, whose activities were enlisted on the American side. Early in 1775 Congress dispatched an emissary, John Brown to make contact with this group and persuade them to send delegates to Congress. A meeting was held in Montreal, at which Brown presented the American appeal and Thomas Walker made a fiery speech in support. But the response was an expression of sympathy accompanied by a refusal of positive action. Congress was informed that the acceptance of the nonimport agreements would ruin the merchants and deliver the fur trade to their French competitors. "We beg to be informed," they said, "in what manner we can be serviceable to your cause, without bringing down ruin upon our own heads." That was hardly the language of ardent revolutionaries who were determined on liberty or death.

The appeal to the French was hardly more successful. In October 1774, Congress issued an address to the Canadians that was intended to expose to them the iniquities of the Quebec Act. It listed the blessings of English institutions that had been promised them by the Proclamation of 1763, of which they were now to be deprived. It appealed to them to join in the struggle for liberty and to send delegates to Congress. It brushed aside the chief barrier with the words: "We are too well acquainted with the liberality of sentiment distinguishing your nation, to imagine that difference of religion will prejudice you against a hearty amity with us." But although the address was widely circulated by Walker and his associates, it made few converts. The French leaders were well aware that Congress only three days earlier had issued an address to the people of Britain protesting against the establishment in Quebec of "a religion that has deluged our island in blood and dispersed impiety, bigotry, persecution, murder and rebellion through every part of the world." The habitant was not emotionally stirred by appeals to the traditions of English liberty. Very few French were prepared to fight against British rule for the sake of absorption in an American republic. By the summer of 1775 it was clear that persuasion had failed, and that Canada was only to be won by force of arms. In June—over a year before the Declaration of Independence—Congress authorized an invasion.

The disadvantages that prevented an attack on Nova Scotia also hampered the effort to conquer Canada. Washington, desperately striving to whip together an army after Bunker Hill, could spare only limited forces and supplies. The lack of sea power meant that an amphibious attack on Quebec was impossible and that the St. Lawrence was open to reinforcements from England. Success could come only as the result of a *coup de main* that would seize Canada before its defenses could be organized and hold it against any British efforts at recovery.

Yet the chance for such a stroke was far from negigible. The defenses of the province were at their lowest ebb. Carleton had advocated the consolidation of the line of the Hudson and the St. Lawrence by the strengthening of the anchor points of New York and Quebec and the restoration of the intervening links at Ticonderoga and Crown Point and Fort George. No steps had been taken to carry out this plan. Ticonderoga and Crown Point, the vital outposts of Canada, were in partial disrepair and were garrisoned by only forty men each. The forces within the colony had been depleted when Carleton, with light-hearted confidence, sent off two of his four regiments to reinforce Gage in Boston. Only about 600 troops remained when Carleton's illusions that the Canadians would rush to the colors were shattered to bits. On the basis of his assurances the home government instructed Carleton to raise 6000 men. The figure proved fantastically impossible. Only a few hundred joined the militia; and Carleton, stricken by this blow to all his calculations, showed himself incapable of improvising effective measures to meet the coming attack.

The initiative was thus left to the Americans, and they quickly took advantage of it. Ethan Allen and Benedict Arnold, whose combined forces of hastily recruited New England farmers totaled eighty-five men, surprised and captured Ticonderoga on May 10, 1775. Crown Point surrendered on the following day. The single armed sloop on Lake Champlain was captured, and the way was cleared for an advance on Montreal. Allen, pushing his advantage too far, was repulsed in his effort to seize St. Johns in May, and a similar attempt to seize Montreal with a raiding party in September led to his defeat and capture. But meanwhile a more substantial expedition had been organized under General Richard Montgomery and had launched the invasion by way of Lake Champlain and the Richelieu.

With the loss of Ticonderoga and Crown Point, St. Johns became the key point in the defense of the colony. Thither Carleton sent almost his whole remaining force of regulars, which with about ninety militia formed a garrison of some 700 men. For six weeks they withstood a siege by nearly six times their number; but by that time their ammunition was virtually exhausted, and there were no troops that could be sent to their relief. On November 2 the surrender of St. Johns wiped out the only organized force that had been available for the defense of Montreal, except for a small and none too reliable body of militia. Carleton abandoned the town and set out for Quebec, barely escaping capture on the way; and on November 12 Montreal capitulated to Montgomery.

It had been Montgomery's intention to go into winter quarters at Montreal. His plans were suddenly changed by the news that arrived from Quebec. In default of naval resources for an assault on that stronghold, Benedict Arnold had conceived the idea of an overland expedition through the Maine wilderness. Struggling up the Kennebec and across the height of land, his starving and exhausted band reached the first settlements along the Chaudière after the loss of all their baggage and provisions. Only their friendly reception by the French settlers saved them from complete disaster. It was with 700 men—little more than half his original force—that Arnold arrived before Quebec. He was too weak to take it by surprise, particularly since he lacked artillery; and even the troops that Montgomery brought down to join him only raised the total American force to around 1000 men.

In Quebec there was now an extemporized and decidedly mixed garrison of about 1800. Over half were militia, supplemented by odds and ends of marines and artificers and ex-soldiers. But Carleton's presence lent inspiration to the defense, and his vigor in directing resistance and purging the town of the leaders of disaffection was in distinct contrast to his indecision during the previous months. It was at this critical point that Carleton and the Canadian militia, in spite of so many shortcomings, made a real and perhaps a decisive contribution to the preservation of Canada.

The Americans on their part were in a difficult position. They lacked siege artillery to reduce the fortifications by bombardment. They had no proper shelter against the winter, which was closing in upon them, and their ranks were weakened by smallpox and other diseases. There was no hope in a protracted siege, for British reinforcements would arrive in the spring. In spite of their inferior numbers, they decided on a surprise assault as the only course that offered any chance of victory. In the very early hours of December 31, under cover of darkness and a raging snowstorm, they attacked the Lower Town from both ends. While Arnold struck at the northern end along the St. Charles, Montgomery drove in from the opposite end to take the defenders in the rear. But the garrison had got wind of the plan and were ready with countermeasures. Montgomery's attack was shattered by a volley of grapeshot. Arnold's force was halted and cut off by an attack from the rear. The failure was complete. It cost the Americans over 100 killed and 430 captured. Montgomery was among the dead, and Arnold was wounded. After such losses, all chance of capturing Quebec by storm had virtually disappeared.

Yet the Americans continued the siege through the remainder of the winter. There were still two possibilities of retrieving the situation. One was the arrival of reinforcements. Some American troops were sent from Montreal, and others were raised by Congress and rushed north. But these did little to improve the position. The men were untrained and short of supplies, and sickness offset the increase in numbers. Though their strength ultimately reached 3000, the besiegers were never again strong enough to take the initiative against Quebec.

The other hope lay in winning over the mass of the population. At the outset the French had shown considerable readiness to welcome the invaders. The Americans offered relief from the grievances that the habitant felt against the government. The first arrivals paid hard cash for the supplies they drew from the countryside. Their initial victories inclined the Canadians to support the winning side. But in the course of the winter these advantages gradually disappeared. American prospects of military victory diminished. Cash ran out, and the habitant was reluctant to accept paper money, with which he had had such sad experience under the French regime. The Americans resorted to forcible requisitions, which gave rise to active hostility. The antagonism increased when the Puritan sentiments of the invaders found expression in insults to the Catholic religion. Congress increased its efforts to win over the population by propaganda. In April three commissioners—Benjamin Franklin, Charles Carroll, and Samuel Chase—arrived in Montreal. They brought with them a Jesuit to counteract the influence of the Canadian clergy and a printing press with a French printer to spread American doctrines. All these measures were futile. The habitant, abused and disillusioned, sank back into a stubborn neutrality, from which he refused to move for either side.

By May 1776, it was no longer a question of conquering Canada but of saving the invading army. British ships bearing a well-equipped force of 10,000 men appeared before Quebec and sent the Americans into hasty retreat. At Sorel they rallied and with new boldness advanced against Three Rivers. This gave Carleton a chance to destroy their whole force by cutting around to St. Johns and taking them in the rear while Burgoyne engaged them frontally. But the fatal ineptitude that marked British military leadership throughout the Revolution descended on Carleton at this critical point. He delayed his advance, and the Americans, becoming aware of their danger, slipped past St. Johns and retreated down Lake Champlain. Even then a vigorous pursuit might have transformed the situation. But Carleton took until October to build the boats he needed; and though he secured command of Lake Champlain and seized Crown Point, he found Ticonderoga too strong to be taken by assault and the season too advanced for a prolonged siege. Having decided to abandon any attempt against that point, he felt that he must relinquish Crown Point as well. In consequence, the Americans were left in possession of the advance defense posts that barred the way to an invasion from Canada.

Such an invasion was Carleton's plan for crushing the Revolution. The British government accepted his idea and had sent him the force he required. But Carleton was not to be its leader. Military etiquette might lead to difficulties over the command when Carleton made a junction with General William Howe, his junior in rank, and it was suggested that General John Burgoyne be detached to lead the expedition. The attitude of the home government was strengthened by the criticisms that were roused by Carleton's conduct of operations in 1776. It was felt that a more enterprising man should be placed in charge, and Burgoyne was given command of the enterprise. His task was made more difficult by the fact that the Americans retained Crown Point and Ticonderoga. The decision of Howe to sail to Philadelphia instead of advancing up the Hudson allowed the whole weight of New England to be turned against Burgoyne. The outcome was Saratoga and the surrender of Burgoyne's whole army.

This was the end of all serious idea of crushing the Revolution from Canada. During the remaining years of the Revolution there was savage warfare along the border, which recalled the French and Indian raids of an earlier period; but though frontier settlements were ravaged by Johnson and Butler, there was never any danger of a full-scale invasion. The weight of the war shifted to the south; and Canada, which ceased to offer any serious threat, was henceforth also free from any serious danger of attack.

This last development was the result of a rather curious combination of circumstances. One of the fruits of Saratoga was an alliance between France and the United States. This was just the situation that Carleton had envisaged as the most serious danger to Britain's position in Canada, against which his main policy had been directed. The entry of France provided not only an army, but the naval strength that the Revolution had lacked, which gave new possibilities of an attack on either Nova Scotia or Quebec. The Marquis de Lafayette drew up and Congress approved a plan for an attack against the frontier posts from Detroit to Montreal in concert with a naval expedition to the St. Lawrence. Admiral d'Estaing issued a proclamation reminding the Canadians of their racial origin and calling them to join the American cause. But in November, 1778, Washington vetoed the project. He had no desire to expel Britain from Canada at the price of seeing the French resume possession. By 1780 his fears on this score had been removed and he was ready to revive the project of invasion. Lafayette issued a new appeal to the Canadians, but this time France imposed a veto. Her desire was to keep the United States relatively weak and thus dependent on French support, and Britain's continued possession of Canada was looked on as an instrument to that end. The mutual suspicions between the allies, and the desire of each to pursue its own advantage and to restrict the gains of its partner, preserved Canada from an attack that might have had far more serious consequences than the earlier invasion. And whatever sentiment may have been stirred by French appeals, it was not strong enough to bring about a spontaneous movement in Canada on behalf of the Revolution. The war ended with the colonies of Quebec and Nova Scotia both firmly under British control.

The Treaty and the Loyalists

At the root of the treaty that closed the Revolutionary War in 1783 was the mutual desire of Britain and the United States to lay a solid foundation for future friendship. The parting had been in anger; but once the independence of the United States was recognized, both sides wished to heal old wounds and to remove all grievances that might threaten a renewal of their quarrel.

These aims were given added urgency by the intrigues of France. This country had entered the war less from affection for the Americans than from an embittered hostility toward Britain. It remained one of her cardinal objectives to weaken and hamper Britain in every possible way, and her policy during the negotiations at Versailles was guided by that fact. American independence would be useful to her only if it meant a new enemy for Britain. It was to her interest to create as many points of antagonism as possible between the two countries. It would further serve her purpose if the United States, instead of being built up in size and power, could be kept relatively weak and thus dependent on France for continued support against British hostility.

This was exactly the situation that both Britain and the United States wanted to avoid. As a result, both of them tended to reject the help they might have had from France in the negotiations. Successes gained with French aid might turn out to be fatal gifts. Each side showed a preference for a compromise that promised to restore amity rather than for gains that would perpetuate hostility and from which France would draw the real advantage.

One of the controversies that illustrated these factors was over the question of the fisheries. By seceding from the British Empire, the Americans had lost their right to fish in British waters, including the Gulf of St. Lawrence and the inshore waters of Nova Scotia and Newfoundland, or to land on British shores to dry their catch and take on supplies. France urged Britain to stand firm for the exclusion of American fishermen. Quite apart from the fact that this might help to reduce the competition with French fishermen on the Banks, it would create endless friction between British and Americans. But these seemed to Britain to be good reasons for generosity. The Americans insisted that access to the fisheries was a vital interest and even tried to present it as an unalterable right. The British realized that there would be practical difficulties in excluding American fishermen and that any such effort would certainly lead to trouble. The treaty in consequence admitted the Americans to the inshore fisheries and gave them the right to land in certain areas so long as these remained unsettled.

When it came to boundary questions, French intrigues were even more active and more dangerous. There were few disputes over the line east of the St. Lawrence, where the boundaries laid down for Nova Scotia and the old province of Quebec were accepted by both sides. The real question was the disposal of the region between the Alleghenies and the Mississippi. The United States was determined to acquire the whole territory. France had no intention of claiming it for herself, but she felt that it would be advantageous for her purposes to confine the United States to the seaboard east of the mountains, hemmed in by powerful neighbors and dependent on French support. As a result, France showed herself ready to support the claims of Spain to the Southwest and of Britain to the Ohio Valley and even to advocate the creation of an Indian buffer state in this whole region under the protection of Britain and Spain.

These maneuvers gained importance from the real conflict of claims between Britain and the United States. Benjamin Franklin started out, like a good bargainer, by suggesting that Britain should give up the whole of Canada as a proof of her desire for American friendship. He came down to a more practical basis with the idea that the frontier should follow the southern boundary of Quebec as defined in 1763. This ran from the St. Lawrence at the 45th parallel to the south end of Lake Nipissing and would thus cut off the Ontario peninsula. The British government was nearly ready to accept when a delay in the negotiations gave rise to second thoughts, which led to a counterdemand for the extension of the boundary to the Ohio. By this time the United States was becoming alarmed at the attitude of France and Spain and the prospect that she might be denied access to the Mississippi. To avoid this the Americans were ready to compromise with Britain. They offered two alternatives—an extension of the 45th parallel westward to the Mississippi or the adoption of the line of the St. Lawrence and the Great Lakes. Britain on her part felt it wise to conciliate the United States in order to detach her from France, even at the price of surrendering the West. She chose the line of the lakes, "which could never be mistaken;" and thus was settled the first stage in the partition of the continent.

These proceedings were illustrative of a situation that was to be of the most fundamental importance for Canada in the future. An independent state, greatly superior in strength, now occupied the southern half of the North American continent. The Revolution left the United States with a legacy of suspicion and hostility toward Britain that the peace settlement did not succeed in removing completely. In any quarrel between the two nations, Canada as the nearest British possession would be the first object of American attack, no matter how innocent she herself might be. One of her basic interests was thus the establishment of a firm friendship between Britain and the United States. But she also had specific interests, which were of little direct concern to Britain, yet which she must depend on Britain to uphold if they were threatened by the United States. Britain on her part was chiefly concerned to avoid any quarrel with America; and if the sacrifice of Canadian interests was necessary to that end, the mother country would naturally be inclined to pay that price.

The treaty was a first example of the working of these factors. The outraged protests by Canadian merchants against the surrender of the West met little response in London. In the long run that may have been just as well. The Ohio Valley could never have been held vacant for the Canadian fur trade against the pressure of American settlement, and the attempt to preserve it would ultimately have endangered the whole of Canada. But these were not the considerations on which the boundary was decided, and in fact the years after the treaty saw Britain engaged in an attempt to reverse that decision. In the meantime, however, a major blow had been struck at the immediate interests of the Canadian merchants. Their commercial ambitions, not only at this period but for several decades thereafter, were continental in scope. They called for free access by way of the St. Lawrence system to the vast interior of the continent. The treaty line cut squarely across the territory on which the Canadian traders depended. The new boundary meant an economic as well as a political partition; and at the same time what remained of British North America was profoundly changed in its nature and structure as a result of the coming of the Loyalists.

The treaty left the Loyalists in a lamentable position. The British negotiators fought hard to gain generous treatment for the colonists who had supported the imperial cause during the Revolution. But the American envoys were hampered by the limited authority of the loose federal government created by the Articles of Confederation. It had no real control over the treatment of the former Tories by the governments of the individual states. Its delegates could only promise that it would make earnest recommendations to the states to refrain from punitive measures and to make it possible for Loyalists to recover their property and their rights.

Such conciliatory counsels had little effect on the state governments. Vindictiveness against the Tories was expressed in fresh confiscations, and

Loyalists who tried to return to their homes or regain their property found themselves in danger of physical violence. Many who would have accepted the outcome of the Revolution found themselves driven into exile, and they looked to Britain to compensate them for the ruin that their loyalty had brought upon them. Many of them went to England or to the West Indies, but the most significant movement, and the one with the most far-reaching consequences, was to the colonies of Nova Scotia and Quebec.

All through the Revolution there had been a drift of refugees to these two provinces. With the end of the war a mass migration set in. A large number of civilian refugees had gathered in New York under the protection of the British garrison, and Carleton insisted on evacuating them before he handed over that city to the Americans. Nova Scotia, accessible by sea and with plenty of vacant land available for settlers, was their most convenient destination. The movement went on through most of 1783, and by the end of the year the governor estimated that 30,000 new arrivals had reached that colony.

This sudden influx, almost double the size of the existing population, raised difficulties on all sides. The governor of Nova Scotia was instructed to issue land grants on a generous scale, ranging from 100 acres for the head of a family, with an additional fifty acres for each member, to 1000 acres for a field officer. He was also charged with supplying the necessary tools and provisions to aid the settlers in building their houses and starting their clearings and to carry them over until they could bring in their first crop. Such a task was utterly beyond his resources. The shortage of competent surveyors resulted in many delays before the newcomers were placed on their holdings and in many inaccuracies in their grants. The destitute condition of the refugees created demands for food and clothing, for tools and lumber, for utensils and farm implements, which far outran the local supply. The settlers contained a high proportion of town dwellers, including many families who had enjoyed wealth and position in the older colonies. Such people, torn from their cultivated existence and thrown into the harsh pioneer conditions of a land where the soil and the climate were none too hospitable, were ill equipped to face the rigors of their new life. Their helplessness threw an added burden on the provincial authorities, whose inefficiency in turn brought bitter recriminations from the settlers. Many of the new arrivals were appalled by the bleak soil and rigorous climate of the province. Often they found themselves in desperate straits for shelter and supplies. Their plight was at times aggravated by their own lack of judgment. An enthusiastic group sought to create a new metropolis at Shelburne; but the soil was poor and the settlement failed to attract the trade on which it had counted, and the population dwindled from a peak of 8000 to a mere 300 in 1818. There were bitter gibes at "Nova Scarcity" and numbers of Loyalists gave up the struggle and drifted to England or returned to the United States after tempers there had subsided. The majority, however, remained in the new land and formed a permanent increase in its population.

Under such conditions the progress of settlement was inevitably marked by difficulties and divisions. The newcomers were openly hostile to the New England element among the earlier settlers, whom they suspected of disloyalty. Loyalist leaders who had held official positions in the older colonies clamored for posts in the government of Nova Scotia, to the natural resentment of the native officeholders. There were rivalries and divisions among the Loyalists themselves; and the officers and men of the Loyalist regiments, who formed a substantial proportion of the new settlers, were particularly indignant at the way in which the most desirable locations seemed to be reserved for civilians, who had made little contribution to the imperial cause.

One outcome of the friction between old and new settlers was the division of the province. Nearly half the new arrivals had settled on the northwest shore of the Bay of Fundy and up the St. John Valley. The population of those regions, formerly only a few hundred, was raised to about 14,000. The new settlements were separated geographically from the older communities in Nova Scotia. They were remote from Halifax, the seat of the government and the law courts. The existing state of communications thus placed them at a real disadvantage and aroused a genuine fear that their interests would be neglected. At the same time a number of their leaders, headed by Colonel Edward Winslow and his friend Ward Chipman, were quick to realize the advantages that would follow on the creation of a separate government. They would have official appointments for themselves instead of having to compete with the inhabitants of the peninsula. They would be able to control the affairs of a district whose extent offered enticing opportunities for exploitation and land speculation. They would create a community in which the Loyalist element was overwhelmingly dominant, and which would be a special bulwark of the imperial connection, a government upheld by abhorrers of republicanism and headed by "the most gentlemanlike executive on earth."

Over in London there were officials who were thinking along similar lines. The lessons of the Revolution were being studied, and among the conclusions was the desirability of keeping the colonies relatively weak and disunited. To partition Nova Scotia, where the New England element remained suspect, and to create a new province founded on the principles of ardent loyalism and lying like a buffer between Nova Scotia and the United States seemed a wise and timely project. It hardly needed the urgings of Winslow and his associates to bring it to pass. In 1784 the division of Nova Scotia was effected. The island of Cape Breton, which had received a considerable influx of settlers, was separated under a governor and an appointed council. This, as it turned out, was a temporary step, for the island was reannexed to Nova Scotia in 1820. But the separation of the peninsula from the mainland was more permanent. The latter was set up as the province of New Brunswick, with an elective legislature of its own; and a new colony came into being as the symbolic aftermath of the American Revolution.

The migration to Nova Scotia was drawn to a large extent from the substantial classes in the seaport towns. It came after the natural northward expansion of population from New England had already shown signs of receding and represented a new movement created by special circumstances. The movement to Canada was quite different. It was drawn very largely from the western frontier districts of New England and New York and Pennsylvania. It was composed of pioneer farmers, who were thoroughly fitted to embark on the task of carving new homes from the wilderness. And while Loyalism provided the first impulse, the migration fitted into the natural expansion of settlement that was now flowing over the mountains into the vast interior of the continent, whose northern fringe continued to lap over into Canada for years after the original Loyalist motive had ebbed.

There was no such mass migration as that which flooded into Nova Scotia. The nucleus was formed by men from the back country who had been driven out because of their opinions or who had crossed the border to enlist on the Loyalist side. Their families came with them or followed at a later date. The followers of Sir John Johnson and of Colonel John Butler, driven from the Mohawk Valley, formed regiments that harried the frontier settlements during the war. Other supporters of the imperial cause found that the conclusion of peace made their position intolerable and moved north to British soil. At the end of the war the Quebec government was faced with the problem of caring for several thousand civilian refugees and of finding new homes for the soldiers and officers whose regiments were now to be disbanded.

Other settlers continued to flow in during the years that followed. In the United States the pioneer urge encountered various obstacles in the years after the revolution. The Indians remained a menace for a decade. Many desirable areas had been engrossed by land speculators. A national land system was only established by the Ordinance of 1787, and even then the settler was called on to take a section of 640 acres at a minimum cash price of $1 an acre. In these circumstances it was not surprising that a considerable number of land seekers turned their eyes to Canada. Loyalists wrote back to friends and relatives telling them that allegiance to the tyrant George III was being rewarded by the grant of a farm, and not a few aspiring settlers were ready to forswear republicanism at such a price. Some indeed were people who had taken no active part during the revolution, but who had sympathized with the Crown and who now found themselves uncomfortable in their old homes. But besides these "late loyalists" there were others whose chief desire was land and who were quite ready to take an oath of loyalty in return for a grant. The government did not try too hard at this stage to distinguish between these various groups. Its policy was to draw into the new colony all those who were ready to renew their old allegiance and to grant them land on the same terms as the original Loyalists.

There was at first some question as to where this land should be found. The government bought the seigniory of Sorel and planted a number of settlers there. In general, however, the newcomers showed a dislike for settling on the old seigniories. Governor Frederick Haldimand on his part hesitated to settle them farther west. He was afraid of trouble with the Indians, and he had the added problem of settling the Mohawk and other Iroquois who under Joseph Brant had sided with Britain during the Revolution. But the local Indians proved quite ready to sell their lands, and both they and the Mohawk looked with favor on the idea of white settlers. With this obstacle removed, Haldimand became enthusiastic in favor of settling the disbanded regiments around the chief posts in the Ontario peninsula and making them the nucleus of new communities. In 1784 the process got under way. Three main districts were laid out—one along the upper St. Lawrence, a second from Kingston to the Bay of Quinte, and a third in the Niagara peninsula. A fourth settlement was projected around Detroit, but the cession of that post to the United States left the settlement of western Ontario for a slightly later development.

The initial grants were on the same scale as in Nova Scotia, though within a few years these were generously enlarged. Tools and clothing and provisions were provided for three years. Even with this help, and with the pioneer experience that many of the settlers already possessed, there were plenty of hardships to be faced. As in Nova Scotia, a shortage of competent surveyors meant frequent delays, and a lack of tools and clothing and implements caused further difficulties. Not all the settlers were self-sustaining when the government rations came to an end in 1786, and some were both inefficient and improvident. The most trying time was the "hungry year" in 1789, when a sudden shortage of food reduced many settlers to actual starvation. But by that time the new settlements had taken firm root. Loyalists, disbanded German mercenaries, and new settlers from the United States together formed a population of some 10,000 in what was to become Ontario, and the numbers continued to increase as the westward migration in the United States lapped over into Canada.

The effect was to transform the structure and prospects of the old province of Quebec. The basic assumptions on which the Quebec Act had been founded now lay in ruins. It could no longer be contended that Canada would remain French to the end of time. A substantial and growing population of British stock had now been planted in the province, and the need to adjust to this new situation resulted in a fresh political agitation and in a new departure in British policy.

The Constitutional Act, 1791

It had been the clear intention of the British government to apply the Quebec Act in a way that would satisfy the majority and still remove the grievances of the minority. The first purpose, embodied in the main provisions of the act, was to conciliate the French. That, however, was only the starting point. The wide legislative powers granted to the governor and council opened the way for an evolutionary process that would modify and adapt the new system to meet the chief desires of the British merchants. The instructions to Carleton in 1775 called his attention specifically to certain changes that were felt to be desirable. The introduction of the main provisions of English commercial law, the grant of *habeas corpus*, the use of juries in civil suits, were all within the powers of the local government, which was expected to take such steps as would satisfy the English merchants without entrenching on the interests and privileges of the French.

Concessions of this sort would have done much to abate the resentment of the "old subjects" against the Quebec Act. Carleton refused to make them. His rigid and unyielding policy made the wide element of flexibility in the Quebec Act a dead letter. Although he was told to communicate his instructions to the council, he deliberately concealed them and kept its members in ignorance of the latitude that the home government intended them to enjoy in applying the new system. Carleton's instructions allowed him to use a board of five members of council for the transaction of routine business. He took advantage of this to keep the direction of the government in the hands of a select group who would support him in his resistance to concessions. When Chief Justice Livius discovered the situation and protested against Carleton's illegal course, the Governor dismissed him from office even though this action left the colony without a judicial head. By Carleton's deliberate perversity the Quebec Act was warped in operation, its healing features set at nought, its reactionary aspects accentuated.

In consequence the colony was torn by political struggles all through the period of the Revolutionary War. The economic dislocation resulting from war conditions, including the partial interruption of the fur trade, aggravated the discontent of the merchants against the Quebec government, and important elements in the council supported their demands for reform. By the end of the war the agitation was so serious that Carleton's successor Haldimand was forced to take some steps. An ordinance establishing *habeas corpus* was adopted in 1784. Juries for civil suits were granted in 1785. But the concessions were grudging and limited, and by this time the merchants had once more embarked on a campaign for a reversal of the Quebec Act.

Their hands were strengthened by the twin circumstances of the recognition of American independence and the influx of the Loyalists. The crisis in colonial affairs, which might have excused the adoption of special measures to assure the security of Quebec, was now over. The Loyalists, who had been driven from their homes because of their attachment to Britain, would certainly expect to enjoy the constitutional and legal rights of British subjects. The merchants pressed these considerations on the home government in a petition put forward in 1783 and again presented with some changes in 1784, in which they requested the repeal of the Quebec Act, except for the guaranties to the Catholic Church and the French law of property, and the grant of an assembly and the general system of English law.

In certain respects the petitioners overshot the mark. In an attempt to strengthen their case to the maximum, they claimed that they spoke for both English and French in voicing popular demands against an oppressive oligarchy. The French leaders were at once up in arms. They had a strong vested interest under the Quebec Act, and they feared that the effect of any changes would be to weaken their position. They in their turn undertook to speak for the whole French population. In a petition at the end of 1784 they repudiated the demands of the merchants. In their eyes an assembly was simply a device for imposing taxes on the province. They asserted that the *corvée* was preferable to taxation and that the jury system was a burden that favored the rich against the poor. They objected to leaving their privileges under the existing laws at the mercy of a local assembly. To bolster their case they secured an address from the Roman Catholic inhabitants, which repeated the objections to an assembly and asserted that the Canadians were in no condition "to bear the taxes which must necessarily ensue." It was a counterattack that revealed the growing cleavage between the two races.

The merchants were also on dubious ground in implying that they could speak for the Loyalists. Undoubtedly the newcomers, with their American background, would not be indefinitely content to forego a system of representative government in spite of their hostility to republicanism. But at the moment they did not share the burning desire of the merchants for an assembly. Their concern was with their immediate economic problems and with those features of the Quebec Act which threatened their economic interests.

The first desire of the pioneers was to get land of their own. They had no wish to live under feudal tenure, yet that was the only tenure available under the Quebec Act. The seigniorial system prevented grants in freehold. The settlers held land on the basis of location tickets, which assured them the right to settle on certain holdings, but they were technically in the position of tenants on Crown seigniories. This assumed a serious practical significance when the question of mills arose. Mills were among the first needs of the settlers once they became established. The Crown was reluctant to undertake the expense of construction. The suggestion was made that private individuals who were ready to build mills should be encouraged by a grant of the seigniorial rights pertaining to them for a period of fifteen years. The settlers, already suspicious that various retired officers aspired to become seigniors and perpetuate the feudal system, protested hotly and increased their agitation for freehold grants.

This was one of the key points in a petition presented by Sir John Johnson on behalf of the Loyalists in 1784. Other requests were for a system of English law, the establishment of local courts, and the creation of a separate government for the new settlements. In 1787 a group of delegates elected from the new townships drew up another petition, which repeated these demands and which added requests for aid in building roads, schools, and churches, for bounties on lumber and potash and hemp, and for the exclusion of lumber and potash from Vermont.

This last point indicated the incipient economic divergence between the settlers and the merchants. The latter, in their desire to expand their commercial interests, reached out to the United States for staples that had a market in England far greater than Canada could as yet supply. Vermont, whose natural outlet was by way of Lake Champlain and the Richelieu, shared the interest of the Canadian merchants in free trade across the border. But the pioneers in the Loyalist settlements depended on lumber and potash to provide them with a cash income while their farms were being cleared, and the success of the merchants in getting free entry for lumber and naval stores from Vermont in 1786 aroused resentment among the settlers at American competition.

There was also a political divergence between the two groups. They shared a desire for English law and the establishment of freehold tenure; but the Loyalists would be satisfied to see these blessings confined to their own communities without worrying about whether the merchants shared in them. Their desire for local courts was met in 1788, when four judicial districts—Lunenburg, Mecklenburg, Nassau, and Hesse—were established for the new settlements. They carefully refrained from supporting the demand of the merchants for an assembly for the whole province. Instead they requested a separate administration for their own region on the model of Cape Breton—a subprovince subordinate to Quebec, but with a lieutenant governor and an appointed council of its own. The political aspirations of the merchants received meager support from the new Loyalist settlements.

The rising agitation within the province, and the serious divisions that it revealed, caused a growing uneasiness in London. It was clear that a major adjustment was necessary, and the government once more turned to Carleton for advice on the course to be followed. He was raised to the peerage as Lord Dorchester and sent out in 1786 as governor of all the colonies of British North America. At his own insistence he was accompanied by William Smith, who had been chief justice in New York and was now appointed to the same position in Quebec.

It was indicative of the difficulties of the situation that neither of these two able and experienced men could offer any workable remedy. Dorchester's political ideas had found supreme expression in the Quebec

Act. That measure had completely miscarried and had left him bankrupt of further suggestions. He was disillusioned with the French, in whom he had placed such high hopes, yet he had not been won over to the side of the merchants. He had no constructive ideas to meet the new situation or provide an alternative to the ill-starred measure that he had fathered.

Smith, on whom Dorchester leaned heavily for guidance, was equally unable to produce a practical solution. He saw clearly the failure of the Quebec Act and the need to satisfy the British element in the population. But his effort to do this by judicial means, in a decision that the "old subjects" had a right to English law even under the Quebec Act, only increased the legal confusion, and on the political side he had little to offer. The great objective that he urged strongly on London was a federation of all the colonies of British North America. In his view the remedy for the unchecked growth of local legislatures was "the erection of a power upon the continent itself, to control all its own little republics, and create a partner in the legislation of the empire." His vision was prophetic but unfortunately impracticable. At that moment the United States, in the face of grave difficulties but under the impulse of urgent necessity, was evolving a federal system that would provide an effective national unity. But the unitary forces that triumphed in the United States were almost entirely absent in the British provinces to the north. The colonies were separated by distance and divided in interests. They had few economic bonds and little sense of cohesion. They had no common feeling of nationalism and had shared no experience comparable to the American Revolution that might counteract the forces of localism. Geographic and political and economic forces were all for the moment adverse to centralization in British North America.

At the same time, Smith's policy was in direct opposition to the views that were emerging in London. There the lessons to be drawn from the loss of America were being pondered by statesmen and officials. Their conclusion was that the fault lay less in too much imperial interference than in too little imperial control. They drew the moral that the powers of colonial legislatures should be checked by a strengthening of the natural bulwarks of authority, the executive, the church, the appointive elements in the government and the aristocratic elements in the colonies. In contrast to Smith's desire for wider unity, the imperial authorities were convinced of the unwisdom of allowing the colonies to become too large and strong. They favored the principle of "divide and rule," and they had already applied it in the Maritimes with the division of Nova Scotia. Representative government could hardly be denied to any colony with a substantial

British population; but the return to the old model was to be modified in a way that would diminish the democratic element and discourage colonial nationalism.

In addition there were special considerations that called for the application of these conclusions to Canada. For one thing a revenue had to be raised, and under the Quebec Act the local government had no power to levy taxes. Britain, under the teaching of bitter experience, had specifically renounced the right of imperial taxation in 1778, except for such duties as were incidental to the regulation of trade. Local taxation was necessary; and in spite of the views of the seigniors, it was felt that even the French would prefer to decide on taxes through their own representatives, while it was certain that any other method would arouse serious discontent among the British settlers.

External factors added their weight to these motives. Though these factors were similar to the ones that had led to the Quebec Act, they led now to radically different conclusions. There was no longer a question of keeping a check on the colonies to the south. The problem was to keep Canada from being absorbed in the American republic. The existence of the United States, with its advanced political institutions, was certain to exercise a profound effect on Canada, whose British settlers would not accept an indefinite denial of representative government. The danger from France had for the moment abated, but its revival might once more threaten the tranquillity of Canada. It was therefore desirable to strengthen the loyalty of the French Canadians; and while this involved the general preservation of their social structure, the revelation of how little real influence the seigniors possessed suggested a direct effort to attach the mass of the population by a free and generous gift of self-government. Finally the geographic division between the main bodies of French and English settlers made it both possible and desirable to divide the colony and thus reduce racial friction while allowing the French to retain the special concessions that had been granted by the Quebec Act.

Such were the considerations that found their embodiment in the Constitutional Act of 1791. The division of the colony into the two provinces of Upper and Lower Canada was forecast and was effected later in the year by a proclamation that placed the dividing line at the boundary of the westernmost seigniory, that of Longueil. This extended slightly west of the Ottawa near its junction with the St. Lawrence, and the remainder of the boundary was formed by the Ottawa itself. This made it possible to provide that lands in the western province, or Upper Canada, should be granted in freehold and to continue seigniorial tenure in Lower Canada, but with the provision that new grants in that province might also be made in freehold if the applicant so desired.

Each province was granted an assembly, to be elected on a fairly wide franchise. A holding with an annual value of 40s. gave the vote in rural districts; in towns it went to those who possessed a residence with a yearly value of £5 or rented one at £10 a year. The assembly was to number not less than sixteen in Upper Canada and fifty in Lower Canada. A legislative council of at least seven members in Upper Canada and fifteen in Lower Canada formed an upper house. In their desire to reproduce in Canada the full structure of the British government, the authors of the bill had originally contemplated the creation of a Canadian peerage with hereditary titles. This was condemned by Dorchester and laughed at in the debates in the British parliament, but it partially survived in the provision that councilors should be appointed for life and that the king might grant hereditary titles and membership. The council was definitely intended to represent the aristocratic principle and to balance the democratic element in the assembly. The authoritative element was further strengthened by the powers of the governor, who was the appointed head of the executive and who could either veto bills or reserve them for the approval of the home government; and London retained the further right to disallow measures even after they had received the governor's assent.

The new measure repealed the Quebec Act only with respect to the structure of government and the provision permitting freehold tenure. The existing seigniorial system was left untouched. It was left to the provinces themselves to decide on the introduction of English civil law —a step that was taken by the first legislature of Upper Canada. The rights of the Catholic Church under the Quebec Act were specifically reaffirmed. But there was a definite desire to strengthen the Protestant establishment, partly as an offset to French Catholicism, and partly as a further element of order and authority. In addition to the right to collect tithes from Protestants, the provincial governments had the obligation to set aside land, in amounts equal to one-seventh of future land grants, for the support of a Protestant clergy. The influence of the church was to supplement that of the Crown in the new system, which Lieutenant Governor Simcoe enthusiastically presented to his first legislature in Upper Canada as "the very image and transcript of the English constitution."

One curious hope was cherished by the government in London. The division of Canada was specifically intended to allow the two races to enjoy their familiar institutions and pursue their own development. Yet Pitt and his colleagues appear to have felt that the outcome would be a gradual assimilation of the French. By following the complete British model of law and government, they felt, Upper Canada would become so happy and prosperous that the French would be moved to envy and emulation and would abandon their older ways in order to share in the full blessings of British institutions. Along with the principle of divide and rule went a belief in the idea of dividing to unite. It was a vain illusion. The French found in the new system new opportunities to consolidate their racial and religious separatism. The seeds of racial friction were not eliminated by the partition of Canada. The older mercantile groups were left within the bounds of Lower Canada, whose essentially French character was acknowledged by the new measure. The merchants had gained their demand for an assembly, but this was completely stultified by the division of the province, which left the English of Lower Canada in a hopeless minority. Yet their economic and political ambitions were not abandoned; and the result was a steadily increasing friction between the two races in that province and the complete failure of the grant of representative government to solve the problems of Canada.

The Attack on Quebec.
The death of General Montgomery while leading the assault.

The Capture of Ticonderoga.
Ethan Allen summoning the fort to surrender.

The Expedition against Quebec.
Arnold's forces marching through the wilderness.

The Assault on Quebec.
American troops attacking on New Year's Eve under cover of a snowstorm.

The Tory's Day of Judgment.
The kind of treatment the Loyalists were apt to experience at the hands of their triumphant neighbors.

The Battle of Saratoga.

Encampment of the Loyalists at Johnstown.   *(Public Archives of Canada)*

Sir John Graves Simcoe.

Joseph Brant (Thayendanegea).
Mohawk leader of the Iroquois allies of the British during the American Revolution.
197

Chapter 9

Adjustment and Consolidation

The Second British Empire

The first British empire in America was shattered by the American Revolution. The populous and stable colonies, which had formed the pillars of the old mercantile system, were lost in 1783. The whole balance of the imperial structure was radically changed; and the loss of the Thirteen Colonies, in combination with the profound changes that were simultaneously under way as a result of the Industrial Revolution, meant a drastic change of outlook and a shift of the center of gravity in imperial affairs.

Britain indeed retained her foothold on the American continent, but the remnants that were left to her could not step into the place left vacant by the loss of the older colonies. By 1791, when the initial reorganization of British North America had been effected, six provinces had come into being. Lower Canada, the most populous and the longest settled, was overwhelmingly French in population. Upper Canada and New Brunswick had only just been created. The settlement of St. John Island—its name was changed to Prince Edward Island in 1799—had barely begun on the eve of the American Revolution. Newfoundland and Nova Scotia were older British possessions, but their population stood at about 15,000 and 40,000 respectively. All were at a much more primitive stage of development than the lost colonies to the south. Their resources were far less varied, their opportunities for expansion were far less extensive. To British eyes the remaining empire in America offered less promise than the sugar islands of the West Indies or the dazzling prospects that were now unfolding in India.

Nonetheless, Britain had an opportunity to build in North America a new empire whose prospects of permanence were much greater than in the original American colonies. The population of the provinces she now held had not been driven from the mother country by religious persecution or economic distress and had no established tradition of resistance to imperial authority. On the contrary, many had fled to British soil to escape persecution at the hands of American radicals. The absence of major grievances, coupled with the Loyalist background, meant that there was in British North America a far stronger element of conservatism than had existed in the older colonies. The structure of the local governments was more strongly weighted on the side of authority. The aftermath of the Revolution left feelings of resentment and even fear toward the United States, which strengthened the sentiment of imperial loyalty. Yet that sentiment could be tried too far. The population was still pioneer in character and American in its environment and to a large extent in its origins. Loyalty did not imply subservience. All the colonies had economic ambitions that would lead to demands for political rights. Unless Britain's imperial policy was favorable to these aspirations, the second empire would ultimately risk the same fate as the first.

In the period between the end of the Revolution and the outbreak of the War of 1812, a process of adjustment and consolidation took place, during which the character of the different provinces gradually emerged. In all of them the spread of settlement and the expansion of population were accompanied by the development of staples based on the exploitation of natural resources. But between the different provinces there was a wide disparity in the rate of growth, due partly to geographic location and partly to the differences in their economic potentialities.

The Maritime Provinces benefited least from any influx of population. The expansion of the United States was now directed toward the west, and the northward thrust along the seaboard found its last expression in the Loyalist migration. There was little emigration from Europe or the British Isles during this period. Distress in Ireland resulted in a number of settlers around the turn of the century, but they were a handful compared to the later movement. Distress in the Scottish highlands, as a result of the clearances that turned the crofters off their small farms to make way for sheep runs, had a somewhat greater effect. The arrival of the ship *Hector* at Pictou with a group of Highland settlers in 1773 was the beginning of a gradual influx, which spread from the mainland of Nova Scotia to Cape Breton and Prince Edward Island. In the latter province Thomas Douglas, Earl of Selkirk, inaugurated his philanthropic efforts to relieve distress by mass immigration to the New World, and his planting of 800 settlers in 1803 was a prelude to his later and ill-starred venture on the Red River. But the influx into Prince Edward Island and Nova Scotia was modest in extent, and New Brunswick received little immigration of importance during this period. In 1814, settlement in the last two provinces was still largely confined to the coastal strip and to a few river valleys such as the St. John.

In the region of the St. Lawrence there was a very different situation. A continuous stream of settlers flowed into the area, not from Europe but from the pioneer migration that was flooding into the American West. Some of this spilled over into Lower Canada as the result of a thrust from northern Vermont into the Eastern Townships. At the close of the Revolution the authorities were reluctant to open this area to settlement. It was felt desirable to keep a wilderness stretch along the frontier as a buffer against the United States, and Haldimand also wanted to reserve the lands in this area for the French Canadians. But after 1791 this attitude was reversed. Land in the townships was open to settlement on the basis of freehold tenure, and by 1812 some 9000 settlers had arrived to establish the nucleus of an English-speaking population.

This movement was not large enough to change the essentially French character of the province. Its growth from 113,000 in 1784 to 335,000 in 1814 was chiefly the result of natural increase. It was Upper Canada that felt the chief impact of the frontier movement, rising in these 30 years from some 10,000 to 94,000, largely as a result of the unchecked influx from the United States.

The attitude of the authorities toward American settlers was somewhat mixed. On the one hand there was a fear "lest they import and diffuse principles adverse to the British constitution." On the other hand there was a feeling that the safety and security of Canada depended on a rapid and substantial increase of population, and that generous offers of land to allure "the repentant sinners of the revolted colonies" was the best method of achieving this end. Governor Simcoe was energetic in his efforts to attract American settlers, and land hunger in the United States brought a favorable response to the inducements he held out. It was estimated that in 1813 fully 80 per cent of the inhabitants of Upper Canada were American in origin and that not more than one-quarter of these were of Loyalist stock.

In nearly all the provinces the aspiring settler found plentiful land available on easy terms. The chief exception was Prince Edward Island, which had been partitioned among sixty-seven proprietors in 1767. The grants, as usual, were conditional on the planting of settlers, and as usual the conditions were almost wholly ignored. The absentee proprietors evaded their obligations and refused titles to settlers who came on their own initiative, and with the establishment of representative government in 1773 the inhabitants embarked on their century-long struggle to free themselves from this incubus. In the other Maritime Provinces there were fewer difficulties of this sort. Although various individuals secured possession of large grants, the real problem was the scarcity of good arable land to which settlers could be attracted or which was even adequate to prevent emigration from Nova Scotia and New Brunswick to Canada and the United States.

In Upper Canada the system of land grants was generous to excess. Any applicant who showed evidence of good faith could secure a grant of 200 acres, which in some circumstances might be increased to 1200. In addition to the original Loyalist grants, the son or daughter of a Loyalist was entitled to 200 acres on coming of age. Disbanded field officers could claim as much as 5000 acres. Members of the Legislative Council were granted 6000 acres each in 1797, and comparable grants were made to other favored persons. A system of granting whole townships to groups of leaders and associates was in vogue for several years toward the end of the century until its abuse led to its abandonment. The grants to Loyalists and other special classes were free of charge. The ordinary settler paid a relatively modest fee. Terms of this sort were a temptation to avarice. By 1798, well over 1,000,000 acres had been alienated, and the figure rose to 4,500,000 by 1804. In a pioneer province where hired labor was almost unobtainable, it was clear that the holders of large grants had no hope of cultivating them but were chiefly interested in their speculative value.

In the history of the expansion that has peopled the continent of North America, the land speculator has played a prominent and in certain aspects a useful part. In Upper Canada, however, his influence was almost wholly bad. Large tracts of land in the most desirable locations lay waste, and the new settler had either to pay excessive prices or to locate in areas remote from markets and transportation. The situation was aggravated by the existence of Crown and clergy reserves. Together they amounted to roughly two-sevenths of the land allocated to settlers. The clergy reserves were to be leased, not sold; but few settlers were inclined to pay rent when they could get free land of their own. The Crown reserves were intended to provide a provincial revenue from the sale of land that had risen in value with the progress of settlement. This involved the government itself in land speculation and largely defeated its purpose by making settlement difficult and purchase unattractive.

Economic and Social Beginnings

As settlement proceeded, the various provinces developed their individual economic structures. In the Maritimes the chief activities were directed toward the forest and the sea. Only on Prince Edward Island did agriculture become the main activity. Neither New Brunswick nor Nova Scotia grew enough food for its own needs. Newfoundland settlement, which West of England fishing interests had long tried to prevent, was scattered in small pockets along the coast and depended on fishing supplemented by sealing, with virtually no agriculture. There was no resident governor until 1818, no elected assembly until 1833. Fishing was the leading activity in Nova Scotia, whose schooners sailed to the Grand Banks and whose valuable coastal fisheries were exploited locally by small boats. Lumbering was mainly an adjunct of shipbuilding, which developed into an industry of major importance. This in turn aided the growth of a carrying trade, and by the nineteenth century the bluenose skipper had become a legendary figure on the seas.

New Brunswick also built ships, largely for the timber trade or for sale abroad, and developed a fishing industry in the Bay of Fundy and the Gulf of St. Lawrence. In that province, however, both fishing and shipbuilding were overshadowed by lumbering. The great forests of the interior, with their virgin stands of white pine, were the paramount natural asset. Rivers such as the St. John and the Miramichi provided the necessary transport routes to carry the logs from the interior to the coast. Lumbering in winter could be combined with farming in summer and offered to able-bodied youths a rough and lusty life, which had certain parallels to that of the *coureur de bois*.

The American Revolution weakened, though it did not entirely break, the earlier trade connection between the Maritimes and New England. There were hopes that compensation might be found in the exclusion of American competition from the West Indies and the acquisition of that lucrative market by the Maritimes. These hopes were only partly realized. There was a measure of happy reciprocity based on the need of the West Indies for fish and the hearty appetites of Maritimers for overproof rum. There were some markets for lumber, but there were few agricultural products to export, and the West Indies needed the greater variety and volume of goods available from the United States. The abandonment of the British mercantile system eventually dashed Maritime ambitions. Trade with the West Indies helped in the development of Nova Scotia shipping; but New Brunswick reaped less advantage and depended largely on Britain as a market for lumber.

In the St. Lawrence region lumber was also rising in importance. The first aim of the pioneer settler was to clear his land. A common method was to kill the trees by girdling and burn them where they fell. But as a market developed, lumber became a cash asset of which the new settler could take advantage, and lumbering gradually became an industry on its own account. From the shores of Lake Ontario, great timber rafts were floated down the St. Lawrence to Montreal and Quebec. The Ottawa Valley developed into a leading area of the lumber industry. The Napoleonic Wars brought an increased demand in Britain for masts and squared timber, particularly after the supply from the Baltic was cut off, and preferential duties on timber after 1794 also provided a stimulus to the industry in both New Brunswick and the Canadas. By the turn of the century, lumber was a leading staple in the Canadas as well as in the Maritimes.

As the forests receded before the advance of settlement, the next stage was to develop a staple crop from the land that had been cleared. In Upper Canada the evolution of agriculture was marked at an early stage by wheat as the chief product. Simcoe had high hopes that the new province, in addition to remedying the deficiencies of Lower Canada's food supply, would become the granary of England. Here, as in the case of lumber, Britain's wartime demands provided a real stimulus, not only to grain growing but to the expansion of the milling industry. Exports of wheat and flour reached a peak of over a million bushels in 1802. But the demand was subject to severe fluctuations; and important as wheat growing was in the initial development of the economy of Upper Canada, the uncertainty made reliance on this single export crop unsatisfactory as a foundation for the growth and prosperity of the province.

There were attendant difficulties of transportation, which hampered the frontier farmer. Among the earliest demands of the pioneers were roads and schools and churches. All of these were expensive to supply. The pioneer was seldom willing to undertake their construction himself or to bear the expense in the form of taxes. He tended to rely on the philanthropy of private groups or on the generosity of the government to provide these benefits without appreciable cost to himself.

The vital need for good roads was an immediate consequence of the advance of settlement, of which adequate roads were themselves important instruments. Yet for a large part of this period the main dependence of all the provinces was on water transportation, and the roads that would link the new settler with mills and markets were primitive or nonexistent. Nova Scotia made slow progress in the construction of roads to connect the coastal settlements and to link the south shore with the Bay of Fundy. There was a postal route through New Brunswick to the St. Lawrence, but this was suitable only for couriers, and transport highways were almost entirely lacking. "Ten miles of road fit for any kind of wheel carriage is not to be found in the province," wrote one surveyor in 1802. In Upper Canada Simcoe initiated work on the main trunk arteries. Yonge Street, running north from York to provide a connection with Lake Simcoe, was partly a military road and was constructed by troops. In 1796 the 35 miles to Holland Landing had been opened, but for many years it was so full of stumps and holes that it was almost useless for heavy traffic. Dundas Street, cutting across the base of the Niagara peninsula from Burlington to the Thames, was undertaken at the same time. By 1800 a highway along the shores of Lake Ontario linked Dundas Street with the road that had already been built from Kingston to Montreal. But even these roads were primitive at the best, and the building of secondary roads lagged deplorably.

One difficulty was the reliance on statute labor for both construction and maintenance. New Brunswick tried to finance roads by land grants to the builders, and Simcoe attempted a modified version of this scheme, but with only moderate success. The regulation that property owners should give at least three days' work a year on the roads was hopelessly inadequate, particularly when large tracts of waste land meant that there were long stretches on which no work could be secured by this means. The situation was particularly serious in Upper Canada, where the farmer had to transport his wheat for considerable distances to the merchant or the mill and to carry back his supplies. It was not until 1804 that funds for road building were appropriated from provincial revenues, and even this brought little improvement in their condition.

The desire for schools also ran into financial difficulties. Grammar schools were established in most of the chief centers by 1800; but the provincial governments showed little interest in primary education, and the scattered pioneer communities were too poor and primitive to undertake it themselves in any satisfactory fashion. The rural settlements depended for the most part on itinerant schoolmasters, whose qualifications were scanty and whose characters were frequently dubious. In 1807 the legislature of Upper Canada provided for a grammar school in each of eight districts, and Nova Scotia followed this example in 1811; but it was not until 1816 that Upper Canada undertook to assist primary education by a grant of public funds.

Like the itinerant schoolmaster, the itinerant preacher was a figure in the early settlements. The Catholic Church sent out missionaries to the frontier districts. The Catholic Highlanders who settled in Glengarry brought their priest with them, and Scottish Presbyterians established their own churches at an early stage. But in most of the pioneer communities it was the more evangelical sects that made the greatest appeal. The Church of England, with its staid approach and its aristocratic tone, found it hard to secure any extensive foothold outside the towns. "I found the lower orders of the people, nearly to a man, Presbyterians or fanatics," lamented one Anglican missionary to Nova Scotia in 1776. And Bishop Jacob Mountain of Quebec, visiting Upper Canada in 1794, found to his horror that the population was largely in the grip of "itinerant and mendicant Methodists, a set of ignorant enthusiasts whose preaching is calculated only to perplex the understanding, and corrupt the morals; to relax the nerves of industry, and dissolve the bonds of society." In the Maritimes, the Congregationalist background of the early settlers was the original basis for the "New Light" movement, which made its contribution to the considerable Baptist element in the population at the beginning of the nineteenth century. The Methodists were also established by that time and had formed a connection with the English Wesleyans. But it was in Upper Canada that Methodism, following in the wake of the settlers from the United States, secured its strongest hold. The indefatigable circuit rider brought the gospel to the frontier settlements. The camp-meeting technique suited communities that had a taste for emotional gatherings and a dislike for Anglican pew rent. In default of permanent churches, such ministrations provided for the religious needs of the pioneers.

In this frontier society the growing towns were emerging as potential centers of culture as well as of commerce. Montreal, with a population of 22,000 in 1801, was the metropolis of Canada and the center of the far-flung commercial system of the St. Lawrence. Kingston had some 2000 inhabitants in 1812 and was the leading town in Upper Canada. Governor Simcoe, in his search for a capital that would be comfortably remote from American attack, had fixed on the wilderness site where London now stands, but in 1793 he was overruled by his superior Dorchester, who decided on the old carrying place at Toronto. That spot, which contained a single wigwam at the time, was christened York and only resumed its older name on its incorporation in 1834. In 1812 its population was still under 1000 and it was only slowly rising toward the position of a commercial as well as an administrative center. Halifax combined the character of a seaport and a garrison town. St. John was the center of the timber trade and the commercial life of New Brunswick. In many ways these small urban communities with their rude living standards and occasional disorderly tendencies—which the large numbers of taverns did nothing to abate—reflected the primitive pioneer society out of which they had sprung; but they also contained the germs of a more cultivated and intellectual life. All of them had groups with social pretensions who sought to constitute themselves an aristocracy, and some of their members including officials and garrison officers, had in fact an aristocratic English background. The emergence of local newspapers gave modest signs of urban intellectual interests. Halifax in the early part of the nineteenth century saw the appearance of three newspapers and a monthly magazine and local newspapers were published in all the chief towns. The *Quebec Gazette* was founded in 1764, the *Upper Canada Gazette* in 1793—the first journals in their respective provinces, to which others were soon added in the various growing centers.

The economy that emerged in British North America during this period exhibited the salient features that were to characterize it throughout the nineteenth century. It was an economy that rested largely on the production of staples for export—fish and lumber in the Maritimes, lumber and wheat and furs in the St. Lawrence region. It was also an economy that from an early date showed tendencies toward the consolidation of capital and control. The production of staples gave the merchant a place of special importance and often made him not only a trader but also an entrepreneur, directly engaged in milling and lumbering and shipping. Large-scale operators began to emerge in Nova Scotia shipping and in lumbering in New Brunswick and the Canadas. In Upper Canada the country merchant was frequently the banker and broker as well as the miller. He bought up the local grain for exporters or government contractors. The farmer depended on him for the sale of his crop in return for goods or credit and was often completely in his grip economically. In his turn the local merchant depended on the large commercial interests in Montreal, who dominated the export and import trade. The fur trade too was in the hands of the Montreal merchants; and it was the fur trade, with its increased demands for capital and growing burden of transportation costs, that offered an oustanding example of financial consolidation at this early stage in the economic evolution of Canada.

The Expanding Fur Trade

The peace of 1783 hastened a reorientation of the fur trade that was already under way by the time of the Revolution. The new boundary severed Canada from the main fur-bearing area south of the Great Lakes. In the negotiations that preceded the treaty, the Americans had offered a reciprocal freedom of trade, which would virtually have assured a British commercial monopoly in the West. But it would also have involved a drastic revision of the British mercantile system for the benefit of the Americans, and this was something to which London was unwilling to agree. As it turned out, the adverse effect of the division of the continent was less immediate than had been feared. Britain held on to the western posts for over a decade, and Jay's Treaty in 1794 at last provided for free trade across the boundary. On the other hand, Britain surrendered the posts, which were so important to the fur trade, and the Americans found ways through adverse regulations and transit tolls to hamper the activities of traders from Canada. The political boundary gradually hardened into an economic barrier. The purchase of Louisiana by the United States in 1803 was followed by a pronouncement that the concessions of Jay's Treaty did not apply to that area and by regulations that confined its trade to Americans. The enterprising John Jacob Astor seized on the opportunity to form the American Fur Company, which aimed at a monopoly of trade in the newly acquired area; and although this was later reorganized into the South West Company, in which certain Montreal interests had a share, it meant the practical end of the Canadian fur trade south of the boundary.

There were, however, other factors contributing to the shift toward the Canadian Northwest. The steady advance of settlement foreshadowed the extinction of the older fur trade areas. Already those areas were being rapidly depleted. But to the north lay the great forest region, the wealth of which had been only partly tapped by the Hudson's Bay Company and where the highest quality pelts were to be found. The French had already made an initial penetration into this region. Almost immediately after the conquest of Canada the first British traders followed in their wake. Their number increased after the relaxation of the restrictions on the fur trade in 1768. The Hudson's Bay Company faced an irruption into its domains of enterprising "pedlars," who set up posts on the Saskatchewan and the Assiniboine, planting themselves athwart the main trading routes and intercepting the Indians on their journey to Hudson Bay.

Hitherto the Hudson's Bay Company had confined its trading posts to the shores of the bay itself. Occasionally, stirred by criticism and by threats to its charter, it had made gestures toward further exploration. Its chief purpose in sending occasional servants into the interior, however, was to make contact with new Indian tribes and persuade them to come down to the bay to trade. It was obviously preferable from the company's point of view that the Indians should bear the toil and expense of the long journey, while the company devoted itself to reaping the maximum profits with the minimum of effort.

This situation was completely changed by the arrival of the pedlars. The fur-trading interests from the St. Lawrence had now extended their activities into the region on which the company depended for its revenues, confronting the company with a competition that was far more serious than any it had experienced from the French since the very early days. The gratified Indians who encountered a white trader while they were still only halfway to their goal were only too pleased to exchange their furs on the spot. If the company was to maintain its position, it too must expand into the interior. "It appears to me," reported one of the leading factors in 1772, "that the only way of increasing the fur trade is to have an inland settlement to supply the natives with necessaries: ammunition, tobacco and brandy." In 1774 the company established its first inland post, Cumberland House, on the portage route leading from the Saskatchewan to the Churchill by way of Cumberland Lake. It was the beginning of an expansion into the interior to keep pace with the rivalry from Montreal.

This countermove by the Hudson's Bay Company in turn imposed the need for new measures on the Montreal traders. Although they, like the company, had English goods with which to trade, the company could trade more cheaply because of far lower transportation costs. The route from Montreal by way of the Great Lakes was long and expensive and became still more so after 1783. One serious effect of the treaty of that year was to leave Grand Portage, the best route from Lake Superior to the northwest, on American soil. An alternative route was evolved by way of Lake Nipigon, starting from the present Fort William, but this was more difficult and more costly. Like the French before them, the Montreal traders found themselves under the continual necessity of outflanking their rivals and of reaching new tribes and new areas in advance of the Hudson's Bay Company.

The result was a steady rise in overhead costs. The exhaustion of successive fur-bearing areas was added to the pressure of competition to drive the traders ever farther afield. Lengthening transport routes called for increased personnel, not merely for transportation, but for depots and supplies. Permanent posts had to be established at strategic intervals for the storage of furs and the distribution of goods to the various brigades. The cost of transporting food into the remote interior was almost prohibitive. It became impossible to rely on hunting or on trading for food along the way. Efforts were made to develop local supply centers that could draw on the surrounding areas for food, usually by trading with the Indians for pemmican instead of for furs. As the source of furs receded, the time lag between investment and returns increased. More and more the conduct of the fur trade demanded an extensive and a permanent organization backed by substantial amounts of capital and aiming at a monopoly position. It was a situation that brought about a steadily increasing predominance of the English—or perhaps more often the Scottish—merchant as the entrepreneur who took the financial risks and realized the profits. French personnel continued to be of vital importance as voyageurs and traders, but French merchants lacked funds on the scale demanded by what had now become big business, and by the turn of the century they had in effect been eliminated from the management and investment aspects of the fur trade.

At an early stage both the traders and their backers discovered the virtues of cooperation. Temporary combinations to finance the expeditions, such as that entered into by Todd and McGill and the Frobishers in 1769, were common almost from the outset. In 1775 the arrival of several large expeditions in the Saskatchewan region brought a realization on the part of their leaders that, if they had to compete with the Hudson's Bay Company, it would be folly to compete among themselves as well. They decided to pool both their stock of goods and the returns from their winter's trading, and this procedure was repeated during succeeding years. In 1779 a number of the principal firms pooled their interests in a sixteen-share agreement, which was renewed yearly until 1783, when a new combination was agreed on for a period of five years. In 1787 a still more important agreement was reached, which brought in new members on a twenty-share basis. Although this too was in the first instance for a five-year period, it proved to be more enduring, for it was the effective establishment of the North West Company, the "lords of the wilderness" for a full generation to follow.

This did not mean the immediate end of independent competition. There were still jealous rivals outside the combination, and there was a constant tendency for discontented partners or winterers to break away on their own. During the next twenty years there were periodic reorganizations to eliminate these difficulties. The most serious threat arose when the loss of the western posts forced the groups who had hitherto traded southward from Detroit and Michilimackinac to turn their attention to the northwest. These groups in their turn drew together in 1800 to form the New North West Company, of the XY Company, as it came to be known from the letters with which it stamped its bales to distinguish them from those of its rivals. For several years a fierce struggle raged between the two groups, until its ruinous nature brought about a coalition in which 25 out of 100 shares were allotted to the XY interests. From 1804 on the new merger held a virtual monopoly of the Montreal fur trade and stood alone in its rivalry with the Hudson's Bay Company.

The North West Company needed all its growing resources to meet its growing burdens. There were now more partners, both winterers and financiers, who had to be satisfied. There was an added urge to seek new and untouched areas; yet the very success of such efforts added to the costs of transport and personnel. Grand Portage, and later Fort William, had at first been the main advance depots, from which the traders spread into the interior and to which they brought back their winter's accumulation of furs. But as the traders penetrated into the far north in the region of the Peace River and Great Slave Lake, it became impossible for them to bring down their furs to Fort William and return with supplies in a single season. The main supply line had to be extended to Fort Chipewyan on Lake Athabaska, which became the distribution center for the northern fur trade. There were efforts at the beginning of the nineteenth century to effect a merger with the Hudson's Bay Company or, failing that, to lease a transport route to the bay. But the older company rejected all overtures, and the North West Company was forced to continue its process of expansion, which carried it eventually to the Pacific.

One of the great figures in this process was Alexander Mackenzie. His Scottish soul revolted against the mounting cost of the long transport route from Montreal. His imagination was stirred by the old dream of a water route through the continent to the Pacific. His first effort to discover such a passage in 1789 led him down the Mackenzie River to the shores of the Arctic. It was a notable contribution to the exploration of the far north, but it was not what Mackenzie had sought, and his attitude was reflected in the name River Disappointment which he gave to his discovery. He fell back on the idea of ascending the Peace River in search of a passage across the height of land to the waters flowing into the Pacific. In 1792, on a journey marked by appalling hardships, he worked his way up the turbulent headwaters of the Peace, along the Parsnip, and across the divide to the Pacific watershed. He journeyed for some distance down the Fraser but soon concluded that its rapids and cascades made it useless for navigation. An overland crossing carried him to the Blackwater, and in July 1793, he reached the waters of the Pacific at Bentinck Arm, a long inlet halfway up the coast of British Columbia. For the first time a white man had completed the overland crossing of the North American continent.

This opened up a completely new fur area, one to which the North West Company was inevitably drawn. Mackenzie had still not found the

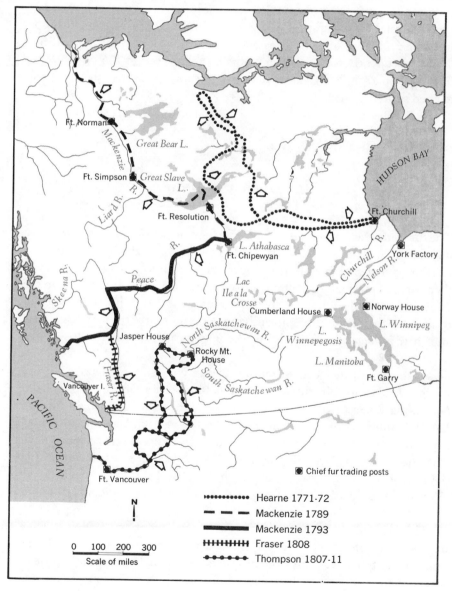

Northwest Exploration, 1771-1811

cheap route that he sought; but within a few years the pressure of competition had carried the fur trade to the Rockies, and by 1807 the Columbia Enterprise of the North West Company had been established on the Pacific slope. In that year David Thompson began his survey of the Columbia River, and in 1808 Simon Fraser explored the river that bears his name. Competition threatened from John Jacob Astor, who tried to set up an establishment at Astoria in 1811. But disaster overtook his ships, and when the War of 1812 threatened the post with capture the Astorian partners prudently forestalled such loss by selling out to the North West Company in 1814. For the few remaining years of existence the company reigned supreme on the Pacific Coast.

The Uneasy Frontier

The fur trade was not merely responsible for competition, at times erupting into physical strife, in the vast wilderness of the Canadian Northwest. Its shift to that region took place over a period of two decades, and even then some contact was maintained from Canadian posts with tribes on the American side. Meanwhile there were trading interests who were reluctant to abandon their establishments and connections south of the new boundary, and their influence contributed to the uneasy situation that followed the peace of 1783.

At the end of the Revolution the British were still in effective control of the American Northwest. They held a series of key posts from Michilimackinac through Detroit and Niagara to Dutchman's Point on Lake Champlain. All these were south of the new boundary, and the treaty stipulated that they were to be handed over with all convenient speed. But the treaty had hardly been signed before the British authorities developed serious misgivings about the unconsidered way in which the West had been given up and began to aim at a postponement, if not an actual reversal, of the surrender.

The fur traders were among the first to urge a policy of delay. They had been unable to prevent the surrender of the area from which the bulk of the trade was still drawn, but they felt that they should at least be given time to collect their debts and recover their investments in the West—the amount was perhaps £200,000—and they asked for a delay of two years in the evacuation of the posts in order to achieve this end. But a more serious consideration immediately rose to trouble the mind of Governor Haldimand. In negotiating the treaty, Britain had neglected to make any provision for the Indians. A number of the tribes had sided with Britain during the war. They claimed full title to all their lands that had not been formally ceded. Yet it appeared that Britain had assumed the right to hand over the possession of these lands to the Americans, who made no secret of their intention to open them to white settlement. Haldimand feared that the Indians would vent their indignation on the British. Even before the treaty was signed, he expressed his "apprehension of the effects which the preliminaries will have on the minds of our Indian allies, who will consider themselves abandoned to the resentment of an ungenerous and implacable enemy."

Until this danger was past, Haldimand with the approval of London decided to take advantage of the vagueness of the treaty and its lack of any time limit to delay the surrender of the posts. Excuses for this course were soon found in the failure of the United States to fulfill the treaty terms, under which the Loyalists were to regain their estates and the British merchants were to have full facilities for recovering their debts. As the occupation was prolonged, still wider objectives emerged. The idea took form of an Indian buffer state, which would check the spread of American settlement and allow Britain to retain her commercial and political dominance in the West. There was even the prospect that the weakness and disunity that the United States exhibited in the years immediately after the Revolution would result in disintegration. Vermont was bringing pressure on Congress to recognize it as a state by throwing out hints of a readiness to return to its British allegiance. Spanish intrigues were active in the new settlements in the Southwest. It was not inconceivable that, by playing for time, Britain might find an opportunity to regain the western territory that she had prematurely given up.

Such calculations were short-lived. The United States adopted a new federal constitution, which checked the forces of disruption. A national government with effective powers and resources replaced the impotent confederation. American diplomacy now had behind it the concerted strength of the republic and could speak with a new weight of authority. The creation of a federal judiciary provided legal means of redress for Loyalists or British creditors whose rights had been denied by the various states. The reasons that Britain had put forward for retaining the posts largely lost their validity, and the unwisdom and danger of continuing such a course became only too evident when the Indians were crushed under circumstances that brought Britain and the United States to the verge of war.

It was natural that Britain's retention of the posts should cause irritation in the United States. Resentment was increased by the belief that the British in Canada were engaged in stirring up Indian hostility. Actually their desire was to prevent an Indian outbreak, which might have serious repercussions on Canada. But this was made difficult by American determination to secure the Indian lands and by British reluctance to risk Indian hostility by abandoning the tribes to their fate. British efforts at mediation irritated the Americans, who felt that such efforts only encouraged Indian resistance. The defeat of two American military expeditions further inflamed these feelings and brought accusations that Britain was arming the tribes against the United States.

The situation was aggravated by the growing dispute over maritime rights. By 1793 Britain was once more at war with France and had become involved in the unhappy controversy over the rights of impressment and blockade. The danger of war with the United States made the Canadian authorities more anxious than ever to hold the good will of the Indians along the frontier and more reluctant to weaken the defenses of Canada by giving up the posts. Lord Dorchester, gloomily convinced that a new struggle was inevitable, added fuel to the flames. In February 1794, with inexcusable tactlessness, he told an Indian delegation that he fully expected war before the year was out, "and if so, a line must then be drawn by the warriors." A week later he took the still more provocative step of ordering the reoccupation of Fort Miami, a small post some distance from Detroit, which had been recently abandoned.

This was pushing matters dangerously far. It meant the extension of British military occupation on American soil. Moreover, it was an aggressive thrust into an area that was about to become a scene of conflict. A new American expedition against the Indians was launched in 1794. The decisive engagement took place at Fallen Timbers, within earshot of Fort Miami. The Indians were completely routed, and the triumphant American force swept to the very walls of the fort. A single provocative act by the small garrison would have precipitated a clash. But fortunately the commanders on both sides confined their exchanges to words, and the danger passed when the American force withdrew.

By this time the American government was gravely worried about the danger of war. British interference with American commerce had roused American feelings. Dorchester's speech added to the indignation that already existed over British policy in the West. In an attempt to ease the tension, John Jay was sent to London as a special envoy to settle existing grievances, and his mission was fortunately arranged before the news of the occupation of Fort Miami arrived to inflame passions still further.

Jay's task was to settle the difficulties arising out of the peace treaty, to solve the problem of maritime rights, and to negotiate a trade treaty with Britain. On the last two points he had little success. Britain refused to give up the right of search, and the clause admitting American ships to the West Indies was so restrictive that the Senate refused to accept it. On the matters most directly affecting Canada, however, a fuller measure of agreement was reached. Britain was at last reconciled to the need to surrender the posts. The battle of Fallen Timbers virtually ended the prospect of creating an Indian buffer state in the Ohio region, which was in fact ceded by the Indians in the following year by the Treaty of Greenville. Provision for a speedier settlement of the claims of the Loyalists and the merchants removed the chief excuses for retaining the posts. Britain agreed to evacuate them by June 1, 1796; and in return the Americans agreed to British commercial access to the West under the provision that goods crossing the boundary from either side were to be subject to no higher duties than those on similar goods imported from Europe.

The first clause of the treaty expressed the high hopes of its authors: "There shall be a firm, inviolable and universal peace and a true and sincere friendship between His Britannic Majesty, and his heirs and successors, and the United States of America; and between their respective countries, territories, cities, towns and people of every degree." These aspirations were sincerely entertained by both sides, but circumstances were already conspiring against their realization. The continuance of the war in Europe, and the reliance of Britain on sea power as her major weapon against France, led to repeated incidents that roused American anger. Britain insisted on searching American ships for deserters from the navy and sometimes seized sailors who claimed American citizenship. This practice led in 1807 to a battle between the British ship *Leopard* and the American warship *Chesapeake*, which nearly precipitated war. A further grievance, which grew in weight after 1806, was over the British blockade of Europe. Britain claimed the right to seize ships carrying contraband to the enemy. The United States insisted that neutral ships made neutral goods and protested against any interference with American commerce. When Napoleon, after the destruction of his fleet at Trafalgar, fell back on the attempt to exclude British goods from Europe by his Continental System, Britain retaliated with her Orders-in-Council, which forbade neutral ships to enter any European port without first going to Britain.

American efforts at retaliation, first by Jefferson's embargo in 1807, which forbade American trade with foreign countries, and then by nonintercourse with the offending belligerents, were ineffective. Maritime grievances continued to mount and to bring the danger of war steadily nearer.

This situation was of the gravest concern to Canada. As the nearest British possession she could expect at once to become a main theater of hostilities if war broke out between Britain and the United States. The sins of the mother country would be visited upon the colony even though the latter might itself be unoffending. But in fact the Americans felt that Canada was also an offender. The danger of war led to Canadian measures of defense, which the United States regarded as signs of hostility and which made their contribution to the renewal of conflict in 1812.

Once again the issues arose in the West. The abandonment of the posts did not entirely break the connection between British traders and the Indians of the American Northwest. Many of the latter continued to bring their furs to posts on the Canadian side, where they traded for ammunition and supplies. The authorities in Canada desired to retain the friendship of the Western tribes, not merely for its commercial advantages but still more from fear of an Indian attack in case of war with the United States. Whenever the threat became particularly acute, special efforts were made to attract the Indians to the Canadian posts and special generosity was shown in the matter of presents and supplies. This in turn alarmed the Americans, who renewed their accusations that the British were stirring up the Indians and arming them against the United States.

The crisis came in the autumn of 1811. It was essentially the outcome of the relentless pressure of American settlement on Indian lands. The Treaty of Greenville was followed by a series of cessions, which pushed the hunting grounds steadily farther west. In an attempt to check these continued encroachments, the able Indian leader Tecumseh endeavored to form a league that would unite all the tribes in resistance to the advance of the whites. To the Americans this seemed a threat of an Indian league that would loose a new and savage warfare against the frontier. Tecumseh's refusal to acknowledge a new cession of lands along the Wabash and his announced determination to resist their occupation brought matters to a head. The West was determined to wipe out the Indian threat; and at the battle of Tippecanoe in November 1811, Tecumseh's followers were routed and his dream of a federation was smashed.

This event came just as a new Congress with a strong body of new Western members was getting under way. The West was now fully convinced that the British in Canada were behind the Indian menace and only the conquest of Canada could remove the threat. In actual fact the Canadian authorities had been acutely aware of the danger and had urged the Indians to peace, and it was the Americans and not the Indians who had precipitated the clash. But the fact that the Indians drew their weapons and supplies from British sources was enough to convince the West of where the real danger lay. The War Hawks, drawn from the new states of the West and from the frontier districts of the older ones, clamored for the expulsion of British power from North America. Without the background of hostility to Britain created by the controversy over maritime rights, their efforts might have met with little success. But a combination of grievances—to which were added the effects of commercial depression and the desire of the South to expel Spain from Florida—gave weight to their agitation, and a fresh naval clash between the *President* and the *Little Belt* in May 1811, had further inflamed the popular temper. Napoleon's specious pretense of modifying his commercial restrictions in 1810 meant that resentment was concentrated more than ever on England. There were last-minute attempts at compromise; but Britain's repeal of the Orders-in-Council came only after war was declared, and in any case her refusal to abandon her impressment of seamen would have made agreement impossible. On June 18, 1812, Congress declared war and the United States embarked on the conquest of Canada.

The War of 1812

The brunt of the war fell on Upper Canada. Along the seaboard the supremacy of the British navy together with the bitter hostility of New England toward "Mr. Madison's war" secured the immunity of the Maritimes from any serious danger of attack. The naval efforts of the United States were reduced to privateering, and that was a game which two could play. Nova Scotia skippers took out letters of marque and preyed enthusiastically on American shipping. Nova Scotia traders and shipbuilders seized on the opportunities presented by the strangling of the American carrying trade. At the same time the British blockade that was clamped down on the Atlantic coast was not applied to New England until the later stages of the war, and traders from the Maritimes were able to continue an active commerce with the northeastern states. For the Atlantic provinces the war was a period of prosperity unclouded by any threat of invasion.

Lower Canada was almost equally immune, though for very different reasons. All through the war the idea of an expedition against Montreal held a central place in American plans. It was symbolic of the whole conduct of the war on the side of the United States that this main objective was never really threatened. The feeble efforts against Lower Canada collapsed at the first sign of opposition from the French volunteers and militia, whose small forces decisively checked the invaders at Chateauguay and Lacolle.

These episodes had far more than a military significance. They symbolized the profound change that had taken place in the French attitude during the past generation. The sullen ambiguity of 1775 had given way to a solidarity of resistance to the Americans in 1812. Even the fact that Britain was at war with France had strengthened rather than weakened the loyalty of the Canadians. For it was a war against revolutionary France, and the revolution was anathema to French Canada. The half century that had passed since the conquest had weakened the tradition of attachment to the mother country. The revolution, with its attacks on the church and its destruction of the monarchy, broke it completely. Efforts by the envoys of the French republic in the United States to stir up trouble in French Canada had only a limited success; and by the time Bonaparte came to power, articulate French-Canadian sentiment—and particularly the influence of the Church—was unreservedly on the side of Britain. "The Catholic Clergy," wrote Governor George Prevost in 1814, "are my firmest supports." And while opinion had turned against the atheist French republic, it had also hardened against the United States. The French had their grievances under British rule, but they also had their privileges. They were fully aware that the concessions they enjoyed in such matters as laws and language and religion would be swept away if they were absorbed into the United States. The Quebec Act may have been of doubtful value in saving Canada in 1775; the real effect, heightened by the later grant of representative institutions, was apparent in 1812.

It was in Upper Canada that the real danger from disloyalty arose. That province had recently been people by American settlers, only a small proportion of whom were of Loyalist stock. The United States fully expected that the invasion would receive a popular welcome and that the conquest of Upper Canada would be a mere military promenade. When General William Hull launched his invasion from Detroit, he issued a proclamation calling on the population to rejoice in their deliverance from British tyranny, and he fully expected his forces to be received with open arms.

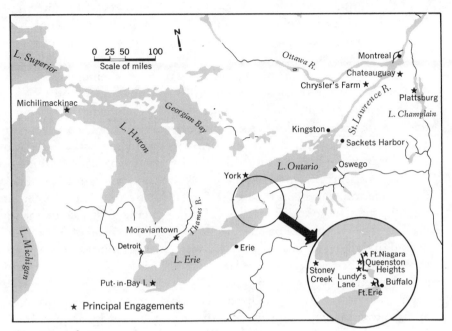

The War of 1812

There were serious grounds for such expectations. The American settlers in Upper Canada were no more anxious to fight their former fellow countrymen than those in Nova Scotia had been during the Revolution. A considerable number, including half the militia assembled for the defense of Malden, deserted to the invaders. Still larger numbers refused to take up arms against them. The Norfolk militia flatly refused to march. The assembly, where American influence was strong, rejected the proposal for martial law and opposed any strengthening of the Militia Act. Sir Isaac Brock, the lieutenant governor and military commander in Upper Canada, was convinced that the bulk of the population was disloyal at heart and that his only hope was to "speak loud and look big" in an attempt to give an impression of confidence that he was far from feeling.

What saved Canada was the combination of American political dissensions and military ineptitude with the initial vigor displayed by the Canadian authorities. The potential strength of the United States, with ten times the population of British North America and an even greater preponderance in resources, was overwhelming. Britain's strength was fully absorbed in the struggle against Napoleon in Europe and she could send little immediate help to Canada. The defense rested on some 4500 regular troops supplemented by militia. At the outset Brock had only 1600 regulars in Upper Canada, and it was essentially this hard core of trained fighting men, superior in quality to anything immediately available to the invaders, that saved the province when the first shock fell upon it.

Fortunately for Canada, the United States never managed to bring anything like its full weight to bear. New England refused to support the war. Its citizens preferred to invest in British securities and to carry on a lucrative trade with the British army. Toward the end of the war, two-thirds of the beef consumed by the British troops came from across the border, largely from Vermont and New York, and without this help from American purveyors the British forces would have been in sore straits for supplies. The southern states were more interested in Florida than in Canada. The enthusiasm of other sections for a declaration of war did not extend to fighting it. The forces raised were disappointing in numbers and quality and their leadership was lamentable. The war never had behind it a resolute effort by a united nation.

In contrast, the leaders in Upper Canada were able to offset the disunity in that province by prompt and effective action. The energy and ability of Brock resulted not only in the successful defense of Canada during the first campaign, but in the actual seizure of the initiative. It appeared that defeat was not inevitable after all. The consequence was a stiffening of resolution on the part of the loyal elements in the population and a check to further defections by the waverers. The more actively disloyal, by committing themselves at the outset, had removed some of the danger from within. A large part of the population chiefly wanted to avoid active participation and to be on the winning side. The decisiveness with which Brock acted in the initial stages of the war cast doubts on the prospect of an American victory and was a paramount factor in saving Canada.

The campaign of 1812 was a rude shock to American hopes of an easy conquest. The main blow was to have been struck at Montreal by way of Lake Champlain, with supporting thrusts from Niagara and Detroit. But the troops who crossed the border above Plattsburg immediately decided that they would be happier at home and fell back ignominiously before they had even encountered the enemy. In the west, Hull's advance from Detroit was hampered by British naval command of Lake Erie and by the resistance of the small post of Malden on the site of the present Amherstburg. On the Niagara frontier the conclusion of a brief armistice allowed Brock to hasten west with the few hundred men he could muster. Meanwhile the surprise capture of Michilimackinac by a British force had turned the wavering Indians of the Northwest against the Americans, resulting in the massacre of Fort Dearborn and a serious threat to Detroit. This, coupled with Brock's advance, not only brought Hull's retreat across the frontier, but led to the ignominious surrender of Detroit to a greatly inferior force. Brock at once hurried back to Niagara to meet the renewed threat from that quarter. The American attack on Queenston was marked by the refusal of the various commanders to support each other and of the New York militia to follow their comrades across the river, and met with a decisive repulse. It was a costly victory for the British, for Brock was killed during the engagement; but the invaders had now been thrown back at every point, and the war had even been carried to American soil.

The campaign of 1813 was only slightly less dismal. The naval balance on the Great Lakes—a pivotal factor throughout the war—shifted toward the American side with Perry's victory on Lake Erie, which enabled the Americans to recover Detroit and to advance into Canada. But though the retreating British force was caught and virtually destroyed at Moraviantown, the invasion was not pressed. It was to have been concerted with an advance from Niagara; and when this was checked at Stoney Creek, the western column fell back after ravaging the countryside, and its victory was reduced to purely local significance.

In this year the main American objective was still supposed to be Montreal. As a prelude a naval attack was made on York, which was looted and burned, and the American squadron then sailed off to support the invasion of the Niagara peninsula. But a British counterthreat to the naval base of Sackets Harbor resulted in the recall of the American ships and the abandonment of the Niagara campaign after the check at Stoney Creek. The offensive against Montreal, however, was launched in two columns, one under General Wade Hampton from Lake Champlain and the other under General James Wilkinson by way of the St. Lawrence. But Hampton turned back after a brush with 800 Canadians at Chateauguay; and on receipt of this news General Wilkinson, part of whose force had already been badly mauled at Chrysler's Farm, promptly abandoned his advance and took his whole army into winter quarters. Canada had gained a respite for another year.

The prospects in 1814 were more formidable for both sides. A new thrust into Lower Canada, it is true, was ignominiously abandoned after a skirmish at Lacolle; but on the Niagara frontier a more serious effort was undertaken. It was halted at Lundy's Lane in the hardest fought engagement of the war. Both sides claimed a victory; but the decisive fact was that the encounter abruptly and conclusively checked the American invasion. It was now the turn of the British to take the initiative. Hostilities in Europe had ended with the first abdication of Napoleon, and Britain was able to turn her attention to America. British forces occupied Maine, captured Washington and burned it in revenge for the destruction of York, and launched an abortive attack on New Orleans. Strong reinforcements were sent to Canada, and in September an army of veterans from Europe advanced by way of the classic invasion route of Lake Champlain. At Plattsburg they confronted an American force; and when an improvised British naval squadron was beaten in its efforts to secure command of Lake Champlain, the British military commander decided that this made it impossible for him to proceed by land and tamely abandoned the effort and retreated to Canada. It was clear that lack of enterprise was not confined to American generals.

By this time both sides were heartily sick of the conflict. Peace efforts had in fact been in progress all through the war, and in August 1814, they issued in a conference at Ghent. The Americans were still desirous of securing British recognition of their maritime claims and of ending the concessions in Jay's Treaty that gave Canada commercial access to the West. But in the military sphere, and consequently in diplomacy, the Americans were now on the defensive. They had not won the war. They would be lucky if they could hold it to a draw. It was the British forces who had a foothold on American territory, and the chief task of the American negotiators was to prevent Britain from making her gains permanent.

Britain on her part saw a chance to modify the boundary settlement of 1783. She was in control of northern Maine to the Penobscot, and her retention of the area would greatly ease the problem of communications between the Atlantic and the St. Lawrence. She hoped to regain both Michilimackinac and a strip of land east of the Niagara River. Her command of the Northwest might be used to modify the ill-defined boundary in that region. By the Treaty of 1783 the line was to run from the Lake of the Woods west to the Mississippi. But it was now known that the Mississippi did not extend that far north. Some new arrangements would have to be made, and Britain hoped that the result would be to shift the boundary much farther south and give access to the navigable part of the Mississippi below the falls of St. Anthony. And for the last time the idea of an Indian buffer state was revived, with the suggestion that the line of the Treaty of Greenville should be accepted as a permanent boundary between the settlers and the tribes.

oundary Settlement of 1818

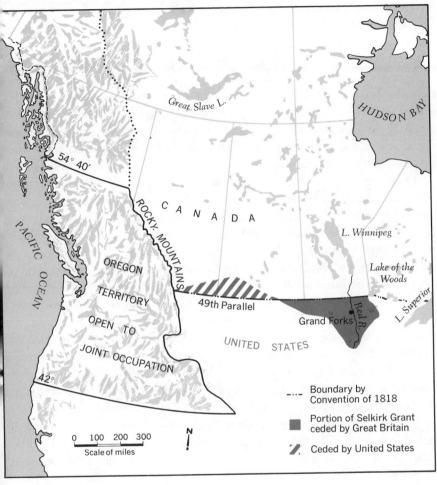

Such demands were far too stringent for the United States to accept. Sooner than surrender any part of their territory, the Americans would renew the war; and that was something for which Britain, wearied by twenty years of conflict, had no desire. Moreover, there were prospects of renewed hostilities in Europe, and the Duke of Wellington bluntly advised his government to make peace with America. In the end it was agreed to return to the general basis that existed before the war, modified by the cancellation of Jay's Treaty and of the American rights in the fisheries of the Maritimes and Newfoundland.

Inconclusive as this outcome might seem on the surface, it actually provided the foundation for the long, unbroken peace that followed. The salient issues that had led to the quarrel soon disappeared. With the world at peace, the maritime controversy lost its importance. The continued retreat of the tribes before American settlement broke their connection with Canada and no longer involved her in Indian troubles. Boundary commissions, set up under the provisions of the treaty, partly settled some disputed points. In 1818 it was agreed that the 49th parallel should form the boundary between the Lake of the Woods and the Rockies and that the disputed territory on the Pacific coast should be under the joint occupation of both countries until they could agree on its disposal.

Even more significant and symbolic was the disarmament convention that was concluded as an aftermath of the peace settlement. The war had shown the importance of naval power on the lakes. Neither the United States nor Canada could allow the other to gain a permanent ascendancy without endangering its own defense. Unless some agreement on limitation could be reached, both countries would be involved in a naval construction race, which might seriously affect their relations. This was something that both Britain and the United States earnestly wished to avoid. The United States, which had suggested disarmament on the lakes as early as 1783, renewed the proposal, and this time it met with a favorable reception. In 1817 the Rush-Bagot agreement was reached, and this limited the armed vessels of either side to the size that was needed for police and protection against smuggling. Fortifications were not mentioned and in fact the decades that followed saw substantial expenditures on permanent defenses by both sides. It was only after the Civil War and the achievement of confederation that diminished fears of any new hostilities led to a tacit renunciation of any further increases and made the undefended border a reality for virtually its whole length across the continent.

A *Coureur de Bois.*
A drawing by
Frederic Remington.

A Bush Road in Upper Canada.

Overland to the Pacific.

(Provincial Archives, Victoria, B.C.)

Rock at Bella Coola marking the completion of Alexander Mackenzie's crossing of the continent.

The Capture of Detroit.
General Hull surrenders to the British commander.

The War at Sea.
HMS Shannon *tows the captured American frigate* Chesapeake *into Halifax harbor.*

The Battle of Fallen Timbers.

The Attack on York.
American ships supporting the landing.

The Battle of Plattsburg.

Chapter 10

The Road to Rebellion

An Expanding Population

The War of 1812 left behind it deep scars, which have never wholly disappeared. In the United States an enthusiastic view of the struggle, which was little in evidence while it was in progress, developed after it was over. Tradition glorified the conflict into a "second war of independence," a new resistance to British oppression, which was spiritually identified with the resistance of 1776 and which added to the strength and permanence of anti-British sentiment. In Canada, on the other hand, the war was looked on as a wanton aggression, which had been motivated by vindictiveness and rapacity and which was only too likely to be repeated at the next opportunity. The result was a potent stimulus to an incipient Canadian nationalism. Pride in the successful defense of Canada against a vastly superior enemy was accompanied by a sense of continued danger from the same quarter and by a feeling that constant vigilance was necessary to guard against it.

One consequence was a serious increase in hostility toward Americanism and everything it implied. The war and its outcome had shifted the balance still further toward the side of conservatism. Many of the more radical elements had been eliminated when they went over to the American side. The doubtful attitude of the American settlers in Upper Canada gave ground for the charge that American origins implied disloyal tendencies. In contrast, the Loyalists vaunted their part in saving Canada from invasion and conquest, and the Loyalist tradition gained a fresh access of strength as a consequence of the war.

If this had been connected solely with the memory of "old, unhappy, far-off things," no serious harm might have been done. In the period that followed, both the British and American governments made earnest efforts to eliminate the remaining causes of friction and to lay the basis for a genuine and lasting friendship. The great bulk of the population on either side of the line had no real feeling of animosity. But the Tories in Canada found in the anti-American cry a political weapon that was too useful to be relinquished. Their control of public affairs was coming under attack from a rising tide of democratic sentiment. It was highly useful to be able to stigmatize reform agitation as republicanism and opposition to the provincial ruling clique as disloyalty to the empire. They used such charges on all possible occasions, and it was largely their zeal in rooting out all American influences, real or suspect, that kept alive this attitude of antagonism and perpetuated it into a cult—not, it must be admitted, without potent aid from chauvinistic American orators, who provided plentiful ammunition to the self-appointed custodians of Canadian loyalty.

One of the first manifestations of the new temper was the prohibition in 1815 of any new land grants to Americans. This was modified to permit a settler who had taken the oath of loyalty to secure land after seven years' residence; but the restriction was still serious, and the authorities were generally hostile to American immigration. As a result, Canada failed to share in the new westward migration that took place in the United States after 1815, much to the discontent of the land speculators and the perturbation of those who hoped for the rapid settlement of Upper Canada. A positive and energetic policy might have diverted part of the westward stream to that province. But the opportunity was rejected, and within a generation the peopling of the new states of the Middle West meant that the tide of migration had swept beyond Ontario and was even beginning to draw emigrants from that region to the prairie lands of the United States.

This curtailment of American immigration was accompanied by an influx from across the Atlantic, which radically changed the composition of the population. For the first time since the American Revolution the provinces of British North America received a substantial immigration from the British Isles. With the end of the war in Europe the full impact of the industrial and agricultural revolutions came home to the people of Britain. Distress and unemployment drove many to seek new opportunities overseas. The tide set most strongly toward the United States, where cheap land was available and where the infant industrial cities offered employment for skilled workers. Some effort, however, was made to divert the flow toward Canada by state aid to emigrants during the decade after 1815. Private charitable organizations in Britain also lent their aid;

but the great mass of emigrants financed their passage with what they could scrape together by themselves or with the aid of their families and friends. The new arrivals were of all sorts and conditions—discharged officers and distressed farmers, Scottish artisans and Irish paupers; but a large proportion arrived destitute or with few resources to take up a pioneer life in the new land.

The Maritime Provinces shared in the influx. There were nearly 40,000 arrivals in Nova Scotia in the decade after 1815. In the same period New Brunswick received an average of 5000 to 6000 a year, over two-thirds of them from Ireland. But this was only a trickle compared to the tide that flowed to the St. Lawrence. It gathered slowly during the early twenties, but by 1826 a rapid increase had set in which was maintained for several years. From around 12,000 in 1828, immigration rose to 30,000 in 1830 and to 66,000 in 1832. Then there was a temporary decline, to be succeeded by a new influx in the forties.

The process of settling the new arrivals on the land was impeded by private rapacity and public ineptitude. In Lower Canada the seigniorial system acted as a barrier. Nearly two-thirds of the seigniories were now in English hands, and legislation was secured that permitted changes in the tenure to freehold. But many of these lands were held for speculative purposes, and access to ungranted areas was difficult because of lack of roads. In Upper Canada the speculative aspect was aggravated by the confusion of policy concerning the granting of land. The system of free grants was extended to militiamen who had served in the War of 1812, many of whom already had land of their own. This, added to the system of Loyalist grants and the corruption and favoritism of the officials, increased the area of waste land held by speculators. Crown and clergy reserves added to the problem. Sale of Crown reserve lands was allowed in 1826, and limited sales of clergy reserves began in the following year. But on the whole the system combined an excessive generosity in free grants with an undue niggardliness in the handling of the reserves. The local authorities pursued a muddled course, torn between the desire for settlement and the hope of revenues from land sales, and the aspiring settler was only too apt to find that land in Upper Canada was either expensive or inaccessible.

Nonetheless, settlement proceeded in spite of all difficulties. New areas were opened up by pioneer farmers. Enterprising individuals and private land companies played a considerable part. Peter Robinson, who was later surveyor general, brought out a group of Irish settlers in 1823 and another in 1825. The eccentric and overbearing Colonel Thomas Talbot, who secured a large tract on the northern shore of Lake

Erie, over which he ruled as arbitrarily as a feudal baron, attracted 30,000 settlers to his domain, and the town of St. Thomas was named for this most unsaintly character. The most ambitious scheme of all was that of the Canada Land Company, which was formed in 1823. Its plan was to take over more than 2,000,000 acres of crown and clergy reserves; but when a dispute arose over the price of the clergy reserves, a tract of 1,000,000 acres on the shore of Lake Huron was substituted. The towns of Guelph and Goderich were founded, and by 1834 the company had disposed of 450,000 acres and the Huron Tract contained a population of 2500. A similar venture was started in Lower Canada, where the British American Land Company in 1833 secured a grant of over 800,000 acres in the Eastern Townships. But comparatively few immigrants were attracted to that area, and it was the expansion of the French population that eventually peopled the company's lands.

In terms of the growth of settlement, the progress of British North America during this period wore an encouraging aspect. Nova Scotia in 1838 had a population of nearly 200,000. Upper Canada nearly doubled in the decade after the war to reach 150,000 in 1824, and in 1838 it was almost 400,000. Yet there were circumstances that gave rise to impatience and discontent. The land system and the lack of roads increased the difficulties of the pioneer and impeded his rise to prosperity. The postwar slump in trade hit the commercial life of the provinces and brought a drastic decline in wheat prices. The uncertain operation of the English corn laws brought serious fluctuations in the exports of wheat and flour. A glut in the timber market in 1825 coincided with a lowering of the timber preference; and though the reduction was not serious—in fact, it still made it profitable to ship timber from the Baltic to the Maritimes and back to England under the preferential rates—it introduced an element of uncertainty affecting the main staple of colonial export trade.

Economic discontent was aggravated by the proximity of the United States. That country too had its depressions, but in the intervals it rose to heights of prosperity never reached by the British provinces. The rapid settlement of the Middle West, the construction of canals, and the growth of manufacturing brought a period of intense activity and a burst of economic progress. The effect on the Maritimes and Canada was directly evident in the movement of population across the border. A considerable proportion of the immigrants who arrived at Quebec continued their journey to the United States, attracted by high wages and cheap land. Probably half the immigrants to the Maritimes moved on across the border, and those who remained were only partial compensation for the continued emigration of the native-born to the United States. The contrast between the economic conditions of the two countries is a constant theme during this period. In a typical passage, a traveler in Upper Canada wrote around 1820: "There, bustle, improvement and animation fill every street; here, dullness, decay and apathy discourage enterprise and repress exertion."

This state of affairs was all the more exasperating because of the general faith in the potentialities of Canada. The blame for such conditions was variously placed. Many of the pioneers felt that it rested on the government, with its lack of energy and its self-seeking officials. William Lyon Mackenzie found the explanation in the baneful grip of British financiers and manufacturers. "A chain of debt, dependence and degradation is begun and kept up, the links of which are fast bound round the souls and bodies of our yeomanry." There were others—and this explanation naturally appealed most to the Tories—who found the fault in the lack of initiative displayed by the mass of the population. "We should be extremely happy," wrote the *Montreal Gazette*, "if our good people of Lower Canada would give up the trade of grievance-mongering, and devote more of their energies to the improvement of the country, like their neighbors to the south."

This last point of view was given unique expression in Nova Scotia by Thomas Chandler Haliburton. Through *Sam Slick,* the itinerant Yankee clockmaker, he employed the weapon of satire in an effort to bestir his countrymen into a more active appreciation of their opportunities. The wandering peddler, with his crude dialect and his sharpness in driving a bargain, expressed in one aspect Haliburton's Tory dislike of American ways; but his shrewd and earthy comments were also designed to arouse Nova Scotians to an awareness of the resources of their province and to greater energy and initiative in developing them.

In addition, *Sam Slick* was the first truly original contribution to Canadian literature. For the most part Canadian literary efforts before confederation took the form of descriptive works of travel or were confined to the ephemeral columns of periodicals. Major John Richardson plunged into the field of historical fiction based on Canadian themes, and in *Wacousta* he produced a lively and bloodthirsty novel of Pontiac's revolt. It was avowedly influenced by James Fenimore Cooper, but Richardson had served in the War of 1812 and had the advantage of knowing the West and the Indians at first hand. But Haliburton struck into still newer ground with a fresh vein of dialect humor, which had a wide success on two continents and which had its influence on such writers as Mark Twain and Artemus Ward.

The Commercial System of the St. Lawrence

While Canada was being transformed into a settled community, its commercial life was also in process of adjustment. The St. Lawrence, the great artery of Canadian commerce, reached out toward the vast interior of the continent, and the Canadian merchants looked beyond the horizon of their own provinces to the vision of a commercial empire that would be continental in its scope.

In the previous period their ambitions had centered chiefly on the fur trade. The loss of the area south of the Great Lakes had been compensated, at least in part, by the shift to the new fur areas of the Canadian Northwest. By a magnificent feat of energy and organization the North West Company had flung a system of trade and transportation across the breadth of the continent. But the very magnitude of this achievement foreshadowed its doom. As the fur trade extended to the Athabaska region and beyond the Rockies to the Pacific coast, the burden of maintaining it steadily mounted. The cost of transporting goods from Montreal to the trading areas rose to double their original value. The cheaper route by way of the bay gradually told in favor of the Hudson's Bay Company; and as competition increased and successive areas were depleted of their best furs, the North West Company found itself facing financial difficulties as a result of its growing overhead.

To add to these difficulties, the bitterness of rivalry led to clashes that threatened serious complications. The North West Company dealt in a highhanded fashion with interlopers into its domain. The struggle with the XY Company in particular was marked by violence on both sides. Relations between the Hudson's Bay Company and the North West Company were somewhat more restrained; but they penetrated into the same area and their posts were often side by side, and the hardy and impetuous traders who sought their fortunes in the far wilderness were ready enough to resort to coercion and menaces to wrest furs from their rivals. So frequent did these episodes become that the Hudson's Bay Company even suspected a concerted plan to force them to terms with the North West Company under threat of ruin.

A climax was precipitated by the planting of the Red River settlement. After his experiment in Prince Edward Island and an unsuccessful venture in Ontario, the colonizing ambitions of Lord Selkirk turned to the prairies of the west. There was considerable opposition in the Hudson's Bay Company to the intrusion of settlers into the domain of the fur trade; but there was also a desire to cut down expenses, and one group felt that this could be helped by establishing a colony as a center of food supplies. A reorganization of the company, in which Selkirk obtained a considerable financial interest, was followed in 1811 by Selkirk's purchase of 116,000 square miles in the Red River area, and in 1812 two parties of immigrants arrived to lay the foundations of the new settlement. Their early privations nearly wrecked the venture at the outset, but new groups of settlers arrived in 1814 and 1815 to keep the colony alive.

The North West Company looked on this development with unfriendly eyes. The new settlement lay directly across their route to the Northwest, and there was fear that it might be used by the Hudson's Bay Company to enforce its territorial claims and to bar the North West Company from access to the fur areas. There was also a fear that the colony would deprive the Montreal traders of the food supply that they had previously drawn from this area, and this took tangible form in January 1814, when Governor Miles Macdonnell, fearing a repetition of the food shortage of the previous winter, placed an embargo on the export of food supplies. The Nor'Westers retaliated by luring discontented settlers away, plundering the settlement, and burning down the buildings. But the arrival of fresh settlers in 1816 showed that Selkirk was determined to pursue the enterprise, and friction grew to the point of open war. The climax came with an armed clash in 1816—the massacre of Seven Oaks in which twenty settlers were killed. A series of arrests and countercharges followed as the antagonists used their conflicting claims of jurisdiction in an effort to destroy each other. The contest threatened to be ruinous to both sides; and, faced with this prospect, the two companies decided to merge. In 1821 the union was arranged, and the Montreal group was absorbed in the Hudson's Bay Company.

This was the end of the St. Lawrence route as a main artery of the fur trade. The cheaper route by the bay had won out, and the Canadian merchants had to seek new products to replace the lost staple. The resources of Canada itself were too narrow for their ambitions. Many of them were already concerned in the timber trade and the export of wheat and flour, but they looked for wider fields to conquer. In the growth of settlement in the Middle Western states they saw an opportunity to restore the system that had been the basis of the earlier fur trade, which might prove equally sound in relation to the new agricultural communities. The St. Lawrence seemed to offer the shortest and most natural route between Europe and the interior of the American continent. With free access to markets in both Britain and the United States, the Canadian merchants would become the middlemen between those two countries, supplying manufactured goods to the western settlers and shipping their produce to Britain and Europe. The St. Lawrence would become the mighty highway of trade between two continents, and Montreal would be the commercial metropolis of the New World.

This was not a result that could be achieved by private enterprise untrammeled and unaided. On the contrary, it revealed the intimate relation in Canada between business aspirations and government policy and the great degree to which Canada's economic fortunes depended on the policies pursued by both Britain and the United States. The merchants needed a combination of a free market in America and a protected market in Britain. In this way British manufactures imported by way of Montreal would flow into the markets of the Middle West, while American grain and other products entering Canada would share in the preferences that Britain extended to colonial products and would thus have the advantage over exports from American ports. At the same time the St. Lawrence route needed improvements to bring its cheapness and efficiency to the maximum, and this called for government aid to canals and similar public works.

These aspirations ran directly counter to the actual trend of events. While the United States after 1815 sought to set up a protective system, Great Britain was taking the first steps toward the abandonment of mercantilism. The restrictions of the old colonial system, which had fostered the growth of British commerce, now appeared as obstacles to British industrial expansion. As a result of her lead in the development of machine industry, Britain had become the workshop of the world. The rising strength of the new manufacturing class was reflected in a demand for the removal of all barriers to complete freedom of trade—a demand to which the theories of the classical economists gave powerful support. Under the influence particularly of William Huskisson as president of the Board of Trade, a series of reforms was carried out between 1822 and 1828. The navigation laws were relaxed to permit direct trade between the colonies and foreign countries. The corn laws were modified and the timber duties reduced. These changes still left a measure of preference to Canadian staples, and the rise of the American tariff was checked by the opposition of the southern states. But the trends were nonetheless perturbing, for they threatened to undermine Canadian commercial ambitions at both ends.

To these external factors were added internal difficulties. The division of Canada into two provinces was a fatal impediment to the adoption of a vigorous and coherent policy on navigation and trade. It left the English merchants of Lower Canada as a minority in the midst of an overwhelmingly French population, which showed itself increasingly hostile to their commercial ambitions. It deprived them of the effective support of the mercantile group in Upper Canada, while it accentuated the growing divergence between the aims of the merchants and the interests of the Upper Canadian farmers.

Between the provinces as such there was comparatively little friction. The chief cause for dispute was the division of the customs revenue. The inclusion of Montreal in Lower Canada meant that Upper Canada lacked a seaport and that the bulk of its imports passed through the sister province—a situation that was only slightly tempered by the prevalence of smuggling across the border from the United States. On the one hand, Lower Canada could impose a provincial tariff that would tax the consumers of Upper Canada without their consent. On the other hand, Lower Canada might make difficulties over a division of the customs revenue and might refuse to levy duties for the benefit of the treasury of Upper Canada. A series of agreements provided for the division of the revenue, first on the basis of population and then on the volume of goods that passed through Lower to Upper Canada. But the latter arrangement lapsed in 1819, and it was not until 1822 that a new basis was provided by the Canada Trade Act, which gave one-fifth of the revenue from customs duties to Upper Canada and provided for the consent of that province to any tariff act passed in Lower Canada. The arrangement was both clumsy and unsatisfactory, and Upper Canada continued to feel that its share was inadequate in view of its higher rate of consumption of imported goods.

In addition, Upper Canada had its own views about trade relations with the United States. The aspirations of the Montreal merchants toward a trade monopoly were looked on without affection. If British goods could be brought in more cheaply by way of New York, or if American manufactures were cheaper and more desirable, the consumers wanted to be free to take advantage of these benefits. On the other hand, the producers had no interest in admitting American farm products to equal competition with their own in the British market, and their desire for agricultural protection was opposed to the aims of the mercantile group.

Most serious of all was the failure of the two provinces to pursue a concerted policy with respect to canals. If the St. Lawrence was to become the commercial highway of the continent, its navigation must be improved. Steamboats made their appearance on the St. Lawrence in 1809 and on Lake Ontario in 1816, but the need to tranship cargoes at various rapids could only be overcome if a series of canals were built.

Sentiment in Upper Canada on the whole favored the work; but in Lower Canada the French were opposed to the spending of public funds for purposes that they felt were of benefit only to the English merchants, and this opposition hardened as the racial conflict became more acute.

It was partly in the hope of overcoming these obstacles that the British government, largely under the influence of the merchants, put forward the union proposals of 1822. They provided for the continuance of two administrations, but for a united legislature in which each section should be equally represented. This would mean that the smaller population of Upper Canada combined with the minority in Lower Canada would be able to secure an English majority; and the racial feature was underlined by provisions that the records should be kept in English and that after fifteen years English should be the sole language of debate. The French at once saw in the new scheme a plot to Anglify them and launched violent protests. In Upper Canada there was some sentiment in favor of annexing Montreal but almost none on behalf of a corporate union with the French of Lower Canada. In the face of the general opposition aroused by the proposals, the bill was dropped by the British government, and only the Canada Trade Act survived from the wider scheme that had initially been put forward.

Thus the Montreal merchants were left virtually powerless to secure the physical improvements of the St. Lawrence, which were so vital to their aims. Upper Canada, under the enthusiastic urging of William Hamilton Merritt, began work on the Welland Canal across the Niagara peninsula. By 1829 it was open to traffic and another canal had been undertaken at Cornwall. But while the smaller and less wealthy province was accumulating a load of debt from these enterprises, Lower Canada lagged in doing its part to make them successful. Work was undertaken on a canal at Lachine, but its depth was only 4 feet, and nothing was done toward the deepening of Lake St. Peter, which was necessary if seagoing ships were to come up to Montreal.

Meanwhile the completion of the Erie Canal in 1825 struck a heavy blow at the hopes of the Canadian merchants. The Erie opened an American route from the seaboard to the growing settlements of the Middle West, circumventing the barriers of the mountains and revolutionizing transport costs. Western grain no longer needed to depend on the St. Lawrence as an export route. At New York it had a port that was open all the year round, in contrast to Montreal and Quebec, which were closed by ice for nearly half the year. Upper Canada, too, found in the new route a cheap and convenient avenue for both its imports and exports. The Hudson had emerged as a major competitor with the St. Lawrence and threatened to capture not only the American but the Canadian West. As in its previous competition with Hudson Bay, so now in its competition with the Hudson River, the St. Lawrence system faced the need of improving its efficiency and extending its range; and the political barriers in the way of this task exasperated the conflict that had already arisen in Lower Canada and was emerging in the other provinces as well.

Oligarchy and Opposition

The provincial constitutions that were established by 1791 were based on the idea of keeping popular movements in check by strengthening the elements of authority in government and society. In this they succeeded only too well. To the power of the governor as the direct and active agent of the British government was added the strength of the local oligarchy, which controlled the executive and legislative councils. In the Maritimes the two bodies were identical in personnel, which meant that the members of the executive enjoyed a virtual life tenure. In the Canadas the membership of the two councils overlapped, though without being identical; and in all provinces the admission of judges to membership in the council brought a fusion of executive and legislative and judicial power in the hands of a small select group of appointees, who were largely independent of popular control.

In both provinces the core of the ruling elite was drawn from the top officials who were responsible, under the governor, for the direction of administration. In Lower Canada the Château Clique worked closely with the leading merchants and with the Anglican hierarchy. Members of the old seigniorial class were included in the Legislative Council and at times in the Executive Council, but played little part in the power structure. "Their attendance was poor, their interest in constitutional issues slight, and their influence on elections negligible." As racial divisions deepened and as the Assembly became overwhelmingly French in character, the councils became the stronghold of the English party with its championship of mercantile interests and its defense of independent executive authority against the pressure for full popular self-government.

The merchants as such had less place in the so-called Family Compact in Upper Canada—a group whose bonds were to be found in a common ideology rather than in any blood relationship. They were by no means hostile to the business element. They actively favored economic development, and a number were personally associated with such enterprises as banks and canals. Their main character, however, was administrative and professional, with strong Anglican affiliations. An outstanding member was the Reverend John Strachan, an Anglican convert from Presbyterianism who rose to become Bishop of Toronto, who attained membership in the Executive and Legislative councils, and who, in his earlier career as schoolmaster, had been the mentor of a number of his younger colleagues. Perhaps half the members of the group were of Loyalist stock, and Loyalist pretensions to special guardianship of the imperial tie and the preservation of the colony against aggressive American republicanism had been heightened by the War of 1812. Their creed has been summed up as "the British tie, a balanced government, and an established church." For the most part these members of the ruling elite were able and conscientious men; but too often, they also showed themselves to be narrow and vindictive in dealing with any opponents or any criticism of their ascendancy.

These tight little oligarchies exercised a firm grip upon public affairs. Through their control of funds and patronage they maintained a monopoly of public office and emoluments. Through their control of the councils they were able to block unfavorable legislation and to assure a privileged position to the Anglican Church, the commercial and financial interests, and the large land speculators. As upholders of the established order they expected the governor to rely on them for advice and support and the British government to uphold them as the sole bulwarks against disloyalty and anarchy. If a governor showed signs of compromising with the reformers, or if the Colonial Office advised moderate concessions to allay popular discontent, the fury of the Tories was at once roused against the imperial authorities; but they were loud in proclaiming their unqualified loyalty so long as their position and policies received unquestioning support.

The attitude of the British government was thus of cardinal importance in Canadian politics. Unfortunately for both Britain and Canada, colonial policy in this period was marked by fumbling and uncertainty. Skepticism about the value of colonies, which was already apparent at the time of the American Revolution, was increased by the changes in Britain's economy. The new industrialists felt little need for special privileges in colonial markets. They showed an increasing dislike for the burden and expense of governing and defending the colonies, which were no longer regarded as economic assets. The relaxation of the mercantile system weakened the political bonds. The radicals were eager for the day when the colonies would gain their independence. The older parties, both Whigs and Tories, accepted the view that the colonies would separate from the mother country when they reached maturity; and if they showed no desire to hasten this development, they were equally without constructive ideas as to how it could ultimately be averted.

The result was a negative policy based largely on indifference and pessimism. Britain's attitude was not actively oppressive. There were no such attempts to tax the colonies or to intervene actively in their internal affairs as had led to the American Revolution. But there was a conviction that the disruption of the empire could only be avoided by a firm maintenance of authority and that this was only possible if the governor and his advisers were kept independent of popular control. There were periodic efforts to persuade these authorities to adopt a more moderate policy which would mollify the local electorate, and the views of the local administration were met at times with reservations or even resistance. Henry Ryland, a leading member of the Château Clique, was moved to report on his visit to London in 1810: "It is really very provoking to see men of fine endowments and excellent natural understanding, too inattentive to make themselves masters of a very important subject which has been placed before them in an intelligible manner." On the whole, however, the British government in the last resort came down on the side of the oligarchy. Without directly being the cause of grievances, it became involved in the struggle over local grievances by siding with the groups that were chiefly responsible for them and thus in the end endangered the unity of the empire that it was striving to maintain.

Against this situation there arose a popular opposition, which varied in intensity in the different provinces. The privileged groups were in a position to stultify representative government. Even if the reformers secured a majority in the assembly, they could not force the executive to adopt the policies they desired, or cut down the expense of government by diminishing the number of placemen and pluralists, or break the grip of the vested interests on the affairs of the community. Out of a desire for the redress of practical grievances grew a movement for more democratic government as the necessary instrument of effective reform.

One persistent cause of discontent was the existence of religious discrimination. Freedom of worship was general in the colonies, but among the Protestant sects only the Church of England had the right to solemnize marriage, and dissenting groups such as Methodists and

Baptists were denied the right to hold property. Resentment over these disabilities was increased by the attempts of the Church of England to monopolize education. In Nova Scotia, the founding of King's College at Windsor under Anglican auspices led to the setting up of Pictou Academy by the Presbyterians and of Acadia College by the Baptists and helped to bring the establishment of Dalhousie University as a nonsectarian institution. In Lower Canada there was an attempt to get control through the establishment of the Royal Institution for the Advancement of Learning; but French Catholic opposition nullified this aim, and the conflict of creeds and races checked the progress of primary education until the confessional basis was adopted in 1846.

In Upper Canada the conflict was particularly acute between the Anglicans and the Methodists. The Anglican leader was Archdeacon Strachan, a member of the Family Compact and a stout champion of Anglican ascendancy. His violent attacks on the Methodists as American in origin and sentiment were among the factors that led the Methodists to sever their connections with the United States and to set up a Canadian conference in 1828. As president of the Board of Education, Strachan pursued the avowed aim of placing education "under the direction and control of the regular clergy" as one means of strengthening British loyalty; and his efforts at a sectarian system, pursued without too many hampering scruples, provoked widespread resentment. In 1827 he secured a charter for King's College with provision for the imposition of religious tests on the teaching staff, and this threat of a monopoly of higher education roused the Methodists to found an academy of their own, which developed into Victoria University. The controversy also enlisted the bulk of Methodist sentiment on the side of reform; and it brought forward in Egerton Ryerson, who was appointed editor of the newly established *Christian Guardian* in 1829, a vigorous opponent of Strachan and of religious privilege.

The question of the clergy reserves added fuel to the conflict. These lands were set aside "for the support and maintenance of a Protestant clergy." The claim of the Church of England to be the sole beneficiary was hotly contested by the other sects, which demanded a share in the revenue from the reserves. In point of fact the revenue was so slender as to be hardly worth the energy expended on the quarrel, but Strachan's aggressiveness helped to keep it actively alive. Various efforts were made to find a compromise, but without success; and by 1826 the reformers were advocating the secularization of the reserves by selling them and devoting the proceeds to education. The urge to find a satisfactory settlement was all the greater because of the economic effect of the clergy reserves. Scattered as they were throughout the surveyed areas, they lay in vacant lots of 200 acres, retarding the consolidation of settlement and impeding to some extent the construction of roads. As settlement gradually filled the older districts, it became possible to lease some of the reserved lands, though confused administration and inconsistencies in terms of lease often gave rise to dissatisfaction on the part of all concerned. To a considerable degree the reserves represented an economic nuisance and an obstacle to advance, aggravating, if they did not overshadow, the similar difficulties imposed by the vacant Crown reserves and the lands held waste by private speculators. In 1827, however, an imperial act allowed the sale of one-quarter of the reserves, with a maximum of 100,000 acres to be offered in any one year. As sales mounted, revenue flowed in and vacant lots were filled, and the effect of the reserves on the spread of settlement ceased to be a serious grievance. What was not solved was the problem of a satisfactory arrangement for a distribution of the revenue between rival claimants, secular as well as sectarian; and the result was the persistence of political and religious resentments which embittered the popular attitude toward both the privileged claims of the Church of England and the oligarchy with which it was allied.

At the same time there arose a growing suspicion of the connection between government and business. The pioneer farmer, despairing over the reluctance of the government to spend money on roads, could not help contrasting this parsimony with the readiness of the government to pour money into canals. The belief that public funds were being used to further private interest seemed confirmed by an investigation into the financing of the Welland Canal, which revealed a fantastic tale of incompetence and extravagance and speculation. The founding of the Bank of Upper Canada, in which the government held a quarter interest, was also regarded with hostility. The dislike of banks, which was so evident in the United States during the Jackson period, was almost equally prevalent in Canada. There were vigorous attacks on the Bank of Montreal, which was founded in 1817, and the Halifax Banking Company, established in 1825. The pioneers of Upper Canada saw in the bank a new addition to the power of the oligarchy and a strengthening of its control over the life of the province. "This great monied engine," charged Mackenzie, "the only one in the colony, is under the thumb of Parson Strachan and his pupils to wield at their discretion."

In Lower Canada the social and economic issues were irrevocably bound up with the racial conflict, which was all-embracing in its scope.

The illusion that the Act of 1791 would be followed by a gradual Anglicization of the French Canadians was dissipated within a few years. Instead, the grant of representative institutions was turned into a potent instrument of French Canadian nationalism. The Quebec Act had consolidated the basic institutions of French Canada. The Constitutional Act placed political power in the hands of a people determined to maintain and strengthen that basis. With no desire to return to French allegiance and with a readiness to accept their position under the British Crown, the French set out to establish their solidarity as a separate and distinct community with their own language and religion and laws.

Behind this lay a concept of society that was in fundamental conflict with that of the English minority. The French sought to preserve a culture that was static and conservative. It is true that, while they repudiated the type of economic progress represented by the English commercial class, they also resented being denied its fruits. The readiness of the English to take the risks inherent in large-scale ventures led to their virtual monopoly of transportation and commerce and banking. The highest and most lucrative positions in the economic life of the province fell to their lot. The French saw themselves confined to humbler roles— the tenants on English seigniories, the lumberers for English timber merchants, the clerks and laborers for English firms—and their sense of grievance grew. Yet their basic aim was the establishment of a stable rural society rather than an expanding commercial state; and the very fact that the encouragement of commerce would strengthen the English element in the province was an added reason for viewing it with hostility.

This defensive attitude in fact found expression in an effort to block every measure that might increase the size and influence of the English population. There was a profound dislike of immigration that would bring in English-speaking settlers and bitter resentment at the cost of public assistance to the diseased and destitute human cargoes that the returning timber ships discharged at the ports of Lower Canada. In 1832, cholera brought by the new arrivals spread through the city of Quebec, and agitators were not above accusing the British government of a deliberate scheme to destroy the French population by infection. At the same time the need for funds to meet the cost of caring for sick and unemployed newcomers was made the occasion for levying a head tax on immigrants, which might also serve to discourage a further influx. All encouragement to new settlement was looked on as a danger. There were protests against the Canada Tenures Act of 1825, which allowed proprietors to change from seigniorial to freehold tenure. The Eastern Townships were not given representation in the assembly until 1829, and were denied land-registry offices until 1830. The chartering of the British American Land Company, with its scheme for bringing large numbers of settlers into the townships, provoked a violent outcry and brought appeals to the British government for its cancellation.

The spokesmen for this emergent nationalism were drawn from a new social stratum that had appeared by the early years of the century. It was composed of members of the liberal professions, particularly the lawyers. Drawn largely from the rural population, they had close affiliation with the mass of the habitants and an understanding of their ways and thought patterns. Few of them were particularly well-to-do, yet by virtue of their superior education, they aspired to the role of elite. Since they could not expect to attain this through wealth or social status, the way to their goal lay through a political career. The influence of the seigniors in this field was rapidly declining. Even the Catholic hierarchy had limited success in imposing its guidance in political affairs. The electorate was largely illiterate at the outset, but as the habitant slowly developed a political awareness, his confidence in these traditional leaders tended to diminish, and rising politicians could evoke a response on issues that touched his interests or his emotions. On their part, aspirants to political careers needed issues that would rally mass support and appeals that would inspire popular enthusiasm. To this might be added the more mundane pressures which George Ramsay, Lord Dalhousie, believed he detected in 1822: "The leaders just now are Lawyers and Notaries of the second order, country practitioners, who have laid the poor people under debt and other obligations and require of them implicit obedience in voting."

The outcome was, as Fernand Oullet observes, that "the liberal professions did not present themselves as a social elite among many others, but as a national elite with a mission to perform—that of protecting the interests and rights of a nation." Their instrument was the Assembly, through which they sought to dominate the whole structure of government. The more earnest members studied British parliamentary procedure as a guide to the methods by which the elected branch might achieve supremacy. The result was a tendency toward political liberalism, on which the Church looked askance as likely to undermine reverence for authority, and, indeed, an element of anticlericalism was by no means absent. At bottom, however, the forms of political liberalism were used as weapons in defense of social conservatism. The structure of French Canada was to be maintained against the hostile influence of English capitalism and English bureaucracy. Politically, as well as socially and culturally, the stratification gradually hardened along racial lines; and even the adherence to the reformers of such figures as the Scottish John Neilson or the Irish Edmund O'Callaghan did little to modify the essentially ethnic character of the confrontation. The French majority in the Assembly sought political control for racial ends, and Governor Craig suspected the presence among them of dark, designing men, exploiting the prevalent ignorance of the bulk of the members to persuade them that the Assembly should govern the province.

The political alignments that had existed before 1791 were drastically changed by these developments. It was no longer a case of the governor allying himself with the seigniors and clergy against the English minority. In fact the seigniors and the more substantial French *bourgeois* continued to work with the government, and so on the whole did the upper clergy. But the governor and officials were now confronted with an assembly in which the French majority sought to gain full control of the machinery of government and to impose a policy adverse to the interests of the English merchants. Both groups drew together to oppose such a development. They entrenched themselves in the councils and used their position to frustrate the rule of the popular majority in the assembly. In Lower as in Upper Canada, representative government was stultified by a privileged oligarchy immune from popular control.

By the 1830s there had arisen in all the provinces a demand for government more responsive to the popular will. The first desire of the reformers was for the full benefit of the British parliamentary system, and at the outset they placed their hopes in an appeal to the home government against the local reactionaries. The delegates from the Maritimes had some success in London; those from the Canadas had almost none. Rebuffed by the Colonial Office, they found sympathy and support among the British radicals, who encouraged them in their demands and who indeed were prepared to welcome a Canadian movement for complete independence. The success of the movement for parliamentary reform in Britain in 1832 was a further encouragement to reform sentiment in Canada, where many of the recent immigrants from the British Isles had already been influenced by radicalism in the old country.

No less important was the influence of the United States. This was the era of Jacksonian democracy, and its stirrings were felt across the border. Distance lent enchantment to the view of the United States as a working example of popular sovereignty, where economic prosperity was combined with economical government and where popular election of officials together with rotation in office prevented the growth of a vested interest in the state administrations. Yet it was only in the last resort that there was any serious desire to adopt the American system. What most reformers wanted was the results of that system achieved through British institutions and under British rule. When the more radical leaders, despairing of such an outcome, advocated the adoption of an American form of government and hinted at separation from Britain, the bulk of their followers drew back from a course that not only involved a break with tradition but was rapidly leading to armed rebellion.

The Struggle for Reform

In the Atlantic provinces during this period political life ranged from dull to disorderly. It was chronically turbulent in Newfoundland, with its embittered antagonisms between merchants and fishermen, Catholics and Protestants, St. John's and the outports. Prince Edward Island's complaints against the absentee proprietors were a growing source of bitterness. There were fewer impassioned issues in the mainland colonies. They were free from various problems that agitated the Canadas—the clergy reserves, the urgent need for internal improvements, the racial divisions that beset Lower Canada. Efforts by the Assemblies to gain full control of the revenue were not pressed to extremes. The demand for the separation of the councils was granted in New Brunswick in 1832 and was soon in prospect in Nova Scotia. The desire for an executive responsible to the popular majority grew only slowly; and it was not until Joseph Howe emerged as a political leader in Nova Scotia with his election to the assembly in 1836 that the reform movement began to gain coherence and to adopt responsible government as its goal.

It was in Lower Canada that political divisions emerged earliest and brought forth the greatest acrimony. The clash was precipitated by the question of taxation. When the need for additional revenue arose in 1805, the government asked that it be raised by a land tax. The assembly rejected the proposal and substituted a tax on imports. The episode brought to light a conflict of economic interests along distinctly racial lines. The French sought to throw the cost of government on the English commercial class. The merchants responded with indignant outcries and public attacks on the French and their majority in the assembly. The racial divisions were intensified; and in answer to the diatribes in the English press, the French founded their own journal in *Le Canadien,* with the slogan: "Our language, our institutions, our laws."

The breach was widened by the growing friction between the executive and the assembly. Sir James Craig, governor from 1807 to 1811, looked with despair on the task of working representative government in the face of an assembly in which there was not a single Canadian gentleman and which was dominated by a partisan French majority. He lent a sympathetic ear to the extreme partisans of the policy of Anglicization. When the assembly tried to reduce government influence in the legislature, Craig replied by dissolving the assembly and dismissing a number of militia officers. The protests of *Le Canadien* brought the seizure of its press and the imprisonment of its proprietors. Such measures only strengthened the French in the election that followed; and the government in London, alarmed at the growing agitation, made an effort at conciliation. Craig was replaced by Sir George Prevost, whose moderation and concessions diminished popular antagonism and helped to assure French loyalty during the War of 1812. But by the end of the war new difficulties were in prospect, and a new French leader had appeared in the person of Louis Joseph Papineau.

Papineau, who began as a lawyer and became a seignior, was the champion and embodiment of French Canadian nationalism. His vivid personality and oratorical prowess made him an outstanding popular leader and gained him early prominence in the assembly. His election as Speaker in 1815 gave him a position from which he could exercise the virtual leadership of the majority. Anomalously enough, this defender of a Catholic feudal society was a liberal in his political outlook and a deist in his religious views. He had absorbed the teachings of the eighteenth-century French *philosophes* and the traditions of English parliamentary government. This approach made it possible for him to work closely with the small group of English reformers led by John Neilson in a common effort at constitutional changes that would make representative government an effective reality. But behind these parliamentary tactics lay Papineau's fundamental aim of consolidating the political ascendancy of his race in order to preserve its distinctive cultural basis. The language and methods of political liberalism became in his hands the weapons of racial separatism and social conservatism.

At an early stage the struggle centered on the control of finance. In addition to its independent revenue from lands and fees, the government had the customs duties under the Quebec Revenue Act of 1774, an imperial measure whose proceeds went to the provincial treasury. To cover the full expenses of the province, supplementary grants were needed from the assembly, but the refusal of such grants did not completely deprive the government of funds. The complete control of all the revenue, whatever its source, therefore became the paramount objective of the assembly.

The practical significance of this aim was made clear in 1819. The assembly asserted its right to decide on all appropriations, and took the opportunity to reduce the salaries of various officials who had incurred its displeasure. Sooner than acquiesce in such a measure, the legislative council rejected the whole budget and took the stand that a permanent grant covering official salaries must be passed by the assembly in return for control of the revenue.

The struggle over this issue raged through successive administrations, aggravated by a series of episodes that accentuated the racial divisions. The union proposals of 1822 seemed proof to the French that their enemies were still plotting to destroy their nationality. In 1827, when the Assembly refused to vote a limited budget, Lord Dalhousie dissolved it, and when the new Assembly met he made a provocative and futile attempt to veto the choice of Papineau as Speaker. Next year the British government, in an effort to find a solution, appointed the Canada Committee to investigate and report. That body advocated, among other things, the placing of the revenue at the disposal of the Assembly in return for a permanent civil list covering the salaries of the governor, the judges, and the executive councilors and the creation of a more independent legislative council by excluding judges and cutting down the number of placemen in that body. But the Assembly rejected these limited concessions; and although in 1831 the British government made a new effort at conciliation by handing over the bulk of the revenue without conditions, tempers by that time had reached a point that made such a gesture too little and too late.

Papineau's tone had now grown more extreme. While still pressing for effective control over the executive, he also put forward demands for an elective legislative council—a proposal that the outraged councilors denounced as a "wicked intention to degrade the local authorities in the eyes of the people" and a threat to the British connection. A climax was reached with the Ninety-two Resolutions adopted by the assembly in 1834. All the grievances and demands of the majority were thrown together indiscriminately—control of the revenue, an elective council, no changes in land tenure, abolition of the British American Land Company, as well as personal accusations against the leading officials. What was more serious, an implied threat of rebellion ran through the whole tone of the document. To expressions of admiration for American institutions, reflected in a practical way in the unprecedented demand for an elected executive, were added unmistakable references to the American Revolution and to the prospect that it might be repeated in Lower Canada. Papineau and his more radical followers were beginning to speak the language of revolt.

By this time the radicals of Upper Canada were moving in the same direction. There had been few political difficulties up to the War of 1812, but the period that followed saw a growing discontent, which needed only focus and leadership to translate it into a movement for reform.

The first coherent expression was provided by Robert Gourlay. As part of a plan to encourage immigration, in which he had a direct interest through his hope of a large land grant in Upper Canada, he sent a circular questionnaire to the various townships in order to get statistical information. The replies gave the pioneer districts an opportunity to express their grievances over the haphazard land system and the lack of internal improvements. Gourlay was roused to a sympathy that was all the more acute because he had in the meantime encountered difficulties over the validation of his own grants. He began an agitation against the selfishness and obstructiveness of the ruling clique, which culminated in a convention of township delegates in 1818 to petition for redress. The Family Compact took alarm. It secured legislation making such conventions illegal and launched a series of prosecutions against Gourlay, which ended with his arrest and expulsion from the province.

These drastic steps showed that the oligarchy was ready to repress popular protests and to class criticism with sedition. The lesson was driven home a few years later over the Alien Question. In 1821 Barnabas Bidwell, a settler from Massachusetts who had taken the oath of allegiance, was elected to the Assembly. His exclusion was demanded on the grounds that he was an ineligible alien and that he had fled the United States to escape charges of maladversion of public funds. The Assembly rejected the claim of legal incapacity but voted his expulsion on moral grounds. When his son Marshall Spring Bidwell presented himself as a candidate at the ensuing election, he was initially debarred as an alien though he later secured a seat. The alien issue brought into question not only the status of the settlers from the United States, who still formed the bulk of the population, but also the validity of their land titles, since aliens were barred from holding property. Attempts at remedial legislation were blocked by the Compact, and it was not until 1828 that a law was passed establishing the rights of the existing settlers. The struggle brought into being a definite reform group, which looked to Marshall Spring Bidwell as its leader.

Meanwhile a more vivid figure had appeared in the person of William

Lyon Mackenzie. This combative little Scot had deserted business in 1824 for the perilous profession of journalism, and his *Colonial Advocate* at once became the leading organ of the reformers. Mackenzie's ideas about the best system of government were highly flexible. He was less interested in forms than in results. He attacked the practical grievances that called for remedies; and as he realized the power of obstruction that the existing system placed in the hands of the Tories, he grew steadily more radical in his demands for a change of institutions. His attack was directed against the clique of merchants and churchmen and officials that dominated the life of the province, and he made himself the champion of the mechanics and freeholders of Upper Canada, whose interests were sacrificed to those of a small privileged group.

Mackenzie's passion for justice and hatred of abuses found expression in a trenchant style that was not sparing of personalities. The virulence of his attacks roused the Tories to fury. In 1826 the office of the *Colonial Advocate* was attacked and its presses wrecked by a mob led by several youthful scions of the Compact families. But Mackenzie secured damages that more than compensated for his loss, and the incident increased his political stature. In 1828 he was elected member for York to an Assembly in which the reformers were for the first time in a majority.

The reformers gained little from their victory. They were not yet a coherent party, and they had little solid organized support in the constituencies. The Tories, entrenched in the councils, were able to block all legislative measures of reform. The electorate was disappointed by the lack of results, and this reaction, together with the popularity of a new governor, Sir John Colborne, restored the Tories to power in 1830. Their victory was followed by certain concessions; but there were also attacks on the radical press, and when full control of the revenue was handed over in 1831, the Assembly voted a generous permanent grant for the civil list. The passage of this "everlasting salary bill," which made the placemen more independent than ever, was hotly attacked by the radicals. Mackenzie accused the Assembly of subservience to a mean and mercenary executive. The Assembly voted the article libelous and expelled Mackenzie from its midst. Four times he was re-elected, only to be again expelled on each occasion. The majority seemed determined to use its power to crush its enemies.

The election of 1834 was held in an atmosphere of excitement and bitterness. The tone of the advanced reformers was becoming more radical, to the perturbation of the moderates. The political broils had been further stirred by Egerton Ryerson, who after his return from England in the autumn of 1833, published a series of impressions in the course of which he stigmatized the English radicals as notorious atheists and republicans. His implied desertion of the reform cause roused many Methodists to protest and infuriated Mackenzie, who was ready to attribute it to the fact that the recent union of the Methodists with the English Wesleyans had admitted them to a share in a government grant for missions. Ryerson, he wrote, "has gone over to the enemy, press, types, and all, and hoisted the colors of a cruel, vindictive Tory priesthood. . . . I was the dupe of a Jesuit in the garb of a Methodist preacher." Within a few months Mackenzie added further fuel to the flames by publishing a letter from the English radical Joseph Hume congratulating him on his latest election and expressing a belief that the approaching crisis in Canada "will terminate in independence and freedom from the baneful domination of the mother country." Such language seemed clear proof to the Tories of the disloyalty of the radicals.

The outcome of the election was a victory for the reformers but no real advance in reform. Once again the councils stood in the way of constructive measures. The reformers fell back on a select committee on grievances, of which Mackenzie was the moving spirit; and in its Seventh Report it summed up all the complaints against the existing system. The lavish system of patronage, the handling of the clergy reserves, the loose system of finances, as well as various economic abuses, all came under attack. The irresponsibility of the executive was strongly condemned, and a direct demand was made for an elective legislative council. The report was a more moderate document than the Ninety-two Resolutions, but it was almost equally condemnatory of the existing state of affairs.

The Rebellion of 1837

By 1835 an explosive situation had developed in the Canadas. The radicals in both provinces, balked of the fruits of their electoral victory in 1834 by the resistance of the councils, were growing more active in their agitation and more extreme in their language. The Tories were drawing tighter together, and in Lower Canada particularly the formation of constitutional associations was accompanied by armed preparations and dark hints of readiness to settle the issue by force.

At the same time the reformers were weakened by a growing split between moderates and extremists. Papineau's increasing glorification of American institutions and invocation of the spirit of the American Revolution alienated John Neilson and his followers, whose aim was constitutional reform on British lines. It also did violence to the basic outlook of French Canadian nationalism. French moderates saw clearly that their desire to remain a separate community with their own language and religion and institutions would be doomed if they were thrown into the arms of the United States; and the higher clergy, alarmed at the growing threat of violence and the anticlerical tone of Papineau's younger followers, issued warnings against any resort to force. In Upper Canada, too, the moderates drew back from Mackenzie's advocacy of the American elective system in all branches of government. Robert Baldwin emerged as the consistent and leading advocate of responsible government as the true alternative—the full extension to Canada of the British cabinet system, with the ministry resting directly on the support of the elected majority in the assembly.

The solution rested in the hands of the British government. So long as it continued to support the local oligarchy, no way out of the deadlock could be found in Canada. In a new effort to find a compromise without surrender, Britain sent out Lord Gosford in 1835 as governor general and as commissioner to investigate and report. The new governor made a show of conciliation, which alarmed the Tories without convincing the French. His instructions in fact debarred him from making any real concessions; and this was revealed when the new lieutenant governor of Upper Canada, Sir Francis Bond Head, published his own instructions, which were known to be on similar lines. The Assembly of Lower Canada in 1836 repeated its demands for reform and restricted its grant of funds to six months. The council refused to accept a limited grant; and, for the fourth year in succession, Lower Canada was left without an authorized revenue from local sources.

Meanwhile Sir John Colborne had been replaced as governor of Upper Canada. He had endeavored to hold a moderate course, but his failure to forward the Seventh Report on Grievances had displeased the Colonial Office, which decided on his recall. In an unfortunate final act, Colborne signed patents for the establishment of forty-four new Anglican rectories in the province. It was a course that was authorized by the Constitutional Act, but it was of the greatest unwisdom in the existing state of affairs. There had been some promise of abatement in the religious controversy. Government grants had been extended to the various Protestant sects, and a bill allowing their clergy to solemnize marriage had been passed in 1829.

But Colborne's action showed that Anglican pretensions had not been abandoned and revived the fears of religious discrimination in favor of the Church of England.

Colborne's successor was Sir Francis Bond Head. His appointment was a mystery to himself at the time and has remained a mystery to posterity. An obscure Poor Law commissioner, he found himself routed out of bed in the middle of the night to be told that he had been appointed governor of Upper Canada. The theory that he was chosen in mistake for Sir Edmund Head is tempting but unsupported, and no alternative explanation has been found. To increase the confusion, his appointment was hailed with approval by the British radicals, who commended him to the reformers in Canada, and Sir Francis was astonished if gratified to find himself greeted on his arrival as "a true and tried reformer."

Head's first steps gave a brief and delusive hope that he might live up to this unearned reputation. Three out of the six places on the executive council were vacant, and Head showed his desire to attract the support of the moderates by offering one of the posts to Robert Baldwin. Baldwin insisted at first that the executive must enjoy the full confidence of the assembly and that this could be achieved only by the dismissal of the three Tories who were already members. He was persuaded reluctantly to waive this demand and to enter the council with two other reformers. His doubts were soon justified. Head was in fact determined to exercise an independent authority and to use it to repress all opposition to the existing system. He consulted the Executive Council only when he chose and ignored them at will, and his cavalier attitude soon alienated not only the reformers but even his Tory advisers. The Executive Council resigned in a body when Head rejected their protests. The Assembly supported their action by a vote of "no confidence" in their successors; and for the first time in Upper Canada the legislature refused to vote funds. Head answered by suspending all grants, even those already available, dissolving the Assembly, and appealing to the electorate.

In the election that followed, Head pressed the attack. In a series of speeches he pointed out that the withholding of funds meant that there was no money for public works and that the electors themselves suffered from their folly in opposing the governor. "Can you do as much good for yourselves as I can do for you?" he asked one group rhetorically. "If you choose to dispute with me, and live on bad terms with the mother country, you will, to use a homely phrase, only quarrel with your own bread and butter." He even raised the specter of a mythical plan for an American invasion as a stimulus to Loyalist sentiment. His campaign won him considerable personal popularity, and the tactics of his supporters contributed to his success. Open voting gave plentiful opportunities for coercion and intimidation. The Orangemen—the bully boys of Toryism—gathered in arms at the polling centers and roared through the streets "crying five pounds for a liberal." The outcome was a Tory majority; and Head, triumphant and self-complacent, rejected all counsels of moderation from London, dismissed several officials suspected of reform sentiments, and refused to obey positive instructions from the Colonial Office that he felt involved misguided concessions to the "low-bred antagonist democracy."

The radicals now despaired of gaining reform by consitutional means. There was no longer any hope in the success of appeals to London. Gosford's report and the subsequent debates in Parliament showed that parliamentary reform in Britain had not shaken the government in its opposition to responsible government in the colonies. This stubborn rigidity found concrete expression in the Ten Resolutions introduced by Lord John Russell in March 1837. There was to be no responsible executive or elective legislative council. The remaining Crown revenue was to be handed over only in return for a permanent civil list; and to offset the deficit resulting from the Assembly's refusal of funds, the government was empowered to use the money it had on hand irrespective of legislative sanction.

The resolutions were both a rebuff and a challenge to the reformers. The indignation that they aroused was sharpened by the depression of 1837. A panic in the United States and a financial recession in England extended their effects to Canada. A crop failure in Upper Canada added to popular distress. Exports fell and prices declined. The tightening of credit was accentuated by Head's refusal to allow the Bank of Upper Canada to suspend specie payment, thus forcing it to call in its loans. Bankruptcies and unemployment and a general commercial paralysis affected all classes in the community and gave powerful stimulus to the existing discontent.

The agrarian crisis in Lower Canada was even more widespread and significant in its effects. Overpopulation in the region of the older seigniories, together with the progressive exhaustion of the soil, had led to a decline in the production of wheat and a shift to coarse grains and potatoes. Attacks by the wheat fly in 1831 further reduced the harvest and left no surplus for export. The habitant, forced to cut down on the consumption of white bread which had previously been the staple in his diet, also saw his cash income reduced and himself gradually pushed from a market to a subsistence economy. His diminished purchasing power had repercussions in the towns, bringing lower prices and a decline in wages. These were developments for which the government could hardly be held responsible, but they nonetheless gave rise to popular restiveness and resentment. As an observer commented a decade later: "When a man is suddenly reduced to more uncomfortable circumstances than customary, he is the more ready to receive the impulse of dissatisfaction infused into him by discontented and designing demagogues."

In Lower Canada, Papineau was now talking the language of revolt, echoing the slogans of the American Revolution and calling for a boycott of British goods. Actually he had neither plans nor desire for rebellion, but his words breathed incitement to violence, and the more ardent French radicals as well as such English extremists as Dr. Wolfred Nelson and Dr. O'Callaghan were prepared for action. Mackenzie had embarked on the same course. He was in close touch with Papineau, and through his new paper *The Constitution* he called on the oppressed people of Upper Canada to strike their blow for liberty. By midsummer the reformers in Toronto had issued a virtual declaration of independence, and in the pioneer districts the forging of pikes and the awkward efforts of farmers to arm and drill themselves illuminated by their very pathos the depth of popular discontent.

The clash was precipitated in Lower Canada. There the rising agitation had found expression in the organization of *Fils de la Liberté* and the holding of a series of mass meetings, culminating with an assembly from six counties at St. Charles on October 23. On November 7 a brawl between rival French and English organizations in Montreal showed the rising danger of disorder. In the hope of preventing further trouble, Papineau and his leading associates left Montreal a few days later. The authorities, tense and on edge, jumped to the conclusion that the radical leaders had gone into the countryside to raise a revolution. Warrants were issued for their arrest. Armed *patriotes* gathered to oppose the troops who tried to support the execution of these orders and repulsed them at St. Denis on November 23. It was the signal for rebellion, but a rebellion that was unplanned and leaderless. Papineau and O'Callaghan fled to the United States. Two days after the check at St. Denis, a military force crushed a hastily assembled group of rebels at St. Charles and brought an abrupt end to the movement south of the St. Lawrence. In December another gathering at St. Eustache, north of Montreal, was bloodily dispersed by 2000 troops, and the movement in Lower Canada was virtually at and end.

The rising in Upper Canada was even more scattered and short-lived. It was precipitated by the outbreak in Lower Canada and by Head's dispatch of all his troops in response to a call from that province. Head boasted that this was a trap to lure the rebels into overt action, which he was sure could be crushed by the forces of loyalty without military aid. He brushed aside all warnings that trouble was impending, while farmers from the back country began to gather at Montgomery's tavern, just north of where Eglinton Avenue now crosses Yonge Street, summoned by Mackenzie to capture the capital and overthrow the government. It was a hopeless enterprise, which was further compromised by a last-minute effort to advance the date of attack from December 7 to December 4. Confronted with actual danger, Head blustered around armed to the teeth, vetoing every plan of action and offering none of his own. At length Colonel James Fitzgibbon, adjutant general and a veteran of the War of 1812, took matters into his own hands. On December 7 he led a force of 1000 volunteers out against the ill-armed rabble of a few hundred that had gathered above the town. A few volleys scattered the insurgents and ended the rebellion in Upper Canada. Mackenzie fled across the border and endeavored to organize an invasion with the aid of sympathizers in the United States; but although there were a few incursions across the border during the winter, by the end of 1838 these last hopeless efforts had collapsed.

The Tories made the most of their victory. They felt vindicated in their persistent claim that the reform agitation was merely a cloak for sedition and republicanism, and they set out to break their opponents beyond recovery. Only two men, Samuel Lount and Peter Matthews, were hanged for their part in the actual uprising, but later frontier raids brought additional arrests and trials, resulting in several more executions and the transportation of over ninety prisoners to Van Diemen's Land.

A number of reform leaders such as Bidwell were frightened into exile, and widespread and indiscriminate arrests gave evidence of a vindictiveness that quickly produced a reaction. "It is a great blessing," wrote John Ryerson to his brother Egerton, "that Mackenzie and radicalism are down, but we are in immediate danger of being brought under the domination of a military and high church oligarchy." In fact the crushing of the rebellion did not decide the fundamental issues. The bulk of the population had refused to follow the radicals in their resort to armed violence, but the demand for reform along constitutional lines and through British institutions remained unabated. The rising was one of those cases where nothing succeeds like failure. It jolted the British government into a realization that only a drastic readjustment could remove the causes of discontent in Canada; and with the appointment of Lord Durham to find a remedy, the first step was taken toward a new orientation, which was of the most profound consequence for both Canada and the British Empire.

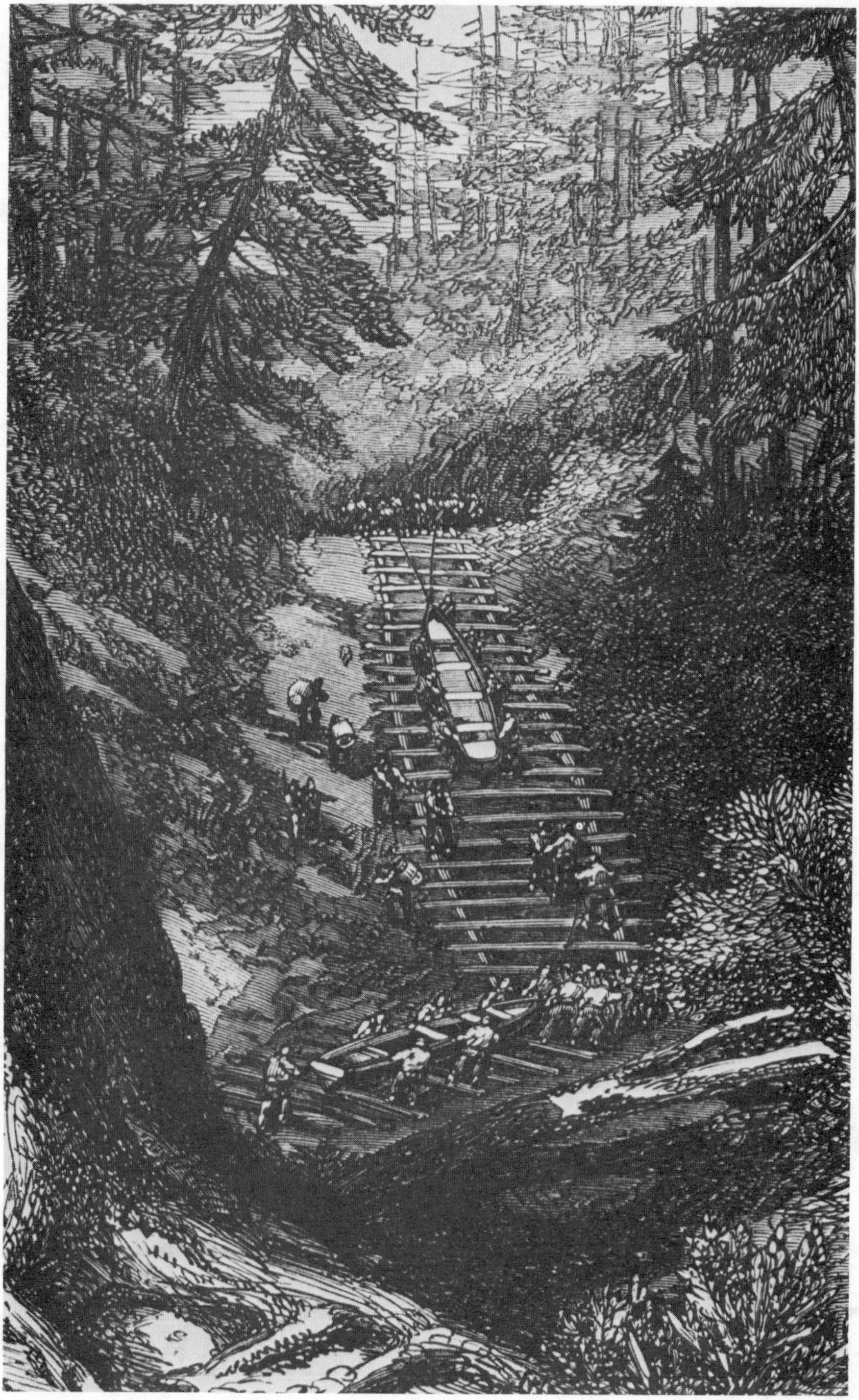

(Public Archives of Canada)

Crossing a Portage.

A Bush Farm near Chatham about 1838.

Immigrants Clearing a Farm in New Brunswick.

Digging the Lachine Canal.

(Public Archives of Canada)

The Lumber Trade.
A square timber raft moving down the St. Lawrence for transshipment at Quebec.

(Public Archives of Canada)

Chapter 11

The Advance of Self-Government

The Durham Mission

The appointment of Lord Durham was one more example of how the fortunes of Canada were affected by the fluctuations of British domestic politics. When news of the rebellion reached London, it presented the tottering Whig government of Lord Melbourne with a fresh threat to its existence. The Tories were certain to use it to attack the ministry for its mismanagement of colonial affairs. The radicals, on whose support the government depended, were already restive, and many of them welcomed the outbreak in Canada as a step toward a release of Britain from her colonial obligations. They would certainly turn against the ministry if it showed signs of adopting a repressive policy; and it was partly to reassure the radicals that Lord Durham—his nickname was Radical Jack—was chosen to deal with the Canadian situation. His advanced liberal views and the prominent part he had taken in the battle for parliamentary reform made his appointment acceptable and promised to rescue the Melbourne ministry from the downfall that threatened it.

It did not, however, save the Whigs from a new crisis as a result of Durham's actions in Canada. He was both high commissioner and governor general, charged not only with investigation but also with the duties of government over all British North America. By a special act the constitution was suspended in Lower Canada, and Durham was given power to govern through a special appointed council. One of the first problems confronting him was the treatment of the many persons accused of taking part in the rebellion. Durham placed his hopes in the healing power of generosity. He issued a wide amnesty, decreed the banishment of Papineau and fourteen other fugitives under threat of the death penalty if they returned, and ordered the exile of eight other admitted rebels to Bermuda. This last provision was hardly an onerous penalty, but it was one which Durham had no authority to impose, and Melbourne's opponents used it as an excuse for a new attack. Melbourne, who had promised Durham "the firmest and most unflinching support," now felt obliged to disavow him; and although this was accompanied by an act of indemnity, Durham's anger flared against the ministry. He sent in his resignation, but he was persuaded by his assistants to complete his mission and to produce the report that is his life's monument.

With Durham a new spirit made its appearance in imperial affairs. In opposition to the prevailing pessimism toward the future of the colonies, a small group of radical imperialists had developed under the leadership of Gibbon Wakefield. They vigorously repudiated the theory that the arrival of the colonies at maturity would inevitably mean their separation from the motherland or that self-government was necessarily a prelude to independence. They believed that a constructive policy would bring into being new and prosperous communities bound to Britain by ties of affection and interest. A policy of carefully selected and assisted emigration, financed by the proceeds of lands sales in the colonies, would end the old haphazard system in favor of a regulated process of settlement. Large numbers of the emigrants who at present went to the United States could be diverted to the colonies to build up British possessions overseas. Far from being a burden, the colonies would become valuable outlets for British capital and markets for British goods; and the full rights of self-government which must necessarily be conceded to them, would be in no way incompatible with imperial unity. These were the views that Durham shared and expressed. He took with him to Canada other leading exponents such as Gibbon Wakefield and Charles Buller, who had an important share in the production of his report; and the result was a document imbued with a new faith in an empire based on the principles of freedom and self-government.

Such views stood in glaring contrast to the situation that Durham found in the Canadas. He was forthright in his condemnation of oligarchic rule and its chronic frustration of the popular will. He gained the impression that the executive, particularly in Lower Canada, was in a state of habitual collision with the elected Assembly and that the Legislative Council was chiefly employed to veto the acts of the majority. "It is difficult to understand," he wrote, "how any English statesman could have imagined that representative and irresponsible government could be successfully combined." Even in Upper Canada the Family Compact lacked any real popular support and relied on "a somewhat refractory and nominal submission to the imperial government" to secure power without responsibility.

But the problem went deeper than the system of government. In

Durham's eyes the racial conflict in Lower Canada overshadowed all other issues. "I expected to find a conflict between a government and a people," he wrote. "I found two nations warring in the bosom of a single state." It was a conflict that extended into every field of activity and left the two races not only divided but irreconcilable. Each sought to use its power to achieve domination—the English through their control of administration, the French through their majority in the assembly. The lack of mutual objectives meant that there was no basis of harmonious cooperation for common ends. Neither side was willing to share power, and neither would accept the ascendancy of the other. Durham discerned that the English, for all their professions of loyalty, would revolt rather than be subjected to French control, and quoted their opinion that "Lower Canada must be English, at the expense, if necessary, of not being British." It was his opinion that while many French would support an American invasion, many English would prefer American annexation to a government in which the French were in control.

Sympathetic as Durham might be to the desire of the French for self-government, he had nothing but condemnation for the basic aims that lay behind it. They sought to maintain "an old and stationary society in a new and progressive world." Their concept of cultural and racial separatism led them to obstruct all commercial development and to oppose every measure that might increase the English population. "They looked on the province as the patrimony of their own race; they viewed it not as a country to be settled, but as one already settled." They sought to establish a narrow nationalism, which to Durham seemed repugnant in its objectives and utterly false in its basis. He poured scorn on the ambitions of an isolated remnant clinging to obsolete traditions and institutions and striving to maintain the distinctive existence of "an utterly uneducated and singularly inert population" in the face of all the forces of modern progress. "There can hardly be conceived," he wrote, "a nationality more destitute of all that can invigorate and elevate a people, than that which is exhibited by the French in Lower Canada. . . . They are a people with no history and no literature." As a result, the mere grant of self-government was not enough. It must be established on a basis that would extinguish the vain hopes of French nationalism and absorb the French population. The time had come, he asserted, to settle once and forever the national character of the province. "I entertain no doubts as to the national character which must be given to Lower Canada; it must be that of the British Empire; that of the great race which must, in the lapse of no long period of time, be predominant over the whole of the North American continent."

In his analysis and recommendations, Durham covered a wide range of details that called for drastic reform. He criticized the system of land grants in Upper Canada and the survival of feudal tenures in Lower Canada; and Buller, in a special report, advocated a tax on waste lands coupled with a system of cash sales, which would provide funds for internal improvement and for assisted immigration. Another special report called for a comprehensive system of primary education jointly financed by local taxation and provincial grants. Durham was highly critical of both the system of justice in Lower Canada and the character of the Legislative Council, though on these matters his recommendations were somewhat indefinite. He attached particular importance to the creation of municipal institutions in Lower Canada. He regarded them not only as an essential training ground for self-government, but also as instruments in the policy of Anglicizing the French. He pointed to the contrast between Upper Canada, where provincial lavishness on public works had forced the localities to raise their own funds for local improvements, and Lower Canada, where the French paid for their reluctance to accept taxation in an absence of police and street lighting, adequate education, and good roads. In a passage that sounds optimistic as well as paradoxical to modern ears, he wrote: "If the Lower Canadians had been subjected, or rather had been taught to subject themselves, to a much greater amount of taxation, they would probably at this time have been a much wealthier, a much better governed, and a much more contented people." But important as these features were, they were overshadowed in significance by the three great recommendations of the report—the union of the Canadas, the grant of responsible government, and the separation of local from imperial affairs.

At the outset of his mission, Durham had been attracted to the idea of a federation of the whole of British North America. Contact with the actual situation in the provinces convinced him that this must be postponed to a later stage. Better communications between the Maritimes and Canada seemed necessary as a prelude to political union. Federation on the existing basis would still leave Lower Canada a predominantly French province, and the racial question was in Durham's eyes the very heart of the problem. The absorption of the French was necessary not only to end the political conflict but also to pave the way for economic progress. With French obstruction removed, the way would be cleared for an active policy of immigration and for the development of the St. Lawrence as a commercial artery. Union would end the existing disputes between the provinces, give Upper Canada secure access to the sea, and make possible a coherent policy of economic development under English direction.

These were the ends which the merchants had hoped to achieve through the union proposals of 1822. Durham accepted their aims but went much further in the methods he proposed. He warned against any mere amalgamation of the existing legislatures that would allow the shadow of separatism to survive. The provinces must be merged in a single community, which would be irrevocably English in character. Durham would confirm the existing religious rights of the French, but the barriers of language and of divergent laws and institutions must be wiped out to pave the way for the absorption of the French into a homogeneous state.

In addition, union on this basis was an essential prelude to the grant of self-government, which was the core of Durham's recommendations. The Tory merchants must accept the inescapable connection between their economic aims and the political program of the moderate reformers. The British government on its part must accept the irrevocable consequences of representative institutions by placing the conduct of government in the hands, not of an irresponsible clique, but of those in whom the representative body had confidence.

This meant responsible government as advocated by the Canadian reformers. To Robert Baldwin, the single-minded advocate of this fundamental reform, goes much of the credit for its central place in the Durham report. Baldwin had gone to England in 1836 to urge its adoption by the imperial government. Rebuffed in his effort to obtain an interview with Lord Glenelg, the colonial secretary, he had sent that gentleman a memorandum containing a clear exposition of his doctrine. Its essence was the transformation of the executive council into a provincial cabinet on the British model, resting on a majority in the legislature and responsible to that majority for the advice that it tendered the governor. This memorandum Baldwin sent to Durham, and Durham's language reflects Baldwin's views. It is not certain that Durham accepted the full doctrine of responsible government as Baldwin understood it. He speaks of instructing the governor "to secure the cooperation of the assembly in his policy, by entrusting its administration to such men as could command a majority." Such phrasing suggests that the initiative in policy might still lie with the governor, and it does not clearly envisage the collective responsibility of the cabinet. But his whole treatment of the topic makes it plain that Durham's essential aim was to place effective control over colonial affairs in the hands of the colonists and their representatives.

The inevitable corollary was the reduction of imperial interference to a minimum. The British government had taken the attitude that its control could only be maintained by upholding the independence of the governor and the executive, even in opposition to the popular will. Durham was scathing in his description of the results in practice—the chronic conflict with the legislature, the efforts of the governors to ease their position by throwing responsibility on London, the lack of stability in colonial policy resulting from the frequency with which the office of colonial secretary changed hands and the lack of actual knowledge on the part of the various incumbents. In consequence, the British government was directly involved in quarrels that sprang from local causes, in which no imperial interests were involved. Durham urged that imperial intervention be confined to the relatively few topics that were of real imperial concern. Constitutional changes, the conduct of foreign relations, control of external trade, and the management of public lands should remain in the hands of the imperial government. On all other matters the colonies should be free to pursue their own course.

This was a policy which Durham urged with all the eloquence at his command. Self-government, he insisted, did not mean secession. The colonies entertained a real affection for the mother country, but the evils under which they suffered could not long be endured and might place an intolerable strain on their loyalty. The remedy lay in a policy of confidence and generosity. The Canadians, he insisted, were a people who could be trusted and to whom power must not be grudged. Their loyalty would be strengthened by strengthening their influence over their own government. "It is not in the terrors of the law," he wrote, "or in the might of our armies, that the secure and honorable bond of connection is to be found. It exists in the beneficial operation of those British institutions which link the utmost development of freedom and civilization with the stable authority of an hereditary monarchy."

Judged by its reception and its immediate results, Durham's report was a failure. Alone among the parties concerned, the Canadian reformers hailed it with enthusiasm. The Tories of Upper Canada disliked the proposed union and fiercely attacked the idea of responsible government. The Family Compact, stung by Durham's criticisms, pointed out that he had spent only eleven days in Upper Canada out of his five months' stay and that his report contained many misconceptions. The French were outraged by the attacks on their race and the revival of a policy of Anglicization. Their anger at the report increased their solidarity and showed how mistaken Durham had been in his hope of extinguishing French nationalism. His chief recommendations were either warped or rejected. The British government refused to draw a clear line between local and imperial affairs. Responsible government was firmly rejected. In the debates on the report, Lord John Russell insisted with triumphant logic that since the governor was an official responsible to the Colonial Office, he could not also be responsible to a colonial body whose advice might be in conflict with his instructions. The union of the Canadas was indeed provided for by an imperial act of 1840, which came into force in 1841; but in the desire to secure an immediate English majority, the two sections were given equal representation with forty-two members each, thus perpetuating that very sense of separate identities which Durham had warned could only be overcome by complete fusion. Yet in spite of this failure to implement his proposals, and of Durham's own errors in judgment and foresight, time was to bring his vindication. The logic of events worked inexorably on the side of his faith in free government as the basis for harmony and imperial unity. Durham's report marks the beginning of the transition from the troubled and precarious Second Empire to the modern British Commonwealth of Nations.

The Struggle for Responsible Government

The failure of the rebellion meant the temporary disappearance of radicalism as a force in Canadian politics. During the decade that followed, the initiative lay with the moderate reformers. Although the Tories tried hard to brand them as the accomplices of treason, leaders such as Robert Baldwin, and Francis Hincks, and Louis Hippolyte Lafontaine were not really open to charges of disloyalty and republicanism. Their essential demand was for the extension to Canada of the full benefit of British institutions. They adopted wholeheartedly Durham's program of responsible government as the rallying ground for their campaign for self-government.

The publication of Durham's report, and its effect in clarifying the lines of political division in Canada, made it plainer than ever that the final decision lay in the hands of the British government. In a straight contest for popular support the colonial Tories had no hope of maintaining their ascendancy. They depended on the power and influence of the governor to uphold their policy and maintain them in office, and the attitude of the governor was determined by his instructions from London. Two objectives dominated the policy of the British ministry. One was to swamp the political power of the French by merging them in a united province of Canada. The other was the firm maintenance of the governor's independent authority, qualified but not weakened by the hope that that authority might somehow be exercised in a way that would satisfy the desires and command the support of the bulk of the population.

The man selected to implement these aims was Charles Poulett Thomson, who came out as governor general in the autumn of 1839 and whose initial success was rewarded in the following year by a peerage that transformed him into Lord Sydenham. He was a Manchester merchant who was particularly interested in the Baltic timber trade and a politician who had held office in the Whig ministry. His business experience made him highly appreciative of the importance to Canada of a progressive economic policy. His skill as a politician, and particularly his lively awareness of the importance of pork and patronage, proved of the highest practical advantage to him in his active dealings with Canadian politics. His energy in administration, his buoyant optimism, and his persuasive personality represented a remarkable combination of qualities, which enabled him to win a striking though transient success in the task he had undertaken.

Sydenham's first problem was to achieve the union of the two Canadas. The measure was not a response to any widespread popular pressure. The decision had been taken by the imperial authorities in the conviction that it was a necessary step toward solving the Canadian problem. Yet the British government, while determined to carry it through, hoped that this could be done with as much evidence as possible of Canadian approval. In Lower Canada the governor made use of the special council to carry a series of resolutions in favor of union. He even convinced himself that these represented the general sense of the province, but he avoided putting his conviction to a popular test, which would certainly have been disillusioning. In Upper Canada he carried a similar measure through the legislature in spite of the opposition of the Family Compact, helped by lavish promises of public works and financial aid. Prospects of this sort carried tremendous weight with a province that was virtually bankrupt. Its existing debt was well over £1,000,000, most of it incurred in the construction of canals. An annual deficit of £75,000 exceeded the whole revenue, which was barely enough to pay the charges on the debt. Commercial depression accentuated the financial crisis and made it almost impossible to secure fresh loans from English private investors. The provision in the union proposals that the debts of the two provinces were to be merged, thus throwing on Lower Canada with its negligible debt a large part of Upper

Canada's indebtedness, and the promise of an imperial loan of £1,500,000 to redress the finances and provide funds for new enterprises made a powerful appeal, which was reflected in a majority vote in favor of the union.

This brought the first part of Sydenham's task to a triumphant conclusion. He now entered on the more difficult enterprise of working the union within the limits laid down by the home government, and this was a continuous process, which called for the full exertion of the governor's political talents. His powers of management had been displayed in the contest over the union proposals. "My ministers vote against me," he had written lightheartedly. "So I govern through the opposition, who are truly Her Majesty's." But this was hardly a sound basis for a permanent system. If Canada was to be tranquilized under a stable government, harmony must be achieved between the different branches; and this meant in practice that the governor must secure a favorable majority in the legislature if his policy was to be maintained.

The elections to the first assembly of the united province in 1841 were thus of exceptional importance. Sydenham entered directly into their management, making use not only of his personal popularity but of more direct and less scrupulous methods of influence. The boundaries of the electoral districts in Montreal and Quebec were gerrymandered to secure the election of English candidates. "Bludgeon men" were active at the polls, especially though not entirely on the government side, and their intimidation played a part in the defeat of the French leader, Lafontaine. These methods achieved a limited success. Out of a membership of 84, only 24 were definitely accounted as supporters of the government; and while the moderate members were in general well-disposed toward Sydenham, his continued management was necessary to keep them in line. He approached the task with characteristic optimism. "The mass of people are sound," he wrote, "but they have been oppressed by a miserable little oligarchy on the one hand and excited by a few factious demagogues on the other. I can make a middle reforming party, I feel sure, which will put down both."

This need for a personal majority was a direct consequence of the rejection of responsible government. The policy to be followed was embodied in two dispatches from Lord John Russell dated October 14 and 16, 1839. The first was a direct pronouncement against a responsible ministry. The governor, Russell pointed out, received his orders from the Crown. The advice of his colonial ministers might be at variance with such orders. "If he is to obey his instructions from England, the parallel of constitutional responsibility entirely fails; if, on the other hand, he is to follow the advice of his council, he is no longer a subordinate officer, but an independent sovereign." The home government had every desire to see the affairs of the colony carried on harmoniously in accordance with the wishes of the people, but in the last resort imperial policy must override colonial desires.

The dispatch of October 16 was concerned with the habit that had developed of regarding places on the executive council as appointments for life. The governor was advised that he had complete freedom to change his advisers "as often as any sufficient motives of public policy may suggest the expediency of that measure." The first purpose of this dispatch was to free the governor from the shackles of the local oligarchy by enabling him to get rid of councillors who opposed his policy. But it clearly made possible a wider use of this power to bring the executive into complete harmony with the majority in the assembly. Durham had already pointed out that no legislation was needed to effect a change of system. All that was necessary was an instruction to the governor to choose ministers who had the support of the majority in the Assembly. The dispatch of October 16 opened the way for such a course if the governor chose to follow it.

The reformers seized on this possibility. In Upper Canada, Baldwin hoped that Sydenham would use the opportunity thus offered to him. In Nova Scotia, Joseph Howe sought to force the carrying out of the full implications of Russell's dispatch. Already in 1837 Howe had secured the separation of the councils in spite of a governor's recalcitrance and had mobilized the reformers behind the demand for responsible government. Russell's opposition to concessions in the debate on Durham's report roused Howe to publish four open letters, which trenchantly rejected the theory that the colonies could only be held if they were denied self-government. On the contrary, he asserted, the surest bond lay in the enjoyment of the full benefits of the British constitution. 'We seek nothing more than British subjects are entitled to; but we will be content with nothing less." The dispatch of October 16 opened the way for the governor to satisfy this desire, and Howe set out to force his hand. In February 1840, he carried a vote of "no confidence" in the existing ministry; and when the governor refused to dismiss his council, the assembly demanded his recall. The outcome was a somewhat barren triumph. The home government decided that a change of governors was necessary, but it still refused to concede the principle on which the demand had been based, and Sydenham interposed to delay its realization.

Sydenham fully accepted the dual position that Russell had laid down. "I have told the people plainly," he wrote, "that, as I cannot get rid of my responsibility to the home government, I will place no responsibility on the council; that they are *a council* for the governor to consult, but no more." But he also told the people that he had "received Her Majesty's commands to administer the government of these provinces in accordance with the well-understood wishes and the interests of the people." How these two things were to be combined was the problem that confronted Sydenham, and he could only solve it by maintaining an unbroken harmony between his policy and the wishes of the majority in the legislature. Either he must secure his own following, or he must ally himself with the reformers at the price of yielding on the basic principle at issue.

The converse of this was the need for the reformers to secure control of the legislature if they were to gain their essential objective, and this meant a union between the French and English reform groups. The supple and practical mind of Francis Hincks grasped this necessity from the outset. Hincks, a rising young figure in the financial world, was the editor of the *Examiner*, which was founded by the reformers in July 1838, for the specific purpose of campaigning for responsible government. Scarcely had the Durham report been published when Hincks made approaches to Lafontaine in anticipation of the coming union of the provinces, appealing for cooperation on the basis of common objectives. "Lord Durham ascribes to you national objects," he wrote frankly. "If he is right, union would be ruin to you; if he is wrong, and that you are really desirous of liberal institutions and economical government, the union would, in my opinion, give you all you could desire. . . . If we all combine as *Canadians* to promote the good of all classes in Canada, there cannot be a doubt that under the new constitution worked as Lord Durham proposes, the only party that would suffer would be the bureaucrats."

These words went close to the heart of the matter. The initial attitude of French Canada toward the union proposals was one of indignation touched in many cases with despair. To the offense given by Durham's avowed desire to extinguish French nationalism was added a resentment at the unfairness of certain specific clauses in the Act of Union—the proscription of French as an official language, the saddling of Lower Canada with a share of the heavy debt of Upper Canada, the grant of equal representation to Upper Canada with its population of 450,000 and Lower Canada with 650,000. Yet there were features that to discerning eyes might offer hope for the future. The laws of the two provinces remained in force at the union. The French had not lost their essential institutions, and by concentrating on their maintenance they might frustrate Durham's policy of Anglicization. Even the equality of representation, unjust though it was at the moment, might ultimately be an asset. Durham had warned against such a measure because of his faith that immigration would soon make the English population numerically superior to the French. By adopting equal representation for the sake of an immediate advantage, the British government in fact raised a barrier to the swamping of the French in the legislature when they became a minority in the population. The way was opened for a policy that would combine acceptance of the union with the continued defense of French nationality. This was the policy adopted by Louis Hippolyte Lafontaine, the acknowledged successor of Papineau as the political leader of French Canada; and by 1840 he had been convinced by the arguments of Hincks and was prepared to join with Baldwin and his followers in a demand for responsible government.

The projected combination collapsed in the first session of the united Assembly in 1841, and its collapse was due to the lack of coherence among the reformers of Upper Canada. The French showed a solidarity that was to become one of the salient features in Canadian politics throughout the succeeding century. The English reformers, in contrast, showed a complete inability to stick together. There was a foretaste of this even before the session opened. At the outset of his administration, Sydenham had persuaded Baldwin to accept office in order that the governor might not be thrown completely into the arms of the reactionaries. But Baldwin made it clear from the start that he would insist on a coherent ministry responsible to the majority in the legislature. On the eve of the meeting of the new assembly he demanded the formation of a reform administration and resigned when Sydenham refused. He had hoped to carry a number of his moderate colleagues with him; but these men now drew back, and Sydenham was able to avoid a major crisis in his ministry.

He followed this by surmounting the threat of a crisis in the Assembly. There Baldwin sought to put matters to the test by offering a series of resolutions that asserted the right of the assembly to hold the ministers "politically responsible for every act of the provincial government." Through one of his moderate supporters, S. B. Harrison, Sydenham put forward an alternative set of resolutions, which, while affirming the need for harmony between the executive and legislature, drew the sting from Baldwin's motion by omitting specific mention of responsibility. It became clear that even if Baldwin defeated Harrison's resolutions, he could not carry his own, for the Tories would vote against both sets. He accepted the amendments, and the governor was once more victorious over the disunited forces of reform.

The truth was, as Hincks charged, that the reformers of Upper Canada did not form a party in any real sense of the word. They were a fluctuating group of individuals, the majority of them "loose fish" who exercised their independent judgment on individual questions and were bound by no common program and no party discipline. However much they might approve of responsible government as a principle, they were more immediately concerned with practical measures, and the active and constructive program of reforms that Sydenham offered won their general support. The negotiation of the imperial loan, the inauguration of of fresh construction under a board of works, the beginning of local government, and new provisions for immigration were things which appealed to the practical politicians as well as to their constituents. Hincks himself had been won over to the support of Sydenham by the close of the session and was shortly to enter the administration under Sydenham's successor.

Nonetheless, Sydenham's success rested on a precarious foundation. He had staved off responsible government in principle only by virtually adopting it in practice. His methods only served to make clearer the absolute necessity of resting the administration on a legislative majority. Unless the governor kept command of that majority himself, he would have to surrender to his opponents. It was a system that left no margin for failure. By becoming his own party manager and acting as virtual prime minister, Sydenham had retained control. But already there were signs that opposition was beginning to rally, and, with the completion of his constructive program, Sydenham faced his real test. His death in September 1841, as the result of a fall from his horse spared him from the approaching crisis and left it as a legacy to his successor.

The Attainment of Self-Government

Sir Charles Bagot came out with every intention of continuing Sydenham's policy. In London the Tories had just replaced the Whigs in office, and Lord Stanley at the Colonial Office was even more determined than Russell to resist responsible government. Bagot was instructed to avoid as far as possible committing himself to any party, but with the significant addition that in the last resort he should fall back on the old Family Compact as a barrier against the reformers.

It was not long before Bagot discovered how remote such views were from the realities with which he had to deal. Sydenham's system was on the verge of collapse. The appointment of moderates unconnected with party did nothing to assure a favorable majority in the legislature. The attempt to balance the administration by including both Tories and reformers was equally ineffective. It was no longer sufficient to win over individuals. Some way must be found of rallying a solid group to the support of the administration, and for practical purposes this meant winning over the French.

Here was a striking demonstration of how utterly the union had failed in its basic purpose. Instead of absorbing the French, it had made them the decisive force in the political situation. Without their aid, no party could act effectively. Even the Tories were prepared to seek an alliance with them for the sake of gaining power. Bagot's ministers unanimously agreed that unless the French were won over, the government could not carry on; and, on the eve of the legislative session of 1842, Bagot made overtures to Lafontaine.

The French on their part were prepared to take practical advantage of their position. With the fruits of office dangling before their eyes, Lafontaine's followers were anxious to accept the governor's offer. But Lafontaine himself was not ready to accept unconditionally. He recognized the importance of maintaining the connection between the French and English reformers, and he insisted that Baldwin must be included in the new ministry. This gave rise to further difficulties. Baldwin felt that he could not hold out for a complete reform ministry at the price of wrecking the negotiations and disappointing the French. But he did insist on a broad reconstruction of the administration that would involve the dismissal of several leading Tories and he refused to agree to Bagot's demand that pensions should be granted to the dismissed councilors. Faced with an imminent crisis, Bagot felt that he had no choice. He accepted a compromise that averted a vote of "no confidence," and in September 1842, five reformers, including Baldwin and Lafontaine, entered the ministry.

Tactically this was a real success for Bagot. He won the support of the reformers at the price of admitting their leaders to office; but the ministry was still a coalition, and the governor retained his independent authority and political initiative. The compromise had staved off the formal acceptance of responsible government. Nonetheless, Bagot recognized that it had been brought one step nearer in reality. "Whether the doctrine of responsible government is openly acknowledged," he wrote Stanley, "or only tacitly acquiesced in, virtually it exists." His concessions roused the fury of the Tories in Canada and the alarm of the government in England; but Bagot defended them as the only possible course, and the home government reluctantly accepted his view in spite of their avowed dislike of his actions.

Yet the expedient was temporary at best. Admitted to a share in the administration, the reformers abated their demand for full control. But Baldwin had not abandoned his principles; and while he and his associates had for the moment accepted half a loaf, they were nonetheless determined to exercise all the realities of power. Among those realities was the control of patronage. Bagot might have been ready to concede this as the necessary consequence of his admission of the reformers to office. But the ill-health that was shortly to prove fatal led to his retirement early in 1843; and his successor, Sir Charles Metcalfe, fresh from the governorship of Jamaica, was determined to resist any further attrition of the governor's authority. He conceived that this involved maintaining his independence against both his ministers and the majority in the assembly. Such an attitude was bound to lead to a crisis, and in November 1843, it broke over the claim of the ministry to approve all appointments. Metcalfe indignantly refused to surrender what he regarded as a prerogative of the Crown. All the ministers except one resigned. The assembly supported their stand in a vote of confidence that was a virtual censure of the governor. Metcalfe responded by dismissing the assembly. The election that followed was in effect an appeal by the governor to the country, very similar in character to the earlier ones by Head and Sydenham and with a comparable measure of success. The election of 1844 was marked by unprecedented violence on both sides; but once again moderate opinion in Upper Canada, including the Methodist followers of Egerton Ryerson, rallied to the support of the governor. The stand of the reformers told against them. It could be supported by constitutional arguments, but it also had a highly practical basis. Patronage was an important element in political power, especially for a government which sought to base itself on solid party support. Not only could it not risk resistance or opposition to its policies within the civil service; it must try to gratify its supporters and strengthen their loyalty by distributing the fruits of office to deserving adherents. It was easy to charge the reform leaders with sordid motives and to raise the cry of loyalty to the governor against self-seeking partisan politicians. Thus the reformers, while victorious in Canada East, experienced a severe setback in Canada West, and Metcalfe and his supporters emerged with a precarious majority.

On the surface this was a repulse to the drive for full responsible government. In the long run it proved to be one more stage toward that goal. Metcalfe had won the support of the electorate, but his ministry was dependent on the resulting majority in the Assembly to maintain itself with difficulty for the next two years. Practically, it functioned as a cabinet whose advice the governor must accept or find an alternative, and there was no alternative short of surrender in principle as well as in fact. Canada could no longer be governed indefinitely by the methods of Sydenham and Metcalfe. Repeated appeals by governors for electoral support against their reform opponents and the growing turbulence that marked these successive contests threatened to lead to a new explosion if the situation was prolonged.

The events that decided the final outcome took place not in Canada but in Britain. There the achievement of political reform in 1832 was followed by an assault on economic privilege, particularly on the special protection to the landed interests afforded by the Corn Laws. When Sir Robert Peel crowned his policy of tariff reform by carrying the repeal of the Corn Laws in 1846 in the face of his outraged followers, he split the Tory party and struck the final blow at the old colonial system. Mercantilism was dead, and the motives for holding the colonies in political dependence were weakened by the relaxation of economic ties. A new spirit entered the Colonial Office with the appointment of Lord Grey, and his dispatches opened the way for the full concession of responsible government.

The results were first made evident in Nova Scotia. There Joseph Howe, after an uneasy participation in a coalition ministry, had resigned in 1843 and resumed his campaign for a responsible executive. The struggle was less turbulent than in Canada, but its lines were similar. Although the reformers were unable to win a majority in the legislature, they forced the governor to rely on the Tories and in effect to adopt a party administration. A Tory defeat would inevitably force a change of ministry, and Grey perceived that the full consequences of such an event must be freely accepted. "It cannot be too distinctly acknowledged," he wrote to Governor John Harvey on November 3, 1846, "that it is neither possible nor desirable to carry on the government of any of the provinces of British North America in opposition to the opinion of the inhabitants." And in a dispatch dated March 31, 1847, he made it even clearer that there was now no obstacle to the full and immediate adoption of the cabinet system in the colonies. Thus when the reformers won the election in the autumn of that year, the governor's course was clear. He accepted the popular verdict; and when the majority in the new assembly declared their lack of confidence in the existing ministry, the governor called the reformers to office on January 28, 1848. It was the formal inauguration of responsible government in the British colonies.

Two months later it was extended to Canada. In January 1847, Lord Elgin was sent out as successor to Metcalfe. A son-in-law of Lord Durham, he shared the latter's views and was eager to apply them, and his path was made smooth by the policy that Grey had by this time laid down. A few months sufficed to convince him that its application was not only desirable but imperative. In a community torn by political and racial dissensions and gripped by economic depression, the continued alliance of the governor with one party in direct opposition to the reformers—and, even more, a reliance on the English to the exclusion of the French—involved the risk of a new rebellion. Elgin was determined to commit himself to no party, and Grey was in full agreement. When the election in January 1848—an election at last free from direct intervention by the governor—resulted in a reform majority, Grey wrote: "I have no doubt that you must accept such a council as the newly elected parliament will support." The assembly at the first opportunity showed that only a reform administration could command its confidence; and on March 11 the first coherent party ministry came into office under Baldwin and Lafontaine.

If any question remained about the reality of responsible government, it was disposed of during the following year. Under Metcalfe an act had been passed to compensate those persons in Upper Canada who had suffered losses during the rebellion of 1837. A similar measure for Lower Canada could hardly be denied, and after an investigation by a commission the Rebellion Losses Bill was passed in 1849. The breadth of its provisions gave rise to a Tory outcry against compensation to rebels and to pressure on the governor to refuse his assent. But Elgin was convinced that, whatever his personal views of the measure, he had no constitutional course but to accept the bill. The fury of the Tories was turned against the governor in person. He was stoned in the streets of Montreal, and riots in that city reached a climax with the burning of the parliament buildings. But the stamp placed on responsible government was now irrevocable; and its extension not only to the other provinces of British North America, but to all the self-governing colonies, became merely a matter of time. The struggle for Canadian self-government had issued in a solution that was applicable throughout the empire and that held within it the possibility of continued evolution toward full and independent national status.

Defining the Boundary

In the political controversies of the forties, not the least significant feature was the decline in the direct influence of American political ideas. The rebellion of 1837 was a crucial landmark in the development of Canadian nationality. Its failure decided the course that Canada would pursue in her effort to establish her position as a distinct community. She showed a resolute dermination to gain full control of her own affairs against the claims of British imperial authority. But that control was to be exercised through institutions modeled on those of Britain. The alternative to colonial subjection was neither absorption in the United States nor the assimilation of the Canadian form of government to that of the neighboring republic, but the evolution of a distinctive national character within the framework of the British parliamentary system.

At the same time the neighborhood of the United States was a constant and pervasive factor, which colored all aspects of Canadian life. The danger of a new conflict that would threaten the existence of British North America had abated since 1814, but it had by no means disappeared. The United States had entered a new expansionist era, the rampant nationalism of which was expressed in the phrase "manifest destiny." The God-given mission of the American republic to extend its sway over the whole continent was a favorite theme for political rhetoric. Fortunately for Canada, the aggressive manifestations of this spirit were directed mainly against Mexico and the coveted regions of Texas and California. In the absence of any urgent motive for armed conquest, the ultimate absorption of Canada in the union was left for the forces of predestination to achieve. But close beneath the surface lay a persistent anti-British sentiment, which was ready to take advantage of any opportunity to expel Britain from her foothold on the American continent, and any controversy between the two countries held possibilities of a crisis in which the fate of Canada would be at stake.

The aftermath of the Canadian rebellion gave rise to an uneasy situation, which showed how easily such a threat might arise. The spectacle of Canadians taking up arms against a British government roused memories of 1776, which were further stimulated by the appeals of Mackenzie and Papineau to the traditions of the American Revolution. This flattering emulation increased the sympathy of those elements in the United States whose dislike of Britain naturally inclined them to support any Canadian movement for independence. The leaders of the rebellion who fled to the United States were able to set about raising an army and planning an invasion of Canada with little interference from either state or federal authorities. The American government was sincerely desirous of avoiding complications, but it felt unable to exercise much effective control along the border, where sentiment strongly favored the rebel cause. Depression and unemployment in that region aided Mackenzie's recruiting campaign. A number of societies were formed for the specific purpose of supporting an invasion of Canada. The most important of these was the Hunters and Chasers of the Eastern Frontier, and Hunters' Lodges spread from Vermont to Michigan and even into the Southern states. In the autumn of 1838 a convention in Cleveland set up a republican government for Canada, organized a bank for the issue of currency, and set about raising an army for invasion.

Little came of these plans. A series of forays across the border collapsed ignominiously. One force of about 1000 succeeded in establishing a foothold near Prescott, where part of it occupied a stone windmill and stood a siege of five days; but the garrison was surrounded and forced to surrender, and this proved to be the most serious effort at invasion. By the end of 1838 quiet had been restored along the border. But such episodes aroused alarm and irritation on both sides and led to incidents that increased the tension. One of these was the burning of the *Caroline,* a small steamer that had been hired to provision the force that Mackenzie gathered on Navy Island in the Niagara River at the end of 1837. A Canadian detachment, sent to destroy the ship, found her moored on the American side. In the attack an American was killed, and the *Caroline* was seized and sent adrift and blazing down-river, where she sank some distance above the falls. American indignation at this counter-invasion led to reprisals, including the destruction of the Canadian ship *Sir Robert Peel*; but the affair would soon have died down if a Canadian named Alexander McLeod, drinking in a Buffalo tavern, had not boasted incautiously—and probably untruthfully—that he was responsible for the death of the man killed on the *Caroline*. He was promptly arrested for murder. The British government intervened and demanded his release. The American government, in the face of revived local passions and the lack of federal jurisdiction, found it impossible to comply. Fortunately an acquittal was secured, but the inherent danger of the situation was shown by the fact that this sordid and relatively trivial affair actually brought two great nations to the verge of war.

This state of affairs emphasized the urgency of settling other outstanding questions, particularly the boundary controversies, which were now growing in acuteness. Foremost among them was the dispute over the boundary between Maine and New Brunswick. This had been defined by the Treaty of 1783 along lines that had been laid down by previous provisions for the boundaries of the old provinces of Quebec and Nova Scotia. The line was to run up the St. Croix River to its source, then directly north to the highland dividing the rivers flowing into the Atlantic from those flowing into the St. Lawrence, along the highlands to the northwest head of the Connecticut, down that river to the 45th parallel, and thence due west to the St. Lawrence.

It soon developed that every item in the description was open to doubt. There were disputes over which of several rivers was meant by the St. Croix. It proved almost impossible to discover the highlands that the treaty assumed existed. It was not certain which was the northwest head of the Connecticut. Even the 45th parallel was wrongly located in the initial surveys, with the result that a fort built by the United States at Rouse's Point was actually a quarter of a mile inside Canadian territory.

A few of these difficulties had by this time been cleared up. The location of the St. Croix was determined in 1798. A commission appointed under the Treaty of Ghent decided on the ownership of the islands in the Bay of Fundy. It was, however, unable to make progress on the question of the main boundary, and in 1827 the matter was submitted to the arbitration of the King of the Netherlands. That monarch found the provisions of the treaty "inexplicable and impractical," and in 1831 he suggested a division of the disputed area that would give the United States two-thirds of the 12,000 miles involved. But the American government refused to accept, and no progress toward a settlement was made during the decade that followed.

Yet the need for a settlement was rapidly growing. Residents were moving into the disputed area. Timber was being cut under licenses from both Maine and New Brunswick. The conflicting claims to jurisdiction by state and province threatened to bring about a serious clash, which was nearly precipitated by the Aroostook War in 1839. Maine sent a party to expel New Brunswick lumbermen from the Aroostook Valley. The New Brunswickers surprised the party, carried off fifty of them to jail in Woodstock, raided the local arsenal, and set out to repel the intruders. Bloodshed was averted in the end by the moderation of the authorities of both sides, but not before Maine had raised funds for defense, Congress had authorized measures in support, and New Brunswick had called for military aid to defend its threatened rights.

The time had come for a serious effort to reach a final settlement. Negotiations were undertaken in 1842 between Lord Ashburton, as the

Maine Boundary Dispute, 1783–1842

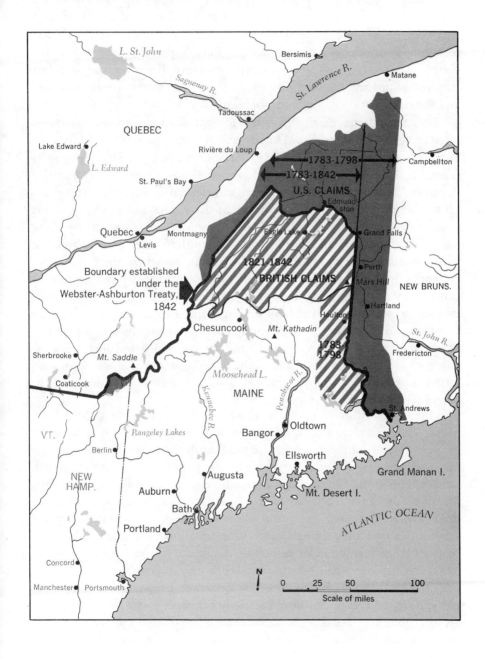

British envoy and Daniel Webster, the American Secretary of State. An effort was made to deal with all outstanding problems. The *Caroline* affair was disposed of by a mild apology on the part of Britain. An extradition treaty was agreed upon. Certain details of the boundary between the St. Lawrence and the Lake of the Woods were adjusted, including a considerable triangle west of Lake Superior, which Ashburton conceded to the United States with little resistance. But it was the boundary between Maine and New Brunswick that was most vital in the negotiations and the chief feature of the resulting agreement.

The chief desire of the British and American governments was to reach an agreement that would finally remove this chronic cause of friction. Subject to that, they wanted chiefly a settlement that would be strategically favorable. The United States wanted to retain Rouse's Point, which guarded the route down Lake Champlain. Britain desired to keep the Americans off the height of land overlooking the St. Lawrence and to gain a secure road for military traffic from St. John to Quebec—a route that was important for overland reinforcement of Canada during the winter months and that was jeopardized by the line that had been suggested by the king of the Netherlands. Ashburton paid relatively little attention to New Brunswick's concern for its forest resources or to its plans for a railway to Quebec, whose shortest route would lie through the area in dispute. Webster was forced to consider more seriously the unyielding attitude of Maine, which wanted not only to retain the timber in the disputed area, but even to regain a strip on the west bank of the St. John, and which was supported by Massachusetts, whose jurisdiction had extended over Maine until its attainment of statehood in 1820.

One episode that helped to produce a solution was the Battle of the Maps. The American search for supporting evidence had disconcertingly brought to light a map that bore out the British claim, which was wrongly suspected of being the map drawn up by Benjamin Franklin in the original peace negotiations. On the British side there was the equally disconcerting discovery of a map that favored the American case. Both sides concealed these awkward items, but both were disposed to moderation by the knowledge that they existed, and Webster found the alleged Franklin map a useful instrument in bringing Maine and Massachusetts to terms. The outcome was a compromise, unsatisfactory in certain aspects to both sides but probably as fair as could be obtained. Britain got five-twelfths of the disputed area and a more southerly line than under the Netherlands award, though the resulting wedge still impeded communications between St. John and Quebec. The United States retained Rouse's Point and a valuable area around the head of the Connecticut and compensated Maine and Massachusetts with a money payment of $150,000 each.

It had been hoped that Ashburton would succeed in settling not only these questions, but also the problem of Oregon, which was rapidly approaching a crisis. His failure left Oregon to be dealt with later and in a much more dangerous atmosphere. In 1818, Britain and the United States had agreed on the 49th parallel as the boundary across the prairies to the Rockies. But they had been unable to agree on its extension to the Pacific, where both countries claimed the Oregon region between California and Alaska. They agreed on joint occupation for ten years, and in 1827 this was extended without time limit.

Actually only a part of this territory was in serious dispute. The United States was willing to extend the 49th parallel to the Pacific. The British held out for the Columbia River as the boundary. Until the end of the thirties the controversy was not of great importance. There was some rivalry over the fur trade, but after 1821 the supremacy of the Hudson's Bay Company met little serious challenge. By 1840, however, the tide of westward migration had crossed the Rockies to the Pacific slope, and the familiar conflict between settlement and fur trade was extended to Oregon.

The new settlers were determined to secure the area for the United States. They formed their own provisional government in 1843 and appealed to Washington for recognition. Next year the issue was injected into national politics. The Democrats coupled their claims to Oregon with their claims to Texas and demanded the whole coast up to Alaska with the slogan "fifty-four forty or fight." Their victorious candidate, President James K. Polk, renewed the compromise offer of the 49th parallel; and when this was again rejected by Britain he announced the end of joint occupation and embarked on war preparations. He had no real desire for war with Britain at a time when war with Mexico was approaching; but neither had Britain any wish for a war over Oregon of which the immediate result would be a threat to Canada. In 1846 the two countries agreed to extend the 49th parallel to the coast, leaving, however, the whole of Vancouver Island to Britain. With this settlement—apart from minor disputes about details—the process was completed of drawing the southern boundary of the future Dominion of Canada.

Quite aside from the territorial results, these episodes in diplomacy held implications that were of the most profound significance in Canada's national development. The province was not immediately concerned with the controversy over Oregon, but its outcome had a real bearing on Canada's future prospects. New Brunswick, and Canada in a lesser degree,

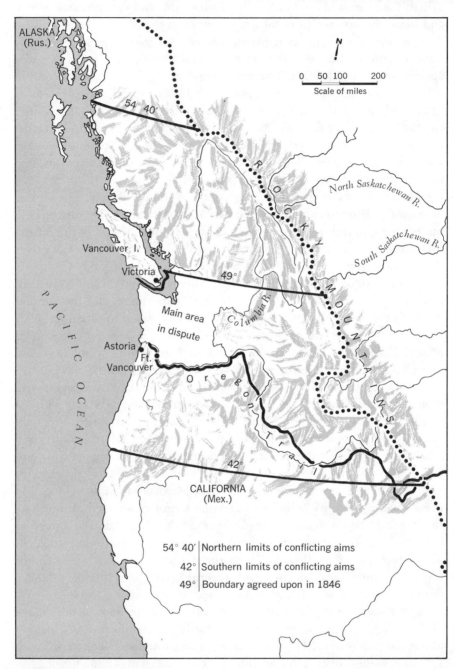

Oregon Boundary Dispute, 1818-1846

had a more direct interest in the decision on the Maine boundary, which left considerable resentment for many years to come. Yet in both cases the negotiations were handled entirely by the British government with only a cursory attention to the views of the provinces. From the British point of view, local colonial claims were necessarily subordinate to imperial interests, among which harmony with the United States occupied a cardinal place. Such an attitude was understandable and even laudable, but it did not prevent the rise of a feeling in Canada that Britain was unduly ready to sacrifice Canadian rights for the sake of American friendship. Given that situation, self-government would obviously be incomplete so long as it was confined to domestic matters. Control of diplomacy, and particularly of relations with the United States, was ultimately necessary as an aspect of full autonomy; and the boundary negotiations of the forties laid the initial foundation for a slowly rising desire for freedom in external as well as internal affairs.

In addition, the Oregon controversy served as an object lesson and a warning. The American settlers of a previous generation who had moved into Ontario were in general content to accept a change of allegiance. But the growth of American nationalism had given rise to a new expansionist spirit, and the settlers who migrated to Oregon acted as the spearhead for the advance of American sovereignty. That same spirit would be equally evident in other areas that were invaded by the advancing frontier. As available free land diminished, it would be impossible to hold large stretches of vacant land north of the border. The tide of settlement would flow irresistibly into the vacuum; and if Canada was to possess the lands that remained above the 49th parallel, she must take steps toward their effective occupation or be forestalled by American pioneers.

Annexation and Reciprocity to 1854

At the end of the forties the pervasive influence of the United States on Canadian politics was once more evident in a way that was all the more striking for being paradoxical. The Tories had steadfastly contended that the reformers were American in sympathies and that surrender to them would mean the disruption of the empire. Surrender came with the grant of responsible government, and still the Empire remained intact. It was now the Tories themselves who in their fury and disillusionment set out to break it up.

At the root of the annexationist movement of 1849 lay the sense of frustration experienced by the English merchants of Lower Canada. The union of the Canadas, which they so ardently desired, had failed to achieve the results that they had hoped to derive from it. The political power of the French had not been nullified. On the contrary, the grant of responsible government had given them a new ascendancy in the affairs of the province. The union had, it was true, made possible the construction of canals to improve the navigation of the St. Lawrence; but the dream of transforming the river into the great commercial highway of the continent was balked by the changes in British trade policy that were simultaneously under way.

The triumph of the free-trade movement in Britain forced a commercial revolution on Canada. The convenience of the St. Lawrence route on which the merchants so hopefully insisted was not by itself enough to draw American export traffic away from New York. A stronger lure was the prospects that American products passing through Canada would share the preference that Canadian products enjoyed in the British markets. This applied particularly to wheat and flour, the staple exports of the Middle West, and the merchants pressed hard for an extension of the British preference accompanied by favorable terms for the admission of American wheat. For a brief moment it seemed that their desires had been granted. By the Canada Corn Act of 1843, the sliding scale of duties, which stood at 5s. a quarter when the price in Britain was under 67s., was changed to a flat duty of 1s. a quarter in return for the adoption by Canada of a 3s. duty on American wheat; and American wheat ground into flour in Canada shared the advantage of a similar preferential relaxation of the British tariffs. The merchants rejoiced not only in the prospect of increased traffic on the canals, but also in the vision of an expansion of the Canadian milling industry.

These bright hopes were dashed in 1846. The repeal of the Corn Laws in Britain ended the preference on colonial grain. As it turned out, this had comparatively slight effects on the Canadian farmer, but it was a severe blow to the milling and transportation interests. Its effect was accentuated by the American Drawback Act of 1845, which allowed free passage of Canadian exports to American ports and which was shortly extended to cover imports as well. Thus while British action reduced the incentive for Americans to use the St. Lawrence route, American action was luring Canadian trade from Montreal to New York. These blows descended at a time when trade was already depressed, and piteous cries of ruin arose from Canadian merchants and investors. "I commenced to build the Welland

Mills and finished them about midsummer last at a cost of eight thousand pounds," one of them lamented in 1848, "but my mill has done nothing since it was finished, 'the glory is departed.' I embarked my all in the enterprise, with now the almost certain prospect that all will be a loss."

On top of these economic setbacks came political desertion. The grant of responsible government demolished the barriers that the Tories, with the support of the home government, had maintained against democracy. The Rebellion Losses Bill showed that the consequence was not merely the victory of the reformers, but the acquisition of power by the French. The Tories had looked to the imperial connection to support the principles of economic solidarity and racial ascendancy. Now both had been thrown over, and the imperial government itself seemed to be moving toward the dissolution of the empire. The merchants had little faith in Canada's ability to maintain economic autonomy in the absence of imperial protection. Political autonomy could only be maintained at the price of yielding to the French. Rather than face that prospect, a section of the Tories preferred annexation to the United States.

The Annexation Manifesto was issued by a group of Montreal leaders in October 1849. The document pointed to the apparent intention of Britain to thrust freedom on the colonies. It found no remedy for economic problems in local protection or in the union of British North America. Reciprocity with the United States would offer only a partial solution on the economic side and none on the political. Annexation suddenly appeared to be full of advantages—higher farm prices, lower import costs, new sources of credit, access to American capital to build up industry and transportation. Entry into the American union would give Canada a voice in the policy of the central government such as she had never enjoyed in imperial policy, and it would achieve the supreme end of swamping the French in an overwhelmingly Anglo-Saxon community.

The response was disappointing. The chief support came from the commercial elements in Montreal and the Eastern Townships. The French, apart from a small group of radicals, were steadfastly opposed. In Upper Canada the only adherents were the extremists among both the radicals and the conservatives. The Montreal leaders had hoped to make use of the British American League, which the Tories had formed to combat the Rebellion Losses Bill and through which they voiced vigorous criticism of both the British and the local governments. But the Tories of Upper Canada hesitated to repudiate their old professions of loyalty. They were further deterred when Britain flatly denied any desire to cast off Canada and stigmatized the Manifesto as little short of treason. Even the United

States, in spite of some enthusiasm in the border regions, showed only a tepid interest. With the sectional conflict rising in intensity and the struggle leading to the Compromise of 1850 already under way, the American government had little desire to aggravate the South by absorbing a region that would strengthen the power of the North. These factors, coupled with a revival of good times, prevented the annexation campaign from making effective headway, and by the early part of 1850 it had virtually collapsed.

Yet, short-lived as it was, the movement was a significant illustration of one persistent current in Canadian life. The idea of annexation to the United States as a solution for political or economic ills was of periodic recurrence. To check it, an alternative remedy must be found, and particularly a remedy for economic difficulties. The idea emerged of a closer economic integration as a means of maintaining political separatism, and the outcome was the movement for commercial reciprocity.

This approach was indicative of the change in both the economic structure and the commercial orientation of Canada. In the ambitions of the St. Lawrence merchants, the development of a trade in Canadian products with the United States had hitherto held little place. Canadian staples had found their export market in Britain. The urge for access to American markets and resources was based on the desire for a middleman position in the exchange of British manufactured goods for American natural products. But by mid-century the United States was growing in attraction as a market for Canadian commodities. The construction activity which accompanied the rise of industrial cities and the expansion of canals and railways meant an increasing demand for materials. The depletion of the forests in the eastern states opened up a growing market for Canadian sawn lumber. By 1849, one-third of Canada's timber exports went to the United States. The growing cities of the East were customers for fish and farm products. The development of freer exchange across the border would not only benefit Canadian producers, but promised to increase the general level of prosperity and offered a new basis for an active commercial development to replace the older system, which had been shattered by Britain's abandonment of mercantilism.

One of the earliest advocates of reciprocity was William Hamilton Merritt. This energetic promoter, who had been the moving spirit in the building of the Welland Canal and whose interests were involved in milling as well as transportation, started an agitation in 1846, which met with a prompt response in the Canadian legislature. In May of that year an address asked the British government to negotiate a treaty of reciprocity.

But an alternative method of procedure was opened up by the imperial measure of 1846, which allowed the colonies to repeal any discriminatory tariffs against foreign countries. Canada could thus take action by legislation, and there was some hope that reciprocal legislation could be arranged with the United States. A bill to this effect was introduced in Congress in 1848, only to be defeated in the Senate; but in the following year Canada adopted a bill offering free admission of a list of natural products whenever the United States should take similar action.

There were, however, complications on the American side. The states of the Northwest were interested in the free use of the Canadian canals, and there was some sentiment along the border in favor of freer trade. But the chief American producers who would be affected by an agreement, including the coal and timber interests, were more anxious to exclude Canadian competition than to gain freer access to a limited Canadian market, and their opposition was strengthened by the rising protectionist sentiment in the North. The issue was also affected by the growing sectional conflict. Northern opinion held that closer trade relations would be a prelude to the political annexation of Canada, and this prospect roused the opposition of the South to a measure whose outcome might be an increase in the strength of the North.

But while the United States was little concerned about trade with the province of Canada, it found itself involved at this time in a crisis over the fisheries of the Maritimes. The War of 1812 brought an end to the privileges that the United States had enjoyed under the Treaty of 1783. A new convention in 1818, while it gave the Americans certain rights along the coasts of Newfoundland and Labrador, excluded them from the inshore fisheries of the Maritimes. But disputes had arisen over what constituted territorial waters. Nova Scotia insisted that the 3-mile limit extended across all bays from headland to headland. The Americans claimed that the limit followed the windings of the coast and made it legal for them to fish inside the wider bays. By 1852 the controversy was so acute that Britain announced the dispatch of a naval force to protect the fisheries, and the United States replied by sending a warship to protect its fishermen. It was a situation perturbing to both sides, and both Britain and the United States were anxious to see it settled.

The fisheries dispute provided a lever for the securing of trade concessions. Canada, with no interest in the Maritime fisheries, was naturally willing to see them opened in return for a reciprocity agreement in which the Maritimes would share. Prince Edward Island and New Brunswick were both prepared to consider the bargain. Newfoundland was more dubious, and Nova Scotia—the chief province in which the inshore fisheries were at stake—voiced considerable opposition to the sacrifice demanded of her. Even the prospect of the free admission of fish and coal from Nova Scotia into American markets was for a time overshadowed by indignation at the neglect of the British government to keep the province informed about the negotiations or to consult the provincial authorities, and approval of the ultimate agreement was accompanied by sharp words about the shortcomings of British diplomacy.

The injection of the fisheries issue meant that the reciprocity agreement must take the form of a treaty negotiated by the British government. For several years after 1846 there were tentative discussions but little progress. By 1852, however, matters had reached the stage of definite proposals, and negotiations were begun over matters of detail. These went forward somewhat haltingly, but by 1854 an agreement was at last in sight. No small part of the credit for the advance went to Israel de Wolfe Andrews, American consul at St. John and special agent during the negotiations. Andrews's extensive knowledge of conditions in the provinces, his wide contacts with publicists and politicians on both sides of the border, and his talent for placing funds where they would have the most persuasive effect were invaluable in paving the way for the adoption of the treaty. Without his manipulations, backed by funds from Britain and the United States and Canada, the enterprise would have encountered much rougher going before it was brought to completion.

As it was, negotiations were far enough advanced by May 1854, for Lord Elgin to be appointed as special British envoy to carry them to their conclusion. His task was not merely to arrange final details, but to contribute to the favorable atmosphere that would secure ratification in Congress. A key development was the change in the viewpoint of the South. Southern representatives were now persuaded that reciprocity, instead of facilitating annexation, would be a barrier to it. One factor in their conversion may well have been the lavish hospitality offered by Elgin during his mission, and his special cordiality toward Southern senators. Even if the treaty was not "floated through on champagne," Elgin's secretary admitted that "in the hands of a skilful diplomatist, that beverage is not without its value." The treaty, signed in June, was carried through the Senate with almost suspicious ease and approved on August 2. Britain on her part submitted the agreement to the provinces involved, and their formal agreement was secured during the year that followed.

The treaty, concluded for an initial period of ten years, provided for the mutual free admission of the principal natural products of both countries, including not only farm produce but also fish and timber and coal. Access to all fisheries north of the latitude of 36°, while reciprocal in form except for the exclusion of the Florida fisheries, was in reality a concession to the United States. So was the inclusion on the free list of such items as turpentine and rice and raw tobacco, which were meant to gain Southern support. Americans were granted the right to use the St. Lawrence canals in return for Canadian access to Lake Michigan—a grant which, while beneficial to the states of the Northwest, was in fact based on a Canadian desire to attract the largest possible volume of traffic away from the Erie and into the St. Lawrence.

The actual effect of the treaty is open to argument. In the course of its operation, trade between the United States and British North America trebled in value, although there were considerable fluctuations from year to year. Recent authorities have pointed to such factors as the railway boom in the United States and wartime demands after 1861 as important elements, and part of the apparent increase was no doubt due to the transformation of smuggling into legitimate trade. Yet the conclusion of the treaty undoubtedly marked, and very probably aided, an orientation of Canadian trade toward the United States that was already in progress before its conclusion. The economic division of the continent had not been eliminated, but it had been modified temporarily; and the result was a period of progress toward closer economic integration, which, paradoxically, strengthened the forces of political separatism and brought still nearer the achievement of a distinct national status by British North America.

Lord Elgin Assenting to Canadian Legislation.

Burning the Houses of Assembly.

(Royal Ontario Museum)

Engagement in the Thousand Islands.
One of a number of border clashes following the rebellion of 1837.

The Burning of the *Caroline.*

(Public Archives of Canada)

Settlement Reaches the Pacific.
John McLoughlin, centre, greeting American arrivals at the Hudson's Bay post at
Fort Vancouver.

The Oregon Dispute.

The Collapse of
Annexation.

(Punch in Canada)

DROPPING A HINT.

Boy.—Hallo, Mister! ye've dropped yer hankercher.

Leaguer.—Ha! my good boy, yes!—I mean no, my blessed little kid, no! not mine, my
excellent little gentleman, not mine—Oh no, no, no, not mine!

Boy.—Well, some o' yis dropped it anyhow, and now none o' yiz 'll own to it.

Punch in Canada, May, 1849.

FAIR ROSAMOND; OR, THE ASHBURTON TREATY.

(Punch in Canada)

The Ashburton Treaty.
An expression of Canadian resentment at the manner and nature of the settlement.

Chapter 12

The Prelude to Confederation

Horizons Old and New

By the middle of the nineteenth century the provinces of British North America were firmly established as distinct communities, which were forging ahead on their own course toward the goal of ultimate nationhood. They had proved their ability to maintain a political existence separate from the United States. They had wrested from Britain the grant of a wide autonomy, which could be developed into complete self-government. The stage was set for an evolution toward full independence in domestic matters and eventually in foreign affairs as well.

The grant of responsible government meant that the initiative in local policy devolved on the provincial ministries. "I have always said to my advisers," wrote Elgin, "'while you continue my advisers you shall enjoy my unrestricted confidence; and *en revanche* you shall be responsible for all acts of government.'" But though the governor ceased to direct policy—from the time of Elgin he no longer attended cabinet meetings except on special occasions—he retained both influence and authority. He was still guided by his instructions from the Colonial Office and could press his own views as well as those of the home government on the ministry. He could reject bills or reserve them for the approval of the imperial authorities, and the British government could disallow colonial legislation. British laws that applied to the whole empire took precedence over local measures. Foreign affairs were still wholly under British control, and defense was largely an imperial concern. In practice, however, imperial interference in matters of local concern grew steadily rarer. The lack of a clear dividing line between imperial and provincial topics resulted in a wide flexibility, which allowed the colonies to extend their activities into ever-broadening fields.

A striking illustration of this process was the establishment of fiscal autonomy. In theory the British government retained control of imperial trade policy. In practice this was greatly modified by the Act of 1846, which allowed the colonies to repeal any duties that discriminated against foreign countries. The intention was to leave the colonies free to follow the mother country in abolishing tariff barriers. But circumstances in Canada led to its application in a very different fashion. Chronic financial difficulties made the customs duties important as means of increasing the provincial revenue. Newborn infant industries made their presence known immediately by lusty cries for protection. These factors combined to bring a succession of tariff increases, which were applied against British as well as against foreign goods. The general duties on manufactures were raised from 10 percent in 1847 to 12½ percent in 1849 and to 15 percent in 1856. New financial difficulties following the depression of 1857 and vigorous pressure by Canadian manufacturers, organized through the Association for the Promotion of Canadian Industry which had been set up in 1858, secured in the budget of that year a tariff of 20 percent on many manufactures and a general level of 15 percent. This neither solved the revenue problem nor satisfied the demands for protection, and in 1859 a further increase to 25 percent on selected items and 20 percent on other imports established a clearly protectionist basis.

British industrialists, already irritated by Canadian policy, protested angrily to the Colonial Office against a measure that they stigmatized as indecent and a reproach, directly contrary to the settled policy of the home government, and destructive of British manufacturing interests. The reply of the Canadian finance minister, A. T. Galt, when these protests were communicated to him, was vigorous and decisive. "Self-government would be utterly annihilated," he wrote, "if the views of the imperial government were to be preferred to those of the people of Canada. It is, therefore, the duty of the present government distinctly to affirm the right of the Canadian legislature to adjust the taxation of the people in the way they deem best—even if it should unfortunately happen to meet the disapproval of the imperial ministry." It was a successful assertion of Canada's independence in the economic as well as the political sphere.

In almost all the provinces a new stage of development seemed to have begun. Newfoundland lagged behind the others in its economic and political advance, but in the remaining colonies the solid foundations had been laid for the construction of prosperous and stable communities. During the forties—the "hungry forties" in Britain—the tide of immigration continued to flow to the St. Lawrence. The numbers, which averaged 25,000 a year during the early part of the decade, were swollen when famine in Ireland sent new waves of destitute and plague-stricken refugees to the New World. In 1847, arrivals at Quebec numbered 90,000; and though there was a slackening during the next few years, the figures showed 41,000 immigrants in 1851 and 53,000 in 1854. Population in Upper Canada—now officially known as Canada West—leaped from 455,000 in 1841 to 952,000 in 1851, outnumbering for the first time the neighboring section of Canada East, which grew in the same period from 697,000 to 890,000. In 1861 the two sections held 1,396,000 and 1,111,000 respectively. Growth in the Maritimes was slower, but by 1861 Nova Scotia had a population of 330,000, New Brunswick 252,000, and Prince Edward Island 80,000.

Although there was still pioneering to be done in all the provinces, as communities they were passing out of the pioneer stage. Settlement was spreading into the remaining arable lands of Canada East and filling in the skeleton outline that had already been marked out in Canada West. In the latter section the clearing of the land was followed by the expansion of wheat as the staple crop, stimulated by high prices and a rising export demand. Towns grew in population as the land filled up, and local industries, chiefly devoted to consumer goods and agricultural machinery, arose to take advantage of the growing markets. The building of canals and railways created a demand for construction materials and brought the beginning of an iron industry. Efforts to develop the copper and silver deposits north of Lake Superior, ineffective during this period, represented the first tentative stabs into the Laurentian Shield. By mid-century there was evidence of the beginning of more diversified activities than had marked the economy of the earlier formative stage.

In the Maritimes this period was to be viewed in retrospect as a golden age. A balance had been struck between lumbering and fishing and shipping, which admirably suited the position and resources of the eastern provinces. Agriculture, the basic activity on Prince Edward Island, increased in both New Brunswick and Nova Scotia to meet the demand of the staple industries. The trade in square timber was on the decline, as it was in Canada, but sawn lumber was in increasing demand for export, and in both Nova Scotia and New Brunswick lumbering was linked with the active shipbuilding that marked the last great days of sail. Shipbuilding was integrated with the expansion of the fisheries, especially the cod fishery, which took place during the period of the Reciprocity Treaty. Clipper ships built in Nova Scotia competed in the world carrying trade, and Bluenose vessels were employed in an active commerce with Britain and the United States and the West Indies.

In all the provinces, trade was still the keystone of prosperity. Their fortunes depended on the export of a few staple products, and particularly on exports to Britain and the United States. Britain's abandonment of colonial preference, while it forced Canadian producers to compete with Baltic timber and American wheat, did not by any means result in their loss of the British market. Half the trade of Canada and over two-thirds that of the Maritimes was with the mother country. The United States offered a growing market to which access was facilitated by the Reciprocity Treaty. The rise of Canada's total exports from $13,000,000 in 1851 to over $36,000,000 a decade later testified to the continued expansion of her economy and her success in adjusting to new trade conditions.

Yet this bright picture had its shadows as well. Dependence on external trade left the provinces vulnerable to sudden alterations in world conditions. There were disturbing fluctuations in trade from year to year. Recovery after the slump at the end of the forties reached new heights of prosperity with the coincidence of railway construction, the Reciprocity Treaty, and the demand for supplies created by the Crimean War. The end of the war and the panic of 1857 brought an abrupt decline, which was succeeded by a new period of activity during the American Civil War. That conflict not only created a demand for Canadian products, but also presented new opportunities to Maritime shipowners. A decline in American shipping gave them an increased share in the carrying trade, and blockade running became a lucrative if hazardous occupation. With the end of the war and the denunciation of the Reciprocity Treaty a new situation developed and new uncertainties again clouded the future.

There were other and equally basic factors that raised serious questions about the future prospects of the provinces. The age of steam heralded the doom of the wooden sailing ships and the end of the balanced economy of the Maritimes. In all the provinces the limits on the further expansion of settlement were approaching with the exhaustion of available land. It was significant that in 1861, in all the areas except Canada West, approximately nine-tenths of the population was native-born. The brief period of immigration into the Maritimes had come to an end. Canada East held few inducements to settlers. The bulk of the land seekers had flooded into the Ontario peninsula, and by 1861 that fertile region had largely been occupied and the fringe of settlement had reached the edge of the Laurentian Shield.

Some margin for expansion still remained. Agriculture slowly expanded in the Maritimes as new lands were cleared of timber. The French of Canada East spread into northern New Brunswick, and provision for the creation of parishes outside the existing seigniories was followed by a steady French infiltration into the Eastern Townships. Pioneers opened new districts

Settlement in Central Canada, 1791-1851

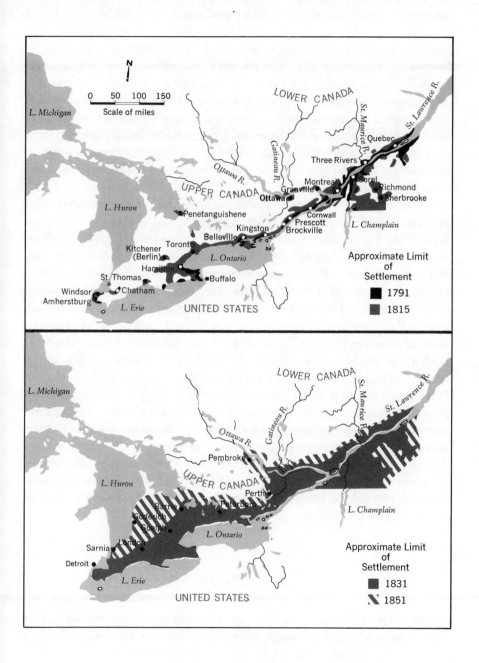

north of the St. Lawrence and the Ottawa. The government undertook the construction of colonization roads in both districts of Canada in an attempt to open up new areas: and vacant lands held by speculators or land companies were available for purchase. But while opportunities for settlement were available, they were no longer adequate to the type of large-scale migration that characterized the advance of the agrarian frontier. The individual settler had to seek out a location in remote and isolated areas where communications were lacking and the prospects of establishing a substantial settled community were often remote. As early as 1856 the Commissioner of Crown Lands admitted that, while various areas still held opportunities for settlers, "the government has now no more land to offer to settlers in the part of the province considered the most favorable for settlement."

By the 1860's, what was needed was a new Canadian frontier. The best lands in the region of the St. Lawrence and the Great Lakes had been taken up. Between that region and the prairies of the Canadian west lay a vast wilderness that was largely unsuitable for cultivation, through which no adequate communications existed. The prairie region of the American Middle West was closer and more accessible, and a regular system of land sales offered farms at reasonable cost and on easy terms. The immigrant into Canada, confronted with a choice between clearing a farm in a remote region or paying a high price for more desirable land, often preferred to continue his journey to Illinois or Wisconsin. Many native-born Canadians showed the same preference. The agrarian frontier, continental in its influence, was drawing off a steady flow of pioneers from the British provinces to the United States; and the flow would increase unless new opportunities were opened north of the border. Not only the land-hungry settlers, but the commercial and transportation groups whose interests were linked with a continued expansion, viewed the situation with increasing concern and embarked on a search for new horizons beyond the bounds that for the moment threatened to constrict the growth of the Canadian community.

The Railway Age

In the effort to expand the Canadian economy, transportation held a central and a vital place. Despite the reorientation of Canada's commercial life that was forced upon her by the revolution in British trade policy, the merchants of the St. Lawrence had not abandoned their wider ambitions. They still sought for commercial prosperity, not merely in the development of Canada's own resources, but in the capture of the transit trade between Europe and the interior of North America. Deprived of the special advantages in the British markets on which they had formerly based so much of their hopes, they fell back on the idea of the natural superiority of the St. Lawrence route. Forced by the loss of privilege to rely on free competition, they still believed that the St. Lawrence could be developed into a more efficient artery of trade than any of its American rivals.

This, however, was a highly expensive undertaking. The construction of canals, and still more the building of railways, called for funds far more substantial than could be provided by Canadian private enterprise. A relatively new land, with a population that was chiefly agricultural and not far removed from the pioneer stage, lacked the accumulated capital that such ventures demanded. English capital helped to finance many of the new developments, either through direct investments or indirectly through the purchase of government bonds. But help from the Canadian government was indispensable to provide the guaranties that would tempt English investors and the additional funds that still had to be raised; and even the imperial government was called on, though with little avail, when local aspirations broadened into a general scheme for an intercolonial system of railways.

Railways indeed were the nodal factor in bringing about a new and closer integration, not only between the leading Canadian commercial and financial groups, but between government and private business. Interlocking interests drew together the Hudson's Bay Company, the Bank of Montreal, the chief insurance companies, and the leading railway and construction interests. Leading government officials held stock and office in railways and other enterprises, and some of the principal promoters held high posts in the government. John Ross, the solicitor general, became president of the Grand Trunk Railway. George Etienne Cartier, leader of the French majority, was its salaried solicitor. Sir Francis Hincks, while prime minister, became deeply involved in the Grand Trunk and connected ventures—so deeply, and with such an eye to his personal advantage, that his activities were the subject of official investigation and led to his temporary retirement from Canadian public life.

An outstanding example of this merging of public and private interests was Alexander Tilloch Galt. His father John Galt, though more widely known to fame as a novelist of Scottish life, had been superintendent of the

Canada Company and a moving figure in the British American Land Company. Alexander Galt entered the latter concern in 1835 and rapidly rose to a leading position. His activities brought him into close contact with the chief business interests in Montreal. He entered politics in 1849 for the specific purpose of forwarding his business interests. He became a leading railway promoter and contractor, and in 1858 he was appointed finance minister of Canada. Throughout the remainder of his life he occupied an outstanding place in both business and politics.

One gets the impression that Galt never felt much enthusiasm about the political side of his activities. In contrast to such a man as Hincks, who was equally at home in the cabinet or a board of directors (and there were occasions on which the two were almost indistinguishable) Galt looked on politics as a necessary but somewhat distasteful aspect of his business career. His political convictions were largely dictated by his desire for wider economic opportunities. In 1849 he supported the Annexation Manifesto. A decade later he emerged as an early and vigorous advocate of the federation of the provinces. In the period after confederation he pressed strongly for the attainment by Canada of full national status, and as first high commissioner to Britain he sought to establish the right of Canada to negotiate her own trade agreements with foreign nations. Such policies, touching the most vital questions of Canada's national destiny, were significant of the viewpoint of Canadian big business. The leaders of the Canadian economy could afford no narrow outlook. They were driven by their own interests to look beyond the bounds of the individual colony and to seek the ever-widening horizons necessary for Canadian expansion and prosperity.

The union of the two Canadas in 1841 had made it possible to throw the full resources of the province behind the first great transportation project—the improvement of the navigation of the St. Lawrence. The Welland Canal was enlarged and improved. The Lachine and Beauharnois canals were constructed. Other canals were built to circumvent the intervening rapids. The Rideau Canal, built by the British government as a military project, provided a subsidiary route linking the Ottawa and the St. Lawrence, and work was begun on another subsidiary, the Trent system, between Lake Ontario and Georgian Bay. The channel through Lake St. Pierre was deepened to allow larger seagoing craft to come up to Montreal. By mid-century a waterway nine feet deep had been completed at a cost of $20,000,000, most of it from public funds.

The hope that this system would draw an increasing volume of trade from the Erie-Hudson route was only partly realized. While the volume of traffic increased, nearly nine tenths of the trade of the American West by way of the lakes continued to flow through New York. The advantages that the waterway itself gave to Montreal over New York were more than offset by other factors. Ocean freight and insurance were lower from the latter port. The difficulty of navigating the lower St. Lawrence added to the risks and the costs. New York was a more efficient distribution center for imports as well as for exports. Not least important, it possessed an ice-free port, whereas Montreal was closed to water transport for half the year. To overcome its limitations, Montreal needed a year-round outlet to the seaboard, and the solution lay in the building of railways.

The first railway in Canada was the St. Lawrence and Lake Champlain —a 16-mile road built in 1836 between La Prairie and St. Johns to circumvent the rapids of the Richelieu. Its first cars were horse-drawn until acquired a locomotive in 1837. Characteristically, this was a portage road; and when a sudden rash of railway schemes broke out during the next decade, they too were dominated by the idea of providing fast through transit between important centers rather than of serving the region through which they ran. A line from Toronto to Collingwood which would link Lake Ontario with Georgian Bay, a line from Buffalo on Lake Erie to Goderich on Lake Huron, the Great Western Railway between Buffalo and Detroit— all these were in essence glorified portage routes cutting across the Ontario peninsula, with the aim of capturing the through traffic from the American West to the main ports and transport centers of the East.

Few of the promoters were greatly concerned about the fortunes of Montreal. They were quite ready to direct their traffic toward the Erie or the railways of the eastern states if they offered more desirable outlets that would encourage traffic over the Canadian lines. The bonding privilege extended to Canadian exports that crossed American territory facilitated such an orientation. The very success of such ventures would be a fresh blow to Montreal unless that port could draw their traffic down the St. Lawrence. The need for a connection with the coast grew in urgency; and at the same time it presented an opportunity to American ports that were ambitious to rival New York. Both Boston and Portland became interested in tapping the trade of the St. Lawrence. The advantage of Portland was not only that it was closer, as its energetic promoter, John A. Poor, demonstrated by racing two sets of teams from Boston and Portland to Montreal; it also offered better prospects of providing railway facilities to the Eastern Townships, which were in serious need of better transportation outlets, and whose claims were strongly pressed by A. T. Galt. In 1845 an arrangement was concluded. A Montreal group, in which Galt was prominent, organized the St. Lawrence and Atlantic Railway Company to build a line to the border, there to meet the Atlantic and St. Lawrence that was to be built by American promoters from Portland. When these roads were opened to through traffic in 1851, they formed the first international railway in the world.

By this time a vigorous and ambitious campaign for railway facilities was also under way in the Maritimes. Hitherto the trade between those provinces and Canada had been meager, and arrangements for intercolonial reciprocity in 1850 brought little increase. While there was some hope that improved transport might result in a greater exchange of products, the prospect of access to each other's markets carried far less weight with the provinces than the desire to capture the import and export trade of the continent. Like the St. Lawrence merchants, the commercial groups in the Maritimes now had visions of attaining a central position in the trade between Europe and North America. Halifax and St. John, closer to Britain than were the American ports on the Atlantic, saw a chance to rival New York and Boston by linking up with the St. Lawrence route and gaining access to the interior of the continent. It was a dream that ignored the greater cost of rail over ocean transport and the fact that the American ports had great markets served by widely ramified transport routes in their immediate hinterland, but it was pursued nonetheless ardently for being based on misconceptions.

As early as 1836 there was a scheme for linking the Bay of Fundy with the St. Lawrence by a railway from St. Andrews to Quebec. This was killed when the Webster-Ashburton treaty left Maine astride the most direct route. By the end of the forties, however, a new project was on foot for an intercolonial railway from Halifax to Quebec; and simultaneously the ambitions of Portland linked with those of the Maritimes and gave birth to the proposal for a railway with the grandiose title of the European and North American, whose route would connect Portland with St. John and Halifax and provide an outlet also on the Gulf of St. Lawrence.

These schemes were far too costly for local resources to carry through alone. Not only must the provinces cooperate to the fullest possible extent; they must also find outside aid, and the most promising source seemed to be the imperial government. The first appeals met with rebuffs, but in 1851 the British cabinet relented and agreed to supplement the joint efforts of the provinces by providing a loan of £7,000,000.

The hopes raised by this success were soon dashed. The commercial aspect of the project, which was the dominant concern of the provinces, was of little interest or advantage to Britain. The appeal to the imperial government had to be on the strategic ground that the railway would provide a military route from Halifax to Quebec. But a military route by way of the St. John Valley lay too close to the border of the United States for safety. The preferred route was one which was surveyed by Major Beverly Robinson in 1848 and which ran through the eastern part of New Brunswick to the Bay Chaleur. The adoption of this route was a condition of the proffered imperial loan. But that threatened to leave St. John out in the cold and made it all the more necessary to couple the Intercolonial with the construction of the European and North American to satisfy New Brunswick. It was initially understood that the loan could be applied to both railways. But the British government shattered this illusion in 1852 by insisting that the funds were for the Intercolonial alone. This attitude wrecked both projects. The Colonial Office refused to accept a change of route through the St. John Valley. Canada withdrew from participation in the Intercolonial. The Maritimes fell back on the construction of such local lines as they could finance from their own resources, and Canada turned to the creation of the Grand Trunk Railway.

The Grand Trunk was the direct outcome of the failure of the Intercolonial. Even while negotiations on the latter project were under way, English contractors—the firm of Peto, Brassey, Betts, and Jackson—had indicated a strong interest in Canadian railways. Sir Francis Hincks was even accused of contributing to the breakdown of the negotiations because of the connection he had formed with this group. When the Intercolonial scheme collapsed, Canada embarked with new energy on the effort to create a trunk railway system paralleling and supplementing the St. Lawrence with the aid of English contractors and investors.

In the last resort, however, the success of this venture depended on the generosity of the Canadian government. Already the principle of public assistance to private construction had been fully established. An act passed in 1849 promised a guaranty of 6 percent on half the cost of construction of any line over 75 miles in length. In 1851 this was restricted to trunk lines; but in the following year further sources of funds were opened up by legislation, which created the Consolidated Municipal Fund and made it easier for the municipalities to raise loans for the assistance of railways. The initial agreement on the Grand Trunk provided that half the construction of the section between Montreal and Hamilton should be financed by bonds guaranteed by the province, while another one-tenth was to be raised from Canadian municipalities or individuals. This of course was only one part, though a vital one, of the whole project. New construction was to be supplemented by the acquisition and amalgamation of existing lines in a single system linking the Detroit area with ocean outlets on the St. Lawrence and the Atlantic, and eventually joining up with the projected railway system of the Maritimes.

The deal roused vigorous protests from certain interests in Canada. Galt and his associates were particularly affronted. They had already built the line from Montreal to Portland and had secured a charter for a road from Montreal to Kingston. There were plans afoot for the stretch from Kingston to Toronto, and still farther west Galt and his partners, organized as Gzowski and Company, secured the contract for a line from Toronto to Guelph. The idea that preference should be given to "strangers and foreigners" brought an indignant outburst. While the Galt group acknowledged the need for English capital, they insisted that they could arrange the financing under the terms outlined by the government and that control of the venture should be in Canadian hands. "We can construct a railroad in less time," they asserted, "for about one-half the declared capital, and with a smaller amount of aid than the parties applying for the charter in question." To reinforce their arguments they secured subscriptions, at least on paper, for the full capital issue of the Montreal-Kingston line. With this stroke added to their control of the St. Lawrence and Atlantic, the Galt group was in a strong position and had to be brought into the wider project. An amalgamation was arranged that involved taking over at par the greatly depreciated stock of the St. Lawrence and Atlantic. When the Great Western held out for unacceptable terms, the Galt-Gzowski group was given the contract to extend its Toronto-Guelph line to Sarnia as the western section of the Grand Trunk; the guaranty was changed from half the cost of construction to £3,000 a mile, and provision was made for a bridge across the St. Lawrence at Montreal and for the extension of the railway down the St. Lawrence to the New Brunswick border.

The Brassey-Jackson group dazzled Canadians with prospects of unlimited English capital at their command and investors with predictions of dividends of $11\frac{1}{2}$ percent. Both promises were delusive. Considerable English capital was raised, but in the end the bulk of the cost fell on the Canadian taxpayer. In spite of Canadian participation in the financing and on the board of directors, the real management remained in London, and English ignorance of Canadian conditions was all too evident in both the construction and the operation of the road. The *Times* even stated that the railway was intended to connect Hudson Bay with the St. Lawrence and that its rails would be laid on tree stumps cut off 18 inches from the ground. The English contractors knew better than that; but

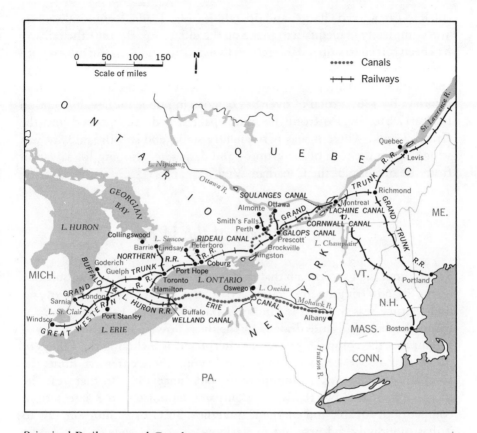

Principal Railways and Canals, 1866

their faulty estimates of costs and the inefficiency of their work created a burden of operating expenses that dogged the railway from the start. The contractors went bankrupt before the road was finished, and by 1855 the Grand Trunk had to appeal for further government aid. A sum of £900,000 was advanced in return for a lien on the whole system; then in the following year the railway was allowed to issue $2,000,000 in debentures with priority over the provincial lien. With this aid the Grand Trunk was enabled in 1856 to begin operation of the longest railway system in the world—a continuous stretch of 1100 miles, which was later extended westward to reach Chicago.

This was only the beginning of difficulties. The railway was initially intended to supplement the canals in a second great bid for the commerce of the West. Instead it competed with them, to the disadvantage of both. The volume of trade diverted from competing American lines was too small to carry fixed charges and operating costs. Traffic from local sources was completely inadequate to make up the difference. By 1861 the railway had been forced to suspend interest on its securities and was confronted with a deficit of $13,000,000. Once more the government stepped in to reorganize and bolster the finances on a basis that reduced its own claims to ninth in priority. By 1867 a total of over $25,000,000 in public money, in addition to nearly $10,000,000 from the municipalites, had been poured into the Grand Trunk, where it was permanently sunk; and still the railway was struggling in the toils of bankruptcy and desperately hoping for salvation from the opening of the Canadian West.

The Problem of the West

Throughout the vast domain that stretched from the shores of Hudson Bay to the islands fringing the Pacific coast, the sole effective authority at mid-century was that of the Hudson's Bay Company. Its charter gave it full ownership of all lands drained by the rivers flowing into Hudson Bay— a grant that the company resolutely interpreted as including the valleys of the Red and Saskatchewan rivers; and beyond those extensive limits the company had enjoyed a monopoly of trade since 1821. In that year the merger with the North West Company eliminated the last serious competition. An able and energetic governor, Sir George Simpson, saw to it that monopoly did not lead to slackness or complacency. By periodic personal visits he kept in touch with the actual operations of the trade, the ramifications of which spread through the wilderness of half a continent, bringing the zeal of an efficiency expert to bear on such questions as the import of European luxuries to provision the posts or the use of fewer men to transport bigger loads and giving short shrift to any interlopers who ventured into the company's domains.

Into that region the company's servants carried law and authority. Whatever jurisdiction Canada might be inclined to claim in theory over the Northwest, practically it exercised none. The barrier of the wilderness and the lack of adequate communications imposed obstacles that cut off Canada politically as well as geographically from that remote area. Yet in contrast to the conditions that accompanied the advance of the frontier in the United States, the rule of the Hudson's Bay Company meant that the advance of the law preceded that of settlement. In the critical situation that was soon to arise, it may be that this factor was just enough to sway the balance and to save the West for Canada. But the margin was slender; and insofar as the company's monopoly delayed the extension of Canadian settlement to the prairies and the Pacific coast, it brought into jeopardy the retention of that vital domain.

The danger arose from the steady westward advance of American settlement. Iowa was admitted as a state in 1846. Minnesota achieved territorial status in 1849. The settlement of the Oregon dispute was followed by the organization of that region into a territory in 1850. The tide of settlement was sweeping around the western extremity of the Great Lakes and flowing into the fertile regions of the Pacific coast. The westward extension of railways foreshadowed the rapid filling up of the remaining prairie lands. A mere political boundary was a fragile barrier against the pressure of the agrarian frontier. It had not prevented the flow of American settlers into Canada after 1783 or of Canadians into the United States after the depression of 1837 to the number of a quarter of a million by 1860. Experience had long since proved that in any conflict between fur trade and settlement, the fur trade was doomed. Vacant agricultural land would inexorably be overrun by the pioneers; and if Canada was to prevent American settlement from leading to American annexation of the West, she must take effective steps to occupy the West herself.

In 1850 settlement on the prairies was confined to the small community that had grown from the Selkirk colony on the Red River. Its population had risen to over 5000, mostly clustered in the vicinity of Fort Garry on the site of the present city of Winnipeg. The handful of original Scottish settlers had been augmented by retired servants of the Hudson's Bay Company, the overwhelming proportion of whom were half-breeds of Scottish or French origin. It was not a Canadian population in any real sense of the word. The merger of the fur companies broke the economic connection between Canada and the West. There were neither ties of sentiment nor community of interest to link the Red River settlers with the eastern provinces. The English-speaking settlers were pioneers devoted to their farms. The French half-breeds, who formed the largest group, combined a more casual agriculture with the roving life of the plains, in which the buffalo hunt played a leading part. All felt themselves to be Westerners with distinct interests and a distinct character that made them almost a tiny nation in themselves.

In 1834 the Selkirk heirs abandoned their interest in the settlement and sold the region back to the Hudson's Bay Company, which organized it as the District of Assiniboia under a governor and appointed council. The company showed little interest in the settlement and exhibited a positive hostility toward any fresh influx. The colony might be useful as a source of food supply, but there was always the danger that it might become a center of unauthorized fur trade. With only the company offering any market for their produce, and with little opportunity for economic advancement, the colonists were in fact tempted to embark on private fur trading, particularly when the American advance into Minnesota opened up new opportunities for an illegal traffic. One of the chief causes of friction between the settlers and the company was the persistent effort by the latter to exclude the inhabitants from the fur trade, and the threat of disturbances over this issue became so great that in 1849 the prohibition was tacitly relaxed in the interests of tranquillity.

The settlers themselves showed no great desire for immigration and still less for absorption in Canada. If their political status was to be changed, they aspired to become a separate Crown colony. Apprehension over the security of their holdings—to which few of the settlers had anything like precise and valid titles—was accentuated in the case of the French by a dislike of any incursion into their hunting grounds. Already they looked on the prairies as their own domain, from which strangers should be excluded. In addition, the French clergy feared the effect of an English-speaking influx on the devotion and docility of their flock, and like their brethren in French Canada they upheld a policy of exclusion and separatism in an attempt to maintain the solidarity of a French Catholic community.

By the 1850s a handful of Canadians, the advance guard of the later migration, had found their way to the Red River. Their character and activities did nothing to increase respect or affection for Canada among the settlers. One of them, Dr. John Christian Schultz, became a storekeeper whose combination of price profiteering and political intrigue soon made him a highly unpopular figure. The poet Charles Mair, whose patriotic doggerel gave lively expression to the newly awakened Canadian national impulses, expressed himself in such tactless terms concerning the country and its population, including the feminine element, that the colony became almost too hot to hold him. Two journalists founded a paper, the *Nor'wester,* which trumpeted the Canadian version of "manifest destiny" with little regard for the susceptibilities of the existing settlers. Around these men there gathered a small and noisy "Canadian party," which stirred up an agitation against the Hudson's Bay Company and defied the authority of its officials; and the resulting unrest, together with the increasing apprehension of the half-breeds at the brutally grasping ambitions of the newcomers, resulted in a growing tension that threatened to erupt in violence.

The activities of the Canadian party were spurred by the growing threat of American absorption. Settlers were filtering across the border, and a small "American party" developed, which began to advocate annexation to the United States. Their sentiments found considerable support in Minnesota, whose legislature celebrated the attainment of statehood in 1858 by passing a resolution in favor of the annexation of the Red River district, and attracted the sympathy of the expansionist elements in the northern states. The advance of communications drew the settlement closer to its neighbors south of the border. The building of a wagon road to St. Paul was followed by the inauguration of steamship service on the Red River in 1859. Railways were pushing westward, and the Hudson's Bay Company itself was finding that its most convenient route for mail and supplies lay through the United States. The Canadian party in 1857 appealed to Canada for action to check this southward trend. "It would seem," their petition asserted, "that we have no other choice than the Canadian plow and printing press, or the American rifle and Fugitive Slave Law."

By this time Canada was exhibiting a steadily rising interest. Agrarian radicalism as embodied in the Clear Grit party was attracted by the prospect of opening up new lands for settlement and immigration. Such a development would serve not only to check the growing drift of Canadians to the United States, but also to provide for the increase in population, which was at present hampered by the exhaustion of land in Canada itself. On the political side there was the added consideration that a fresh wave of British immigration would swing the balance decisively against the French. George Brown in the *Globe* and William McDougall in the *North American* launched their campaigns for the annexation of the West, which gradually attracted a wide popular support. Manufacturers who sought a wider domestic market, railway interests envisaging a line across the continent, financial and commercial groups desirous of wider opportunities, all added their influence. By 1857 the Canadian government had taken up the matter in earnest, spurred on by the growing danger that the United States might secure the area by default.

The grant of a trade monopoly to the Hudson's Bay Company was due to expire in 1859. In anticipation of this, and in view of changing circumstances and prospects, the British government in 1857 appointed a select committee to survey the whole question of the company's position in the West. Canada was thus given an opportunity to state her case, and a delegation was sent to London to present the claims of the province to the possession of the West.

The first tendency in Canada was to attack the validity of the company's charter, on the ground that Charles II had no right to grant territory that had already been claimed and explored by the French. There was, however, a reluctance to take the initiative in submitting this question to a formal legal decision and in general a desire to throw on the British government the responsibility for extinguishing the title of the company and establishing that of Canada. Britain was unwilling at this stage either to invalidate a charter that had stood for nearly two centuries or to undertake the expense of buying out the company. The company on its part asserted that the prairies were quite unsuitable for settlement and fought to maintain its exclusive control. In the end it failed to get a renewal of the legal monopoly of trade beyond its own domain; but its proprietory claims remained in force, and for practical purposes its monopoly was in no danger so long as physical difficulties prevented the assumption by Canada of effective jurisdiction over the remaining western lands. Until these obstacles were overcome, the company was to retain its authority. The development of communications between the two regions seemed an urgent need if Canadian authority was to forestall American absorption.

Beyond the Rockies a comparable situation had developed on the Pacific coast. The Oregon settlement established a dividing line, which left the Hudson's Bay Company in control of what remained to Britain. The British government was aware of how precarious this retention might be if American settlers pushed north of the boundary; and in an attempt to forestall this it created Vancouver Island as a Crown colony in 1849 and sought to establish a settlement there. But Britain was unwilling to bear the expense of such an enterprise; no natural influx could be expected from a region so remote as Canada; and the British government fell back on the hope that the company itself would act as the agent of settlement. The approach was natural but quite anomalous. The company had no incentive to divert its profits to an activity that was at variance with its interest in the fur trade. Although it was granted the island in 1849 on condition that it should undertake the work of settlement, it exhibited little enthusiasm for this costly task, and its combination of high prices for land and low wages for laborers discouraged any extensive growth of population.

The first influx into the region came from the United States. It came not to Vancouver Island but to the mainland, and the incentive was not land but gold. The discovery of gold on the Fraser River in 1856, just when the boom was subsiding in California, brought a rush to the new area. The little port of Victoria, the chief supply center and transit point, suddenly became a frontier boom town, and the rush of population into the new region revived the same danger that had led to the loss of Oregon.

It was averted largely through the prompt action of James Douglas, governor of Vancouver Island and chief factor of the Hudson's Bay Company. He combined the dual capacity of representative of the British Crown and servant of the company, and he was determined to protect the interests of both his masters. But his authority as governor extended only over Vancouver Island. The only authority on the mainland was the somewhat vague control that the company might claim in virtue of its trade monopoly. Faced with an emergency, Douglas brushed aside such legal limitations. He was determined to avert any occasion for self-constituted government by the settlers such as had paved the way for the American annexation of Oregon. He was also determined to preserve the company's trade monopoly. He proclaimed the extension of his jurisdiction over the mainland and imposed a licensing system with high fees on the ships and the miners who went there. The latter restrictions met with the disapproval of the home government; but the policy of Douglas in assuming extended though unauthorized authority was commended, and the position was regularized by the creation of the Crown colony of British Columbia in 1858 under Douglas as governor. A regularly constituted authority had thus been set up. Courts were instituted, and police functions were partly fulfilled by a body of Royal Engineers whose construction of a road to the Cariboo gold fields was a major step in facilitating the settlement of the interior. The danger of a political void was thus averted; but even on the coast, and still more on the prairies, the possibility of a gravitation toward the United States remained alarming and was increased by the new tension that developed as a result of the American Civil War.

The American Civil War

The position that Canada occupied between Britain and the United States involved a triangular relationship, which complicated matters for all the parties concerned. Periodic friction between the United States and Canada drew Britain into the controversy and impeded her efforts to establish harmonious relations with the United States. Occasional threats of serious trouble between the United States and Britain made Canada apprehensive for her own safety. Any grievance that the United States felt against Britain was reflected in an unfriendly attitude toward Canada, and any resentment at Canadian policy was readily translated into fresh bitterness against Britain.

The interplay of these factors was particularly evident during the Civil War. The United States, involved in a desperate struggle to preserve national unity, was acutely apprehensive of foreign intervention on behalf of the Confederacy. With the issue in doubt during the early years of the struggle, the North was ready to view with nervous suspicion every action or expression of sentiment that could be looked on as unfavorable to its cause. Both Britain and Canada came in for a good share of the resulting accusations and recriminations, and the outcome was a sharpening of anti-British feeling and a strengthening of sentiment in favor of the annexation of Canada.

It was Britain that gave the earliest and most serious grounds of offense. However correct the attitude of the government may have been, leading men such as Palmerston and Gladstone made little effort to conceal their sympathy for the South; and the North suspected, not without some reason, that this feeling might find expression in active aid to the Confederacy if occasion favored. Britain's recognition of the southern states as belligerents, though it was a normal consequence of the North's declaration of a blockade, was looked on by the North as deliberately unfriendly. There were fears that it would be followed by a recognition of the Confederate government, which France was urging and which Britain was actually contemplating by 1862. Ships built in British ports for the South were armed at sea and turned into commerce raiders, and there were heated accusations that Britain was fully aware of this purpose from the start. Tension reached its height in 1861 when an American warship halted the British steamer *Trent* on the high seas and forcibly removed two Confederate agents who were on their way to England to press for more active aid. There was an outburst of enthusiasm in the United States at this challenge to Britain's maritime rights, and a wave of indignation in Britain at American disregard for the freedom of the seas. The sharpness of the British demand for redress threatened to precipitate war between the two countries. Lincoln returned a moderate and satisfactory answer, which, together with the release of the Confederate envoys, eased the situation; but memories rankled on both sides, and the two nations continued to eye each other with a wary vigilance in an atmosphere of barely suspended hostility.

The sense of outrage on the part of the United States was directed against Canada as well as Britain. However unoffending Canada herself might be, the very fact that she was a British possession was sufficient to attract American dislike. In their strained and excited state of mind, many groups in the North saw no reason to distinguish between the colony and the mother country. The former was looked on as sharing the sins of the latter; and, in addition, any sign of misconduct on the part of Canadians was seized on and magnified into an example of deep and sinister designs against the North.

In actual fact, Canadian opinions and interests were predominantly on the side of the North in the conflict. There was a similarity of social structure on both sides of the border that led to a considerable similarity of outlook. A pioneer nation composed largely of independent farmers had little reason to sympathize with slavery. Agrarian radicalism and humanitarian sentiment alike dictated an attitude of condemnation. Canada was the terminus of the underground railway, where the escaped slave might at last find security against the operation of the Fugitive Slave Law—a measure that added to the dislike with which the average Canadian viewed the operation and results of American Negro slavery. The economic ties that had been strengthened by the Reciprocity Treaty and the personal ties resulting from the continued ebb and flow of population across the border linked the colonies of British North America with the northern states, and some tens of thousands of volunteers from Canada served in the ranks of the northern armies.

There was, however, a strong and articulate element whose attitude was less friendly. Tory opinion still clung to a belief in the malevolence of the United States, and particularly of the North, with its rampant nationalism and its turbulent democracy. Certain economic groups, particularly among the new manufacturing class, looked on the Yankees not as customers but as competitors and were not displeased at the prospect that the strength of the industrial North might be undermined by the loss of the agrarian South. Certain portions of feminine society were overcome by the charm of southern officers recuperating from their wounds as guests of Canadian friends. These sentiments, largely confined to a few urban centers, were nonetheless more evident to a hasty glance than was the attitude of the less articulate farming class; and their reflection in a few newspapers made more impression than the sustained support of the North by such papers as the *Globe*. Sensational or anti-British newspapers in the North were quick to seize on the slightest evidence of sympathy for the South as an excuse to loose their invectives against Canada, and many Canadians, particularly when emotions were heated by the *Trent* affair, grew cool toward the prospect of a Northern victory.

It was not long, indeed, before Canada faced the danger of armed attack. The *Trent* crisis and the threat of war between Britain and the United States once more raised the specter of an invasion of Canada. Britain embarked on preparations for defense and sent some 15,000 reinforcements to Canada. As usual, the unhappy troops arrived too late to sail up the St. Lawrence and had to undertake a winter trek overland through New Brunswick, offering an involuntary demonstration of the strategic value of the proposed intercolonial railway. The liquidation of the *Trent* episode diminished the danger that British policy would involve Canada in war; but it did not entirely disappear, and a new series of episodes roused the possibility that Canada herself might inadvertently provoke an American attack.

The chief danger arose from the activities of Confederate agents on Canadian soil. As the cause of the South declined after Gettysburg, the desire to relieve pressure by attacking the North from the rear naturally grew, and a number of southern emissaries planned to use Canada as a base for such a diversion. It was to some extent a reversal of the situation on the border after the rebellion of 1837, modified by the fact that Mackenzie had raised troops and funds in the United States, whereas the Confederates hoped at most to be allowed to buy supplies in Canada and to be left alone by the Canadian authorities. In actual fact they received less help from Canadians and less toleration from the government than the exiles of 1837 had enjoyed from the United States in their border forays; but the United States on this occasion was involved in a war and was little inclined to accept any excuses that covered activities by its enemies or to be charitable toward Canadian lapses because of its own past sins.

Few of the Confederate schemes found expression in effective action. There were plans to organize groups of incendiaries to burn northern cities, to rescue Confederate prisoners by raids on prison camps near the border, and even to precipitate an uprising in Chicago. None of these efforts came to anything. The most serious incursion was the raid on St. Albans, Vermont, in September 1864. A band of twenty-five men descended on the village, wounded a couple of citizens, set a few fires, looted three local banks, and fled across the border with their booty. The understandable wrath of Americans at this outrage was increased when a Canadian judge, on very dubious technical grounds, ordered the release of the culprits after they had been apprehended. A perturbed Canadian government rearrested the accused and rushed through new legislation to prevent similar offenses in future. But the damage had been done, and press reports represented Canada as a hostile base from which robbers and murderers operated with impunity. The impulse to retaliate was strengthened in the United States and with it the danger of serious trouble along the border.

The more sober Canadian leaders had little real fear that the United States, at the close of the Civil War, would embark on the conquest of Canada. There was some public apprehension over the possibility that the veteran army of the North might be launched against the province; but this was less real than the risk that the United States, without any immediate aggressive designs, might be provoked into a clash by the deliberate activities of unofficial groups intent on stirring up trouble along the border in the hope of precipitating a conflict between Britain and the United States.

The embodiment of this threat was the Fenian Brotherhood. The purpose of this body, which was organized in New York in 1857 by a group of Irish patriots and exiles, was to revive an active revolutionary struggle for Irish independence and to mobilize sympathy and support in the United States. Much of its energy was devoted to preparations for an Irish rising and found expression in the murder of policemen in Ireland and the bombing of prisons in England; but one group conceived the idea of a more direct stroke at British power by an attack on Canada, hoping for support from both Canada and the United States. The strength of anti-British feeling in the North, the vigor of annexationist sentiment, and the competition of political parties for the Irish vote created a favorable atmosphere; and at a time when the United States was hotly indignant over Canada's failure to curb a handful of conspirators, it was looking with complacency and even approval on an agitation whose mass demonstrations and organizing activities were avowedly directed toward an armed invasion of Canada.

It was this attitude on the part of the American authorities that made the movement alarming. The Fenians themselves were more impressive in bluster than in action. Their plans for conquest dwindled to a few ineffective raids across the border. The most serious effort was in June 1866, when a force of some 800-900 crossed the Niagara frontier and captured Fort Erie. On June 2 they beat off an attack by a body of Canadian volunteers, but the approach of a force of regulars discouraged the invaders and brought their retirement to American soil. The American authorities now intervened to prevent a renewed attack by arresting the Fenian leaders and seizing the arms that had been collected. But the organization was not suppressed, and its continued activities involved the danger not merely of a new invasion, but of border incidents that would provoke a serious crisis with the United States. For another five years the Fenians, merely by existing, created a state of uneasiness along the frontier from Maine to Minnesota, until a ludicrous raid into Manitoba in 1871 marked the collapse of the movement.

The apprehension aroused by this situation was all the more serious because of the new problems of defense with which the provinces were confronted just at this time. This was the period during which imperialist sentiment in Britain was virtually at its nadir. The grant of responsible government inaugurated a deliberate policy of devolving on the self-governing colonies a large part of the duties and costs of government, including the burden of defense. The Crimean War gave a practical occasion for the withdrawal of troops and the inauguration of a policy of reducing the colonial garrisons to a minimum. Canada and the Maritimes were thus called on to make new provisions, not merely for external defense, but for the maintenance of internal order. But it was quite clear that their resources were unequal to the raising of a force large enough to repel an attack by the United States. Imperial help must be forthcoming, all the more so because Canada believed that the danger of invasion, if it existed, arose from imperial policy. The Canadian people, the government asserted in 1862, "have relied for protection in some degree upon the fact that under no conceivable circumstances will they provoke war with the United States, and if therefore Canada should become the theatre of war resulting from imperial policy, while it would cheerfully put forth its strength in the defense of its soil, it would nevertheless be obliged to rely for its protection mainly upon imperial resources."

This issue came to a head over the militia bill of 1862. The need for a reorganization of the militia system, emphasized by the *Trent* crisis, led to a proposal for a force of 50,000 to cost $1,000,000 annually. The proposal was rejected, largely on the ground that the burden involved was unwarranted by the existing circumstances and too heavy for the resources of the province. A new and less extensive measure, more acceptable to general opinion, was carried in its place. The episode led to bitter recriminations in England, where Canada's past offenses in such matters as the tariff and her present reluctance to assume a larger share in the cost of defense were cited as proofs of how valueless and burdensome to Britain was her continued connection with the colony. The spirited defense by the Canadian ministry of the right of Canadians to decide for themselves what forces they needed and could support represented one more step in Canada's advance toward full autonomy. But it did not solve the inherent problem of the relation between local and imperial defense, nor was it a completely satisfactory solution when the Fenians brought a real danger of trouble along the border. Canada, traditionally the province most exposed to attack, was naturally the most concerned; but New Brunswick was also affected, and the desirability of closer cooperation was emphasized by the problem of defense resulting from the new uneasiness in relations with the United States.

The most concrete expression of American antagonism, however, came not in armed threats but in economic reprisals. Under the Reciprocity Treaty the growth of trade between the two countries had been fully as beneficial to American as to Canadian exporters. But the groups most exposed to competition from Canadian products, particularly the fish and coal and lumber interests, resented the treaty and were eager for its abrogation. There were complaints that the increase in the Canadian tariff on manufactures, while it was within the letter of the treaty, violated its spirit. There was resentment at the Canadian attempt to encourage traffic down the St. Lawrence by a rebate in the Welland Canal tolls in the case of through shipments. Above all, the growing protectionist sentiment in the North was at last freed from southern restraint as a result of the secession of the Confederacy. Steps were immediately taken to establish a protective system, and by 1862 a hostile congressional report on the Reciprocity Treaty showed that opposition to it was gathering strength. In January 1865, a resolution demanded the abrogation of the treaty, and notice was duly given, which brought the expiration of the agreement in 1866.

The economic partition of the continent, which Canada had so long sought to modify, was thus to be hardened and confirmed. Supporting this move were the annexationist forces in the United States, who believed that Canada would find it impossible to maintain economic independence and would be forced to seek political union. In addition to the abrogation of reciprocity, other steps emphasized the difficulties that were in prospect for Canada. War necessities were made the excuse for an embargo on certain American products, such as coal and livestock, which were important in Canada's normal trade, and for the introduction of a passport system, which further hampered intercourse between the two countries. Even more serious was the talk of a canceling of the bonding privileges, which would strike a severe blow at Canadian exporters and at the Grand Trunk, whose outlet lay across American soil. A comprehensive series of difficulties was gathering from external sources; and at the same time Canada was facing an internal situation of increasing gravity, which added to the need for a new and drastic adjustment in both political and economic affairs.

Sectionalism and Deadlock, 1849-1864

In the decade following the grant of responsible government, British North America became the scene of a growing struggle between the forces of unity and sectionalism. The coming of the railways brought a powerful new factor, which tended to draw the provinces closer together. The desirability of union for mutual defense became more apparent. But still outweighing these influences were the geographic and economic factors, which made for a divergent orientation. While the Maritime provinces continued to look eastward, Canada's eyes were turning more than ever toward the West. And within the province of Canada there were still strong sectional tendencies, the result of a continued racial separatism that the union had failed to overcome.

The Durham report and the union that followed had in fact contributed to the consolidation of French nationalism. Durham had stigmatized the French as a people with no history and no literature and had prescribed union as a means of extinguishing their vain nationalist pretensions. The French were roused to a determined effort to disprove his cultural aspersions and to do battle for the survival of a distinctive French Catholic community. In his *Histoire du Canada,* the first volume of which appeared in 1845, François Xavier Garneau set out to bring to life the stirring epic of French Canada. His work inspired a succession of historians and a school of fervent historical and patriotic poetry, which found its emotional inspiration in the events of the past and which celebrated the virtues and achievements of the French Canadian race. Cultural contacts with France were strengthened as an incidental aspect of broadening trade relations, and the renewal of direct ties with the old land was symbolized by the visit of the naval vessel *La Capricieuse* to Quebec in 1855—the first French ship to anchor in the St. Lawrence since the surrender of Canada. French romanticism had an evident effect on such poets as Octave Crémazie and Louis Fréchette, but their themes and their spirit were intensely Canadian. At a time when the handful of writers in English-speaking Canada were still groping toward a distinctive national expression, French Canadian nationalism flowered in a literary and historical movement, the basic purpose of which was to vindicate and strengthen the spirit of racial separatism.

This persistent sectionalism was reflected in the working of the political system. Under the form of a legislative union the province of Canada possessed what was virtually a federalist system of government. Canada East retained its own legal system, its special church privilege, its distinctiveness in such matters as land tenure and education, as well as its own language and culture. These divisions were reflected in the operation of government. There was practically a dual administration symbolized by the joint premiership of the leaders of the two racial groups. Every session saw the passage of legislation that applied exclusively to one section of the province. On matters of common interest it became increasingly desirable that support should be obtained from a majority in both sections. Lafontaine was particularly insistent on the principle of the "double majority"; and while only a few of the leaders in politics were prepared to accept this as a dogma, the practical difficulty of imposing laws on one section by the votes of the other was only too evident. Yet there were still greater difficulties in the way of establishing a ministry that had the support of a majority from both Canada East and Canada West. Their diverging orientation was expressed in different political alignments; and a stable party system, so necessary to the working of responsible government, was made impossible by sectional and racial dissension.

The French reformers who followed Lafontaine had sought constitutional concessions that would give them political power. They had allied with the English reformers against the Tories, who were the racial and religious adversaries of the French and who had clung to political privilege as a weapon against them. But once responsible government had been achieved, the essentially conservative nature of the French outlook became apparent. Their desire was not to embark on a liberal program in social and economic affairs, but to erect political bulwarks that would safeguard their racial and cultural privileges. They had little sympathy with the aspirations of the radicals in Canada West. They needed to retain power; but, if the Tories would accept the new situation created by responsible government and abandon their insistence on Anglicization, the French would find them acceptable allies for the purpose of resisting radical demands. When Augustin Morin, the draftsman of the Ninety-two Resolutions, united in 1854 with Sir Allan McNab, the surviving embodiment of the Family Compact and the scourge of the rebels of 1837, it showed how completely the old alignments had been transformed by the coming of responsible government.

Such an alliance involved an abatement of intransigence on both sides. The Tories had to acquiesce in the survival of that French Catholic community which they had so long sought to extinguish. The French had to abandon their overt opposition to English commercial enterprise and to the use of public funds in the interests of economic progress. The union gave them a chance to combine the defense of French Canada against the cultural encroachments of English capitalism with French participation in the fruits of economic development. French politicians discovered the virtues of sharing in offices and patronage and of gratifying their consituents by a generous distribution of contracts and public works. A group of leaders emerged who shared the new and simple creed of Sir Allan McNab: "Railways are my politics." They combined a championship of French separatist interests with an insistence on a full share in the economic benefits of English capitalism. The powerful influence of the church was enlisted on the side of this dual policy; and pragmatic considerations drew French nationalists and the Catholic heirarchy into a working cooperation with those ancient enemies, the Montreal merchants and the Tories of Canada West.

The approval of this combination by the French clergy was motivated to no small extent by their fear of the new radicalism that had emerged, not only in Canada West, but in the bosom of French Canada itself. By the end of the forties a group of young democrats had taken form as the *Parti rouge*. The *Institut canadien*, founded in Montreal as a literary society, became their chief political center and spread to the leading towns in French Canada. They acquired a newspaper in the *Avenir* and founded several other journals to spread their views. They drew their doctrines partly from American republicanism, but still more from the traditions of French radicalism. The return of Louis Joseph Papineau in 1845 after eight years of exile in Paris and the election of the aging orator to the assembly in 1848 provided a tremendous stimulus. The triumph of the Paris radicals in the revolution of 1848 fired their enthusiasm. Papineau, whose unbalanced and unrepentant extremism made him almost an anachronism in the new political scene, shortly retired from public life; but under the leadership of A. A. Dorion the *Rouges* remained the embodiment of a French Canadian radicalism in revolt against the pragmatic conservatism of the majority bloc.

Their creed revealed a curious conflict between democratic principles and racial prejudices. They adopted the doctrine of popular sovereignty and the republicanism that it implied. They called for universal suffrage, elective officials, popular education, and the abolition of seigniorial tenure. But these progressive aspirations were accompanied by attacks on the British connection and bitter invectives against the Act of Union. Though their outlook became more moderate as time went on, their racial resentment made them at bottom enemies of Canadian unity. Their hatred of England and English Canada, joined to their dogmatic republicanism, led them to a paradoxical advocacy of annexation to the United States. Such a policy ran directly contrary to the deepest instincts of French Canada; and, joined with their political radicalism, it ranged the clergy almost solidly against them. The *Rouges* responded with anticlerical outbursts that made the breach irrevocable. The hierarchy, backed by a Papacy whose antagonism to liberalism was completed by its trials during the revolutions of 1848, undertook a sustained campaign against the party. When the *Institut* refused to purge its library or to exclude liberal journals from its reading room, it brought down upon it a formal clerical condemnation, which drastically reduced its membership. For a generation the *Rouge* group maintained its existence in defiance of the unremitting enmity of the hierarchy, but politically it never succeeded in rallying more than a small minority of the electors in French Canada.

Radicalism thus made only slight inroads into the political solidarity of the French bloc. In contrast, its progress in Canada West showed that political divisions in English Canada were as acute as ever. The unity of the English reformers, which gave their party a majority in 1848, scarcely survived the victory. With the winning of responsible government the party began once more to disintegrate, and its breakup contributed not a little to the continuance of sectional and racial antagonism.

The paramount aim of the Baldwin-Lafontaine ministry was achieved with the winning of responsible government. This success was followed by a number of progressive and constructive measures. A comprehensive system of local government was created for Canada West. Reforms were introduced into the system of primary education established in 1841. The long struggle to transform King's College into the nonsectarian University of Toronto was brought to a successful conclusion in 1849, and Bishop Strachan, erupting with pious fury, countered this surrender to infidelity by founding Trinity College to preserve the pure Anglican faith. The French were gratified by the placing of their language on an official equality with English and by an Act of Amnesty for the rising of 1837. Representation in the Assembly was raised from 84 to 130, though without changing the equality of numbers from each section. Yet important as these measures were, they stopped short of the desires of the more radical reformers. The ministry failed to achieve a final settlement of the clergy reserves or the abolition of seigniorial tenure. Educational reforms still preserved separate schools for Catholics in Upper Canada. Judicial reforms retained the Court of Chancery in Canada West, which the radicals criticized as oppressive and expensive. Attacks on this measure brought Robert Baldwin's retirement in 1851, and Lafontaine, harried by demands for patronage and disgusted with the growing dominance of commercialism in politics, followed a few months later. "I am getting too old to form part of the school of 'chiselers,' " he wrote to Baldwin, "that is a bad school; I stick to the old rule, honesty is the best policy in the long run." The new school, under Francis Hincks and Augustin Morin, was increasingly subject to radical criticism; and the drastic decline of its support in the election of 1854 showed that new alignments were in the making.

By 1850 discontent with the limited progress of reform had led in Canada West to a resurgent radicalism which gradually took form as the Clear Grit party. Initially largely agrarian in its support, it reviewed the old demands for government that would be both cheap and democratic and revealed that the appeal of American elective institutions still exercised its attraction. This, however, would wane as the movement evolved. A more pervasive sentiment was "voluntaryism" which opposed any connection between church and state, with particular reference to education and the settlement of the clergy reserves. At an early stage the movement attracted a number of young urban liberals as well as old agrarian reformers, and in due course its ranks were joined by certain businessmen. With urban leadership backed by agrarian support, particularly from the hinterland of Toronto, it evolved into a type of democratic liberalism which, while suspicious of big business and especially of the domination of Montreal interests, was broader and more pragmatic than the agrarian radicalism of an earlier age.

A potent figure in the shaping of the movement was George Brown. An early supporter of Baldwin and an opponent of constitutional change on the American model, he initially dismissed the Grits as "a little miserable clique of office-seeking, bunkum-talking cormorants." Yet he distrusted Hincks, and by the end of 1852 he was attacking the ministry as "the abject vassals of French Canadian priesthood." His belief in secularization, his growing resentment over French Canadian political domination, his attacks on the influence of the Grand Trunk, brought a *rapprochement* with the Grits which ended in their acceptance of Brown as the acknowledged leader of the party. And Brown, the editor of the *Globe,* brought to the support of the Grits the most influential newspaper in English-speaking Canada and a weapon of unmatched political power.

The platform of the Clear Grits called for a wide extension of political democracy. Among the planks were universal suffrage, secret ballot, elective officials, and biennial parliaments. They wanted fiscal reform and free trade, a simplification of the judicial system, abolition of primogeniture, and secularization of the clergy reserves. They viewed with dislike and distrust the growing connection between government and business, and they looked on the Grand Trunk Railway as the special embodiment of the iniquities to which this connection gave rise. As the struggle developed, this antagonism toward big business added to the increasing asperity of Brown's attacks on the French. The Grits found themselves the unavowed heirs of the old Tory policy of racial absorption. The French had abandoned the overt opposition to commercial expansion that had been one ground of Tory hostility. Their alliance with English business interests now brought upon them the enmity of the radicals for their support of a business oligarchy that exploited the farmer. Political solidarity enabled the French to dominate the ministry and to check the progress of reform. Clerical influence was blamed for blocking a settlement of seigniorial tenure and the clergy reserves, and for riveting the system of separate schools on CanadaWest. It was now the Grits who sought means to swamp the French politically and racially. They advocated the annexation of the West for political as well as economic motives. They demanded an end to the equal representation of both sections and the adoption of representation by population.With the population of CanadaWest at last outnumbering that of French Canada, this change would assure an English majority and break French domination and obstruction. "Rep by pop" became by 1857 a major aim of the party and the most popular item in its platform. Its avowed purpose was underlined by the anti-French and anti-Catholic diatribes of the *Globe;* and this feature, added to the political radicalism of the Grits, hardened French resistance and heightened the sectional and racial character of political divisions in Canada.

In consequence the moderate reform ministry under Hincks and Morin was faced with mounting difficulties. It was able at the outset to secure the support of the embryo Grit section, but the French group looked somewhat askance at this combination, and the relations between moderates and radicals in Upper Canada became increasingly uneasy. There was restiveness over the failure to settle the question of clergy reserves. There was rising resentment over the ministry's yielding to the demand for separate Catholic schools, particularly in the School Bill of 1853 which was carried by the votes from Canada East, and over the bills which chartered ecclesiastical corporations under clerical auspices. The acerbity of controversy provoked by these measures not only aroused religious passions but heightened sectional antagonisms. The ministry's difficulties with its allies on the left were compounded by attacks from its opponents on the right, where the old rigid Toryism was gradually being superseded by a more moderate conservatism. Assailed from all directions, the government was defeated on a vote of censure in June 1854. The elections that followed reduced its relative strength in Canada East and left it in a minority in Canada West.

When the ministry, faced with confusion and disintegration, resigned in September 1854, it marked the end of the old reform grouping and a reorientation of party alignments.

The opportunities presented by these political fluctuations were brilliantly seized by a rising young politician, John Alexander Macdonald. whose name was to dominate Canadian politics for half a century. This supple opportunist was a master of tactics with an unrivaled talent for conciliating diverse personalities. Unhampered by dogmatic principles, he had an almost unerring shrewdness of perception of the means that were necessary for practical accomplishments. He had a personal charm that was a unique asset in keeping together a conglomerate and often restive following. He combined a remarkable flexibility with a talent for political effrontery, which left his opponents baffled and raging at his unabashed shifts of policy. His most sustained conviction was his abiding faith in Canada's future as a nation; but he recognized that unity could only be maintained and the practical work of government carried on by an almost day-to-day policy of compromise and concession, and it was on that basis that throughout his career he held the country together, though at times most precariously, in spite of unremitting sectional and racial strains.

Macdonald saw that the confused situation following the election of 1854, which gave no group a clear majority, could be remedied by a combination of forces on the basis of moderate conservatism. If the Tories would abandon their die-hard opposition to all change they could join with the moderate reformers. If they would drop their insistence on racial and religious supremacy they could achieve a working alliance with the French. Largely through Macdonald's efforts, the new arrangement was successfully concluded; and with characteristic ingenuity he appropriated the dual title "Liberal-Conservative" for the party that was thus created. The first ministry that it brought into being was headed by McNab and Morin; but the true leaders were Macdonald for the moderates of Canada West and Cartier for the French majority, and the final emancipation from the Toryism of the Family Compact was symbolized by the formation of a Macdonald-Cartier ministry in November 1857.

The rallying of a majority, fleeting though it proved to be, made it possible to dispose of the chief problems that still lingered from the past. Lord Sydenham in 1840 had carried a compromise on the clergy reserves, which he hoped would settle the matter, only to see it warped in the imperial parliament as a result of Anglican insistence. The outcome was a division of the revenues among the various sects, to the discontent of the radicals, who insisted on secularization. The Hincks government, shortly before its fall, had secured an imperial statute which gave the province itself the necessary authority to deal with the question, but had taken no steps to implement it. The new ministry settled the long-vexing question by accepting the principle of secularization. The vested rights of the churches were abolished, and the revenue from the sale of the reserves was to be divided among the municipalities on the basis of population, saving only the life interest of the present incumbents. A clause allowing the churches to commute this last provision by accepting a capital sum was attacked by the radicals as perpetuating ecclesiastical endowments, but most members accepted with relief a measure which finally disposed of the troublesome and disruptive issue.

The time was equally ripe for the abolition of seigniorial tenure. It had in fact been recommended by an official commission in 1843, and sentiment in its favor continued to grow during the succeeding decade. Behind this was a shift of opinion in French Canada which was not so much a reorientation of basic outlook as a changed view of the value of the system as an instrument of national and cultural survival.

The Union of 1841 was an economic as well as a political merger. The two former provinces were now interdependent; they profited mutually from economic expansion, from improved transport, from progress in industry and investment. French Canadian leaders, abandoning their former obstruction, showed a readiness to share in profits as well as in patronage. Yet compromise and collaboration at the upper level, far from promoting amalgamation of the two racial societies, led on the French side at least to a strengthening of the forces of resistance against any inroads that would diminish the sense of national identity. The political power of French Canada rested on its social and cultural solidarity as a distinct community. That solidarity would be weakened and perhaps in the end destroyed by absorption into the capitalist individualist culture of English Canada. With the encouragement of the political elite and the even more vigorous prompting of the clergy, the habitants, apprehensive of any threat to the familiar laws and institutions to which they were so deeply attached, were urged to find salvation by striking firm roots in the soil. Agriculture, it appeared, was the pious vocation that was the peculiar destiny of the race and that could be deserted only at the risk of submergence; and the cry *emparons-nous du sol* became the slogan of a stubbornly agrarian nationalism.

The seigniorial system was no longer an effective structure for promoting this objective. In the period since the conquest the seigniories had been increasingly commercialized. Their possessors, old as well as new, sought to maximize the financial returns from their domains. By various devices they managed to increase the charges on their *censitaires,* while at the same time delaying the grant of new holdings from speculative motives. More and more the growth of population outran available seigniorial land. The consequence was on the one hand an uneconomic fragmentation of existing holdings, and on the other a migration of the younger generation to the towns and in increasing numbers to the United States. Colonization societies, seeking to check this drift from the land, were forced to look outside the seigniories to such areas as the Eastern Townships or the region around Lake St. John. To the overburdened habitants no less than to the merchant proprietors, the system had ceased to be a bulwark and had become an impediment and an incubus, unsuited either to national aspirations or to the new commercial age, an obsolete survival which French Canada was now ready to discard.

It was generally agreed that abolition must be accompanied by compensation, but at the charge of the community rather than the *censitaires.* The Act of 1854 separated feudal dues as such from charges that could be looked on as in the nature of rent. The validity of the strictly feudal claims was investigated by a commission, and the result was the award of $1,500,000 to extinguish this aspect of seigniorial claims. The sum proved inadequate, and to the wrath of the reformers a further $2,000,000 was voted in 1859; and the simultaneous measure providing for an annual grant to Canada West and the Eastern Townships, where freehold tenure prevailed, failed to mollify the critics. The habitant remained subject to an annual charge on the land he held, but he could achieve full ownership by commuting this for a lump sum. The way was open for the complete liquidation of feudal tenure in French Canada.

Other measures were adopted to satisfy the moderate liberals. The franchise for the assembly was broadened. The appointed legislative council, which had proved a nuisance and an encumberance, was changed to an elective body in 1855 without its usefulness being noticeably improved. Yet in spite of these accomplishments, the stable majority that had seemed in prospect proved difficult to maintain. Party lines were still extremely elastic. Independent members used their position to demand special concessions, and Macdonald complained that even when these had been granted the "loose fish" refused to stay bought. Constant management of the sectional groups, especially the French, was a necessity, and the growing sectional divisions made it hard to attain any stable balance in the legislature.

One persistent difficulty was the inability of any group to secure a majority from both sections. The Conservatives were dominant in Canada East but never attracted more than a minority of the electors in Canada West. The whole policy and temper of the Clear Grits affronted the French majority; and though the Grits had a loose alliance with the *Parti rouge,* it was far from solid, and the *Rouges* were in a distinct minority in Canada East. The consequence was a relatively even balance of forces, which left any ministry at the mercy of shifting opinions and issues.

This political precariousness was forcibly illustrated in 1858 by the controversy over the location of the provincial capital. Montreal had been punished for the riots of 1849 by the removal of the government and the alternation of legislative sessions between Toronto and Quebec. The effort to reach a decision on a permanent capital had been frustrated by sectional jealousies, and a self-governing Canada had been reduced to the ignominious course of appealing to the Queen to decide. When, as expected, it was announced that she had decided on Ottawa, the hopes of the ministry that royal prestige would settle the matter were wrecked by an outburst of local and sectional resentments. The Assembly voted to disapprove of Ottawa, and the government, disheartened by accumulating difficulties, decided to resign.

George Brown as leader of the opposition was now called on to form a ministry, and though the prospect was dubious he felt that he could not refuse to make the effort. He put together a coalition of Grits and *Rouges,* but their slender chance of securing a majority was further diminished by the fact that the new members would have to vacate their seats and stand for re-election. Their first test in the Assembly resulted in an overwhelming vote of no confidence. After a three-day interlude the Conservatives were back in office, still precariously, and threatened with defeat in their turn if ministers had to seek re-election. A technicality showed the way out. The law provided that a minister who entered a new office within one month after leaving an old one need not vacate his seat. Macdonald and his colleagues therefore each took a different office from the ones they had previously occupied, and then, the formalities satisfied, went back to their previous positions. The "double shuffle," as the *Globe* derisively christened it, was one more example of the shifts to which government in Canada had been reduced.

The situation in fact threatened a complete stultification of responsible government. Political and sectional divisions threatened to make the union unworkable, and by 1859 the Grits, like *Rouges,* were prepared to advocate its dissolution. In the party convention of that year, however, outright separation was rejected in favor of a federal arrangement which would create two provinces but link them with "some joint authority" over matters of common concern. An alternative solution on the principle of the "double majority," which would maintain the union but optimistically attempt to produce a ministry that would command a majority of members from each of the two sections, was advocated by a group of moderates under John Sandfield Macdonald and L. V. Sicotte, and these two leaders formed a ministry after the defeat of the Conservatives over the Militia Bill of 1862. By 1863 it had been defeated in its turn; and although the elections of that year followed by a reorganization enabled it to prolong an uncertain existence, it fell in March 1864. The Conservative ministry that replaced it lasted only until June 14. Two elections and three changes of administration since 1861 had failed to give stability, and no possibility of a remedy on the existing basis could be seen. Some new and drastic change was needed; and in a bold effort to meet the accumulating internal and external difficulties, Canada turned to the idea of a federation of British North America.

Sir Alexander Tilloch Galt.

Timber Slide at Ottawa.
The drawing shows the Prince of Wales and party descending the slide during the visit of the Prince, later Edward VII, in 1860.

The St. Albans Raid.
A slightly retouched version from a contemporary newspaper sketch.

Opening of the European and North American Railway.

(Canadian Illustrated News)

Sir James Douglas.

Trading Post, Fort Garry.

Victoria at the Time of the Gold Rush.

(*Harper's Weekly*)

The *Trent* Affair.   *(Public Archives of Canada)*
British reinforcements for Canada on the overland march through New Brunswick.

The Fenian Raids.   *(Public Archives of Canada)*
Skirmish near Cook's Corners.

George Brown. *(Public Archives of Canada)*

Sir George Étienne Cartier. *(Public Archives of Canada)*

John Alexander Macdonald.

341

Chapter 13

The Confederation of Canada

The Framework of Unity

In the opening years of the decade of the sixties the simultaneous emergence of a whole series of problems confronted the provinces of British North America with a crisis that called for prompt and effective action. The political and sectional deadlock within Canada, the growing urgency of the western problem, the unsolved and expanding problem of railways, the drastic change in the trade situation that seemed likely to follow the abrogation of the Reciprocity Treaty, the troublesome question of defense, all converged within this brief period. External factors weighed heavily in the situation. Britain, while placing strict limits on provincial autonomy, had followed her withdrawal of trade benefits by a retreat from the burden of imperial defense and seemed half willing to abandon her American possessions rather than undertake any serious effort on their behalf. The influence of the United States pervaded almost every aspect of the external difficulties. The threat to the West, the blow to trade, the complications that increased the gravity of the railway problem, all rose to no small extent from American attitudes and policies; and in addition there were the dangers embodied in the Fenian movement and the vociferous annexationist sentiment throughout the northern states.

These were problems which were largely beyond the competence of any single province to solve. Canada was far more vitally affected than the other provinces and more urgently impelled to a drastic effort at solution. Her internal difficulties had no parallel in the Maritimes, which were untroubled by serious racial divisions and whose political basis was not threatened with stultification by party instability. It was Canada that was most acutely concerned over the future of the West and most exposed to threats of attack from across the border. The other provinces, however, were not wholly indifferent to such matters and were directly involved in questions concerning trade and railways. A combination of circumstances gave unprecedented strength to the forces favoring unity and presented a unique opportunity. But it was a fleeting situation, and the chance once missed might not soon recur. Canada's whole destiny was transformed by the men who seized this transient opportunity with boldness and decision and used it to weld the scattered communities with a population of less than 4,000,000 into a nation whose dominion should extend from sea to sea.

The idea of a union of British North America had been put forward as early as 1790 by Chief Justice William Smith. It was not until the 1850s, however, that a number of journalists and political leaders embarked on a serious effort to bring it about. Sectional difficulties in Canada motivated a search for some alternative basis other than a mere dissolution of the union. Federation was discussed during various negotiations over the Intercolonial Railway and was brought forward in connection with the agitation for control of the West. Galt pressed it in the debates of 1858 and made its acceptance a condition of his entry into the ministry in the autumn of that year. But although the matter was raised with the British government, no serious effort was made to secure its adoption. Galt's colleagues failed to share his enthusiasm. The Maritimes showed little interest, and the British government was cold to the idea. There were leaders in the various provinces who preferred limited regional unions to a general federation. It took more urgent circumstances to bring the project into the forefront of the political scene.

Three developments were of special importance in precipitating the issue. The first was the outcome of the political deadlock in Canada. The fall of the Taché-Macdonald ministry in June 1864 brought prospects of a new election but little hope of any substantial change in the political balance. Only some new combination offered a promise of the way out of the impasse, and the key to any such combination was now George Brown.

Though Brown was unrivaled as the leader of the Upper Canada reformers, he had limited success in welding them into a coherent party. He had little appreciation of politics as an art and little talent for the management of men. There were chronic divisions in the ranks—Grit radicals, Toronto liberals, right-wing moderates—and relations with the *Rouges* of Lower Canada were tenuous and uneasy at best. Yet no other figure commanded such personal loyalty or could have rallied a solid following in support of the great enterprise which was emerging through his own initiative.

By 1864 Brown had reached the conclusion that "rep by pop" was not by itself a practical solution for the difficulties of the Union. French Canada was adamantly opposed to being swamped by an English majority, and

343

Brown had come to appreciate the legitimate desire of Lower Canada to maintain its own institutions and handle its own affairs. Yet the alternative of a simple dissolution of the Union was one to which he was utterly opposed. That left only federalism as the device for reconciling cultural duality with continued political unity. Powerfully reinforcing this view was his growing concern over the need to acquire the west for Canada, and to this end, a solution of Canada's political difficulties seemed essential. Federation might open the way to satisfying Lower Canada, to releasing Upper Canada from French political domination, and to securing the great western domain. "Let us endeavour," he pleaded in the *Globe*, "in carrying on the affairs of our common country to arrive at some basis on which we may all stand in peace and contentment."

It was with this aim that he secured in May 1864 the appointment of a legislative committee to examine the constitutional problem and to devise a remedy. On June 14 the committee reported a strong feeling "in favor of changes in the direction of a federative system, applied either to Canada alone or to the whole British North American Provinces." On the same day the Taché-Macdonald ministry fell, leaving no assurance that the project would not expire with it.

In actual fact the crisis opened the way to its realization. Brown made it known that he would support any ministry that would sincerely try to solve the constitutional question. John Alexander Macdonald, though he had publicly dissented from the federal proposals of the committee, grasped at the prospect of a coalition that would avert the threatened breakdown of government. The governor general, Lord Monck, used his influence in favor of negotiation rather than dissolution of the Assembly, and helped to persuade a reluctant Brown that he must personally enter the ministry if it was to succeed. In the discussions Macdonald dropped his insistence on legislative union and agreed to seek a general federation, while Brown, though skeptical about the immediate prospects, consented to the attempt provided that a federation of the two Canadas was accepted as a possible alternative if the wider scheme should fail. With the entry of Brown and two of his supporters into the ministry, the Great Coalition came into being on June 30. This was the event that actually set in motion the process that led to the formation of the Dominion of Canada.

A second motivating force was provided by the Grand Trunk. Even the substantial help that it received from the government in 1862 had not brought salvation to the railway. Edward Watkin, sent out by the London financial interests to investigate, discovered that "the management of this railway is an organized mess—I will not say, a sink of iniquity." The appointment of a new manager, C. J. Brydges, brought some order into affairs, but the real need was for a fundamental change of basis. The hope of capturing the trade of the American West had fallen through. The Canadian West, toward which the eyes of Canadian business leaders had now turned, seemed to Watkin the new land of promise, where the Grand Trunk would find relief from its woes. The remedy for a railway that was too expensive for the existing population was to build a railway several times the existing length into regions that were still unpopulated. In addition to opening the West for settlement, a line to the Pacific would give access to the trade of the Orient and provide a fast military route between Britain and her possessions in the Far East. The old dream of Canada as the entrepôt between Europe and the interior of North America was replaced by the still more grandiose vision of British North America as the halfway house between Europe and Asia. Its realization involved not merely the construction of the long-deferred Intercolonial as well as of a transcontinental railway, but the political union of the provinces that would facilitate the acquisition of the West. In the end the Grand Trunk took no part in the tremendous construction project that was thus projected; but its influence was enlisted on the side of the new political departure, which seemed a necessary prelude, and was of no small importance in making it a reality.

The third development was the emergence of a scheme for Maritime union. Here, too, railways were an important factor. For a decade after the setback to the plan for the Intercolonial in 1852, the provinces continued to negotiate on the project and to seek the aid of the imperial government. By 1861, with the new influence of the Grand Trunk now enlisted and the *Trent* affair providing a fresh illustration of the military importance of the railway, the British government was persuaded to renew its earlier offer of a financial guaranty, and the construction of local lines in the Maritimes had diminished their earlier objections to the Robinson route. A conference in 1862 led to an agreement on the share of the cost to be borne by each province. It seemed that the building of the Intercolonial was at last assured, when Canada suddenly raised objections to that part of the financial provisions which provided for a sinking fund and which was a condition of the imperial guaranty. Once more the arrangements collapsed amid recriminations that added to the long-standing dislike and distrust of Canada in the Maritimes. The disappointment that gave rise to these emotions also lent an impetus to the idea of Maritime union, which had been tentatively put forward from time to time, and Nova Scotia in 1864 took the lead in initiating the first official discussion of the project. Even then the response of New Brunswick and Prince Edward Island showed little enthusiasm. The Nova Scotia resolution as originally drafted provided for the appointment of delegates to a conference to *arrange* a plan of union. The two other provinces agreed to meet to *consider* it, and even then they were in no haste to arrange the actual meeting.

They were jolted into action by a message from Canada. On June 30 a formal communication was sent by the governor, Lord Monck, asking whether a Canadian deputation might attend the forthcoming conference to present their wider proposals. The Maritimes agreed to accept an unofficial delegation and proceeded in a somewhat leisurely fashion to make definite arrangements for the conference to meet at Charlottetown on September 1. It was perhaps typical of the very casual interest aroused by the prospective discussions that, when the appointed date arrived, members of the Island government as well as the general public were less interested in the arrival of the delegations from the mainland than in the rare presence of a circus in Charlottetown. The delegates from Nova Scotia found no one to welcome them, and the reception to the Canadians took the form of a self-sacrificing provincial secretary rowing out in a small boat to meet the ship in which they arrived.

It was the Canadians who took the initiative in the discussions and whose proposals dominated the conference. Maritime union, which the meeting had officially been called to consider, received scant attention. It proved to have few strong advocates, and it encountered the rooted reluctance of Prince Edward Island to see its legislature abolished and a demand that in any case the capital should be at Charlottetown. Theoretically, Maritime union was quite compatible with the larger federation; but in practice, the broader scheme weakened still further the slender prospect of a merger of the three eastern provinces. After a few brief discussions, consideration was postponed until after the Quebec conference, and ultimately at a meeting in Toronto the plan was shelved indefinitely. Its vanishing wraith trailed the conference as it moved on to Halifax after a week's discussion at Charlottetown and thence for oratorical festivities at St. John and Fredericton. These ambulatory proceedings issued in an agreement that a confederation of all British North America would be highly advantageous if it could be arranged on equitable terms and in a decision to meet at Quebec to discuss precise details. On October 10 the delegates from the provinces, including two representatives from Newfoundland, embarked at Quebec on the momentous discussions that laid the foundations for the new Dominion.

The essential outlines of the new scheme had already been drawn at

Charlottetown. The starting point was a recognition that the union must be federal in structure. John Alexander Macdonald was strongly in favor of a legislative union that would extinguish the separate governments of the provinces, but this was beyond attainment. The Maritimes were unwilling to see their identity submerged, and they lacked the general municipal instutitions that would be necessary to provide an effective system of local government under a unitary system. French Canada was an equally serious obstacle. Restive as they were under the existing union of the Canadas, the French were unlikely to accept a still wider union, which would accentuate their minority position. The price of their consent to any new arrangement was the creation of a predominantly French province in which their special rights would be guaranteed and their control of local affairs assured. "We had either," said George Brown in the subsequent debates, "to take a federal union or drop the negotiation. . . . There was but one choice open to us—federal union or nothing."

Having accepted this necessity, however, the delegates at Charlottetown were generally agreed on a strong central government, which should be vested with all the powers outside the list of strictly local topics to be left to the provinces. The governor of New Brunswick reported that, according to his information, it was contemplated that the powers of the local government "should be carefully restricted to certain local matters, to be specified and defined by the Act establishing the confederation, whilst all general legislation should be dealt with by, and all undefined powers reside in, a central legislature, which should in fact be not only a federal assembly charged with the consideration of a few topics specially committed to its care, but the real legislature of the country, the local assemblies being allowed to sink to the position of mere municipalities."

There was little tendency at Quebec to depart from this fundamental basis. The conference met under the shadow of the terrible conflict that was being waged for the existence of the American union. To Canadians the Civil War seemed the disastrous outcome of the doctrine of states' rights and an object lesson that they took deeply to heart. Although the expressed desire was "to follow the model of the British constitution so far as our circumstances will permit," the federal nature of the proposed structure inevitably invited attention to the Constitution of the United States. But the tendency was less to copy its salient features than to avoid the defects that experience had so glaringly revealed. Its most significant expression was in the deliberate reversal of the American provision that restricted the powers of the federal government to those specifically granted and reserved all others to the states or the people. Both at

Charlottetown and at Quebec there was general agreement on the desirability of vesting in the central government all residuary power outside the list of local subjects specifically assigned to the provinces; and this feature was further strengthened by the provision that gave the federal government a veto over provincial legislation.

The composition of the federal legislature gave rise to more serious controversy. There was no objection to a two-chamber system, and it was generally agreed that the lower house should be based on population, in spite of Prince Edward Island's objections to having only five members out of 194. But the upper house was the subject of heated arguments. The proposals outlined at Charlottetown envisaged the division of Canada into two provinces and the amalgamation of the Maritimes into one and gave equal membership to each of these three units. Although it was soon clear that Maritime union was highly unlikely, the ideas was retained of treating them as a single section and basing the upper house on sectional rather than provincial equality. This roused considerable protest. There was no serious support for the suggestion that all provinces should have equal numbers, as had the states in the American Senate, but there was a strong demand that the Maritimes be given a larger representation. The presence of Newfoundland at Quebec provided the basis for a modest compromise. The three Maritime provinces were still left with twenty-four members, the same number as Ontario and Quebec, but Newfoundland was to have an additional four if she entered the federation. It was a somewhat delusive concession, but it settled a question that almost threatened to wreck the conference. There remained the question of how the members of the upper house should be chosen, and this too was sharply debated. There was no real support for an elective basis, and Prince Edward Island was the chief advocate of appointment by the provinces. But there was some fear that the first appointments, if left to the federal government, might be on a partisan basis; and it was only after an agreement that the initial members should be nominated by the provincial governments from the existing councils, with due regard to the fair representation of all parties, that the general principle of life appointment by the federal government was conceded.

There was another hard battle over financial arrangements. A federal government that was charged with all the great functions outside of local affairs, and that was to assume the cost not only of administration and defense but of an expensive program of railway construction, must necessarily have at its disposal the bulk of the revenue; and the need was increased by the decision that the provincial debts should be assumed by the central government. The provinces, left with little more than municipal functions and relieved of their debts, were expected to get along on an extremely frugal budget. Even so, it was a real question where they would find the money for education and roads and other local obligations. The federal government took over the customs duties, which provided one main source of revenue, and such publicly owned enterprises as railways and harbor works as could occasionally be regarded as paying assets. Yet it was reluctant to share its taxing power, and it was only after considerable opposition that the idea of federal subsidies to the provinces was accepted as an alternative.

The result was a somewhat complicated adjustment. The difference in provincial debts was equated by crediting each province with an amount roughly equivalent to $25 per head; and each was to pay or receive interest at 5 percent on any difference between this amount and the debt actually assumed by the central government. Their revenue from local license fees was to be supplemented by a federal grant. Taking the most economical estimate of future provincial expenses—that provided by Tupper of Nova Scotia—the conference worked out a system of grants-in-aid calculated on the basis of 80 cents per head. If the provinces still needed money, they were to raise it by direct taxation, and it was fully expected that the unpopularity of such a proceeding would act as an effective curb on any tendency toward extravagance on the part of provincial governments.

On October 27 the work of the conference was finished. It was embodied in seventy-two resolutions, which laid down in detail the proposals for the new scheme of government. In the first flush of enthusiasm there had been some talk of submitting the draft constitution to popular approval. But second thoughts brought doubts about the wisdom of this course and a decision to agree with Britain's preference for ratification by the provincial legislatures rather than by the electorate. Even this, as it turned out, was in most cases impossible to attain, and the returning delegates found themselves involved in a struggle that delayed the establishment of Canadian federation for nearly three more years.

Carrying Confederation

The motivating forces behind the movement for confederation showed themselves strongest in English-speaking Canada. The threat of political deadlock, accompanied as it was by the fear of economic stagnation, roused a widespread desire not merely to escape from present ills, but to open the way for future progress. The hope of westward expansion was particularly strong in rallying the support of both agrarian and business interests behind the proposals. This did not mean that opposition was absent. Although the Grits had approved the idea of federation in their convention of 1859, Brown and his followers thought chiefly of a purely Canadian federation accompanied by the annexation of the West. Brown looked on the inclusion of the Maritimes as more likely to be burdensome than advantageous, and he was particularly hostile to the Intercolonial Railway, which he viewed as another Grand Trunk scheme at the expense of the Canadian people. He had yielded to necessity when he realized that the inclusion of the Maritimes was needed in order to satisfy the French, who believed that it would redress the balance in their favor against Canada West, and that Maritime consent could only be won by a promise to build the Intercolonial.

His surrender was attacked by radicals from both sections of Canada. "The confederation of all the British North American provinces," Dorion charged, "naturally suggested itself to the Grand Trunk officials as the surest means of bringing with it the construction of the Intercolonial Railway. Such was the origin of this confederation scheme. The Grand Trunk people are at the bottom of it." There were also sharp attacks by the radicals on the conservative nature of the proposed structure; but Brown succeeded in winning the bulk of his followers to the support of the Quebec resolutions. With Galt assuring the English of Canada East that their minority rights would be protected within the new province of Quebec while their economic interests would be forwarded under the federal government, and with Macdonald's careful and persuasive exposition giving full satisfaction to the Conservatives, opposition in English Canada was confined to a small though able minority.

French Canada was much more divided. Quite apart from the *Rouges*, who disliked the whole idea of a broad federation, many Conservatives were gravely concerned over its effect on their racial and cultural prospects. French Canada was torn between fear of absorption into a united Canada with an English majority and fear of annexation to the United States if Canada continued weak and disunited. It was the task of the French leaders to minimize the first of these fears and to take full advantage of the second. Cartier and his associates stressed the protection that French institutions and culture would enjoy under the new provincial arrangements and insisted that American annexation was the inevitable alternative to confederation. The new scheme at last offered the means of reconciling racial diversity and national unity. To this view the clergy gave a somewhat guarded support, their desire to erect stronger bulwarks against the United States outweighing their reservations about the adequacy of the guaranties offered to French Canada.

Even so, the controversy was violent, and a number of French Conservatives went over to the opposition. The situation moved George Brown, during the debates in the assembly, to an eloquent appeal to the spirit of mutual generosity. He reminded his hearers:

> One hundred years have passed away since these provinces became by conquest part of the British Empire. Here sit today the descendants of the victors and vanquished in the fight of 1759, with all the differences of language, religion, civil law, and social habit nearly as distinctly marked as they were a century ago. Here we sit today seeking amicably to find a remedy for constitutional evils and injustice complained of—by the vanquished? No, sir, but complained of by the conquerors! Here sit the representatives of the British population claiming justice—only justice; and here sit representatives of the French population discussing in the French tongue whether we shall have it.

The debates in the Canadian assembly on the Quebec resolutions opened on February 3, 1865. In the early hours of March 11 the main motion was carried by a vote of 91 to 33. In contrast to the overwhelming majority of English members who supported the Quebec plan, the French were closely divided, with 27 in favor against 22 opposed. Nonetheless, Canada registered its approval in a decisive fashion and with a majority of votes from both sections. It was the only province that gave formal ratification to the confederation proposals. In none were they approved by popular vote, and in the Maritimes an opposition developed that threatened to wreck the whole project.

The situation revealed the relative weakness of unitary forces in the face of the deep-rooted localism of the lower provinces. The Quebec resolutions pledged the federal government to secure without delay the completion of the Intercolonial. Supporters of federation painted glowing pictures of increased trade between the provinces, of a great industrial expansion based on Maritime resources in coal and iron, of the ports of the Maritimes rivaling those of Britain as centers of world trade. But many of their hearers took a skeptical view of these prospects and were unconvinced that the benefits from the Intercolonial would outweigh the burdens and the loss of independence that the Quebec plan foreshadowed. The Maritimes had little interest in the acquisition of the West. They foresaw a costly program of transcontinental railway construction added to expenditures on communications and defense works in Canada, with a considerable part of the expense falling on the Maritime taxpayer. They envisaged the drift of their industries and other enterprises to the more populous region of the St. Lawrence and an imposition of the Canadian protective tariff on the Maritime consumer. It was easy to magnify what would be lost and to minimize prospective gains. The delegates, returning from Quebec full of satisfaction with their work, were met by angry charges that they had sold their constituents to Canada for 80 cents a head. "They gave the whole province away," asserted a Nova Scotia critic even after union had become a reality. "We had a well-working constitution; we made our own laws, raised our own revenues, and taxed ourselves. We owned railways, fisheries, and other public property, but they gave them all away for nothing. We can at any moment be taxed to any extent arbitrarily by an oligarchy in Canada."

This threat of taxation without recompense, coupled with the prospective curtailment of provincial authority, roused a storm of criticism. Both Prince Edward Island and Newfoundland rejected the Quebec proposals. In New Brunswick the premier, Samuel Leonard Tilley, felt forced by circumstances to risk an election on the issue. His party was overwhelmingly defeated, and under a new administration the New Brunswick Assembly passed a resolution asserting that "the consummation of the said scheme would prove politically, commercially and financially disastrous to the best interests of this province."

This was a serious defection, all the more so because of its effect on Nova Scotia. In that province the powerful influence of Joseph Howe had been thrown against confederation. Howe had on previous occasions expressed a somewhat vague approval of federation as an ultimate goal. He had been invited to form part of the delegation to Charlottetown; and though he alleged that his duties as imperial fisheries commissioner prevented his acceptance, he promised that he would be "very happy to cooperate in carrying out any measure upon which the conference shall agree." But it was his Conservative opponents under Dr. Charles Tupper who were responsible for the negotiations, and there is little doubt that this made it all the easier for Howe to convince himself with perfect sincerity that the scheme they had sponsored would be disastrous for Nova Scotia. He threw himself ardently into the campaign against federation, and became the leading spirit in the Anti-Confederation League that was formed to combat it. The violence of the opposition made it risky for Tupper to submit the resolutions to the legislature, let alone to the electorate; and without New Brunswick's adherence it would be almost physically impossible for Nova Scotia and Canada to join. Tupper marked time, reviving the proposal for Maritime union and delaying all further action until the situation was clarified.

The time had now come to invoke the overriding authority of the British government. At first Britain had been dubious about the desirability of Canadian union, which it was feared might result in a further weakening of the imperial tie. Maritime union was favored as a necessary prelude, and the Colonial Office looked with disapproval on the intrusion of the Canadians at Charlottetown. With the progress of the negotiations, however, it began to dawn on Britain that a strong federation might go a long way to solving the problem of Canadian defense, particularly since it would also facilitate the building of the Intercolonial. Important British financial interests, fearing a decline in their Canadian securities, pressed the government in London to lend positive aid to the federation proposals. Thus when a Canadian delegation arrived in the autumn of 1865 to discuss the situation, it met with a favorable reception. A counterdelegation from Nova Scotia under Howe found itself unable to persuade the British government that it should protect the province against being forced into union. Indeed, the imperial authorities now threw their influence on the side of confederation in none too subtle a fashion. The governor of Nova Scotia was replaced by a more energetic partisan of union. The governor of New Brunswick, who shared the earlier preference of the Colonial Office for Maritime union and had used his influence against the wider scheme, was ordered in no uncertain terms to give confederation his full support; and in pursuit of this new policy he succeeded in the spring of 1866 in maneuvering the anticonfederation administration out of office and clearing the way for a new election.

Already there were signs that opposition was weakening in New Brunswick. There had been a year in which to give fuller consideration to the Quebec proposals, and the advantages of union were underlined by the massing of a Fenian force just across the border and its threat of an irruption into the province. No means were spared to encourage the conversion of the electorate. The Fenian threat was played up heavily. Volunteers were called out to meet it and were kept under arms—and under pay—to maintain their patriotic fervor until the elections were over. Urgent appeals for election funds went to Canada, not without response.

The Grand Trunk Railway lent support in a distinctly practical way. From the inception of the movement for confederation the leading railway officials had been assiduous in their support, arranging excursions of press and politicians from one section to another, shepherding the delegations to London, mobilizing their financial connections in England to bring pressure on the British government. Tilley's appeal for "the needful" was generously answered, and he and his followers were returned with a handsome majority.

This success opened the way for the final stage of the negotiations. Once it was clear that New Brunswick was moving back into the fold, Tupper took steps to bring Nova Scotia into line. His task was made easier by a suggestion from one of the opponents of the Quebec resolutions that some arrangement should be sought on a more acceptable basis. Tupper succeeded in carrying a resolution that authorized the appointment of delegates to arrange with the British government for a scheme of union. A similar resolution was passed in New Brunswick; and in December 1866, delegates from the two Maritime provinces joined with those from Canada in a conference at the Westminster Palace Hotel in London.

The Quebec resolutions were the starting point for the new negotiations. Although they had received no approval in Nova Scotia and had been rejected in New Brunswick, their main provisions were accepted by the representatives of those provinces; and although they had been formally accepted in Canada, the Canadian delegates held themselves free to make such alterations as seemed necessary. The changes were not in fact extensive, though several of them were important. Subsidies to the provinces were increased by a provision for fixed grants in addition to the earlier provision of 80 cents a head. Construction of the Intercolonial was made more definitely mandatory. The Quebec clause on education, which safeguarded the separate schools of the religious minorities in Canada, was widened to apply to all provinces, and minorities were given the further right of appeal to the federal government if they felt unable to secure a redress of grievances from the provincial governments. Still other modifications were introduced at the instance of Britain when the London resolutions, sixty-nine in number, went through the process of being translated into a draft of legislation. The power of pardon was taken from the lieutenant governors and concentrated in the hands of the governor general. To provide some measure of flexibility in case of a deadlock between the two houses of the legislature, power was given to add either three or six members to the Senate. Not least important, the title "Kingdom of Canada" which Macdonald strongly favored was objected to on the ground that it might give offense to the United States, and the result was the dropping of a designation that would have expressed more effectively the aspirations behind the new union.

It now remained to give effect to the new constitution by securing its adoption as a statute of the imperial legislature. In the form of the British

North America Act it was introduced into Parliament in March 1867, and passed with hardly more than formal attention. Anti-confederation delegates from Nova Scotia, who had kept up their unavailing battle to the end, remarked bitterly on the scanty attention that the measure attracted in the British House of Commons, compared to the eagerness with which members plunged into the debate on a new dog tax immediately afterward. On July 1, 1867, a proclamation brought the Act into force for the four provinces of Nova Scotia, New Brunswick, Ontario, and Quebec, and the Dominion of Canada entered into the first stage of its existence.

The British North America Act, 1867

The constitution that established the confederation of Canada was a product of both heredity and environment. It was founded on the British system of parliamentary government, whose traditions the provinces had inherited and on which their own institutions were modeled. Yet the British system, which had already been modified in operation to suit local conditions, had to be adapted still further to satisfy the need for a federal rather than a unitary structure. This was the first example of a federal government within the British Empire, and those who framed it inevitably looked for guidance to the Constitution of the United States. The combining of the British parliamentary system with American federal principles was a symbolic Canadian achievement—all the more so when both elements were freely adapted to Canada's own particular needs.

The influence of the American Constitution pervaded the discussions at Quebec and the subsequent debates in the Canadian legislature. Repeated references to the history and literature of American constitutional development revealed the close attention that had been paid to it by the Canadian fathers and their recognition of its intimate bearing on the task in which they were engaged. The broad objectives that they sought were similar to those which animated the delegates at Philadelphia in 1787—the creation of a strong national government, which could act directly on the individual citizen without the intervention of the states or the provinces and which would have full and adequate powers to deal with all matters of truly national concern. But it is significant that in implementing this aim through specific provisions, the Canadians laid far more emphasis on their departures from the American model than on their adoption of its basic features. They emerged with a firm conviction that their plan represented a tremendous improvement on the American system. Macdonald said:

> It is the fashion now to enlarge on the defects of the Constitution of the United States, but I am not one of those who look upon it as a failure. I think and believe that it is one of the most skillful works which human intelligence ever created. . . . We are happily situated in having had the opportunity of watching its operation, seeing its working from its infancy till now. . . . We can take advantage of the experience of the last 78 years, during which that constitution has existed, and I am strongly of the belief that we have, in a great measure, avoided in this system which we propose for the adoption of the people of Canada, the defects which time and events have shown to exist in the American Constitution.

The result was a Canadian federal structure that, superficially similar in outline to that of the United States, was actually profoundly different in a number of vital respects. It made provision for a federal legislature combining the two features of regional and proportional representation. It contained a scheme for the distribution of power between the federal and provincial governments. It embodied these provisions in a written document whose application was subject to judicial review. Yet in all those features it differed widely in practice from the American system, and in various other aspects such as the nature of the executive it showed a deliberate departure from American institutions.

The adoption of the title House of Commons for the popular branch of the federal legislature was in itself significant. Not only did it imply a conscious adoption of the British model, which had in fact been followed to a large extent by the United States; it emphasized also the claim to the full status conveyed by the provision that "there shall be one Parliament for Canada." Quebec was made the standard for representation. It was given the fixed number of sixty-five seats—the same number as it had had in the assembly under the old union—and members were to be assigned to the other provinces in the same proportion to their population as this figure bore to the population of Quebec. There was to be a redistribution after each decennial census, with the qualification that no province should have its representation reduced unless its proportion of population to that of the whole Dominion showed a decline of at least one-twentieth. There were provisions for annual sessions and for a maximum term of five years, subject to dissolution within that time. Provincial franchises were accepted in the first instance, but Parliament had the right to establish a federal franchise and qualifications for membership.

The upper house was given the title of Senate and was nominally the embodiment of the federal aspect of representation. Such apparent similarities to the American system were largely misleading in this case. Quebec and Ontario each had twenty-four members, but the Maritimes had to divide twenty-four between them. Initially Nova Scotia and New Brunswick received twelve each, but with the provision that each must surrender two members to Prince Edward Island when that province entered the federation. A fourth district, also with twenty-four members, ultimately came into being as a result of the admission of the western provinces. In spite of the fact that senators were to be resident in the provinces for which they were chosen, and that in Quebec they were even to be selected for individual districts, the provision that they were to be appointed by the federal government further weakened their status as representatives of the provinces. In this, and in the provision that their appointment should be for life, the model was not that of the American Senate but of the legislative councils under the old colonial system with their somewhat shadowy resemblance to the House of Lords; in fact, it is the title of Legislative Council that is given to the upper house in both the Quebec and the London resolutions.

While a nominal concession was made to the idea of federal representation, the real purpose of the Senate, like that of most second chambers, was intended to be the guardianship of property rights. "There should be a large property qualification for the upper house," said Macdonald, "which is then the representative of property. It should be an independent body as far as property goes." Actually the qualification was limited to the possession of real and personal property worth $4000; but the Senate has probably been more effective as the protector of property than of provincial rights. Even then its effectiveness has been limited. Though the Senate possesses all the powers of the House of Commons except the origination of money bills, its right of initiation has been comparatively little used and it has been extremely cautious in blocking or even revising legislation sent up from the lower house. The very basis of the Senate has given it little independent authority and even less prestige. While occasional members have been elder statesmen who no longer feel like facing the hurly-burly of election campaigns, appointment has more usually been used as a political reward to faithful adherents worn out in the service of their party or fallen on evil days. The Senate has not been a stage in the rise to the highest public positions, but a haven where political warriors may find refuge—formerly for a tranquil longevity, but since 1965, only to the age of seventy-five. Periodic demands for reform of the Senate, or even for its abolition, keep alive the consciousness of its members that the institution is held in relatively light esteem and restrain their natural desire for a more influential role in government from leading them into activities that might precipitate a conflict with the representative branch or a challenge to popular sentiment.

When it came to providing for the executive, about the only question involved was that of phraseology. The real decision had been taken a generation previously when the radical demand for the American system of elective officials was rejected in favor of responsible government on the model of the British cabinet system. Time had confirmed the wisdom of that choice, particularly in the eyes of the Conservatives, who saw in monarchical institutions a desirable source of authority and stability. The vesting of the executive power in the sovereign was looked on not only as a distinct affirmation of Canada's desire to retain the imperial connection, but also as a bulwark against that turbulent democracy whose manifestations in the United States were regarded as an object lesson. Macdonald stressed the desirability of placing the head of the state above party politics. Cartier voiced the French adherence to the monarchical tradition and identification of republicanism with the rule of the mob. The unbroken authority of the Crown was emphasized by the clause declaring the executive authority "to continue and to be vested in the Queen," while at the same time Canada's aspirations toward an advanced status were symbolized by the provision for a Privy Council for Canada to act with the Queen's representative.

These formal provisions ignored the practical reality—the exercise of executive power by a cabinet responsible to the House of Commons. It rested not on any specific provisions, but on the clause in the preamble that expressed Canada's desire for "a constitution similar in principle to that of the United Kingdom." That single phrase covered the unwritten yet vital part of Canada's constitution—the vast and somewhat indefinite agglomeration of prerogatives and conventions, of customs and statutes and judicial decisions, which underlie the British system of government. There is no Bill of Rights in the British North America Act. The rights of British subjects rest on the common law and on the great concessions wrested from the Crown through a long series of constitutional struggles, and Canada is heir to the full body of these privileges and safeguards.

The judicial system was a compromise, which on balance was still highly favorable to the central government. The organization of courts and the administration of justice remained with the provinces, but all judges above the county court level were to be appointed and paid by the Dominion, which also had the right to establish a court of appeal and "any additional courts for the better administration of the laws of Canada." This clause, coupled with provincial control over property and civil rights, safeguarded the retention by Quebec of French civil law. But it was provided that the federal Parliament might create a uniform system of civil law for the English-speaking provinces, subject to their ratification, and criminal law was made a federal matter. Macdonald pointed with particular satisfaction to the provision for a single criminal code, in contrast to the United States, where each state had a code of its own. Duality was avoided not only in this field, but also in the administration of justice. The only specifically federal courts established under confederation were the Supreme Court and the Court of Admiralty. With a single criminal law for the Dominion, a single system of courts with federally appointed judges, and the possibility of a uniform civil code covering all provinces except Quebec, the new constitution went far toward placing the judicial system on a national level.

This was an important illustration of one of the key features of the act—the distribution of powers between the Dominion and the provinces. Here was perhaps the most deliberate and significant departure from the American model. Over and over again the discussions revealed a desire to avoid any issue comparable to the disruptive conflict over states' rights and a determination to establish the authority of the central government over everything except purely local matters. Both the Quebec and London resolutions called for "a general government, charged with matters of common interest to the whole country, and local governments . . . charged with the control of local matters in their respective sections." Lord Carnarvon, explaining the measure to the House of Lords, stressed the fact that its object was "to give to the central government those high functions and almost sovereign powers" which would vest in it authority over matters of common concern, leaving to the provinces an "ample measure of municipal liberty and self-government." Macdonald summed it up in the simplest terms. "In the proposed constitution," he said, "all matters of general interest are to be dealt with by the general legislature, while the local legislatures will deal with matters of local interest, which do not affect the confederation as a whole."

The basic scheme of distribution is contained in Sections 91 and 92 of the act. Under Section 92 are listed 16 topics over which the provinces have exclusive control. They include such matters as public lands, municipal institutions, licenses, local public works, prisons and hospitals and charitable institutions, and the solemnization of marriage; and the final clause gives general control over "all matters of a merely local or private nature in the province." Throughout this section the recurrence of the qualifying words "in the province" emphasizes the general intention. Education is given to the provinces, with certain safeguards, by Section 93; and Section 95 provides that provinces and Dominion shall have concurrent powers over agriculture and immigration, with Dominion legislation prevailing in case of conflict.

All powers not specifically given to the provinces are assigned to the Dominion. Section 91 establishes this comprehensive residuary power "to make laws for the peace, order and good government of Canada," and goes on to declare that "for greater certainty, but so as not to restrict the generality of the foregoing terms" exclusive Dominion authority extends to twenty-nine specific matters. These include the regulation of trade and commerce without restriction—that is, not merely interprovincial or foreign; the unrestricted right of taxation; currency, banking, interest, and bankruptcy; marriage and divorce, though solemnization of marriage is a provincial matter; and certain subjects exempted from provincial control under Section 92. These last include communications extending beyond provincial boundaries, steamship lines between the provinces or connecting with foreign countries, and "such works as, although wholly situate within the province, are before or after their execution declared by the Parliament of Canada to be for the general advantage of Canada or for the advantage of two or more of the provinces." These sweeping powers are reinforced by the right of the Dominion to disallow provincial legislation even when it deals with provincial matters; and federal appointment of the lieutenant governors was expected to provide a further check on any tendency by the provinces to use their powers in a way that might be adverse to federal policy or the general public interest.

Macdonald was satisfied that these provisions drew a clear and unmistakable line between local matters and those of general concern. Pointing to the American mistake in leaving residuary power to the states, he went on:

Here we have adopted a different system. We have strengthened the general government. We have conferred on them, not only specifically and in detail, all the powers which are incident to sovereignty, but we have expressly declared that all subjects of general interest not distinctly and exclusively conferred upon the local governments and local legislatures, shall be conferred upon the general government and legislature. We have thus avoided that great source of weakness which has been the cause of the disruption of the United States. We have avoided all conflict of jurisdiction and authority, and if this constitution is carried out... we will have in fact, as I have said before, all the advantages of a legislative union.

Time and the Privy Council were to play sad havoc with these expectations; but the framers of the act had some ground for believing that they had expressed, as plainly as words could do, the fundamental purposes of the new national structure.

If there seemed to be no opening for the doctrine of provincial rights, there seemed even less for the development of a compact theory of confederation. The Dominion was not the outgrowth of a popular movement, but the work of a small group of political leaders supported by important economic interests, and the final scheme was never submitted to popular ratification. Neither was it submitted to or accepted by the provincial legislatures. The provincial governments had been given a general mandate to arrange a scheme of union; but the real authority behind the British North America Act, and the only one which could give it statutory effect, was that of the British Parliament. The provinces had no independent power to make a binding contract; and although the word "treaty" was used in discussions, it was for tactical purposes in an attempt to head off any demand for alteration in the original proposals.

Confederation was the outcome of an attempt to create a stronger nationalism capable of dealing with common problems. In a large measure it was a response to the dangers that loomed from the direction of the United States; but it was also, though less obviously, an effort to strengthen Canadian national autonomy against imperial authority. Macdonald failed to get the desired title of "Kingdom of Canada," but he made clear his aim at full national status within the British Empire. Canadians would become a people, he asserted:

able from our union, our strength, our population, and the development of our resources, to take our position among the nations of the world. . . . The colonies are now in a transition state. Gradually a different colonial system is being developed. . . . Instead of looking upon us as a merely dependent colony, England will have in us a friendly nation—a subordinate but still a powerful people—to stand by her in North America in peace or in war.

It was a vision of Canada controlling her own destiny, retaining a free association with the mother country but standing on her own feet and embarking on a bold course of territorial and economic expansion and on the continental destiny that now lay before her.

"Dominion from Sea to Sea"

The four provinces whose federation was proclaimed in 1867 were only the nucleus of the transcontinental dominion upon which Canadian

361

ambitions were fixed. Unless confederation was followed by the acquisition of the West, one of its central purposes would be frustrated. In the east the insular provinces of Prince Edward Island and Newfoundland might be allowed to stand aloof without vitally endangering the future prospects of Canada. But it was the West that held the promises of economic expansion and population growth that had so largely motivated the movement toward unity; and if these were dashed, the Dominion would be balked of one of the main achievements for which it had been brought into being.

Even the limited union was precarious at the outset. The Maritimes were still filled with resentment over the highhanded methods that had been used to bring them into confederation. Emotions were particularly strong in Nova Scotia, where an outraged electorate avenged its sense of betrayal at the first opportunity. In the first election to the federal legislature, Dr. Charles Tupper alone out of nineteen members was returned as a supporter of confederation. In the provincial elections the Conservatives were overthrown, and opponents of confederation were returned for thirty-six out of thirty-eight seats. A repeal resolution was introduced into the Nova Scotia legislature, and a delegation was sent to London to plead the case of the province.

These efforts came to nothing. The British government refused to sanction the secession of Nova Scotia from the Dominion, and without British consent little could be done. There was fiery talk of resistance to federal authority and even of seeking annexation to the United States, but this only weakened the movement by alienating the moderates and affronting Loyalist sentiment. Macdonald and his colleagues took advantage of this weakening opposition to hold out a gilded olive branch. In 1869, negotiations resulted in an agreement on "better terms." Although the financial grants to the provinces under the British North America Act were to be "in full settlement of all future demands," the subsidy to Nova Scotia was increased from $63,000 to $82,000 a year for ten years. As part of the bargain, Joseph Howe entered the federal cabinet, thus undermining the opposition by removing its chief pillar of strength. There were bitter accusations of betrayal, and a legacy of resentment remained in Nova Scotia, but for the moment the chief threat of disruption was brought to an end.

By this time the tortuous negotiations over the West were at last approaching a conclusion. From the start they were closely linked to the problem of communication, with which private interests as well as the Canadian government were concerned. As early as 1852 a project had been launched for a route from Lake Superior to the Fraser River, only to collapse from lack of backing. A short-lived postal service, inaugurated in 1858, proved unable to compete with the American route by way of St. Paul and was abandoned in 1862. By that date, English financial interests as well as the Grand Trunk and the Canadian government had become interested in a telegraph as well as a railway line. Next year the Canadian government offered a grant of $50,000 toward a postal and telegraph connection, and the indefatigable Edward Watkin, organizing the Atlantic and Pacific Transit and Telegraph Company, brought pressure on the Hudson's Bay Company as well as on the British and Canadian governments to aid in the venture.

The company was horrified at the prospect. "What!" burst out its governor, "sequester our very tap-root! Take away the fertile lands where our buffaloes feed! Let in all kinds of people to squat and settle and frighten away the fur-bearing animals they don't hunt and kill! Impossible. Destruction—extinction—of our time-honored industry. If these gentlemen are so patriotic, why don't they buy us out?"

The suggestion that the company might sell opened up new vistas. The British government still refused to bear the expense of purchase, but Watkin formed a private group, including some of the existing members of the company, and carried through the deal in 1863. The reorganized company was still desirous of making the most lucrative terms it could; but at least it saw in land sales to settlers a possible alternative to the fur trade, and to that extent the change facilitated a bargain with Canada. There were still serious obstacles. Canada wanted Britain to buy the West and present it to the Dominion. Britain showed no enthusiasm for the idea. The company raised a further obstacle when it insisted on retaining a substantial amount of fertile land as part of any agreement. Eventually the Colonial Office cut through the tangle and practically dictated terms to all parties. Britain would provide a loan to help Canada buy out the company. The terms were £300,000 in cash and the retention by the company of 45,000 acres around its posts and, in addition, the right to claim blocks of land up to one-twentieth of the fertile belt. Under this agreement, dated November 19, 1869, the company surrendered its lands to the British government, to be transferred to Canada as soon as the Dominion was ready to take effective possession.

These negotiations over the property, however, virtually ignored the fact that the inhabitants went with it. The Red River settlers looked on the new prospects with alarm. They felt that they were being bartered like cattle without their wishes being consulted or their rights safeguarded.

The local officials of the Hudson's Bay Company also felt aggrieved at the way the company was passing from one hand to another without proper consideration for their interests. Their resentment, coupled with doubts about the extent of their authority after the region had passed to Britain, made them dubious about taking vigorous action when trouble began to brew. The Canadian government on its part ignored with unforgivable levity repeated warnings about the growing seriousness of the situation until it found itself confronted with a virtual rebellion against its assumption of control.

Serious signs of trouble had in fact developed in 1868. In that year the devastation of crops by a plague of grasshoppers brought appeals to Canada for aid. The government responded by sending a party under John A. Snow to build a road from Fort Garry to the Lake of the Woods, even though Canada had not yet assumed title to the region. This effort to combine the construction of communications with the provision of employment was unfortunately compromised in its benevolent aspect by the conduct of the Canadian party. They stayed with Dr. John Christian Schultz and they employed Charles Mair as paymaster, and these were two of the most unpopular men in the settlement. Comparatively few natives actually found employment on the road, and they discovered that they were hired at low wages and paid in orders on Schultz's store, which were filled at exorbitant prices. To cap the climax, Canadians began to survey lands that they claimed to have purchased from the Indians, disregarding the settlers who were already there. The rising fear on the part of the half-breeds that their farms were in danger soon received full confirmation. With the terms of the transfer from the company agreed upon, Canada sent surveyors, who proceeded to run rectangular surveys, completely disregarding the river-lot boundaries of the existing farms. In October 1869, a band of half-breeds prevented the continuance of the survey across the farm of one of their number and threatened violence unless the whole proceeding was stopped. It was the first step toward organized resistance.

The leadership and inspiration that was needed to give the movement coherence came from Louis Riel. A native of the settlement, of French descent with a dash of Indian blood, he had been educated under clerical auspices at the College of Montreal. His intelligence, his vigorous personality, and his power of oratory made him a natural leader in the critical situation that was now developing. When a group of French-speaking settlers met on October 20, it was decided to set up an organization that would band together all their compatriots in defense of their rights. A committee was established whose nominal president was John Bruce, but

Area of the Red River Rising, 1869-1870

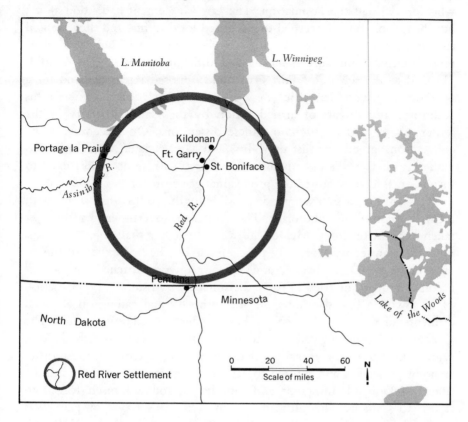

it was Louis Riel, first as secretary and then as Bruce's successor, who was henceforth the moving spirit.

The first step was to prevent the assumption of authority by Canada until a suitable agreement was reached. Already, in anticipation of the transfer of the territory, the new governor, William McDougall, was on his way to the Red River. His route lay through the United States; and when he reached the border, he found his way barred by a group of forty half-breeds who prevented his entry into the settlement. That was on October 21, and the event hastened the effort by Riel and his associates to secure effective control over the colony. On November 2, in a bloodless coup, they seized the Hudson's Bay Company stronghold at Fort Garry; and on the sixth they issued a call for delegates from the English-speaking population to join with the French in a convention that would represent the whole colony.

Hitherto all initiative had been taken by the *métis*, or French half-breeds, who formed half the population. The English element had stood aloof; but they, too, were concerned to safeguard local rights, and they wanted to find some peaceable solution to the problem. They sent their representatives, but agreement proved difficult to reach. The English objected to the seizure of Fort Garry and opposed Riel's demand for a provisional government. But new efforts by McDougall to assert his authority, and threats of armed action by the Canadian party in the settlement, helped to overcome these dissensions. On December 1 the convention agreed to a list of rights, and a week later, after an armed gathering of Canadian sympathizers had been surrounded and forced to surrender, Riel proclaimed the provisional government.

This important step was made possible by the confused situation with regard to constituted authority. The Canadian government had not yet taken over the territory. McDougall was fully aware that he had no status until the transfer was formally proclaimed. But he had expected this to take place on December 1; and when no word reached him of its accomplishment, he tried to force the situation by issuing a proclamation of his own on that date asserting his authority and calling on all loyal elements for support. The step was both ineffective and unwarranted. The Canadian government had no intention of taking over a rebellion along with its new territory. It insisted that the British government must assure tranquil possession and refused to accept the transfer until this could be done. McDougall, impotent and humiliated, found himself forced to return to Canada. The authority of the Hudson's Bay Company was doubtful after it had surrendered the territory to Britain, and British authority was not directly represented. The result was a political void, which the new provisional government undertook to fill.

The Canadian government now made an effort to regulate matters. Bishop Alexandre Antonin Taché, the embodiment of ecclesiastical authority in the colony, was summoned back from Rome, where he was attending the Vatican Council. Two French Canadians, Grand Vicar Thibault and Colonel de Salaberry, were sent off to the settlement with an official proclamation asserting the conciliatory intentions of Canada. They were followed by Donald Smith, head of the Hudson's Bay Company in Canada, as special commissioner to report on the situation and explain matters to the settlers. Smith put the case before two public mass meetings on January 19 and 20 and so impressed his hearers with the possibility of compromise that a convention was chosen, which drew up a fresh list of rights and appointed delegates to negotiate with Ottawa.

This promise of a tranquil outcome was unhappily vitiated by new threats of violence. The Canadian party had been chafing under Riel's ascendancy, and their desire for action was stirred up by a number of escaped prisoners from the party that had surrendered in December. Early in February an expedition was organized at Portage la Prairie to rescue the remaining prisoners. By the time it reached Fort Garry, Riel has been persuaded to release the arrested men, and the frustrated deliverers turned back toward home. But the French had been stirred by the threat of attack; and as part of the returning expedition passed Fort Garry, it was assailed by a party of *métis* and its members taken into custody. Riel, whose touchy and uncertain temper had hitherto been kept under remarkable control, was violently exasperated by the new challenge that had been offered to his authority and was determined to make an example in the interests of discipline. His choice fell on Thomas Scott, who had escaped after his earlier arrest in December and whose conduct during both his periods of imprisonment was uniformly insulting and provocative. Riel decided to treat him as a rebel. Scott was tried by an improvised court-martial whose proceedings added haste to irregularity. Riel remained adamant to appeals to either humanity or reason, and on March 4, Scott was executed by a firing squad.

This was a disastrous blunder. On the settlement, it is true, the execution seemed to have a tranquilizing effect by showing Riel's readiness to deal sternly with overt resistance. But in Canada, and particularly in Ontario, news of this action provoked an explosion of wrath. Scott, an Orangeman and a native of Ontario, had been done to death by a French Catholic who was himself widely regarded as a rebel. All the ugly passions of racial and religious enmity flared in a cry for vengeance. Fortunately it did not prevent the conclusion of a satisfactory agreement between the government and the delegates from the Red River, in spite of the short-lived arrest of the latter on their arrival in Canada; but it roused once more the sectional animosity that confederation was meant to allay, and it increased the clamor against a negotiated settlement and a demand for forcible measures.

Preparations for a military expedition were in fact already under way. The possibility of serious disorder and the fear that Riel might call on the aid of the United States seemed adequate reasons for the dispatch of a force to the Red River. With the agreement between the government and the Red River delegates the urgency disappeared, but the agitation over Scott's execution made it impossible to abandon the plans. Efforts were made to avoid any appearance of a punitive measure. The force under Colonel Garnet Joseph Wolseley was composed of a small body of British regulars and two detachments from Ontario and Quebec, and its announced purpose was to assure order and "afford equal protection to the lives and property of all races and of all creeds." Actually the settlement was quiet when the expedition, after backbreaking toil through the wilderness west of Lake Superior, arrived at Fort Garry. Riel had all along professed his loyalty to the British Crown. He was satisfied with the agreement that had been reached and was prepared to hand over his power to the new governor who was being sent from Canada. It was only the warning that his life might be in danger that drove him into flight at the last minute. The loyalty of the bulk of the *métis* was demonstrated when with Riel's approval they rallied to repulse a Fenian raid in October 1871. But neither this attitude nor the efforts of Wolseley to preserve discipline could keep the Ontario militia from regarding the expedition as a punitive one. Their arrogance and violence and the highhanded conduct of the triumphant Canadian party created resentment and bitterness and sowed the seeds of later and even more serious trouble, which was to have a prolonged and disruptive effect on the whole of Canada.

Meanwhile the status of the Red River settlement was settled by an act of May 1870, which provided for its admission as the province of Manitoba —a measure that was followed by the formal transfer of the West to Canada, effective July 15. The list of rights drawn up by the settlers demanded provincial status, respect for existing customs and property rights, an adequate financial arrangement, equality of French and English as official languages, and representation by two senators and four members in the Commons. Although certain other requests, such as provincial control of public lands, were rejected, most of these demands were met by the Manitoba Act, which transformed the District of Assiniboia into the new province. The remainder of the West was to be administered as the Northwest Territories under an appointed governor and council. Because of doubts about the constitutionality of certain provisions, an amendment to the British North America Act was passed by the Imperial Parliament in 1871, validating in full both the Manitoba Act and the legislation on the Northwest Territories and specifically giving the Dominion the right to create new provinces and to determine the terms of their entry.

The acquisition of the prairie region by the Dominion had a vital bearing on the situation on the Pacific coast. There the colonies of Vancouver Island and British Columbia, which were united into a single province in 1866, were going through a difficult period. The earlier outburst of prosperity had come to an end with the subsiding of the gold rush. A serious decline in population set in, which accentuated the burden of the debt that had been incurred during the brief period of expansion. Half the provincial income went to pay the interest on a debt of $1,000,000. With a scattered and dwindling population, heavy taxation, and a few outlets for its natural products, the province faced a serious question as to its future development.

The alternatives that presented themselves were entry into confederation or annexation to the United States, and it was far from certain that the first of these would be chosen. There were comparatively few ties of sentiment or interest with so remote a community as Canada. So long as the prairies remained under the Hudson's Bay Company, a political connection between Canada and the Pacific coast was almost impossible. This fact, and the dangers inherent in delay, gave Canada an added motive for speeding the acquisition of the West; but even when this was assured, the tremendous problem of communications remained to be solved, and the benefits that union would bring to the province were still uncertain. British Columbia had adopted a high tariff to protect the mainland producers from American competition, and the farming and lumbering interests wanted to preserve the local market against the United States; but the local market was not large enough to assure prosperity, and it was doubtful whether Canada would provide an outlet for British Columbia products. The influence of the governor and the local officials was in general hostile to a union with Canada. When in 1867 a resolution in favor of such a step was carried through the legislature—a mixed body containing both elected and appointed members—the governor described it to the Colonial Ofce as merely "the expression of a despondent community longing for a change."

In addition there existed within the province an active sentiment in favor of annexation to the United States. In no other province was annexationist feeling so strong or so vigorously expressed. There was a growing connection with the Pacific states, which was strengthened by the progress of the transcontinental railway, whose completion in 1869 offered a transportation link with the East. Commercial interests saw new prospects of trade if the province became part of the United States. Victoria in particular had visions of becoming the chief port of trade between America and the Orient. The annexationist group was encouraged by the agitation in the United States, where leaders such as William Henry Seward and Charles Sumner were advocating the absorption of British North America and where a bill was introduced by Senator Banks in 1866 providing for the entry of any or all of the provinces into the American union. In contrast, British public sentiment was avowedly indifferent and prepared to let the colony choose its own course. The annexationists were emboldened to

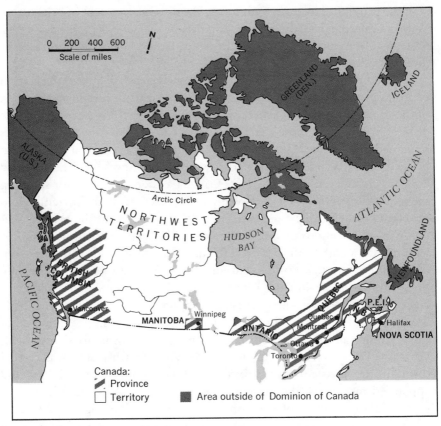

Dominion of Canada, 1873

petition the Colonial Office for virtual release from the empire in 1867. Two years later the legislature reversed its earlier stand and asked that British Columbia be left out of confederation, and a petition was circulated for a request to President Ulysses S. Grant to arrange the transfer of the colony to the United States.

Against these proposals the advocates of union with Canada launched a vigorous countercampaign. One of the most active figures was the editor of the *British Colonist,* a gentleman whose high aspirations had led him to change his name from Smith to the more grandiloquent appelation of Amor de Cosmos. Under his inspiration a series of mass meetings was held throughout the province, beginning in January 1869, to press for entry into confederation, and these culminated in September in a popular convention at Yale, which criticized the obstruction of the local government and adopted an address to the Queen in favor of union with Canada. By this time the British government had decided to throw its influence on the side of union, as it had previously done in the Maritime Provinces. A dubious and lethargic governor was succeeded by a more energetic appointee. His active influence with the official element resulted in still one more change of mind by the legislature and an agreement on the terms on which British Columbia would consent to enter confederation. Negotiations at Ottawa resulted in a definite arrangement. The debt of the province was to be assumed by the Dominion, a favorable subsidy granted, full responsible government introduced into the province with a federal representation of three senators and six members in the Commons, and a railway to the coast to be begun in two years and completed in ten. A provincial election produced a legislature that unanimously ratified the proposal, and British Columbia entered as a province on July 20, 1871.

Prince Edward Island followed two years later. The feeling that the original scheme of federation would be both politically unfair and economically disastrous to the Island began to wane with the rise of new economic difficulties. The province had shown itself reluctant to share the cost of railways on the mainland, but when it embarked on a railway program of its own it soon found itself in need of help. The Island confronted a debt that had suddenly risen from $250,000 in 1863 to $4,000,000 a decade later. The provincial finances were strained, and the stability of the banks, loaded down with railway debentures, was in serious danger. The province turned to the Dominion for rescue. An agreement was made that a federal grant of $800,000 should be given to buy out absentee landed proprietors and extinguish that long-standing question. The Dominion was to take over the railway guaranty, assure communications between the Island and the mainland, and grant a generous subsidy. On July 1, 1873, Prince Edward Island was added to the Dominion.

In Newfoundland in contrast, popular opinion, undecided at the outset, continued to harden against confederation. The island's outlook was oriented toward the Atlantic and the British Isles, and there was little communication or economic connection with the mainland. Despite indigenous poverty and wild fluctuations in the economy, the prospect of economic relief through union was too uncertain to offset the fear of added taxation and the imposition of protective tariffs. Newfoundland lapsed into stubborn and distrustful aloofness; and though overtures were renewed in the eighties and nineties, it was not until the twentieth century that Newfoundland was persuaded to enter as the tenth province of Canada.

The Citadel at Quebec. *(Public Archives of Canada)*
The view at about the time of the Quebec Conference.

The London Conference, 1866. *(Public Archives of Canada)*
The conference that completed the drafting of the British North America Act.

The Charlottetown Conference, 1864.

The First Dominion Day.

The Execution of Thomas Scott.

Red River Transport.
Carts from Fort Garry stopping in St. Paul.

Chapter 14

The Sinews of Nationalism

The Treaty of Washington, 1871

With the completion of confederation a political framework was established through which Canada's growing sense of nationalism could be more definitely and more effectively expressed. The political achievement, however, was only a first step. The process of unification itself had revealed the limited strength of the forces of nationalism. The new ties must be strengthened by the development of a transcontinental economy that would overshadow the forces of sectionalism by opening up new and wider opportunities under the auspices of the Dominion. The settlement of the West, the creation of a national system of transportation, and the stimulation of manufacturing by the development of resources and markets were among the salient purposes for which the Dominion had been created and for which the federal government had been given such extensive powers. Upon its success in carrying out these tasks the fortunes and even the continued existence of the Canadian federation largely depended.

There were external as well as domestic aspects to these problems. Canada had been forced into a greater reliance on her own potentialities, and consequently into a more effective organization for their development, by the simultaneous growth of indifference in Britain and hostility in the United States. It was of the utmost importance that both of these should as far as possible be overcome. Canada's prosperity as a trading nation and her security as a distinct community were bound up with her relations to the two great English-speaking nations. Her continued connection with Britain was desirable not merely to facilitate access to British markets and capital, but also from motives of defense. Britain, it is true, was calling home the legions—the last British troops, except for a small garrison at Halifax, were withdrawn in 1871—and her determined policy of friendship toward the United States made her extremely reluctant to become embroiled for the sake of Canada; but if a crisis should arise, Canada would have to count on Britain for adequate military help.What was still more desirable was that any real danger of a crisis between Canada and the United States should be eliminated. Canada had to share the continent with her powerful neighbor in reasonable amity if she hoped to maintain her separate existence. Trade relations with the United States formed one cornerstone of Canada's prosperity. A restoration of harmony after the strained relations that had accompanied the Civil War was one of the most immediate problems confronting the new Dominion.

The circumstances were far from propitious. The spirit of "manifest destiny" still lingered in the United States. In some quarters it was even accentuated by the outcome of the Civil War and the impetus it gave to expansionist elements in the triumphant North. The purchase of Alaska in 1867 eliminated Russia from North America and strengthened the desire to expel Britain from the continent. Anti-British feeling, which had increased during the war, could find a focus in the disputes that had now arisen over the *Alabama* claims and the San Juan boundary. The latter arose from differences over the demarcation of the channel south of Vancouver Island, which brought into question the possession of the strategic island of San Juan. The former was concerned with American claims for damages resulting from the depredations of Confederate commerce raiders that had been built in British ports, of which the *Alabama* was the most famous. There was a deliberate attempt by annexationist leaders in the United States to use these claims as a lever and to demand that Britain settle them by handing over her remaining possessions in North America.

Canada was thus vitally concerned in the relations between Britain and the United States. With the expansion of the Dominion to the Pacific, the San Juan dispute involved her territorial interests. She was less directly affected by the *Alabama* claims; but so long as that issue remained alive, it offered a pretext for American hostile designs against Canada. Confederation had not diminished that hostility. Americans were less impressed by Canada's efforts to attain a more independent status than by the fact that the new national structure was monarchial in its basis and a reaffirmation of the ties with the British Crown. Difficulties between the United States and Britain were reflected in strained relations between the United States and Canada and made more difficult a settlement of the questions of trade and fisheries that were directly at issue between the two countries.

These two questions were intimately connected. Canada's immediate desire was to secure a renewal of the reciprocity agreement that had expired

San Juan Water Boundary Dispute, 1872

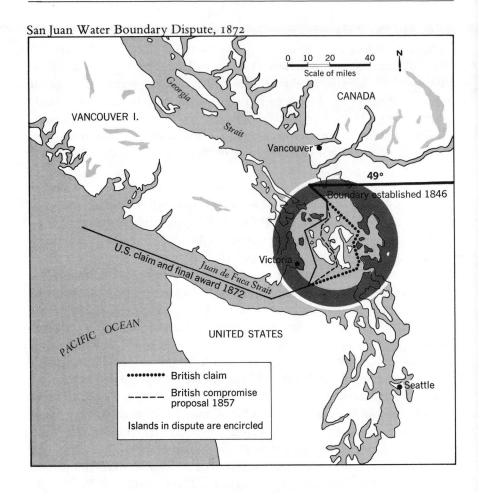

in 1866. The United States, where northern protectionist sentiment was now in the ascendant, was averse to any new trade agreement. There was a rooted conviction that reciprocity had operated to the advantage of Canada rather than of the United States, and no offer of trade concessions by Canada seemed important enough to motivate a relaxation of the American tariff or to overcome the opposition of such special groups as the coal and lumber interests to the admission of Canadian products. If Canada was to secure an agreement, she would have to find other bargaining weapons than reciprocal trade advantages.

One such asset was to be found in the Canadian canals, whose use was particularly desired by the western states. Canada on her part wanted to attract American traffic; and while the exclusion of American shipping from the Welland and the St. Lawrence canals could be used as a form of pressure, it was far from a desirable policy from Canada's point of view. The fisheries were far more important factors in the situation. The abrogation of the Treaty of 1854 forced American fishermen back to the less favorable basis of the Convention of 1818, which excluded them not only from inshore fisheries, but also from the ports of the Maritime Provinces, "except for the purpose of shelter and of repairing damage therein, of purchasing wood, and of obtaining water, and for no other purpose whatever." American fishing interests felt that it was vital to them to have access to both the ports and the fishing grounds, and their pressure induced the Grant administration to seek a renewal of the arrangements of 1854 and presented Canada with a chance to demand trade concessions as the price of American admission to the fisheries.

From 1865 on a number of efforts were made to reach an agreement. They failed because the United States was unwilling to pay the price that Canada desired. The Americans wanted the fisheries with only nominal concessions in return. To Canadian suggestions of reciprocal free admission of natural products, the Americans in 1866 replied with an offer of a moderate tariff level and free admission of five articles—millstones, rags, firewood, grindstones, and gypsum! That was too derisive to be considered seriously. Within a short time after the lapse of the Reciprocity Treaty it became apparent that Canada's trade with the United States, while it might be reduced, would not be completely ruined, and Canadians felt that they could await a more satisfactory offer without the risk of economic collapse.

Meanwhile, however, American fishermen were unwilling to give up the advantages they had hitherto enjoyed, and which were now legally forfeit. Canada did not press the matter so long as there was hope of a new agreement. American fishermen were admitted to the inshore fisheries on payment of a moderate license fee, and there was a lenient attitude toward unlicensed ships. But as it became apparent that conciliation was ineffective in moving the United States to a comparable generosity in trade matters, and as Americans persisted in evading the license regulations, Canada decided to try firmness. When new conversations on reciprocity in 1869 came to nothing, Canada announced that the license system would be ended in 1870 and sent her own ships to enforce the exclusion more effectively than British patrols seemed ready to do. The result was the seizure of 400 American vessels in Canadian waters during the season of 1870 and an outburst of wrath in the United States against Canada's audacity in enforcing her rights. "This semi-independent but irresponsible agent," said President Grant in a message to Congress, "has exercised its delegated powers in an unfriendly way." Threats of American retaliation and the prospect of renewed friction during the fishing season of 1871 gave fresh incentives for an attempt to reach an agreement.

The way was opened by American overtures to Britain. A convention for the settlement of existing difficulties had been rejected by the Senate in 1869, but a fresh approach was made in 1870. The United States agreed to accept arbitration of the *Alabama* claims if Britain would arbitrate on the San Juan boundary and to negotiate on trade concessions in return for the opening of the fisheries. An agreement was reached providing for a joint high commission to meet in Washington in 1871 and to tackle the accumulated controversies of the past decade.

Canadians looked on the prospect with mixed feelings. Galt expressed a prevalent view when he objected to the mingling of Canadian and British interests in the negotiations. Memories were still fresh of the occasions when Britain had sacrificed Canadian claims for American friendship, and there were fears that the surrender of the fisheries would be the price paid for a settlement of the *Alabama* question. But Canada's advance in strength and importance, and the new status she had achieved through confederation, placed her in a stronger position to defend her cause. Although the treaty-making power still lay solely with the imperial government, it was recognized that any agreement on the fisheries must have Canada's consent and that Canada must be associated with the negotiations. She was not to be separately represented, but the inclusion of a Canadian member in the British delegation was nonetheless a distinct advance toward a voice in diplomatic matters that directly affected the Dominion. The fate of an American suggestion that the governor general should act for Canada symbolized her growth in stature since 1854. The precedent of Elgin's role in the reciprocity negotiations was now obsolete. Only a responsible political leader could be accepted as a spokesman for Canada, and that meant in effect that Macdonald must be the Canadian member of the commission.

Macdonald accepted the necessity with reluctance. He was fully aware of the pitfalls that lay before him. "If things go well my share of the kudos will be but small," he wrote, "and if anything goes wrong I will be made the scapegoat at all events so far as Canada is concerned." He knew that he would have to stand up, not only to American pressure, but to his British colleagues as well. Britain might concede Canada's right to dispose of the fisheries; but she was determined to reach a settlement with the United States and would certainly urge Canada to make the concessions that were necessary to achieve this end. Her own difficulties over the *Alabama* could be settled with relative ease. Canada did not dare wreck the settlement by appearing intransigent. Macdonald hoped that the *Alabama* claims would be disposed of first, leaving the British delegates free to take a more vigorous stand on behalf of Canada. But the Americans, fully aware of its tactical importance, insisted on putting the *Alabama* question later on the agenda and disposing of the fisheries first. Although the agreement to arbitrate the *Alabama* claims was the most celebrated outcome of the Washington negotiations, it was over Canadian questions that the chief struggle took place, and the Canadian delegate was the unhappy focus of all the major difficulties.

Macdonald recognized that there was no hope of excluding the Americans from the fisheries or the canals. It was not indeed in Canada's interest to do so. His essential objective was to get the most favorable bargain possible in the form of trade concessions. He was up against a determined effort by the Americans to get what they wanted and to pay little or nothing in return. They demanded compensation for the *Alabama* but refused to consider any compensation to Canada for the Fenian raids. They insisted on retaining San Juan Island as a right and on admission to the fisheries as a necessity that it would be unfriendly of Canada to refuse. The threat that a rejection of American demands would result in the loss of American friendship was wielded with particular vigor against Britain in an effort to enlist British pressure against Canada. Macdonald, battling on two fronts, could do little except use Canada's nuisance value to the limit, and that limit was circumscribed by a haunting fear that too unyielding a stand would play into the hands of the British anti-imperialists, who already looked on Canada as a liability. He concentrated on wringing what concessions he could from the Americans and on laying the foundations for a claim to compensation from Britain if these concessions proved inadequate.

Macdonald's basic aim was a renewal of reciprocal trade in return for the fisheries. In the face of protectionist sentiment in Congress it was almost hopeless that such an agreement could be carried. Instead the Americans offered a million dollars for the fisheries in perpetuity, together with free entry of Canadian coal, salt, fish, and lumber. They rejected Macdonald's proposal to add admission to the coasting trade or a cash equivalent. A hot discussion raged within the British delegation, with Macdonald's colleagues making speeches at him in an effort to persuade him to abate his demands. Macdonald, backed by messages from the cabinet in Ottawa, insisted that any such surrender would be rejected by the Canadian Parliament. A deadlock was reached, and it seemed that the negotiations must break down, when a new American offer opened the way for settlement. It was a proposal that arbitration should be accepted not only on the San Juan boundary and the *Alabama* claims, but also on the value of the fisheries. Under British urging the Americans agreed to add free entry of fish. Even then Macdonald was inclined to refuse, and even to resign from the Commission; but a British offer to compensate Canada for the Fenian claims which the United States would not meet induced him to acquiesce in the proposal after he had lodged with Britain a formal protest against its inadequacy.

The Treaty of Washington admitted Americans to Canadian inshore fisheries for a ten-year period. In return for free navigation of the St. Lawrence the United States allowed Canada free navigation of the rivers of Alaska—a privilege to which the Hudson's Bay Company attached considerable importance. Free navigation of the canals was not directly conceded, but the United States was to urge this concession on the individual states, and Britain was to make similar recommendations to Canada. Canadian fish was to be admitted to the United States free of duty. The United States and Canada agreed to mutual bonding privileges for twelve years and to limited reciprocity in the carrying trade on the Great Lakes. The most notable feature of the treaty was the acceptance of the principle of arbitration in relation to the chief questions. Under this the United States secured a favorable settlement of the San Juan boundary and the payment of $15,500,000 in settlement of the *Alabama* claims, and Canada was awarded $5,500,000 in payment for the opening of the fisheries.

Not all the problems were immediately solved by the treaty. It roused considerable oppostition in Canada, and Macdonald had to give opinion time to cool before he secured approval in Parliament. The slowness of Congress in implementing the terms by legislation delayed the removal of the tariff on fish, and consequently the opening of the fishing grounds, until 1873. Arbitration on the value of the fisheries was not completed until 1877, and British protests over the size of the *Alabama* award were paralleled by American resentment over the excessive valuation placed on their admission to Canadian inshore fishing grounds. Yet such causes of friction were minor compared to the dangerous possibilities that had been disposed of by the treaty. A relative harmony tempered by occasional bickering was restored between the United States and Canada; and the Dominion, freed from external danger, could turn its energies more fully to the work of internal expansion.

The National Policy

One of the salient economic purposes behind confederation was the expansion of commercial prosperity through a new orientation of trade relations. The abrogation of the Reciprocity Treaty threatened a serious curtailment of the markets that the provinces had enjoyed in the United States. To offset this loss they were thrown back on their own resources. Political union, by bringing them together in a single free-trade area, was expected to increase the interchange of products between the Maritimes and the St. Lawrence region. The acquisition and settlement of the West was counted on to provide new and growing outlets for eastern production. The flow of traffic north and south across the border was threatened with interruption by the American protective tariff. The remedy seemed to lie in the creation of a new trade system on east-west lines, which would knit the political structure together by the close ties of an integrated national economy; and the achievement of this aim involved the most intimate relation between commerce and transportation and settlement.

This did not mean a renunciation of the hope of new trade arrangements with the United States. Even after the ending of reciprocity, that country was still Canada's largest customer, and increased access to American markets seemed the surest road to commercial expansion. This was an aim that successive Canadian administrations pursued at every opportunity during the remainder of the century. It was not incompatible with a growing volume of east-west trade; but a more active domestic commerce, however desirable as a supplement to wider trade with the United States, was hardly a satisfactory substitute. It was, however, the only alternative that offered itself; and the question arose whether Canadian producers, denied free access to the markets of the continent, could find compensation in the home market if they had to compete freely in that limited field with their protected American rivals.

This question was of special importance to Canadian manufacturers. At that time of confederation the bulk of Canadian industry consisted of small shops, usually with fewer than five employees, producing consumer goods for a purely local market. Woolen textiles, the boot and shoe industry, and harness manufacture were examples of enterprises that were engaged in the processing of local raw materials to meet local demand. Processing for export was largely confined to the lumber industry, where the decline of the trade in square timber was accompanied by a rising demand for sawn lumber in markets abroad. Sugar refining and the slowly developing cotton textile industry were among the few important branches of manufacture dependent on imported raw materials. Nonetheless, the pattern was in process of change. The coming of the railways not only created a demand for construction materials and stimulated the rise of an iron industry, but began the breakdown of the system of local distribution, enabling the manufacturer to reach out toward wider markets and favoring the growth of larger establishments and the concentration of industry in the chief urban centers. The small firm supplying local needs was in a relatively sheltered position. The manufacturer who reached out toward more distant areas was more exposed to competition, not only from Canadian rivals, but from the more advanced industries of Britain and the United States. The aspirations of the infant Canadian industries to secure a larger domestic market, and particularly their dream of new and expanding outlets in the West as settlement advanced, had to take these facts into serious consideration. If they could trade freely in a continental market, Canadian manufacturers professed a belief that they could compete successfully with their American rivals. But if they were confined by the American tariffs to the more restricted Canadian field, their natural impulse was to keep it to themselves.

The first organized pressure for a protective tariff developed in 1858 and secured a considerable measure of satisfaction in the tariffs of 1858 and 1859. In the negotiations over confederation, however, the high level of Canadian duties roused objections in the Maritimes, and it was partly to mollify this sentiment that Galt in 1866 lowered the general level of duties on manufactured goods to 15 percent and considerably enlarged the free list. The next few years were marked by the effort to secure a new reciprocity agreement with the United States; and except for a few short-lived changes in 1870, the Canadian tariff remained at a revenue rather than a protective level.

In 1873 the defeat of Macdonald as a result of the Pacific scandal meant the fall of the Conservative government and its replacement by a Liberal administration under Alexander Mackenzie. The Grit tradition of free trade and a tariff for revenue only was strong in the Liberal ranks. George Brown remained a power in the party, though after his resignation from the coalition at the end of 1865 as a result of his opposition to Galt's reciprocity proposals he had largely withdrawn from active politics. Yet he retained a connection with public life through his subsequent appointment to the Senate, and his interest in political issues and his abiding distrust of the Conservatives still found forcible expression through the columns of the *Globe*. Brown's personal antipathy toward Macdonald sharpened the edge of his attacks. He had vigorously assailed the failure to secure a renewal of reciprocity with the United States and the supineness with which Macdonald had surrendered Canadian interests in the Treaty of Washington. With the full operation of the treaty postponed as a result of the delay over arbitration on the value of the fisheries, the door still seemed open for negotiations to substitute trade concessions for cash compensation. The American administration seemed to have grown more receptive toward the idea. Brown convinced himself that this change in attitude amounted to a positive eagerness for a commercial agreement and that this eagerness was now shared by Congress. In a mood of rosy optimism he saw a chance for a personal triumph over his rival; and in 1874 he set out to negotiate the renewal of reciprocity that Macdonald had so lamentably failed to secure.

Unfortunately these hopes were based on illusions. An agreement was indeed negotiated that offered substantial advantages to both sides. For a period of twenty-one years there was to be reciprocal free trade in sixty specified natural products, a wide range of agricultural implements, and thirty-seven categories of other manufactured goods, and provision was made for reciprocal navigation of canals. But the American enthusiasm in which Brown placed such glowing hopes was entirely imaginary. Hamilton Fish, the American Secretary of State, favored an agreement in principle but was highly dubious about its acceptance by Congress. He was quite sure that a treaty confined to natural products would have no chance of ratification; and Brown, in his determination to secure an agreement, found himself consenting to successive extensions of the list of manufactures and to the demand that the Canadian canals should be enlarged to accommodate ships with a 14-foot draft. Even these concessions made little impression on Congress. The protectionist forces showed little disposition to accept any inroads on the high tariff system that was being built up, and the advantage to American interests of tariff concessions by Canada was not great enough to rally solid support. Indifference rather than positive hostility determined the fate of the agreement. President Grant sent it to the Senate with a somewhat tepid message of approval; but the Senate after considerable delay decided to refuse consideration, and the rebuff made it clear that the United States had no real interest in the idea of reciprocity with Canada.

Meanwhile circumstances had brought into the forefront the question of tariff readjustment in Canada. The depression of 1873 hit Canada at a time when substantial revenues and credits were both needed to carry an expensive program of expansion, particularly in railway construction. Falling prices and a slump in commercial activity were accompanied by a tightening of the money market, which made the raising of loans more difficult. Customs and excise duties, which provided five-sixths of the federal revenue, were hit by the decline in imports and in the consumption of luxuries. To meet the financial crisis that confronted it, the Mackenzie government in 1874 raised the general level of duties on manufactures to $17\frac{1}{2}$ percent and imposed a moderate duty on semimanufactured goods.

It was obvious that a rise in the tariff level, even though the initial aim was increased revenue, could be made to serve the purpose of protecting home industry. A considerable protectionist sentiment developed among the urban Liberals in Ontario. The rising hopes of the protectionists were increased when continued deficits led the government to contemplate further changes in 1876. But Liberal members from the Maritimes, already uneasy over the rise in rates, intervened with a strong protest against further increases. The government abandoned the project, and in the budget debate of 1876 the Liberal leaders rejected the idea of protection and announce their firm adherence to a tariff for revenue only.

Macdonald watched these developments with the shrewd eye of an opportunist. His own convictions were as flexible on this as on other issues. He did not believe that unreciprocated free trade on the British model was a suitable policy for Canada. But although he had been impressed by the growing protectionist sentiment in Ontario in the early seventies and by the political possibilities that it offered, he had not committed himself to protection as a policy. He was thinking rather of a readjustment of the tariff that would attract support to the party, while still professing that the protectionist effect was purely incidental to the revenue aspect of the tariff.

The Conservative tactics were in fact determined by the attitude of the Liberals. Macdonald and his followers had shared the general expectation that the government would raise the tariff in 1876. Tradition has it that they were prepared to attack the idea of protective duties and to advocate a continued search for reciprocity as an alternative. When the Liberals reasserted their attachment to the principles of free trade and left the duties unchanged, Macdonald promptly shifted his ground. Here was an opportunity to rally to the party those industrial groups, not only of capital but of labor as well, whose expectation of favors from the Liberals had been disappointed. Macdonald is reported to have remarked that protection had done so much for him that he must do something for protection. He recognized that the word itself, with its odious connotation to so many elements in the country, must be avoided, "but we can ring the changes on National Policy, paying the United States in their own coin, etc." The need for a tariff adjustment that would remedy the depression in trade, foster a national economy, prevent Canada from becoming a "slaughter market" through the dumping of foreign goods, and encourage native industry by harmonizing its needs with those of the public revenue suddenly became a matter of burning concern to the Conservative party. If the United States refused reciprocity of trade, it must accept reciprocity of tariffs. The phrase "National Policy" conveyed the idea of benefits in which all groups in the nation would share and became the chief slogan in the attack that the Conservatives now launched against the policies of the government.

The resulting protectionist campaign was vigorous and sustained. The traditional bonds between the business interests and the Conservative party were drawn tighter than ever. A convention of the Manufacturers' Association of Ontario voiced a demand for duties equal to those imposed by the United States. The Dominion Board of Trade came out in favor of protection. A National Policy League was organized to support the cause. Macdonald unfolded its merits to the electors at a series of political picnics, while he and his party continued to champion it in Parliament against the resistance of the Liberal government. It made a growing appeal to a public that found in the negative policy of the Liberals no remedy for its economic ills and no response to the awakened nationalist sentiment. In the election of 1878 the Conservatives won a sweeping victory, with 137 seats against 69 for the Liberals. It was a clear mandate for a policy of tariff protection.

The outcome was the tariff of 1879. Samuel Leonard Tilley, the new finance minister, introduced it with the explanation that the government had endeavored to meet every possible interest and had invited all those who felt an interest to make their wants known. The result, he felt confident, "would give ample protection to all who are seeking it, and who have a right to expect it." The new levies provided a rate of 10 percent on partly manufactured goods and an average of around 30 percent on finished articles. The principal beneficiaries were textiles and iron and steel products, but other enterprises that were exposed to competition from abroad were given generous consideration even when their production met only a small fraction of the Canadian demand. Nova Scotia coal was protected by a duty of 50 cents a ton. The small petroleum industry in western Ontario was covered by a tariff of over 35 percent. For the benefit of a single firm making cheap clocks, a duty of 35 percent on all clocks was levied. Other and more important products were favored in varying degrees. While steel ingots and rails entered free, other iron and steel products were taxed at rates ranging from $12\frac{1}{2}$ percent on pig iron to

25 percent on castings and forgings, and the latter rate was also applied to machinery and agricultural implements. Duties on cotton textiles ranged from 20 to 34.4 percent. Woolen textiles carried rates averaging over 30 percent, and blankets were taxed at the equivalent of 41.4 percent. Whatever the consumer might feel, few industrial producers had serious reason for complaint.

The advocates of the National Policy asserted that a protective tariff would provide a remedy for economic depression, check Canadian emigration by providing increased employment, attract fresh capital to Canadian enterprises, encourage a more active interchange of products between the various sections of Canada, and even increase the prospects of reciprocity with the United States. At best these hopes were only partly realized. The new tariff may have done something to check the fall in prices and the decline in production and to bring about the establishment in Canada of American branch plants. But it did little to restore the general level of prosperity or to halt the exodus of population to the United States, and Americans remained as indifferent as ever to the idea of a reciprocal trade agreement. Yet the National Policy did express the desire of Canadians to build a vigorous and independent national economy as the bone and sinew of political unity; and in spite of party changes and party professions, the protective tariff has ever since remained a cardinal feature of Canadian national life.

The Canadian Pacific Railway

Among the bonds that were counted on to cement the new Dominion, railways held a place of the highest importance. Political union had been achieved in the face of geographic barriers that could only be overcome by a nationwide system of transportation. The hope of facilitating the construction of a transcontinental railway had been a potent factor in the movement for confederation. Its realization was essential if confederation was to succeed. Railways were needed not only to open the West to settlement and to create a national commercial system on east-west lines, but to bind together the diverse and widely separated sections into a single state. They were political as well as economic necessities; and even if they were commercially unprofitable, they still had to be built as part of the basic framework of Canada's national structure.

A salient illustration was provided by the Intercolonial Railway. This road, connecting the St. Lawrence with the Atlantic seaboard, was the necessary price of the entry of the Maritimes into confederation. The strength of their insistence was shown when the railway was written right into the Canadian constitution. The accomplishment of this long-deferred project depended directly on the initiative of the federal government and on the provision of public funds. A loan of £3,000,000 was raised in Britain, aided by an imperial guaranty of 4 percent interest on three-quarters of the total amount. The rest of the ultimate cost of $34,000,000 came from the Canadian treasury. The lines already built in the Maritimes were taken over; construction was extended on the general line of the Robinson route by way of the Bay Chaleur; still other lines were taken over east of Quebec, and arrangements for running rights over the Grand Trunk eventually extended the complete system from Halifax to Montreal.

The choice of the route was made largely on strategic grounds. Britain still wanted the line to lie a safe distance from the border, and other considerations were not strong enough to offset this view. Advocates of a route up the St. John Valley were unable to prove conclusively that the cost would be substantially less than by the Chaleur route or that the commercial advantages would be greater. Indeed, the chief engineer, Sandford Fleming, feared that traffic would be diverted to the existing line from St. John to Bangor and cherished a hope that the new railway would create an ocean port on the Bay Chaleur. But in either case the line would run through large stretches of sparsely settled territory, and local traffic was bound to be of secondary importance. It was as a through route that it was desired and that it served its purpose. Commercially it was never a paying proposition, and the Grand Trunk, which had been so eager to get the Intercolonial built, saw no purpose in taking over its operating losses when it was available in any case as an alternative to its American outlet. The government was left to operate the road and to assume its annual deficits, finding consolation in its service as an instrument for national unity—and, on a lower level, as a highly useful source of political patronage in the Maritimes.

A railway stretching across the prairies to the Pacific was a problem of equal urgency and far greater magnitude. Circumstances called for prompt and speedy action. British Columbia's entry into Confederation was conditional on the completion of the railway within ten years. The early settlement of the prairies depended on adequate transportation. American lines were reaching out in that direction, and the Northern Pacific in particular threatened to establish itself as the main route to the Canadian West unless it were forestalled by a Canadian road. Yet there were serious obstacles. The estimated cost of $100,000,000 was to prove highly optimistic, but it was still too vast for either government or private enterprise to contemplate without qualms. The Liberals were alarmed by the prospects of such an expenditure and deeply suspicious of any scheme that brought railway interests and John Alexander Macdonald into combination. Even their desire for western settlement did not weigh against their growing hostility toward the project, which the *Globe* attacked as "a rash and maybe disastrous step at the dictation of a handful of people 2,500 miles away." The Grand Trunk, originally an enthusiastic advocate of the Pacific railway, soon became its bitter opponent and used both its political influence in Canada and its financial influence in London to create difficulties. American railway and financial interests created similar difficulties in New York. Indeed, the engineering problems that the railway encountered, great as they were, sank into insignificance in comparison with the political and financial obstacles that loomed in its path.

There was one asset on which the government counted heavily to meet the problem of financing. In the United States, land grants had been used lavishly as incentives to private railway companies. The Canadian government had at its disposal a vast imperial domain to be used for the purposes of the Dominion. By offering substantial tracts of land, it hoped to tempt private capital into undertaking the railway. An initial cash subsidy would have to be added to help the company through the initial stage before land sales began to bring in revenue, but the government expected to recoup this outlay from land sales to settlers. Thus the work of construction would be thrown on private enterprise, and the Canadian taxpayers would be spared any share of the burden. It was an optimistic vision in view of the past record of the canals and the Grand Trunk, but it resulted in a government offer of a subsidy of $30,000,000 and a grant of 50,000,000 acres.

Two groups entered into competition for the contract. One was formed in Toronto under the presidency of Senator D. L. Macpherson, and among its leading figures were a number of Grand Trunk officials including C. J. Brydges. The other was formed in Montreal under Sir Hugh Allan, who enlisted the support of American capitalists. Their competition was marked by a strong element of sectional rivalry, which made the government extremely reluctant to choose between them and which even forced the selection of the geographically neutral point of Callendar on Lake Nipissing as the Eastern terminus of the proposed road. National feeling was also summoned to the aid of the Toronto group, which charged that Allan's company was really composed of directors of the Northern Pacific and was under American financial control. When the government tried to get an amalgamation of the two companies, the Toronto interests refused on these grounds. Efforts to overcome the hostility of the Grand Trunk to the Montreal company were also unsuccessful, and Cartier's connection with the Grand Trunk made it likely that his influence in the government would be thrown against Allan and his associates.

Allan took vigorous steps to deal with this situation. "I satisfied myself," he wrote to one of his New York backers, "that the whole decision of the question must ultimately be in the hands of one man, and that man was Sir George E. Cartier." He set out to bring Cartier to terms by building a political backfire against him in his own constituency. He described with some gusto his resulting activities:

I employed several young French lawyers to write it up for their own newspapers. I subscribed a controlling interest in the stock, and proceeded to subsidize the newspapers themselves, both editors and proprietors. I went to the country through which the road would pass, and called on many of the inhabitants. I visited the priests, and made friends with them, and I employed agents to go amongst the principal people and talk it up.

I then began to hold public meetings, and attended to them myself, making frequent speeches in French to them, showing them where their true interest lay. The scheme at once became popular, and I formed a committee to influence the members of the Legislature.

This succeeded so well that, in a short time, I had 27 out of the 45 on whom I could rely, and the electors of the ward in this city, which Cartier himself represents, notified him that unless the contract for the Pacific Railway were given in the interests of Lower Canada, he need not present himself for re-election. He did not believe this, but when he came here and met his constituents, he found to his surprise, that their determination was unchangeable.

Even with Cartier brought to reason, there were still difficulties. The election of 1872 was looming, and the government considered it unwise to take any action until the results were known. Cartier in his turn made it plain to Allan that his true interests lay in the return of a friendly government; and as an aid toward that end, Allan parted with some $350,000 for campaign funds. The return of the Conservatives was followed by fresh efforts on the part of the government to eliminate American control and to bring in the Toronto group. A reorganization of Allan's company was carried out on a basis that ostensibly satisfied both these aims, and it was granted the charter for the Canadian Pacific Railway in 1872.

The success was ephemeral. In the session of 1873 a Liberal member,

L. S. Huntington, launched the charge that the contract had been granted in return for campaign contributions to which American capitalists had subscribed. Concrete evidence was shortly forthcoming when G. W. McMullen, the representative of the disgruntled American interests, that found themselves excluded from the final contract, gave to the press an account of the negotiations and copies of various letters and telegrams bearing on them. A royal commission was appointed to investigate, and further documents were brought to light. Among the most damaging items of evidence were a list of contributions requested by Cartier to the amount of $110,000, of which $35,000 was for Macdonald; a further request to Allan's representative for $20,000 for Cartier and $10,000 for Macdonald; and a telegram from Macdonald marked "Immediate, Private" and reading "I must have another ten thousand; will be the last time of calling; do not fail me; answer today." Macdonald stoutly denied that there was any corrupt bargain. He insisted that these were simply normal political operations, and that sums of this size were quite usual for a man as wealthy as Allan. But an aroused public sentiment was reflected in a motion of censure in Parliament, and as it saw its support evaporating the government chose to resign before the matter came to a vote. The Liberals took office and early in 1874 appealed to the electorate. In a contest that the *Globe* excitedly described as "the Thermopylae of Canadian virtue" the Conservatives were defeated and the Mackenzie government received an overwhelming majority.

These events meant the end of Allan's contract but brought no immediate alternative into view. The depression of 1873 on top of the Pacific scandal made it more difficult than ever to interest private capital in Canadian railway ventures. The Mackenzie government decided to proceed with construction as a public undertaking, building the road by sections as the advance of settlement warranted, and using water routes and American lines to fill in the intervening stretches. It was a policy calculated to relate the rate of expenditure to the resources of the government, but it was too slow and cautious to meet the needs of the situation. British Columbia was particularly restive over the delay, which threatened to violate the terms on which the province had entered confederation. A sharp controversy developed, on which the government, in due course, reluctantly accepted the arbitration of the governor general. Even this proved only partially successful, and there was rising talk of western secession. Boldness was needed on this as on other aspects of the new national economy, and the lack of that quality did much to bring the defeat of the Liberals in 1878.

For a time after the return of Macdonald and the Conservatives to power they continued the policy of piecemeal government construction inaugurated by their predecessors. But it was clear that this would not meet the needs and the problems they had inherited, and they seized the first opportunity to fall back on private enterprise. A temporary revival of prosperity at the end of the decade increased the prospect of raising capital in Britain and the United States. At the same time a group of Canadians emerged from a profitable if none too scrupulous transaction involving the St. Paul, Minneapolis and Manitoba Railway in the United States. They included the railway promoter J. J. Hill, Donald Smith of the Hudson's Bay Company, and George Stephen of the Bank of Montreal. It seemed desirable that their funds and their experience should be taken advantage of by Canada. "Catch them while their pockets are full," Macdonald was advised by his confidant John Henry Pope. Negotiations were successfully undertaken, and in 1880 a new syndicate with financial connections in London and Paris as well as in New York was given the contract for the Canadian Pacific Railway.

The company combined a predominantly Canadian personnel with the somewhat delusive appearance of international financial backing. Reliance was still placed on the combination of government subsidies and extensive land grants. Both were somewhat lower than the earlier proposals. The cash grant was $25,000,000. The land grant was reduced to 25,000,000 acres, but this was offset by provision for "indemnity selection," which allowed the syndicate to choose fertile land in place of any part of its grant that proved unsuitable for settlement. In addition the government handed over to the company the 700 miles of road already built, allowed its materials to come in duty free, exempted it from taxes on its land for twenty years and on its property forever, forbade the construction of any competing line to the south or southwest during the next twenty years, and promised that there would be no regulation of rates until the company was earning 10 percent. The work was to be completed by 1891. The generosity of these concessions roused a Liberal outcry and brought into being a rival syndicate, which offered to build the road on much easier terms. But the government used its majority to push the contract through Parliament, and the company embarked on the construction of a railway with a total length of 1900 miles.

The task proved to be a formidable one. Construction difficulties were greater than expected. Additional expense was incurred in securing eastern lines connecting with Montreal and Toronto. The fact that the work was pushed forward speedily only added to the difficulties, for it reduced the chances of raising funds from land sales during the construction period. A new slump made it harder to raise loans, and the influence of both the Grand Trunk and rival American roads was adverse to the effort. By the end of 1883 the company, in desperate straits for ready funds, was appealing to the government for a loan of $22,500,000. Macdonald told them they might as well ask for the planet Jupiter. He was sure his cabinet would never consent and that the party would break if they did. The situation was only saved by the intervention of J. H. Pope, who roused Macdonald in the middle of the night to recall him to political realities. "The day the Canadian Pacific busts," he asserted, "the Conservative party busts the day after." Macdonald saw the light and fought the loan through Parliament at the price of paying blackmail to sectional interests in both Quebec and Ontario in the form of fresh subsidies. Even this did not end the problem. Within a year the railway was again in trouble and even lacked funds to meet its pay roll. Its request for a fresh loan of $5,000,000 threw the government into despair and almost decided it to take over the road. This time the outbreak of the Northwest Rebellion saved the situation. The transport by rail of a military expedition from Ottawa to Winnipeg in six days, in contrast to the two months taken by the Wolseley expedition in 1870, was a spectacular demonstration of the value of the railway. The loan was granted, and on November 7, 1885, the last spike was driven in the Canadian transcontinental system. Macdonald's lighthearted assertion that the road would cost Canada nothing was to prove optimistic. Apart from more than 26,000,000 acres of the best prairie lands, the company received the equivalent of $63,500,000 in public subventions, direct and indirect, as well as loans to a further amount of just under $35,000,000; but the ensuing burden was the price for a vital artery of national commerce and for a system of transportation that would make possible the settlement of the Canadian West.

Western Policies and Problems, 1870-1885

When Manitoba was created a province in 1870, all ungranted lands within its borders were retained by the federal government to be administered "for the purposes of the Dominion." In that phrase lay the very heart of the policy that was to be adopted toward the West. The resources of that vast domain were to be utilized by the central government, not for local purposes, but for the benefit of the nation as a whole. Upon the settlement and the development of the West rested the chief hope of national economic expansion. The cost of that expansion was to be defrayed from western lands.

In evolving its land policy the Dominion could draw on the experience of the United States over a period of nearly a century. The problems were similar; the process of settlement was expected to follow much the same lines. Two of the most salient features were the regular system of surveys and a uniform system of grants to settlers on easy terms, and both were adopted by Canada. The basic unit, as in the United States, was the township 6 miles square, divided into 36 sections of 640 acres each. The homestead system of free grants provided that a settler could secure 160 acres on condition of three years' residence and cultivation and the payment of a $10 patent fee. Not all the land, however, was open on these terms. In addition to setting aside two odd-numbered sections in each township for the support of schools, the government hoped to combine free grants with the raising of a revenue from land sales. The remaining odd-numbered sections were set aside for railway and other grants or for sale at a minimum price of $1 an acre. Homesteading was thus to be confined to the even-numbered sections, and even there it was restricted by the alienation of considerable quantities of land for other purposes.

For although the Western domain that the Dominion had acquired was vast in extent, the quantity of arable land was relatively limited. Yet it was from this arable portion that the Dominion sought to discharge its mounting obligations. Part of the purchase price to the Hudson's Bay Company consisted of a grant of one-twentieth of the land in the fertile belt, and two even-numbered sections in each township were set aside to meet this provision. The 25,000,000 acres granted to the Canadian Pacific Railway initially consisted of alternate sections in a 24-mile belt on either side of the railway. But it was stipulated that the land should be "fairly fit for settlement," and provision was made for indemnity selection of lands outside this belt to compensate for the deficiencies within it. Further railway grants were made to branch or colonization lines. All these lands, as well as what remained to the government in the odd-numbered sections, were for sale at comparatively easy terms in the early years. The average price that the Canadian Pacific Railway got for its land up to 1906 was under $5 an acre. But with such quantities set aside for railways and the Hudson's Bay Company, for schools, and for government sale, what remained for homestead purposes amounted to barely one-quarter of the fertile belt. As the consequences of this situation became apparent, the government's hope of direct revenue from land sales rapidly dwindled. Its chief concern was to get settlers into the West—a policy that the railways and the Hudson's Bay Company, whose holdings would increase in value with the spread of settlement, heartily endorsed. "It is worth while," concluded one Minister of the Interior in 1905, "for the Dominion to spend hundreds of thousands of dollars in promoting immigration and surveying and administering these lands, and then to give them away."

At an early stage the Dominion embarked on an active immigration policy in an effort to bring settlers to the West. Agents were sent to Europe, and special fares were offered to immigrants. The provinces and the Canadian Pacific Railway added similar inducements. The results, however, fell short of expectations. While a flood tide of settlement was pouring into the last unoccupied lands of the United States, only a trickle of population flowed into the Canadian prairies. The American West was easier of access and more familiar as a goal to immigrants and even to large numbers of Canadians. A revival of prosperity about 1880, followed by the advance of the Canadian Pacific Railway brought a brief rush to Manitoba; but by 1883 the boom had collapsed and many homesteads were abandoned. The population gradually increased during the subsequent decade. In Manitoba it rose from 25,000 in 1871 to 152,000 in 1891, while the remainder of the prairies grew from a handful of half-breeds to approximately 50,000 during the same period. But this was a slow advance compared to the spectacular progress of the American West and represented a serious blow to the hopes of a rapid influx that had been entertained at the time of confederation.

To the original dwellers on the plains, however, any progress of settlement gave cause for perturbation. The efforts of the *métis* to preserve the Red River region for themselves were based partly on a fear that the growth of settlement would mean the doom of their seminomadic way of life. That fear was justified when the settlement of Manitoba broke the earth to the plow and brought an end to the buffalo hunt. Farther west along the Saskatchewan, not only the *métis* but the Indians faced the prospect that the same fate would overtake them as the coming of the railway forecast the advance of settlement into the Northwest Territories.

In contrast to the United States, the provinces of British North America had hitherto been relatively free from serious Indian troubles. In the East the opening of the land to settlement had been achieved with relative ease by a series of Indian treaties. In the West there had been none of that chronic warfare between Indians and settlers that marked the advance of the American frontier. Before 1870 the settlers had been few in number, and the majority of them had blood ties with the tribes. The Hudson's Bay Company carried the principles of law and order into the Far West and provided an economic outlet for both *métis* and Indians, which helped to avert any fundamental conflict between fur trade and settlement. These factors were not completely wiped out by the transfer of the West. The company continued as a trading corporation in close relations with the Indians. Its civil authority was replaced by that of a territorial government. The Royal North West Mounted Police, organized in 1873, imposed a restraining yet beneficent control over Indians and white men alike and protected the tribes from the frontier desperadoes and whiskey traders whose incursions from Montana presented one of the earliest and most serious problems. The gradual advance of settlement meant that there was little forcible intrusion on Indian lands, and the government had a margin of time in which to negotiate amicable treaty arrangements. Beginning in 1871, a series of treaties was concluded, which provided for the surrender of most of the fertile belt, the retention by the various tribes of reserves in their traditional locality, the payment of annuities to the Indians, and government assistance in education and agriculture. It was a process the object of which was to prepare the Indians for the transition from a hunting to a farming mode of life.

Not all the Indians were reconciled to the change. They continued to follow the buffalo hunt, interspersing it with occasional horse-stealing raids against other tribes on either side of the border. But the buffalo was rapidly disappearing, partly as a result of mass slaughter. By 1878 the animals were almost extinct, and the Indians who depended on them were on the verge of starvation. Pressure of necessity forced the Indians to acquiesce in the government's policy and to settle on the reserves; but there was much discontent over the abrupt change from the old way of life, and this was aggravated by the economy—and occasionally the inefficiency—with which the government managed Indian subsidies and supplies. By 1884 a sullen resentment had developed against the whites and their attitude toward the tribes.

By this time the *métis* also had developed serious grievances, many of which were shared by the white settlers in the territories. A considerable number of half-breeds had moved west from Manitoba and settled in the valley of the Saskatchewan. There they were soon beset by the same difficulties that had provoked the Red River uprising. Once more the government system of square survey ignored the boundaries of river-lot farms and brought their titles into question. Once again these grievances were brushed aside and a rising demand for political self-government was ignored. And once again the *métis,* with the initial support of the white settlers, turned to Louis Riel to lead their struggle against the government at Ottawa, whose apathy and indifference had not been overcome by the lesson of fifteen years before.

Riel's career during that period had not been wholly reassuring. Elected to Parliament, he appeared in Ottawa in 1874 only long enough to sign the members' book and then disappeared before his vengeful enemies could lay hands on him. Macdonald strove to avoid embarrassment by secretly subsidizing Riel to stay out of Canada while publicly vociferating a desire to bring him to justice. In 1875 Riel and two associates were banished for five years as a condition of their ultimate admission to the general amnesty that was extended to the participants in the Red River uprising. Riel's mental aberrations grew more apparent as the years passed and landed him for a time in mental asylums, though they did not prevent him from later becoming a schoolteacher in Montana. His religious obsessions increased until he became convinced that he was an instrument of divine revelation. But in spite of his lack of balance he was a leader to whom the *métis* looked for help in a crisis and an orator who could stir his followers to desperate action.

At the end of 1884 a petition to Ottawa embodied the grievances and demands of the territorial inhabitants. These included more generous treatment of the Indians, more favorable land terms to both whites and half-breeds, local control of natural resources, lowered tariffs, and a railway to Hudson Bay. On the political side there were requests for local self-government and adequate representation at Ottawa. Prompt attention to the petition would have averted trouble. A bribe of a few thousand dollars would have secured Riel's withdrawal and at least delayed the crisis. But Macdonald, whose tendency to postpone decisions until problems had solved themselves had earned him the soubriquet of "Old Tomorrow," took no action in spite of increasingly urgent warnings from the local authorities, and Riel's impatient followers moved rapidly toward violence.

The agitation took a long step toward rebellion with the formation of a provisional government in March, 1885. This step, and the growing danger of an armed outbreak, alienated the English element that had originally supported Riel. The clergy, too, had swung against him as a result of his religious aberrations, which culminated in his decision to found a new church and his persuading his council to declare him a prophet. But the *métis* remained loyal in spite of clerical efforts to detach them; and at their headquarters at Batoche, Riel and his associates pushed forward their preparations for armed action.

Area of the Northwest Rebellion, 1885

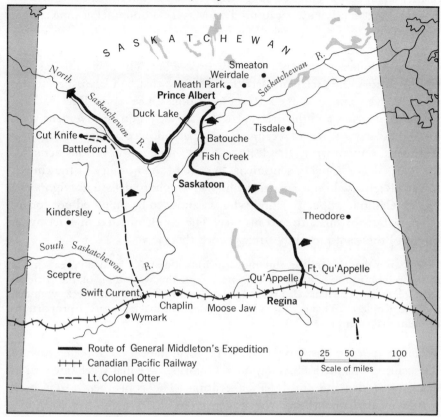

The struggle was precipitated by a clash between half-breeds and police at Duck Lake on March 26. The police were routed, and the engagement was the signal not only for a *métis* rising, but also for an Indian outbreak. On March 30 a band of Cree under Poundmaker pillaged a Hudson Bay post and laid siege to the town of Battleford. On April 2 another band under Big Bear sacked the little settlement at Frog Lake and massacred the inhabitants. News of these events at last aroused the federal government to action. A force of over 5000 troops was despatched to the West. Its arrival, together with belated redress of the most immediate grievances, localized the rebellion and prevented a general Indian uprising. On May 12, following an initial check at Fish Creek, General Frederick Dobson Middleton captured the rebel headquarters at Batoche and scattered the leaders. Another column relieved Battleford, and though its further advance was checked at Cut Knife, the back of the uprising was by that time broken. Riel was captured on May 15, Poundmaker on May 26, Big Bear on July 2. The rebellion was at an end and with it all further danger from either *métis* or Indians.

Its consequences were not so easily disposed of. The new outbreak had fanned to fury the racial and sectional passions that had been smoldering uneasily ever since the Red River uprising. Once again Riel had led resistance in arms, and the grievances that lay behind the movement were lost sight of in the storm of recriminations that followed. Ontario Protestant sentiment, remembering the death of Scott, burst out in furious demands for Riel's death. Quebec sentiment, in spite of the hostility of the church toward Riel, saw him as a patriot who had sought to defend the rights of a French Catholic population and who was now to be punished not for his offenses, but for his faith and his race. The condemnation of Riel by an English Protestant jury only strengthened this view.

Why is it that this traitor, this apostle, this madman . . . holds so great a place in the public mind?" asked *La Minerve.* "It is the wounding of the national self-esteem. . . . The hand that placed the gallows rope around his neck wounded a whole people. . . . That is why the death of this criminal takes on the proportions of a national calamity.

When an appeal to the Privy Council failed, agitation was directed toward the securing of a pardon. Agitation in Ontario was equally vehement in its determined demand for Riel's execution. The controversy split both parties in Parliament; but the government stood firm, and Riel was hanged on November 16, 1885. Few events so profoundly shook the Dominion or had such long-standing results. Riel became a symbol of all the deep-rooted antagonisms that continued to divide Canada along racial lines and that contributed in a major degree to the revival of sectionalism which marked the final decades of the century.

The Canadian Pacific Railway.
Donald Smith, later Lord Strathcona, driving the last spike.

The Treaty of Washington.
The renewed friendship of Britain and the United States meant the end of the Fenian threat.

Calling Home the Legions.
Departure of the British garrison from Quebec, 1871.

Alexander Mackenzie.   *(Public Archives of Canada)*

Chapter 15

The Years of Hope Deferred
1873-1896

Stagnation and Sectionalism

The bonds that were essential for the creation within Canada of a genuine national unity were first of all those of material interest. In the campaign for confederation there were orators, not least among them the eloquent Thomas D'Arcy McGee, who gave expression to the higher vision of a community united by spiritual ties and imbued with a passionate sense of Canadian patriotism, and these ideals were sincerely held by large numbers of Canadians. But such emotional aspirations were not by themselves of sufficient strength to weld the new Dominion into a single coherent whole. The difficulties that had been encountered in bringing about confederation showed how slender were the ties between sections that were separated by physical barriers and in certain instances were at a relatively young stage of development. Questions of material advantage had bulked large in the controversy over the scheme of federation. Its success would be judged largely by the tangible blessings it conferred on the component communities.

From that point of view the quarter century after 1867 was an era of disappointed hopes. It was a period of great efforts and in certain respects of great achievements, but the rewards seemed sadly out of proportion. The acquisition of the West and the construction of a transcontinent railway had opened the prairies to settlement, but the expected flood of settlers had yet to materialize. Industrial growth was retarded by the slowness with which the domestic market expanded, and a protective tariff was only a partial compensation. Failure to secure a renewal of reciprocity with the United States was not offset by the limited increase in trade between the provinces, and no alternative foreign markets were opened from which Canadian export staples might derive any substantial benefits. In spite of political unity, the Canadian economy remained dependent on an active world market, and the depression of the seventies struck it a body blow from which it did not recover for over twenty years.

In the long-term perspective the period recorded a more substantial over-all advance than was appreciated at the time. Real output expanded; industries such as steel and agricultural implements established solid foundations; unadjusted estimates of gross national product rose from $459 million in 1870 to $803 million in 1890. "From 1870 to 1890 the Canadian employment in manufacturing rose by 76 percent and output in constant dollar terms 138 percent." Yet progress was uneven, and a brief upsurge of prosperity between 1879 and 1883 was preceded and followed by discouraging slumps that seriously retarded, even if they did not wholly check, the economic advance on which such hopes had been placed.

Among the immediate effects of the depression were a fall in prices and a contraction of international credit; and Canada, as an exporting and a debtor country, was hard hit by both. From its peak in 1872, the price level showed an almost unbroken decline until 1897, when the index of wholesale prices stood at barely 56 percent of its earlier high. Falling prices and contracting markets brought a decline in both the value and the physical volume of Canadian staple exports. Foreign sales of lumber were cut in half by 1879. Exports of wheat and fish were also reduced, though less drastically, and there was a brief recovery at the beginning of the eighties; but this was followed by a fresh slump and a steady downward course. Between 1882 and 1889, wheat exports fell from over 6,000,000 to less than 2,000,000 bushels, bacon from 10,000,000 to under 4,000,000 pounds, butter from 15,000,000 to just over 2,000,000 pounds. Part of this decline was offset by changes in Canada's pattern of exports, which saw a considerable increase during this period in cattle and cheese and corn, as well as in lobsters and salmon to offset the decline in other branches of the fishing industry. In spite of many fluctuations, Canadian exports increased from $48,000,000 in 1868 to $88,000,000 in 1891. This growth, however, did little more than keep pace with the increase in population from slightly over 3,000,000 to almost 5,000,000 during the same period. Such figures represented, not a realization of objectives, but the frustration of Canadian hopes for broadening prosperity and expanding opportunities.

Even in the matter of population the significant thing was not the actual growth but the slowness of the rate of increase. In the older provinces the spread of agrarian settlement had almost reached its limit. In Ontario the institution of free land grants and the opening of the Muskoka district in the sixties pushed the frontier into the region of the Laurentian Shield. In Quebec the building of colonization roads gave access to new lands in the Eastern Townships and north of the St. Lawrence. Such measures, however, had a relatively meager effect on the basic situation. Any substantial increase in population must be absorbed by the prairie West and the urban centers of the East; and when prairie settlement was retarded, urban industry was also held back by the lack of that expanding home market on which its growth depended.

During this period the economic structure of the older provinces was in a state of transition. Its significance was illustrated by the shift in the proportion of rural to urban population. During the decade after 1881, rural population in the five Eastern provinces remained almost stationary and even showed a slight decline in Nova Scotia and Ontario. In contrast, urban population in Nova Scotia increased by 13,450, in Quebec by 121,000, in Ontario by 243,000 for a gain of more than 50 percent. In the generation after 1867, approximately three-quarters of the increase in Canada's population was absorbed by the towns. By 1891, Montreal had 250,000 inhabitants, and Toronto, with 181,000, had outdistanced Quebec to become the second city in Canada and to develop a growing commercial and financial rivalry with Montreal.

Behind these shifts in distribution lay changes in the pattern of rural as well as urban life. In central Canada particularly the era of wheat as the leading staple crop was drawing to a close. The West was soon to replace the older region as the great wheat-growing and wheat-exporting area. Ontario and Quebec gradually turned to mixed farming and the provisioning of the local markets created by the growing towns, and this phenomenon was to a certain extent paralleled in the Maritimes. There was a rise in dairying and fruit farming and livestock production, and this was reflected in the export trade as these products sought foreign markets to supplement the ones that were nearer at hand.

These changes, however, did not enable the rural areas to support an expanding population, and their failure was only partly offset by the absorptive capacities of the towns. In industry as in agriculture there were limitations and fluctuations, which hampered the revival of prosperity. Although the gross value of Canadian manufactures rose from $221,000,000 in 1871 to $370,000,000 in 1891, industrial growth was distinctly uneven. The depression of 1873 was marked by bankruptcies and unemployment. The rising tide of business failures reached a peak in 1879, when assets involved were approximately $30,000,000. There was a temporary recovery during the next few years, but 1884 saw the effect of a new slump in bankruptcies to the value of some $20,000,000, and difficulties continued throughout the next decade. Weaker firms failed or were absorbed by stronger rivals. The completion of the main railways and the decline in general construction diminished the demands for both products and workers. Thousands of Canadians, finding the doors of enterprise closed to them at home, turned to the United States in search of the opportunities that their own land seemed unable to offer.

In consequence, the long period of the depression saw a steady drain of population from Canada southward across the border. Of all the aspects of the depression, this was the most galling to Canadians. The United States itself was not without its troubles during this period, which saw severe fluctuations in business and active manifestations of agrarian and labor unrest. Nonetheless it offered a wider range of opportunity than could be found in Canada. Farmers from central Canada, discontented with their prospects in their native province, found Nebraska and Dakota more attractive than the remote Canadian prairies. Maritime youths joined the New England fishing fleet or migrated to the cities along the Atlantic seaboard. French Canada sent workers to the lumber camps and the mines and to the mill towns of New England. Skilled industrial and railway workers found their services in demand in the United States, and many an aspiring young professional man found it easier to make a start in that country than in the overcrowded field at home. While Canada was seeking to attract immigrants who would people her empty spaces, she was losing some of her best stock to her southern neighbor, and many of her immigrants proved to be mere birds of passage who moved on or returned to their native land. Perhaps half a million people, natives or immigrants, left Canada in the decade after 1871; perhaps a million in the succeeding decade. During these twenty years, the actual increase in Canada's population fell below the estimated natural increase, apart altogether from 1,200,000 immigrants during the period—a figure that by itself was slightly in excess of Canada's population gain.

In the face of these conditions, the various sections of the Dominion felt only a restrained satisfaction with the individual benefits that political union had conferred upon them. In certain provinces, such as Nova Scotia and British Columbia, there was even a strong feeling that confederation had brought more burdens than advantages. To the general feeling of frustration induced by the depression there was added a growing exasperation at the inequality with which it seemed to bear on different regions. Both the Maritimes and the West attacked the domination of central Canada; and all sections directed their resentment against the federal government, whose policies seemed to favor certain groups and regions and to deny to the individual provinces the power to work out their own salvation.

The West had a wide variety of grievances. British Columbia had been induced to enter the Dominion by the promise of a railway within ten years; and when it became clear that this was impossible of fulfillment, an agitation developed that raised a serious threat of secession. An appeal to the imperial government brought an offer of mediation from the colonial secretary, Lord Carnarvon—a well-meaning gesture that was far from appreciated by the federal government. The view of the Mackenzie administration was that the matter was one between the provinces and the Dominion, in which the British government had no right to interfere; and irritation was increased when Carnarvon sought the aid and advice of the governor general, Lord Dufferin, in reaching his decision. The government's insistence on modifying the Carnarvon award embittered the controversy, which only subsided when definite arrangements for the completion of the Canadian Pacific were at last concluded under Macdonald. Meanwhile a further controversy over Oriental immigration, consequent on the influx of Chinese in the wake of the gold rush, contributed to friction with the Dominion as provincial efforts at restriction were balked by the central government.

The railway situation also caused trouble on the prairies. The monopoly clause in the Canadian Pacific charter was hotly resented, but efforts by Manitoba to charter competing lines were repeatedly disallowed by the federal government, and the issue remained acute until the Canadian Pacific Railway was persuaded to surrender this offending privilege in 1888. A chronic grievance was the retention by the Dominion of control over Manitoba's natural resources as one of the terms on which the province was admitted—a provision that was denounced as unconstitutional and was all the more resented because of the relative slowness of settlement under Dominion auspices. The grievances of the territories that led to the Riel rebellion and the controversy over separate schools in Manitoba, which developed into a national issue, were further examples of the persistent friction between the West and the government at Ottawa.

The Maritimes were also restive, and for even deeper reasons. Their economy, like that of the central provinces, was in a state of transition. The age of wood and sail was giving place to the age of steam and steel. The great days of the sailing ship were over by the eighties, and the Maritimes were being by-passed by modern transportation and commerce. With fishing and lumbering and agriculture nearing the limits of their expansion, the Atlantic provinces had to seek new activities to replace the decline in shipbuilding and commerce, and the disappointing results of that search brought a growing discontent with their lot under confederation.

The depression of the seventies coincided with the beginning of the decline in shipbuilding; and that decline was accompanied by a gradual loss of the carrying trade, in which Nova Scotia had formerly been so active. One of that province's own sons, Samuel Cunard, provided a vivid illustration of the effect of the coming of the age of steam. In the period after 1815 he was active in both shipping and shipbuilding, securing mail contracts and conducting regular services between Halifax and Liverpool. By 1830 he had become interested in steamships, and he was one of the shareholders in the *Royal William*, which made one of the first steam crossings of the Atlantic in 1833. A steamship line between Halifax and Liverpool was inaugurated in 1838, and Cunard conducted regular services after the founding of his own line in 1840. For nearly a generation Halifax, the closest to England of all the major ports on the Atlantic seaboard, dreamed of becoming a leading entrepôt of trade. But the pull toward ports with a more prosperous hinterland was too strong. The Cunard terminus was shifted to Boston; their ships soon ceased to make regular calls at Halifax; and by 1876 it was only in winter that Halifax was a regular port of call. The building of the Intercolonial Railway did little to redress the situation; for while it gave a transit route for winter traffic, trade during the summer preferred to seek the St. Lawrence; and while the port of Halifax was to some extent sustained by the railway, the lesser ports along the coast lost much of the trade they had enjoyed before the railway brought competition with coasting ships.

The trade advantages that confederation brought to the Maritimes were thus limited. The stimulus to other branches of Maritime economy was varied in character and somewhat dubious in value. There was little market in the St. Lawrence region for such natural staples as timber and fish. Coal found an increasing market in the province of Quebec and was favored by a protective tariff after 1879; and by the eighties the foundations had been laid for a steel industry that also came under the protective system. In general, however, the hope of industrial development in the Maritimes proved as vain as the hope for wider markets in the rest of Canada. The industries of Ontario and Quebec, with larger markets nearer at hand, were able to keep control in their own provinces and to compete successfully in the Maritimes. Although industrial production increased during this period, most manufacturing was by small firms for local markets, and these felt the constant pressure of competition from the larger industries of central Canada. In consequence, the Maritimes felt that the balance of trade with the rest of the Dominion was distinctly to their disadvantage and that the National Policy imposed additional costs on them without compensating advantages. When this was accompanied by declining markets abroad and by the failure of the Dominion government to renew reciprocity with the United States, it was not hard for disgruntled Maritimers to convince themselves that they could make better arrangements for themselves outside the Dominion than within it; and this feeling found expression in the Nova Scotia legislature in 1886 in an abortive resolution in favor of secession.

At the same time the central provinces, the objects of so many recriminations, had troubles of their own. If they were accused of exploiting the rest of Canada, they could retaliate with complaints about the cost to their taxpayers of the constant demands for increased subsidies, which rose from what one embittered speaker called "the shreds and patches of confederation." In both Ontario and Quebec, a growing resistance developed to the control by the central government over policies and resources. In addition, the chronic issues of race and religion arose once more to embitter the relations of those two provinces and to embroil both of them with the federal government as these issues were injected into Dominion politics.

The Conservative Ascendancy

The dominant force in national politics in the quarter-century following confederation was the Conserative party of Sir John Alexander Macdonald. The organization that had been knit together in the old province of Canada was carried over into the broader field provided by the new Dominion. The forces that had been chiefly instrumental in bringing about confederation were enlisted in the effort at national expansion that followed the attainment of political unity. With his genius for opportunism, Sir John was able to rally to his side most of the leading political figures and to identify his party with the main policies that affected the Dominion as a whole.

The foundations of the party still rested on those two anomalous elements, the big business interests in English-speaking Canada and the French Catholic hierarchy in Quebec. It was above all the leading business groups whose interests cut across sectional lines and whose aspirations embraced Canada as a whole. Financial groups such as the Bank of Montreal were concerned with the construction of railways and the expansion of industry and the settlement of western lands. Railway projects could only be realized with substantial government assistance; and although the struggle over the Pacific Railway lost the Conservatives their alliance with the Grand Trunk, the former *bête noire* of the Grits, its opposition only served to cement more closely the identity of the Canadian Pacific Railway with the Conservative party. Manufacturers were attracted by the Conservative adoption of a protective tariff and the hope of greater security in an expanding domestic market. By the seventies the party had evolved a program calculated to attract all those whose fortunes were bound up with the development of economic nationalism.

The appeal to Quebec rested on an entirely different basis. Its starting point was the unrelenting hostility of the hierarchy to liberalism and all its works. The effort of the Papacy to strengthen its spiritual authority in compensation for the loss of its temporal power was reflected throughout the whole Catholic world, and not least in Quebec, where the struggle against the forces of secularism and intellectual independence was waged with increasing intensity. The determination to crush the *Rouges* and the resentment aroused by the anti-Catholic and anti-French attitude of the Grits ranged French clericals on the Conservative side. It was an uneasy alliance with a party that found one of its most stalwart bulwarks in the Orange order; but the very fact that Quebec had a voice in Conservative councils gave some guaranty of restraint on the more extreme Protestant elements, and the alignment of Catholicism with the party of property was based on a common hostility to radicalism in the political and social spheres. So long as the Church felt that rougism was a danger—and this was a convenient specter, which haunted Quebec politics long after the body had departed—the influence of the hierarchy was thrown on the Conservative side.

With all these advantages, however, Macdonald found that the task of maintaining a coherent national party taxed to the utmost the ingenuity and resourcefulness with which he was so highly endowed. The electorate—and, for that matter, their chosen members—could not always be counted on to reverence the judgment of business leaders or even to follow their spiritual shepherds. Businessmen had constantly to be mollified by contracts or tariff concessions. Special interests in Quebec had to be placated by appointments and appropriations. In the Maritimes and the western provinces, where the party had no deep roots, subsidies and patronage formed the uncertain cement that held its supporters in line. The skill with which Macdonald carried on the work of reconciling incompatibles in the face of constant threats of disruption wrung a grudging admiration even from his critics. "When this man is gone," wrote Goldwin Smith, "who will there be to take his place? What shepherd is there who knows the sheep or whose voice the sheep know? Who else could make Orangemen vote for Papists, or induce half the members for Ontario to help in levying on their own province the necessary blackmail for Quebec? Yet this is the work which will have to be done if a general break-up is to be averted. Things will not hold together of themselves."

It was against this process of sordid bargaining for sectional advantages that a young group of nationalists in the early seventies raised the standard of revolt. The Canada First movement, which was launched by a manifesto by the Toronto barrister William A. Foster in 1871, expressed a desire to subordinate the existing sectional outlook to a truly Canadian nationalism and to make the existing political parties more adequate instruments of Canadian national interests and sentiments. It was an ideal that rallied a lively group of enthusiasts, chiefly in Ontario. The National Club was started in 1874 as a meeting place, and in the same year a weekly journal, the *Nation*, was founded to inaugurate a public campaign. In 1874 also the formation of the Canadian National Association signalized the entry of this group into politics with the avowed intention of supporting whatever elements in the existing parties were prepared to accept and implement their ideas.

The aims of the movement were extremely general; the means by which they were to be attained were vague and in some respects contradictory. The essential desire was to achieve a distinctive Canadian national character and status, accompanied by the evolution of a constructive program that would develop the resources and build up the population of the Dominion. Specific proposals for internal reform ranged from the extension of the franchise to the reorganization of the Senate and from pure and economical administration to a revenue tariff that should manage to be protective as well. It was, however, the question of Canada's external relations that provided the most vital as well as the most controversial aspect of the movement. At its heart lay the problem of developing in Canada a national personality that would set her apart from both Britain and the United States, the two great nations with which her fortunes and her destiny were so intimately linked. The Treaty of Washington provided a vivid example of the disadvantages to Canada of her continued colonial status. The desire for a more independent position, which would reduce Canada's subjection to Britain without leading to absorption in the United States, was expressed in the plank "British connection, consolidation of the empire—and meanwhile a voice in treaties affecting Canada," and the idea of full autonomy within a federated empire was one which attracted many members of the movement.

This was an issue that caused divergences within the movement and attacks upon it from without. From both the old parties came cries of republicanism and annexationism. Foster might protest that "we no more advocate independence than we advocate the day of judgment," but he made clear his belief that Britain was loosing the ties of empire and that Canada must prepare for the time when she would be forced to strike out for herself. The adherence of Goldwin Smith, an English radical who firmly believed in the inevitability of Canada's separation from Britain and her continental destiny in association with the United States, gave an intellectual leadership that strengthened this aspect of the movement. By the end of 1875, a series of disappointments and the failure to rally any large measure of popular support brought the end of Canada First as an organized movement, though the ideals that it had voiced survived as a persistent undercurrent in Canadian life.

The most damaging blow to the movement was the defection of Edward Blake. This brilliant if unpredictable leader, who now stood in the front rank of the Liberal party, had withdrawn from the Mackenzie administration in 1874 after a brief term as minister without portfolio. On October of that year, speaking at Aurora, he pronounced in favor of the chief planks in the Canada First program, with special stress on the need for greater autonomy. "The time will come," he asserted, "when we shall realize that we are four millions of Britons who are not free"; and when he described himself as "one who prefers to be a private in the advance guard of the army of freedom, to a commanding place in the main body," he seemed to be indicating his readiness to lead a crusade for the conversion of the Liberal party. The impression was strengthened when Blake lent his influence to the founding of the *Liberal*, a paper that appeared as a rival of the *Globe* and an ally of the *Nation*. But the hopes raised by these developments were dashed in the following year. Blake made his peace with his party and returned to office as minister of justice; the *Liberal* went out of existence; its editor moved over to the *Globe*. It was a desertion that crushed at one stroke the whole Canada First movement.

It was also a blow to the prospect that the Liberal party might find a solid national basis that would enable it to rival the appeal of the Conservatives. Blake in office made a real contribution to the definition and extension of Canadian autonomy. But he did little to associate his party with the work of national reconstruction and expansion, which was so much more urgent a problem for the Dominion, or to overcome the negative outlook and the parochial basis that characterized the Liberal party during this period.

The Liberal tradition of individualism, which had hampered the effectiveness of the reform movement in the past, remained a barrier to party coherence and solidarity. Party discipline sat lightly on many professed members. Internal restiveness divided the Liberal ranks, with one group looking to Blake for more vigorous leadership, while another remained under the influence of George Brown and looked with distrust on any innovations in policy. Ontario provided the dominant element in the party, and concern for Ontario interests strengthened an innate distrust of centralized government. To this was added a continued suspicion of big business and its connection with government, accompanied by a greater concern for honesty and economy than for a broad program of economic expansion.

The influence of these factors was evident during the administration of Alexander Mackenzie. This former stonemason, with his rigid integrity and his lack of imaginative vision, had been chosen leader when Blake refused to accept the position; yet Blake remained a power in the party, and his independent attitude and his reluctance to assume any real responsibility created repeated difficulties. Mackenzie himself provided little inspiration as leader. In his determination to assure honesty of administration, he himself took over the Ministry of Public Works; and while his watchfulness no doubt benefited the taxpayers and the treasury, it burdened him with a mass of routine duties and distracted his attention from broader policies. To add to his troubles, he was confronted with the economic and financial crisis resulting from the depression of 1873. In a situation that called more urgently than ever for bold constructive measures, Mackenzie's natural instinct dictated increased caution and economy. His failure to solve the railway problem, his inability to secure reciprocity with the United States, and his refusal to adopt a protective tariff left him with no remedies to offer the country in its time of distress and led to his decisive defeat in the elections of 1878.

The decade that followed saw the Liberals still groping for an effective national basis and still plagued by troubles over leadership. When Mackenzie retired in 1880, Blake consented to replace him; but his dislike of responsibility, and the intellectual aloofness that separated him from the rank and file, brought happiness neither to himself nor to his followers. The loss of the election of 1887 brought his resignation. Largely through his influence the mantle of leadership fell on Wilfrid Laurier, who still had to win the unreserved loyalty of the party and who in his turn found himself hampered by Blake's continued prestige and unpredictable actions. In federal politics the Liberals seemed reduced to a party of chronic opposition.

In the provincial field their efforts were more successful; and this fact strengthened their tendency to support local autonomy against the central government. Unable to break Macdonald's ascendancy at Ottawa, they were ready to seize on any opportunity to reduce the limits of his power and to enlarge the authority of the provincial governments that they controlled. In consequence, provincial rights became one of the main tenets of the Liberal creed; and this was particularly evident in central Canada, where the issue came to overshadow the older aspects of the Liberal tradition. The long career of Sir Oliver Mowat as Premier of Ontario after 1872 was marked by the quiet abandonment of the element of radical reform that had been evident in the Clear Grit party. The accession of Honoré Mercier to power in Quebec in 1887 marked the extinction of the last flicker of the old *Parti Rouge*. In the federal sphere a certain legacy from the past was evident in that wing of the Liberals which adhered to free trade and continued to distrust big business; but this group steadily dwindled in influence, and under Laurier the party at last discovered its true future in the capture of the chief positions and policies on which the Conservatives had built their success.

The Rise of Provincial Rights

It had been the clear intention of the fathers of confederation to confer on the federal government full control over all matters affecting the general interests of the Dominion as a whole. A legislative union had been impossible of attainment, but there was a deliberate effort to approach it as closely as was compatible with a federal form of government. The distribution of powers under the British North America Act was designed to confine the provinces to purely local matters; and Macdonald showed an intention in practice to treat the provinces not merely as inferior in status, but as definitely subordinate to the government of the Dominion.

A potent instrument to this end was the federal power of disallowance. The right to nullify provincial legislation made it possible for the central government to restrict the power of the provinces even over those matters allotted to them by the constitution. The Liberals, with their tendency toward strict construction, took the attitude that disallowance should be invoked only when a provincial measure was *ultra vires*, thus making it a shortcut to an end that could be equally—and perhaps more legitimately—attained through judicial review. But the Conservatives felt the power should also be used to prevent a conflict between federal and provincial legislation or any intrusion by the provinces upon the interests of the Dominion, and that it should be invoked against undesirable measures "contrary to reason, or to natural justice, or equity." In practice these terms were very broadly interpreted. Manitoba railway legislation was disallowed when it infringed on the privileges of the Canadian Pacific Railway. A Prince Edward Island land act was disallowed because it seemed unfair to the proprietors. When Ontario passed a Rivers and Streams Act to enable upstream lumbermen (who happened to be Liberal) to make use of timber slides and similar improvements erected by other lumbermen (who happened to be Conservative) in floating their logs downstream, the Dominion three times interposed its veto before it decided to let the measure become law. Between 1867 and 1896, sixty-eight provincial laws were disallowed; and in many cases the power was used to achieve much the same effect as that attained under the contract and due-process clauses in the American Constitution.

Other means of keeping the provinces properly subservient were also attempted. There was considerable hope at the outset that the lieutenant governor would prove an effective agent of the Dominion government in imposing restraints on provincial policies. It was also believed that a useful influence could be exercised through the dual mandate that allowed a member to sit in a provincial assembly as well as in the federal Parliament. The possibility of using these and other resources for party advantage was not lost on Macdonald. At the outset the franchise for federal elections was based on that of the provinces; but when these showed a tendency toward increased democracy—Ontario, for example, adopted a low income franchise in 1874 and moved by cautious steps to full manhood suffrage in 1888—Macdonald countered by invoking the Dominion's power and establishing a federal property franchise in 1885. Distribution of seats and electoral boundaries were also arranged with a shrewd eye to party advantage, notably in the gerrymander of 1882, which was designed to increase Conservative chances in doubtful constituencies by a process of "hiving the Grits." Yet few of these devices proved of lasting effectiveness. It is doubtful whether either the gerrymander or the change in the franchise seriously affected election results. The holding of a seat in more than one legislature was forbidden by a federal law in 1873. The provinces resisted all efforts to increase the authority of the lieutenant governor at the expense of the tradition of responsible government. When that issue was put to the test, it was by a Liberal incumbent, Letellier de St. Just, who was accused of seeking to aid his party by dismissing a Conservative ministry in Quebec on the eve of the elections of 1878; and it was the outraged Conservatives whose cries for vengeance brought the dismissal of the offending governor and virtually ended the prospect of vesting this office with independent authority.

The plain fact was that Macdonald's centralizing policy outran the forces that could be marshaled behind it. Popular support had to be attracted to the national government on the basis of interest and sentiment, and neither was as yet strong enough to break down the old sectional loyalties. There was still a strong feeling in the different provinces that their fortunes could best be served by the development of their own resources under their own authority. In spite of their restricted powers, the provinces had many opportunities within their own spheres, and they were reluctant to see those opportunities reduced by further federal encroachments. In addition, there were concrete political reasons for a provincial government to resist any intrusions that would deliver further resources of patronage into the hands of a rival party at Ottawa. Behind the controversies between the provinces and the Dominion lay a struggle for control over very tangible assets. The issuing of charters to railway promoters and land companies, the granting of timber and mining concessions were stakes of no mean importance. In the boundary controversy between Ontario and Manitoba, involving an area of some 144,000 square miles northwest of Lake Superior, important timber and mineral rights were at stake, and Macdonald's unsuccessful intervention on the side of Manitoba was an attempt to keep these lucrative assets out of the hands of Mowat and the Liberals. The withdrawal of railway lines from provincial control by declaring them to be "works for the general advantage of Canada" struck at the political as well as the economic resources of the Ontario government. Rival legislation in the Dominion and Ontario respecting liquor licensing involved the issue of patronage as well as of temperance and led to an attack by Sir John on "Mr. Mowat, that little tyrant who had attempted to control public opinion by getting hold of every office from that of a Division Court bailiff to a tavernkeeper." The battle for provincial rights was intimately bound up with the struggle for party advantage.

The gathering strength of these forces found a tangible expression in 1887. In that year, the twentieth after confederation, a conference of provincial representatives was held at Quebec "for the purpose of considering questions which have arisen or may arise as to the autonomy of the provinces, their financial arrangements, and other matters of provincial interest." The Dominion was invited to send representatives, but Macdonald replied that no good purpose would be served, and British Columbia and Prince Edward Island also held aloof. Four of the five provincial premiers who attended were Liberals, and this gave grounds for the Conservatives to dismiss the affair as a political maneuver by their opponents. Political motives were certainly not lacking, but the issues went deeper than that, and the conference was a warning symptom of internal maladjustments within the Canadian federation. Resolutions were passed demanding a readjustment and stabilization of provincial subsidies, a voice by the provinces in the selection of senators, provincial consent for the transfer of local works to Dominion jurisdiction, better machinery for determining the validity of provincial laws, and the removal of the power of disallowance from the Dominion to the imperial government. The provinces were not merely drawing together in their resistance to centralization, but were even venturing on a tentative counterattack.

Although the conference gave expression to a trend that was to increase in significance at a later period, it had no immediate results. The federal government ignored its proceedings. The issues that it raised were not acute enough to rally the degree of popular support that was necessary to bring about the desired changes in the face of resistance at Ottawa. But this failure on the political level was more than compensated by the impetus to the cause of provincial rights that came through the body of constitutional decisions now being built up by the Judicial Committee of the Privy Council.

There had been an effort during Mackenzie's administration to eliminate appeals to the Privy Council and to make the Supreme Court that was created in 1875 the final judicial authority for Canada. Edward Blake as minister of justice from 1875 to 1878 showed himself particularly concerned to define and enlarge Canada's sphere of autonomy. The activity of Dufferin and Carnarvon in the dispute between the Dominion and British Columbia was an irritating instance of interference by the imperial authorities in internal Canadian affairs. When Dufferin on his own responsibility commuted the death sentence imposed on Riel's lieutenant Ambroise Lépine, he raised the constitutional question of whether the governor could exercise the right of pardon without the advice of his ministers. Looking further into the matter, Blake discovered that the form of the governor's instructions dated from the days before responsible government and included a long list of the classes of bills from which he was to withhold his assent. Blake succeeded in getting the instructions changed to a form more in keeping with Canada's status. The list of legislative topics was eliminated. The governor's power of pardon was to be exercised only on ministerial advice. In addition, Canada secured the right to establish courts of admiralty jurisdiction, which enabled her to exercise authority over shipping on the Great Lakes. When, however, Blake tried to secure assent to a provision in the Supreme Court bill that would abolish appeals to the Privy Council, he encountered resistance and even a threat that the measure would be disallowed if this feature were included, and he felt reluctantly obliged to drop the matter. His failure was critical. It came just when the process of judicial interpretation of the Canadian constitution was getting under way; and it left that process in the hands of judges outside Canada, with results that were of the gravest consequence for Canada's future.

In the beginning there seemed little cause for alarm. The early decisions of the Judicial Committee started from the sound premise that the Dominion's power of general legislation was restricted only by the subjects assigned exclusively to the provinces under Section 92 and that even this restriction must not operate as a barrier to legislation that was for the benefit of the Dominion as a whole. When the validity of the Canada Temperance Act was challenged as an infringement on provincial authority over property and civil rights, the judges replied with a clear statement of the "aspect doctrine" of interpretation (*Russell v. The Queen*, 1882).

> Few, if any, laws could be made by Parliament for the peace, order and good government of Canada which did not in some incidental way affect property and civil rights. . . . The true nature and character of the legislation in the particular instance under discussion must always be determined. . . . Parliament deals with the subject as one of general concern to the Dominion, and the Parliament alone can so deal with it.

In the following year the question of regulating the liquor traffic was dealt with from a somewhat different angle. This time the judges decided (*Hodge v. The Queen*, 1883) that an Ontario act was valid because it dealt with a purely local matter and that it was not inconsistent with the Dominion's power of legislation in the interests of uniformity. What gave this case a special interest was less its illustration of the two-sided working of the "aspect doctrine" than the fact that the judges undertook to clarify the status of the provinces in terms that were highly favorable to them. "They are in no sense delegates of, or acting under any mandate from, the imperial Parliament." The British North America Act conferred upon the provincial legislatures "authority as plenary and ample within the limits prescribed by Section 92, as the imperial Parliament, in the plenitude of its power, possessed and could bestow." Thus the provinces were in no way subordinate to the Dominion or to the British legislature, but exercised full authority so long as they remained within the sphere allotted to them.

However sound this may have been from a legal point of view, it represented the beginning of a shift of outlook that was to have serious consequences. Hitherto the judges had tended to look at the British North America Act from the aspect of the authority it intended to confer on the Dominion. From now on their attention was more and more directed to the powers assigned exclusively to the provinces. It was a shift in standpoint that was reflected in an increasing concern to prevent any unwarranted intrusion by the federal government into the provincial sphere. Its consequences were seen when once more the liquor question came before the committee in the Local Prohibition case (1896). In upholding an Ontario act providing for local option, the decision seriously modified the basis laid down in *Russell v. The Queen*. It implied that the general and residuary powers of the Dominion under Section 91 were separate from and supplementary to the powers specifically enumerated, although the section plainly stated that the enumerated powers were illustrative "for greater certainty, but not so as to restrict the generality of the foregoing terms." It also laid down the doctrine that the general residuary power "ought to be strictly confined to such matters as are unquestionably of Canadian interest and importance and ought not to trench upon provincial legislation with respect to any of the classes of subjects enumerated in Section 92."

Here was the beginning of a trend that developed steadily during the next half century and profoundly altered the original balance of the Canadian constitution. The powers assigned to the provinces were lifted to a paramount position. The fact that they were meant to be exclusive only in their application to local matters was brushed aside. The general power of the Dominion to legislate for the welfare of the nation as a whole was reduced to something that could only be justified in extreme emergencies. Provincial control over property and civil rights took supremacy over peace, order, and good government; and the result was virtually to wipe out the residuary power of the Dominion and to restrict its authority for ordinary purposes to the enumerated subjects under Section 91. By a process of attrition the plain intent of the framers of the constitution was nullified, and the federal government found itself confined by a constitutional strait-jacket and unable to deal with the broad national problems that were to confront it as the twentieth century advanced.

Commercial Union

Among the varied factors that made for internal restiveness during this period, not the least was the slowness of the growth of Canada's external trade. The hope that confederation would be followed by expanding markets abroad had not been realized. The National Policy under Macdonald did little to remedy the situation; for, although it gave domestic interests protection in the home market, it failed to provide the outlets that the producers of natural staples needed for their prosperity, while the protective tariff on manufactured goods added to their costs of production.

The dominant factor in this situation was the desire to improve commercial relations with the United States. Canada saw little immediate prospect of a substantial expansion of trade with continental Europe or Latin America. The British market already absorbed half Canada's exports, and no great increase could be expected in that quarter so long as Canadian products had to compete on a basis of equality with those from foreign lands. Among the more ardent imperialists there were a few optimists who dreamed of a restored system of colonial preference, under which Britain would grant a privileged position to the other parts of the empire by imposing tariffs against the rest of the world; but the practical possibility that Britain would abandon free trade was too remote for serious consideration. The United States, Canada's other major customer, already had a high tariff system, which restricted the entry of goods from other countries as well as from Canada. If Canada could breach that wall by a special agreement, she would open up a wider market in which she would enjoy a distinct advantage over foreign competitors.

Thus the desire for a renewal of reciprocity remained active in Canada in spite of successive rebuffs, and in 1887 it burst out in the new form of a campaign for commercial union with the United States. The movement was encouraged by President Grover Cleveland's efforts to secure the reduction of the tariff to which his party was pledged and stimulated by the activities of a number of interested individuals. Samuel J. Ritchie, an American businessman with interests in Canadian mines and railways, and Erastus Wiman, a New York financier who was a Canadian by birth, became active advocates of closer commercial relations. Hezekiah Butterworth, a congressman from Ohio, made himself the spokesman of the idea in Congress. Wiman conducted an active publicity campaign in both the United States and Canada; the Toronto *Mail*, and with more hesitation the *Globe*, rallied behind it; Goldwin Smith lent vigorous support; and by 1887 the enthusiasm that had been roused, particularly in Ontario, gave rise to an organized movement and made commercial union a major political issue.

It was an issue that ranged the interests of Canadian manufacturers against those of the staple producers. Attempts were made to convince Canadian industrialists that they would profit from access to a wider market, but without success. They preferred their protected position within the Dominion to the risks of competition in the larger continental field. The Canadian Manufacturers' Association flatly asserted its opposition to any measure that would allow the free admission of American manufactured goods. The potent influence of the Canadian Pacific Railway was thrown on the same side. In 1888 the Canadian Pacific Railway was forced to surrender its monopoly of the West; but the entry of American lines into that region made the Canadian road all the more determined to support every circumstance favorable to the east-west traffic on which it depended, and not even its own decision to build and acquire branch lines in the United States in any way weakened its opposition to a trade system that would encourage the exchange of goods on north-south lines.

The staple producers, dependent for their fortunes on active export markets, were naturally more receptive. Free access to American markets had long been the desire of the lumbering and fishing and coal-mining interests, who had not ceased to regret the loss of the benefits they had enjoyed during the period of reciprocity. Agrarian unrest was an even more potent factor. Faced with poor markets and declining prices, the farmers turned their wrath against the interests that they accused of oppressing them. In the West they battled against the Canadian Pacific Railway, which was held responsible for the high rates that placed the prairie farmer at a disadvantage in the world market. In the East they turned against the middlemen, implement manufacturers, and financial institutions, which were held responsible for the high cost of credit and supplies, and against the tariff, which sheltered the large corporations. The Grange, the embodiment of agrarian revolt in the United States, spread into eastern Canada, and a somewhat similar movement made its appearance in Manitoba. Its activities were largely economic in form, with particular stress on cooperative organization. There was nothing parallel to the political side of the Granger movement, for the Canadian farmer was still inclined to work through the old parties. But the Farmers' Institutes in Ontario were among the most important groups that rallied to the movement for commercial union, and this evidence of widespread rural support made Ontario the chief battleground of the campaign.

The opponents of the proposal rallied emotion as well as interest to their aid. The charge was freely made that commercial union was an annexationist scheme, and all the deep-rooted sentiments of loyalty to Britain were invoked in appeals against any weakening of the imperial tie. At the same time appeals were made to the sentiment of nationalism, not only by raising the specter of annexation, but also by the assertion that the removal of the customs barrier and the assimilation of the Canadian and American tariffs would leave Canada subservient to a fiscal system dictated from Washington. These were shafts directed at vulnerable spots. The supporters of commercial union argued that Canada's independent position would be strengthened rather than weakened by wider trade opportunities. "The only temptation to annexation," asserted the *Globe*, "is that which arises from existing restraints upon reciprocal trade. Canada, if commercially united with the States and politically with Great Britain, would be a living link of friendship between the greater communities." In its essence the movement embodied the long-cherished aim of reconciling political separatism with the economic unity of the continent. Nonetheless, there were advocates who were prepared to contemplate political unity as well. Goldwin Smith, who was one of the most vigorous and active figures in the movement, might deny that it necessarily entailed the sacrifice of Canada's independence; but it was no secret that he regarded annexation as Canada's logical destiny and that many of his associates viewed it as a desirable solution for Canada's difficulties.

One of the real difficulties was that the United States had little interest in trade concessions that would strengthen Canadian nationalism or in relaxing the protective system for the sake of the limited advantages that the removal of Canadian tariff barriers would offer. Cleveland failed to secure a downward revision of the tariff. The Republican victory of 1888 and the McKinley tariff of 1890, which raised duties to a new height, gave a serious setback to Canadian hopes. But they also gave new urgency to the problem of a trade agreement with the United States; and the reaction against the McKinley tariff in that country, expressed in the Democratic gains in 1890, made it appear that there was still a prospect of an acceptable arrangement.

This was an issue that caused considerable searching of heart by both political parties in Canada. With the adoption of the National Policy the Conservatives had made themselves the champions of the protective system, and they had a strong body of support that was loath to see that system impaired. Yet Macdonald, fully aware of the temper of the rural areas and the strength of the traditional desire for reciprocity, was not prepared to renounce all efforts to satisfy it. Even the adoption of protection had been presented as a method of persuading the United States to make trade concessions, and in theory the door was held open for reciprocal concessions whenever the United States was ready to agree.

This opportunist approach was illustrated by the negotiations of 1887. Two years earlier the United States had denounced the fisheries clauses in the Treaty of Washington. Canadians thus lost the free admission of fish to American markets, and American fishermen lost the privileges they had enjoyed under the treaty. Access to the inshore fisheries of the Maritimes had lost its former importance; but some American fishermen continued to resort there, and the loss of the right to enter Canadian ports and buy supplies was much more keenly felt. When Canada proceeded to enforce her treaty rights with untactful vigor, excluding American fishing vessels from her ports and seizing those which trespassed on the fishing grounds, an outcry arose in the United States and retaliatory measures were threatened by the American government. The Cleveland administration, however, had every desire to avoid trouble; and, as the result of a suggestion that the question should be amicably negotiated, Britain and the United States appointed commissioners to meet in Washington in 1887.

Sir Charles Tupper was included in the British delegation as Canadian representative; and Tupper embarked once more on an effort to link trade concessions with a fisheries agreement. But this procedure, which had succeeded in 1854, had failed in 1871 and was now even less likely to be acceptable to the United States. For that matter, his proposals, which he summed up as "an unrestricted offer of reciprocity," would have been anything but welcome to a large section of his own party. As it was, the best he could secure was a clause providing that Canada would restore the right of American fishermen to use her ports whenever Congress should agree to reciprocal entry of fish and fish products. Even this was unacceptable to the American Senate, which refused to approve the treaty. Canada, however, chose to end friction over the fisheries by continuing a *modus vivendi*, adopted as a temporary measure during the discussions, by which American ships were admitted to her ports on payment of a license fee; and Macdonald, though hopefully assuring Tupper that "commercial union is a dead duck," watched carefully for any new opportunity to renew trade negotiations.

The Liberals for their part were by no means at one on the issue. A section of the party held distinctly sympathetic views toward the protective system and pointed out how difficult it would be to sacrifice tariff revenue at a time when government income was already seriously depleted. Edward Blake, in particular, was firm in repudiating free-trade ideas.

In the campaign of 1887 he insisted that the tariff was not an issue and that no serious changes would be undertaken by the Liberals. Laurier took a cautious attitude, professing a support to the principle of reciprocity but refusing to commit himself to commercial union as an immediate and specific policy. But the free-trade wing, led by Sir Richard Cartwright, was still strong in the party. While it could not carry endorsement of commercial union, it did succeed in 1888 in committing the party to a policy of "unrestricted reciprocity"—a policy that was somehow expected to enable Canada to keep her separate tariff system and at the same time to open free trade in both natural and manufactured products with the United States.

This was the issue that dominated the election of 1891. At the outset Macdonald seemed bent on stealing the Liberal platform by convincing the electorate that reciprocity could best be secured through a Conservative government. To strengthen this contention it was announced that new reciprocity negotiations had been undertaken and that the first overtures had come from the United States. What had actually happened was that Canada had intervened to demand a share in negotiations on trade and fisheries that had been initiated between the United States and Newfoundland. James G. Blaine, the American secretary of state, hastened to repudiate the report that his country had taken the initiative. "There are no negotiations whatever on foot for a reciprocity treaty with Canada," he asserted, "and you may be assured no such scheme for reciprocity with the Dominion confined to natural products will be entertained by this government." Macdonald was equal to the occasion. With an unabashed about-face he launched an attack on unrestricted reciprocity as a policy designed to break up the empire. "A British subject I was born, a British subject I will die," he trumpeted in his election manifesto. "With my utmost effort, with my latest breath I will oppose the 'veiled treason' which attempts by sordid means and mercenary proffers to lure our people from their allegiance." His followers rallied with enthusiasm behind this familiar battle cry, and with the slogan "The old flag, the old man, and the old policy" they threw themselves into the fray on behalf of patriotism and the protective tariff.

The earlier perturbation of the Liberals at the prospect that their chief issue would be filched by their opponents was hardly greater than their shock at this sudden shift of the attack. Their plight deepened when the Conservatives secured possession of a private pamphlet written by Edward Farrer, editorial writer on the *Globe*, which suggested methods of economic pressure by which the United States might force Canada into annexation.

This was flaunted as clear proof that the Liberal policy was in truth "veiled treason." The protests of Farrer and the Liberals that private views had nothing to do with party policy were drowned by Tory cries of outraged patriotism. To add to the Liberal embarrassment there was the mute disapproval of Edward Blake. That veteran leader had even drafted a manifesto whose phrasing was highly ambiguous but whose tone clearly indicated a dissent from the Liberal policy on reciprocity. He was persuaded to suppress the document until after the election, but his silence in the interval was eloquent and undoubtedly damaging to the party.

With all these factors the Conservatives were able to gain victory only by a somewhat reduced margin. The patriotic cry and the personal prestige of Macdonald helped to save the party, and even then its majority of thirty-one rested on the smaller provinces. The Maritimes were held by pressure and patronage. The West was held largely through the influence of the Canadian Pacific Railway, whose need for favorable conditions to facilitate new financing had been one of the reasons why the Conservatives decided to spring an election in 1891 and get full advantage from Canadian Pacific Railway support. But Ontario was almost evenly divided, and in the former stronghold of Quebec a Liberal majority of five was a still more ominous symptom of the Conservative decline.

Race, Creed, and Party

The death of Sir George Etienne Cartier in 1873 removed one of the pillars on which Macdonald's political structure had been built. There was no one to take his place as the acknowledged leader of the French majority, whose vital function it was to reconcile Quebec solidarity with national unity. The system of dual leadership on a racial basis that the Conservatives had carried over into confederation was now at an end. Henceforth Macdonald had the more complex task of holding Quebec through secondary figures backed by federal patronage, and his success during the next fifteen years was made possible by the fact that until the end of that period no dominant figure emerged to rally the forces of race and creed on the side of the Liberal party.

The coming of confederation, together with the effects of the subsequent depression, wrought important changes in the scope and outlook of French Canadian nationalism. While there were extremists who dreamed of a distinct French Canadian state on the banks of the St. Lawrence, this idea of a separatist and isolationist Laurentia was not easy to reconcile with the wider sympathies that developed from the new conditions. It was borne in upon the advocates of racial solidarity that French interests were by no means confined to Quebec. The Red River uprising awakened concern over the lot of the French Catholic elements in the West. Quebec rediscovered the existence of the Acadians and showed an increasing interest in them. In Ontario there was a growing French population, which numbered 100,000 by 1881. In addition, there was the acute alarm over the continued emigration to the United States, and strenuous efforts were made to preserve the French Catholic character of the expatriates wherever they formed a community. Quebec sought to become a racial fatherland within North America, championing its compatriots throughout the Dominion, holding the loyalty and affection of its sons in exile, and striving whenever possible to draw them back within its borders.

This policy involved a potential dilemma between minority claims and provincial rights. The first impulse was to protect the racial and religious privileges of Quebec by setting strict bounds to the power of the federal government. Yet it was through its influence on federal politics that Quebec sought to protect the French minority in other provinces, and more than once it found itself calling on the federal government to use its power to nullify provincial measures. When New Brunswick abolished separate Catholic schools in 1870, there was unsuccessful pressure on Ottawa to intervene. The question of separate schools in Manitoba gave rise to a major political crisis. On the whole, however, Quebec sentiment was on the side of provincial rights and against the centralizing tendencies that were felt to be characteristic of Macdonald and his party.

Religon went hand in hand with racial nationalism and was one of its main bulwarks. Language and religon were closely allied, and the maintenance of the French language was not only an instrument of racial separatism, but also a barrier against the subversive ideas of Protestantism or of modern secular thought. The separate-school issue was linked with the demand for French-speaking schools in areas of French settlement outside Quebec, and there were heated protests against proposals to abolish the equality of the French and English languages in the courts and legislature of the Northwest Territories. Yet here too a potential dilemma could be detected. The French clergy were nationalists, but they were also anti-Liberal; and their adherence to the Conservatives was sometimes carried to a point that the more ardent nationalists felt involved the sacrifice of racial interests.

In the seventies the relentless assault of the hierarchy on the *Rouges* was pushed to a triumphant conclusion. A formal condemnation of the *Institut Canadien* was secured from Rome in 1869, and Bishop Ignace Bourget of Montreal followed this up by announcing that any Catholic who continued to be a member would be refused the sacraments. The lengths to which clerical hostility could go were shown in the case of a member named Guibord, who died in 1869. When he refused on his deathbed to renounce his membership, his priest denied him the last rites, and the Church that rejected his soul refused to have anything to do with his body. For six years Guibord lay unburied while his friends fought through to the Privy Council their claim that he was entitled to rest in consecrated ground. Their victory did not end the matter. A mob turned back the first funeral procession at the gates of the cemetery. A second attempt under military protection laid Guibord to rest, though without religious rites, and slabs of iron and concrete were placed over the coffin to protect it from the vandalism of outraged piety. But the bishop, having acceded to the letter of the law, proceeded to deconsecrate the ground in a final stroke at the dead man who had dared to question his edict. It was a repellent example of the arrogance and vindictiveness of which the extreme clericals were capable.

Meanwhile their claims to authority were pushed deep into the sphere of politics. In 1871, with clerical approval, a group of ultramontanes drew up a Catholic program that condemned such pernicious doctrines as the separation of church and state and called on the electorate to support only those candidates who would uphold the interests of religion as defined by the bishops. It was specifically explained that in nearly all cases this meant supporting the Conservatives. In 1875 a joint pastoral letter warned against the hypocrisy of Catholic Liberalism and defended the right of the priests to intervene in politics and to brand as sin a vote for an unacceptable candidate. Some moderate members of the hierarchy viewed these doctrines with grave misgivings as likely to do the Church more harm than good, but they found themselves unable to curb the ultramontanes, who threw the weight of the Church into the elections of 1876 on the Conservative side. Macdonald, warned by Galt that trouble would come of these activities, professed to believe that they were only a passing phase. "Use the priests for the next election," he counseled, "but be ready to fight them in the Dominion parliament." It was a policy that the Conservatives may have had later cause to regret, but in the short run it was profitable. The clerical assault was virtually a death blow to the *Parti Rouge*. A handful of unrepentant members kept its ideals alive, but the party as such was swallowed up in a moderate Liberal party, which in provincial politics had little to distinguish it from its rivals except a more lively opposition to Ottawa.

This distinction, however, was of growing importance. In spite of all Macdonald's skill, the alliance of the French bloc with the English-speaking Conservatives rested on precarious foundations. Successive controversies over school questions and the language issue brought Orange outbursts against French Catholic pretensions; and the resentment thus roused in Quebec led to an increasing feeling that the Conservatives were at bottom antagonistic to French Canada. Even the ultraclericals, though bitterly hostile to Liberalism, viewed the Conservatives with hardly less distrust and gave them a grudging support only so long as the alternative seemed to be a surrender to the *Rouges.*

These smoldering passions burst into full fury over the case of Louis Riel. To Ontario, Riel was a rebel and a murderer whose hands were twice stained with innocent blood and who must not be allowed a second time to escape the penalty of his crimes. To Quebec, he was the champion of an oppressed minority whose death was nothing short of martyrdom. In the emotion that swept the latter province, Riel's execution seemed a deliberate and calculated blow at the whole French race. A mass meeting in the Champ de Mars in Montreal protested against it as an act of odious cruelty and branded the French ministers in the cabinet as national traitors for their failure to resign rather than acquiesce. The English press answered with recriminations that were equally unbridled. Not since 1837 had the racial cleavage been so deep as it now became under the shadow of the Regina scaffold.

The political opportunities that this situation presented were seized on by Honoré Mercier. This leader of Quebec Liberalism had long sought to orient his party away from its radical past. Fifteen years before he had been associated with an abortive effort by a group of moderate Liberals to win over the clericals by purging themselves of the *Rouge* taint and transforming themselves into the *Parti national.* Now the time had come for the Liberals to make themselves the champions of race and creed and to mobilize Quebec sentiment against the supine followers of Macdonald. With the support of a dissident section of the Conservatives, Mercier once more announced the formation of a *Parti national,* which renounced "certain traditions considered as dangerous and certain ideas condemned by respected authorities" and summoned French Canada to form a solid unity in defense of its rights. The outcome showed that for all the emotional outburst over the Riel affair, it had not yet generated a widespread political revolt, but the beginning of a new trend was nonetheless evident. In the provincial elections of 1886, Mercier and his allies from the former Conservative ranks gained a narrow majority, and in the following January, Mercier became premier of Quebec.

One of his first tasks was to win the confidence of the clericals who were still wary of anyone associated with the name of Liberal. As steps to that end he permitted the reconstitution of the Jesuit order and took measures to settle the long-standing question of the Jesuits' estates. The extensive property that the order possessed at the time of the conquest had been taken over by the Crown, and its distribution had been a matter of controversy for nearly a century. Mercier sought to settle it by extinguishing the Jesuit claims in return for a sum of $400,000, to be shared by the Jesuits with other Church bodies in such proportion as the Pope might decide. Protestant schools were to be compensated for the loss of the revenue they had formerly enjoyed from the estates by a grant of $80,000.

The basis of settlement was not unreasonable. There was some murmuring on the part of Quebec Protestants, but no serious opposition. Nonetheless, the measure symbolized a tendency alarming to militant Protestants elsewhere, particularly in Ontario; and the submission of a Canadian matter to the jurisdiction of the Pope was a special ground for offense. A press campaign with strong support from the Orange Lodge was launched to compel the federal government to disallow the measure; and when this failed, an Equal Rights Association was formed to carry on the crusade under the leadership of an ardent Conservative, D'Alton McCarthy. The attack was directed not only against Mercier and Quebec, but also against Mowat in Ontario for his concessions to the separate schools and to the use of the French language in primary education, and against the federal government for admitting French as an official language in the territories. The assault on French domination and ultramontane encroachments, which had formerly been conducted by the Clear Grits, had now been taken up by the Conservatives, and the campaign added fresh bitterness to the racial and religious feuds.

A new political alignment was clearly in the making. The open enmity from Conservative sources was making it increasingly difficult for that party to hold Quebec. At the same time Ontario Liberalism had shed much of the old Grit antagonism and had formed a close connection with the Irish Catholics, who had been alienated from Conservatism not only by their religious feuds with the Orangemen but also by their racial feuds with the French. The real danger was that the new movement for French racial solidarity would isolate Quebec politically and might even threaten to disrupt the Dominion. In this situation Laurier was a figure of vital importance. A sincere Catholic and a true French Canadian, he was at the same time a firm though moderate Liberal and an ardent advocate of Canadian national unity. Though he had turned away from the *Rouge* doctrines that had attracted him during his early career, he stood resolutely against any surrender of intellectual and political freedom to ultramontane domination. He based his creed on the English Liberal tradition of gradual reform, with liberty of the individual as its basis and its goal. Against the narrow racial nationalism of Mercier he insisted on an outlook that would embrace the whole Dominion and on a common patriotism that would be shared by all races and creeds. When Mercier was forced from office in 1891 by charges of corruption (the common fate of Quebec ministries) Laurier was left without a rival in French Canada and was steadily gaining the confidence and loyalty of the English section of his party. He was perhaps the one man in Canada who at this critical time could bridge the widening gap between the two races.

The Conservatives on their part were falling victims of the forces of disruption. The campaign of 1891 was Macdonald's last battle. Worn out by the struggle, he died three months after the election, and his death removed the only trusted leader who could hold the jarring factions together. A procession of prime ministers—John Abbott, Sir John Thompson, Mackenzie Bowell—struggled unhappily with the personal rivalries that disrupted the party and the cabinet and the charges of corruption against one department after another. In 1896, after seven disgruntled members of the Bowell ministry had resigned their offices and picketed the trains against possible political strikebreakers, the veteran Sir Charles Tupper was called on to head the government and to assume its legacy of difficulties, of which the most pressing was now the problem of the Manitoba schools.

The issue was in part an outcome of the Equal Right agitation. When Manitoba was admitted as a province, a clause in the act safeguarded the existing denominational schools. This was followed by provincial legislation, which adopted the Quebec system of separate schools and a proportional division of funds. There was some restiveness under this system as the English-speaking population increased, but the Liberal party that came into power in 1888 was understood to have promised to respect the existing rights of the French Catholics. In the following year, however, D'Alton McCarthy carried his campaign against French Catholic influence into Manitoba, and the Liberals suddenly announced their decision to reorganize the educational system. In 1890 an act was passed that abolished separate schools in favor of a uniform and nonsectarian basis, with permissive nondenominational religious exercises during school hours.

Once again the emotions of race and religion were involved in a question that was bound up with provincial rights and brought them into conflict with minority claims. The federal government had not only the right to disallow the measure; it had also, under the Manitoba Act, the right to pass remedial legislation in case the province violated the provisions respecting education. The ministry at Ottawa sought to evade any responsibility for action by allowing the matter to be tested in the courts in the belief that the new Manitoba school law would be declared unconstitutional. But the Privy Council overruled the Supreme Court and declared the provincial law to be valid. The question of the right of the Dominion to intervene was next raised; and again, the Privy Council reversed the decision of the Supreme Court and declared that the federal government could take action. With all excuse for evasion thus removed, the Conservative ministry reluctantly brought forward a bill providing for separate schools in Manitoba. But time was too short to carry it in the face of the opposition it roused. The life of Parliament expired before it could be passed, and the issue was carried into the election of 1896.

Laurier's task in this controversy was to reconcile minority and provincial rights, and to do so under peculiarly difficult circumstances. The hierarchy was strongly in favor of the remedial bill, even though it was imposed on the province by Ottawa. The full authority of the church was thrown behind the measure; and Laurier was solemnly warned that, if the Conservative government was overthrown on this account, "the episcopacy, like one man, will rise to support those who may have fallen in defending us." Laurier refused to swerve from his course. He believed that the grievances of the minority must be redressed, but that this could be done more effectively and with less coercion than by the means proposed by the government. His stand brought down upon his head the wrath of the Quebec clergy. Not only were Catholics instructed, by a *mandement* read in all the churches, to vote only for candidates who would support remedial measures; the clergy made it clear that this meant voting for Conservatives, and the faithful were warned that a vote for Laurier and his followers would be disobedience to the bishops and thus a mortal sin. But racial loyalties triumphed over religious obedience. In the face of clerical condemnation, Quebec returned a Liberal majority. There was an almost equal split in Ontario, where economic discontent as well as religious resentment worked against the government. The Maritimes broke even; the West, with the somewhat paradoxical exception of Manitoba, voted Liberal. The long Conservative ascendancy was broken, and the Liberals under Laurier came into power with a majority of over 30.

There was a bitter aftermath as the enraged clericals continued to fight a rear-guard action against the man who had braved their censure. The Manitoba schools question was settled by negotiations between the province and the Dominion. Separate Schools were not restored, but provision was made for denominational religious instruction and for bilingual teaching when ten pupils in any school had a native language other than English. The province was satisfied, and so were most Protestant leaders elsewhere. But the Quebec bishops poured their wrath on this "indefensible abandonment of the best established and most sacred rights of the Catholic minority" and continued their diatribes against the Liberalism that Laurier embodied. It took a mission of Quebec Liberals to Rome, and the visit of a papal legate to Canada, before counsels of moderation from the Vatican brought a subsidence of the attack and allowed the new ministry to turn its full attention to the work of national revival.

Edward Blake.

(Public Archives of Canada)

Thomas D'Arcy McGee.
The orator of the Confederation.

(Public Archives of Canada)

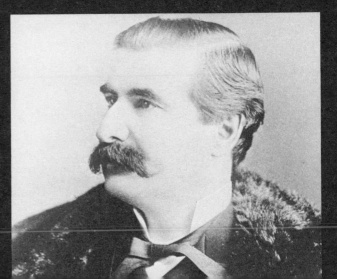

Honoré Mercier.

(Public Archives of Canada)

(Public Archives of Canada)

The Cunard Steamship Calabria.

Chapter 16

The Age of Laurier, 1896–1911

"Canada's Century"

The accession of Laurier to power coincided with a new upsurge in world economic activity. A rapid increase in the supply of gold resulted from new discoveries, particularly in the Transvaal. The expansion of the world's monetary reserves was accompanied by a rise in prices, which stimulated the new productive forces that had been building up all through the depression. Countries such as Germany and the United States emerged as highly industrialized states. Manufacturing expanded in Britain and France. Industrialism took root in Russia and eastern Europe. The search for new products and markets and investment outlets, which brought a wave of imperialism in the latter part of the nineteenth century, resulted in the opening up of new regions in Africa and Asia. In old as well as new areas, construction and development gave rise to large-scale demands for capital goods, which in turn increased the demand for raw materials, while the urbanization of western Europe and the United States created growing markets for outside food supplies. The clouds of the depression were swept away, and a world that was more closely integrated than ever entered a new era of activity in investment and production and trade.

The effect of these developments on Canada was profound; and in addition there was a special factor, which was basic to the new stage in her evolution. This was the exhaustion of free land in the United States. The westward march of the agrarian frontier had almost reached its limits. On the whole of the North American continent, the only substantial area of cultivable soil that remained for occupation was that of the Canadian prairies. The land seeker from the older settlements, the immigrant from Europe in search of free land grant, must now turn to the Canadian West. The tide of settlement, which had so long and so persistently flowed toward the United States, now swung north across the border, and Canada at last received the influx of population for which she had been hoping ever since confederation.

In the quarter century after 1891, Canada's population expanded from 4,800,000 to 8,000,000. Manitoba rose from 152,000 to 554,000, British Columbia from 98,000 to 456,000. The remainder of the Northwest, the population of which was just under 100,000 at the beginning of the period, held over 1,000,000 at its close, and the two new provinces of Saskatchewan and Alberta had overtaken their older sister communities of the West. This rapid growth had a tremendous and invigorating effect on the whole national economy. The rise of a new home market, the railway expansion that was stimulated by western settlement, the construction activity that resulted, all gave new impetus to commerce and industry; and outside capital, American as well as British, was available at low rates to finance the growth of manufacturing and the extension of transport routes. During the years from 1900 to 1913, investments from British sources were estimated at $1,753,000,000 and American investments at over $629,000,000. Even then the bulk of the expansion was financed by Canadian capital, with private investments lavishly supplemented by government credit and expenditures; but the influx of foreign capital gave an added stimulus to the growth of Canadian manufacturing and the expansion in mining and lumbering. The gross value of manufactured products rose from $368,000,000 in 1891 to $1,381,000,000 in 1916. The value of field crops more than quadrupled during the same period. And overshadowed for the moment by the spectacular expansion of the West and the accompanying industrial activity, yet adding elements of growing importance to the pattern of the national structure, were the developments in mining and lumbering that marked the initial exploitation of the riches of the Cordilleras and the Canadian Shield.

Fundamental to this whole development was the revival of world markets and the growth of Canada's export trade. The industries of the United States and western Europe offered a growing outlet for Canada's primary staples. Of paramount importance was the growing dependence of an industralized Europe on overseas food supplies to support a growing urban population. It was this that made possible the growth of the Canadian West and its transformation into one of the great granaries of the world. Canada's export trade as a whole rose from $88,000,000 in 1891 to $741,000,000 in 1916; and exports of wheat, which amounted to barely 2,000,000 bushels at the beginning of this period, were over 150,000,000 bushels at its close, when wheat and flour exports together reached a value of $200,000,000. Though products of the forests, and still more of the mines, also showed tremendous advances, it was above all on the West as a wheat-exporting area that the prosperity of the Dominion now rested.

This situation held sobering implications, which might well have tempered the optimism generated by the boom. There were distinct limits to the expansion of prairie settlement. By 1913 the great bulk of the lands fit for cultivation had been occupied, and the prospects of a continued mass increase in population were checked by the virtual disappearance of the agrarian frontier. The forest frontier remained, and the exploitation of the mining frontier had only begun; but these regions could absorb only a relatively limited number of settlers, and their development—particularly the development of the mineral areas of the Shield—was a slow and expensive task. Moreover, the continued dependence of Canada on primary staples for export left her in a highly exposed position. A fall in world prices, the development of new and competing wheat areas, the discovery of richer mineral areas, new industrial techniques that called for new raw materials instead of those which Canada produced—any of these might deal a major blow to the Canadian economy. But at the turn of the century such prospects seemed remote. In the flush of expanding prosperity, Canadians were ready to believe that the world would always want Canadian products in increasing quantities and that they possessed a land of unbounded natural resources with unlimited opportunities for settlement, whose full development would place the Dominion in the front rank of world states. It was Laurier who summed up the prevailing attitude and assumptions in the assertion: "The nineteenth century was the century of the United States; the twentieth century will be the century of Canada."

In view of this lively sense of a broadening national destiny, the effort to evolve a distinctive Canadian culture was bound to receive a new stimulus; and this too was significant not only for its high aspirations, but for its limitations as well. The racial duality that colored every aspect of Canadian life was the most immediate and perhaps the most stubborn obstacle to the development of a common national culture. But the task was also complicated by external factors; and while French Canada might feel that it had a cultural unity peculiar to itself, the remainder of the Dominion found difficulty in giving satisfactory expression to the sense of individuality that distinguished Canadians from the two great English-speaking communities to which they were so closely akin.

The internal problem of reconciling diversity with unity was nowhere better symbolized than in the field of education. The gradual establishment of free and universal primary education was beset by the repeated intrusion of questions of language and religion. In the English-speaking provinces the principle of secular education under state control was accompanied in various instances by concessions to religious minorities, and these were paralleled by concessions in the matter of language as well. Quebec's rooted opposition to secular instruction resulted in the placing of Catholic education under clerical control but leaving the Protestant minority in charge of its own separate schools. These compromises, evolved to meet the necessities of the situation, sacrificed complete uniformity for a relative measure of harmony. There have been occasional outbursts of friction, but no recurrence of anything comparable in intensity to the Manitoba schools crisis. Yet the system has led to diversities in standards as well as in outlook, and the search for national unity has involved as one of its aspects an effort to minimize these differences and to widen the area of common ground. The secular aspect of higher education was held within narrower limits. State-supported universities were established in six of the nine provinces; but in the older areas, particularly, the private foundations clung to their independence even when they became increasingly reliant on public funds. Not only the Catholic Church, but the various Protestant creeds maintained the colleges they had established during a period of opposition to either Anglican domination or completely secular instruction. By the twentieth century, however, their survival in many cases was based on pride in tradition or on local interests far more than on any fundamental diversity of aims. The federation of three Church colleges—Anglican, Methodist, and Catholic—with the secular University of Toronto was uniquely symbolic of the working compromise that in a less formal way was coming to characterize the relations of the diverse institutions of higher learning. This was a sphere in which, while the various branches of knowledge might tend toward increased specialization, there was a basic common inheritance that took little account of the boundaries of creed and race; and this factor was strengthened by the growing place that professional training occupied in the universities. It might be possible to teach philosophy on a confessional basis or to use the social sciences as instruments of nationalism and religion; it was pointless and hampering to inject these elements into the teaching of medicine or the physical sciences. In these fields the period laid the foundations for later Canadian contributions to the advancement of science, of which the discovery of insulin by Frederick Grant Banting and Charles Herbert Best was an outstanding example. The search for new knowledge was a common ground that drew scholars of all sections ever closer together and strengthened the intellectual bonds that might contribute to national unity. On a different plane it also contributed to national intellectual independence. Canadian education had been profoundly affected by both

British traditions and American methods. Canadian universities had drawn on scholars from both countries, as well as from continental Europe, in a way that was fruitful and invigorating. Nonetheless, the emancipation of Canadian scholarship from its previous dependence on outside sources was a vital element in Canada's advance toward maturity; and in education, as in many other fields, Canada was in process of evolving a system based on an amalgam of British and American influences but adapted to her own conditions and needs.

The search for a distinctively Canadian expression in literature and art was actively pursued during this period, with rather mixed success. French Canada was still largely preoccupied with the virtues of its own past and the desire to preserve them unaltered. Writers in English, who looked on the record of New France as one distinctive part of Canada's national heritage, were in a better position to lay the foundation for a synthesis of her dual culture. Novelists who sought distinctively Canadian themes were attracted to the romantic aspects of the French regime. William Kirby used this setting for *The Golden Dog*, which was published in 1877 and which enjoyed an unusually long vogue for a Canadian novel. Gilbert Parker produced a novel of old Quebec in *The Seats of the Mighty*, and Charles G. D. Roberts turned to old Acadia for several of his stories. Parker worked another romantic vein in *Pierre and His People*, the theme of which was the Canadian Northwest, with its Mounties and Indians and half-breed trappers; and another aspect of the Canadian wilds was developed in the animal stories of Roberts and of Ernest Thompson Seton. The pioneer community of Glengarry, and the rough life of the mining and lumbering frontiers, were pictured in the novels of Ralph Connor. By and large, however, Canadian fiction in this period was of slender merit, either as literature or as an expression of Canadian life. More serious consideration could be claimed for the school of lyric poetry that had its inception with the publication of *Orion and Other Poems* by Charles G. D. Roberts in 1880. During the next two decades there emerged a group of poets—Archibald Lampman, Bliss Carman, and Duncan Campbell Scott among them—who deliberately strove to speak with Canadian accents. In spite of this conscious effort, much of their work remained conventional and derivative. It is minor verse; but much of it is sensitive and appealing, and through it runs especially a feeling for the Canadian landscape that is possibly its most distinctive quality.

Like the poets, the painters found in landscape a theme that was characteristically Canadian. There were occasional efforts to depict Canadian life, notably the studies of habitant life by Cornelius Krieghoff during the earlier part of the century; but it was to nature that most of the artists of ability were attracted. It was in particular the discovery of the rugged beauty of northern Ontario and the Laurentians that produced a vigorous and original movement in Canadian art. Tom Thomson was to some extent the pioneer and the leader; but associated with him were a number of young men, ardent in their love for the northern wilds and influenced in their technique by the Impressionists, whose bold use of design and light resulted in paintings that were at once distinctive and unconventional. By the end of World War I a number of intimates had formed the Group of Seven, which represented the nearest approach yet achieved to a specifically Canadian school of art.

It was of some significance that writers as well as artists tended to turn for their subjects either to the primitive and remote aspects of Canada or to the distant past. In both cases there was a romanticism of approach, an escape from the nearer realities, which largely evaded the task of giving expression to the inner core of Canada's emerging personality. A few historians, among those whose work was embodied in the series *Canada and Its Provinces,* were exploring the roots of Canadian social life. Stephen Leacock, in his *Sunshine Sketches of a Little Town,* looked with the shrewd and kindly eye of a humorist at small-town life in Ontario. But it was left for a postwar generation of creative writers to initiate the serious attempt to explore the underlying social forces and to depict them in literature; yet it was by this process, rather than by dwelling on the romantic past, that the sense of a basic Canadian community underlying the duality of culture was most likely to emerge and grow.

National Expansion

The broad internal policies of the Laurier government illustrated the permanence—indeed, in certain aspects, the rigidity—of the factors that conditioned the lines of Canadian development. The relation between world trade and the exploitation of natural resources, between the expansion of settlement and the expansion of industry, between all these and the problem of transportation, were the determinants in any program of national advancement; the intimate relation between government and private enterprise was fundamental to the methods adopted. External conditions at last made possible the achievement of the basic objectives that lay behind confederation. There was no difference between the major political parties on these objectives as the ultimate goal, and relatively little as to methods. There were certain variations in detail, but on such major questions as immigration and railways and the tariff the policies of the Liberal administration showed little departure in principle from those of its predecessors.

It was Clifford Sifton as minister of the interior who was charged with the twin topics of emigration and western settlement, which were so vital to the whole program; and Sifton was symbolic of the dynamic forces that largely dominated the early Laurier era. Coming from Manitoba, he was one of a succession of western figures whose course led through politics to a leading place in the activities of Canadian big business. His interest in the opportunities offered by the West brought links with the financial and industrial groups in central Canada and ultimately gained him a fortune and a knighthood. His philosophy on public affairs can be illustrated by two quotations. Opposing the idea of government control and management of the Yukon at the time of the gold rush, he wrote: "One of the principal ideas western men have is that it is right to take anything in sight provided nobody else is ahead of them. As a rule, it is sound policy for the government to fall in with this idea and encourage the people to go ahead." And opposing the admission of American vessels to coasting trade on the Great Lakes, he stated: "I would favor the government spending any sum of money, or pledging its credit to any extent necessary, to place upon the lakes a Canadian marine fit to carry our grain between Canadian ports." Here was the dual approach toward public finance and private enterprise that had long been traditional in Canada, which was calculated to appeal fully as much to eastern corporations as to western men.

Sifton's immediate purpose was to fill up the West by attracting suitable settlers and creating conditions that would encourage them to stay. Circumstances favored his success. Land seekers from the older provinces, no longer lured to the United States, turned to the vacant lands of western Canada. Settlers from the United States, driven by the same urge, flooded into the Canadian prairies. There was an active effort to repatriate Canadians who had settled in the United States; but Sifton also realized that the American pioneering urge could be turned to advantage, and an active propaganda campaign was conducted in the chief centers across the border. Government publicity was supplemented by the efforts of private interests. The railways had land to sell on relatively easy terms and were eager to encourage settlement, particularly after government pressure induced them to select definitely the lands to which they were entitled under their grants. The policy of railway land grants was brought to an end, and in 1908 such odd-numbered sections as remained were thrown open to homesteaders. The effect was somewhat modified by grants to land companies and the speculative element that was thus encouraged, but these too were vigorous in seeking settlers, and Sifton was quite satisfied that the reward of private profit could be used as an efficient instrument for public purposes to the advantage of all concerned.

In the years from 1897 to 1912, 784,000 persons, perhaps half of whom were returning Canadians, entered from the United States. During the same period there were 961,000 immigrants from Britain and 594,000 from continental Europe. The last source was of increasing importance. Though settlers were sought from the British Isles, it took a policy of careful selection—not always in practice as careful as could have been wished—to secure from that highly industrialized area the sort of people who would make successful pioneer farmers. Western Europe also presented limited opportunities, but the agricultural population of central and eastern Europe offered a more hopeful field, and incentives for emigration existed in economic distress and in racial or religious discontent. Enlisting the aid of such interested parties as steamship agents, the government created the North Atlantic Trading Company with headquarters in Hamburg to seek out "the stalwart peasant in a sheepskin coat" in whom Sifton placed great faith. Group settlement, which had its precedent in the colonies of Icelanders and Mennonites that were planted in the West during the seventies, had now a rather less happy example in the transplanting of the Dukhobors from the Russian Caucasus. The West became a melting pot for a conglomeration of racial groups with widely varying habits and standards; and while the policy succeeded in its economic aims, it also created social problems that in some cases were more enduring than had been realized.

The growth of population on the prairies also brought to the fore the political questions involved in their transformation from territories to provinces. The Northwest Territories, which had been organized under a governor and council in 1875, had secured a completely elective assembly in 1888 and formal recognition of responsible government in 1897. Now there was a strong desire for the admission of the settled region as a single province with full control over its natural resources. The federal government decided to create two provinces, Saskatchewan and Alberta, and to retain control of their resources, as had been done in the case of Manitoba. A generous federal subsidy helped to salve the disappointment of the territorial leaders and kept these points from being the cause of serious controversy. The question of education, however, was more difficult, and for a brief time it threatened a crisis similar to that over the Manitoba schools.

In 1875 a separate school system on the model of Ontario had been established in the Northwest. Successive acts of the territorial government had, however, considerably modified the situation, restricting the establishment of new Catholic schools and the place of religious instruction and standardizing curriculum and administration in a way that approached closely to a unified system. This was the situation that the territorial leaders and their supporters in Ottawa wanted continued. But Catholic sentiment was naturally restive over the way in which the earlier privileges had been whittled down, and Laurier saw an opportunity to mollify this feeling. When the Autonomy Bill creating the new provinces was introduced in 1905, it contained a clause restoring the separate school system of 1875. It was a serious miscalculation on the part of the usually shrewd Laurier. Widespread opposition at once broke out, not only in the territories and in Protestant quarters elsewhere, but also in the cabinet. William S. Fielding, the minister of finance, objected strongly; and Sifton, who had gone south in the belief that the school question had been settled on the existing basis, hurried back to enter a strong protest and to resign his office when it seemed that Laurier intended to persist. With trouble rapidly brewing, Laurier modified his course. An amended draft, which defined the rights of the minority in terms of the existing situation, averted the threatened crisis; but Sifton failed to return to the cabinet, and Laurier's initial course left an aftermath of uneasiness in the ranks of English-speaking Liberals.

The settlement of the West, and the dawning opportunities in the new mining areas, gave new urgency to the problem of transportation and presented new opportunities, which enterprising promoters were eager to exploit. The rapid increase in western wheat exports outran the facilities of the Canadian Pacific Railway, which was still the only trunk system serving the West. The building of local roads to tap new areas threw an added burden on the main line and only partly satisfied the need for access to new regions. There was a rising western demand for better facilities and lower rates and livelier competition, and the responsibility for securing these ends was laid on the federal government.

In their attitude toward such questions the Liberals had come a long way since the days of Alexander Mackenzie. They no longer doubted the desirability of a national system of transcontinental transportation. They were converts to the views of their Conservative predecessors on railways as the essential foundations for a national economy and were fully as prepared to back private enterprise with public funds in the interests of national expansion. The Canadian Pacific branch line to the Crowsnest Pass mining area was subsidized by the government, in return for an agreement to reduce rates on shipments to and from prairie points west of Fort William. To improve the water outlet by way of the Great Lakes and the St. Lawrence, the canals were uniformly deepened to 14 feet. With somewhat less enthusiasm the government accepted the idea, in which Manitoba particularly placed great hopes, of a railway to Hudson Bay. These, however, were still piecemeal measures. The need was growing to widen the slender southern band to which Canada's population and activities had hitherto been restricted, and this could be done only by a major expansion of Canada's railway system.

The issue was brought to a head by the Grand Trunk. It had just emerged from one of its more successful receiverships affecting its subsidiary to Chicago; and with reduced charges, growing revenues, and new and vigorous management it had a fresh access of energy and a rush of ambition to the head. The opportunities offered by the growth of the West tempted it to revive its dreams of a transcontinental railway and to challenge the Canadian Pacific Railway in that lucrative area. In 1902 it petitioned for a charter for a line from North Bay to the Pacific and for a government subsidy of 5000 acres a mile and $6000 a mile.

This proposal raised a whole complex of considerations. Quite apart from the unacceptability of the suggested terms, in view of the settled decision of the government to end the policy of railway land grants, the project as it stood would satisfy neither sectional interests nor national needs. The fact that the eastern terminus of the Grand Trunk was at Portland was a serious objection. The railway's professed willingness to link with the Intercolonial was viewed with skepticism. The government wanted an all-Canadian road, which would carry traffic to Canadian ports and which would at the same time provide a shorter route than the Intercolonial; for though the Canadian Pacific Railway had built a short line to St. John, that too ran across American soil. There was also a desire for a line from Quebec through northern Ontario, which would give access to the newly discovered clay belt and the mining areas in that region. In addition, the Grand Trunk had to some extent been forestalled in the very sections that it hoped to exploit. An enterprising firm of contractors, Mackenzie and Mann, had embarked upon a spectacular career of acquiring charters and building local lines throughout the West, creating in the process a tangle of subsidiaries and holding companies whose complexities were as baffling to the investors as they were dazzling to outsiders. By 1902 they were in control of a railway network, the Canadian Northern, with an outlet on the Great Lakes at Port Arthur, and were ambitious to extend both east to the St. Lawrence and west to the Pacific.

The natural thing was to arrange a connection between the Grand Trunk and the Canadian Northern. Efforts were made by the government to secure an agreement between the two railways, but their mutual jealousies and conflicting ambitions stood in the way. Both systems needed government help to realize their plans, and this might have been used to force them to come to terms. But in the optimistic atmosphere of the times the need did not seem urgent. The prospect of unlimited national expansion made it seem that Canada could carry all the railways she could build, and the government was reluctant to discourage any private help that was available. Laurier suddenly discovered that immediate action was vital. "This is not a time for deliberation, this is a time for action," he asserted. "The flood-tide is upon us that leads on to fortune; if we let it pass it may never recur again." But circumstances gave ground for the suspicion that it was the interests of the Grand Trunk rather than of the Dominion that called for haste and that Grand Trunk influence was once more a determining factor in government policy.

The scheme that was adopted in 1903 was a curious combination of public and private enterprise. The Grand Trunk was to construct a subsidiary line, the Grand Trunk Pacific, west from Winnipeg to the coast at Prince Rupert, aided by a government guaranty of bonds up to $13,000 a mile on the prairies and 75 percent of the cost through the mountain section. This was to connect with a government-built line, the National Transcontinental, from Moncton through Quebec to Winnipeg. Laurier asserted that it was desirable to keep this eastern exit in government hands in order that all railways might get the benefit from it, but this was to be achieved by the somewhat curious method of handing the completed line over to the Grand Trunk Pacific on lease at 3 percent of cost with the rental remitted for the first seven years. The arrangement caused some qualms inside the Cabinet. Both Sifton and Andrew George Blair, the minister of railways, felt that the Grand Trunk and the Canadian Northern should have been forced to agree, and Blair, who because of his contracts with Mackenzie and Mann had been kept in the dark about negotiations that directly concerned his department, resigned in indignation. In the end the Canadian Northern too got government help to extend east to Montreal and to give Canada a third transcontinental system.

This was carrying optimism to fantastic lengths. New railways were needed to open Canada's territory and resources; and even if they were not commercially profitable, they were part of the price of nation building.

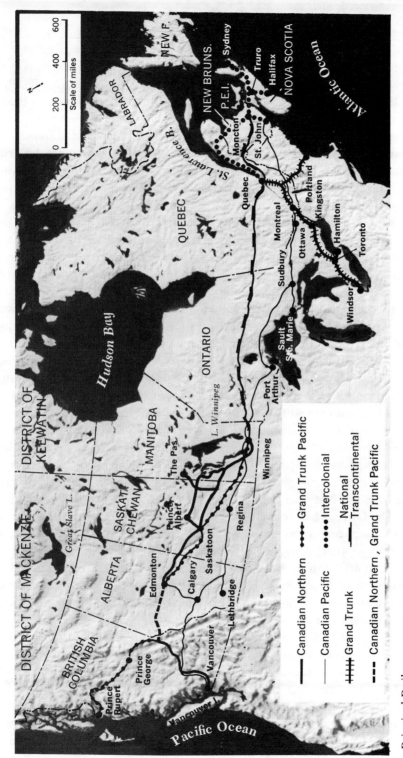

Principal Railways, 1914

447

But the price resulting from these unrestrained policies was excessive and unwarranted. Three main lines ran almost side by side through hundreds of miles of unproductive wilderness and found themselves involved in ruinous overcompetition in the areas they were meant to serve. Miscalculations and mismanagement, soaring costs, and dishonesty in construction added to the burden. The Grand Trunk, once more drained of funds by the reckless greed of its shareholders, fulfilled none of its promises. It refused to take over the lease of the National Transcontinental. It allowed the Grand Trunk Pacific to collapse into bankruptcy. Bankruptcy was also the fate of the Canadian Northern; and the roads that were to have been carried by private enterprise with the backing of public credit fell with their load of debts on the shoulders of the Canadian taxpayers, a legacy from the public recklessness and private deceptions and dishonesty that marked this phase of national expansion.

In their attitude toward western settlement and railway extension, those two activities so vital to the creation of a strong national economy, the Liberals departed little from the aims and the basic methods of their predecessors. Toward the growth of manufacturing, the third major element in the economic purposes of the Dominion, they showed much the same outlook as the Conservatives. Not merely were they content to see Canadian industry stimulated by the growth of the home market and the demands of railway construction; they were also desirous of preserving these advantages from undue foreign competition, and their tariff policies maintained the principle of protection to a degree that, except for the inauguration of imperial preference, was virtually a continuance of Macdonald's National Policy.

The Liberals had actively attacked the protective system in the election of 1896. Once in office, however, their urge to destroy it dwindled to the vanishing point. A commission was appointed to hold public hearings in the chief centers; but when the findings were incorporated in the budget of 1897, it became clear that the idea of moderate protection had triumphed over the old Liberal doctrine of free trade. Some concessions were made to the farmer in the removal of duties on binder twine, wire fencing, and other items, and agricultural implements in general were subject to lower rates. But the duties on binders and mowers were unchanged; the promise to remove the duty on coal was not carried out; and, while duties were lowered on iron and steel to satisfy one group of manufacturers, the producers of these articles were compensated by increased bounties. The most important feature was the introduction of maximum and minimum duties, the latter to be extended to countries giving favorable terms to Canada. This was in reality the first step toward imperial preference; and by making possible a reduction of the rates on British goods by one-eighth—later increased to one-third—it opened the way for lower levies on important items in the cost of living. The revision of 1897 has rightly been described as an able compromise, but it did nothing drastic in the way of impairing the protective system.

The West and the railway question each cost Laurier a cabinet minister; the tariff was responsible for still another casualty in the ministerial ranks. It was Israel Tarte, the minister of public works, who undertook to scrap what remained of the old Liberal tendency toward free trade and to commit the party openly to a policy of high protection. Tarte had for years been a key figure in Quebec journalism and politics, where successive factions and leaders of both parties had fallen victim to his trenchant pen and his talent for intrigue. In federal office he was increasingly attracted to a policy of vigorous economic nationalism that would rival that of the United States. In 1902, when Laurier was absent in Britain and when it seemed that ill-health might make his retirement imminent, Tarte seized the chance for a bold stroke, the success of which might win him the leadership of a transformed party. On his own responsibility he suddenly launched a protectionist campaign with a whirlwind speaking tour through Ontario and Quebec. Strong elements of the party were at once up in arms. Increased protection, Sifton declared, would "meet with the strenuous opposition of every Liberal elected west of Lake Superior." Laurier hurried back, dismissed the aspiring usurper, and reasserted his authority. Yet Tarte had given expression to tendencies that were by no means ignored in later tariff revisions. In 1904 the preference on British woolens was reduced, and dumping duties were adopted to reassure the manufacturers without unduly arousing the consumers. There were signs that a general upward revision was contemplated in 1907 under the guise of retaliation against countries with a hostile trade policy. This was checked by the strong low-tariff sentiment which farmers made vocal in hearings before the tariff commission; and when the new tariff introduced an intermediate schedule to apply to countries that had a trade agreement with Canada, it was lower than the existing maximum rates though higher than the British preference. Even then its effect fell far short of any general lowering of the tariff, while certain preferential rates were increased against British goods. The government clearly had no desire to make any major inroads on the protective structure.

It was these tariff policies that illustrated most clearly the new orientation of the Liberal party and the resulting strains within its ranks. Like the

Conservatives under Macdonald, the Liberals under Laurier sought to win the support of both English capitalists and the Quebec forces of religion and race. In both cases they had a somewhat qualified success. The habitant was loyal to Laurier, but the ultraclericals were never completely won over. National economic expansion drew the party into close relations with financial and railway interests, and the tariff policy gained a measure of support from the industrialists; yet the manufacturing interests were only partially reassured, and most of them still felt more confidence in the Conservatives as supporters of protection. On the other hand, there was a strong undercurrent of restiveness among the older Liberal elements, particularly in the rural areas, over the government's resistance to more drastic tariff reductions. When these divergences over trade policy became entangled in questions of external and imperial relations, the explosive forces thus generated were to rend the party asunder when they were touched off by the reciprocity issue in 1911.

An Evolving Society

The return of prosperity brought a remarkable easing of the sectional strains under which the Dominion had labored. It was true that the benefits were still unevenly distributed. The Maritimes in particular remained almost stationary, in contrast to the expansion of the rest of the country. The steel industry expanded, helped by bounties and protective duties and stimulated by railway and other construction. But smaller industries made relatively little progress in the face of competition from central Canada and the increasing concentration of manufacturing in that region, while fishing and lumbering struggled to hold their own by adjusting to new techniques and new markets. In central Canada the racial issue continued to smolder, fed by the growing controversy over imperial relations. In general, however, the surge of activity and expansion diverted attention from sectional disparities and diminished their importance. Controversies over provincial rights also declined in acerbity; and the federal government, which under the Liberals had less inclination as well as fewer reasons to intrude on the provinces, rose in the general esteem as the architect of national prosperity.

In the work of development the provinces and the Dominion were in fact moving on parallel lines and had few occasions to collide. National economic policies gave a profound stimulus to the economic life of the provinces. Provincial policies of expansion supplemented those of the Dominion and gave further impetus to the exploitation of provincial resources. Construction demands and the settlement of the treeless prairies brought a great increase in lumbering, particularly in British Columbia, which was closest to the prairie market. British Columbia's fisheries almost doubled in value between 1900 and 1914. The exploitation of the forest wealth of the Cordilleras and the Shield entered a new stage with the expanding demand for pulpwood toward the end of the nineteenth century, and this in turn provided a basis for the growth of the Canadian pulp and paper industry, which increased rapidly after 1900. A new basic industry was emerging whose direction was almost wholly under the control of the provinces.

The penetration into Canada's vast storehouse of mineral wealth was also largely the affair of the provinces, even though the phase that made most impact on the public imagination fell within the federal sphere. The discovery of gold in the Klondike section of the Yukon in 1896, and the feverish rush that followed from all over the continent, provided a spectacle of drama and adventure that revived the waning color of the American frontier. Its varied human aspect was a rich theme for popular fiction and for the verses of Robert W. Service, which stamped this passing episode with so deep an imprint on the public mind. The Yukon was a literary success even if its economic significance was somewhat qualified in the final outcome. It gave an added impetus to the development of transportation and the westward movement of goods and supplies, but the rush petered out and the population dwindled as placer mining gave way to commercial operations and as production declined. From a peak value of $12,000,000 in 1903, Yukon gold production fell to slightly over $5,000,000 in 1914, and its downward trend continued through the years that followed. By 1916 its peak production had been surpassed by that of the Kootenay region in British Columbia, whose development was aided by the building of the Crowsnest line and whose resources in lead and zinc ultimately became more important than its precious metals. In northern Ontario the construction of the Canadian Pacific Railway brought about the discovery of the copper and nickel resources of the Sudbury region; and by 1914, with the development of new uses and new techniques, Canada was on the way to a near-monopoly of world nickel production. The building of the Temiskaming and Northern Ontario to open up the lands of the clay belt resulted in the discovery of the rich silver deposits around Cobalt in 1903, and during the decade that followed the mining frontier advanced steadily northward to Kirkland Lake and the Porcupine district. The settlement of the clay belt made only moderate progress, partly as a result of its remoteness from the markets of the older settled areas; but mining and lumber camps provided local markets, which helped to encourage the growth of agriculture, and in the newly discovered mineral resources of the Shield, not only the Dominion, but Ontario and later Quebec and Manitoba found sources of wealth that bulked increasingly large as their extent was gradually revealed.

The effort to realize these assets involved the provinces, like the Dominion, in an expansion of public expenditures and activities. Access and essential facilities often had to be provided at a stage when the prospects of profits were too remote to tempt private enterprise or on a scale beyond the resources of private capital. The federal program of railway construction was supplemented by provincial building of roads and railways to reach new areas of settlement or to aid the development of new mining districts. The growing importance of electric power in the evolution of mining and the pulp and paper industry turned attention to the utilization of water-power resources under public control, and this was further stimulated by the remoteness of Canada's coal deposits from the chief industrial areas. In 1906 the Ontario Hydro-electric Commission was created, first for the distribution and later for the production of electricity. Other provinces followed this example in the field of public distribution and ownership. In the prairie provinces the rapid expansion of settlement was accompanied by heavy expenditures, not only on roads and railways and power plants, but also on provincially owned telephones and grain elevators. Provincial as well as federal expenditures quadrupled between 1896 and 1913 while Canada's population increased by only 50 percent. These fifteen years saw the nation mortgaging its credit on the basis of its future prospects and taking on extensive public obligations as the price of a national expansion that could not be achieved through unaided private enterprise.

In addition, there were features accompanying this expansion that laid further burdens on public authority. While old frontiers were being settled and new ones opened up, there was a simultaneous urban and industrial growth, whose implications were far-reaching. Under the stimulus of construction demands and the expanding home market there was a rapid increase in both heavy industry and the production of consumer goods. Iron and steel products trebled in value from 1900 to 1910; textile production doubled; other products from shoes to liquor and from chemicals to newsprint showed comparable gains. Three-quarters of the net increase in manufacturing took place in central Canada, increasing its dominance as an industrial area and the urban concentration in Ontario and Quebec. In spite of the great influx of agrarian settlers into the West, rural population increased by less than 600,000 while urban population grew by 1,260,000 and the proportion of urban to rural for the whole of Canada rose from 36 to 45 percent. In the light of the general situation, this was a striking trend, whose consequences were felt at all levels of government. Not only were the municipalities involved in increasing expenditures on public services; both the provinces and the Dominion were faced with problems arising from the growth of industry and labor and with new questions affecting their respective authority and responsibilities in matters of social policy and economic control.

One element in the situation was the growing concentration in finance and industry. The large corporation was a tradition in Canada, where even monopoly had been a recurrent phenomenon, and the habitual leaning by large-scale enterprise on government aid had involved the acceptance of a certain measure of government oversight and regulation. In transportation particularly the two had gone together, and the assumption by the government of a general power of control over all railways was merely an extension of the authority that it already possessed in practice over a considerable part of Canada's railway system. Controversies over rates resulted in 1903 in the establishment of the Board of Railway Commissioners with power to regulate charges, and its authority was later extended over telegraphs and express companies. Banking provided an example of a somewhat different type. In contrast to the decentralized system in the United States, where branch banking was viewed with hostility, Canada favored the development of strong centralized institutions under proper legal restraints. The Bank Act of 1871 laid down a minimum capitalization, restricted note issues to the amount of capital subscribed, and made certain stipulations as to reserves. Revisions at ten-year intervals tended to strengthen these safeguards, and in 1900 the Bankers' Association was set up with legal powers of supervision and investigation. These were conditions that tended to encourage the growth of the larger and more stable institutions and the absorption of their weaker competitors. The 41 banks of 1886 had become 22 by 1914, with 3000 branches spread throughout Canada.

Even in these fields, in which the government was involved, there had long been popular opposition to large corporations. The industrial combinations that emerged in the early years of the twentieth century aroused further hostility. The process of large-scale consolidation that marked the maturing of industrial capitalism in Britain and the United

States was repeated in Canada and gathered speed, particularly after 1907. Expanding markets offered greater opportunities for mass production and merchandising; domestic as well as foreign capital was available in growing volume, and growing speculative tendencies added to the ease with which new combinations could be financed. Nearly every important branch of industry saw the emergence of new corporations—Dominion Steel, Canada Cement, Dominion Textiles, Maple Leaf Milling—which grouped together enterprises that had formerly competed, and in some cases established almost a monopoly. Between 1909 and 1911, 196 firms were absorbed into 41 combinations; and the rise of the capital involved from $125,000,000 to $335,000,000 suggested a certain amount of stock watering at the expense of the investing public. Here was a field in which government finances were not involved and government restraint was not immediately exercised, while at the same time the government's tariff policy was one of the factors that encouraged the process. These were also cases in which the interests not only of the consuming public, but also of other productive enterprises, seemed affected by the threat of monopoly. The demand for public intervention arose from conditions similar to those which had produced the antitrust campaign in the United States, and that movement itself undoubtedly had its effect on Canada. As early as 1889 an act had given statutory form to the old common-law prohibition of conspiracies in restraint of trade. In 1910 a new measure, the Combines Investigation Act, undertook to strengthen the earlier legislation by providing simpler and speedier machinery for investigating complaints about combinations detrimental to the public interest, though the initiative was still left to private complainants.

Parallel with the growth of large corporations came the growth of trade unions. It was not until the seventies that union activity became important in Canada or that unions gained legal recognition. But British craftsmen had carried their union experience to Canada, and organization seems to have been particularly strong in the printing trade. In 1872 the printers of Toronto struck for a nine-hour day. The employers, with George Brown of the *Globe* prominent among them, retaliated by arresting the leaders on a charge of criminal conspiracy. Sir John Macdonald, inspired by the passage of the British trade union act in the previous year and happy to deal a blow at his old adversary Brown, at once secured the passage of an act that freed trade unions from the danger of criminal charges on the ground of conspiracy and gave them a legal status. Under the stimulus of this development, an effort was made to form a national body in 1873. The depression brought its collapse within two years;

but unionism survived through the next decade, and a new effort resulted in the formation of the Trades and Labor Congress of Canada in 1886.

Unity in the movement was not easily achieved. While many of the ideas and leaders were British in origin, more immediate influences came from the United States, where conditions were similar and contacts were more direct. Many of the Canadian unions were linked with the Knights of Labor; but during the eighties the struggle between that body and the American Federation of Labor was reflected in Canada, and in addition there were organizations, such as the Provincial Workmen's Association in Nova Scotia, which stood aloof from international connections. By the turn of the century, however, the American Federation of Labor was in the ascendant. The Congress in 1903 decided in favor of exclusive relations with that body and expelled from its ranks the remaining adherents of the Knights of Labor, who formed a new body of their own known later as the Canadian Federation of Labor. It was distinctly a minority group. By 1914, out of a trade union membership of 166,000, over 140,000 belonged to international unions. But the total was not impressive out of a labor force of nearly half a million in manufacturing, 246,000 in the building trades, and over 100,000 in the forests and the mines. These figures revealed the narrow skilled-craft basis of the existing unions as well as the obstacles presented by the hostility of employers and the indifference if not actual antipathy of the public. The Canadian Federation maintained an active existence in spite of its small numbers, and the emergence of Catholic unions added a further disruptive element to the labor situation.

At the same time the growing number of industrial workers, added to the labor situation in mining and lumbering, called for new measures on the part of governments. The federal government concerned itself chiefly with the settlement of disputes. Machinery was created by the Conciliation Act of 1900, and a Department of Labor was set up to administer it. In 1903 a Railway Labor Disputes Act was passed, and in 1907 a stronger measure, the Industrial Disputes Investigation Act (Lemieux Act), forbade strikes or lockouts until the dispute had been dealt with by a mediation board. The Department of Labor, hitherto under the postmaster general, now became a separate ministry. Meanwhile the provinces were taking their first steps in social legislation. Ontario passed a Factory Act in 1884 and was followed by every province except Prince Edward Island. Measures were adopted to safeguard workers in mines and to regulate conditions in shops and small industries. Ontario provided workmen's compensation in 1886, and most of the other provinces adopted similar legislation.

These were significant initial steps. Most of these measures, however, were tentative in their provisions and limited in their effects. Only a single prosecution was carried out under the Combines Investigation Act up to 1913. Social policy was largely confined to the regulation of working conditions and was not yet concerned with economic security or minimum standards of living. The prevalent social philosophy in Canada was still based on the individualism of a pioneer background and on the belief that unlimited prospects of expansion offered full opportunities to the enterprising individual. It was only when the traditional form of expansion was abruptly checked by the disappearance of the agrarian frontier, and when the nation found itself evolving along the characteristic lines of a capitalist and industrial society even in the exploitation of its natural resources, that the full implication of this situation would be reflected in a more comprehensive program of social legislation.

Nation and Empire

The world situation that lent such an impetus to Canada's economic growth also gave rise to external problems on a new political level. The revival of world prosperity was accompanied by an intensification of international rivalries and of imperialist competition. The great nation-states, whose growth in size and power was an outstanding feature of the nineteenth century, dominated the course of world politics. As their interests became world-wide, so did the scope of their antagonisms. Gradually the leading states ranged themselves in a new balance of power and drew in after them the smaller countries, whose interests bound them to one or other of the great powers. Canada, her horizon bounded chiefly by Britain and the United States, had little awareness of the underlying issues and little direct concern with the European situation; but as Britain became increasingly involved in the European system of alliances, the whole empire was affected and the question of imperial relations took on a steadily heightened significance in Canadian domestic politics.

The indifference to empire that colored British policy during the heyday of mid-Victorian prosperity gave way to a renewed interest when the depression of the seventies revealed Britain's changing world position. The emergence of competitors such as Germany and the United States challenged British industrial supremacy. Protective tariffs curtailed the markets for British goods, and competition in exports cut still further into

Britain's foreign trade. It could no longer be assumed that *laissez faire* would automatically assure Britain's ascendancy in world markets. There was a tendency to entrench more firmly the privileged position that Britain had attained in various dependent areas; and this was accentuated by the scramble for colonies after 1880, which ushered in a new and intense period of imperialist rivalry. The resulting international tension, and Britain's growing isolation in the face of powerful rivals on the European continent, called for a drawing together of her imperial resources to strengthen her hand in the game of power politics. Along with the emergence of these motives went a novel sense of pride in Britain's imperial achievement. Writers such as Charles Dilke and John Seeley and James Froude inaugurated a reaction against the Little Englandism of the Manchester School. Politicians such as Benjamin Disraeli awakened latent popular emotions by appeals to the glories of empire. The formation of the Imperial Federation League in 1884 marked the beginning of a movement for consolidation on the basis of a centralized federation; and with the appointment of Joseph Chamberlain as colonial secretary in 1895, the advocates of greater solidarity found a champion who embarked on vigorous efforts to give practical form to their ideals.

Thus Britain, whose interests at mid-century seemed to call for an extensive devolution of responsibility and expense on the self-governing colonies, now found that her welfare demanded a reversal of that trend and a tightening of the bonds that she had once been almost ready to cast off. This new approach ran headlong into the forces that had developed in the colonies during the past half century. A broadening autonomy was accompanied by the growth of a nationalist sentiment that demanded continued progress in the direction of ever greater freedom. The embryo dominions were not prepared to sacrifice the control they had gained over their own affairs or to merge their semi-independence and their opportunities to extend it in a rigid imperial constitution through which the mother country might regain her lost authority. Canada was the first of the self-governing colonies in both size and seniority; and Canada, which had pioneered the path to self-government within the empire, continued to lead in the evolution that transformed the empire into the British Commonwealth of Nations.

This process, however, gave rise to acute controversies that did much to conceal the fundamental solidarity of Canadian opinion. The great bulk of Canadians wanted to reconcile two cardinal aims—the maintenance of the British connection and the exclusion of the British government from interference in Canadian affairs. It was only on the fringes of public opinion that any serious dissent could be found, and any widespread discussion centered on details rather than on principles or policy. Unhappily these discussions roused profound emotions, which transcended the concrete issues and resulted in cleavages out of all proportion to the practical differences involved.

The Conservatives were naturally the most vocal advocates of the imperial connection. Deep-rooted sentiments were reinforced by considerations of practical interest. Britain was looked on as a bulwark against the political or economic absorption of Canada by the United States and as a support to English Protestant ascendancy against the threat of French Catholic domination. Both these assumptions were of increasingly dubious validity in the period after confederation, but they were held nonetheless ardently for being unreal, and Macdonald found that a vigorous waving of the Union Jack evoked a response that was invaluable at election time.

Yet the fact was that relatively few Conservatives were prepared to take any practical steps that would sacrifice Canadian interests on behalf of imperial unity. Under all his imperialist pretensions, Macdonald was a consistent Canadian nationalist. He would have nothing to do with a scheme of imperial federation that might set bounds to the development of Canadian autonomy. The economic nationalism that found expression in the Galt tariff of 1859 was even more evident in the National Policy with its protective duties against British as well as foreign imports; and the Canadian Manufacturers' Association, that stalwart ally of the Conservative party, showed no enthusiasm for tariff concessions as instruments of closer imperial trade connections. On the question of imperial defense, Macdonald repeatedly asserted that Canada would give her full support to Britain if she were endangered; but even this was the expression of a national interest, which recognized that Britain's strength was an essential element in Canada's security. Macdonald took care to avoid any commitment that would limit Canada's freedom of decision as to the form and extent of her military contribution, and he resolutely refused to become involved in minor imperialist ventures. When the proposal was made that Canadian troops should take part in the expedition to the Sudan in 1885, Macdonald would have none of it. "Why should we waste money and men in this wretched business?" he wrote to Tupper. "Our men and money would be sacrificed to get Gladstone & Co. out of the hole they have plunged themselves into by their own imbecility."

Far from being prepared to curtail Canada's sphere of separate action, Macdonald sought to broaden it in both domestic and external affairs.

The creation of the office of High Commissioner for Canada in the United Kingdom in 1880 was a deliberate expression of Canada's new relation to the mother country. Since she had "ceased to occupy the position of an ordinary possession of the Crown" and was growing in status as a self-governing community, there was need for more direct contact between the governments in Ottawa and London than was provided through the medium of the governor general. In addition she felt an increasing need for direct access to foreign nations in matters of Canadian concern, and the wish was expressed that the High Commissioner should be accredited as a diplomatic representative when negotiations affecting Canada were undertaken. The British government, clinging jealously to control of diplomacy on behalf of the whole empire, refused to see this formally impaired; but in practice, a system was worked out whereby the details of trade discussions between Canada and foreign states were left in the hands of the Canadian representative, while the British ambassador was in formal charge of the negotiations and signed the completed agreement for ratification by the imperial government. Under this method a trade treaty between Canada and France was negotiated in 1893; and in a further treaty in 1907 the negotiations were carried on by the Canadian envoys, and the British ambassador merely appended his signature. Political negotiations still remained solely under British control, but for practical purposes Canada had secured the right to regulate her own trade relations with foreign states.

In the Liberal ranks there were those who wished to press more rapidly along the road to full autonomy, and a few who looked to the goal of complete independence. But the bulk of the Liberals of both races favored the maintenance of formal connections with Britain combined with the practical exclusion of any interference from London. Laurier was able to steer a middle course along much the same lines as Macdonald had followed, with some shifts not of direction but of emphasis arising out of changing conditions. If Liberal low-tariff sentiment made it easier for them to adopt imperial preference, Liberal traditions in the matter of self-government made resistance even more determined to the new centralizing tendencies that had appeared in British policy.

The issue in its broadest form confronted Laurier at the Colonial Conference in 1897—an event that was itself a landmark in the evolution of the self-governing empire. There had been an informal gathering of the colonial premiers and British cabinet leaders during the celebration of Queen Victoria's Golden Jubilee in 1887, at which matters of common interest were discussed; and in 1894 a meeting was held in Ottawa on

Canada's invitation, chiefly to consider the development of imperial communications. Now the Queen's Diamond Jubilee provided the occasion for a full-dress conference, in which the self-governing units of the empire could deal with common matters on the basis of free discussion. It was an implicit recognition of a new type of relationship, which called for new methods of dealing with imperial problems. If the empire was to be drawn closer in matters of trade and defense and government, it must be done on the basis of free consent rather than by the use of Britain's overriding imperial authority.

For Laurier the occasion, with its pageantry and its majestic symbolism and the flattering attention paid to him personally—including the grant of a knighthood, which he was none too eager to accept—was a heady experience. In the first flush of his enthusiasm, he gave utterance to phrases that raised the hopes of the imperial federationists. But his native caution soon reasserted itself, and his emphasis shifted to Canada's growing national stature. To Chamberlain's suggestion of an imperial council, he opposed a firm refusal if this meant a reduction of Canada's legislative independence; and the outcome was a conference resolution which asserted—without too much regard for strict facts—that the present system of relations was "generally satisfactory under the existing condition of things."

In the matter of trade relations, Canada was already giving a lead toward imperial preference as the alternative to a customs union. It was all the more striking because it accepted Britain's free-trade policy and offered tariff concessions without demanding any favors in return. Even so, Britain was unable to accept without some sacrifice on her part. Her trade treaties with Belgium and the German *Zollverein* promised those countries most-favored-nation treatment throughout the empire, and Canadian tariff concessions to Britain would have to be extended to them as well. This Canada was unwilling to do, and it was only by denouncing the treaties that Britain could take advantage of Canada's preferential offer. The loss involved in abandoning the treaties was far greater than any immediate economic gain from Canadian preference; but there were long-run political considerations to be weighed as well, and these brought a decision to denounce the treaties in 1898. The aftermath was not only Britain's loss of important trade privileges, but a tariff war between Canada and Germany that lasted until 1910; but meanwhile Canada was able to apply preferential rates to British imports, first of 25 and later of 33 percent.

This was the method of voluntary independent action instead of formal and rigid commitment. The same attitude was applied to the question of imperial defense. Laurier recognized that when Britain was at war, Canada also was legally at war and in theory liable to attack. But he was determined that Canada should be the sole judge of the action to be taken by the Dominion, and he refused to join in any concerted plan that involved specific commitments in advance.

The Boer War put this attitude to a severe test. As the conflict approached, Chamberlain saw in the rising emotion throughout the empire a unifying force that should be utilized to the full. He inquired about prospects of Canadian military aid in terms that virtually assumed that it would be forthcoming. The new governor general, Lord Minto, who "was absolutely untrained in constitutional practice, knew little but horses and soldiering," raised the question of a volunteer force at the instance of the colonial secretary, although he reported that "I have myself carefully avoided any appearance of pressing for troops, but I have put what I believe to be the imperial view of the question strongly before Sir Wilfrid." The commander of the militia, General Edward Hutton, went further and asserted that a definite force would be offered. Laurier repudiated Hutton, resisted Minto's urging, and remained completely noncommittal as to the government's course in case of war. The only satisfaction Chamberlain could secure at this stage was a resolution expressing Canadian sympathy for Britain's efforts to secure justice for her subjects in the Transvaal.

It was a relatively simple matter to put the imperial authorities in their place. It was a much more serious problem to deal with the internal situation in Canada that resulted from the actual outbreak of war in 1899. If there was little dissent from the principle that Canada must decide for herself what action to take, there were bitter arguments over what the decision should be, and the deepest divisions were along racial lines. In English-speaking Canada there arose a loud clamor for immediate military aid to Britain. From French Canada came protests against the sacrifice of men and money when neither British security nor Canadian interests were at stake, especially when the issue seemed to involve the forcible suppression of a racial group seeking to maintain its independence. The controversy loosed unbridled passions, particularly on the imperialist side. Accusations of French disloyalty were accompanied by assertions that Canada must be maintained as a British country. The French reacted by accusing their compatriots of divided loyalties, which placed British interests ahead of those of Canada, and French Canada became more convinced than ever that it alone stood for a truly Canadian nationalism.

Thus the issue that Laurier had to face was not what action was demanded by the external situation as such, but what policy would best avert the threatened cleavage within Canada. His course was inevitably a compromise. The French must accept the necessity of sending Canadian troops; the English must be satisfied with a relatively modest contribution. He announced that the government would equip and transport volunteers up to the number of 1000, to be paid and maintained by the British government. The initial setbacks of Britain in South Africa, culminating in the defeat of three separate forces during the "black week" of December 1899, resulted in the raising and dispatch of a second contingent. Other forces were raised under private auspices or through direct recruiting on behalf of the British government; and ultimately a total of 7300 Canadians took part in the campaign. The policy was attacked by English imperialists as belated and limited and by French nationalists as a yielding to British pressure. The election of 1900 gave the Conservatives a chance to fan the flames; and Tupper, who struck a high imperialist note in Ontario, announced in Quebec that "Sir Wilfrid Laurier is too English for me." It was a tribute to the success of Laurier's policy that these reckless tactics, while they gained the Conservatives some seats in Ontario, failed to detach Quebec from the Liberals or to prevent the return of Laurier to power. But the crisis had planted new seeds of division; and Canada, now emerging onto the world stage, had to reckon with a situation in which every major decision in external policy would involve the threat of internal disruption.

One inevitable result was to increase Laurier's resistance to any strengthening of imperial authority. Chamberlain held the optimistic view that common participation in the Boer War had laid the foundation for closer ties between Britain and the self-governing colonies; and in the Colonial Conference of 1902, at the time of the coronation of Edward VII, he pressed for greater solidarity in government and trade and defense. But Laurier refused to agree to any military contribution or to tread the path toward federation, and clung to his belief in trade preference as an alternative to a customs union. When Chamberlain, convinced that stronger trade ties were the only possibility immediately in sight, launched his campaign in favor of the abandonment of free trade by Britain, he split his party and brought the Liberals to power in 1905. It was the end of the idea of an imperial *Zollverein* but not of pressure for a closer organization in other respects. The suggestion of an imperial council received some support from Australia and New Zealand in the conference of 1907; but Laurier was suspicious even of the title, and while he accepted the desirability of more regular consultation, it was under the title of Imperial Conference that provision was made for the establishment of a permanent secretariat and for meetings at four-year intervals. Even the scope of consultation was something on which Laurier showed increasing caution. He wished for fuller control by Canada over her relations with foreign countries; but Britain resolutely refused to impair the unity of imperial diplomacy, and Laurier felt that consultation on foreign affairs would involve Canada in implied commitments without giving her any effective influence over decisions. When in the conference of 1911 Sir Edward Grey gave the colonial delegates a guarded and confidential view of the European situation, it marked the nearest approach to an admission of the colonies to a share even in information on the workings of British foreign policy.

Yet in spite of the effort to avoid responsibility for the consequences of actions in which she had no share, Canada found it impossible to remain aloof from questions of imperial defense. The growing tension in Europe, and particularly the increasing danger from Anglo-German naval rivalry, called for some positive decision on the nature of Canada's armed forces and their relation to those of the empire. Laurier stood steadfast in his refusal to make a direct contribution, but it was almost unavoidable that the organization and equipment of Canada's armed forces should be integrated with those of Britain. The practice of having a British commander of Canadian forces ended in 1904 after the dismissal of Lord Dundonald who, with the support of Lord Minto, had tried to interfere in the organization of the militia and had publicly criticized the government's policy; but there was close contact with the Imperial General Staff, and consequent decisions that laid down the lines of cooperation in case of war.

It was naval rather than military policy, however, which raised the most serious problems. The Admiralty was insistent on the importance of unified command in case of war and pressed strongly for direct contributions from the colonies. Australia and New Zealand had acquiesced, but Canada held back. It was not until a special conference on naval affairs in 1909, at a time when tension with Germany was running high, that the Admiralty relaxed its former stand in the hope of securing greater cooperation. Australia by this time was in favor of a separate naval force, and Canada decided to create her own naval unit with an initial strength of five cruisers and six destroyers.

The Naval Service Bill, introduced in January 1910, brought a discussion that raised anew the whole question of imperial relations and showed that the divisions of a decade before were if anything more acute than ever. From the Conservative side came demands for a direct contribution to the

British fleet and sneers at Laurier's "tin-pot navy." From Quebec came even more serious indications of disaffection. The extreme forces of clericalism and racial nationalism, temporarily in abeyance during the early period of Laurier's ascendancy, were once more on the upswing. Prominent among their champions was Henri Bourassa, a grandson of Louis Joseph Papineau, with much of his ancestor's power of oratory and charm of personality. A strong ultramontane and an intense French-Canadian patriot, he devoted his gifts to inflaming the passions that centered on a narrow devotion to race and creed. Laurier, who long clung to personal friendship with Bourassa in the face of increasing political divergence, finally recorded his verdict: "Bourassa is a man of great ability, but his ability is negative and destructive. He will never accomplish anything constructive or of benefit to any cause which he may espouse." He had resigned his seat in Parliament in protest against Canadian participation in the Boer War and had been triumphantly returned by acclamation. He had protested against the school settlement in Alberta and Saskatchewan and against the Lord's Day Act of 1906, whose effort to enforce Sabbath observance was represented as an interference with the religious customs of Quebec. Now the naval proposals gave a focus for all the resentment against the British connection and the ascendancy of the English-speaking element in Canada, which burned so deeply in the breasts of Quebec extremists. Laurier was denounced as an enemy of his race and his religion, and the specter was raised of French-Canadian youths compelled to shed their blood on foreign fields at the bidding of British imperialists. Neither this campaign nor the attacks of the Conservatives prevented the passage of the naval bill; but the storm signals had appeared, and their significance was to be manifest in the new crisis that arose in 1911.

Alaska and Reciprocity

The process of defining Canada's position within the empire went on against a background of increasingly close integration with the United States. The similarity in technology, which arose out of similar conditions during the pioneer stage, was strengthened rather than weakened as the economy of the continent broadened in variety and complexity. The first settlers used American-type plows and axes. Their descendants used farming techniques and implements, and traveled on railways, and lived in cities, which showed few basic differences on either side of the boundary. The development of communications and the growth of the popular press increased the similarity of culture and outlook. Canadian newspapers relied for their foreign news primarily on the Associated Press, whose dispatches were available first through the Canadian Pacific wire service, and after 1911, through the Canadian Press. American popular magazines and novels had a wide circulation in Canada. New York and Hollywood purveyed the bulk of Canadian entertainment in the fields of the theater and the movies. American influences ran through Canadian institutions from schools to trade unions and from service clubs to political machines. Canadians might be sentimentally attracted to Britain, but in this era of mass production and mass distribution the neighboring United States had a direct and pervasive impact on Canadian life immeasurably greater than that of the mother country across the seas.

The effects were evident in the relations of the two countries. Although Canada still lacked the right of direct diplomatic representation, informal contacts between Ottawa and Washington grew in frequency, and consultations between ministers and officials from either side encouraged the habit of cooperation. More than one long-standing controversy was settled during this period by arbitration or by working arrangements. When the United States canceled the fisheries clauses of the Treaty of Washington, the situation reverted to that established by the treaty of 1818, whose provisions had aroused so much controversy. Among the matters in dispute were the right of Canada to exclude American fishermen from bays along the coast and to draw the 3-mile limit from headland to headland, and the right of commercial access by American fishermen to Canadian ports. In 1909 the whole complex matter was submitted to the Hague tribunal, whose award in the following year broadly upheld the Canadian case. The controversy over pelagic sealing in the North Pacific, in the course of which the United States sought to protect the seal herds by closing Bering Sea, had been submitted to arbitration in 1893, again with results favorable to Canada, and in 1911 Canada joined in an international convention, which at last established effective regulations over the sealing industry. The interest of both nations in traffic facilities and water levels in the Great Lakes system led to the Boundary Waters Treaty in 1909 and the establishment of a permanent International Joint Commission, whose activities, as valuable as they were unspectacular, presented a particularly happy example of two nations working in friendship and harmony in matters of practical concern.

Such a temper, however, was not invariably displayed by either side.

Although each had a sincere desire for friendship and a conviction of its own friendly intentions, and although the danger of war between them had now all but vanished, there were still periodic episodes that exasperated their relations and revived old feelings of distrust and antagonism. American pronouncements on Canada's place in the scheme of "manifest destiny" were now relatively rare, and American interests, with access to Canada's markets and resources, were content to let predestination take its course without forcible extraneous aid. But by the turn of the century the United States had embarked on the course of empire in the Caribbean and the Pacific, and the aggressive attitude thus engendered—expressed in the dictum of a secretary of state that the fiat of the United States was virtually law on the whole American continent—was inevitably reflected in any dealings with Canada that involved American national interests. Canada, when she felt her own rights threatened, was occasionally driven to an intransigent stand in the face of this highhanded approach. When in 1898 an effort was made to settle various matters at issue by means of a joint high commission, it was wrecked on just these grounds. Most of the dozen topics under consideration could have been disposed of with relative ease; but all others were overshadowed by the Alaska boundary controversy, which at this stage threatened to reach the proportion of a major crisis.

The controversy was precipitated by the Yukon gold rush. Successive efforts had been made to establish the boundary during the two previous decades, but they had run into both geographical and political difficulties, and neither side had felt any great urgency about pushing them to a conclusion. All that was changed by the rush to the Klondike. The gold seekers needed outfits and supplies, and prospects of a lucrative trade aroused the cupidity of both American and Canadian merchants. In the rivalry that resulted between Vancouver and Seattle especially, the boundary question became vital. Its importance lay not in the possession of territory as such, but in its bearing on the Canadian desire for direct access to the Yukon. The best route lay through the long coastal inlet known as the Lynn Canal, on which lay the ports of Dyea and Skagway, and across the passes to the Yukon River. If the head of the Lynn Cnal lay within Canadian territory, goods from Vancouver could enter freely; otherwise they must pass through American customs houses, to the great advantage of Seattle. This was the essential issue behind the discussion of boundary lines and treaty terms; and the fact that local commercial rivalry could so embitter the relations of two friendly countries showed how shallow that friendship was when questions of profit were involved.

The basic provisions respecting the boundary were laid down in the

Anglo-Russian Treaty of 1825. From Portland Channel at the 56th parallel it was to run north along "the summit of the mountains situated parallel to the coast"; but if these lay more than 10 marine leagues inland, the line was to follow "the windings of the coast" at that maximum distance, until it reached 141° west longitude. The clear intention was to create an unbroken coastal strip; and in fact the efforts of the Hudson's Bay Company to secure a coastal outlet had been resolutely rejected by the Russians, who refused to accept any treaty embodying that concession. In contending for an unbroken *lisière*, which would exclude Canada from the Lynn Canal, the Americans were thus on sound ground. When it came to applying the terms of the treaty, however, insuperable difficulties arose. There was a plethora of mountains, but no range that conveniently ran parallel to the coast. An attempt to draw a line parallel to the sinuosities of that deeply indented coastline would soon send any surveyor into a nervous breakdown. The treaty provisions could be applied only in the most general way; and practical circumstances thus gave Canada a chance to contend for a line following the general bearing of the coast at a maximum distance of 10 leagues inland—a boundary that would leave the head of the larger inlets, including the Lynn Canal, in Canadian hands.

In 1899 the Americans countered by suggesting that Canada be given a fifty-year lease of Pyramid Harbor on the Lynn Canal. This would have maintained American boundary claims and still given Canada the access she desired; but such an outcry was raised in the Pacific coast states that this fair and generous offer had to be withdrawn. Canada then suggested arbitration on the same basis that the United States had recently forced Britain to accept in the controversy over the Venezuela boundary; but this involved a tribunal with an outside arbitrator, and the United States refused to accept that feature when her own case was in question. The American government favored judicial settlement by a tribunal of three from each side; and at length Canada, seeing no prospect of any better arrangement, accepted this proposal, which was embodied in an Anglo-American convention in 1903.

The prospect that this arrangement, under which it was virtually impossible for the United States to lose, might nonetheless result in an amicable settlement, was gravely jeopardized by Theodore Roosevelt. The President had throughout been unyielding in his insistence on the American claim and his belief that the Canadians had not a leg to stand on. He had secretly ordered troops to Alaska and announced his intention, if the tribunal failed to reach a decision, of asking Congress "to give me the authority to run the line as we claim it, by our own people, without further

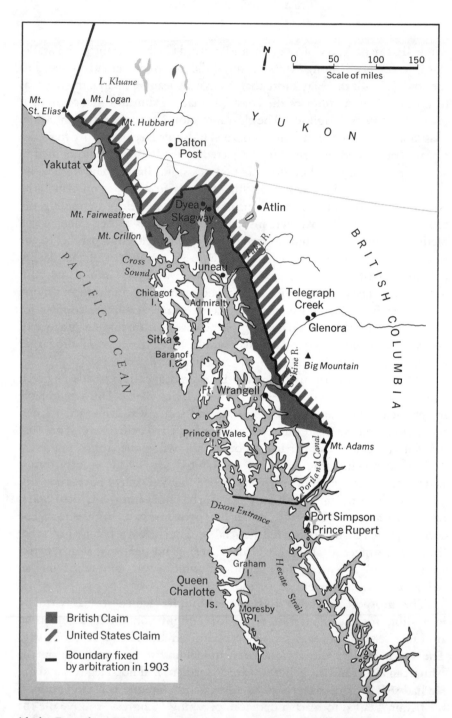

Alaska Boundary Dispute, 1903

regard to the attitude of England and Canada." He made it clear that the American appointees would be expected to reject all compromise—an attitude which in fact was necessary to secure the consent of the Senate to the agreement—and he made this doubly sure by the nature of his appointments. According to the convention, each side was to appoint three "impartial jurists of repute," who were to take an oath to consider impartially the arguments and evidence. Roosevelt showed how he interpreted these obligations when he named Elihu Root, Henry Cabot Lodge, and Senator George Turner of Oregon. Whatever the repute of these men, they were anything but impartial. All three had expressed themselves publicly and vigorously on behalf of the American claim. Roosevelt's action at one stroke compromised the whole proceeding by violating the spirit if not the actual letter of the convention and aroused bitter resentment on the Canadian side.

Canada was in a difficult position. She was unwilling to retaliate in kind, yet she faced a situation in which the best she could hope was a deadlock, and then only if the British and Canadian delegates held firm. It was chiefly on Lord Alverstone, the British Chief Justice, who along with two Canadians constituted the remainder of the tribunal, that the outcome depended. This unfortunate gentleman was placed in an almost intolerable situation. On the one side he was under the watchful suspicion of Canada, which recalled Britain's repeated sacrifice of Canadian interests for the sake of harmony with the United States and feared a similar surrender in this case. On the other side was the direct pressure from the American members of the tribunal, reinforced by indirect but sustained pressure through Alverstone's own government, whose members were warned of the unfortunate effects of an award adverse to the United States and undoubtedly allowed the Chief Justice to understand his responsibility for averting these potential difficulties.

The outcome seemed to Canadians a confirmation of their worst fears. Lord Alvertsone, after openly expressing agreement with certain aspects of the Canadian case, came down completely on the American side. Whatever the practical merits of the final decision—and the general American case was undoubtedly the sounder—it was quite clear that in its details it was a political compromise rather than a judicial award. The arbitrary selection of the mountains that were to mark the boundary and the arbitrary award to the United States of four islands in the Portland Canal provoked heated protests from the Canadian delegates and violent criticism in the Canadian press and Parliament. Indignation at Alverstone and Britain almost overshadowed the earlier wrath at Roosevelt and the

United States. Laurier found in the episode renewed proof of Canada's need to control her own external relations, though on cooler second thoughts he refrained from insisting on this advance. But the underlying bitterness against the United States left a legacy behind, and its fruits were apparent when the issue of reciprocity arose a few years later.

Prospects of a trade agreement with the United States were dim at the outset of the Laurier regime. The ideas of commercial union and unrestricted reciprocity had met no response. The real answer came with the defeat of Grover Cleveland and the adoption of the Dingley tariff in 1897, with its increased protective rates. On the Canadian side, signs of reviving prosperity brought a decline in the agitation for closer trade links. When Laurier's exploratory visit to Washington in 1897 ended without results, he seemed more relieved than disappointed. "There will be no more pilgrimages to Washington," he announced. "We are turning our hopes to the old motherland."

But if Liberal leaders were prepared to forget their former dalliance with free trade, the rank and file had longer memories. The farmers in particular refused to be content with moderate tariff reductions or the gesture of imperial preference. Their agitation had checked the trend toward higher tariffs in 1907; and when Laurier embarked on a speaking tour of the West in 1910, he found himself confronted with vigorous demands for lower duties and for renewed efforts at reciprocity with the United States.

In the United States itself there were at last signs of a changing temper. William Howard Taft and the Republicans had fought the election of 1908 on a platform of tariff revision. Hopes that this would mean a real downward revision, which would ease the cost of living, were dashed by the Payne-Aldrich tariff with its high protective rates. A group of insurgent Republicans revolted against this betrayal and joined with the Democrats in attacking the administration, and popular outbursts of protests—egged on by newspaper interests, who were denied the expected cut in the cost of newsprint—gave the administration a strong political motive for seeking a trade agreement that would mollify the rising opposition. As it was, the President was barely able to avert the imposition of still higher rates against Canada. The new tariff embodied retaliatory duties to be applied against any country that discriminated against the United States. Canada had concluded a trade agreement with France, which admitted that country to the intermediate instead of the maximum tariff schedule. The United States insisted on being granted a similar concession, even though nothing was offered in return, under threat of applying its new maximum rates against Canada. Taft, anxious to avoid such action, accepted a series of nominal Canadian concessions in 1910, but this only emphasized the desirability of a much more comprehensive agreement.

A casual episode brought matters to a head. The editor of the *Globe*, holidaying in Washington, had an interview with Taft in which he found the President receptive to the idea of a trade agreement and desirous of a meeting with Laurier. The excited editor, seeing new vistas opening before him, hurried back to inform the Prime Minister. Laurier was cautious and skeptical, but Fielding was anxious to follow up the matter. Discussions were initiated that ultimately led to a draft agreement in 1911. Reciprocal free entry was accorded to a wide list of natural products; low identical rates were imposed on another list of agricultural products and manufactured goods; still other articles benefited from nonreciprocal concessions by one side or the other; and at Canada's desire the agreement was to take the form of concurrent legislation rather than of a treaty.

In the United States the agreement was pushed through Congress in spite of an opposition reluctance to accept any measure that might reflect credit on the Taft administration. In Canada, however, it met with a resistance as virulent as it was unexpected. The first feeling was that Laurier had scored an overwhelming triumph. Robert Laird Borden, the Conservative leader, described the divisions in the party caucus and the insistence of western members that they did not dare oppose reciprocity. "The atmosphere that confronted me was not invigorating; there was the deepest dejection in our party, and many of our members were convinced that the government's proposals would appeal to the country." As signs of opposition appeared, however, the Conservatives took heart. They embarked on a course of obstruction designed to force an appeal to the people and made it impossible for Laurier to force the measure through Parliament without invoking the closure, which he was unwilling to do. The somewhat bewildered Liberals soon found themselves on the defensive; and the victory that might have been won had the election followed immediately on the announcement of the proposals was jeopardized by the time given its opponents to mass for the assault.

A formidable array of vested and protected interests rallied to defeat reciprocity. At the first hint that it was in the air, the Canadian Manufacturers' Association had launched a campaign against any weakening of the tariff structure. The president of the Canadian Pacific Railway announced that he was "out to bust the damned thing." Clifford Sifton threw the powerful weight of his influence and resources into a skillfully organized campaign, with the backing of interests connected with the Canadian Northern. Eighteen Toronto Liberals, closely linked with the banking and insurance interests, broke with their party and attacked its policy. Other factors were also at work against the government. Impatience with a government long in office was aggravated by widespread rumors of corruption in various departments. In Quebec there was violent opposition to Laurier's naval and imperial policies; in Ontario a new outbreak of sectarian resentment revived the old cry against French-Catholic domination. These crosscurrents worked against the Laurier government; but all were overshadowed by the violent struggle over the reciprocity proposals.

There was relatively little discussion of these proposals on their merits. Perhaps the most serious objection was against their dependence on mutual legislation, which left Congress free to change the whole basis after Canada had become dependent on its continuance and which Sifton described as "putting our heads in a noose." The most telling appeals, however, were to emotion rather than reason. The Conservatives discovered that reciprocity was a mere prelude to annexation and launched almost hysterical invocations to the spirit of loyalty to the empire. Unguarded and ill-judged utterances by American leaders gave them plentiful ammunition. Champ (James Beauchamp) Clark, Speaker of the House of Representatives, avowed his desire to see the American flag wave over British North America clear to the North Pole. Taft wrote to Roosevelt that closer trade relations would make Canada a mere adjunct of the United States. Such words were galling evidence of the lack of either understanding or consideration in high American quarters. Even so, the exaggerated lengths to which the campaign was carried showed that scruples had been cast to the winds in the desire for office. A party that, in the face of Canada's inescapable economic dependence on the United States, could trumpet the slogan "No truck nor trade with the Yankees," was reckless in its dishonesty; and a party that, while ostensibly battling to defend the imperial connection against mythical dangers, could ally itself in Quebec with Bourassa and the ultra-nationalists, stultified all claims to sincerity.

But whatever might be said of the morality of these tactics, they were a striking political success. The Liberals held the Maritimes and the western prairies, but lost British Columbia and Manitoba. Ontario went overwhelmingly Conservative, with seventy-two seats to fourteen for the Liberals; and in Quebec the Conservative-Nationalist alliance captured twenty-seven out of sixty-five seats. The Conservatives were returned with one hundred and thirty-three seats to a Liberal total of eighty-six. Laurier blamed religious rather than economic issues for the outcome. "It is the province of Ontario which has defeated us," he wrote. "It was not reciprocity that was turned down, but a Catholic premier." That, however, was oversimple. Dislike of the United States, translated into an access of Loyalist fervor and unscrupulously allied with the extreme anti-imperial elements in French Canada, lay behind the election results. After long years of alternate bullying and indifference at the hands of their stronger neighbors, Canadians seized on an opportunity to assert their independence of spirit, and, under an emotional upsurge that had nothing to do with logic, they rebuffed the United States by rejecting an agreement that Canada had been seeking for the past seventy years.

Sir Wilfrid Laurier.

Sir Clifford Sifton.

Settling the Prairies.
Land seekers leaving a Saskatchewan town for the pioneer area.

The Colonial Conference, 1897.

Prairie Agriculture Mechanized. *(Public Archives of Canada)*
An early binder at work on a Manitoba farm.

Setting the Prairies.
Land seekers leaving Minnesota for western Canada in 1902. *(Public Archives of Canada)*

Chapter 17

Armageddon: Act One

Canada at War, 1914-1918

The Robert Laird Borden ministry, which was swept into power on a wave of imperialist emotion, was to find itself caught up in the storm of a world conflict in which the destinies of Britain and the empire were at stake. Not only was it confronted with the task of mobilizing Canada's full resources for the struggle. It also faced the new problems in imperial relations that arose in the course of the war and the consequent adjustments that were to initiate the final transformation of the empire into the British Commonwealth of Nations.

At bottom the issues were those which had emerged in embryo under Laurier, sharpened to new urgency by the war and its aftermath. There could be no better illustration of the continuity of Canada's political evolution than the fact that Borden adopted a policy that differed in very few essentials from that of Laurier. There was a greater willingness to contemplate positive steps in the direction of imperial unity, in contrast to Laurier's cautious and rather negative attitude. But there was no less insistence that unity must be reconciled with the fullest measure of freedom; and it was largely through Borden's initiative that not only Canada, but the other Dominions as well, took a major stride forward on the road to full national status.

In domestic affairs there was a different sort of legacy. Here the prospective task was not the carrying on of a previous course of development, but a drastic readjustment to abruptly changed conditions. The boom that had marked the Liberal era collapsed in 1913. Curtailed investments from abroad, accompanied by a decline in wheat prices, deflated the speculative anticipations that had contributed to economic expansion. Farm incomes fell off, construction activity declined, urban employment fell by one-quarter. Canada, which had been pledging its credit and expending its activities in laying the foundations for a continued and indefinite growth, found the anticipated lines of growth suddenly blocked. With the occupation of the bulk of the agrarian West, the chief element of flexibility in the Canadian structure disappeared. For many individuals Canada would still remain a land of opportunity, but a new type of opportunity, which was less widespread and whose fruits were harder to grasp. National outlook and government policy alike had to be adjusted to the fact that the mold was beginning to harden. The war and its demands on production partially concealed the full implication of these developments; but they were accentuated by the war and its effects and were to emerge in their full gravity in the years that followed.

The political aftermath of the election of 1911 found the naval issue, which had figured so prominently in the campaign in Quebec, very much in the foreground. Borden himself, although he criticized Laurier's general outlook as isolationist, had differed from many of his followers in approving the principle of Canada's control of her own naval forces. But a visit to England, in the course of which he had interviews with Sir Edward Grey and Winston Churchill, convinced him that more immediate measures were necessary. Anglo-German tension had increased as a result of the Agadir incident. Churchill's proposal of a naval holiday, and Richard, Viscount Haldane's exploratory mission to Berlin in 1912, proved ineffective in checking the growing naval rivalry. Facing the specter of a German navy that threatened within a few years to equal that of Britain in dreadnaught strength, the Admiralty embarked on a construction program of two keels for one and was more anxious than ever for aid from the rest of the empire. In 1912, therefore, Borden proposed an emergency contribution of $35,000,000 to cover the cost of three battleships to be built and manned in Britain. The measure passed the Commons, only to be blocked by the Senate in one of its rare interventions on a major matter of policy. With its overwhelming majority of Liberal life appointees, the upper house refused to accept the Borden naval program until the people had been consulted. No newly elected government, tasting the sweets of office after fifteen years in the wilderness, was likely to accept such a condition even on so important a matter, particularly when it would involve fighting an election in the midst of a depression and would risk the loss of that anomalous alliance with the French nationalists which had proved of such service in Quebec. The Borden program was dropped. The Laurier program remained in suspense. At the outbreak of war, Canada possessed one heavy and one light cruiser, and no plans were on foot either for the development of the Canadian navy or for a direct contribution to Britain.

The outbreak of war in August 1914, brought an immediate decision by Canada to range herself fully beside Britain in the struggle. Steps were at once taken to raise an infantry division; and in addition the Princess Patricia's Canadian Light Infantry, a special regiment composed of reservists with previous military experience, was formed and dispatched overseas. Slightly over two months after the outbreak of war, the first contingent of Canadian troops landed in the British Isles. They were the forerunners of a growing army. The original call for 25,000 men was expanded to 250,000 in 1915 and to half a million in the following year. In the end over 600,000 men were raised to form a corps of four divisions with ancillary units from medical services to forestry and railway units. Naval strength was expanded through the addition of small craft, chiefly for coastal patrol, and the enlistment of over 8000 personnel. Another 8000 serving in the Royal Air Force added a particularly bright chapter to Canada's fighting record. Of over 400,000 troops who served overseas, two-thirds became casualties of one sort or another, and Canada's toll of war dead was 60,661—barely short of the comparable total for the United States.

While small special forces served in a variety of theaters—railway troops in Palestine, a tiny detachment in Mesopotamia, other troops in northern Russia and Siberia—the overwhelming bulk of the effort was on the Western Front. The record was one of high distinction. In April 1915—barely two months after their landing in France—the Canadians were involved in the first gas attack that the Germans launched against the Ypres salient. When the French-African troops on their left broke before the dreadful and asphyxiating cloud that rolled over them, the Canadians plugged the gap, and in spite of continued attacks blocked the road that had momentarily been opened toward the Channel ports. The struggle for Festubert in the following month added to their laurels. The arrival of the second division in France in September resulted in the creation of the Canadian Corps, which was augmented by the third division during the winter and the fourth in August 1916, and which in the interim was placed under the command of Sir Julian Byng. The spring of 1916 brought bitter struggles at St. Eloi and Sanctuary Wood in the Ypres salient; and then, in the summer came the prolonged and costly Allied offensive effort on the Somme. Here, where the capture of Courcelette added to their battle honors, the Canadians definitely established their record as shock troops. "For the remainder of the war," wrote David Lloyd George, "they were brought along to head the assault in one great battle after another. Whenever the Germans found the Canadian Corps coming into the line they prepared for the worst."

That reputation was clinched at Vimy in April 1917. The capture of this dominant feature, the key to the Arras sector, was a masterpiece of massive preparation, precise timing, and dashing assault; and as the first predominantly Canadian operation no less than by the decisiveness of its success, it occupies a uniquely symbolic place in Canadian military annals. It was followed during the summer by the prolonged struggle for Hill 70 slightly farther to the north and in the autumn by a return to the Ypres salient and the bloody and disheartening struggle in the mud around Passchendaele. The Corps now had a Canadian commander in Sir Arthur Currie. With the coming of 1918 and the failure of the last desperate German drive, in which the Canadians were not directly involved, the Allies passed to the offensive, and the Canadians entered on their hundred days of almost continuous action and of unbroken triumph. At the battle of Amiens on August 8, with the Australians on their left and the French on their right, they formed the spearhead of the breakthrough. This was "the black day of the German army," which marked the beginning of the end. Late in August came another blow when the Canadians, shifted to the Arras sector, broke the most formidable bastion of the Hindenburg Line, drove on to the Canal du Nord, crossed that barrier in a brilliant example of timing and execution, captured Cambrai early in October, and embarked on an uninterrupted advance, which carried them into Mons on Armistice Day. It was a record that need yield to none established by the Allied companions in arms.

Canada's entry on the world stage thus involved a military effort without precedent in her history, conducted thousands of miles from her own shores. Accompanying this was a program of war production that had profound and lasting effects on the development of the Canadian economy. The first impact of the war brought a dislocation that deepened the existing depression and aggravated the problem of unemployment. Shortly, however, a new period of expansion set in under the impetus of two simultaneous factors—the rising demand for war materials, and the opening of markets that the chief European nations had formerly occupied but were no longer able to supply.

One salient aspect was the expansion in primary commodities. Demands for food by the European Allies, especially Britain, lent a tremendous stimulus to agriculture. Prairie acreage under cultivation increased by four-fifths between 1913 and 1919. Exports of wheat and flour doubled in value; meat exports rose from $6,000,000 to $85,000,000, livestock from $10,000,000 to $35,000,000. Lumber, depressed at the outset of the war, was later in demand for wooden ships and airplane frames. The curtailment of Swedish exports opened new markets for Canadian wood pulp. The demand for minerals, especially base metals, led to the opening of new deposits and the development of new methods for processing low-grade ores. Nickel production was almost doubled; copper and lead and zinc showed substantial gains; and with rising prices the production of these four metals advanced in value from $29,000,000 in 1913 to $74,000,000 in 1918.

Superimposed on these developments was the growth of war industry. Canada, which had no munitions plants at the outbreak of war, embarked on the extensive production of ammunition and light weapons, and by the end of the war was engaged in the manufacture of steel ships and airplane frames. One-third of her industrial capacity and a labor force of nearly 300,000 were absorbed in war production, and turned out munitions to the value of over $1,000,000,000. Canada took rank among the leading industrial states, and the wartime activity in construction and production revived the demand for consumer articles and capital goods, and incidentally contributed to a price inflation that raised the cost of living 60 percent by 1918 and by June 1920, shot it temporarily to double the prewar level.

The direction of this comprehensive effort imposed new burdens on the federal government; the nature of the emergency enabled it to secure the constitutional powers that were needed to meet it. The Privy Council, when the question was put to the test, conceded that the external crisis justified the Dominion in exercising the internal authority originally vested in it. In 1914 a War Measures Act was passed giving the government sweeping powers of action. Authority over harbors and ship movements and transportation generally, control of trade and production, the right to seize and expropriate property, the power of arrest and deportation, could all be exercised by order in council. Potential control of the national economy was thus placed in government hands.

In practice there was no considered attempt at over-all direction and integration. Establishment of new government agencies and restrictions on the civil population were alike motivated by the need to deal with specific problems. Even within these limits, however, there was a striking advance in government activity and intervention. Munitions production was brought under the direction of a Shell Committee established by the minister of militia; and when this became involved in charges of patronage and profiteering, it was replaced by an Imperial Munitions Board acting under the British Ministry of Munitions, which established factories of its own as well as issuing contracts to private firms. In 1915 a War Purchasing Commission was set up, and a Munitions Resources Commission was created to report on available supplies of raw materials and the best means of conserving them. In 1918 export and import licensing was placed in the hands of a War Trade Board. The threat of a fuel shortage that followed the entry of the United States into the war in 1917 was met by the appointment of a fuel controller to handle imports and shipments, stimulate domestic production, and allocate available supplies. Food control was instituted in 1917 and placed under the Canada Food Board early in 1918. Civilian consumers were not rationed, but millers and food dealers were licensed, the use of grain in distilling was prohibited, public eating places were placed under restrictions, and a campaign against wastefulness was accompanied by the encouragement of victory gardens and regulations against hoarding. The most drastic and significant step of all was the government's assumption of responsibility for the handling of Canada's basic crop. In June 1917, a Board of Grain Supervisors was appointed to handle the whole wheat crop, controlling the marketing and fixing export and import prices; and in 1919, the Canada Wheat Board took over the exclusive marketing of that year's crop, which it sold at an average of $2.63 a bushel—a price that was soon to seem utopian to the Canadian farmer.

The financial burden imposed by the war was heavy for a nation of barely 8,000,000 people. It was particularly onerous for a country that for most of a century had consciously been living beyond its income, relying heavily on outside credits to build the foundations of its future advance, and on that advance to enable it to carry its accumulated obligations. Canada, like other belligerents, found it impossible to finance its war expenditure out of current income, in spite of increased taxes. The first year saw the imposition of new customs and excise duties on such articles of consumption as coffee and sugar, liquor and tobacco. In 1915 came special taxes on a variety of sources, from railway and steamship tickets to the gross income of loan and trust companies, stamp taxes on checks and similar instruments, and tariff increases of a flat $7\frac{1}{2}$ percent on the general and immediate rates and 5 percent on the British preference schedule. In the following year the Dominion at last invaded the field of direct taxation, which had hitherto been left to the provinces, with the imposition of a business profits tax, and in 1917 the first Dominion income tax was introduced—developments that were portentous for the future relations between the provincial and federal governments.

In the years from 1914 to 1920, Canada raised by taxation $1,121,000,000. But war costs alone were $1,670,000,000, on top of ordinary and extraordinary federal expenses, and the new war taxes brought in only one quarter of this amount. The remainder had to be raised by borrowing. It was a significant indication of Canada's growing capacity that the bulk of the necessary loans, to the amount of over $2,000,000,000, was raised within the country, although the federal government had never before the war floated a long-term loan for even as much as $5,000,000. To make up the remainder, Canada first turned to Britain; but by the end of the war it was Canada who was supplying Britain with credit, and her financial reliance for outside funds had shifted to the United States. Even then only $150,000,000 in new money was raised in that quarter by the federal government. Provinces and municipalities also resorted to New York, and a flood of American funds into Canadian manufacturing and mining aided expansion in those fields and trebled American investments in Canada to an estimated $2,300,000,000 by 1921.

Arthur Meighen, solicitor general in the Borden cabinet, exclaimed in a burst of emotional loyalty that he was ready if necessary to bankrupt Canada in order to save the empire. Things did not come to quite that pass, but the reality was serious enough. With railway expenditures added to war borrowings, the federal debt of $520,000,000 in 1913 had become $3,520,000,000 in 1921. With provincial and municipal debts added the net totals for these respective years were $1,298,000,000 and $4,882,000,000—a per capita increase from $170 to $556. Canada emerged from the war with a greatly expanded productive capacity; but this would need to be matched by greatly expanded economic opportunities if her people were to be enabled to carry the burden they had inherited from the conflict.

Wartime Politics and Conscription

On the political front the outbreak of war brought an atmosphere of unity born of a sense of the tremendous responsibilities into which the nation had plunged. Laurier pledged his full support to the government in its efforts to prosecute the war effectively. A political truce marked the early stages of the conflict. With the passage of time, however, old impulses reasserted themselves. The government's shortcomings in the handling of the war became the target for mounting criticism. Favoritism by officials and frauds by contractors sullied the record of war production. Boots with paper soles, horses that had been rejected for the South African war, graft in the production of shells—these were some of the things the government found on its hands. Some of the harshest criticism was directed at the minister of militia, Sir Sam Hughes, a man whose energy was as dynamic as his conduct was unpredictable and whose organizing ability was largely stultified by his irresponsibility. The scandals involving the Shell Committee could largely be traced to his stubborn trust in the intimate adviser who profited from the unscrupulous manipulation of contracts. His equally stubborn defense of the Ross rifle with which Canadian troops were armed—a fine target rifle, but one which failed to stand up to the rough conditions in the trenches— was dangerously exasperating when Canadian soldiers were throwing away the Ross and salvaging the sturdier British Lee-Enfield. By 1916 his feuds with his colleagues and insubordination toward his leader led Borden to demand his resignation, but his dismissal did little to retrieve the government's dwindling reputation. In the provincial field too the revelation of corruption in the Conservative governments in New Brunswick, and Manitoba, and British Columbia reflected on the party in power and even on some of its federal ministers. By 1916 the initial harmony was breaking down under accumulated strains, and the feeling was growing that a major readjustment was needed to deal with problems present and in prospect.

This sentiment took the form of a rising agitation, particularly in certain Liberal quarters, in favor of a union government. Only a coalition, it was felt, could take the steps that now appeared necessary to increase the war effort to full effectiveness. As the conscription crisis loomed, Borden himself became convinced that an all-party government should be attempted. In May 1917, he made approaches to Laurier with the suggestion of a cabinet in which the two parties should have an equal number of seats apart from the office of prime minister. The Liberal leader was dubious and aloof. He suspected that the proponents of the idea desired not merely to strengthen the war effort, but to save the railways, which were on the verge of bankruptcy, and to coerce Quebec into the acceptance of compulsory service. The discussions dragged on for nearly a fortnight, but Laurier became increasingly firm in his belief that conscription should not be imposed without either a referendum or a general election, and ended by rejecting Borden's coalition proposal.

Quebec was by this time the pivotal factor in the situation. In contrast to the position at the time of the Boer War, the decision of Canada to participate in the European struggle was supported at the outset by French as well as English Canada. Laurier's attitude was a powerful force on the side of unity. The hierarchy called for full and loyal support to Britain in the struggle. Even the nationalists acquiesced at first. Their earlier intransigence had been considerably modified by their alliance with the Conservatives. Bourassa refused a seat in the cabinet, but several of his followers entered with his approval and did not scruple to support Borden's naval program after having fought with the utmost bitterness against Laurier's. And in the early days of the war, Bourassa himself asserted that it was Canada's national duty "to contribute, within the bounds of her strength and by the means which are proper to herself, to the triumph, and especially to the endurance, of the combined efforts of France and England."

Here was a unique opportunity to advance Canadian unity, to submerge the elements of racial and religious friction in a common effort for a common national end. The chance was let slip, with grave and enduring consequences. Within a short time, old irritations had been stirred into new and more dangerous antagonism. Already Protestants were protesting against the Catholic attitude toward mixed marriages as embodied in the *Ne Temere* decree, and Quebec was deeply stirred by Ontario's promulgation of Regulation 17, which placed restrictions on French-language schools. Agitation over these matters gave added bitterness to the recriminations and rebuttals that were being exchanged with rising vehemence between the two races over the question of their respective readiness to bear their full share of the war effort.

In the initial rush of volunteers to the armed forces, the greatest eagerness was shown by men who had been born in the British Isles. Even as late as October 1917, this group formed just under one-half of the total volunteers. Among the native-born the French, long cut off from their mother country and with no feeling for any homeland other than Canada, were possibly less ardent than their compatriots in other sections. But there is no sure basis for comparison in the early stage, and the quality at least of French-Canadian recruits was amply testified by the record of the 22nd battalion—the "Vandoos" of affectionate memory. By the end of the second year of the war, the drain on manpower inevitably meant a slowing down of recruiting throughout the Dominion; but by that time too there were special reasons why this should seem particularly evident in Quebec.

Many of these arose from the ignorance and blundering with which recruiting was handled. Little account was taken of the language factor in organizing and training French Canadian volunteers. There was an unexplained reluctance to meet the desire of the French for distinct French units. The small proportion of French-speaking officers appointed, particularly in the higher ranks, gave rise to charges of discrimination. The grotesque stupidity with which the situation was handled was illustrated by the fact that the chief recruiting officer in this predominantly French Catholic community was an English Protestant clergyman. No real effort was made to educate the habitant in the issues and needs involved or to break down his traditionally parochial outlook. Nothing effective was done to hold and satisfy the leaders who could rally the full support of French Canada; and when these were discouraged or alienated, the two races once more began to drift rapidly apart.

Quebec apologists insisted that the French record in enlistments was not much behind that of other native-born stocks proportionally, especially when the rural nature of the province was taken into account. Conclusive statistics are lacking, but informed estimates of 30,000 to 35,000 volunteers from French-speaking Quebec suggest that the gap was a real one even when all the qualifying factors are weighed. In any case, large sections of English-speaking Canada were firmly convinced that the French were lagging in their contribution. The result was an outburst of criticism, at times rising to intemperate abuse, which ended by alienating the French still further. All the old fears and suspicions of English designs against the survival of French Canada as a distinct nationality were revived. There was a growing tendency to fall back once more within the bulwarks of race and language, concentrating on domestic problems and on the maintenance of French solidarity. By 1916 Bourassa was openly condemning the war, riots against further recruiting had broken out in a number of French cities, and a renewed racial split threatened the progress of Canada's war effort.

This came at a time when a manpower crisis was rapidly approaching. At the end of 1916 enlistments were still 70,000 short of the goal of 500,000. Recruiting figures of 30,000 a month at the beginning of the year had dwindled to 6000 at its close. Farm production and the expanding munitions industry competed for manpower with the armed forces, and there were rising demands that skilled workers should be exempted from military service. The unexpected length to which the war was dragging out, the heavy losses incurred by Canadian troops overseas, the prospect of even more strenuous efforts during the year ahead, made the problem urgent and acute. The government had hitherto clung to the system of voluntary enlistments and had voiced its opposition to compulsory service. But Borden, returning from England in the spring of 1917, was deeply impressed by the critical situation on the battlefront and the need to strain every nerve to bolster the Allied effort. He and his colleagues were fully aware that conscription would meet with opposition that was not confined to any one section. Labor disliked the idea of compulsory service. The farmers, already hard pressed for help, were vigorously opposed to the drafting of their sons into the army. But it was from Quebec that the most serious dissent was to be expected, and it was the desire to carry conscription in spite of these minority objections that gave new impetus to the agitation for a union government and brought Borden's abortive overtures to Laurier.

The issue was sharpened by the introduction of the Military Service Bill in June 1917. In the face of the need for positive decision presented by the measure, a split in the Liberal ranks became virtually inevitable. The decline in the government's popularity was more than offset by the inability of its opponents to hold together when confronted by this disruptive issue. The divergence of sectional views was irreconcilable, and it was the Liberals who bore the brunt. The Conservatives held together, though at the price of losing their French nationalist allies. But the Liberals could support conscription only at the price of alienating their Quebec followers, or oppose it and risk wrecking their party in the other provinces. The party was unable to make the choice. Laurier, sore at heart, saw himself deserted on the issue by an important body of his former supporters. In opposition to the bill he pleaded the cause of national unity for which he had struggled during his whole career and proposed a referendum as the course most likely to avert a split. His amendment was defeated, and the bill was carried with the support of more than a score of Liberal members.

The movement for a union government now gathered impetus. By no means all the Liberals who favored conscription were prepared to support a coalition, but the division in the party weakened resistance to the proposal. Under the inspiration of Clifford Sifton a sustained effort was undertaken to break down the resistance of the rank and file. When union government was rejected by conferences of Ontario Liberals in July and western Liberals in August, Sifton mobilized the supporters of the project and secured an agreement to serve under a Conservative leader other than Borden. The Prime Minister was prepared to retire in favor of Sir George Foster, but neither Foster nor the party would hear of it. An effort was next made to persuade Laurier to retire in favor of an English-speaking leader. The delegates believed they had succeeded; but Laurier, irritated by a premature announcement and stiffened by advice from his loyal followers, eventually refused to give way. By this time, however, the end was in sight. A Wartime Election Act, which enfranchised women who were next of kin to soldiers serving overseas and disfranchised all former citizens of enemy countries who had been naturalized since 1902, struck at the western Liberals, who relied heavily on the votes of the foreign-born. The Westerners were brought to terms. A group of Liberals entered into conclusive negotiations with Borden. On October 12, 1917, a union cabinet was announced, with Borden as prime minister and with Liberals to the ultimate number of ten in the government.

By this time Parliament had been prorogued and preparations for a general election were under way. The government had already secured the extension for one year of the normal term of Parliament, but the recent political upheaval made a popular mandate desirable, and the combination of the Liberal split and the new franchise made victory certain. Conscription was the issue, and the outcome revealed how deeply it had divided the country. Laurier carried 62 out of Quebec's 65 seats, but he won only 8 in Ontario and only 20 in the whole of Canada outside of Quebec. Against these 82 Liberals were 38 Union Liberals and 115 Conservatives. The popular vote showed a far more even division of opinion. There were roughly 842,000 civilian ballots cast for government candidates and 750,000 for their opponents. But the overseas soldier vote was overwhelmingly on the government side, and it was manipulated to give the government the benefit of doubtful seats. Consequently the cleavage between Quebec and the rest of the Dominion, serious though it was, was made to appear all the more glaring, and the feeling was accentuated on both sides that the two races were irreconcilably at odds.

The victory was dearly bought. Conscription was upheld, but at the price of a profound deepening of the racial gulf and without any major effect on the manpower situation. By 1918 the government was obliged to go back on its pledge to exempt farmers' sons, and an angry demonstration by thousands of farmers in Ottawa showed that the French were not the only group who disliked military compulsion. In the end conscription raised some 60,000 effectives, few of whom ever got overseas. The price was a new and lasting bitterness between the two major races, which was to color Canadian politics throughout the whole of the generation to follow.

Advance to Nationhood

The part that Canada played in the war as an autonomous member of the British empire gave added emphasis to the changes that were under way in imperial relationships and to the need for defining these relationships in new and more definite terms. The conflict lent a tremendous impetus to an evolution that was already under way. It clarified and crystallized the salient issues; it heightened Canada's confidence in her stature as a separate community and her insistence on removing the remaining marks of political subordination; it accelerated the process of transition from colony to nation, and the end of the war found Canada standing in her own right among the company of free and self-governing states.

The military aspect itself gave rise to questions that were quite unprecedented. In the Boer War, the only previous occasion when Canadian troops had been sent overseas, the forces had been in the pay and under the command of the British authorities. The situation was quite different when Canada undertook to maintain a force of nearly half a million men on the European battlefront. From the start Borden insisted that this force should constitute a distinct formation. The initial desire of the British authorities to break up Canadian units and use them as replacements was firmly and successfully resisted. The Corps was built up as a distinctively Canadian body and was ultimately brought under a Canadian commander when Sir Arthur Currie succeeded Byng in 1917.

It was, however, one thing to have control over the composition and organization of the Canadian Corps; it was quite another matter to have any voice in determining how it should be used. For operational purposes it came under the British commander in chief, and at that point its direction passed out of the hands of the Canadian government. Borden found that he had no share in the decisions on general military policy and no way of determining or even of knowing where and how Canadian troops might be employed. His protest at the end of 1915 that "we deem ourselves entitled to fuller information and to consulation respecting general policy in war operations" was met with expressions of sympathy, professions of British inability to see any practical way of meeting Canada's desires, and suggestions that, since nothing effective could be done, nothing embarrassing should be said. Borden found this attitude unsatisfactory. "It can hardly be expected." he wrote vigorously, "that we should put 400,000 or 500,000 men in the field and willingly accept the position of having no more voice and receiving no more consideration than if we were toy automata. Any person cherishing such an expectation harbors an unfortunate and even dangerous delusion. Is this war being waged by the United Kingdom alone, or is it a war waged by the whole empire?"

By the end of 1916 more acceptable arrangements were in prospect. Lloyd George had come into power in Britain at the head of a coalition, and under his leadership a new vigor and coherence was infused into the war effort. A critical situation was in prospect during the year to come. Britain's resources in both men and money were now under severe strain. The German submarine campaign was taking a heavy toll of shipping and reducing food supplies to a perilously narrow margin. A military effort on an unprecedented scale was accompanied by a tremendous expansion of war production. Britain had reached the end of her manpower reserves. France was in an equally serious plight. If new sources of strength were to be found, they must be sought overseas; and with the United States still neutral, the chief hope lay in the British Dominions.

It was thus vital that the Dominions should be convinced of the need to intensify their war effort, and one means to this end was to associate them more fully as well as more formally with the general direction of the war. The outcome was the formation of the Imperial War Cabinet, consisting of the Dominion prime ministers or their deputies sitting with the British war cabinet, the inner group that had been constituted for the over-all direction of war policy. In the nature of the case the Dominion prime ministers could not take part in continuous discussions. They could attend only at intervals and for relatively short periods. The weight of authority still rested with the British war cabinet, and its responsibility to the British legislature rather than to any wider imperial body remained fundamental. Yet none of this detracts from the significance of the new development. The Dominions at last found themselves admitted to the inner councils and were able to exercise a genuine influence on decisions in which their own interests were so deeply involved.

The importance of this advance was demonstrated when the organization of the Imperial War Cabinet was virtually carried over into the making of the peace. This had not been the original intention of the British government. With the war brought to a successful conclusion, Britain expected that the main task of peacemaking would rest in the hands of the Allied Great Powers, with the smaller states consulted only on matters directly affecting them and with the Dominions accorded only a nominal share in the proceedings. Borden, arriving in London for consultations in 1918, shortly discovered that Britain had embarked on preliminary consultations with France and Italy and that there was to be a single delegation on which he himself would symbolize the interests of all the Dominions. Borden was roused to strong protest. He had not come over, he asserted, to take part in a light comedy. He was insistent that the Canadian people, in the light of their war effort, fully expected to have a share in the making of the peace and could not imagine that they would be excluded. His demand gained weight from the protests of other small states at the minor role assigned to them and from the fact that it would clearly be difficult to admit a state of the rank of Belgium and still to maintain that a country that had made such a contribution as Canada was not entitled to a seat. In the end, Canada and the other Dominions were not only admitted in their own right, but enjoyed the added privelege of being included on the British Empire panel for purpose of representation on committees. The new status thus conceded was jealously insisted on to the end of the formalities of peacemaking. The Dominions fought for and won the right of separate signature to the peace treaties. Borden stood out for submission of the treaties to the Canadian Parliament and imperial ratification only after the Dominion legislature had given its approval, in spite of British perturbation at this unprecedented course and the delay it involved. It was ironic to find Canadian Liberals voicing the charge, which the Conservatives in their place would have trumpeted even more vociferously, that Borden by this action was threatening the disruption of the empire.

In the actual negotiations at Paris, Canada played a minor though on the whole a commendable part. With little stake in the details of the peace settlement, she was free to use her influence in the more general cause of a sound and workable peace, and Borden's temperate manner was seen to good advantage in committee discussions. Canada had no desire for territory, in contrast to some of her sister Dominions, who were avid to the point of intransigence. When Lloyd George advanced the idea that Canada might take over the West Indies, he found Borden "deeply imbued with the American prejudice against the government of extraneous possessions and peoples." The suggestion from an American source that the Alaska panhandle might be handed over to Canada in lieu of territory in the Caribbean was not followed up. Where the Canadian delegates felt that their country was directly affected, they could be as firm as those of other nations in resisting interference. They opposed the draft international air convention on the ground that it was unsuited to conditions in North America and that Canada should be free to make her own arrangements with the United States, and they opposed the insertion in either the League Covenant or the labor charter of clauses on racial equality that might have curtailed Canada's right to restrict Oriental immigration. In the main, however, their chief attention centered on the new international organizations that were being set up and, particularly, on the place of Canada in the League of Nations and the International Labor Organization.

In the discussions of the League Covenant, Canada found herself strongly opposed to Article X, with its universal guaranty against aggression, and Borden fought to have it struck out or at least drastically amended. To the Canadian delegates it presented the perturbing prospect that the Dominion would be inextricably entangled in European quarrels with which it had no concern and called on to give military aid in defense of boundaries that were neither wise nor just. As a young nation engaged in setting its house in order and a secure country unlikely to call on foreign states for help, Canada objected to being saddled with an unlimited liability. "Though the risks be unequal—in some cases startling so—the same premium is to be paid by all the members," said a Canadian memorandum. "Can anything be more manifestly unjust?" At most, the guaranty should be given only to the states reconstituted or created by the peace settlement and assumed by the states responsible for the settlement or benefiting from it. Here was an expression of that North American distrust of European entanglements which was soon to be even more evident in the United States. To Wilson, however, Article X was "the heart of the Covenant," and he resisted stubbornly and successfully all attempts, whether by his opponents at home or his associates in Paris, to have it modified or eliminated.

A more vital objective for Canada, however, was the securing of full membership in the League of Nations. It was a continuation of the battle for an independent national status that had been waged in connection with Canada's right to sit in the peace conference, and it involved not merely her admission to the League, but her equal right with other small states to be elected to a nonpermanent seat on the Council. It was typical of the difficulties involved that the chief opposition came not from Britain but from the United States. Borden consciously sought to make Canada a link between the two great nations whose harmony was so essential to her own welfare. When he discovered on the eve of the peace conference that certain British leaders were thinking in terms of a balance of power that would curb America's postwar influence, he entered a vigorous dissent. Good relations with the United States, in his view, were the best asset that could be brought home from the war. "If the future policy of the British Empire meant working in cooperation with some European nation as against the United States," he asserted plainly, "that policy could not reckon on the approval or the support of Canada."

On the American side, however, there was little appreciation of this attitude or of the value inherent in the emergence of Canada as a distinct entity with a distinctive policy. Quite apart from the myth, which played so large a part in later American opposition to the League, that the admission of the Dominions meant six seats for Britain there was a real dislike of the prospect that Canada would have to be dealt with directly as a nation in her own right. It was much simpler for all diplomatic questions affecting her or any other part of the empire to be channeled through an amenable Foreign Office in London. American delegates, including Colonel Edward Mandell House, stoutly opposed Canada's pretensions. "She is to be first in the line of battle," Borden complained bitterly, "but not even in the back seat of the Council. The submission of such a proposal to our Parliament would, in my opinion, be wholly futile." In the end an appeal to

Wilson secured a pronouncement by the Big Three in favor of Canada's full right of election to the Council and assured her a comparable status in the International Labor Organization. Her place in the latter body had been the occasion for an even harder battle with the Americans, even though there was a much stronger case for her claims. The chief American member of the commission, while professing sympathy, felt that it would be impossible to persuade public opinion in the United States that the interests and outlook of the Dominions were distinct from those of Britain. Events bore out this judgment only too well, but Borden could hardly agree that Canada's legitimate aspirations should be blocked by the determined ignorance of her neighbors. "The Dominions have maintained their place before the world during the past five years through sacrifices which no nation outside Europe has known," he protested to Lloyd George. "I am confident that the people of Canada will not tamely submit to a dictation which declares that Liberia or Cuba, Panama or Hedjaz, Haiti or Ecuador must have a higher place in the International Labor Organization than can be accorded to their country which is probably the seventh industrial nation in the world, if Germany is excluded from consideration." It was an argument unanswerable in logic, and one which eventually prevailed.

The conclusion of peace thus brought with it a transformation of Canada's status in both the imperial and the international spheres. If a common war effort had strengthened the sentiment in favor of imperial unity, Canada's pride in the part she herself had played resulted in an even greater strengthening of her nationalist outlook and aspirations. If these two elements were to be harmonized, a new orientation was needed; and one of the tasks of the postwar period was to clarify and develop the unique relationship that had transformed dependence into partnership and the empire into the Commonwealth.

Postwar Readjustment

Canada emerged from the war with her productive structure greatly expanded and its pattern considerably modified. While agriculture had grown tremendously, the limits of its expansion were in sight, with the Peace River Valley marking the far northern fringe of the agrarian frontier. Wheat remained a paramount factor in the economy, but the emphasis was growing on manufacturing and extractive staples. Capital invested in industry grew from $127,000,000 in 1911 to $2,000,000,000 in 1916 and over $3,000,000,000 in 1921; the net value of manufactured products increased during the same decade from $564,000,000 to $1,366,000,000. Pulp and paper rose to the rank of a major industry, and its growth, together with the continued expansion of mining, was linked with a parallel expansion in the development of hydroelectric power. Like the agrarian frontier, the forest and mining frontiers were pushing steadily north, and Canadians were beginning to look with new and hopeful eyes toward the vast stretches reaching to the Arctic, under whose barren surface lay virgin wealth in minerals and oil.

Along with expansion went diversification. The wide variety of wartime demands brought into existence new types of manufacturing plants and developed new skill for application to postwar needs. The virtual cessation of imports from Europe in many lines of goods provided an incentive and an opportunity for domestic producers. Textiles, chemicals, and secondary industries processing iron and steel were among the groups to profit by the new conditions. The multiplication of industrial plants had its reflection in the increasing trend toward urbanization. By 1921 the urban population of Canada almost equaled the rural and exceeded it in the two chief industrial provinces of Ontario and Quebec. Canada had become an industrial state, with consequent effects on its social structure and profound implications in the field of public policy.

One of the immediate tasks at the end of the war was the reabsorption into civilian life of half a million veterans. This very process contributed to a postwar demand for consumer goods, which, while it led to serious price inflation, nonetheless aided in the transition to peacetime production and helped to avert any immediate problem of unemployment. There was a postwar slump in the latter part of 1920, but by 1923 production was again on the upgrade. The Dominion and the provinces cooperated in establishing an employment service for returned men. In addition to discharge gratuities, interim unemployment relief was provided, loans were made available for vocational and university training, and vocational instruction was undertaken for disabled veterans. Above all, the long-standing North American tradition that land was the appropriate reward for military valor was once more invoked in the dying stages of the free-land era. All remaining lands within 15 miles of any railway were reserved for veterans, who could claim a quarter section in addition to the normal homestead grant. A Soldier Settlement Board was set up with power to buy agricultural land and to issue loans for stock, equipment, and buildings. The project had a somewhat limited success. In 1921 the board reported that 43,000 returned men had been settled; but many were inexperienced, and some of the lands were in the dry belt that was unsuited for wheat growing, and in the end the numbers sank to 25,000. The wastefulness in human and material resources that marked the whole history of the North American frontier continued to the end.

This paternalistic effort was exceptional in the postwar period. With the end of hostilities the government hastened to divest itself of its wartime functions and controls. The war period had provided a striking though limited illustration of the possibilities of central control and direction when the federal government was invested with full constitutional powers; but with the coming of peace the government lost both the authority and the will to continue activities on the same scale. There was an effort to curb the inflationary trend in 1919 with the passage of a Combines and Fair Prices act, to be administered by a Board of Commerce; but this was declared unconstitutional by the Privy Council as exceeding the Dominion's general power over trade and commerce. The Wheat Board was dissolved after disposing of the 1919 crop, in spite of protests from the western farmers. One burden, however, the government was unable to cast off. The war had thrown the problem of the railways on its hands, and the Dominion found itself committed to a vast and burdensome experiment in public ownership.

The war dealt a ruinous blow to the grandiose and optimistic railway policy that had been sponsored by the Laurier administration. The curtailment of credit from abroad and the rising costs of materials and labor accentuated the difficulties that had already arisen from miscalculations and mismanagement. By 1916 both the Canadian Northern and the Grand Trunk Pacific were staggering into bankruptcy, and the Grand Trunk was once again in financial difficulties as a result of the greed of its shareholders and the inefficiency of its absentee management.

The crisis reached a head when the Canadian Northern, which in 1914 had been granted a government bond guaranty on $45,000,000 on the understanding that this would enable it to raise the remaining capital it needed, came back in 1916 with a request for further government aid. This time the government, whose early concession had aroused serious criticism even among its own supporters, limited its help to a loan of $15,000,000. At the same time it appointed a commission of three to investigate the whole railway situation. The report disclosed a gloomy situation. Of all the private lines, only the Canadian Pacific was really solvent. The others had reached a point where they were unable to carry on unaided. Once more the federal government was confronted by a major question of policy in relation to the transportation system of the Dominion.

In their recommendations the commissioners were agreed on the folly of trying to maintain both the Canadian Northern and the Grand Trunk Pacific as separate and competing systems. Three transcontinental lines were too many for the traffic available, and such competition could only lead to ruinous results. The question of an alternative course, however, found the commission divided. One of them, in a minority report, recommended the amalgamation of the Canadian Northern and the Grand Trunk Pacific west of Winnipeg and the leasing of the lines between Winnipeg and North Bay to a private company. Admitting that the lines would still need government aid, he felt nevertheless that this scheme would be less costly and dangerous than any other plan. His two colleagues, Sir Henry Drayton and W. M. Ackworth, disagreed. The combination of private management and public financing had after all had a long and sad history in the record of Canadian transportation. The majority report advocated that the government, which had to pay the piper, should be enabled to call the tune by taking over all the major railways with the exception of the Canadian Pacific.

The simplest way would have been to allow the railways to lapse into bankruptcy and to foreclose the government's own mortgage. The Borden ministry, however, shrank from this forthright procedure. It feared the effect, not only on Canada's credit abroad, but on financial stability at home as a result of the large holdings of railway securities by the leading financial concerns. The Bank of Commerce in particular was deeply involved in the Canadian Northern, and the government was reluctant to endanger its stability. Instead of taking over the railways free of debt, as the majority report recommended, the government decided to submit the value of Canadian Northern stock to arbitration. A private agreement with the bank and the company introduced a certain safeguard by accepting a maximum valuation of $10,000,000; and when the arbitrators conveniently arrived at a figure that was only slightly higher, the matter was settled to the satisfaction of all the interested parties with the possible exception of the Canadian taxpayer.

This disposed of the problem of the Canadian Northern. As for the Grand Trunk Pacific, it was allowed to go into receivership and was taken over in 1919. There remained the Grand Trunk, whose chronic difficulties through a period of seventy years had now reached a point where it was kindest to put that ailing corporation out of its misery. In the autumn of 1919 it too was taken over. The government agreed to continue the payment of 4 percent interest on the guaranteed stock and to submit the value of the remaining securities to arbitration The arbitrators showed a wide divergence of views. Chief Justice William Howard Taft of the United States, a profound respecter of property rights, held the belief that the shareholders in this bankrupt corporation still had an equity to the value of $48,000,000. His two colleagures, Sir Thomas White and Sir Walter Cassels, in a majority report that the government accepted, pronounced the securities in question completely worthless. There were anguished and indignant outcries in England, where the bulk of the stock was held and where this brusque treatment was contrasted with the tenderness extended to Canadian investors in the Canadian Northern. Judicial proceedings challenging the award were instituted before the Privy Council; but that body dismissed the case, and the shareholders were left with no recourse but to nurse their wrongs and to boycott any further Canadian securities that might be offered them.

In the final outcome the handling of the railway problem diverged considerably from the course recommended by the Drayton-Ackworth report. This had advocated the immediate taking over of the roads in question; in fact the process of acquisition was spread over the better part of five years. Instead of being taken over free of debt, the railways were still burdened with external obligations, and in addition the government's loans were left on their books as claims against their earnings. Their full unification took place only in 1923, when the Grand Trunk, Grand Trunk Pacific, and Canadian Northern were amalgamated with the National Transcontinental and the Intercolonial to form the Canadian National Railways. The government found itself in possession of a system embracing 22,000 miles of track and stretching clear across the continent and involved in a vast public enterprise that was to present serious political as well as financial problems in the years that lay ahead.

Sir Robert Borden. *(Public Archives of Canada)*

The Battle of Vimy.
Germans surrendering to the advancing Canadians.

(Department of National Defence)

The Imperial War Cabinet.

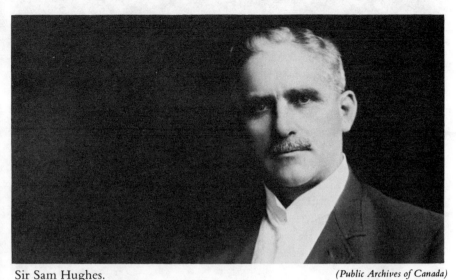

Sir Sam Hughes.
Canadian Defence Minister during World War I.

Canada in Flanders.
Sir Sam Hughes (centre) with officers watching an air attack.

Sir Arthur Currie.

(*Public Archives of Canada*)

Commander of the Canadian Corps in the latter stages of World War I.

Chapter 18

The Quest for Stability
1918-1935

The Dominion and the Provinces

World War I was a cataclysm that thrust Canada abruptly from a stage of development that was nearing completion into a new and drastically different one, which was already in sight when the war broke out. The war years were not so much a period of transition as a violent interlude that greatly accelerated the inevitable transformation. The agrarian pioneer phase had all but ended by 1920. The future expansion of the Dominion was now linked to the development of industrial capitalism, not merely in manufacturing but in the exploitation of such natural resources as timber and minerals and water power. It was not merely a change in the balance of the Canadian economy; it was the virtual end of that type of individual opportunity made possible by the availability of free land for settlement. Although most Canadians continued to think in terms of the traditional pattern, a stage had been reached that called for the charting of new paths and for the adaptation of Canadian society to the limitations as well as the possibilities with which it was now confronted.

This in turn imposed a new role on the federal government. Under Laurier the basic original purposes of confederation had at last been achieved. A flood of settlers had filled in the vacant lands of the West. The national need for transcontinental transportation had been more than amply met. Transportation facilities and an expanding home market guarded by a protective tariff had brought into being a substantial manufacturing industry, and all these had lent fresh stimulus to the exploitation of Canada's forest and mineral wealth. The further contribution that the federal government could make to these forms of activity was relatively limited. Its task was to round out the structure that had already been created, to assure favorable conditions for continued economic expansion, and to resolve the divergences in economic and social interests through policies that would contribute the maximum to national unity and national welfare.

The changing outlook was reflected in immigration policy. There was still a desire for settlers who would go on the land, but there was no longer a wide-open door for homeseekers from other countries. The free lands that remained were in most cases remote from the railways, and the government, struggling with the legacy of past transportation problems, was not eager to incur new expenditures. In the immediate postwar period immigrants were restricted to those who could buy land or who would take farm or domestic employment. After 1923, with stability achieved and prosperity rising, a wider but still selective policy was adopted, but the flood never again reached the peak of the prewar years. Its high point was in 1929, when 165,000 immigrants arrived in Canada. By that time almost no free land remained; and with the advent of the depression, new restrictions were imposed that cut down arrivals to a few thousand a year.

These years completed the filling up of the prairies. In the decade ending in 1931, Saskatchewan's population grew by more than 160,000 and Alberta's by over 140,000, while occupied land in these provinces increased by one-quarter and one-third respectively. Wheat was still the settler's main crop; and out of the problems of the western wheat farmer grew a unique experiment in cooperative marketing. Agricultural cooperatives in Canada had a history dating back to the middle of the nineteenth century. In fruit, dairy, and wool products they were conducting successful operations on a relatively large scale by the time of the war. By that time, too, the western wheat growers had already entered the field with the establishment of cooperative elevator companies and of the Grain Growers' Grain Company for storage and marketing. The Wheat Board during the war met a vital need; and when this was abolished, provincial marketing and elevator pools were organized, and the Wheat Pool as a central selling agency was set up in 1924. Here was one more example of the inevitable pressure toward large-scale organization in Canadian staple production. The pool endeavored to carry out a program of orderly marketing that would secure the maximum price for its members. By 1939 it had over 140,000 members and was selling 100,000,000 bushels of wheat in the world market. Prices during the twenties had stabilized at around $1.45 a bushel after the postwar slump; acreage and yields had expanded; new and hardy varieties of grain had been developed, enabling the wheat-growing area to push steadily north; and a peak crop of 567,000,000 bushels in 1928 marked the mature fruits of Canada's policy of western settlement.

In transportation, too, the task was now chiefly to round out the existing pattern, but here the federal government was still committed to substantial efforts and expenditures. The insistent demand in the West for a railway to Hudson Bay was at last met by the construction of a line from The Pas to the port of Churchill at a cost of $50,000,000. The champions of the project believed that the old route, which had been of such advantage to the fur trade, would be of equal service to the western grain grower. But the outgoing cargoes of the Hudson's Bay Company had been articles of high value in small bulk, and the demand for supplies at the company's posts had provided a two-way traffic. These factors were now absent; and the shortness of the season, the dangers to navigation, and the high cost of insurance, all weighed against the advantage of the Bay route as the shortest sea route between Europe and western Canada. The six vessels that docked at Churchill in 1939 carried away less than 2,000,000 bushels of wheat, while their incoming cargoes amounted to 1,262 tons. Even the construction of this alternative to the St. Lawrence route did not relieve the government of the need to spend $100,000,000 between 1921 and 1929 to improve the latter by deepening the canals— indeed, the postwar years saw the growth of the project of a St. Lawrence waterway, which would enable ocean-going ships to traverse the whole Great Lakes system from Montreal to the head of Lake Superior.

These activities, however, were overshadowed by the railway problem that the government found on its hands during the postwar period. Having taken over the bankrupt lines, the Dominion was virtually committed to their operation as a public enterprise. The Canadian Pacific, alarmed at the prospect, eventually suggested that it should take over the paying portions of the roads and that the rest should be abandoned. But opposition to a Canadian Pacific Railway monopoly, especially in the West, which nursed resentful memories of that state of affairs during the early years of its development, made such a scheme impractical. An almost equal hostility to government monopoly stood in the way of the creation of a single public-owned system by the absorption of the Canadian Pacific Railway. The compromise course of two competing systems, one public and one private, brought the greatest satisfaction to the greatest number, even if it did not eliminate a strong and vocal body of dissenters.

The Drayton-Ackworth report, in recommending government amalgamation and ownership of the lines involved, sought to keep the railways out of politics. It advised the creation of an independent corporation under a board of five members. Their tenure of office was to be permanent, and the board was to be self-perpetuating; its members were to renounce all political views, and the government was to refrain from interference in policy. The fatal obstacle to this scheme was that the government was called on to shoulder the anticipated deficits in the operation of the roads. A Parliament that was called on to vote funds for such a purpose was bound to insist on its right to scrutinize policy and lay down conditions. A ministry that would be held responsible for the use of public funds could not divorce itself from the management of its own possessions. As a result, the Canadian National Railway Company was created with a board of fifteen members appointed by the government and removable at will and was placed under a Department of Railways, which was answerable to Parliament.

The man chosen as head and director of the company was Sir Henry Thornton. An able executive with extensive railway experience in Britain and the United States, he entered on his task with vigor and enthusiasm. His experience and his dominating personality resulted in his securing virtually a free hand with little interference from the board. He was determined to vindicate the efficiency of the public-owned system and to make it an effective competitor of the Canadian Pacific Railway. It was a logical and in many aspects a desirable attitude, but it necessarily involved further capital expenditures. Many of the roads were in parlous shape as to both roadbeds and rolling stock. New feeders were needed to tap new areas. Competition with the Canadian Pacific Railway led to the establishment of luxury services, the building of hotels, the acquisition of steamships. Thornton's bold and imaginative policy knit the lines into a coherent and well-run system, which showed a gross operating surplus. But earnings still fell short of meeting interest obligations, including those which were claimed by the government itself. Annual deficits were made the grounds for a sustained campaign by interested groups against the extravagance of government policy and the financial burden it entailed. Once more Canada's transportation needs involved the pledging of her immediate credit in anticipation of future returns.

The prosperity of the railways depended to a very large extent on the prosperity of the western farmer. Wheat for export provided the bulk of eastbound freight over the long haul. The westbound volume of manufactured goods was directly related to prairie purchasing power. This situation was of equal significance to the Canadian industrialist. Canadian manufacturers, it is true, were now finding markets abroad. A number of American branch plants were established in Canada for the purpose of taking advantage of imperial preference in their exports to Britain and the Dominions. But Canadian industry was still primarily dependent on the home market and particularly on that portion of the home market which in its turn depended on world trade. In these circumstances the direct contribution that the federal government could make to the growth of industry was distinctly limited. Tariffs might be devised to reduce costs or protect the domestic market. Freight rates might be adjusted to stimulate the flow of goods within the Dominion. Trade treaties and immigration policies might play their part in opening new markets or expanding old ones. By and large, however, the dominating emotion of Canadian industrialists was less the hope of favors yet to come than the fear of interference and impositions in the form of social legislation or tax burdens, and demands for economy and nonintervention were particularly directed against the federal government.

The role of the provinces, in contrast, was becoming increasingly positive. It was within the framework of their powers and policies that a large part of any further expansion must take place. The occupation of the agrarian frontier had been completed under federal auspices; the development of agriculture and the solution of its problems now rested to a growing degree with the provinces. The northward extension of the boundaries of Quebec, Ontario, and Manitoba in 1912 and the handing over to the prairie provinces in 1930 of control over their remaining natural resources extended their power over timber concessions and the granting of mineral rights. The development of water power fell within the provincial sphere, and this linked up with the location and development of industry, which looked to the provinces for suitable facilities and for favorable policies in such matters as taxation and labor legislation. While business chiefly required the federal government to refrain from action, except when higher tariffs were in question, it looked to the provinces for tangible contributions to the success of rugged individualism.

The widening of provincial functions was paralleled by the broadening of provincial jurisdiction. In its work of judicial interpretation the Privy Council steadfastly developed the trend that had become evident by the turn of the century. With the end of the war emergency the work was resumed of enlarging the powers of the provinces and drawing tighter the bonds that restricted the authority of the Dominion. The judgment of Lord Haldane invalidating the Industrial Disputes Investigation Act of 1907 (*Toronto Electric Commissioners v. Snider,* 1925) carried this process to a new extreme. "It does not appear," it stated, "that there is anything in the Dominion Act which could not have been enacted by the legislature of Ontario, excepting one provision. The field for the operation of the Act was the whole of Canada." Since that exception is the very heart of the residuary power in Section 91, Lord Haldane's dismissal of it seemed a trifle cavalier. He went even further and boldly tackled the difficulty that had faintly haunted the Privy Council ever since 1882, when *Russell v. The Queen* accepted the original scope of the power of peace, order, and good government. In an imaginative reconstruction of the mental process of his predecessors, all the more striking for being totally unsupported, he reached the conclusion that they must have thought "that the evil of intemperance at that time amounted in Canada to one so great and so general that at least for the period it was a menace so serious and pressing that the national parliament was called on to intervene to protect the nation from disaster. An epidemic of pestilence might conceivably have been regarded as analogous."

After Haldane's retirement there were brief signs that the Privy Council might repent of its intellectual aberrations. In two cases in 1932 it was decided that the Dominion had the right to exercise control over the fields of civil aviation and radio broadcasting—two functions completely new since the passage of the British North America Act, yet now brought within the field of federal powers. But these glimmers of modernity were quickly extinguished. The decisions of 1937 on the validity of the social legislation recently passed by the Bennett government reaffirmed the earlier attitude toward the balance of the constitution and tightened the strait jacket on the federal government. The Dominion was to enjoy the full powers originally assigned to it only in such extreme cases as war, pestilence, or a nationwide orgy of drunkenness. For all lesser exigencies it was virtually restricted to the illustrative heads enumerated in Section 91, and even then, to the narrow meaning within which the Privy Council had by this time confined them.

The result was not merely to invest the provinces with new authority, but also to burden them with new responsibilities. The broad interpretation given to their control over "property and civil rights" virtually barred the Dominion from the whole field of social policy. From education to highways, and from labor legislation to liquor control, the main burden fell on the provinces, and it was steadily increasing with the expanding functions of government. The advent of the automobile, which lifted the tourist industry to major rank among Canada's activities, involved the provinces in heavy expenditures on roads. Improved standards of education, the adoption of old-age pensions and mothers' allowances, the tentative beginnings in the establishment of maximum hours and minimum wages for certain classes of workers, threw added burdens on provincial budgets. Yet the provinces lacked the financial resources to carry out these duties effectively; and action on a purely provincial basis made it difficult to achieve the uniform national level that was so desirable in such fields as labor standards and health services.

Thus the federal government, denied the right to act directly, was forced to find other ways of serving the national interest, for which it could not escape ultimate responsibility. One method was to encourage the provinces to expand their services by providing federal grants-in-aid to ease the financial burden; and it was sometimes possible to make these contingent on the adoption of standards laid down by the Dominion in the interests of uniformity. A salient example was the Old Age Pensions Act of 1927, by which the federal government was authorized to make uniform agreements with the provinces and to bear half the cost. At best, however, this was a cumbersome procedure; and it was even more unsatisfactory in the case of grants for a term of years such as were made to assist the development of technical and agricultural education. When these subsidies came to an end, the provinces found themselves committed to expanded services that it was difficult for them to abandon. To some extent new sources of provincial revenue—corporation and income taxes, motor licenses and gasoline taxes and profits from liquor sales— helped to fill the gap. Yet there remained the basic anomaly of a situation in which the bulk of the taxing power lay with the Dominion while the chief social functions were jealously retained by the provinces; and the problem of redressing this warped constitutional balance, largely resulting from the decisions of the Privy Council, emerged as an issue of growing urgency.

It was aggravated by the persistence not only of the doctrine of provincial rights, but also of a sectionalism that that doctrine helped to bulwark. Even while the different regions were becoming increasingly interdependent, they were increasingly conscious of special and divergent interests. The Maritimes were chronically aggrieved at their lack of progress under confederation. The stimulus to shipbuilding and the steel industry that arose from wartime demands subsided with the coming of peace; manufacturing declined while industry in central Canada continued to expand; the development of a trade in fresh fish failed to compensate for declining markets for dried cod. The recommendations of the Duncan Commission on Maritime Rights, appointed in 1926, led to a 20 percent reduction in freight rates between the Maritimes and other sections, and efforts were made to encourage shipping and harbor development; but these concessions only partly overcame the basic disadvantages of geography. The prairies, like the Maritimes, looked with jaundiced eyes on the protective tariff and sought repeated concessions in the matter of transportation. When the Crowsnest Pass agreement was canceled in 1921, a clamor arose that was not stilled by the promise of the Hudson Bay Railway but brought the re-establishment of the agreement in 1922 and reduced rates on shipments of prairie wheat. British Columbia, whose trade position had been vastly improved by the opening of the Panama Canal, felt less dependence on Canadian railways or on the markets of central Canada. All these sections looked on central Canada as a region that exploited them for the benefit of concentrated financial and industrial interests. In their turn the central provinces regarded the outlying areas as responsible for the debt and the rising expenditures that threatened Canada's stability and as enemies of the protective system that Canadian industry needed in order to survive. The basic interests of Ontario and Quebec placed them in diametric opposition to the rest of the country on some of the most vital economic issues, while racial friction continued to divide these two provinces and to present a major obstacle to Canadian national unity.

Parties and Policies

The end of the war brought the decline of the Union government and saw the old parties reconstituting their ranks under new leaders. Ill health brought Borden's retirement in the summer of 1920 and his replacement as prime minister by Arthur Meighen. By that time the government was breaking up. Liberals who had supported the wartime coalition were drifting back to their old allegiance. Laurier, heartsick at the sectional antagonisms that threatened his lifelong effort on behalf of national unity and at the desertions from the Liberal ranks that undermined his leadership, nonetheless rallied his strength in an attempt to reunite his party. He felt deeply the way in which his race and creed had been used to the disadvantage of the Liberals and insisted that the next leader must not be a Catholic. His death in the spring of 1919 necessitated the choice of a successor, and the Liberals called a national convention attended by 1400 delegates and no less than eight provincial premiers—the first occasion on which a major Canadian party adopted the American method of choosing a leader. Among the older figures, W. S. Fielding was outstanding; but Quebec was cool toward him because he had supported conscription, and there was much sentiment in favor of a younger man. This feeling rallied to William Lyon Mackenzie King, a grandson of the old rebel leader and a faithful supporter of Laurier; and with the support of the Quebec delegates he was chosen to head the reunited Liberal party.

This was the man who was to dominate Canadian politics for the next quarter of a century and to hold the office of prime minister longer than any of his predecessors. He was a somewhat unlikely figure to leave such a mark on history. Though a skilled debater, he lacked the personal charm and oratorical powers of Laurier or the profoundly human warmth of John Alexander Macdonald. He had been trained in political science and labor relations and had been Canada's first minister of labor in the Laurier cabinet, yet he never won a personal following as a social reformer or a champion of the downtrodden and exploited. His personality seemed much like his person—rather commonplace, even flabby, with few outward signs of intellectual endowment and with a tendency toward a profuse and uninspiring sentimentalism. Probably no major political figure ever evoked so little spontaneous affection among his followers or such baffled rage among his opponents at his persistent success in persuading the electorate to return him to power.

His success was a profound commentary on certain basic and inexorable realities in Canadian politics. The desire for positive accomplishments, badly needed as these frequently were, was almost as frequently overshadowed by the fear of troubles in store. If there was need for a leader who would strike out with a vigorous and constructive program, there was at least an equal need for one who would avoid any steps that might increase to the breaking point the already existing strains in the structure of the Dominion. It was in this negative yet highly necessary role that King excelled. There were positive accomplishments as well, but his long ascendancy rested less on these than on his tactical astuteness, on his skill in avoiding dangerous decisions until the most pressing demand for decisions had subsided, on his ability to portion out half a loaf in a way that mollified the recipients without outraging too many of the involuntary donors. It was an unheroic role, but any attempt to govern Canada by heroics would have split the country. Genius might have found more inspiring solutions; but genius is rare in politics as in other fields, and with all King's shortcomings, it is probable that no available leader could have achieved more and still have held the nation together. A man may deserve well of his country not only for the things he brings to pass, but equally for the things he keeps from happening.

The Liberal convention that selected a leader who was young and full of vigor also produced a platform whose high promises were more delusive. In the forefront stood a pledge of substantial tariff reduction, with farm implements and supplies to be admitted free, and lowered duties on clothing and other articles affecting the cost of living. Faith in the reciprocity proposals of 1911 was reaffirmed; a comprehensive program of social insurance was outlined; representation of labor in the management of industry was endorsed; control of natural resources was to be returned to the provinces; and proportional representation was endorsed as the basis for the House of Commons. It is an adequate comment that a full generation later Canada was still waiting for tariff reductions on anything like the promised scale, proportional representation seemed further away than ever, unemployment insurance was only enacted in 1940, and effective representation of labor in industry was still a distant goal.

But while there were doubts even at the time about the sincerity of the Liberals, such skepticism worked to the advantage of the newer parties rather than of the Meighen government. The election of 1921 was disastrous for the Conservatives. Quebec in particular nursed bitter memories of the conscription issue and resentment against Meighen as one of its foremost champions; and for the first time Quebec's 65 seats went solidly Liberal. The only province in which the Conservatives showed a majority was British Columbia. The party was reduced to 50 members in the House of Commons. The Liberals, with 117 seats, came into power. But their tenure was precarious, for they lacked a solid working majority. The prairies had swung against both of the older parties, and they newly formed Progressive party, which had swept the West and captured 24 seats in Ontario, now held the balance of power.

The new party was primarily an expression of agrarian discontent. The similar movements that had swept the United States toward the end of the nineteenth century, which found expression in the Granger and Populist parties, had hardly been reflected hitherto in Canadian politics. The Grange spread north of the border but refrained from political activity. The Patrons of Industry entered Ontario in 1889, but their incursions into politics were brief and none too successful, and their main attention was turned toward the encouragement of cooperatives and pressure for government aid in transportation and marketing. In 1909 the Canadian Council of Agriculture was formed in an attempt to bring together all farm organizations, but this, too, confined its political activities to pressure on the federal government for measures favorable to agriculture.

The fact was that in spite of many apparent similarities in conditions, the circumstances and motives behind the rise of third parties in the United States operated much less strongly in Canada. There was a comparable resentment at the domination of big business and at the tariff as a bulwark of monopoly and a burden on the farmer. But the clamor in the American West for the dissolution of large corporations and the compulsory restoration of free competition had relatively few parallels in Canada before 1914. Quite apart from the fact that industrial capitalism was at a less mature stage, the large corporation was a traditional and in certain fields a necessary feature of the Canadian economy. This was particularly true in the case of the railways, against which the farmers in the American West directed their earliest and bitterest attacks. In Canada, too, there was a dislike of private monopoly, but the alternative in many cases was not private competition but government control. The limited resources of private capital had repeatedly been shown by the extension of government aid to large undertakings. The direct activity of government in business was evident in the development of transportation and water power. Dissolution of existing combinations in cement or farm implements might restore free competition; but by and large there was no assurance, in view of the limited resources of private capital, that the abolition of near-monopolies would in fact open the field to competitors who were both willing and able to enter into it.

By 1914, however, the mounting grievances of the farmers were finding expression in a revolt against the old parties as tools of vested interests and in the emergence of new political organizations based on local and class interests. In Ontario a general provincial organization, the United Farmers of Ontario, was set up. In 1918 it resolved on direct political action, spurred on by grievances over broken pledges to exempt farmers' sons from conscription and by the adoption of a political program by the Canadian Council of Agriculture. This document, which provided the basic platform for the new agrarian movements in general, bore a strong resemblance to the Populist program in the United States over twenty years previously. It attacked the protective tariff as fostering trusts and creating a privileged class at the expense of the masses. It demanded taxes on profits and incomes, public ownership of such utilities as transportation and power, the extension of cooperative methods to the whole field of marketing, and a series of political reforms, including abolition of the Senate and direct legislation through such methods as the initiative and referendum.

In 1919 the United Farmers of Ontario swept the provincial elections in Ontario and installed a farmers' government under E. C. Drury. By this time a similar movement was taking shape in the West. United farm organizations were formed in all the prairie provinces where the refusal of the federal government to continue the Wheat Board or to promise a reduction in the tariff showed the need for direct influence on federal politics. Western labor, too, was restive under postwar conditions. Trade-union membership in Canada had doubled during the war; but the increased cost of living resulting from inflation and from wartime taxes on articles of consumption had caused discontent, and the government's repression of radical opinions, together with its participation in military intervention in Russian against the Bolsheviks, brought protests from the more advanced sections. The conservative leadership of the eastern trade unions also came in for criticism from western organizations, which had been influenced by the Industrial Workers of the World and the doctrines of revolutionary syndicalism and which sought unsuccessfully to transform Canadian unionism from its existing craft basis to the broader form of industrial organization. By 1919 these western groups had launched the One Big Union movement, whose avowed aim was the achievement of socialism by means of a general strike. The projected national strike was never launched, but a strike of metalworkers in Winnipeg in May 1919, unconnected with the One Big Union, was transformed into a citywide strike under the leadership of the local Trades and Labor Council. A citizens' committee was formed to meet the emergency; the federal government rushed through legislation aimed at the repression of radical organizations and giving wide arbitrary powers of deportation; the strike leaders were arrested and charged with seditious conspiracy; and a protest parade brought a clash in which one man was killed and thirty injured. In July the strike ended when the metalworkers accepted a formula providing for collective bargaining; but the movement revealed serious depths of discontent as well as grave divisions in the ranks of organized labor.

There was, however, little effective link between the radical elements in the ranks of labor and the protest movement among Canadian farmers. The agrarian organizations in general disliked the idea of an alliance with the urban workers, while the older established unions showed little desire for independent political action. It was the farmers who, stimulated by political success in Ontario and by the activities of the Non-Partisan League spreading from North Dakota, met at the call of the Canadian Council of Agriculture in convention at Winnipeg in January 1920, and launched the National Progressive party. Its platform was the program that the Canadian Council of Agriculture had issued in 1918 under the title of "the New National Policy." Its first leader was T. A. Crerar, who had a successful record as president of the United Grain Growers and who after serving in the Union cabinet had resigned in protest against its refusal to lower the tariff; and when Crerar later retired to devote his energies to the United Grain Growers, his place was taken by Robert Forke. The strength of the party rested on rural Ontario and the three prairie provinces, and it was in these regions that it captured 65 seats in the election of 1921 to become second in strength to the Liberals, whose tenure of office was dependent on Progressive support.

The fruits of this success were disappointing. The Progressives, instead of acting as effective critics and goads, found themselves drawn into a virtual working alliance with the Liberals, whose professed policies on tariffs and taxation and social reform coincided with many of their own aims. When it came to implementing these professions, however, the Liberals found lavish excuses for delay. Mackenzie King took the view that the 1919 platform was merely a general chart to indicate a future course. Many of his followers denied that its pledges had any binding effect. William S. Fielding, challenged on his failure to carry through the promised tariff reductions, stoutly maintained that the platform had played no part whatever in the election campaign. Wartime tariff levies were gradually removed, but it was only in 1924 that Progressive pressure secured a general reduction on agricultural implements. The government was content to play for position and avoid the risks attendant on bold and controversial measures, and many Progressives seemed satisfied to accept occasional crumbs at the hands of the Liberals. By 1924 a "ginger group," dissatisfied with this attitude, had seceded from the party, launching an attack on its tactics and organization and on the old party system, which was branded as an instrument of large-scale financial interests.

The election of 1925 revealed a widespread disillusionment with both the Liberals and Progressives—a trend already revealed by the defeat of the Drury government in Ontario in 1923. The strength of the Progressives sank to 24 seats. The Liberals were reduced to 101, and among the defeated candidates was the Prime Minister himself. The Conservatives, with 117 seats, emerged as the largest group, but they still fell short of commanding a clear majority. Nonetheless, they felt justified in claiming that the Liberals had been repudiated by the country and that the government should resign. King, however, stood on his constitutional right to meet the House of Commons (he was shortly returned at a by-election) in the belief that continued support from the Progressives would enable him to carry on the government.

He did in fact succeed in retaining power for six months, although by the slenderest of margins. The Progressives were held by a series of concessions—a budget that reduced taxes and tariffs, a scheme of rural credit, a bill on old-age pensions, which passed the Commons only to be rejected by the Senate. But western support was weakened when the government postponed the promised return of natural resources to Alberta and was finally alienated by the customs scandal. An inquiry revealed that customs officials had connived not only at the smuggling of liquor into the United States—an offense toward which many Canadians were prepared to take a charitable view—but also at large-scale smuggling into Canada, which was much more heinous in the eyes of Canadian merchants and taxpayers. The government fought to avert any motion in which censure was implied, but in a turbulent all-night session on June 25 a series of votes went against it, with the Progressives voting in opposition. This was a decisive shift of alignment, which ended all prospect that the government could retain a majority. The Prime Minister decided to appeal to the electorate and requested the Governor General to dissolve Parliament. But Lord Byng took the view that the Conservatives should be given a chance to govern with the existing House of Commons; and on Meighen's assurance that they could form a working government, he refused King's request. On June 28 the government resigned and the Governor General called on Arthur Meighen to form a ministry.

These events raised constitutional issues of major importance. The extent of the royal prerogative in general, the degree to which it could be exercised by the governor general as the king's representative, the question whether it included a discretionary right to refuse a dissolution when this was requested by a responsible minister, were all controversial matters over which lawyers could spend long and happy hours of debate. In the final analysis the deciding factors were not legal but political. Byng's action depended for its vindication on Meighen's ability to form a fully functioning government, and Meighen let him down. In his eagerness to gain power for his party and restore his own waning ascendancy, he had committed himself to a gamble when failure was virtually foreordained. Meighen needed all the forces he could rally, including support from the Progressives, to command a majority. But cabinet ministers were still required by law to vacate their seats on the acceptance of office—a stipulation that was not abolished until 1931—and their retirement to seek re-election would fatally jeopardize the government. The Prime Minister fell back on the device of appointing acting ministers, who drew no salaries and took no oath as heads of specific departments. This shift was at once attacked by the Liberals as unconstitutional, and it alienated the Progressives, whose promise of support was predicated on the ability of the Conservatives to constitute a government that was regular in form. After barely three days of office the ministry succumbed to an adverse vote, and Byng was now obliged to grant to Meighen the dissolution he had refused to King. The latter was presented with an issue that he exploited with unrivaled skill, and his denunciation of the unconstitutional interference by a British official in the processes of Canadian government appealed strongly to national sentiment in the Dominion. The Conservatives were reduced to 91 seats. The official Liberals with 119 were still short of a clear majority, but 11 Liberal-Progressives had been elected with the endorsement of both parties, and the support of these and in general of the 24 independent members who were returned assured the Liberals of an adequate working margin. Meighen recognized defeat by resigning ten days after the election, and King was once more called to power.

The election was virtually a death blow to the Progressive movement. The forces behind it remained rooted in western politics, particularly in Alberta, where a farmers' government remained in power until 1935. In the federal sphere, however, it disintegrated into fragments, with one section being absorbed into the Liberals—Robert Forke himself entered the new King cabinet—others adopting various independent labels, and only a handful keeping alive the Progressive name until it too was merged in a new and wider movement.

The Conservative defeat was also a blow to Meighen's leadership. It brought to a head the smoldering discontent in the party ranks at his repeated errors in judgment, which had jeopardized the chances of victory. The implacable hostility of Quebec to Meighen personally was a serious handicap. Many stalwart Conservatives had been deeply offended by Meighen's Hamilton speech in November 1925, in which he advocated a general election before any Canadian troops were sent overseas in future wars. Meighen insisted that this was desirable in the interests of national unity, but to the imperialists among his followers it seemed a desertion of the empire in a vain effort to conciliate Quebec. Meighen himself accepted the outcome of the election of 1926 as fatal to his leadership and resigned as head of the party. A convention in Winnipeg in 1927 chose as his successor Richard Beford Bennett, a western lawyer who had built up a substantial personal fortune and who had been prominent in federal politics since 1911. A vigorous personality, he gave promise of providing the rough fighting spirit for which the party yearned, as well as a healthy contribution to the funds of which it stood in need.

The Liberals on their part gained only a limited infusion of strength from their absorption of the bulk of the Progressive party. Their record during the next few years showed modest progress in fiscal and social reform, including the establishment of old-age pensions and the negotiation of a number of trade treaties. Prosperous times were marked by favorable trade balances and reductions in debt and taxation, and the urge for constructive social readjustment temporarily diminished. The advent of the depression in 1929, however, presented the Liberals with problems with which they were temperamentally and traditionally unsuited to deal. The government was reluctant to take direct steps to remedy agricultural distress or provide adequate unemployment relief. Funds for relief were doled out grudgingly to the provinces, and criticism of the government's parsimony, particularly from the Conservative premier of Ontario, provoked the normally cautious King into an unguarded outburst against his political opponents. "I might be prepared to go a certain length possibly in meeting one or two of the western provinces that have progressive premiers at the head of their governments," he said "but I would not give a single cent to any Tory government." And when this was met by shocked exclamations in the Commons, he reiterated: "With respect to giving moneys out of the federal treasury to any Tory government in this country for these alleged unemployment purposes, with these governments situated as they are today, with policies directly opposed to those of this government, I would not give them a five-cent piece." This "five-cent speech," stressed by the delighted Conservatives in the election campaign of 1930, typified only too well in the minds of the electorate the bankruptcy of the government's policy. Bennett launched vigorous attacks on King's failure to exclude foreign competition or to retaliate against recent increases in the American tariffs and promised to use the tariff as a means of blasting Canada's way into world markets. The election results showed the desire for a more positive policy than the Liberals had to offer. Their numbers fell to 87; the various independent groups were reduced to a total of 20; and the Conservatives, with 138 members, entered into power with a clear majority and a mandate to carry out their promise to end unemployment by the methods of economic nationalism.

The Conservatives and the Depression

The vulnerability of Canada's economic position was starkly revealed by the world depression, which was in full swing by 1930. Under its impact the world-wide conflict of economic nationalisms took on a new intensity. Mounting tariffs, curtailed purchasing power, depreciated currencies, and attempts at a greater degree of national self-sufficiency became general throughout the western world. The Dominion, dependent for its prosperity on a reasonable price level and an active demand for its staple exports, faced curtailed markets and a drastic drop in the world prices of primary commodities. Mining was somewhat cushioned by the irrational persistence of a stable market for gold at a time when nearly all currencies had thrown over the gold standard and by Canada's retention of a virtual monopoly in nickel production. Nonetheless, there was a serious fall in the price of silver and the leading base metals, and such staples as lumber and fish and newsprint fell in price by from 30 to 60 percent by 1933, with a corresponding drop in export values.

Most disastrous of all was the slump in wheat. Even before the depression there were signs of difficulties ahead. Canadian wheat faced competition from other exporters such as Australia and Argentina. Markets diminished when European production revived after the war and still more when the efforts of European countries to achieve a favorable trade balance led to restrictions on food imports. The depression accentuated the trend toward autarchy. Italy was striving for self-sufficiency through the battle of the grain. France and Germany raised their tariffs and adopted regulations requiring the use of a certain proportion of domestic grains in the making of bread. Russia, in urgent need of foreign credits, added to the dislocation by throwing wheat on the world market in 1931. The consequence of all these factors was seen in a decline in world wheat shipments and a rise in the world carry-over from 528,000,000 bushels in 1925 to 1,200,000,000 in 1934.

Canada suffered not only from declining demand and falling prices, but from blows dealt by nature as well. Drought in 1934 and again in 1937 ruined many prairie crops and left many farmers without even the scanty income that a normal yield would have brought at prevailing prices. Production, which reached a peak of 567,000,000 bushels in 1928, sank to 276,000,000 in 1934, and in 1937 it was down to 182,000,000—the lowest yield per acre ever recorded. Wheat prices, which stood at $1.60 a bushel in 1929, had collapsed to 38 cents at the end of 1932 and were only a fraction of the cost of production. Farm incomes on the prairies were cut by as much as three-quarters, and the threat of bankruptcy hung over the whole of the West.

This situation struck at the very foundation of the national economy. The decline in wheat exports had immediate effects on the railways. Revenues were cut in half. The deficits of the Canadian National Railway rose to more than $60,000,000 annually. The Canadian Pacific Railway also ran into difficulties, and when it was forced to pass its customary dividend a shock of consternation ran through Canadian financial circles. Industry was equally hit by the decline in farm purchasing power; and the curtailed market for consumer products was accompanied by a slump in construction activity and in the demand for capital goods. Unemployment in the cities was added to distress on the farms; and by 1935 one-tenth of the population, rural as well as urban, was in receipt of public relief.

Such a condition of affairs outran the resources of individual initiative or private charity. So long as the continent had remained in the agrarian pioneer stage, free land had provided an element of flexibility in times of economic distress. That had now been lost, and the only thing that could take its place was organized community action expressed through government policy. The initial responsibility rested on the provinces and municipalities, but the burden soon outran their financial capacities, and the ultimate responsibility fell on the federal government.

The first and almost automatic response of the Bennett administration was an increase in the protective system. The new ministry was ready to believe that its promise to end unemployment at home could be implemented by excluding competition from abroad. The adoption by the United States of the Hawley-Smoot tariff in 1930, with its new high rates affecting Canadian primary products, was a particularly serious blow, which provoked a desire to retaliate in kind. The new tariff schedules adopted between 1930 and 1932 were deliberately designed to exclude from Canada not merely articles of a type already produced there, but any products that Canadians might conceivably be inclined to produce. New duties were placed on agricultural products. Virtually every industry of any importance was granted increased protection, and the general tariff level was raised by almost 50 percent. In addition such special devices as dumping duties, arbitrary valuations for customs purposes, and arbitrary fixing of exchange rates in the case of depreciated foreign currencies were employed to raise the level still further. Never since the inauguration of the National Policy had there been such a sweeping change in the Canadian tariff system.

This drastic policy of trade restriction was of mixed benefit to the Dominion. By contributing to a heavy reduction in imports, it helped to transform a trade deficit of $125,000,000 in 1930 into a surplus of $187,000,000 in 1935. By increasing the share of Canadian manufacturers in the domestic market, it helped to moderate the fall in unemployment. But it did little by itself to increase domestic purchasing power; rather it imposed higher costs on large groups of both producers and consumers.

The benefits accrued chiefly to the sheltered industries producing for the domestic market. Staple producers dependent on exports found themselves burdened with increased costs without any compensating increase in their sales abroad. A Nova Scotia submission in 1934 calculated that while the tariff represented per capita subsidies in Ontario and Quebec of $15.15 and $11.03 respectively, it imposed burdens on the remaining provinces that ranged from $11.67 in Nova Scotia to $28.16 in Saskatchewan. Manitoba estimated that the cost of the tariff amounted to $100 a farm. The tariff was of no help to the basic producers unless it was used, not as a barrier, but as a lever to force trade concessions from other countries.

This was the professed intention of the Bennett government. Retaliatory duties were to be the means of blasting a way into world markets. In practice, however, the protective aspect of the tariff continued to overshadow its usefulness as a bargaining weapon. Trade treaties with France and Germany did relatively little to increase the volume of Canadian exports. Negotiations with the United States bogged down over the reluctance of Canada to make substantial concessions. It was chiefly on the British market, however, that the eyes of the government were fixed. While the Conservatives professed to be ardent advocates of imperial preference, they had always disliked the Laurier basis of Canadian tariff concessions without favors from Britain in return. Now a situation arose that offered more acceptable prospects. The economic crisis that led to the formation of the National Government in Britain in 1931 was followed the next year by Britain's abandonment of free trade and her adoption of an avowed policy of strengthening imperial economic ties. At last there was hope of regaining the privileged position in the British market that had been lost nearly a century before, at the price of a minimum impairment of the Canadian protective system.

In the Imperial Conference of 1930, Bennett launched a strong plea for a general system of empire preferences. At the same time he made it quite clear that this must be reconciled with the fullest protection for Canadian producers against competition, not only from foreign lands, but from Britain and the other Dominions. Announcing that he stood foursquare behind the doctrine of "Canada first," he asserted that other Commonwealth members would have to take a similar stand, and then all could get together to work out an agreement. His specific suggestion was that after Canada had decided on the level of protection she needed, she should add an extra 10 percent against non-British countries, with a certain flexibility in this margin in the case of specific products. Such a step would have done little to increase the Canadian market for British goods, and it involved concessions in return that the Labor government in Britain, which was still reluctant to adopt protection, refused to contemplate. "There never was such humbug as this proposal," asserted one British minister in the course of a subsequent debate. Yet Britain had political as well as economic reasons for striving for an agreement. Her declining trade position, and the gathering crisis in foreign affairs with its inherent threat to Britain's strategic situation, called for a new rallying of the Dominions in support of the mother country. The economic approach was an initial and inevitable part of this process. A special conference was called at Ottawa in 1932, and by that time the change of government in Britain and the decision to adopt protection had created an entirely new situation.

Nonetheless, the conference produced an agreement only after the most strenuous efforts. If Britain was none too eager to impose high duties on foreign food and raw materials in order to assure a preferred market to the Dominions, Canada balked at the extensive tariff concessions to British manufactured goods that were asked in return. A preliminary conference between the cotton producers of the two countries broke down completely. Canada's sheltered industries exhibited a stout opposition to any impairment of their protected position. Britain's demands for reduced duties on textiles and iron and steel products produced heated discussions, and Canada's insistence that Britain impose an embargo on Russian lumber and other competing materials was strenuously resisted. At one stage it seemed that the conference would break down over these issues. But Britain could not afford to see it fail completely, and a last-minute compromise saved the situation. Britain agreed to free entry of a substantial list of Canadian goods, including a variety of manufactures as well as food and raw materials, with duties ranging from 10 to 33 percent imposed on competing foreign products. Wheat enjoyed a preferential advantage of threepence a bushel; meat and dairy products, fruit and tobacco, fish and timber and minerals, all benefited in varying degrees. In return, Canada increased the margin of preference on 223 British products, either by lowering the existing preferential rates or by raising the general tariff, with textiles, iron and steel products, leather goods, coal, and chemicals among the chief beneficiaries. Britain agreed to take effective steps against foreign dumping. Canada agreed to restrict protection to industries that had a reasonable prospect of success and to allow British representations before the tariff board on the administration of the tariff or any proposed changes in rates. A number of bilateral agreements with the other Dominions supplemented these arrangements with the mother country and gave promise of wider access to empire markets in general.

There were distinct advantages for Canada in these arrangements. Increased markets in Britain offered some compensation for the decline in other quarters, while Canada's changes were less at the expense of domestic production than at that of imports from the United States. During the next six years, the proportion of Canada's exports that went to Britain rose from 28 to 38 percent, and for the empire as a whole the increase was from 36 to 48 percent. In the light of the resentments left behind by the hard bargaining at Ottawa, it is doubtful whether this growth of trade carried with it any increase in affection within the Commonwealth, and the Ottawa agreements aroused some resentment among other nations including—not altogether logically—the high-tariff United States. So far as they were based on a restriction of trade with other nations, the agreements helped to accentuate the dislocation of world trade and the trend toward autarchy; but in view of the extremes to which that trend had been carried in other quarters, there was some merit in the effort to abate it within the far-flung area of the Commonwealth. At the same time, the agreements from Canada's point of view were not so much a step toward imperial consolidation as a triumph of economic nationalism under the guise of imperial solidarity, carried out by the party that professed itself most ardent in the cause of imperial unity.

The next few years brought a limited amelioration of conditions. The world struggled out of the worst depths of the depression, and Canada profited from this general revival as well as from her own efforts at economic readjustment. Between 1932 and 1937 the wholesale price index rose by nearly one-third, and exports increased from $500,000,000 to over $1,000,000,000. But this was followed by a new recession, and the recovery was too restricted to bring permanent relief. Unemployment remained an urgent problem. Low wheat prices and crop failures meant continued distress on the prairies. The government was forced to supplement its trade and tariff policies by steps to provide relief for those groups within the community on whom the heaviest burden of the depression had fallen.

As part of the effort at adjustment, a new attempt was made to deal with the perennial problem of the railways. The fact that the Canadian Pacific Railway as well as the national roads had encountered difficulties which obliged it to seek a temporary loan of $25,000,000 from the government in order to tide it over, gave new impetus to the pressure for an amalgamation of the two main systems. The desire of the Canadian Pacific Railway shareholders for a resumption of dividends and of large groups of taxpayers for relief from railway deficits met with considerable sympathy from the party in power, whose members shared these interests and whose representatives wanted to ease the burden on government finances. In 1932 the Duff Commission, appointed to look into the whole railway problem, issued a report that only partly satisfied these desires. It was critical of Canadian National expenditures under Sir Henry Thornton, who had resigned in the meantime, but it pronounced against the merger of the railways. It recommended instead that the capitalization of the Canadian National Railways be reduced by $1,000,000,000 and its luxury services curtailed; that waste and duplication be eliminated by closer cooperation with the Canadian Pacific; and that the existing directorate be replaced by a board of three trustees who would be independent of political pressure. Even these proposals were only partly implemented. The governing body necessarily remained subject to the ministry and through it to Parliament. Revision of the capital structure was delayed until 1937 and was then limited to the cancellation of some $262,000,000 that had been kept on the government books. Cooperation with the Canadian Pacific Railway was confined to a limited adjustment of schedules and joint use of facilities and the joint operation of a few pool trains between Toronto and Montreal and Ottawa. The impossibility of surrendering public ownership to private monopoly was again made evident, and the railways continued to struggle against adversity until the war brought new and expanded demands that strained them to capacity.

The wheat situation compelled the federal government to grapple with a still more vital problem. The Wheat Pool's effort to carry out a policy of long-range orderly marketing broke down with the collapse of world markets. To save the agency from collapse, the government stepped in and assumed responsibility for the initial payments set for the 1930 crop. The next year the Pool was dissolved and the system of initial payments was abandoned, but the government still felt compelled to make some effort on behalf of the prairie farmer. A bonus of 5 cents a bushel was offered on wheat marketed in 1931. The next year this was dropped, and the government entered on an effort to uphold prices by purchases in the open market. It was only in 1935, after the government had accumulated holdings of 205,000,000 bushels, that the need for a more direct and comprehensive policy was accepted, and the Wheat Board was established to handle the whole marketing problem. Short crops and a rise in world prices helped its operation, and by 1937 it had liquidated its holdings at a loss for all these types of activity of the relatively modest sum of $20,000,000.

But such examples of government intervention, striking though they were in themselves, did little to remedy the fundamental difficulties. Rural distress and urban unemployment remained chronic, and neither federal nor provincial governments had any coherent plans for dealing with them. Some public works were undertaken, including the construction of a trans-Canada highway, but the expense of any comprehensive program was a deterrent to its adoption. Work or subsistence camps for transients and single men proved unsatisfactory, and conditions in some of them provoked serious riots by the unemployed. The bulk of the responsibility for policy and administration fell on the provinces and municipalities, and there were some efforts to provide public employment or to relieve agricultural distress by programs of rehabilitation and resettlement. In the last analysis, however, the main dependence was on direct relief in the absence of any constructive alternative, and this meant that the financial responsibility was largely thrown on the shoulders of the federal government. Total expenditures on relief rose from $18,000,000 in 1930 to $173,000,000 in 1935, with the Dominion assuming over 40 percent of these costs by direct expenditures or grants-in-aid to the provinces, and in addition extending loans to various provinces to help them carry their share. At best the results were uncertain and unsatisfactory and offered the distressed groups in the population neither decent living standards nor security for the future. By 1934 it was clear that bolder and more drastic policies were needed to meet the emergency and that fundamental adjustments in the Canadian economy were urgently desirable in the interests of social welfare.

Arthur Meighen.

Richard Bedford Bennett.   William Lyon Mackenzie King.

Chapter 19

The Gathering Crisis

Crosscurrents in the Thirties

The burden that the depression laid on the provinces was all the more resented for being borne unequally. It was on the prairies that it fell with the most crushing weight. The Maritimes, having soared less high than the other sections in prosperity, had less far to fall in adversity; and while they experienced a drastic cut in cash income, subsistence agriculture was sufficiently widespread to provide some cushion for the shock. On the west coast the effect was more severe. In British Columbia such staples as lumber, fish, and minerals were largely dependent on outside markets and were in general exploited by large firms rather than by small-scale individual operators, and the collapse of prices and markets resulted in widespread unemployment and distress. Even so the general decline in income was less drastic than on the prairies, where dependence on a single cash staple proved disastrous when the bottom fell out of world wheat markets. Saskatchewan was particularly hard hit by crop failures as well as falling prices, but in both Manitoba and Alberta the prevalence of urban unemployment on top of rural distress threatened a general bankruptcy that was only averted by federal financial aid.

Central Canada presented a mixed picture. The industrial heart of the Dominion, it bore a heavy burden of unemployment in the chief manufacturing cities, and it was hit by the decline in exports of lumber and pulp and paper. Low farm prices and curtailed exports brought rural distress and a considerable increase in farm debts. Yet the high proportion of mixed farming in Ontario and Quebec as compared with the prairies meant that these provinces were spared the widespread rural destitution that existed in the West. Continued expansion of mining, especially in Ontario, helped to moderate the impact of the depression on other basic activities. Even industry, badly hit though it was, managed to keep alive in a sheltered market under the protective tariff. Not least important, there were accumulated reserves on which these provinces could fall back through borrowing or taxation to meet the emergency. The West had no comparable resources; and the feeling that the heaviest burdens fell on the sections least able to bear them aggravated the sectional strains already inherent in the Canadian structure.

The result was a new series of crosscurrents, manifested first of all in provincial politics. The separate character of federal and provincial issues had frequently led in the past to divergent alignments by the electorate in these two spheres. Ontario, for instance, could give a consistent federal majority to Macdonald and still keep a provincial Liberal administration under Sir Oliver Mowat in power for twenty-five years. Until World War 1, however, these shifts had taken place within the framework of the two major parties. The rise of the United Farmer movements in Ontario and the West were the first signs of an effort to create new parties as a result of discontent with the old ones. The unrest that accompanied the depression stimulated the desire for still more drastic departures from the old ways and brought into being new groups, which expressed significant and novel trends in both the federal and the provincial fields.

Occasionally this took place even under the old party labels. In Ontario the United Farmers decided to withdraw from political activity after the discouraging collapse of the E. C. Drury government in 1923. But a considerable element of rural dissatisfaction remained; and this, accentuated by the depression, was capitalized on by the local Liberal party under the leadership of Mitchell F. Hepburn. His reliance on rural support was supplemented by a less overt alliance with Toronto mining interests, who wanted immunity from interference in their speculative activities. His stringent economies, particularly in relief expenditure, and his bitter hostility to radical labor movements appealed to both these groups. His zeal for the taxpayer's welfare was demonstrated by his cancellation of electric-power contracts with Quebec interests and his drive to collect full succession duties on large estates that had been leniently assessed under the preceding Conservative administration. But friction over social policies and financial relations embroiled him with the federal Liberal government after 1935, and the development of a growing personal antagonism between Hepburn and King placed the provincial Liberal administration in bitter opposition to the same party in power in Ottawa.

Alberta was the scene of a more drastic departure from traditional politics. In that province the United Farmers, who had held power since

1921, succumbed to their inability to cope with the depression and to the personal scandal in which the premier became involved. In their desperate search for a new panacea the farmers of that distressed province turned to the gospel of Social Credit as preached by William Aberhart. This was a doctrine that held that the basic flaw in the economic system lay in the inadequate distribution of purchasing power and that the remedy lay in the distribution of periodic "social dividends" to bring supply and demand into a more even balance. Aberhart, a school principal and the head of a fundamentalist religious group known as the Prophetic Bible Institute, had already won a wide following as a radio evangelist. He now stepped forward as a prophet of economic as well as spiritual salvation, holding out the prospect that every citizen would be paid a social dividend of $25 a month. The appeal of such promises to a community in which cash had become almost a curiosity was naturally potent, and religious fervor combined with economic desperation led to the elevation of the Social Credit party to power in 1935.

In the sequel Aberhart proved unable to translate his theories into practice. Banking and currency were federal matters beyond the control of the province. Attempts to circumvent these restrictions by imposing licenses on banks, by taxing their reserves, by issuing provincial scrip for a limited period, and by subjecting business enterprises to regulatory codes were either disallowed by the federal government or declared unconstitutional by the courts. The prospect of social dividends gradually receded into limbo. Attempts to prevent appeals to the courts and to muzzle an unfriendly press were also invalidated. In questions of social and international policy outside their own peculiar theories, Social Credit leaders gradually revealed themselves as reactionaries of the deepest dye. Nonetheless, the party consolidated its hold by giving Alberta a reasonably honest and efficient administration and retained its power even after Aberhart's death in 1943.

In Quebec, economic discontent gave rise to new manifestations of racial divergence. Although the bitterness that had been aroused over the wartime issue of conscription gradually abated during the twenties, its memory was not erased, and few positive steps were taken to bridge the dangerous underlying gulf that wartime controversies had revealed. Events had long since shown the folly of envisaging racial amalgamation as a practicable goal. The only workable basis was one which accepted Canada as a biracial state and strove for voluntary cooperation and harmony on the broad common ground of national interest. To achieve this, both sides must make concessions. English extremists must abandon their insistence on an unattainable uniformity and concede to the French the fullest cultural autonomy that was compatible with national unity. French extremists must recognize that the industrial revolution was irrevocable, that Canada was inescapably a part of the modern and highly integrated world, that the ancient traditions of French Canada were not the only traditions cherished by the people of the Dominion, and that a way of life that ran counter to every trend in modern society could not be insisted on by one section at the price of stultifying the progress of the nation as a whole.

There was little evidence of any widespread recognition of these necessities among either French or English. A few groups among both, aware of the inherent perils, sought earnestly for closer contacts, but few responsible public leaders joined in the effort. The Conservatives, anxious though they were to recover lost ground in Quebec, were too closely identified with the forces of imperialism and Anglicization to be capable of a constructive policy of compromise. The Liberals under Mackenzie King clung stubbornly to a policy of letting sleeping dogs lie. The belief that if difficulties are ignored they will eventually disappear was nowhere more evident than in King's attitude toward the racial issue. Because of a fear that any discussion would revive old irritations, the vital need for leaders of both races to forestall new conflicts by a studied and patient campaign of education was deliberately neglected. A policy of negation allowed twenty vital years to slip by without any real attempt to extinguish the fires that smoldered underneath and left these alive to be fanned once more into flames when a new crisis should arise.

The depression produced new strains, which were all the more serious because of the changing pattern in Quebec. That province was no longer the predominantly rural area that so many of its leaders hopefully imagined. Increasing numbers were being drawn into the growing industries of the province. The growth of industry in Montreal was marked by the addition of 200,000 to its population between 1921 and 1931 and the concentration of nearly 40 percent of the population of the province in this one metropolitan area. Smaller towns like Quebec, and Sherbrooke, and Three Rivers grew steadily in size. In the region north of the St. Lawrence, with its resources in pulpwood and minerals and water power, large electrical and metallurgic and pulp and paper establishments created new communities and gave employment to thousands. These developments not only made Quebec increasingly dependent on national and export markets for its prosperity; they also meant that the habitant was being transformed into a wage earner, with consequences that were perturbing to his mentors. The church found it harder to maintain intimate contact with the individual when he moved from the rural parish to a large urban center. In his new surroundings he was exposed to influences, both moral and intellectual, that were a serious threat to his faith. In an industrial environment he risked exposure to trade union doctrines and even to socialist ideas and encountered economic problems that might rouse new aspirations and weaken his docile acceptance of the existing order. There was an effort to counteract the attractions of the international trade unions and their Anglo-Saxon outlook by encouraging the formation of Catholic syndicates; but the effectiveness of these bodies as instruments of religious and racial separatism was hampered by their frequent reluctance to follow a vigorous policy in labour disputes, particularly when the Church so often shared the dislike of the employers for collective bargaining backed by the weapon of the strike.

In one aspect the absorption of the French into industrial society offered the greatest prospect of breaking down the religious and cultural barrier. In another the immediate effect was to create new areas of friction. Quebec authorities deliberately encouraged the influx of industrial capital by maintaining low labor standards and a docile labor supply. Yet this was accompanied by a rising resentment at the exploitation of the French population by large corporations whose control was in the hands of English capitalists, and still more at the fact that the better paid posts were only rarely held by French Canadians. Sober minds recognized that the latter fact was at least partly the result of deficient qualifications, and this realization was reflected in increasing attention to technical education at both secondary and higher levels. The more ardent nationalists, however, combined a dislike for industrialism as such with a desire for the fullest share of the opportunities it offered and identified the cause of French Canadian survival with hostility to English capitalism. To these groups the idea of a corporative system under Catholic auspices made a strong appeal, and the evolution of European fascism—and particularly the struggle in Spain, where Franco was looked on as the champion of Christianity against Bolshevist materialism—gave a strong stimulus to this outlook and roused a definite spirit of emulation.

Efforts at a full-fledged fascist movement, however, attracted only minor support. The sense of economic dissatisfaction and racial resentment, with the accompanying discontent directed against the two old parties, found its chief expression through the *Union nationale* led by Maurice Duplessis. It was a revival of the trend toward a self-contained autonomous French state, with a strong tendency toward autarchy. Duplessis rejected the separatist ideas of the extreme nationalists and did not commit himself to a full corporative program, but he showed considerable sympathy with the aspirations behind these movements. He stood for maximum racial and provincial rights and resistance to centralization, for the exclusion of Anglicizing influences with their alleged subservience to British imperialism, for the retention of Quebec's natural resources for the benefit of its population in place of their exploitation by "alien" capitalists, for the intimate connection between church and state and the suppression of communism or radicalism. The decline of the long Liberal ascendancy in the province, which was hastened by the efforts of a discontented younger group to form a new Liberal party on more nationalist lines, was shown by the reduction of Premier Louis Alexandre Taschereau's majority to a bare margin in the election of 1935; and next year the continued disruption of the old party brought the fall of the government and the accession of Duplessis to power. His outlook was illustrated by labor legislation which subjected the trade unions to close state control and seriously curtailed the right of collective bargaining, and by the notorious "padlock law," which enabled the attorney general to seize and close any places that in his opinion were used for communist propaganda—an activity that was deliberately left undefined and gave wide scope for action against any organization that incurred the dislike of the government or the church. Pressure on the federal government to disallow the law brought no results; and this lack of action on behalf of civil liberties was inevitably contrasted with the promptness of federal intervention in Alberta when property interests were at stake.

Few of these provincial movements had any serious reflection in organized national politics. Quebec was not yet ready to cut itself off from the sources of patronage at Ottawa, and the popularity of Ernest Lapointe, minister of justice and Mackenzie King's principal lieutenant, did much to keep the province in the Liberal fold. In Ontario the Liberal organization remained loyal to King in federal politics in spite of Hepburn's envenomed personal attitude. The mystic creed of Social Credit won few converts outside Alberta; and although the party captured 15 seats in that province in the federal election of 1935, its efforts to invade other provinces were uniformly rebuffed.

It was the West, however, which gave birth to a new national party. Although the Progressives had virtually disappeared, the handful of members who survived in the Dominion Parliament had gained in ability and experience. They continued to urge a federation of autonomous regional and economic groups that would end the domination of special interests working through the old party system. Economic distress revived the interest of Western farm organizations in political action on a national scale. A definite stimulus was given in 1932 by the appearance of a manifesto, in which the United Farmers of Alberta announced their readiness to work with other groups whose object was to end distress and establish a cooperative state controlling all essential resources. This met with considerable response from both farm organizations and labor groups. In August 1932, delegates from these bodies in the four western provinces laid the foundation for the Cooperative Commonwealth Federation—popularly abbreviated to CCF—and in 1933 a convention at Regina drew up a definite program. It included emergency measures such as slum clearance, rural electrification and other public-works projects, and long-range objectives embracing the socialization of finance and public utilities, security of farm tenure, encouragement of cooperatives, and social legislation to establish economic security and decent living standards. It represented a philosophy of evolutionary socialism that in many of its features showed a conscious similarity to the basis of the Labor party in Britain. The acknowledged leader of the new party was James Shaver Woodsworth, a former Methodist preacher who had turned social reformer and who as a Labor member from Winnipeg since 1921 had won the trust and respect of the advanced reform groups in the Dominion Parliament.

Although the initiative behind the new movement was predominantly rural, it differed from the earlier Progressive movement in the seriousness of its efforts to draw workers as well as farmers within its ranks. Canadian labor, hard hit by unemployment and wage cuts and the lack of any regular system of unemployment insurance or adequate relief, was hampered by its weakness in organization and the continued divisions within its own ranks. Trade union membership, which had reached a peak of 378,000 in 1919, suffered a serious postwar decline; and although it recovered to a strength of 322,000 in 1930, the depression brought a slump to 280,000 in 1935. This was less than 15 percent of the industrial employed. The unskilled workers were almost wholly unorganized. Somewhat over half the organized unions belonged to the Trades and Labor Congress, which was affiliated with the American Federation of Labor; most of the remainder were divided among the All-Canadian Congress, the Federation of Catholic Workers, and the Communist-sponsored Workers' Unity League. The spread of the Congress of Industrial Organizations to Canada, signalized in 1937 by a strike at the Oshawa plant of General Motors, which provoked Premier Hepburn to a one-man crusade against "foreign agitators," introduced a new element into the picture and one somewhat more sympathetic than most of the older bodies to the idea of political action. There was, however, no general swing by trade unionism to the new party.

Catholic unions were hostile; the older international unions were dubious; the Communist organizations oscillated between outright opposition and efforts to bore from within. Nonetheless, a number of individual unions pronounced in favor of the CCF and affiliated with it; but its solid core of support lay in the agrarian West rather than industrial Ontario, and it made almost no inroads in either Quebec or the Maritimes.

There were still elements in the Canadian population that were dissatisfied with existing conditions under the old parties but were not prepared to accept socialism as an alternative. The impact of the depression on the middle class was reflected in a vague resentment against the forces of big business and an equally vague desire for government intervention in the interest of free competition. These sentiments, which had contributed to the third-party movements in the United States during a previous generation, were brought to a head by the revelations of the Royal Commission on Price Spreads in 1934. Appointed to investigate the gap between prices to the consumer and costs to the producer and the effect of mass buying by chain and department stores, the commission brought out a startling picture of high profits and large bonuses at the top and starvation wages and sweatshop prices at the bottom. Stock watering at the expense of both employees and the general public; wholesale evasion of wages and hours legislation, with weekly earnings as low as $3 in a Quebec textile firm, and hours as high as 72; serious disparities in standards, especially as between Ontario and Quebec; monopoly buying by large department and chain stores, which mercilessly forced down the prices to primary producers and small manufacturers—these were some of the features brought out in the evidence. "It has been difficult not to be impressed by the fact," reported the commission, "that the corporate form of business not only gives freedom from legal liability, but also facilitates the evasion of moral responsibility for inequitable and uneconomic practices."

These features of rugged individualism, which the public had resolutely ignored in times of prosperity, suddenly became shocking in the midst of economic distress. The chairman of the commission, Harry H. Stevens, then minister of trade and commerce, launched a series of attacks on the iniquities of big business, which culminated in the publication of one of his more comprehensive indictments as a pamphlet. This was a line that his cabinet colleagues were not ready to follow. The pamphlet was suppressed; the minister was taken to task by Premier Bennett; continued dissension led to his resignation in October 1934, and shortly afterwards to the launching of a Reconstruction party under his leadership, with a somewhat vague program of fair wages, restraint of unfair competition, limited public works, and the adjustment of the system of tax collection. It was a platform of carefully restrained paternalism designed to make capitalism safe for small business.

Balked Enterprises

By the time the Bennett administration entered its fifth year, economic distress and political disruption were rampant throughout the Dominion. The promised end of unemployment seemed as remote as ever. The markets of the world had not yet yielded to blasting by Canadian high tariffs. The accumulated strain and disappointment within the nation had sharpened sectional and class divisions and recoiled against the federal government. New and bold courses were needed if the party in power was to redeem its record and retrieve its fortunes. It was to meet this growing emergency that the Prime Minister suddenly launched a broad and unprecedented program of economic and social reforms under state control.

Paternalism was no new element in Conservative policy. Canada, even more than other countries, had witnessed the paradox of a party devoted to private enterprise becoming the instrument for extending public ownership. Conservative governments at Ottawa had built the Intercolonial Railway and laid the foundations of the Canadian National. A Conservative administration in Ontario had created the public-owned hydroelectric system. Though a preferred method was to assist private enterprise with public funds, there were times when this proved inadequate and when the needs of private business combined with the pressure of public opinion obliged the government to step directly into the field of large-scale economic activity.

Under Bennett this activity had been considerably extended. Large grants had been made to the provinces for purposes of relief. The Dominion had increased its share of the cost of old-age pensions from 50 to 75 percent. Government ownership and control had been broadened to take in new areas. The ruling of the Privy Council in 1932 that control of radio communications lay with the federal government was followed by a decision to engage directly in broadcasting. In 1932 the Canadian Radio Broadcasting Commission—reorganized in 1936 as the Canadian Broadcasting Corporation—was set up, with supervision over the whole field of radio and with power to acquire and operate its own stations. Private stations were not abolished, but their use was made subject to the public interest as expressed through the regulatory power of the corporation. Here was that large-scale mixed type of organization that was already so familiar in Canada, steering between government monopoly as in Britain and complete private ownership as in the United States, but embodying uniform national standards and the machinery of national control.

The airways, too, were brought under government regulation. Federal control, established by the Aeronautics Act of 1927, was validated by judicial decision in 1932, and the way was open for complete government ownership. This, however, was not established by the Conservatives; and when the Liberals came to power, they went only so far as to establish Trans-Canada Airways as a subsidiary of the Canadian National Railways, leaving in private hands not only Canadian Pacific Airlines but the numerous "bush" lines whose activities in freight carrying and exploration were so important a factor in extending access to Canada's northern regions. Again the pattern was that of centralized regulation accompanied by partial government ownership, the latter, however, emphasized by the policy that was later announced of keeping the international air routes in government hands.

There was a similar approach to the question of a central bank. The drastic fall of commodity prices and the competition of countries with depreciated currencies brought some agitation in Canada for a policy of currency inflation. Although there was some expansion in the Dominion note issue, the government was in general reluctant to endanger Canada's credit by an avowedly inflationary policy. But the problems of controlling the volume of currency, of keeping the Canadian dollar on a reasonable exchange basis in relation to both the American dollar and the British pound, of providing the credits that the government needed in a period of heavy deficit financing, turned serious attention to the existing system of banking and currency. As the outcome of an inquiry by the Macmillan Commission in 1933, the Bank of Canada was set up in the following year. It was a reserve bank to which all private banks had to turn over their gold holdings and ultimately to surrender their power of note issue. Its functions were to regulate the volume of currency and credit, to serve as a bank of rediscount for governments and private banks, and to act as agent and adviser to the federal government. The government controlled the appointment of its officials. The capital was initially subscribed by private investors; but the privately owned stock was taken over by the government in 1938, and this institution ceased to be one of the customary mixed type and became wholly government-owned.

These steps, however, were only a prelude to much wider efforts in the field of social policy and government intervention. The growing domestic unrest provided a strong motive for a progressive policy that would satisfy the demand for reform and counteract the appeal of socialism. The dynamic example of the New Deal across the border in the United States attracted keen interest in Canada and gave rise to a spirit of emulation. W. D. Herridge, who had become almost simultaneously Mr. Bennett's brother-in-law and Canada's minister to Washington, was profoundly impressed by Roosevelt's program, and his influence over the Prime Minister was widely believed to be a salient factor in the latter's conversion to a policy of sweeping reform.

There were tentative steps in this direction in 1934. A Natural Products Marketing Act provided for the creation of a federal marketing board, with control over the export of any product of farm, forest, or sea and with the right to regulate interprovincial trade in these products. Any group of producers in these categories might apply to come under the operation of the board, which might bonus or compensate them for any losses suffered as a result of its orders. A Farmers' Creditors Arrangement Act provided machinery for settlements between the farmers and their creditors on a scale that would reduce the burden of agricultural debt. The appointment of the Price Spreads Commission was an initial step toward wider regulation of business practices; and the revelations before that body, followed by the secession of H. H. Stevens and the new danger of a party split, added further urgency to the adoption of bold and far-reaching measures.

The new departure was announced by the Prime Minister in a series of radio talks in January 1935. Declaring that the capitalist system must be reformed and that this meant government intervention and control, he outlined a series of measures that would constitute a scheme "more comprehensive, more far-reaching, than any scheme of reform which this country has ever known." In the legislative session that followed he pushed through a group of bills designed to implement this promise. Amendments broadened the earlier measures on farm credits and the marketing of natural products. Minimum-wage legislation, the establishment of the 48-hour week, a weekly day of rest, and a scheme of unemployment and social insurance were all adopted. Fair trade practices were to be enforced through amendments to the criminal code and the Companies Act, with a Trade and Industry Commission set up to regulate trusts and control business standards; and an advisory National Economic Council was also created to assist the government in dealing with future problems.

Whatever criticisms might be offered of these measures on their merits, they were at least directed toward some of the basic problems that beset the Dominion. There were, however, grave obstacles to their full acceptance. At the very outset they ran into the constitutional barrier. In his effort to rally popular support through a bold and constructive policy, Bennett deliberately ignored the rigid limitations that judicial decisions had placed on federal authority. The measures intruded on the sphere that the Privy Council had assigned to the provinces in virtue of their control over property and civil rights, and the greater part of the Bennett legislation was in fact declared unconstitutional in 1937.

It was upon this aspect that the Liberals concentrated in opposing the new program. They were careful to avoid any attempt at an alternative remedy, apart from such generalities as advocacy of wider trade agreements and opposition in principle to the growth of state intervention. No doubt the lesson of the 1919 program and the subsequent embarrassment it had caused was still fresh in the minds of Liberal leaders. A more recent embarrassment was the Beauharnois scandal, which had been one aftermath of the election of 1930. The Beauharnois power company, in connection with the development of a new project on the Quebec section of the St. Lawrence, had applied to the federal government for permission to divert the necessary flow of water from the river. There was opposition from rival power companies and criticism of possible interference with navigation; but in 1929, after assurance had been given that navigation rights would be safeguarded and that the canal to be built could if necessary be taken over by the Dominion, the company was allowed to proceed under an agreement that foreshadowed the placing of the whole flow of the river at its disposal. In the process of gaining its ends, the company had felt it necessary to deal with a number of influential officials and party leaders, and there were curious transactions in the form of gifts of stock and personal loans and alleged campaign contributions. Under pressure from one of the western farm members in the Commons, an investigation was undertaken by the Bennett government, and its results moved King to describe his party as being "in the valley of humiliation." But the Conservatives showed no desire to push the inquiry to possibly awkward lengths; their view on the basic soundness of the project as such was indicated by the renewal of the Beauharnois agreement with certain modifications; the Liberal party soon lifted its head and found ground for trust that the electorate would forget the Beauharnois affair as it had already forgiven the earlier customs scandal.

It was thus on the sins of their opponents rather than on their own virtues that the Liberals concentrated as the 1935 elections drew near. There were good reasons for trusting in such negative tactics. Bennett's dictatorial tendencies toward the Commons, and even toward his Cabinet colleagues, who were to a large extent excluded from his counsels, had won him a growing personal unpopularity. His overbearing manner and his earlier resistance to reform had roused widespread resentment, which his last-minute conversion failed to overcome. Moreover, the new program was a shock to large numbers of his followers. The groups in the United States who bitterly opposed the New Deal had their counterparts in Canada, and these were especially strong in Conservative ranks. These elements failed to share their leader's new-found belief that capitalism needed reform or his sudden passion for state interference. His bold course failed to win any large numbers of new adherents, while it affronted and alienated considerable numbers of his former supporters.

The results were seen in the election of 1935. The Conservatives suffered a disaster that was nation-wide. The Liberals secured a sweeping majority in every province except British Columbia and Alberta, and in the latter the Social Credit party was supreme. The Conservatives were reduced to 40 seats, and the Liberals with 179 had a majority that was unprecedented since confederation. Yet it was significant that this ascendancy was gained with only a minor increase in the Liberal vote since 1930. It was the drastic decline in Conservative support and the scattering of numerous votes among the newer and more radical parties that was responsible for the result. It was true that these parties won relatively few seats. The concentration of Social Credit strength in Alberta allowed the party to capture fifteen seats in that province but only two more outside. The CCF, with twice the number of votes, returned only seven members; the Reconstruction party, with support almost equal to the CCF, elected only its leader and shortly disappeared as a separate group. Yet the fact remained that these new parties attracted almost one-quarter of the voters and that the overwhelming Liberal majority in the Commons was won with the support of less than half the electorate.

In his victory pronouncement, Mackenzie King hailed the outcome as a triumph for democracy and promised that his party would banish poverty and adversity. The means by which this happy result was to be achieved, however, remained obscure. The question of the validity of the Bennett legislation was submitted to the courts, and pending a decision its operation was held in abeyance. Yet circumstances still demanded the adoption of a substantial measure of social reform to meet internal problems and the improvement of Canada's external trade if prosperity was to be restored.

The Conservatives had tried to improve conditions by curtailing foreign imports. The Liberals reversed this course in an effort to strike some of the shackles from international trade. The negotiations that the Bennett government had initiated with the United States were resumed and carried to completion. By the agreement of November 1935, United States imports were placed under the intermediate tariff rates rather than the higher general schedule, and in addition there were further reductions on a number of commodities such as farm machinery and automobiles. The various devices adopted by the Bennett government, such as arbitrary valuation for duty purposes, were also removed, thus making the effective reduction still greater. Canada secured in return concessions on over 200 items embracing her principal natural products, though on some of these such as cattle and lumber the reduction applied only to a maximum quota of imports into the United States. This was the starting point for a still wider arrangement embracing Britain as well. In 1937 the Ottawa agreements were revised by the lowering of Canadian duties on a considerable list of consumer articles, in return for some minor adjustments on the part of Britain and a promise to maintain free entry for Canada's principal staples. In the following year, by agreeing to certain concessions such as the sacrifice of the preferential duty on wheat, Canada facilitated a trade pact between Britain and the United States and was rewarded by a revised agreement with the United States in which further reciprocal tariff reductions were provided. In the final outcome the agreements provided for reduced duties on over half Canada's imports from the United States and on articles that accounted for more than four-fifths of her exports to that country. After more than seventy years a reciprocal trade agreement had at last been achieved between the two neighbors.

In domestic affairs the future path was much more uncertain. To a large extent it hinged on the fate of the Bennett legislation, upon which the Privy Council passed judgment in 1937. The decisions clarified and emphasized the restrictions on the Dominion's authority in the fields of social and economic legislation. The Farmers' Creditors Arrangement Act and the criminal code amendment enforcing fair business practices were upheld, as were certain powers of the Trade and Industry Commission. But unemployment and social insurance were declared to be matters for the provinces, and the judges brushed aside the idea that they came within the Dominion's power of peace, order, and good government with the curious assertion that "the Act does not purport to deal with any special emergency, but founds itself on general world conditions." The Natural Products Marketing Act was invalidated on the ground that "the regulation of trade and commerce does not permit the regulation of individual forms of trade and commerce confined to a province." Even more serious were the grounds for invalidating the laws on minimum wages, the limitation of hours, and a weekly day of rest. These had been passed to give effect to conventions of the International Labor Organization to which Canada was a party and which the Dominion claimed the right to implement under Section 132 of the British North America Act. By this clause the federal government was given power to fulfill the obligations "of Canada or of any province thereof, as part of the British empire, toward foreign countries, arising under treaties between the empire and such foreign countries." Since the framing of that clause, Canada had secured the right to negotiate her own treaties, and the labor agreements were signed by Canada as a separate party. The Privy Council refused to admit that this advance in status had been accompanied by a corresponding advance in legislative power or that the federal government by making a diplomatic agreement could secure jurisdiction over matters that normally belonged to the provinces. Apparently only the imperial government could bring this about by negotiating a treaty that would be applicable to Canada. The Dominion could make its own agreements, but only the provinces could implement them when they dealt with matters outside Section 91; and the Dominion would have to revert to a colonial status in the sphere of diplomacy in order to secure authority to legislate fully on treaty matters. As their lordships remarked with ineffable complacency: "While the ship of state now sails on larger ventures, she still retains the watertight compartments which are an essential part of her original structure." There was clearly no disposition to recognize that the compartments, far from being part of the original structure, had been inserted by the Privy Council itself in complete disregard of the basic design.

However gratifying these decisions may have been to the Liberals as a vindication of their criticism of the Bennett measures, they made the task of framing an effective policy more difficult than ever. It was clear that legislation covering such matters as labor standards and social insurance and fair trade practices was urgently desirable, and that national uniformity could only be attained if these measures were adopted under federal auspices. In theory something might be done by cooperation between the Dominion and the provinces; but if this broke down in practice, the alternative was to amend the British North America Act in such a way as to remove the barriers created by judicial decisions, and to bring it more into line with the intention of the framers and the exigencies of modern conditions. Here, too, however, the cooperation of the provinces was needed. On previous occasions, amendments had been passed by the British Parliament on the request of both houses of the Dominion legislature, and the Dominion had felt no obligation to consult the provinces before making such a request. But previous amendments had neither affected the balance of powers between the provinces and the Dominion, nor trenched on the interest of any important groups within the community. The changes that were now envisaged were likely to do both; and substantial backing would be needed for any scheme that would make it possible for Canada to amend her own constitution, even more than for the amendments themselves.

In 1927 a Dominion-Provincial conference had been held at which the question of the possible method of amendment occupied a prominent place. The Dominion proposed that ordinary amendments should be passed by the federal government after the provinces had been consulted and the consent of the majority had been secured, and that more fundamental changes affecting provincial or minority rights should be carried only by unanimous consent. It was soon apparent that no agreement to this basis could be secured. Not only were there vague fears that the door might be opened to extensive intrusions by the federal government on existing provincial fields or to the coercion of one province or section by the rest of the Dominion; there was also a strong tendency, particularly on the part of Ontario and Quebec, to put forward the compact theory of confederation and to hold that no changes could be made in the federal pact except by unanimity. A trenchant exposition of this theory was put forward in 1930 by Premier G. Howard Ferguson of Ontario, who held that the prospective Statute of Westminster introduced changes into the Canadian constitution that violated the original compact by which the provinces had created the confederation. It was a view without any historical foundation, and one which was refuted by experts during the parliamentary hearings on the topic in 1935; but it steadily gained ground in the provinces, and for practical purposes it was impossible to ignore the need for general agreement in any alterations that were proposed.

The return of the Liberals to power was followed by the calling of a new conference at the end of 1935. While the need for certain amendments was accepted, there was complete failure to reach an agreement on a method that would allow Canada herself to exercise the amending power. In 1936 the government sought through the existing channel to secure amendments that would widen the taxing powers of the provinces to cover indirect taxes and would create loan councils to give the Dominion a measure of control over provincial borrowing; but these were dropped when the first proposal was overwhelmingly defeated in the Senate. For the moment the possibility of any further advance seemed exhausted. It was becoming increasingly clear, however, that the distribution of financial powers was one of the crucial points at issue, and one which had a vital bearing on the constitutional balance and its adequacy under modern conditions; and the government decided to appoint a royal commission to re-examine "the economic and financial basis of confederation and the distribution of legislative powers in the light of the economic and social developments of the last seventy years," and to recommend such changes as seemed necessary to effect a more balanced relationship.

The commission was set up in 1937 under the chairmanship of Newton W. Rowell, who was succeeded after ill health forced his retirement by Joseph Sirois. The commissioners traveled through Canada, holding hearings at the principal centers in the course of a year of activity, while their archives bulged with briefs from bodies both public and private and their research staff accumulated and digested a mass of material. There were warnings of difficulties ahead in the refusal of three provinces—Quebec, Ontario, and Alberta—to cooperate fully with the work of the commission, and these were borne out by the reception of the report when it appeared in 1940. It contained a brilliant summary and analysis of the basic trends in Canada's development since confederation and a series of recommendations embodying five main points. The Dominion was to assume full responsibility for unemployment relief; provincial debts were to be taken over by the federal government; the provinces were to surrender to the Dominion the sole right to income and corporation taxes and succession duties; the existing system of provincial subsidies was to be wiped out; and in their place there was to be a new system of adjustment grants, which would enable the provinces to maintain a satisfactory and uniform standard in administration and social services.

The report met with a mixed reaction. There was some dislike of increased centralization, particularly in Quebec. There was some reluctance on the part of the wealthier provinces to see their powers curtailed and their resources used for the benefit of others. There was particular opposition in Ontario, which was to receive no adjustment grant, to the idea of subsidies that would help to support Catholic schools in Quebec. The federal government was prepared to negotiate on details and called a conference earlier in 1941 with the report as a basis of discussion. But Premier Hepburn of Ontario refused even to consider the report, and he had the support of Alberta and British Columbia, which like Ontario would receive no adjustment grants under the proposed scheme. With Hepburn's refusal to continue the discussions after the first day, the conference broke up, and the report was laid aside for the moment. The Dominion had already secured an amendment giving it the right to establish a scheme of unemployment insurance, and the outbreak of war had vested the government with emergency powers, which allowed it to postpone the effort at constitutional change. But the respite was merely temporary; and if Canada was to solve her underlying problems, she would have to find some more satisfactory way of working the existing constitutional balance or achieve a new balance more suited to the demands of a modern industrial state.

The Advance of Nationhood

The failure of the Dominion to break free of its own constitutional shackles stood in striking contrast to its success in throwing off the remaining restrictions in the sphere of imperial relations. World War I gave Canada a new national stature. The decade that followed was marked by the translation of this practical advance into formal changes in status. The outcome was the virtual renunciation by Britain of any right of interference in Dominion affairs. Canada was left completely free to follow her own course and to solve her own problems, and any failures sprang from her own incapacity rather than from any external restraints.

In 1920 Canada was still technically a colony subject to the overriding authority of the imperial government. The British Parliament could pass laws applicable to the whole empire. The government in London could disallow any measure adopted by the Dominion Parliament. The governor general, appointed by the British government and under instructions from the Colonial Office, could reserve any bills for approval by London. Control over merchant shipping was a function specifically reserved to the imperial authorities. The Dominion was denied the right of extraterritoriality—that is, the right to extend the operation of its laws over its citizens beyond its own borders. The Privy Council remained the final court of appeal, and Canada's attempt to bar appeals in criminal cases was declared *ultra vires* in 1926; and the Canadian constitution was a British statute, which could be altered only by the Parliament at Westminster. Diplomatic control was exercised by the British government on behalf of the whole empire, and the Dominion could neither conclude its own treaties with foreign countries nor establish diplomatic missions abroad.

Many of these restrictions were more nominal than actual. The last instance of imperial disallowance of a Canadian law was in 1873. Amendments to the British North America Act, though formally dependent on Britain, were actually determined by the Canadian Parliament. The governor general was becoming increasingly a cipher in the structure of government, though the Byng episode provided a rare but highly significant example of the disadvantages arising from his existing and anomalous status. Even the retention of appeals to the Privy Council, in spite of the resultant ravages to the Canadian constitution, was looked on by a considerable body of opinion as a safeguard to property interests or minority rights. On the other hand, the lack of ability to control its own registered shipping was of real inconvenience to the Dominion, and the removal of the barrier to extraterritorial legislation was something that had been sought repeatedly and in vain. In addition, an imperial statute, the Colonial Laws Validity Act of 1865, imposed limits on the scope of even domestic legislation. Originally it had been passed to curb the overenthusiastic tendency of certain judges to invalidate colonial measures on the ground that they were contrary to the laws of England. But what had initially been a liberating measure had become a restrictive one as the powers of the Dominion grew, and its restraints were no longer compatible with the full freedom of action that Canada now claimed.

It was, however, the question of control over external relations that was of most immediate and practical concern. It was in this field, where the powers of the Dominion had hitherto been most restricted, that the postwar period saw the greatest practical advance. Starting from the new position that was attained with participation in the peace conference and membership in the League of Nations, the member states of the Commonwealth embarked on the process of securing full freedom in the sphere of foreign relations and on an effort to harmonize this freedom with continued imperial unity.

At the Imperial War Conference of 1917 a resolution was adopted that envisaged the calling of a constitutional conference to adjust and define the new relations that had arisen between the Dominions and the mother country. As part of that adjustment, which was to be based on full Dominion autonomy, the resolution called for an adequate voice in foreign policy and "effective arrangements for continuous consultation in all important matters of imperial concern and for such necessary concerted action founded on consultation as the several governments may determine." This was the approach that Robert Laird Borden, along with Jan Christian Smuts of South Africa, envisaged as the basis of the postwar Commonwealth. Unity was to be maintained in foreign affairs, not as hitherto through the retention of all major decisions in the hands of the British government, but through the free participation of all the Dominions in the framing of policies that would still be implemented through the Foreign Office acting for the Commonwealth as a whole. As Lloyd George expressed it in 1921: "There was a time when Downing Street controlled the empire; today the empire is in charge of Downing Street."

However desirable such a procedure might be in theory, the difficulties in practice were almost insuperable. The widely scattered units of the Commonwealth had widely varied interests. All were concerned with the promotion of world peace and world prosperity. But while Great Britain had specific interests to promote or defend in almost every quarter of the globe, the interests of the individual Dominions were much narrower and more selective. To suppose that Ottawa, Canberra, and Pretoria would follow with a keen and active interest the policies pursued by Britain in remote areas where none of their vital interests were involved, and would provide a constant stream of considered and constructive advice for the guidance of the Foreign Office, represented a highly optimistic view of human nature. The idea that Great Britain would be content or even able to delay action until the possibly conflicting views of Commonwealth members had been harmonized ignored the need for continuous direction and prompt decision in matters of major diplomatic importance. Even with the best will on the part of all involved, the machinery envisaged was too cumbersome to meet the exigencies of the troubled international scene in the years after 1919.

The false premises behind the Borden-Smuts basis were vividly revealed by the Chanak crisis of 1922. The reinvigorated Turks had repudiated the Treaty of Sèvres, and their armies were approaching the zone of the straits that was garrisoned by a small British force. The British government, with ill-judged impetuosity, cabled the Dominions to ask what aid might be expected from them in case of war. The responses showed varying degrees of readiness to participate and a more general uncertainty about the nature of the crisis that had motivated this sudden appeal. In particular, Canada's reluctance to commit herself without fuller knowledge was accentuated by the fact that the British summons had been published in the press before it officially reached the Prime Minister. King replied asking for further information and stating that it would be for the Canadian Parliament to decide what action should be taken. Fortunately the crisis blew over, but it had served to disclose the inadequacy of the existing machinery of consultation as a basis for concerted action in an emergency. The conference that was called at Lausanne to negotiate a new peace treaty with Turkey brought a further and highly significant development. Largely as a result of French opposition, the Dominions were not invited. Canada seized the opportunity to make it clear that she did not regard herself as committed by the outcome of negotiations to which she was not a party. "In our opinion," the British government was informed, "the extent to which Canada may be held to be bound by the proceedings of the conference or by the provisions of any treaty or other instrument arising out of the same, is necessarily a matter for the Parliament of Canada to decide."

While Canada was thus freeing herself from any obligations arising solely out of British policy, she was simultaneously establishing her right to make her own agreements without British intervention. The occasion was the Halibut Treaty concluded with the United States in 1923. The negotiations were conducted entirely by the Canadian envoy, Ernest Lapointe. The British ambassador in Washington, however, expected to append his signature as had been customary in the past. But Canada insisted that the treaty should be signed by her representative alone, and the British government ultimately acquiesced. There was a further hitch when the United States Senate tried to extend the scope of the treaty to cover the whole empire, but this too was eventually overcome. For the first time a Dominion had concluded a formal treaty with a foreign power on its own responsibility and solely on its own behalf. It was a step that not only signalized the attainment by the Dominion of the long-desired control over foreign relations, but marked the deliberate abandonment of the idea of unified diplomacy within the empire. The appointment of a Canadian minister to Washington in 1927 emphasized the new departure. Canada's right to take such a step had been conceded as early as 1920, but the Canadian representative was to be associated with the British embassy in a way that would maintain imperial diplomatic unity. With the lapse of time, developments made possible a more satisfactory basis. The Canadian minister now had his own establishment, with no connection with the British embassy and no interference from it; and his appointment was a precedent for the subsequent establishment of ministries in France, Japan, and the Low Countries.

By 1923 it was clear that the Borden-Smuts basis had broken down. The consequences were faced in the Imperial Conference of that year at which a new concept, associated with the names of King of Canada and James B. M. Hertzog of South Africa, was given formal expression. The idea of a single policy common to the whole empire was abandoned. Diversity of interest was recognized in the acceptance of the right of each Dominion to conclude its own treaties with foreign states. It was recommended that when negotiations were likely to affect the interests of another member of the Commonwealth it should be informed in advance and given an opportunity to express its views; but this shadowy tribute to family courtesy was all that remained of the aspiration toward a common policy expressed with a single voice. The new approach was given practical application in the Treaty of Locarno, by which Britain became a guarantor of the frontier between France and Germany. The Dominions, which had not been associated with the negotiations, were specifically exempted from the terms of the treaty unless they chose to accept them of their own volition—a step that no Dominion showed any inclination to take. The Imperial Conference of 1926 laid down the principle that "neither Great Britain nor the Dominions could be committed to the acceptance of active obligations except with the definite consent of their own governments" and tacitly abandoned the hope that continuous consultation and concerted action could be embodied in a workable system. For all essential purposes, Canada and her sister Dominions had attained the rank of independent states in the community of nations.

Meanwhile the idea of a conference to frame a new constitution for the empire had long since been abandoned. The conference of 1921 showed no enthusiasm for the idea or even for the continuance of the centralized direction of policy that had been implicit in the imperial war cabinet. As a substitute, the Imperial Conference of 1926 tried to reach an acceptable definition of the new relationship. The result was the Balfour report, a document whose subtlety of phrasing no less than its specific content made it a landmark in the evolution of imperial relations. Recognizing that the Commonwealth "defies classification and bears no real resemblance to any other political organization which now exists or has ever yet been tried," the report proceeded to describe its component parts as "autonomous communities within the British empire, equal in status, in no way subordinate one to another in any aspect of their domestic or external affairs, though united by a common allegiance to the Crown, and freely associated as members of the British Commonwealth of Nations." A series of specific recommendations followed. The governor general was henceforth to cease to be an official of the British government and was to be simply the representative of the Crown; disallowance and reservation should be exercised only in accord with the views of the Dominion concerned; imperial legislation should not apply to a Dominion without its consent; and committees should be set up to consider the various statutory limitations by which the Dominions were still bound.

To a large extent the evolution of Dominion status, including those aspects expressed in the resolutions of various imperial conferences, rested on the development of accepted conventions rather than on positive constitutional enactments. A point had been reached, however, where some statutory change was needed to bring the legal basis into line with the changed situation. A special conference on this problem was called in 1929; its report was adopted by the Imperial Conference of 1930, and a number of its recommendations were embodied in the Statute of Westminster, which was passed by the British Parliament in 1931. The preamble asserted as an established principle that any change in the royal title or succession should have the assent of the Dominion Parliaments—a provision that associated Canada with the formalities attendant on the abdication of Edward VIII in 1936. The Dominions were freed from the provisions of the Colonial Laws Validity Act and might change or repeal any imperial law that was in force within their borders, and no future imperial statute was to apply to a Dominion without its consent. The restrictions on control over merchant shipping were lifted, and the right of extraterritorial legislation was specifically recognized.

The Statute of Westminster did not embody a complete constitution for the Commonwealth, nor did it put an end to all imperial authority. The British Parliament could still legislate for the whole empire under certain conditions and was the only body that could do so. It was also the only body that could alter or repeal the Statute of Westminster; and if it chose to exercise its power in defiance of the wishes of the Dominions, there was no legal means of redress. The power of reservation and disallowance was not abolished, but remained subject to self-restraining conventions. The right of the Dominions to abolish appeals to the Privy Council depended in part on existing provisions in their constitution, and it was specifically laid down that the statute gave no power to Canada to change the British North America Act. Yet few of these theoretical restrictions were of practical importance. Canada could secure the right to amend her constitution as soon as she could make up her mind on how she wanted to do it. The legal right of Britain to go back on the provisions of the statute was virtually nullified by the political impossibility of coercing any Dominion into accepting any imperial law against its will. Even the idea of the common Crown as a bond within the Commonwealth had a somewhat mythical character. Lawyers might discuss whether this made it legally impossible for a Dominion to remain neutral when Britain was at war or whether it barred the right of secession from the Commonwealth. But Eire did in fact remain neutral during World War II, and the offer of Dominion status to India during the war was accompanied by a specific recognition that it carried with it the right to secede. The Commonwealth continued to defy classification. It worked out its relationship by a process of compromise and evolution, in the course of which the formal bonds of unity were gradually abandoned, and freedom of association received a steadily broadening interpretation. It was a process in which Canada throughout took a leading part, and which by the time a new world crisis developed had resulted in her attainment of full and untrammeled freedom, with all the powers and status of an independent sovereign state.

Canada in World Politics

In Canada's relation with the outside world, her attainment of the full right of independent action was much more striking than her manner of exercising that right once it had been gained. The new status was not sought in order to clear the way for the application of a specific policy, but primarily to free Canada from responsibility for policies that were not peculiarly her own. This negative and defensive attitude was reflected in her conduct of external relations and in policies designed much more to avoid definite commitments than to bring about positive results.

There were circumstances that helped to explain this attitude. Mackenzie King in 1936 stressed "the unparalleled complexity of our position as a member of the League, a member of the British Commonwealth of Nations, and one of the nations of the American continent," and added the comment that "if some countries have too much history, we have too much geography." There was in fact a task of harmonizing a number of divergent factors, which was far from easy. Yet other small countries had similar problems of far greater gravity and were nonetheless able to evolve a positive line of policy. It was of the utmost concern to Canada that harmonious relations should exist between Britain and the United States, yet no falling out between those two nations was likely to be so serious as to jeopardize Canada's security. Internal problems and domestic divisions of opinion were probably more immediate obstacles to a vigorous policy abroad, though these were by no means insuperable. However real the difficulties, they still left scope for a broader and more constructive activity than Canada showed any desire to undertake. Neither Canada nor any other small state could have done much to alter the disastrous course of world politics in the era between wars, but she exhibited at times an undue readiness to make her undeniable limitations an excuse for sustained inaction.

The most consistent element in Canadian policy was the determination to cultivate good relations with the United States; and this was one of the few matters on which Canada was prepared to attempt to influence the policy of Britain. Borden had given vigorous expression to this viewpoint in his discussions with British leaders at the close of the war. Meighen, his successor, applied it in a concrete fashion when the renewal of the Anglo-Japanese alliance came under discussion in 1921. Britain favored the continuation of an arrangement that had proved of real value in the years before 1914. Australia and New Zealand found in it a measure of reassurance. But a considerable body of opinion in the United States—much of it uninformed or irrelevant—viewed the alliance with apprehension and hostility, and this was decisive for Canada. Meighen opposed any step that might create difficulties with the United States and advocated the substitution of some new arrangement in which the United States should be included. His view prevailed with the British government, and the calling of the Washington conference on disarmament in 1921 presented a chance to substitute for the alliance a more general guaranty of the *status quo* in the Pacific. It was characteristic of the American attitude toward the Commonwealth that neither Canada nor any other Dominion was invited to the conference; but Borden was included in the British delegation, and Canada's essential aim was achieved when the decision was taken to allow the Japanese alliance to lapse. It was almost the only effective example of a concerted policy on behalf of the whole empire, founded on the method of consultation envisaged in the Smuts-Borden approach.

The direct relations between Canada and the United States in the decade after the war were marked by a general atmosphere of friendship but few tangible signs of mutual esteem. Such minor disputes as arose were settled amicably. Direct contacts, which for a long time had been maintained on a semiofficial level, were facilitated by the exchange of envoys in 1927. The renewed emigration of Canadians to the United States, the growth of American tourist traffic into Canada, the influx of American capital into the Canadian economy and the multiplication of American branch plants, the steady expansion of trade during the boom years, all contributed to an increasing integration, which was reinforced by the spread of American cultural influences through the movies and the radio and the press. Yet there was relatively little disposition on the part of the American government to make any real concessions for the sake of cultivating Canadian good will, and the high tariff policy of the postwar era illustrated American indifference to the economic interests of a neighbor who also happened to be a customer rivaled in importance only by Great Britain.

A further illustration was the fate of the proposed St. Lawrence waterway. This was a project that combined the construction of a seaway into the heart of the continent with the development of hydroelectric facilities to produce 5,000,000 horsepower. It involved not only problems connected with water diversion, but cooperation in the development of navigation and power facilities on the international section of the St. Lawrence, with the total cost estimated at something over $500,000,000. After years of investigation and negotiation, a treaty was concluded in 1932. There was considerable opposition on both sides of the border. Montreal and the American seaboard cities feared a serious loss of traffic. New York power interests disliked the project. Ontario and Quebec insisted that the flow of the river was the property of the provinces and not of the Dominion. In both countries there was a certain support for the idea of a wholly national route in preference to an international undertaking. In general the strongest opposition came from the East and the strongest support from the West. In the end the American Senate refused to approve the treaty; and although a new and more limited agreement was concluded in 1941, the exigencies of the war prevented any steps being taken to put it into effect.

With the accession of Franklin D. Roosevelt to the presidency a new spirit was infused into relations between the two countries. The Good Neighbor policy that the Roosevelt administration assiduously pursued toward Latin America was equally evident in its attitude toward Canada. Opinion in Canada as elsewhere was divided on the merits of the New Deal, but there was a growing recognition of the fact that for the first time the government of the United States, which so often in the past had been either overbearing or indifferent, was prepared to treat Canada not only as a friend but as an equal. Roosevelt's struggle against the private monopoly of electric power made him a staunch advocate of the St. Lawrence waterway, though he was unable to secure Senate approval. His desire to broaden the basis of international trade meant that Canada, so often rebuffed in her overtures for reciprocity, was at last able to secure a trade agreement that relaxed the barriers to the flow of goods between her and the United States. Perhaps most important of all, Roosevelt's efforts to moderate American isolationism and to impose restraints on the aggressor nations struck a sympathetic chord in the Dominion, which viewed with concern the gathering crisis in international affairs.

The threat of a new world conflict brought an increasing recognition in both Canada and the United States of their mutual strategic interests. Almost imperceptibly the last vestige of fear that either country might be attacked by the other had been dissipated in the course of a generation. The source of danger lay on other continents; the potential enemies were the same for both nations. Their policies might differ, but their interests aligned them with the other democratic nations and with all states who were threatened by fascist aggression. The problem of security was not national but continental. The conquest of Canada by a foreign power would place a new potential enemy on the northern border of the United States. An attack on the United States would make it essential for Canada to prevent the attacker from using her territory as a corridor for invasion. The implications if not the formal terms of the Monroe Doctrine extended to Canada, and in return Canada had implied obligations to defend herself against external aggression.

These inescapable realities were stated and accepted in official pronouncements in 1938. "I give you the assurance," said Roosevelt during a visit to Canada, "that the people of the United States will not stand idly by if domination of Canadian soil is threatened by any other empire." A few days later Mackenzie King replied: "We too have our obligations as a good friendly neighbor, and one of them is to see that, at our own instance, our country is made as immune from attack or possible invasion as we can reasonably be expected to make it, and that, should the occasion ever arise, enemy forces should not be able to pursue their way, either by land, sea or air to the United States, across Canadian territory." Implicit in this pronouncement was a new and significant emphasis on Canada's position as an American nation, with its consequent effect on policy; and two years later this factor found its embodiment in a specific defense agreement between Canada and the United States.

In the broader international sphere the approach was much less positive. Canada had never felt any direct concern with European continental politics nor shown any desire to become entangled in them. There was an indirect interest through the fact that Britain was inescapably involved in the affairs of Europe and that Canada would inevitably be affected if Britain became embroiled. This, however, was reflected less in any active attempt to remove the causes of European quarrels than in a determined effort to escape from any automatic commitment to the consequences of British policy. Practical commitments, however, were more difficult to avoid than were formal obligations. Any crisis that threatened Britain's security was of major concern to Canada. Any threat to world peace and stability, indeed, had a direct bearing on Canada's own interest. As an exporting nation dependent on world trade and a small state incapable of defending herself against a major aggressor, she was part of an integrated world, and any upheaval would jeopardize both her prosperity and her security.

Canada thus had a vital stake in the efforts of the League of Nations on behalf of world peace. Her admission to the League marked a significant advance in status; her presence there gave her an opportunity to take an active part in the work of collective security. Yet these privileges carried with them obligations that many Canadians viewed with alarm. The possibility that Canada might have to aid the League in its coercive activities against aggression involved the risk that the Dominion might be drawn into European quarrels in which it had no direct interest. This was a prospect that Canada consistently tried to reduce to a minimum. The outcome was a negative policy in which Canada more and more tended to follow the lead of Britain in concessions designed to avert a quarrel but showed an attitude of reserve toward any measures designed to increase the power and vigor of the collective system.

. Undoubtedly the absence of the United States from the League accentuated this attitude. As a Canadian delegate told the Assembly, Canada when she entered the League "was then far from thinking that she would have the whole burden of representing North America when appeals would come to our continent for assistance in maintaining peace in Europe." The possibility of having to choose between divergent policies pursued by the League and the United States laid a constant restraint on Canadian policy. Yet in the last analysis this only added emphasis to a point of view that was indigenous to Canada itself. The increasing emphasis on her American position was reflected in both imperial relations and external policy and was fundamental to her activities within the League of Nations.

The result was a persistent effort to limit Canada's liability within the collective system. The consciousness that Canada was unlikely to call on Europe for military aid, or to get it if she should need to call, strengthened the feeling that the Dominion should not have to share the same burdens as states in the immediate danger zone. As Senator Raoul Dandurand told the League, Canada lived in a fireproof house far from inflammable materials. As a first-class insurance risk, she was inclined to feel that she should pay a minimum premium. This sentiment was evident in Canada's opposition to Article X and her repeated efforts to get it eliminated or modified. In 1923, failing in these aims, she submitted a resolution that called on the Council to take into account the special circumstances of each member when demanding military aid, and affirming the right of each state to decide for itself what forces it would send. The single adverse vote of Persia defeated the formal resolution, but it was generally accepted as the statement of the guiding principle that would be followed if military sanctions were ever invoked.

There was a similar resistance to all efforts to strengthen the coercive side of the League machinery. The Draft Treaty of Mutual Assistance drawn up in 1923 and the Geneva Protocol, which replaced it in the following year, were both unacceptable to Canada. The first embodied even wider obligations than Article X; the second brought objections to "its rigid provisions for application of economic and military sanctions in practically every future war." Canada professed a desire for the fullest use of the methods of consultation and arbitration, but had no enthusiasm for joining in the exercise of an international police power. She accepted the application of economic sanctions against Italy during the crisis over Ethiopia, but carefully avoided taking any initiative of her own. When the Canadian delegate, Dr. Walter A. Riddell, proposed the application of oil sanctions, the government at once issued a statement that made it clear that he did so simply as a member of the League committee on sanctions and not as a spokesman for Canadian policy. The failure of the effort to halt Italy, and the dangers inherent in the effort, increased the reluctance of the government to join in coercive measures in future disputes. Speaking at Geneva in 1936, Mackenzie King stressed the need for placing the emphasis on conciliation rather than coercion and asserted that "automatic commitments to the application of force is not a practical policy." The growing danger of war had increased rather than diminished Canada's desire to avoid all outside commitments.

This, however, was becoming increasingly difficult. The decline of the League solved nothing. The emergence of a new balance of power, in which the Western democracies were ranged against the fascist aggressors, found Canada virtually committed by her position and her interests to the support of Britain and France. As the prime minister clearly stated in 1936: "We do not believe that isolation from interest in world affairs is possible for Canada. The world today is an interdependent world. No happening of any magnitude abroad is without its repercussions on our fortunes and our future." For practical purposes, however, it became increasingly clear that Canada's action would be determined by Britain's course. Whatever her interest in the general balance, it was hardly conceivable that she would intervene in a European war on the side of France or any other state if Britain remained neutral. And if Britain became involved in a major conflict it was becoming increasingly unlikely that Canada could hold aloof.

As a consequence, questions of external policy once more raised acute problems of internal unity. A large and highly vocal section of Canadian opinion looked to Britain as the touchstone in foreign affairs and insisted that British policy should receive unquestioning support from Canada. This view, however, commanded far less acceptance than it had in the previous generation. In English-speaking Canada there was considerable criticism of British policy under Stanley Baldwin and Neville Chamberlain, with its betrayal of the collective system and its dismal and ineffective record of appeasement. The feeling that Britain would fight only for her own imperial interests strengthened the demand for a clear assertion of Canada's right to remain neutral if she chose and helped to bring into being a limited but definite sentiment of North American isolationism. These views were even more pronounced in Quebec. In that province a considerable section of opinion rejected the view that Canada was part of an integrated world or that her interests extended beyond her own shores. A feeling that the League had somehow become the instrument of freemasons and communists, a devotion to the Papacy that was reflected in sympathy toward such Latin Catholic countries as Italy and Spain, an attraction toward the idea of the corporative state that was reinforced by religious sentiments and hostility to communism—all these factors strengthened the isolationist attitude that was traditional in French Canada. To the French extremist, as to the English imperialist, British policy was the touchstone. Both refused to broaden their horizon to embrace the wider issues; but in the case of the French this resulted in a rooted conviction that any participation by Canada in foreign wars would be the result of colonial subservience to the dictates of British imperialism and that Canada's military efforts should be confined to the defense of her own shores rather than directed to meeting the threat while it was still remote.

These divided sentiments were a constant preoccupation of Mackenzie King in his conduct of foreign affairs. Like Laurier before him, he looked on the maintenance of national unity as a paramount aim, which conditioned every aspect of policy. "A strong and dominant national feeling," he asserted in March 1939, "is not a luxury in Canada, it is a necessity. Without it this country cannot exist. A divided Canada can be of little help to any country, and least of all to itself." And in an outburst that revealed the depth of his apprehensions, he added: "The idea that every twenty years this country should automatically and as a matter of course take part in a war overseas for democracy or self-determination of other small nations, that a country which has all it can do to run itself should feel called upon to save, periodically, a continent that cannot run itself, and to these ends risk the lives of its people, risk bankruptcy and political disunion, seems to many a nightmare and sheer madness."

It was clear, however, that a mere policy of isolation was no answer. Quite apart from Canada's basic interest in Britain's survival as a bulwark of the democratic way of life, isolation would arouse disruptive forces in English Canada as much as subservience would provoke them in Quebec. The only adequate course seemed to be one which resolutely avoided any advance commitments to any course whatever and left the decision to Parliament in the light of existing circumstances. Even this was qualified by the underlying knowledge that an actual threat to Britain's existence would make it virtually impossible for Canada to stand aside. The difficulty was that Britain, by pursuing shortsighted and disastrous policies, might bring catastrophe upon herself and that Canada in spite of her changed status would again be involved in the consequences of actions in which she had neither responsibility nor share. Consultation and concerted action were impractical as bases for a united Commonwealth policy; but the King-Hertzog formula of individual freedom held nothing adequate to the inexorable realities that transcended formal relationships when Britain, for whatever cause, became involved in a struggle for existence.

There is no indication of any serious effort on the part of Canada to influence the main course of British policy. There was a general support of the policy of appeasement in the hope that by postponing a clash it might ultimately avert it altogether. There is no record of official Canadian dissent from Britain's attitude toward Japanese aggression in China. Canada followed Britain in lifting sanctions on Italy, in recognizing Italian sovereignty over Ethiopia, in acquiescing in "nonintervention" in Spain. The Prime Minister was ready to call for support to Britain if war had broken out over Czechoslovakia, even though this might have split his Cabinet; but he hailed the Munich settlement with relief and asserted even in the following spring that Chamberlain "made emphatically the right choice." But all hopes for peace by negotiation were vain. With the German invasion of Poland, and Britain's entry into the war on September 3, 1939, Canada was faced with the need for positive decision. The decision was taken in her own capacity as a nation and on the basis of her own independent judgment. For a week after Britain entered the conflict, Canada remained technically neutral. Parliament was summoned and the issue laid before it in the form of a Speech from the Throne calling for a declaration of war. On September 9 the Commons gave its support without a division; and on September 10 the King, on the advice of his Canadian ministers, proclaimed war against Germany on behalf of the Dominion.

William Aberhart.

(Canadian Illustrated News)

Mitchell Hepburn.

(Public Archives of Canada)

Vincent Massey.
*Canada's first Ambassador to
Washington and first Canadian-born
Governor General.*

(National Film Board)

James Shaver Woodsworth.
*One of the founders and first party
leader of the Cooperative
Commonwealth Federation (CCF).*

(Public Archives of Canada)

Chapter 20

Return to Armageddon

World War II: The Military Effort

The world war that Hitler launched with his aggression on Poland was not only the most destructive conflict in the history of mankind; it was also the most all-embracing. Its global scope brought every continent and every ocean into the arena of hostilities. Its impact was felt, directly or indirectly, by the whole population of every organized community. The industrialization of warfare made it a total activity in which the armed forces were simply the spearhead of a concerted national effort. It was a struggle in which the price of defeat might literally be annihilation and in which all the resources, moral as well as physical, of the nations engaged had to be directed toward the one overriding aim of a decisive military victory.

The democracies were slower than their adversaries to accept the implications of total war. They had sought to avoid it by a policy of appeasement, hoping by minor sacrifices to avert a major cataclysm. The mentality that resulted in this ineffectual diplomacy was equally evident in their strategy. There was a natural desire to keep the cost and the effort to a minimum. Emphasis was to be placed less on military might than on economic power. The Allied leaders took to heart what they believed to be the lessons of World War I—the bloody losses resulting from offensives on the Western Front against fixed positions, the ultimate military collapse of Germany when the home front crumbled under the pressure of the blockade. This time they hoped to win the war in the factories and the shipyards rather than on the battlefield. The Germans in their search for a quick decision would be compelled to waste their strength against impregnable fortifications, while the superior productive power of the Allies would be brought to bear with crushing supremacy behind the stranglehold imposed by Allied command of the seas.

These views inevitably conditioned Canada's initial views of her prospective war effort. She was an auxiliary rather than a principal in the struggle. The basic decisions inevitably lay in the first instance with Britain and France. Canada's contribution would be most effective if it was subordinate to and integrated with the plans of these two Great Powers. She might be critical of their plans, though of that there was in fact no indication; but even if she dissented, she had no reason to suppose that her views would carry any great weight. The most she could do—and this would call for a foresight far superior to that exhibited by any other democratic state—would be to direct her own preparations toward the possibility of a disastrous failure and to lay the foundation for the new type and scale of effort that the resulting crisis would necessitate.

Actually the outbreak of war found Canada without any long-range plans on the military side and with only the sketchiest foundation for a major military effort. Defense expenditure more than doubled between 1935 and 1939, but even then it reached only a modest figure of less than $35,000,000. During the same period there was a reorganization of the militia along more modern lines and a tripling of funds for the air service and the navy; but expansion of the last two services was still in embryo, and Canada's permanent army remained at the figure of 4000 men. What the changes evidently envisaged was the creation of small cadres of specialists in the more technical branches of warfare, which could be expanded for service at home or overseas, rather than the raising of forces on the scale of World War I. The Prime Minister himself expressed the opinion that the day of large expeditionary forces had passed. Canada's main contribution was to be in the field of war production rather than in the dispatch of large forces abroad.

This approach was made plain in the plans announced at the outset by the government. Canada's program was to be coordinated with that of Britain, with particular emphasis on the provision of war supplies. Armed assistance at the outset was chiefly to take the form of trained technicians, of naval craft and personnel, and of airmen. Although it was implied that no expeditionary force was actually contemplated, the government refused to give a promise that parliamentary approval would be sought before any troops were sent overseas; and in announcing immediate plans for the raising of an infantry division, with a second to follow, the Prime Minister stated that these forces would be available for overseas service should the need arise.

In the latter part of September 1939, there came the announcement of a further project, which was in fact expected to represent Canada's main contribution to the Allied armed effort. Some time before the outbreak of war the British air force had made overtures for the establishment of air training schools in Canada. The Dominion took the stand that, while it was ready to assist, any establishments must be under its own control. Out of the negotiations that followed emerged the British Commonwealth Air Training Plan, which in December was embodied in a formal agreement between Britain, Canada, Australia, and New Zealand. It called for the construction of 64 schools over a period of three years, with the objective of training some 20,000 pilots a year. Canada was to supply four-fifths of the recruits and to bear $350,000,000 of the initially estimated cost of $600,000,000. It was in the air rather than on the ground that Canada's combat strength was to be most in evidence.

On paper these plans represented an effort toward a balanced program that would channel Canada's war effort along the lines best suited to her capacities in relation to Allied needs. "We determined," said one government spokesman, "that Canada's war effort should be practical rather than spectacular." Within a few weeks, however, this neatly designed balance had been completely overthrown. On the one hand, the anticipated expansion in war production largely failed to materialize, and Canadian industry waited in vain for the flood of orders that had been expected from Britain. On the other hand, a considerable section of the public—the most vocal element of which was naturally found among the Conservative opponents of the government—refused to be content with an unspectacular war. The tradition that an effective war effort was measured in masses of troops marching off to faraway battlefields was clung to stubbornly, and no explanations of the changed character of warfare or of Canada's desire to fit in with Allied plans could mollify the demand for more evidence of martial zeal. An unreasoning emotion demanded satisfaction, and the government yielded to the clamor. In December 1939, the 1st Division, still largely untrained, landed in Britain, to the mixed gratification of the imperial military authorities, and in the following month it was announced that the 2nd Division was to follow. Canada had committed herself to an expeditionary force and to an army expansion whose wisdom and usefulness were at that stage of the war in very grave doubt.

Within a few months, however, the whole picture had changed in the most drastic fashion. The German drive through the Low Countries, followed by the fall of France, swept aside all the earlier Allied calculations and the illusions on which they had been based. The Maginot Line had gone; the French army had been knocked out of the war; the British army had escaped from Dunkirk only by sacrificing all its heavy equipment; the enemy stood for the moment triumphant and unchallenged on the continent of Europe. Britain, her bulwarks gone and her army in desperate straits, lay in imminent danger of invasion. For a full year the British Commonwealth was to stand alone against the Axis, except for the brief interlude of resistance by Greece and Yugoslavia. From the fall of France until Hitler's invasion of Russia, Canada stood second only to Britain herself in the ranks of the opponents of fascism, and the 1st Canadian Division, the only fully equipped division in the British Isles in the weeks after Dunkirk, suddenly found itself one of the pillars of defense against the expected assault from across the Channel.

Thus thrust suddenly into the role of a major participant, Canada was compelled to discard all the previous calculations on which her plans were based. There was no assurance that either American or Russian manpower would be thrown into the scale. Britain's factories were menaced with annihilation from the air, and until the adoption of Lend-Lease the availability of American war supplies was curtailed by the Neutrality Act. The lack of any great demand for Canadian troops or Canadian munitions was replaced by an urgent need for both. The result was a transformation of the Dominion's war effort. While every available rifle and plane was shipped to Britain and Canadian industry embarked on a frantic expansion under maximum pressure, energetic steps were taken to increase Canada's armed forces for home defense and for dispatch overseas. The air training plan was expanded and accelerated. Plans to raise two new divisions were announced in the latter part of May 1940. By the end of the year a complete Canadian corps was on English soil, plans for additional armored formations were under way, 25 air squadrons were to be added to the 3 that had so far gone overseas, and in August 1941, it was announced that still another division—the sixth—would be mobilized.

A force of this size would be somewhat unwieldy if organized in a single corps. If it was to be divided, however, it was still desirable to keep its over-all direction in Canadian hands; and that meant organizing the command at higher than corps level. The desires of the military leaders for bigger and better promotions, of both military and political leaders for greater authority and prestige for the Canadian command in the operations that lay ahead, of the public at large for an even more shining role than the Canadian forces had played during the last war—all these contributed to a decision that would give the Canadian forces a higher and more independent status than they had previously enjoyed. In January 1942, it was announced that the overseas forces would be reorganized as the First Canadian Army, composed of three infantry and two armored divisions and two armored brigades; and in the following April, army headquarters was set up under General A. G. McNaughton.

It was another fifteen months before the ground forces were to see action on anything like a major scale. Until they joined in the Allied invasion of Europe, it was the sister services that had most opportunity for contact with the enemy. The navy expanded from a prewar strength of some 5000 to over 90,000 and from 17 craft to over 900, of which 373 were combat ships. Toward the end of the war the navy acquired a few cruisers and aircraft carriers; but throughout the main period of hostilities its chief task was convoy escort and its strength was confined to smaller ships—destroyers, frigates, and corvettes. At the height of the battle of the Atlantic, nearly half the convoys were under Canadian escort, and in the final stages of the war the proportion rose to four-fifths. In the air, Canada's expansion was even more striking. A personnel strength of 4000 was expanded to over 200,000. More than half the 131,000 air crew graduates of the British Commonwealth Air Training plan were Canadians, and Canada's share in the cost of the enlarged scheme mounted to $1,281,000,000. By the end of the war there were 45 Canadian squadrons overseas. Canadian fliers saw action in every major theater of operations, and by the spring of 1944 they comprised one-quarter of all the air crews operating under British command in the assault on Germany from Britain and the Mediterranean.

For the army, in contrast, much of the war was a period of waiting. Detachments were sent to relieve British forces in the West Indies and to garrison Newfoundland, and for some time Canadians were in occupation of Iceland. A battalion that was sent to reinforce Hong Kong arrived just in time to be involved in the fall of that base, under circumstances that gave rise to considerable criticism in Canada. After the outbreak of war with Japan, which increased the need for home defense forces on the west coast, a token force was sent to Alaska, and a small body of Canadians later participated in the occupation of Kiska. The great bulk of the Canadian troops, however, were subjected to the prolonged strain of inaction in Britain, where they stood as one of the pillars against invasion and steadily prepared for their part in the assault on the Continent. The preparatory phase involved occasional small raids on the European coast, including a landing on Spitzbergen and the destruction of its mining installations in September 1941. The most striking interlude, however, was the attack on Dieppe in August 1942. This large-scale raid, whose primary purpose was to test the German defenses of the Atlantic Wall, came on the eve of the invasion of North Africa and served as a diversion to pin down the enemy along the Channel coast. The main assault force was composed of 5000 troops of the Canadian 2nd Division, supplemented by commandos and paratroops. The attackers succeeded in establishing themselves ashore and maintaining their foothold for ten hours; but tank and artillery support was too light to enable them to make a serious breach in the German defenses or to penetrate far into the town of Dieppe, and Canadian casualties totaled 3371, more than half of them prisoners. It was a costly lesson on the strength of the German defenses and the formidable preparations that would be necessary for a successful assault.

All through the period of waiting there was an insistent demand from certain quarters in Canada that Canadian troops be sent into action. Apparently there were groups who needed the emotional satisfaction that they derived from casualty lists in order to feel that Canada was bearing her proper share in the war. Repeated assertions by government spokesmen that the army was being kept in Britain by the desire of the British authorities did little to diminish the criticism directed at Ottawa. The active share of troops from the other Dominions in the campaigns in Greece and Libya and the Far East aroused envy and a desire for emulation. The paramount role of the Canadians at Dieppe failed to satisfy these emotions, while the shortcomings in the direction of the operation, with the resulting heavy losses, gave rise to further discontent. The absence of Canadians from the forces that invaded North Africa in November 1943, increased the public restiveness. Quite apart from a natural if unreasoning desire to see troops from the Dominion in the forefront of the struggle, there was the fact that the Canadian army was preparing to engage in a great and hazardous enterprise without previous battle experience. The government felt obliged to yield to these considerations. In July 1943, the 1st Division was dispatched to take part in the invasion of Sicily under the command of General Montgomery of the British Eighth Army; and in November, after the landing in Italy, the 5th Armored Division was added to form the I Canadian Corps.

These events brought a crisis in the Canadian command. General McNaughton looked on the Canadian army with its heavy proportion of armor as a special shock formation designed to spearhead the invasion of western Europe. He described it publicly as "a dagger pointed at the heart of Berlin," and he was reluctant to see its purpose diverted or its coherence impaired. He opposed the inclusion of Canadians in the invasion of North Africa. He acquiesced in the dispatch of the 1st Division to Sicily, but on the understanding that this was part of a plan to give Canadians battle experience by sending units to the front temporarily and in rotation. With the establishment of a corps in Italy, however, the diversion of troops to that front took on a character of permanence that was at variance with McNaughton's whole plan. He suspected that the army was being deliberately broken up and his own prospects undermined. Behind this lay a background of friction between McNaughton and General Bernard Law Montgomery as well as between the Canadian commander and the British War Office. He now became convinced that British intrigues against him had succeeded and that the Canadian government had been won over by his adversaries. The outcome was his resignation in December 1943, and his replacement by General Henry Crerar, who had been briefly in command of the I Corps.

Although the army command remained in being, it was not until the final stages of the war that all Canadian troops came under its control. Until the early part of 1945 the I Corps remained in Italy as part of the British Eighth Army. Its record in that theater, which at times seemed the stepchild of Allied efforts, bore out the reputation of Canadians as shock troops. The 1st Division won its spurs in Sicily as the spearhead of Montgomery's left hook against the Etna line and landed with the Eighth Army in Italy and advanced north through Potenza and Campobasso. As the Germans in Italy settled down to the defense of their winter line north of Naples, the Canadians found themselves engaged in the slogging drive across successive rivers on the Adriatic flank. They took part in the forcing of the Sangro and the Moro, and by Christmas were engaged in a bloody struggle for the little coastal town of Ortona, whose capture virtually closed this phase of the campaign. Through the remainder of the winter the right flank was relatively quiet while the Allies battered ineffectively against the western sector with its pivot at Cassino and clung to the flanking beachhead they established an Anzio early in the new year. The spring of 1944, however, saw the massing of forces for an all-out drive on Rome. The Canadians were thrown in to exploit the initial breach in the center and swept up the Liri Valley to break the next defense line before the Melfa River and drive the Germans back toward Rome. They were withdrawn from the line before that city was entered and had only a minor share in the pursuit that followed; but autumn and winter found them once more on the Adriatic flank and battering against the last major defense line guarding the Po Valley. Once more it was a battle of rivers, in which the Canadians pushed foward past Ravenna to the Senio—their last advance before the corps was called from Italy to join their comrades in western Europe.

In the invasion of Normandy the 3rd Canadian Division, serving with the British Second Army, was one of the five Allied divisions which took part in the assault on the beaches, and a Canadian parachute battalion was engaged in the advance landings from the air as part of the 6th British Airborne Division. In the course of the following month the 2nd and 4th Divisions and an armored brigade were added, bringing the II Corps into operation. This corps embraced all the Canadian troops immediately available for the First Army, which came into operation on July 23, 1944. The retention of the I Corps in Italy dislocated the original plans of organization, and led to a British corps, as well as a Polish division and smaller Belgian and Czech units, being placed under Canadian command. The actual composition constantly shifted during the subsequent campaigns, throughout which the First Canadian and Second British Armies acted in the closest integration; and at one stage during the battle of the Rhineland, virtually every British division on the Western Front had been fed into the Canadian formation.

Through practically the whole of the struggle, from the invasion of Normandy to the collapse of Germany, the Canadians held the left flank of the Allied line. It was a position of great and at times of critical importance, involving hard and dogged fighting for pivotal positions. There were few opportunities for the sweeping and spectacular advances that took place on other sectors of the front. The Canadian task was to help to make those advances possible by pinning down German strength and sapping key points in the German defense system. The first month in Normandy found the Canadians involved in the tough and bloody struggle for Caen, to which the Germans clung desperately, and where, in General Eisenhower's words, "every piece of ground was worth more than diamonds." Beyond Caen, captured early in July, the Canadians battered toward Falaise while the Americans broke through on the right flank and swept around the German forces to trap and shatter their armies in Normandy. In the advance that followed, which carried the Allies across the Seine to the German frontier, the Canadians and the British forces attached to them were assigned the task of securing the Channel ports, which were so urgently needed to solve the mounting supply problems. By autumn these problems had slowed the advance and given the enemy a chance to rally, and further operations hinged on the opening of Antwerp by clearing the approaches of the Scheldt, which the Germans still held. The Canadians were committed to this task, which involved a series of difficult and intricate operations over flooded land and which cost some 40,000 British and Canadian casualties. In February 1945, after the defeat of the last German offensive in the Ardennes, the Canadians opened the struggle for the Rhineland with an attack in the Cleve area on the flank of the West Wall. Reinforced by almost the whole of the British Second Army, they battled for a month through the stubborn defenses of the Reichswald and the Hochwald, paving the way for the series of American thrusts that cleared the Germans from the Rhineland and carried the Allies across the Rhine itself. While Allied forces swept into central Germany toward a junction with the advancing Russians, Canadian forces cut off Holland and settled down once more to stubborn fighting against the Germans isolated there; and in this final phase the transfer of the I Corps from Italy at last brought the original Canadian Army together once more.

In the course of the struggle the Canadian armed forces raised over a million men and women, five-sixths of them by voluntary enlistment; and of these the ground forces accounted for 687,000 and the air force for over 220,000. The cost included 41,700 dead and missing; and while this was less than the toll in the First World War, the intensity of the conflict was indicated by the fact that the bulk of the losses occurred during the final year of the fighting. In scale as well as in quality, the military effort was creditable to a nation of less than twelve million people, all the more so when it was set against the background of an economic effort that was even more remarkable in its scope, and that conditioned the scale of the military effort by its demands on man power and resources.

The War Economy

In Canada, as in all other belligerent countries, the impact of total war brought a tremendous increase in state activity and state control. The mechanization of modern armies meant a vast increase in the demands that war made on all branches of production. The need to make the most efficient use of the national resources in supplies and man power and productive facilities called for central planning and direction of the national economy. With a maximum war effort as the paramount aim to which all other activities were secondary, the individual citizen found himself subject in both his property and his person to the regulatory power of the state. The dislocation of ordinary life was far less serious in Canada than in the belligerent countries of Europe, but in degree and scope it was nonetheless unprecedented in the Dominion, and perhaps even on the whole continent of America.

The outbreak of war automatically conferred on the federal government constitutional powers far in excess of those normally conceded to it. Under the War Measures Act of 1914, which was still on the statute books and was proclaimed in effect on the eve of the formal declaration of war, the executive had extensive powers that could be exercised through orders-in-council. In the initial phase these were used chiefly to place the armed forces on an active footing and provide for their expansion, to suppress organizations and arrest persons regarded as subversive, to institute censorship and similar controls, and to lay the foundation for the organization of the war economy. A Wartime Prices and Trade Board was created to ensure adequate civilian supplies at reasonable prices, a Foreign Exchange Control Board was set up, and a War Supply Board was organized to oversee war production. The transformation of the economy from a peace to a war footing, however, proceeded relatively slowly. British firms revealed a reluctance to place substantial war orders in Canada or to deliver plans and specifications, and the British government was more interested in buying food and raw materials than in encouraging the development of Canadian war industry.

All that was changed by Dunkirk and the fall of France. These events, and the bombing assault on Britain that was designed as a prelude to invasion, transformed the supply as well as the strategic situation. Britain desperately needed to replace the lost equipment of her armies and to supplement on a tremendous scale the production of her own threatened industries. German occupation of Denmark and Holland cut off former sources of food supply, and the intensification of the German submarine and air blockade increased the gravity of the situation. Canada, at a time when she was embarking on a rapid expansion of her armed services, found herself confronted by urgent demands on her productive capacities as well. If these were to be met, a new and more far-reaching system of controls must be established for the efficient mobilization and use of the country's resources and energies. What was more, the Dominion, hitherto accustomed to look to more powerful neighbors and associates for guidance in major matters of policy, now had to chart its own course according to its own needs. European experience in wartime organization could offer only the most general guidance in view of the difference of conditions in Canada. The United States, still clinging to neutrality and a peacetime economy, was of no help whatever as a model. For almost the first time in her history, Canada had consciously to strike out boldly along an individual line of her own without waiting for precedent and example from outside.

A symbolic step was the passage of the National Resources Mobilization

Act in June 1940. Although it added relatively little to the war powers already possessed by the government, its sweeping authorization of full control by the executive over persons and property was an expression of the national desire for an all-out war effort. Meanwhile a Department of Munitions and Supply had replaced the War Supply Board and embarked on the expansion of war production. To the controllers who had already been set up over such civilian commodities as wool, sugar, and leather there were now added others over basic materials such as lumber, and steel, and oil, and the number was steadily expanded until almost every article entering into either war production or civilian consumption was brought under official regulation. A Defense Purchasing Board was set up to place orders for war supplies, British as well as Canadian. Private industry was encouraged to expand for war purposes by credit and tax concessions. Government funds were invested in the expansion of existing plants, and government corporations were set up to build and operate new ones. By the end of 1944, over $1,500,000,000 had been invested directly by the government in war industry.

These activities were greater in range as well as in magnitude than similar developments during World War I. Canadian production was no longer confined largely to shells and small arms. An entire new series of industries, from tanks and ships to optical glass and from artificial rubber to radar equipment, came into being. Canadian scientists were closely allied to war production and to the vital work being carried on in the laboratories of the Allies. They made their contribution to the evolution of radar and the development of new explosives. They were associated directly with the work on atomic power, and the government by taking over the uranium deposits at Great Bear Lake brought under control the chief North American source of that vital material. By the end of the war, Canada's manufacturing production had more than doubled and her industrial structure had become more comprehensive and diversified. New industries had been added; old ones such as steel and motor vehicles had greatly expanded in capacity. Canada had risen to fourth rank as a producer among the Allies, and only the United States excelled her as an arsenal from which other Allied states could draw munitions and equipment. Only one-third of Canada's war production was absorbed by her armed forces; the remainder went to their comrades in arms. Her war plants produced goods to the value of over $10,000,000,000 and the end of hostilities found her at a completely new stage of maturity as an industrial state.

This increased industrialization had a varied effect on other aspects of the Canadian economy. On the one hand it meant increased consumption of raw materials and fuel and electric power; on the other hand, by its growing demands for power and labor, it had a restrictive influence on certain aspects of mining and lumbering. In the course of five years, production of electricity increased by 50 percent. Mineral production reached its peak in 1942, when its value was one-fifth above that in 1939. Thereafter it showed a decline, partly as a result of curtailed production of gold, but also as a consequence of labor shortages in the base metal group. Nonetheless, Canada was the source of all but a fraction of the nickel available to the United Nations, as well as of three-quarters of their asbestos and one-third of their aluminum, and supplied substantial quantities of copper and lead and zinc. And although lumber, too, was restricted by labor and power shortages, forest production rose by two-thirds and production of wood pulp more than doubled in the course of the war.

In agriculture the story was one of combined expansion and readjustment. Initially the coming of the war accentuated an already serious wheat problem. The surplus had been rising since 1937, and the loss of European outlets meant a continued increase, which brought the carry-over to 500,000,000 bushels by mid-1941. Several factors combined to ease the situation during the next two years. Apart from somewhat increased demands by Britain, shortages in the United States offered some outlet for Canadian wheat, and the prospective demands of liberated Europe made it clear that Canada's surplus would be drawn on heavily for postwar relief. Even more important was the deliberate policy of the government of using the methods of bonus and subsidy to bring about a reduction in wheat acreage and a shift to coarse grains and livestock. With Europe cut off and the shipping situation hampering supplies from Australia and the Argentine, Britain relied heavily on Canada as a source of essential food. The prairies were encouraged to turn to mixed farming. Agricultural production increased by 40 percent during the war; hog production had nearly doubled by 1943, as the government took special steps to meet Britain's urgent demands; production of cattle and sheep and dairy products all showed substantial increases. Like other producers, farmers were hampered by shortages of labor and equipment, but their efforts to comply with wartime needs were rewarded by a doubling of farm income in the course of the war.

These strenuous efforts at increased productivity in all essential branches, coupled with the desire to turn the highest possible proportion of the nation's energies and resources into channels that would contribute directly to the war effort, meant that the individual citizen was subject as never before to restrictions and compulsions imposed by the state. The basic aims were to cut down on nonessential goods and services, to divert materials and man power from civilian to war production, and to prevent the resulting dislocations from giving rise to a serious increase in the cost of living. As a result the individual found his freedom of choice and of activity progressively curtailed. Exchange control, supplemented by import and export licensing, imposed barriers to foreign travel and restrictions on foreign trade. Certain classes of imports were prohibited in order to conserve foreign exchange. In October 1941, quotas were imposed that curtailed the production of a number of lines of consumer goods. In December a price ceiling was imposed on nearly all goods and services, and in January 1942, rationing was introduced for certain basic foods. Wages were also brought under control in October 1941, by a regulation that stabilized them at roughly the existing level and tied any increases to changes in the cost of living.

The labor policy, of which wage stabilization was a part, evolved rather slowly and tentatively. The 400,000 unemployed at the outbreak of war were largely absorbed as war production got under way, and by 1941 the problem was to meet the steadily increasing demands of war industry on top of those of the armed services. National registration of all citizens in August 1940, was intended to provide a comprehensive picture of available manpower resources, but the widely varied information thus accumulated never seems to have been seriously used as a guide to future policy. Early in 1942 the handling of the problem was entrusted to National Selective Service, whose powers of compulsion were used cautiously and to some extent indirectly. The curtailment of civilian production involved certain shifts in employment, and advantage was taken of this to forbid any able-bodied worker entering a nonessential job without permission. Later regulations brought nearly all changes of employment under the control of Selective Service, and there was some tightening up of prohibitions against leaving essential work or entering certain nonessential jobs. But while there were attempts to persuade men to shift from less vital to more essential activities and to draw on the potential supply of women for war industry, these rested for the most part on persuasion rather than on compulsion. Nonetheless, over a million Canadians were engaged in war production by the autumn of 1943, four-fifths of them directly in war manufacturing.

Along with restrictions on the choice of employment and limitations on wage increases went regulations against strikes and lockouts. At the beginning of the war the Industrial Disputes Investigation Act, forbidding strikes and lockouts pending conciliation proceedings, was extended to cover all war industries. In operation it did not prevent a steady rise in the number of disputes. Discontent with wage limitations or working conditions, demands for union recognition, the relative ineffectiveness of mediation machinery in the early stages of controversies before they resulted in strikes, all contributed to the restiveness that in 1943 led to the loss of a million man-days through industrial stoppages. In February 1944, an attempt was made to deal with the situation through a new series of regulations, which provided for collective bargaining between employers and the agencies chosen by majority vote of the workers, defined and prohibited unfair practices, and established a central Wartime Labor Relations Board together with provincial boards to apply conciliation procedure. The result was a very considerable drop in the number and seriousness of strikes. But while labor showed a real desire to avoid any serious interruption of war production, there was a restiveness under restraints and a desire for improved standards and increased security that was likely to find vigorous expression when the war came to an end.

At the foundation of all these activities lay the government's financial policy, the solid rock on which the whole war effort was based. It was a policy whose prime objective of defraying the cost of the war was intimately integrated with the effort to maintain a stable economy and avert wartime inflation. Price ceilings and rationing were the immediate defenses against a rise in the cost of living; but with the growing scarcity of consumer goods, and with a rising national income, which more than doubled during the war, there was increasingly grave danger that the pressure would wreck the price ceiling or ruin controls by encouraging the black market. To prevent this there was a deliberate policy of draining off purchasing power by high taxes supplemented by heavy government borrowing from the general public. These steps were successful to a striking degree. The first two years of war, before controls were fully applied, saw a rise in the cost of living by over 15 percent; and with the end of the preparatory period toward the close of 1941 and the beginning of expanding production, the danger of an accelerated upward spiral became acute. The inauguration of price ceilings and rationing, combined with the new scale of borrowing and taxation, abruptly halted the rise in living costs. In the remaining three and one-half years to the end of the European war the increase was barely 3 percent. No belligerent nation was more successful than Canada in maintaining a controlled level of prices and a working system of restricted distribution of goods and services.

In the raising of a revenue for war purposes, the main reliance was placed first of all on direct taxes on individuals and corporations. There were special war increases in customs and excise duties and levies on luxury articles, but in many cases these were intended almost as much to reduce consumption as to bring in funds. To facilitate federal financing the provinces were persuaded to vacate the fields of income and corporation taxes for the duration of the war and were compensated either by subsidies based on their previous income from these sources or by federal assumption of their debt charges. Income taxes were drastically increased and exemptions lowered, raising the levies in the middle-income levels even higher than those in Britain. Corporation taxes were also increased and excess profits taxes added. The result was to increase revenue from these sources alone from $145,000,000 in 1939 to $1,200,000,000 in 1944, and the total federal revenue for the latter year was $2,765,000,000. This amounted to slightly over half the total expenditure—a relatively high proportion, which again was deliberately sought in order to reduce inflationary pressure and to keep the burden of debt as low as possible. The remaining funds were raised by domestic loans. For a short period the budget included compulsory savings, but this was abandoned after 1943 and reliance was placed on voluntary loans. Over $12,000,000,000 was borrowed in the course of six years, of which slightly under half was raised from individuals.

These heavy financial demands arose not merely from Canada's own war needs, but also from the necessities of her associates. Two-thirds of her war production went to other nations, the great bulk of it to Britain, and problems of payment soon loomed large. By the end of 1940 Britain's reserves of gold and outside currency had dwindled to a point that made it almost impossible for her to continue payments to Canada in these forms, and her export to Canada of goods and services was far outweighed by the flood of supplies that Canada was providing on British account. Various procedures were adopted to overcome the difficulty. Britain's $200,000,000 investment in Canadian war plants was taken over by the Dominion. British-held Canadian securities to the amount of $800,000,000 were repatriated. The accumulated sterling balances in London, resulting from purchases in Canada on credit, were consolidated into a loan of $700,000,000 free of interest during the war. When the situation outran even these measures, an outright gift of $1,000,000,000 was placed to Britain's credit in 1942 for the purchase of supplies in Canada. Some of these supplies were transferred to other Allies, including Russia; and Canada therefore decided in the following year to deal with these countries directly. The result was the appropriation of $1,000,000,000 for mutual aid in the form of war supplies, with no stipulation as to repayment; and in 1944 another $800,000,000 was set aside for the same purpose.

Far from being a recipient of Lend-Lease, Canada was extending the same sort of aid on her own account to an amount which in one form or another was in the vicinity of $4,000,000,000, apart from the transfer of investments and securities. All told, Canada's war and demobilization expenditure amounted to more than $20,000,000,000, and by the end of the war the federal debt had risen to $13,000,000,000—over four times the prewar figure.

Politics and the War

The magnitude of the war effort imposed heavy strains not only on the economic resources of the Dominion, but on its political structure as well. Only a handful of people—the veteran pacifist J. S. Woodsworth, who felt unable to abandon his lifelong principles even for the sake of party unity, was one of the outstanding—openly opposed Canada's entry into the conflict. But different groups and sections varied widely in the degree of their enthusiasm or acquiescence, and there were equally wide divergences of views as to how the war should be conducted. There were no controversies comparable in intensity to those which rent the Dominion in 1917; but the tensions were serious enough and revealed once more the added difficulty of maintaining internal unity in the face of an external crisis.

The first storm signals appeared in Quebec. Almost all the federal members from that province had supported the declaration of war; but Duplessis alone among the provincial premiers had refrained from giving full assurance of support to the federal government, and within a few weeks he was attacking participation on the ground that it was being made an excuse for infringing on Quebec's autonomy, and issuing an appeal to the electorate to rally for the preservation of the rights of French Canada. In view of the background of intensified isolationism and the fascist undercurrents that were evident in Quebec on the eve of the war, there was a real danger that his stand would lead to a definite breach between Quebec and the rest of the Dominion, with consequences of the most disastrous sort. Ernest Lapointe, denouncing Maurice Duplessis' course as "an act of national sabotage," announced that he and his three French colleagues in the Dominion Cabinet would resign their seats if the Quebec government was upheld, and the federal administration threw its whole weight into the provincial electoral campaign. It was a critical gamble, which was crowned with success. The Liberals won a clear majority of the votes and an overwhelming majority of the seats. Even so, the result did not express unreserved French support for the war policy, but it was a decisive repudiation of any desire to isolate Quebec from the rest of the Dominion.

The next challenge came from Ontario and from the opposite extreme of opinion. Premier Mitchell F. Hepburn's feud with Ottawa was only briefly stilled by the coming of war. Within a short time his hostility flared up again, and he joined in the mounting cries of the Conservatives for a more active and spectacular war effort. His bitterness reached the point where he banned the showing of an American film on Canada's war effort on the ground that it was propaganda for the federal administration. Unlike Duplessis, however, he was not so rash as to stake his own political position on the issue. Instead he secured in January 1940, the adoption of a resolution by the Ontario legislature regretting "that the federal government at Ottawa has made so little effort to prosecute Canada's duty in the war in the vigorous manner the people of Canada desire to see." This challenge from the largest and wealthiest province was almost impossible to ignore. It came as the life of the federal Parliament was drawing to a close and presented an issue on which it was highly desirable that the people of Canada should decide. In March 1940, a federal election was held in which the government was emphatically endorsed. The Conservatives were unable to increase their numbers by a single seat; the Liberals secured a larger popular vote than in 1935 and gained several seats at the expense of the minor parties. It was a triumph that left Mackenzie King and his party firmly in power for the remainder of the war.

Behind these struggles were two issues that played a prominent part in current controversies. One was the demand for a coalition government; the other was the question of conscription. The two were not entirely unconnected. The belief that a national government embracing all parties could adopt a more vigorous course with less risk of serious opposition was naturally connected with the realization that conscription could be imposed only in the face of strong protests from Quebec. In addition, the natural desire of Conservatives for office was heightened by the patriotic belief that they could infuse fresh vigor into the war effort. The Liberals, secure in their majority and satisfied with their ability to direct the war effort, had no motive for surrendering part of their power to their opponents, particularly when such a step might increase the danger of national disunity. In their attempt to force the issue, the Conservatives tried to make it the paramount question in the campaign of 1940 and even adopted temporarily the name National Government party. Their repudiation by the electorate did not at once end the campaign, and its continuance moved the Prime Minister to a gesture designed to satisfy the sentiment behind it without surrendering effective power. When he reorganized his Cabinet in 1940, he offered a number of posts to individual Conservatives, and he announced his readiness to admit leading members of the opposition to the discussions of the War Committee of the Cabinet. Both offers were rejected. What the Conservatives wanted was not consultation but authority, and they still insisted on full admission to office. But the election of 1940 had in fact delivered a death blow to the movement for a national government. It died hard, but it died in the end from sheer exhaustion in the face of the impregnable position in which the Liberals were entrenched.

The conscription issue was less easily disposed of. On a number of occasions before the war, the Prime Minister had given a pledge that he would never impose conscription for service overseas, and this was repeated in the debate on the declaration of war and during the election campaign of 1940. Without such a pledge, more serious opposition would have appeared in Quebec, and there would almost certainly have been a split in the party and the cabinet. Yet it could only be maintained subject to the overriding needs of the war situation; and if this became grave enough, a refusal to adopt compulsion might equally split the country by provoking an outburst in English-speaking Canada. The overriding need to maintain national unity was the deciding factor; and in the constant effort at a compromise course that would attain this end, the government found itself gradually moving in the direction of compulsory service, first for home defense and ultimately for service in the overseas forces.

The first step was little more than a gesture, partly to meet criticism at home but even more to head off criticism in the United States, where a peacetime draft law was adopted in September 1940. The National Resources Mobilization Act had added little to the powers already possessed under the Militia Act and contained an explicit prohibition of conscription for service outside of Canada, but it did represent authority conferred by the existing Parliament, which included the right to call up men for home service. The national registration in August 1940, was opposed by Mayor Camillien Houde of Montreal who advised his constituents not to register on the ground that this was an unauthorized step toward conscription; but he was promptly arrested and interned without any serious disturbance resulting, and French Canadians, who continually professed their readiness to defend Canadian soil, were relatively acquiescent in the steps that followed. At first these were modest enough. In the autumn of 1940 the first selected draft from the twenty-one-year-age group was called up for a thirty-day period of training, which was intended to be applied to all single men between twenty-one and twenty-four. In a series of changes the age limit was ultimately lowered to eighteen, the period of training was lengthened to four months, and in 1941 it was announced that the draftees would be kept in service for home defense after their training period ended.

Such a compromise, designed to meet political necessities, was distinctly unsatisfactory from every other point of view. No large forces were needed for home defense once the threat of a Japanese landing on the west coast receded. The draft for home service did not provide men for overseas, while it withdrew man power from war production, where it was urgently needed. Indirectly it no doubt aided recruiting. The fact that the draftees were to be kept in service anyway was used to press them into volunteering for general service, and boredom may have accomplished what patriotism could not do unaided. But such a procedure was galling to national pride and resented by those subjected to it. Some of them showed a stubborn resistance to either pressure or blandishments, and this in turn led to resentment by the active volunteer forces against the immobility of the "zombie army." Not least significant was the charge that the French were particularly reluctant to "go active" and the consequent persistence of racial and sectional irritation over alleged inequalities of contribution to the war effort.

By 1942 the possibility was looming that Canada would have to adopt full conscription if she was to fulfill the military plans to which she was now committed. In the way stood the Prime Minister's repeated pledges that no such measure would be put into effect. But these pledges had gradually been qualified. In March 1939, the Prime Minister asserted: "So long as this government may be in power, no such measure will be enacted." By 1940, however, he was implying that the promise was not rigid and unalterable, but would hold until the people had been consulted. With industry and the armed forces competing on an increasing scale for available man power, it became highly desirable that the government should no longer be fettered in its course; and in April 1942, a plebiscite was held in which the electorate was asked to release the administration from its past commitments.

This was a device that misfired. Whatever hopes there might have been that the plebiscite would bring an expression of united national sentiment were falsified by the results. For the whole country the plebiscite showed 64 percent of the vote in favor of giving the government a free hand. But while the percentage of "yes" votes was 80 in Manitoba and British Columbia and 84 in Ontario, it was only 28 in Quebec. The vote had revealed and sharpened the lines of division and crystallized Quebec's opposition to compulsion. And although the government insisted that the only issue in the plebiscite was whether it should be free to use its own judgment, the bulk of the voters, whatever their views, undoubtedly believed that they were voting for or against conscription. When the outcome was the removal of the restrictive clause in the National Resources Mobilization Act but a refusal to adopt full conscription at once, the controversy was exacerbated rather than abated. A French cabinet minister resigned rather than accept the amendment to the act. In English-speaking Canada there were violent criticisms of the government's refusal to act and its yielding to the French minority. Racial friction became more serious than ever, and once more Quebec found itself in an isolated position and in opposition to the rest of the Dominion.

In the autumn of 1944 it was brought out that 22 percent of Quebec's male population between the ages of eighteen and forty-five was in the armed forces, as compared with 37 percent from Canada as a whole. There seems little doubt that at the outset of the war, recruiting in Quebec was more successful than it had been in the earlier struggle. The government paid more attention to the natural desire for French-speaking territorial regiments that could be reinforced from the districts in which they were raised. Nevertheless, language remained a hampering factor, and lack of skilled qualifications barred many French from the more technical and specialized branches of the army and the air force. Both the expansion of industry in Quebec and pressure for greater agricultural production attracted man power into civilian war activities. Yet there were other and even more basic factors that accounted for Quebec's relative lack of enthusiasm. Agitation during the period preceding the war had helped to strengthen and consolidate the isolationist elements. While the fall of France was a shock that stirred profound emotions in French Canada, the establishment of the Vichy government with its tendencies toward corporatism and its stress on discipline and religion struck many a sympathetic chord and gave fresh indication of the divergence in attitude between Quebec and the rest of Canada. Admiration for Britain's resistance did little to overcome the dislike of the British connection, and hostility to communism meant a dislike for Russia as an ally. The two sections found themselves at issue over some of the most fundamental concepts connected with the war; and as attacks on the laggard contribution of Quebec grew in volume, the French once more fell back on the defensive and hardened in their resistance to any form of compulsion and to any interference with provincial autonomy.

So long as the inaction of the ground forces kept over-all casualties reasonably light, the government could continue its resistance to the demand for conscription. With Canadian participation in the invasion of Europe, and particularly with the progress of the Normandy campaign, the problem of replacements began to present serious problems. The hard struggle for Caen, the desperate fighting at Falaise, the campaign against the Channel ports, all took heavy tolls. The month of August 1944, which saw the fighting around Falaise, was the costliest of the whole war for the Canadian ground troops, which sustained 9368 casualties; but figures for July and September were not far inferior, and October brought the struggle that led to the opening of the Scheldt, in which the Canadians were again heavily engaged. To aggravate the situation, infantry losses had been much greater than had been expected—a situation that was common to all the Allied forces in the west, but which was particularly serious for the Canadian army with its high proportion of mechanized troops. By the last months of 1944 the infantry replacement pool was at a low ebb, and drastic action was needed to overcome the temporary lag.

The minister of defense, Colonel James Layton Ralston, visited Europe to survey the situation and came back convinced that the normal flow of volunteers would come through too slowly to meet the situation. In Canada, however, there was a home army of 60,000 draftees whose training was well advanced, and Ralston proposed that these should be drawn upon for the numbers necessary to fill the prospective gap. The Prime Minister was unconvinced of the necessity and rejected the idea of compelling drafted men to go overseas. The consequence was the resignation of Colonel Ralston on November 1, and the threat not only of a cabinet split, but of a major crisis between Quebec and the rest of Canada.

The Prime Minister weathered the storm, but only by the use of all his remarkable talent for political agility. To replace Ralston he called to office General McNaughton, who had resigned from the command of the Canadian Army a year previously. This gave him the backing of expert opinion, for McNaughton asserted his conviction that voluntary recruiting would meet the situation, and King was thus able to persuade those cabinet ministers who had been inclined to back Ralston to reconsider then inclination to resign. McNaughton's acceptance of office, in fact, was of better service to the Prime Minister than to himself. Events made it clear that he was not fully informed about the situation. He may have been moved by personal feelings to reject Ralston's judgment and replace him in office because of previous friction between the two men over policy.

He may also have counted on his own personal appeal to stimulate voluntary recruiting. But while recruiting did in fact pick up, that did not solve the problem of providing trained men at once. Within three weeks a new cabinet crisis threatened, and King and McNaughton were both forced to abandon their earlier stand. On November 23 it was announced that 16,000 home defense troops would be made immediately available for overseas reinforcements. The Air Minister, who sat for a Quebec constituency, resigned in protest against even this limited departure from the voluntary system, and there were demonstrations in Quebec and among French troops. But the fact that this was an exceptional step that still avoided unlimited conscription prevented opposition from attaining serious proportions, while relatively light casualties during the next few months allowed the crisis to pass and the conscription agitation to die down. The prospect that a new crisis might be provoked by the government's plans for the Far East, which envisaged a force based on voluntary re-enlistment after the close of the war in Europe, was averted by the collapse of Japan. The whole controversy cast a shadow over the creditable aspect of Canada's military record, which involved the raising of all but a fraction of her armed forces on a voluntary basis. But while the shifts and compromises at times verged on the ignominious, they enabled Canada to come through a potentially dangerous internal situation with no irreparable damage and with no scars as deep and permanent as those left behind by the previous war.

It was quite possibly this service of the Liberal leader to the cause of national unity, as much as any other factor, that enabled him to retain power at the close of the war. The election of June 1945, brought a serious decline in party strength. Official Liberal candidates captured only 119 seats out of 245, though the virtual assurance of support by 14 nominally independent members from Quebec enabled the government to count on a clear majority. But while the Conservatives might take some heart from this reduction in numbers, they had otherwise little cause for rejoicing. Though they increased their numbers from 40 to 66, they were still disappointingly far from carrying the country as a whole in spite of serious efforts to reinvigorate the party. Ever since 1938, when R. B. Bennett retired to England and a peerage, they had been plagued by the problem of leadership. Bennett's successor, Dr. R. J. Manion, though well liked personally, provided neither vigor nor inspiration. In desperation the party turned once more to Meighen after the election of 1940, only to have their hopes shattered at the outset when a CCF candidate defeated Meighen's attempt to win a Commons seat in a by-election in 1942. Meanwhile a group within the party had become convinced that there was no future in trying to compete with the practical conservatism of the Liberal party and that the only hope lay in the conversion of the Conservatives to a vigorous policy of reform. An unofficial convention at Port Hope in 1942 outlined a program that tried to reconcile the new and the old outlooks. On the one hand it reaffirmed a faith in individual initiative and freedom from bureaucratic control; on the other it called for active state intervention to secure full employment and decent living standards, and—most shocking of all to the traditionalists—it expressed a readiness to abandon the sacred cause of protection. It was followed in December by an official gathering in Winnipeg, which adopted these planks with some modification and which showed the Conservative plight by going outside the party ranks to choose a leader. The choice was John Bracken, who had been drawn into Manitoba politics first of all as a Progressive, had evolved into a Liberal leader, and at the moment was head of a coalition government. His progressive background appealed to the reformers; his tenure of power for twenty years as premier of Manitoba showed a skill in practical politics that appealed mightily to the older Conservative elements. These latter even consented to prefix the word Progressive to the name Conservative in the hope that the new leader would at last show them the way to power.

The election of 1945 was a serious blow to these hopes. The party captured only 19 seats outside of Ontario, and only a single one of these was in Quebec. There was scarcely more comfort to be derived from the provincial scene. Ontario had a Conservative government, but Premier Drew showed a distinct tendency to go his own way without too much attention to the policies of the federal party. Elsewhere the nearest approach of the party to power was through coalition governments in Manitoba and British Columbia, and in the Maritimes it had almost been wiped out. What was apparent in both federal and provincial politics at the end of 1945 was a swing away from both the old parties. Social Credit retained its hold on Alberta; the CCF had captured Saskatchewan and had made inroads in the other western provinces, and a year before it had shown a striking though temporary surge of strength in Ontario. In Quebec an extreme racial-clerical party, the *Bloc populaire*, failed to win widespread popular support, but its agitation undoubtedly contributed to a swing back toward Duplessis, which placed him once more in power in the autumn of 1944.

These events revealed an underlying restiveness, a desire for social change and for better and more secure economic standards, a growing doubt about the adequacy of either of the old parties to deal with postwar problems. These undercurrents were reflected in the Liberal party itself.

The war had forced it to embark on extensive measures of state control and had helped to convert it to a limited policy of state paternalism. From a billion-dollar plan of social security, drawn up by the Marsh committee in 1943, the government selected a number of measures, which it sought to implement. Family allowances were introduced in 1945; negotiations for a comprehensive labor code were undertaken with the provinces; a national health insurance scheme was under consideration. Under pressure of changing conditions the Liberals were being driven from their old individualist basis into the paths of state intervention, and any party that came to power in the Dominion would be under similar compulsions.

External Relations

A notable feature of World War II was the increased unity that it brought to the English-speaking world. The United States and the British Commonwealth drew together in a common effort on behalf of a common cause. The sense of a north Atlantic community, in which Canada was one pillar along with the United States and Britain, was heightened and made explicit by the common danger from an Axis-dominated Europe. The necessities that bound Canada to her two great associates were tremendously increased by the demands of war; the closeness and solidity of her ties were reinforced by the fact that the war efforts of Britain and the United States were closely coordinated and that Canada's military and economic activities were directly integrated with those of her larger partners.

The new type of partnership that had evolved within the Commonwealth was reflected in Canada's wartime relations with Britain. In contrast to the situation in 1914, there was on this occasion no problem of status to be met and overcome. There were suggestions in certain quarters of an effort to revive the movement for imperial centralization or at least to secure imperial unity in the sphere of foreign policy. It was particularly urged by Lord Halifax in a speech in Toronto in January 1944. But this was really the last gasp of the champions of imperial federation. The issue had long since been decided, and there was no real chance that the decision would be reversed. When an Imperial Conference was held in May 1944, there were discussions of postwar issues as well as of the existing military situation; but these were exchanges of views among close associates, designed to discover common ground among their several foreign policies rather than to impose a single policy on them all, and by its silence on the subject of any new machinery within the Commonwealth or even any arrangements for regular meetings in the future, the conference tacitly rejected any idea of a move toward consolidation. It was significant that there was not even an attempt to revive such an institution as the Imperial War Cabinet. Coordination of policy was achieved, not through any formal body, but through constant communication and frequent contacts between the departments and the officials concerned with particular aspects of the war effort. The Dominion sought to harmonize its plans and activities with those of Britain, but it retained full independence of control over both its economy and its armed forces—an independence that was at times exercised in a manner that was not wholly welcome to British authorities.

This attitude, however, was linked with a lively sense of Canada's community of interest with a Britain that was holding the front line against the threat from the European aggressors—a feeling that found tangible expression in strenuous efforts to provide Britain with the tools of war and in the financial generosity that accompanied them. These policies in turn added emphasis to the growing closeness of Canada's relations with the United States, with their unprecedented reflection in the strategic as well as the economic sphere. Even during the period of American neutrality, the two countries were drawn closer by a recognition not only of common interests, but of a growing degree of mutual dependence. During those two years there was laid the groundwork for the most intimate cooperation, which was widely extended and developed after Pearl Harbor brought the United States fully into the conflict.

At the outset of the war, Canadians were acutely conscious of the delicacy of their position in relation to their neighbors. The great debate on foreign affairs was raging in the United States, with the isolationists battling strenuously and not always scrupulously to strengthen American sentiment against participation in the struggle. So great was the fear that any apparent attempt by Canada to influence American opinion would do more harm than good that the government and the press were reluctant even to defend Canada's war record against the persistent misrepresentations that were current in the United States. Throughout this difficult time, however, there were close contacts between Washington and Ottawa and a complete awareness of mutual sympathies in outlook and ultimate objectives. The crisis after the fall of France, when for a time it was uncertain whether Britain too might not go down, increased the sense of identity of interest. The traditional bulwarks that had sheltered the Western Hemisphere were crumbling, and their collapse would leave the American continent exposed as never before to foreign aggression. It was a common peril, which called for increased unity of policy and effort. On the one hand there were efforts to strengthen Britain's powers of resistance, expressed in Canada's expansion of her military strength and her war production, and in Franklin D. Roosevelt's policy of all aid short of war, which resulted in the destroyers-for-bases deal and the brilliant device of Lend-Lease. On the other hand there was a renewed emphasis on hemispheric solidarity and on the need for a continental system of defense.

The latter point found striking expression in the Ogdensburg agreement of August 18, 1940. Ever since 1937 there had been periodic discussions between President and Prime Minister on the topic of joint defense arrangements. Such an agreement followed logically from the recognition by both countries that their strategic interests were inseparable. Under pressure of the critical situation in 1940 it was now given tangible form. The agreement provided for the creation of a Permanent Joint Board on Defense to "consider in the broad sense the defense of the north half of the western hemisphere." It was an advisory body, and its function was perhaps less to formulate policies than to provide a definite symbol of cooperation and to give formal sanction to the plans worked out by the military authorities in Canada and the United States, in which the views of the stronger nation would inevitably carry the greater weight. Nonetheless, it served as the embodiment of a completely new relationship whose enduring character, at least in intent, was emphasized by the deliberate use of the word "permanent" and by King's assertion that the agreement was no temporary axis, but "part of the enduring foundation of a new order, based on friendship and good will."

Meanwhile the problem of economic relations was becoming even more vital. The coming of the war had accentuated certain disparities in Canada's trade relations, which even in normal times were marked by a surplus of exports to Britain and of imports from the United States. Britain's demand for war supplies meant an increase in Canada's export balance to that country. Canada's dependence on the United States for many essential materials meant that her imports increased with no corresponding increase in American purchases of Canadian goods. By the end of 1940 a serious situation had resulted. Britain ceased shipping gold to cover the balance of her purchases in Canada, and her dwindling supply of dollars had to be conserved for direct purchases in the United States. Yet Canada had to buy in the United States in order to fill British orders, and this at a time when her expansion of war industry involved heavy purchases on her own account of a wide range of articles from raw materials to machine tools. Her reserves in American currency were falling rapidly, and during the year in prospect she faced an anticipated deficit of over $300,000,000, in spite of her efforts at conservation through exchange control.

The situation was saved by the Hyde Park agreement of April 20, 1941. The United States, even in this precarious period of neutrality, was expanding her own war production, and this gave an opportunity for a measure of integration with Canadian war industry to the advantage of both countries. The agreement provided for a certain amount of specialization on either side. Canada would continue to buy such articles as airplane engines in the United States, instead of embarking on the complex and costly task of creating an industry of her own. The United States on her part would buy such things as ammunition and small arms from Canada, which was by this time producing a surplus. Such purchases were expected to ease Canada's exchange position to the extent of $250,000,000 a year, and in fact exceeded that amount during the next few years as American war demands increased. In addition, the obligations that her acceptance of British orders had hitherto imposed upon Canada were to be greatly eased. Canada accepted no Lend-Lease for herself, but materials that she drew from the United States for the purpose of filling British orders were to be charged against Britain's account under Lend-Lease. The agreement was thus not merely a step to ease Canada's problem; it was also, in the Prime Minister's words, "a joint agreement between Canada and the United States for aid to Britain."

Such a measure had implications that could conceivably extend beyond the war. The division of productive functions in the interests of maximum efficiency in utilizing the resources of the continent might have equal advantages in peace; and Hyde Park was in fact followed by successive steps toward closer integration, which increased the prospect of a permanent modification of economic barriers. Most significant was the creation of Joint Economic Committees, whose purpose was not only to study the more effective utilization of the combined resources of the United States and Canada, but to reduce the prospective postwar dislocation in the two countries. A number of other committees were created to coordinate food production and distribution, the supply of raw materials, and the production of war supplies. With the entry of the United States into the war, the process was broadened to integrate the productive facilities of Britain with those of North America; and the distinct tendency to treat the continent as a unity in this latter process was a revealing comment on the progress of economic relations between the United States and Canada.

The acceleration of this progress after the entry of the United States into the war was paralleled by the advance of cooperation in the strategic sphere. Pearl Harbor raised at once the problem of continental defense, and Canada's action was prompt and definite. There was an immediate declaration of war against Japan, and an assurance by the Prime Minister that Canada's forces would be fully available for service anywhere on the continent. More immediately important from the practical point of view was the provision of facilities on Canadian soil for American bases and communications. The question of a secure route between the United States proper and Alaska was particularly pressing. Already steps had been taken early in 1941 to provide a chain of air bases as a staging route east of the Rocky Mountains, together with a line of fighter bases connecting with the Alaska panhandle. The outbreak of war with Japan gave new urgency to the question of the Alaska highway, which had been under consideration for some years. In March 1942, an agreement was reached that provided for the construction by the United States of a road following roughly along the line of the air staging route; and by November this gigantic project, involving construction over nearly 1,500 miles of mountains and muskeg, had been completed at a cost of approximately $115,000,000. The controversial Canol project, involving the building of a pipeline from the Norman oil wells in the Arctic reaches of the Mackenzie Valley to a refinery at Whitehorse at a cost of $134,000,000, was undertaken at the same time to assure fuel supplies to Alaska. And while concern for the security of the west coast was uppermost during the early stages of the war with Japan, there were also developments along the Atlantic frontier. Both Canada and the United States were vitally concerned to prevent the stepping stones to Europe from falling into enemy hands. Both participated in the garrisoning of Newfoundland and Iceland. Canada established air bases in Newfoundland and Labrador for ocean patrol and air ferry service. The United States built up extensive air establishments in Newfoundland and set up four bases in Canada's far northeast on the Great Circle Route to Britain. By the end of the war, substantial armed forces of the United States were making full use of facilities on Canadian soil.

These were developments that gave new emphasis to Canada's position as a North American state. Even more than in the First World War, events made it clear that the productive capacities and the strategic interests of Canada and the United States were inseparable. The fact that in two major conflicts Canada had been forced to rely extensively on American sources for war equipment and productive tools increased the desirability of intergrating her military structure with that of the United States rather than of Britain. The division of function and accompanying exchange of goods that marked the organization of the war economy on a continental basis held important lessons for the future. The progress of the air age, which brought Canada into a strategic position during the war, would have an important bearing on the future of civil aviation and the role of Canada in air traffic between the continents. The physical ties between Canada and the United States were drawn tighter than ever, with political consequences that were almost inescapable.

The task that now confronted Canada was to evolve the fullest possible cooperation and at the same time retain her independence of policy. Only by this means could she avoid becoming a subordinate satellite of the United States, whose economic and strategic interests would demand favorable concessions from Canada. It was significant that at the close of the war Canada concluded agreements for the purchase of all American-built facilities within her borders. The Dominion by a process of evolution had worked out a relation with Britain based on the advance from subordination to complete freedom. Her future relations with the United States demanded another sort of evolution, which while safeguarding her independence and equality of status would be marked by increasing recognition of mutual interests and its expression in practical measures of cooperation for the mutual benefit of both countries.

While Britain and the United States were thus pivotal in Canada's external relations, there were wider horizons of which the war had made her increasingly aware. Twice within a generation the lesson had been driven home that small nations could not hope to be full masters of their own destiny in a world in which the ultimate standards were war standards. The task of creating a world in which peace standards would prevail, based on the rule of law, rested in the first instance with the Great Powers. Yet states of the rank of Canada had a vital interest in the process and were not ready to abdicate their right to influence it. Peace and war might rest in the hands of the larger states, but the contribution of Canada to deciding the outcome of the struggle was far from negligible. In fighting strength and in war production she ranked next to the three leading Allies. She would be called upon to make a substantial contribution not only to any international organization for the maintenance of future peace, but also to the work of world rehabilitation and stabilization. She was one of the three partners in the development of atomic energy, and in November 1945, she joined with Britain and the United States in proposals for international control of this terrible and unpredictable force. She was a major contributor through United Nations Relief and Rehabilitation

Administration to the postwar relief of liberated countries and an important member of the organizations created under the Bretton Woods agreements for international credit and currency stabilization. She had functions and obligations of no light importance in the postwar world, and she could hardly be denied an effective voice in world policy.

In contrast to the situation at Paris in 1919, there was on this occasion no question of Canada's right as an independent nation to a place in the coming world organization. Her acceptance as a state in her own right was indicated not only by her invitation to the San Francisco conference at which the charter of the United Nations was framed, but by the expansion of her representation abroad during the war. Envoys were exchanged with Russia and China and a number of Latin American states, and Canada's legations were raised to the rank of embassies. Her close connections with both Britain and the United States, particularly the former, made it possible for her to keep fully informed about the preliminary discussions at Dumbarton Oaks, in which the Great Powers drew up a preliminary draft of the charter, and to make her views known in Commonwealth discussions as well as in personal talks between King and Roosevelt.

It remained a question, however, whether Canada had any decided or original views of her own with respect to world policy. At San Francisco her immediate concern was to establish the right of states of her rank—the Middle Powers, in current phraseology—to due consideration in the structure of the United Nations, particularly when it came to the selection of members for nonpermanent seats on the Security Council. "Power is not exclusively concentrated in the hands of any four or five states," the Prime Minister asserted at the outset. "Experience has shown that the contribution of smaller powers is not a negligible one, either to the preserving of peace or to its restoration when peace has been disturbed." Evidently the concern was still with status rather than with policy. There was little inclination to take a lead in urging the drastic departures from old ways that new conditions made urgent. At the same time, Canada did not press too hard her desire for special recognition or her dislike of the veto power as embodied in the charter. She was prepared to cooperate in arriving at compromises that would make it possible to get a working international system established, trusting to time and experience to make it increasingly effective once it got under way.

The interest of the Dominion in the creation of a peaceful world was in fact one that could hardly be exaggerated. Two world wars had seriously burdened her economy and had raised threats to her national unity. It would take all her energies and resources to carry the resulting legacy, and for this she would need not only a peaceful but a prosperous world in which she could trade actively and freely. The balance of her economy had been shifted by the war. Manufacturing industry now accounted for nearly half her production, and its structure was broader and more diversified than ever before. At the same time the production of natural staples had shown itself capable of an expansion even beyond that brought about by the war. Some of the increased productivity in the latter field could no doubt be absorbed by an expanded industry, and prosperity and full employment would increase domestic consumption of manufactured goods. Basically, however, the expansion in both manufacturing and raw materials was based on a tremendous expansion in export demands. The Canadian economy, traditionally dependent on world markets, had become more dependent than ever.

The Battle of the Atlantic. *(Department of National Defence)*
Ships in Bedford Basin, Halifax, awaiting convoy.

Canada in the Alliance. *(Public Archives of Canada)*
Mackenzie King with Roosevelt and Churchill at the Quebec Conference, 1943.

Chapter 21

A Decade of Expansion

Nation on the March

The years that followed the Second World War brought an upsurge that affected almost every aspect of Canadian national life. There was a spectacular expansion of the economy, not only in levels of production but also in the scope and diversity of natural resources. Economic growth was paralleled by a new and striking increase in Canada's population. Internally the growth in strength and stature was reflected both in a broadening range of national activities and in a sense of self-confidence and solidarity that temporarily mitigated, even if it failed to eliminate, the old racial and sectional divisions; externally it was manifested in the positive and constructive policies that marked Canadian participation in world affairs.

Not least among these phenomena was the growth in population. The figures rose from eleven and a half million in 1941 to approximately sixteen and a half million by the middle of 1957. The accession of Newfoundland in 1949 added roughly 350,000; the remainder came primarily from natural increase supplemented by a steady stream of postwar immigration.

In both respects there was a reversal of the trends that had marked the prewar years. The earlier period had seen both a curtailment of immigration and a progressive decline in the birth rate such as had become characteristic of most Western industrial countries. By 1937, births were down to 20.1 per thousand. With the war, however, a sharp change set in that carried over into the postwar period. Young people began to marry earlier, to produce families earlier, and to produce more children per family. By 1947 the birth rate had risen to a peak of 28.9 per thousand, while the death rate steadily declined to a rate of 8.2 by 1954. Canada's natural increase was thus around 2 percent a year—one of the highest in the world, not excepting the prolific and overcrowded lands of Asia.

On top of this there were the newcomers. Between the end of the war and the middle of 1957, approximately a million and a half immigrants entered Canada. Nearly a third of these were of British origin; around 100,000 came from the United States; the remainder, except for a sprinkling of Asiatics, were from Continental Europe. The numbers fluctuated from year to year, primarily because the rate of admissions was based on a cautious estimate of how many Canada could absorb during any given period. Apart from the fixed quotas assigned to the three Asian members of the Commonwealth (India, Pakistan, and Ceylon) there were no rigid numerical limitations applied to individual countries as was the case under the United States system. There were certain basic restrictions on grounds of health and character, geographic origin, and economic capacity, and these applied with particular narrowness to non-European countries; but they still left considerable flexibility, which was used to regulate the flow in accordance with the ups and downs of the Canadian economy.

Up to a point the restrictive aspect was modified by humanitarian concern for the mass of postwar refugees. The problem of dealing with millions of displaced persons was an acute and heartrending one, and Canada could possibly have given even more help in solving it if agreement on concerted international action had proved easier to reach. As it was, Canada stood fourth among the recipient countries under the operations that were conducted through the International Refugee Organization, and accepted something like 100,000 refugees during the immediate postwar period. When a new crisis resulted from the aftermath of the Hungarian revolt in the autumn of 1956, Canada again opened her doors, organizing a special airlift and admitting approximately 36,000 Hungarian refugees by mid-1957—the largest figure for any receiving country. Yet such generosity did not escape domestic criticism, particularly in periods when there were threats of increased unemployment; and it was significant that the first positive act of the newly installed Conservative administration in the summer of 1957—the first time the party had attained power since the depression of the 1930s—was to cut down drastically the issuance of visas for the remainder of the year.

The new arrivals were no longer "the stalwart peasants in their sheepskin coats" of Sifton's day half a century earlier. Canada still had a place for the pioneer, but a pioneer of a very different kind. Free land of a quality that would attract the homesteader had long been all but exhausted. The new frontier was the tough and isolated one of the far north with its subsoil wealth of base metals, or the prairies with their expanding oil resources that supplemented and in places overshadowed the earlier agrarian base. But these new activities, highly significant as they were in value, could absorb only a limited number of new settlers. Many of those who came were skilled craftsmen and professional men who flocked, not to the frontier regions, but to the rapidly growing cities that were equally the magnets for native-born Canadians.

Canada was in fact involved in an accelerating shift from an agrarian and rural to an industrial and urban society. Although farm production countinued to increase, thanks to the progress of mechanization, the strictly farm population actually declined by 10 percent between 1941 and 1951, and this decline continued in the decade of the fifties, though at a somewhat slower rate. The agricultural province of Saskatchewan showed an absolute decline in population during this period; the net growth in Manitoba and the three Maritime Provinces was substantially less than their natural increase. It was Ontario and British Columbia, and in a somewhat lesser degree Quebec and Alberta, that drew both immigrants from abroad and native-born from other regions, and drew them particularly to the expanding urban centers.

By mid-1956, one-third of Canada's population was concentrated in the fifteen leading centers; almost one-half lived in cities of 40,000 or more. Over half of the population of British Columbia lived in Vancouver and Victoria; more than one-third of the people of Quebec were crowded into the enormous hive of greater Montreal; metropolitan Toronto contained approximately one-quarter of the residents of Ontario. Observers drew particular attention to the mushrooming of the suburban areas that fringed the great cities and that, in the case of the fifteen main metropolitan centers, increased by two-thirds in the decade beginning with 1941.

An inevitable result was a rapid rise in the demand for urban amenities, cultural as well as physical. There was need for housing and transportation; there were also desires for entertainment and recreation, for art galleries and museums and concerts as well as for schools and libraries. Television was added to radio as a new vehicle for amusement and instruction, and these mass media in particular made it possible to reach out beyond the urban centers and to bring to rural dwellers and frontier settlers elements of enjoyment that in an earlier generation would have been utterly beyond their reach.

At the beginning of the 1950s the Massey Commission, surveying the cultural needs and facilities of the nation, reported: "We were conscious of a prevailing hunger existing throughout the country for a fuller measure of what the writer, the artist and the musician could give." The increased interest in the arts, a natural outcome of changed social conditions, no doubt received further stimulus from the European immigrants who added their Old World tastes and talents to the existing Canadian pattern. Ballet in particular showed a remarkable development in the forties, which led to the founding of the Royal Winnipeg Ballet and the National Ballet of Toronto. Symphony orchestras were by this time firmly established in Canada's four largest cities, and a number were organized in other centers during the postwar years. Montreal and Toronto successfully experimented with short seasons of opera. The fortunes of the theater were more varied, but there were persistent efforts to maintain repertory companies in the main urban centers, and the annual Dominion Drama Festival, inaugurated in 1933, remained a major stimulus to theatrical effort. A notable new venture was the establishment of the Shakespeare Festival at Stratford, Ontario, in the summer of 1953—a successful experiment which was soon broadened to include musical presentations as well as classical drama.

At the same time, the record would indicate that in these fields Canadians during the postwar period were more successful as performers than as creators. The impulse was there, and it found expression in every major field of artistic endeavor. The results, however, varied widely in degree of maturity. "Canada's reputation in the arts, both at home and abroad, is based mainly on her painting," the Massey Commission asserted. "Serious music by Canadian composers is still too little known in Canada . . . the writing of plays . . . has lagged far behind the other literary arts. . . . Neither in French nor in English have we yet a truly national literature."

There were, of course, qualifications as well as explanations to soften these judgments. If Canadian composers had yet to produce the kind of first-rate work that would compel attention, there was nonetheless a healthy striving for original expression in the face of many practical difficulties. The limited number of established symphony orchestras, combined with a natural public taste for the familiar masterworks, presented obstacles to the Canadian composer who sought an adequate hearing. One significant medium was the Canadian Broadcasting Corporation, which not only gave hospitality at intervals to Canadian compositions in its serious musical programs, but also provided an outlet for composers of incidental music. Even more than the musician, the aspiring dramatist had to rely largely on the CBC as a vehicle for his talents in the absence of anything resembling a national theater. To a lesser degree the musician and writer could look also to the National Film Board, which was established in 1939, and which through its production of documentary films soon earned an international reputation in its field.

In fiction the relative lack of distinctive literature related rather to the level of achievement than to the range of effort. Canadian novelists were in fact searching with commendable persistence for ways to express the essentials of Canadian life, both past and present. Perhaps, as one commentator asserted, there was a "crisis of orientation" that made it difficult to fix firmly the basic elements in a period of social and economic evolution, and accounted for the fact that many Canadian novels were still in a minor key. Yet there were writers in both languages who were serious and sincere in their approach. Roger Lemelin looked with a sharp eye at social relations in the city of Quebec; Gabrielle Roy dealt with the working-class sectors of Montreal; Hugh MacLennan probed various aspects of Montreal and smalltown Ontario. These were examples of a search which, tentative and incomplete though it was in many instances, illustrated the desire to give creative expression to the currents that were shaping the national character.

The idea that these various efforts to enrich the national culture should be encouraged by public support found expression in 1949 in the appointment of a Royal Commission on National Development in the Arts, Letters, and Sciences under the chairmanship of Vincent Massey, who shortly afterward became the first native-born governor general of Canada. The Commission's mandate, which laid down the principle that "it is in the national interest to give encouragement to institutions which express national feeling, promote common understanding and add to the variety and richness of Canadian life," entrusted it with a whole series of matters for investigation, from the broadcasting system to the eventual scope and character of a national library, and from the preservation of historical monuments to Canada's relations with the United Nations Educational, Scientific, and Cultural Organization (UNESCO).

The report, issued in 1951, dealt faithfully with all these topics, and even went beyond them in its constructive proposals. Two of its main recommendations were of particular significance for the future. One dealt with federal support for higher education; the other envisaged the creation of a Canada Council for the encouragement of the arts, letters, humanities, and social sciences.

The prospect of federal aid came as a ray of hope to the universities, whose financial plight was already critical and might soon become desperate. By mid-century, virtually every Canadian university of standing was dependent on public funds in one degree or another. It was becoming increasingly difficult to secure additional money to meet the needs of higher education, either from private donations or from provincial grants. Yet those needs were expanding at an alarming rate. Between

1942 and 1951, undergraduate enrollment rose from 35,000 to 58,000. Even this represented only about 7 percent of the college-age population, as against nearly 20 percent in the United States. Yet without any change in this proportion, it was calculated that the effect of the wartime upsurge in the birth rate would bring an enrollment of over 110,000 by 1965 and at least 183,000 by 1974. As one university president pointed out, these were not hypothetical figures. "The children who will knock at our doors in the early nineteen-sixties have been born. They are in elementary schools." And if a higher proportion of eligible students should go on to the universities, the tidal wave might become overwhelming.

Backed by the sanction of the Massey Report, the federal government in 1951 embarked on the first modest steps to relieve the situation with a grant of $8 million to be distributed to the universities through the provinces on the basis of population. The action involved some political risks. Under the constitution, education was one of the subjects specifically reserved to the provinces, and one that Quebec in particular guarded with a special jealousy. The consequences were seen in the outcome. Quebec accepted its share of the federal grant during the first year, but by the end of that period Premier Maurice Duplessis was convinced that a continuance would menace provincial control over one of the main bulwarks of French-Canadian culture. He rejected any further subsidies and turned a minatory eye on any of the universities in the province that showed signs of yielding to the temptation of the federal flesh pots. In this, however, he stood alone among provincial leaders. All the others accepted federal aid with gratitude, which was heightened when, in October 1956, the Prime Minister announced a doubling of the federal grant and followed this early in 1957 by taking steps to establish the long-delayed Canada Council.

The timing of this action was officially attributed to a particularly substantial windfall. Two multimillionaires had recently died, and their large estates—not depleted to any appreciable extent by charitable donations during their lifetime—provided almost the whole of the $100 million with which the Canada Council was now endowed. Half of this sum was designated a University Capital Grant Fund to aid the building programs which the universities would be obliged to undertake in the years immediately ahead. The remaining $50 million would be an Endowment Fund whose interest would be used for scholarships, loans, and grants in aid of cultural activities. In addition, the Council would act as the Canadian national body to work with UNESCO, and would play a part in making fuller information about Canada available in other lands.

An Expanding Economy

In its editorial columns of March 30, 1952, the *New York Times* spared a friendly and admiring glance for Canada. Noting that the Canadian population of fourteen million was "just about what the United States had in 1830 when our annual output was $925 million," the writer commented on Canada's gross national product of over $21,000 million, and added in a slightly avuncular tone: "From our own eminence of a $328 billion annual national output it is nostalgic to see the sap rising in a younger economy."

The sap was indeed rising. From a gross national product of $5.7 billion in 1939, the figures rose to $12 billion in 1946 and to something over $30 billion in the first half of 1957, by which time the United States on its part had climbed to around $430 billion. Some of this increase was, of course, the result of the price inflation that every Western country experienced after the war. Taking the base date 1949 as 100, the Canadian index rose from 69.6 in 1941 to 120.3 in January 1957. Yet this still meant a substantial gain in the physical volume of production and a general rise in the real standard of living.

This rise in production was accompanied by changes in the economic pattern. By 1955, service industries accounted for one-half the national income; one-sixth came from advanced manufacturing and construction; the remaining one-third was supplied by the extraction and the initial processing of primary products. Agriculture still led among the primary industries, but forest and mineral products showed a rapid expansion during this period, and the increased processing in Canada of primary products that had formerly been exported in their natural state represented a significant step in Canada's progress toward industrial maturity.

For manufacturing of all kinds the gross value of products rose from $8 billion in 1946 to approximately $20 billion in 1955. Much of this, including the development of relatively new industries such as petrochemicals, rested on the expanding production of natural resources. Of the eight leading industries, seven were engaged in the processing of primary products. The exception was the automobile industry, which relied to a considerable extent on the import of component parts. Leading all others in value was the pulp-and-paper industry, which now supplied over half the world's newsprint, and whose total production rose in value from $528 million in 1946 to more than $1,600 million in 1955. Steel manufacturing grew from a capacity of two and a half million tons in 1940 to five and a half million in 1956. By that date Canada ranked second to the United States in the production of aluminum, and the new smelter at Kitimat was the largest in the world. In the case of pulp-and-paper and aluminum in particular, the availability of cheap and plentiful hydroelectric power was a vital factor, supplementing the advantage of extensive forest resources in the one case, and in the other offsetting the cost of bringing in bauxite from abroad.

While industry showed a growing diversification during the postwar years, this was far overshadowed by the spectacular enlarging of Canada's range of natural resources. Four products in particular—oil, natural gas, iron, and uranium—were discovered in major quantities, and transformed Canada's economic prospects, not only as a primary producer of world commodities, but as a growing industrial power.

Prior to 1947, Canada's slender resources in oil were drawn chiefly from the declining Turner Valley field and accounted for no more than 10 percent of the national consumption. In February of that year, however, persistent and costly exploration by the leading oil companies was rewarded by the strike at the Leduc field a few miles southwest of Edmonton. It was a first revelation of tremendous subsoil wealth whose horizon steadily widened. A larger discovery was made in 1948 at Redwater north of Edmonton; and in 1954 fresh discoveries at Pembina, west of Leduc, opened what within two years became the largest producing field in Canada. By 1956, oil led all other minerals in value and supplied the equivalent of 75 per cent of domestic requirements. In the decade after Leduc, $4 billion was invested in oil development in Canada; new development was being pushed at the rate of over $500 million a year; and with oil there was associated the rapidly increasing reserves of natural gas that added a further element in the revolution that was taking place in Canada's energy resources.

In the same period the picture with regard to iron ore was also transformed. Before the war the principal deposit was at Wabana in Newfoundland. In 1942, production of newly opened deposits was begun at Steep Rock, north of Lake Superior; but even with this expansion, Canada's production in 1947 amounted to only two million tons. In the following year, serious investigation was undertaken of the deposits that were known to exist in the Ungava Peninsula in the vicinity of the Quebec-Labrador boundary. The result was the establishment of a major ore body at Knob Lake and the formation of a Canadian-American syndicate to exploit it. The first shipment of ore went out in July 1954. By 1957, Canadian production had risen to 22 million tons, and the operations at Knob Lake had opened the door to the riches of the Labrador

Trough—a fabulous storehouse of mineral wealth running northward to the tip of Ungava and loaded with nonferrous base metals as well as further deposits of iron.

CANADA'S ECONOMIC GROWTH

Subject	Unit	1946	1956	1966*
Mineral production	$	502,816,000	2,084,906,000	4,003,840,000
Newsprint production	tons	4,162,158	6,445,110	8,418,793†
New dwellings completed		60,600	135,700	162,200
Motor vehicle registrations		1,622,463	4,265,437	7,035,261
Value of shipments of goods of own manufacture	$	8,035,692,000	21,636,749,000	33,889,423,000‡
Gross national product	$	11,850,000,000	30,585,000,000	57,781,000,000
Personal income	$	9,719,000,000	21,958,000,000	42,712,000,000
Capital expenditure	$	1,674,000,000	8,034,000,000	14,897,000,000
Electric power generated	kwh	41,736,987,000	88,383,301,000	158,135,232,000
Retail trade	$	5,787,377,000	14,773,722,000	22,107,709,000

*Preliminary figures.
†Figure is from the "Monthly Bulletin of the Pulp and Paper Industry" and approximates the DBS figure, which will not be available for some time.
‡1965 figure is the latest available.

Source: The Dominion Bureau of Statistics.

And, finally, there was uranium. The opening of the atomic age gave a tremendous stimulus to the intensive search for this new and vital element, which it was soon evident that Canada possessed in abundance. The initial discoveries at Great Bear Lake in the far Northwest, which had been brought into production before the war, were followed by the opening of the deposits at Beaverlodge in northern Saskatchewan, and these in turn were overshadowed by the discoveries in the Blind River area of northern Ontario in 1953. By the mid-fifties, large-scale production was actively under way, and known reserves were steadily expanding. Initially, all the product was exported to the United States in the form of uranium oxide, and such refined metal as was needed for Canada's experimental reactors was brought back from the United States. But in January 1955, it was announced that Canada had decided to build an atomic power station, and this was followed a year later by the decision to undertake her own refining of uranium metal. It was confidently predicted that within another two years Canada would outstrip both the United States and South Africa to become the leading producer of uranium, with an annual output of the value of some $250 million.

The influence of these developments was even wider than the addition of new key natural resources to the Canadian economy. There was a

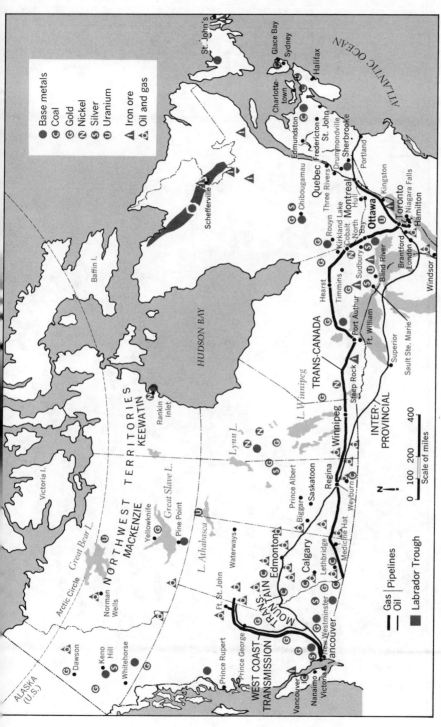

Mineral Resources

Manufacturing

Legend:
- Aluminum
- Autos, machinery
- Iron, steel, metallurgy
- Light industry
- Oil refining
- Pulp and paper

ALASKA (U.S.A.)

YUKON
Whitehorse

NORTHWEST TERRITORIES
MACKENZIE
KEEWATIN
Great Bear L.
Arctic Circle
Great Slave L.

BRITISH COLUMBIA
Prince Rupert
Kitimat
Prince George
Cumberland
Nanaimo
Victoria
Vancouver
New Westminster
Powell River
Trail
Nelson
Lethbridge

ALBERTA
Edmonton
Calgary
Medicine Hat

SASKAT-CHEWAN
Biggar
Moose Jaw
Saskatoon
Prince Albert
Swift Current
Regina
Brandon
Winnipeg

MANITOBA
L. Winnipeg

HUDSON BAY

ONTARIO
Port Arthur
Ft. William
Sault Ste. Marie
Kirkland Lake
Sudbury
L. Superior
L. Michigan
L. Huron
Windsor
London
Toronto
Oshawa
Hamilton
Kingston
Belleville
L. Erie
L. Ontario
Ottawa
Hull

QUEBEC
LABRADOR
Baie Comeau
Chicoutimi
Arvida
Jonquiere
Three Rivers
Quebec
Montreal
Shawinigan
Falls
Sherbrooke

NEWFOUNDLAND
Corner Brook
Grand Falls
St. John's

NEW BRUNS.
Bathurst
Chatham
Edmundston
Fredericton
St. John
Yarmouth

NOVA SCOTIA
Charlotte-town
Moncton
Sydney
Glace Bay
Halifax

ATLANTIC OCEAN

N
0 100 200 400
Scale of miles

602

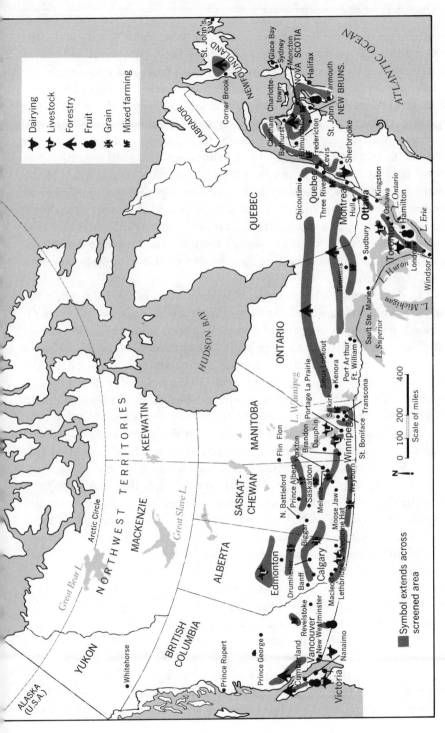

Forestry and Agriculture

broadening of the "filling-in" activities concerned both with the exploitation of existing primary products and the development of processing facilities based on them. There was a fresh and major incentive to exploration in the attempt to enlarge the knowledge and open up the deposits of Canada's vast subsoil riches. And although this was in one aspect a response to the growing demand of world industry for raw materials in increasing quantities, in another it was an added stimulus to the growth of Canadian industrial development to sustain the expansion in the field of primary products. Many of these lay in the heart of the northern wilderness. Transport had to be developed to get machinery in and bring the products out. Power had to be provided, houses and schools had to be built, roads and sanitation and other necessary amenities had to be supplied. The new communities started from scratch, and their needs gave new opportunities to the construction and manufacturing industries that could meet them.

The developments were particularly impressive in the fields of power and transportation. Installed capacity of hydroelectric plants rose from 8.6 million horsepower in 1940 to 18.4 million in 1956, and projects to provide a further 3 million were by then under construction. Some of the more spectacular were designed to expand the productive capacity of the aluminum industry, which along with the pulp and paper industry depended on massive quantities of electric power for its operations. In the East, facilities at Arvida in northern Quebec were expanded, and new construction was begun at Baie Comeau. On the West coast, a bold and imaginative operation was undertaken 500 miles north of the settled area around Vancouver. The Nechako River was dammed to create a reservoir 135 miles long; a 10-mile tunnel was driven through the Coast Range to carry the flow to Kemano, where it dropped 2600 feet to an underground powerhouse; and the electricity thus generated was transmitted 50 miles north to the smelter at Kitimat, whose initial capacity of 83,000 metric tons of aluminum could ultimately be expanded to 500,000 tons.

Many of the new mining developments were also remote from the settled areas and needed both power and transportation to make production practical. The airplane was invaluable in the early stages of exploration and development, when it was frequently the only means of transport and supply, but railways or waterways were essential when quantity production was involved. This meant building new lines to the nickel deposits at Lynn Lake in northern Manitoba and the new copper-producing areas in Ontario and Quebec. To reach and develop the iron deposits at Knob Lake it was necessary to build a railway through 360 miles of wilderness, and to

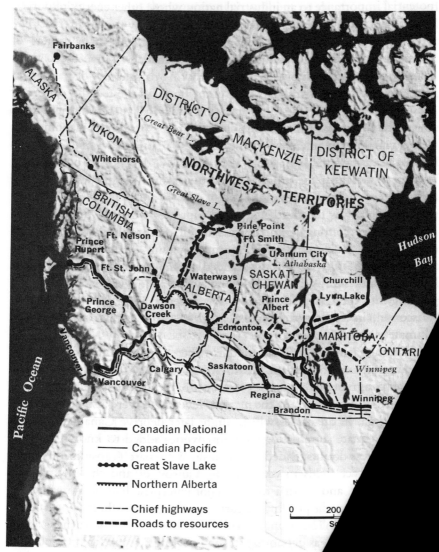

The West: Main Roads and Railways, 1967

construct a harbor at Seven Islands at the mouth of

all the facilities needed for handling and shipping

remained one of the major items of overhead i

particularly with the adoption of new and lar

and gas pipelines and the St. Lawrence Seaw

The postwar discoveries of oil and ga

Finally, and perhaps most decisive of all, was the announced determination of Canada to end the long delay by going ahead with the Seaway on her own. This would be more costly than a joint undertaking but was otherwise perfectly feasible. The main links in the existing seaway, including the Welland and Lachine canals, were purely Canadian undertakings. A canal by-passing the International Rapids on the Canadian side would mean an all-Canadian seaway. In Canada the idea caught the imagination and roused widespread enthusiasm. As Minister of Trade and Commerce C. D. Howe reminded an American audience:

> The bottleneck in the seaway—fourteen-foot navigation in the International Rapids section—would have been removed by Canada long since had your government extended the necessary cooperation.
>
> It should be noted at this point that the St. Lawrence is, and always has been, a Canadian seaway. Every improvement has been built and paid for by Canada, …om Lake Erie down. The cost of operating and maintaining the seaway is paid …lly by Canada. . . .
>
> …ership by the United States of a very long seaway would not only add to …onstruction cost but would complicate problems of maintenance and … canal system.

… 1951, a Canadian statute authorized the creation …ay Authority and empowered it to undertake …ce of the Seaway either as an all-Canadian … States. The door to cooperation was thus …es on June 30, 1952, Canada secured … her own, and in the following …she was no longer interested

…g patience in the face …resident Harry S.

… Lawrence … the United …eration and …y and our … take part

…urther action … the beginning … took form as the … it became law.

the St. Lawrence with the ore. Transportation the Canadian economy, …ge-scale projects such as oil …y. … were clearly of tremendous

There was little jubilation in Canada about this particular measure. The bill did not provide for a genuinely joint undertaking. Instead, it authorized the building of a canal on American soil in the International Rapids section at a maximum cost of $105 million. It seemed that the United States was seizing control of a single bottleneck which at a minimum cost would secure it an equal voice in the Seaway as a whole. Moreover, the bill carried the stipulation that tolls should be set at a level which would provide for the liquidation of the cost within fifty years. The possibility that this could only be done by setting tolls so high as to be uneconomic, thus giving a fresh lever to American railway and port interests in their continued battle against the Seaway, was increased when rising costs during the period of construction meant that still higher revenue would be needed to meet the terms of the bill.

There was in consequence considerable agitation in Canada for going ahead with the all-Canadian route irrespective of what the United States might do. Lester B. Pearson told an audience in Rochester, New York: "To be perfectly frank, many Canadians didn't think too highly of this last-minute participation—either of its timing or of its nature." In the end, however, the spirit of good neighborliness—helped perhaps by the chance to save or at least defer the expenditure of an extra $100 million—prevailed. On August 13, 1954, an exchange of notes defined the new basis. Canada, while accepting responsibility for improvements in certain sections including the Lachine and Welland canals, agreed to defer any construction in the area of Cornwall in favor of a canal on the American side, though reserving the right to build a Canadian canal at a later date if conditions warranted. In return, Canada was to build a canal and lock at Iroquois, and the United States agreed to refrain from duplicating these works. The possibility of an eventual all-Canadian route was thus kept open; in the meantime the essential work could at last proceed. Construction began on November 17, 1954, with completion in the spring of 1959 the target date.

These large-scale undertakings called for very substantial amounts of capital; and Canadians—a frugal as well as a prosperous people—provided the bulk of it from their own resources. In the postwar decade their savings approximated one-quarter of the gross national product, and up to 1950 were enough to finance nearly 95 percent of domestic requirements. This proportion, however, declined as requirements continued to increase, and by 1956 it was down to 79 percent. Moreover, some of this saving was invested in foreign enterprises and securities, to the amount of $7 billion, with the result that Canada became dependent on foreign funds for an increasing proportion of the capital that financed the expansion of the economy.

The overwhelming bulk of this came from the United States. In the course of fifty years there had been a complete reversal of Canada's relations with London and New York as sources of outside capital. In 1900, 85 percent of external investments in Canada were held in the United Kingdom as against 14 percent in the United States. By 1954, 80 percent of foreign investments were American, while the British share had sunk to less than 18 percent. And by 1956, out of a total of nearly $16 billion, the United States owned $11.7 billion and was investing a further $900 million a year—a stake that rivaled American investment in the whole of Latin America.

Out of this total, $7.5 billion represented direct investment in key sectors of the Canadian economy. By 1954, foreign investors controlled nearly three-quarters of the oil industry, one-half of the mining, and over two-fifths of the manufacturing in the country; and over four-fifths of all foreign-controlled business in Canada was American-owned. In the eight years from 1946 to 1953 inclusive, 307 United States firms established branches in Canada; moreover, American funds provided the bulk of the financing for the development of the new resources of oil and iron ore.

There was some uneasiness in Canada over this situation. It was feared that American interests, particularly those controlled by parent companies in the United States, might distort Canada's economic development through greater concern for their own business profits than for Canadian national interests. There was also some resentment against American firms that established wholly owned subsidiaries and thus debarred Canadians from participating directly in businesses that drew their profits from the Canadian market. Yet these sentiments did not offset the realization that Canadian economic expansion, even though it was financed initially from Canadian sources, depended to a vital degree on substantial funds from abroad. It took large-scale capital to carry on oil exploration or to open up the Knob Lake iron deposits, and Canadians were in no position to provide hundreds of millions of dollars for individual ventures of this kind. As C. D. Howe told the Hamilton Chamber of Commerce in April 1956:

> Let us face facts. Had it not been for the enterprise and capital of the United States, which has been so freely at our disposal in postwar years, our development would have been slower, and some of the spectacular projects about which we are so proud and so rightly proud, since they are Canadian projects, would still be far in the future.

To carry such large-scale borrowings, and to sustain the expanding production which they made possible, Canada needed export markets on an ever-increasing scale. The needs of the postwar world, and especially the demand for the primary products that Canada produced in abundance, provided the answer. By 1956, the value of Canada's exports had risen to just under $5 billion out of a total foreign trade of $10.6 billion. For most of the postwar decade, Canada ranked third among the trading nations of the world, and was displaced in the mid-fifties only by the spectacular economic upsurge of West Germany.

In trade as in finance it was the United States that played the dominant part. Although exports to Britain increased in value over the prewar years, their proportion of the total of Canadian exports declined from 32 to 17 percent. In contrast, 60 percent of Canada's exports went to the United States, and nearly 75 percent of her imports came from that country. In 1956 Canada's sales to the United States were $2819 million and her purchases rose to a formidable $4167 million. The two nations were each other's best customers, and Canada bought more from the United States than did all of Latin America or the whole of Continental Europe.

There were changes in the composition as well as in the direction of Canada's postwar exports. Wheat was still a key commodity, but it no longer held pride of place. By 1956 it was in third rank, exceeded by both newsprint and lumber. Other foodstuffs also declined in proportion as minerals and forest products rose, while such formerly important products as cheese and bacon and cattle sank almost to insignificance as far as exports were concerned.

Until 1952, Canada's external trade showed a favorable over-all balance. In spite of the dollar shortage that curtailed overseas markets, and particularly the important British market, the excess of exports over imports was of significant help in partially offsetting the mounting trade deficit with the United States, which reached $1348 million at the end of 1956. The remaining gap was closed by the influx of American capital, to such an extent that the Canadian dollar rose to a premium over the American dollar after exchange was freed in October 1950. This, however, meant in effect that Canada was relying on borrowed funds in maintaining a high level of buying from the United States. One consequence was a growing restiveness over Canada's inability to sell more goods to the United States in return, and trade relations between the two countries formed a subject of major Canadian concern throughout this period.

In the twenty years after the passage by the United States Congress of the Reciprocal Trade Agreements Act in 1934, the incidence of American levies on dutiable goods dropped from 46.7 percent to 12.5 percent. The benefit to Canada was, however, less substantial than these figures would suggest. Many of the concessions were on raw materials which were needed by American industry and on which the duties were already relatively low. There were few concessions on manufactured goods that would have allowed entry of Canadian products on a competitive basis and thus encouraged the growth of Canadian industry by giving access to a continental market. Even on primary products, moreover, there was a tendency to invoke the escape clauses in American legislation for the benefit of domestic producers. Although most of the demands for greater protection were resisted by the administration, positive action in certain cases was averted only by Canada's agreement to restrict exports, as in the case of oats, and continued uncertainty about American commercial policy had an inhibiting effect on Canadian enterprise. There were repeated protests from Ottawa against such acts as the imposition of restrictions on dairy products, which was viewed as a violation of treaty commitments; and Canadian irritation over American attitudes was typified by the outburst of the *Financial Post* in April 1955:

The Americans are always talking to us about integration of continental defence and continental resources. They are ready to take our gas when it happens to suit them. They are indignant when we propose to keep our own waterpower—whether on the Yukon or the Columbia—for our own use. Yet their Cabinet itself recommends an exclusion of our oil.

A further cause of friction arose from the adoption by the United States of the Agricultural Trade Development and Assistance Act in 1954. This was designed to liquidate the large surpluses that had accumulated as a result of the United States program of agricultural subsidies. These commodities might be given away as part of the foreign aid program, or bartered for materials needed for stockpiling, or sold for local currencies. The professed intention was to avoid cutting into the normal export markets of other producers, but Canada vigorously denied that this intention was carried out, and her protests were particularly heated in the case of wheat.

In the postwar period Canada's annual wheat crop averaged around 500 million bushels and reached a peak of almost 700 million in 1952. Until that year, foreign demand held up well, and the carry-over of 200 million bushels did not seem unmanageable. The wartime Wheat Board was continued in existence as the sole export marketing agency, and Canada participated in the International Wheat Agreement in the hope of stabilizing world sales and prices. Although this policy resulted in export sales at prices below the free world markets, it still meant steady returns at an average to the farmer of $1.83 a bushel, and in 1952 farm income rose to an all-time peak of $2800 million.

The decline set in next year. Export demand dropped as foreign countries increased their domestic production; plentiful supplies in the various exporting countries meant increased competition; resistance of importing countries, and particularly of Britain, to the renewal of the International Wheat Agreement reduced its effectiveness. This was the point at which the American surplus disposal program injected a further element of instability. Successive representations from Ottawa failed to secure a modification of American methods. Wheat was added to the other grievances that Canada felt over American commercial policy, and to the problems of Canadian-American relations that bulked so large in Canada's external affairs.

Canada and the Cold War

The years following World War II saw a transformation in Canada's external policies. The preoccupation with status which had arisen from Canada's struggle for independent control over foreign relations during the twenties had at last vanished with the establishment of her sovereign freedom of action. The negative and timorous approach to world politics during the thirties was replaced by an active initiative over a widening range of world affairs. An increasing national strength was accompanied by an increasing stake in a prosperous and stable and peaceful world, and was reflected in the new position that Canada attained on the world stage.

Several basic factors accounted for this change. Foremost among them was the new spirit of harmony between Canada's two main ethnic groups. In the early twentieth century the most acute quarrels between French- and English-speaking Canadians had arisen over issues concerned with external affairs. Little of this conflict was evident in the period after the war. The threats from the inseparable forces of Soviet imperialism and materialistic communism were evident to all sections of the nation; the necessity of taking vigorous steps in defense against them was accepted with only minor dissent. Canada's foreign policy in these years was a truly national policy whose fundamentals commanded almost universal national support.

This support extended with only slight modifications to means as well as to ends. The kind of nation that Canada could hope to create was conditioned by the kind of world she would have to live in. There were not only limitations on the national resources that Canada had at her command; there were also limitations on the extent to which world conditions could be altered in ways that would be favorable to Canada's aspirations, and still more on the effective actions that Canada herself could take to bring such changes about. These limitations were accepted realistically by the great bulk of Canadians; and although there were occasional criticisms of specific actions in the field of foreign policy, that policy as such never became a major issue in Canadian political controversies.

A second development of supreme importance was the emergence of the United States from isolation to active world leadership. This meant the release of Canada from many of the doubts and dilemmas that had inhibited her foreign policy in the prewar years. It meant that the two countries could now act closely and in mutual confidence in pursuit of agreed policy. Beyond this, it brought a new intimacy of association between the United States and Great Britain and relieved Canada of any need to choose, at least in matters of general policy, between the two major powers with whom her interests were inescapably linked.

The uniting factor was the sense of a common danger confronting the whole of the Free World. The aggressive hostility of the Soviet Union destroyed the wartime hopes that victory would be followed by continued cooperation between the leading allies in the establishment of a stable and peaceful world. Canada was alerted to the direct implications of the situation in September 1945, when the defection of Igor Gouzenko, a cipher clerk in the Soviet Embassy in Ottawa, led to the uncovering of a spy ring directed by Soviet officials, and to an investigation by a Royal Commission followed by judicial prosecution of the Canadians involved. Soviet actions in Eastern Europe, culminating in the *coup d'état* in Prague in 1948, finally convinced the democracies that a firm stand must be made against the pressure of communist imperialism, and Canada showed her readiness to play her full part in the common defense of the West.

The extent of the transformation from her prewar role was graphically illustrated by the expansion of Canada's foreign service. The 32 officers in the Department of External Affairs in 1939 had expanded to 364 in 1957; the number of missions abroad had increased from seven to sixty. Not only had Canada established direct relations with most of the states in Europe and the Western Hemisphere and with a growing number in Asia and Africa, including the newer members of the Commonwealth; she was also involved in the numerous international organizations that had proliferated since the end of the war, and in the frequent and prolonged international conferences that had become a normal feature of postwar diplomacy.

This was not the kind of establishment that could any longer be run as an appendage to the Prime Minister's office. Mackenzie King, who had for so long kept foreign policy firmly in his personal grasp, at length relinquished it to Louis St. Laurent in September, 1946; and St. Laurent, who at that time was also Minister of Justice, gave up that post in the following December to become Canada's first full-time Minister of External Affairs. And when St. Laurent became leader of the Liberal party at the retirement of Mackenzie King, he turned to one of the top professionals in this burgeoning department for his own successor with the appointment of Lester Bowles Pearson on September 10, 1948. For most of the next decade, it was Pearson who embodied Canada's external policy and who was the architect of Canada's postwar role in world affairs.

A major avenue for the expression of Canadian views and interests was the United Nations. Support for this organization was one of the main elements in Canadian postwar policy; and although Canadians shared the general disappointment at the failure of the United Nations to fulfill all the high hopes that had initially been entertained, they still held to a firm appreciation of its usefulness within the limits that experience had revealed. Canada's reputation in the General Assembly was reflected in the election of Lester Pearson as President in 1952. Canada was elected to a seat on the Economic and Social Council for three separate terms beginning in 1946, 1950, and 1955, and to the Security Council for the two-year terms beginning in 1948 and 1958. She was a member of every one of the important specialized agencies, and held a permanent place on the Disarmament Commission by virtue of her status as an atomic power.

When the Charter of the United Nations was framed at San Francisco in 1945, Canada's representatives laid particular stress on the functional principle as a desirable basis for the organization. There was at that time in Canadian thinking the concept of a special category of Middle Powers, lacking the strength of the Great Powers yet capable of—and, indeed, obligated to—a far more significant contribution to international peace and stability than was the mass of smaller states. In this situation, Canadian leaders sought to secure in international affairs a voice and status commensurate with the demands that Canada could expect to be faced with as a member of the world organization. "Some compromise must be found," said Mackenzie King, "between the theoretical equality of states, and the practical necessity of limiting representation on international bodies to a workable number. That compromise can be discovered, especially in economic matters, by the adoption of the functional principle of representation."

In this aspect the Charter gave a little satisfaction to Canadian desires. Even the concession that nonpermanent members of the Security Council should be selected "in the first instance" on the basis of their ability to contribute to peace and security received scant attention in practice. The ambitions of the smaller states, in this as in other respects, were better served by putting the emphasis on geographic and regional representation. Canada and the other states of middle rank continued to be saddled with responsibilities, yet denied commensurate influence in international decisions; and the lesson was brought home when Canada found herself drawn into areas beyond her sphere of direct interest because of her general concern for the maintenance of international order.

An outstanding example was the Korean War. Canada had served on the United Nations commission that attempted to arrange for elections to a single Korean assembly. When the Russians barred the commission from visiting North Korea, the Canadian representative opposed the holding of elections for South Korea separately, on the ground that the commission's mandate was to "facilitate and expedite" the election of a national assembly for the whole of Korea, and not just for one part of the country. He was overridden, and Canada subsequently acquiesced in the formation of a South Korean government and its recognition by the United Nations. It was this step that gave the United Nations a direct responsibility for action when the invasion from North Korea was launched in June 1950. Canadian opinion at once recognized the need to uphold the Charter by resisting aggression against a government recognized by the United Nations. Canada was one of sixteen nations that provided troops in response to the appeal of the Secretary-General. A special force of brigade strength was organized and dispatched to Korea; naval forces and air transport were also made available; and by the time the forces were withdrawn in April 1955, they had suffered 1642 casualties, including 406 dead. Among United Nations members, only the United States and the United Kingdom made larger military contributions. Meanwhile, within the United Nations, Canada played an active and a constructive part in the efforts to localize the conflict, and in the attempts to end hostilities which issued in an armistice in June 1953.

Korea demonstrated with inescapable clarity that Canada's international obligations extended beyond the areas of her immediate interests and were likely to involve her increasingly in regions with which she had little or no direct connection. The lesson was underlined in 1954, when Canada reluctantly agreed to serve on the commissions that were set up to supervise the cease-fire agreements in Indo-China; and these commitments in Asia were followed in 1956 by an added involvement in the Middle East as a result of the Suez crisis.

Although the root of the chronic unrest in the Middle East was the creation by the United Nations of a separate state of Israel—a decision that the Canadian delegation avowedly accepted with many misgivings as the least objectionable of the alternatives available—the short-lived outbreak of violence in the autumn of 1956 stemmed also from the clash between Western interests and Arab nationalism under the aegis of the Egyptian leader, Colonel Nasser. The Egyptian nationalization of the Suez Canal Company, without warning, in July aroused the alarm and resentment of Britain and France; the sudden Israeli invasion of Egypt in October presented those powers with an opportunity to intervene in defense of their threatened rights.

The outbreak of hostilities placed Canada in a difficult position. Not only was the United Nations Charter involved; there was also a deep rift between Canada's two closest associates in consequence of the vigorous disapproval of Britain's action on the part of the United States. The Canadian government shared Washington's opposition to the use of force, but went further than the American administration in its desire not merely to end the fighting, but to strive for a new approach to a permanent settlement instead of merely returning to the *status quo ante*.

This larger aim proved to be beyond attainment. There was widespread support in the United Nations for pressure to achieve a ceasefire, but virtually none for any further steps to end the chronic state of tension between the Arabs and the Israelis. Yet it was Canadian initiative that brought into existence a United Nations Emergency Force to secure and supervise a cessation of hostilities, and thus paved the way for the withdrawal of the invading forces from Egyptian soil; and it was Canadians who provided the largest component of the force when it came into being.

Long before this episode, however, it had become clear that the United Nations could not be counted on to secure its members against armed aggression. The Security Council, which was especially charged with the maintenance of international peace and security, was early paralyzed by the veto in the hands of the Soviet Union. The relentless advance of Soviet power, culminating in the Communist coup in Prague in February 1948, convinced the leading Western statesmen that other and more effective means must be found for halting Russian imperialism. In April 1948, Louis St. Laurent publicly called for "the creation and preservation by the nations of the Free World under the leadership of Great Britain, the United States and France, of an overwhelming preponderance of force over any adversary or possible combination of adversaries." This was the prescription which, given further and powerful impetus by the Vandenberg Resolution in the United States Senate in the following June, found its realization in the North Atlantic Treaty of April 4, 1949.

Canada's membership in the North Atlantic Treaty Organization (NATO) meant the assumption of far-flung overseas commitments and of heavy financial obligations. Under the original treaty she was joined in mutual defense arrangements covering most of Western Europe from Norway to Italy and including Iceland and Portugal. In 1951 she accepted a further extension of obligations with the addition of Greece and Turkey to the alliance. In 1954, after serious searchings of heart, the Canadian Parliament ratified the protocol providing for the rearmament of Germany and her admission to NATO. Meanwhile the Communist aggression in Korea had given fresh impetus to Western rearmament and brought a heavy increase in defense efforts and expenditure. Canada provided a brigade of infantry for service in Germany and twelve air squadrons under NATO in Europe, as well as some forty naval craft for defense in the North Atlantic. In addition to these direct costs, Canada contributed to the building of defense facilities and bases in Western Europe, and to the provision of mutual aid to her European allies in the form of arms and an air training program. In 1951 an initial three-year rearmament program was inaugurated at an estimated cost of $5 billion, and defense expenditure at its peak reached approximately $2 billion a year, or just under half the total national budget.

It was hoped at the outset that NATO would be something wider than a purely military alliance. In calling for an overwhelming preponderance of force, St. Laurent emphasized that "it must be economic; it must be moral." It was with this in mind that Canada was particularly insistent on the inclusion of Article 2 with its provision for social and economic cooperation among the signatories. As things turned out, NATO was not the appropriate instrument for implementing such aims, which could be more effectively achieved through other existing bodies such as the Organization for European Economic Cooperation (OEEC). Their membership was wider than that of the Western alliance, and there were few things that the latter could undertake in the economic sphere without overlapping with the work of other international organs. In consequence, NATO as an organization remained almost entirely military as far as its actual functioning was concerned. Yet Canadian opinion remained strongly desirous of establishing a wider basis, and there were repeated demands that more positive efforts be made to translate Article 2 into a working reality. The hope that NATO might be the first step toward the creation of a true Atlantic Community was a significant indication of

Canada's conviction that her own national destiny was inseparable from the fortunes of the North Atlantic region of which she was so integral a part.

In this wider grouping, Canada's dual position as a North American state and a member of the Commonwealth of Nations could now be maintained with relatively few difficulties or dilemmas. The North Atlantic Treaty Organization was the common base for the global policies in the Cold War in which Canada's closest associates, the United States and Great Britain, shared common objectives; and while Canada's connection with Britain was the initial basis for her Commonwealth connections, postwar developments gave her an increasing sense of direct interest in the broadening evolution of that unique institution.

The most striking event was the emergence of the new Asian members and the new geographical and racial diversity that resulted within the Commonwealth. The grant of independence to India in 1947 was accompanied by partition into four separate units; and although Burma opted out, the three remaining states—India, Pakistan, and Ceylon—all chose to retain their Commonwealth connections. Self-government was no longer confined to the settled Dominions with populations of predominantly European stock—indeed, the ranks of these older members were reduced when Ireland, in what may have been an over-hasty decision, withdrew to become an independent republic in April 1949. The trend was now toward an increasingly multiracial basis as Britain pursued her proclaimed policy of leading the colonies progressively along the road to self-government. In 1957, Ghana and Malaya attained full Commonwealth membership, and Nigeria, the West Indies, and Central Africa were approaching the same goal.

This process brought with it certain formal changes that were symbolic of the changed situation. The designation "British Commonwealth" was quietly dropped in favor of "Commonwealth of Nations." The convenient word "Dominion" also disappeared from usage in deference to a feeling that it somehow implied domination. Most significant of all, the common crown, on which the Balfour Report of 1926 had laid such stress, failed to survive as a symbol of Commonwealth unity: India, on achieving independence, resolved to adopt a republican form of government; Pakistan and Ceylon, in due course, reached a similar decision; republican sentiment was growing in South Africa. The question of how republicanism could be reconciled with Commonwealth membership was resolved at the Prime Ministers' Conference in 1949. India was recognized by the other members as a sovereign independent republic, and India on her part accepted "the King as the symbol of the free association of its independent members and as such the Head of the Commonwealth." This had the consequence that while Commonwealth members remained "freely associated" they were no longer "united by a common allegiance." Even the older members who continued to recognize the monarchy were ultimately obliged to realize that there was no longer a common crown, and that the king was separately sovereign over each of his realms. When Elizabeth II came to the throne in 1953, the Canadian proclamation described her as "of the United Kingdom, Canada and Her other Realms and territories Queen, Head of the Commonwealth." The title signified that Canada was now a monarchy in her own right, and it was as Queen of Canada that Elizabeth opened Canada's Parliament during her visit in 1957.

Canada's attachment to the Commonwealth was marked by a favorable attitude toward the flexibility that made it possible to reconcile new republics with an ancient monarchy and to maintain a free and sovereign association between lands of differing cultures and many diverse races. There was particular concern to cultivate close and friendly relations with the new Asian members. In the tensions of the Cold War the attitude of the uncommitted nations outside Europe could be of decisive importance. Through the Asian members of the Commonwealth the West could seek a bridge to Asia in general, accepting the right of such a country as India to maintain a policy of noncommitment, but seeking in return to encourage a greater understanding of Western policies and to strengthen the bonds of common interest. The world tour of Prime Minister Louis St. Laurent in 1954 was particularly designed to strengthen Canada's links with her Asian associates, as was the later visit of Minister of Health Paul Martin in 1956.

These impulses found concrete expression in Canada's contribution to the Colombo Plan. The contrast between plenty in the West and poverty in the East aroused humanitarian consciences; it also offered a ground on which communism could present a serious challenge to the appeal of democracy. Various aspects of the problem were already being tackled by the specialized agencies of the United Nations, and their efforts were supplemented by the adoption of an expanded program of technical assistance in 1950, to whose budget Canada was by 1955 the third largest contributor with a grant of $1.8 million. The sums involved were, however, meager in relation to the vastness of the needs; and by 1950 the efforts of India in particular to embark on a large-scale plan of development, and the impossibility of carrying it out in full without substantial aid from outside, stimulated the formulation of a specifically Commonwealth program at a meeting of the foreign ministers in Colombo.

The plan initially envisaged the provision of some $5.2 billion over a period of six years. Its scope was soon extended beyond the Commonwealth proper to cover the countries of Southeast Asia and to associate the United States and its Point Four Program with the Colombo Plan operations. Next to the United States, Canada provided the largest cash contribution, with an initial annual grant of $25 million for capital developments plus $400,000 for technical assistance—amounts that were increased in 1957 to a total of $35 million. These funds helped to finance a wide variety of projects—a cement plant in Pakistan, a nuclear reactor in India, power and irrigation and transportation developments in several countries—that were significant contributions to the efforts to raise the general standard of living in South and Southeast Asia.

These varied enterprises, from NATO to the Colombo Plan, exemplify the position of Canada which, second in rank to the Great Powers, has the obligations that go with that status yet lacks the full resources that would enable her to undertake major projects on her own initiative in the field of world affairs. To make her aims effective, she must count on working in close cooperation with her major associates and on a basis which they are prepared to accept; and of all those associates, the one whose importance is paramount for Canada is the great neighbor with whom she must live in such close and continuous contact.

It is hardly too much to say that, for the majority of Canadians, relations with the United States during the postwar era were matters of almost daily concern. In economic relations, in cultural influences, in the multiplicity of personal contacts back and forth across the border, there were woven those ties of interdependence that made for a common outlook and for common action in virtually every significant sphere. Inevitably, such contacts were of more importance to the smaller and more dependent country than to the larger and more self-sufficient one. Complaints that seemed trivial to the United States were serious to Canada, and their frequently cavalier treatment by Washington was a recurrent cause of Canadian irritation. In trade policies especially, and to a lesser degree in matters concerning international waterways, there were controversies that might seem minor in the larger perspective, but that nonetheless gave rise to a measure of friction between the two countries.

More than these direct relations, however, American conduct in the field of world politics attracted Canadian interest and concern. In the Cold War, the fortunes of the common cause rested to a very large extent in the hands of the United States. The wisdom and effectiveness of American policy could affect for good or ill the safety and stability of the whole Free

World; and Canada, like other smaller associates, had a vital stake in American actions which she could not control and which she could only rarely hope to influence.

This interest extended to various American domestic policies which had obvious external consequences. The system of farm price supports, for instance, created agricultural surpluses which then had to be disposed of abroad by methods to which Canada took strong exception. In the political field, any manifestations that weakened the moral position of the United States as a champion of democratic freedoms were of legitimate concern to countries that regarded the strength of the United States as a major element in their own security. In the eyes of Canadians, the atmosphere of persecution and repression that developed during the brief ascendancy of Senator Joseph McCarthy of Wisconsin was not only odious in itself, but also a cause of real perturbation because of its damage to American prestige abroad. To this was added the widespread indignation on Canada's own account, resulting from the reckless way in which the Senate Internal Security Subcommittee bandied about the names of Canadian citizens and officials and treated with indifference the assurances as well as the protests of the Canadian government. The resentment reached its climax in the spring of 1957, when the suicide of E. Herbert Norman, Canadian ambassador in Cairo, was widely attributed to the Subcommittee's persistent repetition of unfounded accusations, and the tragedy contributed to an upsurge of anti-American sentiment in Canada that found some reflection in the subsequent election campaign.

In the general field of world politics there was a wide measure of harmony. Canadians fully appreciated the massive contribution of the United States to world security and stability. The Marshall Plan for aid to Europe was hailed for its imaginative generosity. The willingness of the United States to shoulder the main burden in the common defense effort was the indispensable foundation of NATO. These were matters in which Canada had a vital stake, and in which her own objectives could not have been achieved without the assumption of leadership by the United States.

Outside the Atlantic area there was somewhat less identity of viewpoints. In particular, American policy toward China, with its insistent support of Chiang Kai-Shek and its refusal to consider recognition of the communist regime on the mainland, found relatively meager support in Canada. Recognition of Communist China by Canada, which was under consideration in 1950, was put off when the Korean War broke out; but Canada made it clear on a number of occasions that she was in no way committed to support the Chinese Nationalists in their possession of

Formosa, and formally dissociated herself from American military measures in that area.

It was, indeed, American pronouncements and actions in the Far East that aroused the most vocal doubts in Canada about the reliability of American world policies. Advocacy by some American leaders of the use of atomic weapons in Korea, and of forcible intervention at the height of the crisis in Indo-China, and the possibility of war in defense of the Nationalist foothold on the offshore islands of Quemoy and Matsu were viewed with considerable apprehension. Individual actions by the United States, and particularly action which seemed to risk bringing a new world war down on the heads of all the free nations which looked to America as their leader, could only arouse doubts and uncertainties on the part of an associate who would have to bear the full disastrous consequences of a fatal misstep.

None of these considerations, however, seriously disturbed the solid basis of Canadian-American cooperation in world affairs or the close coordination of measures for the defense of North America. Through the Permanent Joint Board on Defense, established in 1940, the close coordination that had been achieved during the war was maintained and developed after the close of hostilities. It found expression in 1947 in an agreement for coordination of training methods, a measure of standardization of equipment, reciprocal access to various defense facilities, and joint exercises for specialized training and experiment in such problems as Arctic defense. In particular, cooperation for air defense on a continental basis moved steadily closer to complete integration, and reached a climax in 1957 with agreement on a common air command (NORAD) under an American commander with a Canadian deputy. No two countries in the Western Hemisphere or the Atlantic Alliance had such close arrangements on a direct bilateral basis as had the United States and Canada in the field of mutual defense.

Among other things, this involved the grant of facilities for the stationing of United States armed forces on Canadian soil. To some extent this was a legacy of the wartime agreements that granted to the United States a number of leased bases on British territory. When Newfoundland entered the confederation in 1949, Canada took over the arrangements that provided for American bases at St. John's, Argentia, and Stephenville. The new situation called for a renegotiation of certain aspects of the original agreements which were looked on as impairments of Canada's sovereignty, including the tax exemptions granted to civilians connected with the American military establishments and the jurisdiction by American military authorities over Canadian civilians in the base areas.

With good will on both sides, a satisfactory agreement on these and other minor matters was reached on May 1, 1951. The United States continued in full possession of the bases, and other United States forces in due course were stationed at various radar installations whose development was one of the outstanding examples of Canadian-American cooperation.

The possibility of a long-range bomber attack, whose logical route would be over the polar regions, brought pressure from the United States for the joint development of a radar system that would cover the northern approaches. By 1955 the Pinetree Line in the general vicinity of the Canadian-American border was in operation, and this was supplemented by a series of automatic warning stations—the mid-Canada line or McGill Fence—along the 55th parallel. The latter was operated and paid for by Canada; the Pinetree Line was jointly financed and was manned in part by American personnel. A more formidable project was the Distant Early Warning System (DEW-line) across the top of the continent. Canada was frankly skeptical of its value and balked at the cost of some $600 million in addition to her existing defense burden. When, however, the United States continued to insist that the line was vital for security, Canada felt that she could not stand in the way. By an agreement on May 5, 1955, the United States assumed the full cost of construction. The line was originally manned by American personnel, but Canada reserved the right ultimately to take over its operation. Some apprehensions were expressed that this might mean the abdication of effective Canadian authority over the Arctic, but on the whole the arrangements worked with relative harmony, and the fears abated as the line gradually lapsed into desuetude with the replacement of the manned bomber by the intercontinental missile as the main weapon of long-range attack.

Federalism and Politics, 1945-1958

Behind these varied activities on the international stage stood a nation that was steadily growing not only in strength but in national coherence and unity. Ethnic and sectional differences still lingered, but for the moment they seemed to be subordinated to the new sense of national identity that had evolved during the war and postwar years. Never in the entire course of Canada's history had there been less chronic friction between internal groups or a more pervasive sense of community throughout all sections of the population.

The physical extent of the community was enlarged when Newfoundland at long last abandoned its stubborn aloofness and entered as the tenth province. Confederation had been rejected in 1867, and negotiations in 1894 broke down over the financial terms of union. Newfoundland remained a separate colony with its own responsible government, and attained Dominion status for a time after World War I. The depression, however, brought on a financial crisis, from which Newfoundland was rescued by the United Kingdom at the price of suspending self-government and accepting the rule of an appointed commission.

The economic situation improved during World War II. Newfoundland became a key strategic area, and the establishment of Canadian and American bases and various other wartime activities brought about a temporary prosperity that was reflected in a series of budget surpluses. By the end of the war, Newfoundland was in a position to consider whether the island should remain under commission government or resume control of its own affairs, and in 1946, a national convention was elected to decide on the future course.

By this time the idea of union with Canada was once more in the air. Canadian interest had been stimulated by strategic considerations and wartime contacts; Newfoundland's economic orientation toward Canada had been growing with the development of trading, financial, and transportation connections, as well as contacts in such fields as education and religion. Mackenzie King in 1943 and St. Laurent in 1946 had hinted at Canadian willingness to consider union if Newfoundland wished; but Canada tactfully refrained from pressing for any such step and left any initiative to Newfoundland itself.

The convention at first showed little enthusiasm for the idea. A motion by Joseph R. Smallwood, an energetic journalist who became the leader of the confederation movement, proposing that a delegation be sent to Ottawa to discuss terms, was initially voted down. The leading alternatives were to continue under the commission or return to responsible government. But support for commission government gradually waned; the United Kingdom refused to promise continued financial aid in restoring separate self-rule; and in the summer of 1947 the Convention sent a mission to Ottawa to investigate the prospects of union on a "fair and equitable basis." By the end of October, draft proposals were worked out, and in the following year the voters of Newfoundland were called on to make their decision.

It took two separate votes for a conclusion to be reached. In the first referendum on June 3, 1947, three choices were involved. Commission government received a relatively small number of votes, but neither responsible government nor confederation attracted a clear majority, though the former obtained a slight margin of preference by winning 44.5 as against 41 percent of the vote. A second referendum, this time presenting a clear choice between responsible government and confederation, was held on July 22, and brought a majority of just under 7000 votes in favor of union with Canada. The margin was slim, but it meant that 53 percent of the voters had pronounced in favor of the proposal, and the Canadian government decided to accept this as an adequate expression of the popular will. Negotiations, which went on from October 6 to December 11, settled the final terms of entry, and the formal union took place on March 31, 1949.

The terms were not ungenerous. Although Newfoundland gave up the revenue from customs duties and came under the higher Canadian tariff system, the new province would get the benefit of such Canadian welfare services as family allowances and old-age pensions. Canada would assume the provincial debt and pay the customary annual subsidies as in the case of other provinces, and would in addition provide transitional grants totaling $42,750,000 on a descending scale over a period of twelve years. These terms were to be reviewed within eight years; in fact, when a Royal Commission was appointed for the purpose in 1957, it was evident that Newfoundland's economic needs were even more extensive than the original agreement envisaged.

The addition of one more province extended the range but in no way altered the essential pattern of federal-provincial relations. Experience had by now developed a tacit demarcation of spheres of action that translated the terms of the constitution into practical application and presented relatively few occasions for any serious conflict of interests. If there was an exception to this, it was in Quebec, where Maurice Duplessis continued to use the defense of French-Canadian culture as a political stock in trade and to demand eternal vigilance against the centralizing tendencies of Ottawa. Yet in the prevailing atmosphere of general national harmony it was often hard for the premier to find concrete threats against which to crusade, and his colorful campaigns at times had the air of a popular emotional indulgence rather than a battle over issues of genuine significance.

In fact, the extension of federal constitutional authority in this period took the form of removing nearly all the remaining vestiges of external restraint. Appeals to the Privy Council were abolished in December, 1949, following a Privy Council decision of 1947 that such action now lay within

Canada's power. Leave to appeal might still be granted in cases that were already in process, but in any new cases the Supreme Court of Canada was henceforth the final resort—which meant that the judicial interpretation of the Canadian constitution was at last vested in Canada's own courts.

A step, though still only a limited one, was also taken toward the right of constitutional amendment when a British statute in 1949 conferred on the Canadian Parliament the right to amend the British North America Act where purely federal powers were concerned. This did not extend to any alteration of the distribution of powers as between the federal and provincial governments, and legislation affecting the use of English or French or the duration of the House of Commons was also excluded. This left a broad and important field in which amendments still had to be sought from the Parliament of the United Kingdom. In January 1950, a federal-provincial conference met to explore the possibility of devising a satisfactory process of amendment that would cover the whole constitution. The conference defined six broad categories, each of which would call for a different type of amending procedure, and set up a continuing committee of attorneys general to discuss details. The report of the committee when the conference reconvened in September revealed a considerable measure of agreement on the less controversial aspects, but on such matters as the distribution of powers and the protection of fundamental rights the difficulties were still unsolved. The committee was instructed to continue its efforts, but at the end of 1950 these were suspended pending a settlement of federal-provincial financial issues, and the question of the amending power remained in abeyance for the rest of the Liberal regime.

Yet while the amending power that had been secured was thus confined within relatively narrow limits, it was not without its usefulness. It was first exercised in 1952 to effect the decennial redistribution of representation in the House of Commons, whose basis had already been altered by a United Kingdom amendment in 1946. The original basis, by which Quebec was given the fixed number of sixty-five seats and the other provinces were represented on a proportional basis according to population, had by that date given rise to dissatisfaction. Quebec in particular felt that successive readjustments over a period of eighty years had left that province underrepresented, and a new formula was therefore adopted. Instead of fixing the standard by taking Quebec as a criterion, the new measure laid down the total number of members for the Commons and divided this number among the provinces on a population basis. Since this was a constitutional provision, it must be amended whenever redistribution involved the need for a change in the total membership, and such a change could now be effected at the necessary intervals on the sole authority of the Canadian Parliament. The result of the redistribution in 1952, together with the provision for seven members from Newfoundland, was to bring the total membership of the Commons to 265; while the Senate, with six members added from Newfoundland, now stood at 102.

In the strict field of federal-provincial relations, the most serious and persistent controversy was concerned with public finance. The Rowell-Sirois Report, with its proposals for a readjustment of revenues as between the provincial and federal governments, had not itself been implemented, but much the same result was achieved by the wartime tax agreements under which the provinces agreed to refrain from levying income and corporation taxes in return for compensation on the basis of federal revenue from these sources. This temporary arrangement proved useful in economizing on administration and in equalizing the burden among the provinces, and efforts were made to continue it on a more permanent basis after the end of the war.

The matter was discussed in a federal-provincial conference which met in August 1945 and held a second session in April 1946. The federal government proposed that the provinces relinquish succession duties as well as income and corporation taxes in return for federal subsidies, and that Ottawa extend its responsibility for social security. It proved impossible to reach any general agreement. Ottawa fell back on fresh tax rental agreements with all the provinces except Ontario and Quebec, and Ontario in 1952 made a separate agreement to hand over corporation and income tax revenue while retaining succession duties. It was a scheme which on the whole worked to the general advantage, in spite of periodic rumblings of discontent from the various parties involved.

There was in this period a growing tendency for the political complexion of the provinces to diverge from that of the central government. The Union Nationale in Quebec, the Progressive Conservatives in Ontario, the CCF in Saskatchewan, Social Credit in Alberta—all retained power with fluctuating but still comfortable majorities. The virtual collapse of the older parties in British Columbia provincial politics left the main battlefield to Social Credit and the CCF and brought a Social Credit ministry to power in 1952. New Brunswick swung from Liberals to Conservatives in 1952; Nova Scotia followed suit in 1956. By 1957 only the two easternmost provinces of Newfoundland and Prince Edward Island were under Liberal rule, though Manitoba, with a Liberal-Progressive majority, might be counted as a doubtful third.

Yet this decline of the Liberals at the provincial level found little reflection in federal politics, where the Liberals maintained their ascendancy through three successive postwar elections. If one explanation for the continuance in power of other parties in the provinces was their record of satisfactory administration combined with a general level of prosperity, the same reasons could be given for the success of the Liberals in the federal field. The competence and energy that the government showed in its handling of wartime problems were also displayed in its postwar activities. The transition from war to peace was accomplished without major dislocations. Wartime controls were gradually abolished as the need disappeared. Social services were extended with the inauguration of family allowances in 1945, the broadening of old-age pensions in 1951, and the formulation of a scheme for hospital services in cooperation with the provinces in 1956. An expanding and prosperous economy at home, an increase in Canada's stature in the world outside, could be at least partly attributed to sound policies on the part of the national government.

The long reign of Mackenzie King now drew to its close. On June 9, 1946, he surpassed the nineteen-year record of Sir John Alexander Macdonald in length of service as Prime Minister of Canada; on April 20, 1948, he exceeded that of Sir Robert Walpole—twenty years and ten months—as Prime Minister of any country in the Commonwealth. It was an achievement on which his heart had clearly been set, and which satisfied him as the climax of his political career. He resigned as leader of the Liberal party on August 5, 1948, and as Prime Minister in the following November. Two years later, on July 22, 1950, death came to him at the age of seventy-nine.

His successor as party leader was Louis St. Laurent, who had been personally persuaded by Mackenzie King to enter public life in 1941, when the death of Ernest Lapointe deprived the party of its veteran federal leader in Quebec. St. Laurent, a highly successful corporation lawyer who had previously shown little interest in politics, proved admirably fitted to fill this vital spot and to hold Quebec to its Liberal allegiance. His unquestioned integrity, his attachment to liberal principles in the Laurier tradition, and his staunch devotion to Canadian national ideals rather than to any local attachment, quickly gained the respect and loyalty of his followers, while his moderation in partisan conflicts combined with his benevolent manner won him the affectionate popular title of "Uncle Louie." On November 15, 1948, he was sworn in as Prime Minister of Canada; and in spite of persistent reports that he meant to retire after a brief and temporary tenure, he continued to lead the party until defeat overtook it in 1957.

Meanwhile the Conservatives remained the official party of opposition. Although the CCF and Social Credit parties maintained their foothold in national politics, their strength was largely regional, and neither one showed any prospect of displacing either of the older parties as a major political force with a truly national appeal. Even the Conservatives found it hard to offer a successful challenge to the Liberals on the basis of either policies or leadership. In the election of 1945 the Liberals lost 59 seats, but the Conservatives gained only 28, while the remainder were distributed among minor parties and independents, and the Liberals retained a comfortable lead with 125 seats to 67 for the Conservatives.

Leadership remained a chronic problem. John Bracken was generally liked and respected, but he failed to infuse the party with a new dynamic spirit or provide it with any fresh popular appeal. When he resigned as leader in 1948, the party chose as his successor George Drew, a vigorous campaigner who had demonstrated outstanding political talents as Premier of Ontario. But Drew's transfer to the federal field brought no improvement in the fortunes of his party. In 1949 the Conservatives won only 41 seats to 190 for the Liberals; in 1953 the corresponding figures were 51 and 170.

Ill-health brought George Drew's retirement in 1956. His successor was John Diefenbaker, a Saskatchewan lawyer, who first entered Parliament in 1940. The new leader at once embarked on a vigorous campaign, covering the country from coast to coast and assailing the government in rolling oratorical phrases whose fervent rhetoric reflected his Baptist background. Yet on the eve of the elections of 1957, few observers expected a Conservative victory. It was conceded that the Liberals would lose a number of seats; but on June 9, the day before the election, so detached a commentator as the editorial writer in the *New York Times* remarked of the Liberals that "it would take a political miracle to defeat them and there is no reason to expect such a spectacular overturn."

It was in fact the unexpected that happened. The Conservatives emerged as the leading party with 112 seats; the Liberals were reduced to 105. Neither party had a clear majority, and any government would be dependent on the votes of the minor parties. The Liberals decided not to try to continue on this basis, but to hand over the reins of power to their opponents, who had the larger number of seats. On June 21, 1957, John Diefenbaker was sworn in as Prime Minister and head of the first Conservative administration in twenty-two years.

Hindsight suggested a variety of explanations for the outcome. Farmers, and particularly the western farmers burdened with a mounting wheat surplus, felt that Ottawa had not been properly sympathetic toward their plight. Rising prices brought demands for larger social benefits, and the government's action in raising old-age pensions by only $6 a month evoked more resentment than gratitude. There was a feeling that the federal government was unduly slow in implementing the promised hospital plan for which several provinces were pressing. The government's efforts to curb inflation by restricting credit created a good deal of resentment, while the failure of the latest budget to reduce taxes in spite of successive surpluses, though it may have been economically sound and politically courageous, brought no increase in popularity.

This accumulation of widely scattered discontents produced an atmosphere of restiveness that developed into active hostility as a result of the debate over the Trans-Canada pipeline. The government's determination to push through its own particular scheme in the face of all criticism and protest, the use of closure to curtail debate in the Commons, the heated criticism of the Speaker for allegedly partisan rulings—all contributed to an impression that the Liberals had grown arrogant in their long tenure of power and needed to be taught a lesson. A particular focus for resentment was C. D. Howe, Minister of Trade and Commerce, who had a record of notable achievement as Director of War Production and Minister of Trade and Commerce, but whose impatience with parliamentary procedures and contempt for both political and popular opposition were all too open and evident. As chastened members of the defeated government were prompt to confess, the party had lost touch with its constituents during these years in office. The time had come to build anew; and while the Conservatives embarked on the complex task of consolidating and extending their new and precarious ascendancy, the Liberals began the search for new policies and new leadership that would retrieve the errors of the past.

The mantle fell to Lester B. Pearson, whose stature as an international figure was underlined by the award to him of the Nobel Peace Prize at the end of 1957. St. Laurent had announced on September 6 that he meant to retire as soon as a convention could choose his successor. During the remainder of the year he was almost ostentatiously inactive in either parliamentary or party affairs. The convention met in Ottawa in January 1958, and on January 16, "Mike" Pearson was chosen leader by 1074 votes against 305 for his close associate and only serious rival, Paul Martin, the former Minister of National Health and Welfare.

The echoes of the convention had scarcely died away before the party was plunged into a new election campaign. The Conservatives had shrewdly decided to take the tide of fortune while it was still at the flood. They had shown in their first test of office that they could form an administration of reasonable competence in spite of a lack of previous experience. They had come through their first parliamentary session with considerable credit and without serious mistakes that might alienate any substantial section of the electorate. The Liberals, thrown into disarray by the June debacle and deprived of effective leadership through the months that followed, had been relatively ineffective in opposition. It was a propitious time for John Diefenbaker to appeal for a clear majority that would enable him to embark on a positive and constructive program. On February 1, Parliament was dissolved, and a new election was called for March 31.

The decision was triumphantly vindicated by the outcome. In a tremendous electoral sweep the government was returned with the largest majority that any party had ever received since Confederation. The Conservatives, with 208 seats, carried every province except Newfoundland. The Liberals were reduced to 49 seats, almost wholly from Ontario and Quebec. Not one Liberal was returned from the West, and in the Atlantic provinces there were only three from New Brunswick in addition to the five from Newfoundland. The CCF was down to eight members, and not a single Social Credit member survived.

One of the most significant features was the turnover in Quebec. That province, which had been Liberal in federal politics for over half a century, now swung decisively with the tide, helped by the unavowed but highly effective support accorded to the Conservatives by the Duplessis machine. The 9 seats that the Conservatives had won in 1957 rose to 50 in 1958; the Liberals sank from 64 to 25. Yet it was further significant that the success of the Conservative party throughout the rest of Canada placed it in the almost unique position of being able to command a clear majority even without the support of the members of Quebec. A new pattern was evidently emerging in Canadian politics that would set its mark on the second half of the century.

A Prairie Oil Well, early 1950s.   *(George Hunter)*

A Newsprint Mill at Powell River, B.C, as it looked in the early 1950s.

(George Hunter)

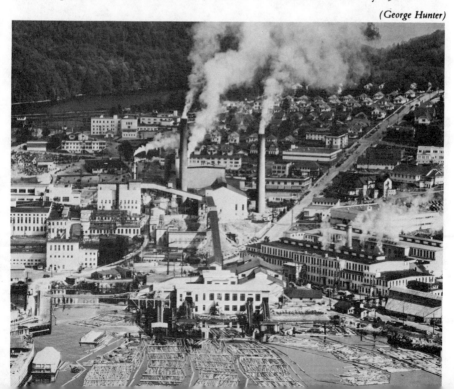

Power from Niagara.   *(Ontario Hydro)*
Sir Adam Beck generating stations six miles below the falls near Queenston.

Canada in NATO.   *(Department of National Defence)*
Canadian troops in Germany engaged in a ground-air training exercise.

Louis St. Laurent. *(Public Archives of Canada)*
Acknowledging the cheers which greeted his election as Liberal leader in succession to Mackenzie King.

Power from the Seaway. *(Ontario Hydro)*
An international project built jointly by Ontario Hydro and Power Authority of New York.

The Queen in Canada.
Elizabeth II, with Prince Philip on her left, reads the Speech from the Throne at the opening of the Canadian Parliament in 1957.

Chapter 22

Troubled Centennial

Economic Aspects of the Sixties

In 1967 Canada celebrated the completion of its first century as a federated state. A royal visit commemorated the occasion; operas were commissioned and literary works subsidized; civic cultural centers proliferated across the land; canoe teams traversed the routes of the fur brigades, and mountain climbers assailed hitherto unconquered peaks in the Rockies. The national focus was a world's fair, Expo 67, at Montreal on two islands in the St. Lawrence, one of them wholly man-made—a spectacular triumph that attracted over 50 million visitors, statistically if not individually more than double the population of Canada.

The exuberance behind these activities might have seemed somewhat restrained in the eyes of less phlegmatic nations. The century had seen many striking achievements. There was a deep if quiet pride in the record of Canada's accomplishments and in the kind of nation that Canadians had built. Yet there seemed to be lacking a sense of climax, a confidence that a definitive stage had been brought to completion which would provide a solid and assured foundation for an advance to further triumphs in the decades ahead. The preoccupations were less with the past than with a troubled and uncertain present and with perplexities as to the course which conflicting factors, internal as well as external, would dictate in a future that was still obscure.

In material terms Canada had reason to feel that it was among the most favored of nations. Gross national product had risen to a rate of almost $65 billion by early 1968 and was still growing. In spite of a moderate decline in the rate of natural increase, population continued to expand to over 20 million. Immigration slumped during the recession of the late fifties to a postwar low of 71,689 in 1961—barely in excess of the estimated exodus from Canada—but better times brought a new influx which once more exceeded 200,000 in 1967.

It may reasonably be speculated that the newcomers added their

637

influence to the changes that were taking place in social attitudes. Throughout the Western world the inhibitions of the Victorian era had now all but vanished. Canada experienced with other lands the results of the relaxation of manners and morals, the revolt of youth against formal conventions, the disregard of law and authority, that marked the postwar era. There was no reason to suppose that New Canadians, inheritors of traditions that differed in many respects from the puritan background that had been especially strong in English Canada, would act as impediments to these trends. The cautious modifications of provincial liquor laws and the relaxation of Sunday observance with the permission of Sunday sports and commercial entertainment were inhibited more by a lingering native distrust of anything savoring of sinful indulgence than by influences intruded from abroad. And in the enrichment of cultural life through increased interest in music and ballet as well as the preservation of traditional folk cultures, the mounting diversity of recent racial origins had a discernible effect.

The political consequences, while not easy to document with precision, were not to be neglected. Adult immigrants granted full citizenship, and thus eligible to vote, ran around 50,000 a year. While this was small compared with the number of native-born who annually reached voting age, it had a real significance. Nearly nine-tenths of the immigrants had flocked to urban centers. They comprised a substantial proportion of the voters in certain urban constituencies. In an era of minority governments, the capture of a few such seats could be decisive. The new voters, unattached by habit or upbringing to any specific party, were a floating electorate open to various forms of influence or persuasion, and added to the factors of uncertainty in any political contest.

The urban orientation of the migrants was a national consequence of the policy of selection based on the skills that were needed and could be absorbed in the current state of the Canadian economy. To the extent that this was implemented, their advent added to the fund of skills so essential to economic progress. There were occasional grumblings by organized labor about foreign competition for Canadian jobs, but the new workers were also customers who increased the domestic market for Canadian products and thus provided new employment.

Between 1957 and 1964, the labor force rose from 6 to 7 million. This period saw the decline of agricultural employment from 740,000 to 630,000, so that more than the net increase was absorbed in the production of other forms of goods and services. There were, of course, fluctuations in the ability to provide full employment. A temporary recession brought a rise in unemployment to a postwar peak of 11.3 percent in 1961, and a crisis in which the unemployment insurance fund faced imminent bankruptcy; but recovery eased the threat, and by the end of 1965 unemployment had receded to a more tolerable 3.6 percent.

Recovery also brought with it an upsurge of labor restiveness. The continued rise in consumer prices, which led to a short-lived campaign by women shoppers against a number of supermarkets, spurred demands for higher wages, accentuated in the case of certain international unions by efforts to attain the same wage levels as their counterparts in the United States. The accompanying strikes, which affected a variety of groups from postal workers to school teachers, were particularly worrisome in the vital field of transportation. Rail and air services both suffered from interruptions. A seaway strike was barely averted in 1966 by a substantial pay rise, and resistance to further demands brought a damaging halt to traffic by a strike in 1968. Strikes by longshoremen in 1966 closed Quebec ports for five weeks during the early summer and British Columbia ports for three weeks in late autumn, seriously disrupting the flow of exports and jeopardizing the important contracts for wheat shipments to China and the Soviet Union.

The serious consequences of industrial conflict produced in certain instances the intervention of public authority. Several provinces tightened the provisions governing mandatory conciliation procedure and the definition of legal strikes. The Newfoundland government secured authority to dissolve a union whose officers had engaged in criminal activities. Alberta outlawed secondary boycotts and picketing in jurisdictional strikes. Quebec in 1967 passed legislation ordering striking teachers back to their classrooms. The federal government intervened in the rail strike in 1966 with a bill demanding a return to work and the resumption of negotiations leading to a settlement. More far-reaching in its implications was the measure to end hoodlumism and violence on the Great Lakes, which accompanied the bitter conflict between rival unions, by placing all the maritime unions in Canada under federal trusteeship—a step which, significantly, had the official support of the Canadian Labor Congress. The rights of labor to organize and to strike remained basically unimpaired; but these measures were warnings signs that the exercise of such rights must take responsible account of the public interest or be further restricted to minimize the harm to economic stability and social harmony.

An expanding economy called for a labor force that was adequate not only in numbers but in quality. Modern industrial states had less and less place for the unskilled and the incompetent; and Canada, combining plentiful natural resources with access to the most advanced Western techniques, sought not merely to increase its volume of industrial output but to raise progressively the level of sophistication of its industrial structure. The limits to which this process could be carried, given full exercise of initiative and ingenuity, arose more from restricted opportunities than from any lack of potential. The domestic market was often too small for profitable ventures in highly specialized products, while political as well as economic barriers at times impeded access to foreign markets. Canadian technology could produce a highly successful atomic reactor, fueled by natural uranium and using heavy water as its coolant, but to be commercially profitable it must find customers abroad in competition with rival types. A striking illustration of the problem was the case of the CF–105 military airplane commonly known as the Arrow. This was a supersonic interceptor, designed to give a much-advanced efficiency to continental air defense against the still existing threat from the manned bomber. But the United States preferred to develop its own counterpart of this weapon rather than rely on Canadian sources; for technical reasons the weapon did not fit the air defense structure of Western Europe; and with the intercontinental missile likely to replace the bombers within a few years, the cost of development and production of a weapon doomed to early obsolescence seemed too formidable for Canada alone. The project was cancelled early in 1959, at the price of the loss to Canada of a large part of the force of skilled technologists who had been engaged on it.

Here was an example of the economic limitations that placed the higher reaches of modern industrial enterprise beyond Canada's grasp. In compensation, world demand for a wide range of Canadian products, both primary and manufactured, continued to mount. Exports expanded from less than $5 billion in 1957 to over $10 billion in 1966, and from 1961 on there was a favorable balance of exports over imports in commodity trade. A series of massive wheat sales to China and the Soviet Union from 1958 on contributed substantially to this rise. Exports of wheat and flour soared from $473 million in 1960 to $1124 million in 1964, and wheat resumed its role as a leading staple in Canada's trade abroad.

The United States remained Canada's best customer and the chief source of Canada's imports. Sales to the United States in 1966 were $6226 billion; purchases of $7132 billion left a trade deficit of just under a billion dollars. While this situation brought a revival in some quarters of the old advocacy of economic continentalism, stimulated by the establishment of the

European Common Market and by proposals for other regional groups, these never reached the level of official policy. What did emerge was a selective approach to the mutual reduction of trade barriers in the case of certain specific products. A starting point was the automotive industry. Imports of cars and trucks, mainly from the United States, represented a major element in the adverse trade balance with that country. In January 1965 an agreement was reached under which selected firms in both countries, subject to prescribed conditions, could import and export cars and parts duty-free; and on the Canadian side it was understood that the industry had undertaken to expand its North American sales by some $260 million during the next three years. Hotly attacked by various groups on both sides of the border, the pact was defended with equal vigor, and on balance it seems to have produced concrete benefits from the Canadian viewpoint. In June 1967 the Ministry of Industry was claiming that it had created 15,900 new jobs during the past year, and that exports to the United States had risen to $845 million in 1966 from $99 million in 1964. By that time wider adjustments were in prospect as a result of new multilateral agreements for tariff reductions under the General Agreement on Tariffs and Trade—the so-called Kennedy Round—and authorities were looking hopefully to increased sales abroad to offset the increased competition of foreign goods in domestic markets that could be expected to result.

The centennial year thus saw a Canada with an expanding economy, a standard of living second only to that of the United States, a rank in world trade close to that of the industrial Great Powers, and a country whose natural resources and productive capacities held every promise of continued expansion. If the accompanying mood was less of ebullient self-confidence than of sober questioning, it was partly due to a recognition of Canada's vulnerability to changing conditions in a troubled and unstable world, but still more to the besetting problems in domestic affairs which challenged the existing national structure and foreshadowed the need for extensive yet still undefined adjustments in the not too distant future.

Federalism and the Welfare State

Like most other advanced countries, Canada was now firmly committed in principle to a broad system of social security. Its range and levels might vary somewhat from one region or province to another, but the need for public action in such fields as health and education, pensions and welfare services, was all but universally accepted, and imposed new tasks and obligations on governments at all levels from federal to municipal.

The trend found expression in both the adjustment of existing benefits and the expansion of government activity into new fields. Old-age pensions were raised to $75 a month and the age progressively lowered from 70 to 65. The Canada Assistance plan provided supplementary aid for the aged and indigent, and in 1966 a federal measure established a guaranteed minimum income for needy pensioners. Provincial schemes for hospital insurance were inaugurated with federal support. A comprehensive plan for medical care was introduced in Saskatchewan in 1962, to the accompaniment of a three weeks' strike by the doctors in the provinces. Other provinces followed with medicare plans, though more often on a voluntary than a compulsory basis; and federal legislation in 1966 offered financial aid to provincial plans that were universal in coverage and nonprofit in administration under public authority. Meanwhile a Canada Pensions Act, financed by contributions from both workers and employers and applying to earnings between $600 and $5000 a year, further strengthened the prospects of financial security after retirement.

Most of these new functions fell within provincial jurisdiction; and the provinces, already confronted with rapidly rising costs in education and public works, faced demands for health and welfare services that went far beyond their existing available resources. Already, in spite of substantial growth in federal spending, provincial expenditures were rising much more rapidly. As an example, Ontario's appropriation of $575 million for education in 1966 almost equaled the whole provincial budget of a decade earlier; when health and welfare were added, the total was over $754 million. By 1968 the estimates for education alone had soared to $1.1 billion. With the federal government in control of the most important sources of revenue, cooperation between Ottawa and the provinces was indispensable if the dichotomy between jurisdiction and resources was to be reconciled.

As a result, the years beginning with the mid-fifties saw a marathon series of conferences between the federal and provincial governments, interspersed with conferences between the provinces themselves. They ranged over the whole field of social welfare as the negotiators sought to hammer out mututally acceptable arrangements on such matters as pensions and medicare, provincial participation in the trans-Canada highway system, and federal aid to higher education. Basic to every issue was the question of finance; and linked with this were the constitutional problems arising from the federal system, and particularly from the existing distribution of powers.

By 1960 it was clear that the postwar system of tax rental agreements was breaking down. Quebec in particular was demanding that Ottawa withdraw from most of the joint welfare programs and hand over a larger share of tax revenue to the provinces. Other provinces, while readier to cooperate in social projects, were hardly less insistent on more generous contributions from federal revenues. Successive conferences worked out the compromises that replaced tax rental by a proportional sharing of the yields from succession duties and income and corporation taxes, accompanied by equalization grants to the less prosperous provinces which would bring their income closer to the national average. Arguments, however, continued over the percentages demanded by the provinces; and by 1966 Ottawa was offering to withdraw from certain fields such as hospital insurance and hand over to the provinces the revenues devoted to their cost. If the provinces wanted more, they must raise it themselves. The resulting criticisms and complaints made it clear that this could be no final solution and that fiscal relations would remain a persistent and worrying problem in the federal structure.

On the surface it might seem that the simple answer would be to let the provinces decide on their own programs and find the money as best they could. It was not a method that had any serious advocacy, at least outside Quebec. Economic disparities between the various regions were far too great; the resources available to all but the wealthiest provinces were far too limited. There was a conviction that the national well-being demanded a reasonable equality in health, education, and social security throughout the whole community. Only the federal government could assure this, and only the federal government could adopt and implement the policies that would give vigor and direction to the national economy as a whole. Premier John Robarts of Ontario, while demanding revenues adequate to the needs of the province, stated forthrightly: "I doubt very much whether Ontario can accept a federal system which is not based on the principle of a single national economy, and, furthermore, a single national government which has control over that economy."

Yet the stubborn fact remained that the growth of the welfare state had brought with it a major and permanent shift in the balance between federal and provincial responsibilities, with consequent strains upon the century-old constitutional framework. The strains could be minimized in practice by close and continuous federal-provincial cooperation, but the arduous task of securing the unanimous consent of eleven different governments on every major issue that arose was all to often productive of friction and delay as well as of imperfections inherent in the inevitable compromises. If political relationships were to be brought into harmony with existing realities, either the federal government should have wider powers of independent action in fields hitherto reserved to the provinces, or the provinces must have larger independent resources to discharge their functions, with Ottawa perhaps serving as coordinator in the national interest. Neither approach found the backing of anything resembling a national consensus, and until this emerged the prospect remained dim for any basic revisions of the British North America Act.

A current catchword in the later 1950s was "repatriation of the constitution." Continued dependence on the Parliament at Westminster for constitutional amendments seemed increasingly an affront to national self-respect. Yet there remained the question of how to handle the constitution once it had been brought home, and particularly the still unsolved problem of devising an acceptable method of amendment before there could even be any practical discussion of what amendments were in fact desirable. Until this hurdle had been surmounted, all questions of specific changes were largely academic.

The problem was tackled in a series of conferences that began in the autumn of 1960. The arguments were stubborn and protracted, but by 1964 it seemed for a time that a solution was actually in sight. A procedure that was christened the Fulton-Favreau formula—the names of the two Ministers of Justice associated with its invention—was unanimously accepted by all provincial premiers at a meeting in October. In essence it provided for the entrenchment of such matters as language rights and provincial legislative authority by requiring unanimous consent for any change; other amendments might be carried with the consent of two-thirds of the provinces representing 50 percent of the population; provincial powers might be delegated to the federal government by a minimum of four provinces which would adopt the specific measure involved, and the federal government might devolve specified functions on any four provinces that signified their acceptance.

The proposals aroused heated criticism, particularly from students of politics and constitutional lawyers. In spite of the flexibility which the provisions for delegation sought to provide, the formula was attacked as confining the nation henceforth to a constitutional strait-jacket. It was branded as the Balkanization of Canada, an unmitigated constitutional disaster, the fixing of constitutional fetters on Canada's greatness as a nation. The outcry did not prevent its endorsement by nine of the ten provinces, but it led Quebec to back away. Quebec nationalist opinion, while firmly insisting on a veto on any change which the province disliked, now raised objections to any veto by other provinces over changes which Quebec desired. Premier Jean Lesage had accepted the formula and submitted it for legislative ratification, but his zeal quickly evaporated in the face of opposition. By January 1966 he resigned himself to abandoning the effort to get it endorsed; and Prime Minister Lester B. Pearson, protesting sharply against this retreat, made it clear that the federal government felt unable to go forward when unanimous consent was lacking. The work that had been done would certainly provide the starting point for future efforts, but for the moment the most promising approach yet devised to the amendment problem had to be laid aside.

Among the significant features of the controversy, not the least was the change in the balance of pressures that had taken place within a generation. At the time of the Rowell-Sirois commission the champions of provincial rights were active and vocal, but they were overshadowed by the advocates of a return to the strong central authority which the framers of the constitution thought they had established, but which had been weakened and distorted by later judicial decisions. The rapid changes in conditions in the past quarter-century had brought things to a point where it was the provinces that now held the initiative. They claimed the right to opt out of federal-provincial projects at will; they insisted adamantly on title to offshore mineral rights in defiance of the federal government; they even pressed for the partition of ownership of Hudson Bay among the adjacent provinces. Most of them still wanted the federal government to be an effective authority for national purposes, but those purposes were being defined with increasing narrowness, and it was now the believers in a strong central government who found themselves on the defensive in the controversy over constitutional change.

Foremost in the assault was the province of Quebec. Lured by the appealing slogan of "masters in our own house," French Canadian nationalism had burst out in a fresh resurgence which carried it to new extremes, and which gave concrete if not always attractive substance to the assertion, so insistently reiterated, that Quebec was not a province like the others.

Maîtres Chez Nous

The death of Maurice Duplessis in September 1959 broke Quebec politics wide open. For fifteen years the Union Nationale, with its firm grip on a corrupt political machine and with Duplessis as unchallenged boss, had held the affairs of the province virtually static. His stubborn resistance to any interference from Ottawa was designed rather to maintain a power monopoly than to use that power for any constructive purposes. Any restiveness of a younger generation impatient for a more positive advance was repressed by the ascendency of the paramount chief. With his death the party lost its head, as well as the discipline and direction which his rule had provided, and all the bottled-up impulses and aspirations burst out in a frenzied variety of manifestations.

The subsequent disarray of the Union Nationale, torn by dissentions and desertions and deprived of effective leadership, opened the way for a Liberal victory in the elections of June 1960. Around Jean Lesage, a vigorous younger minister in the former federal government who moved to the provincial field after the election of 1957, had gathered a group of nationalist intellectuals determined both to modernize the social and political outlook of Quebec and to instill a new dynamism into the French-Canadian community. "It is the hour of restoration that is starting for the province of Quebec," Lesage announced on the news of victory, and under him the new government plunged into the effort to lift Quebec by main force into the twentieth century.

The so-called "quiet revolution" that resulted—remarkably clamorous at times—exhibited three salient facets among numerous secondary ones. There was a determined effort to secure control of the economic instruments that would give the province effective control of its own material development. There was a sweeping program of educational reform designed to equip the youth of French Canada with the knowledge and skills demanded by the modern world. And there was a heightened pressure not merely for the full exercise of provincial rights independent of the federal government, but for a further extension of provincial authority accompanied by the acceptance of a theory of racial partnership whose implications profoundly challenged the existing constitutional basis.

The economic problem was not easily mastered. Most of Quebec's basic industry was controlled by English-speaking groups, either American or Canadian. The province itself was none too well endowed with private investment capital or private entrepreneurial initiative. Funds to take over existing corporations must come from government credit, from public funds such as those arising from Quebec's separate version of the Canada Pension Plan, from accumulated small savings in banks and credit unions. It was possible to buy out private power companies and incorporate them in Quebec Hydro and to purchase shares through government agencies in a number of private firms. But ambitious plans to create a major steel complex bogged down through lack of investment funds as well as available technical personnel, and enthusiasm on the part of savings funds for investment in provincial enterprises proved tepid at best. A change in both climate and attitudes was needed if Quebec was to realize its dreams of economic nationalism, and this was a transformation that could hardly be achieved overnight.

Far more striking were the changes in the educational structure. This was organized on a confessional basis, with the Catholic schools offering instruction in French and the Protestant in English. French-speaking Protestants, English-speaking Catholics, not to mention Jews and other non-Christians, had to fit in by whatever compromises were least intolerable. On the French side the preparation for higher education was traditionally directed toward the professions—medicine, the law, or the Church. This did not prevent periodic outcries at the alleged small proportion of French Canadians appointed to higher posts in business or the federal administration. In recent years such universities as Laval and Montreal had expanded into the fields of politics, science, and engineering —a tacit recognition of the need for adequate training as the basis for advancement in the more modern occupations—but primary and secondary education was still archaic as preparation for a future career.

The Royal Commission of Enquiry on Education in the Province of Quebec (the Parent Commission) reported that public opinion "attributes the only real prestige to the humanities, ranks the sciences a poor second and considers the technical and commercial courses as mere last resorts." It recommended a drastic revision of pre-university education which would democratize administration, create a complete system of public education to which all children would have access, and eliminate the existing rigidities by providing a wide range of options to the student in the process of deciding on his choice of a future career.

An important first step was the establishment in 1964, for the first time in Quebec, of a Ministry of Education with comprehensive supervision over the whole field. The confessional basis of the schools remained, but the possible establishment of neutral schools was not excluded; and the Catholic and Protestant committees, hitherto the effective administrative bodies, were now largely restricted to regulating religious and moral education. This was followed by measures to establish a complete system of regional schools, both primary and secondary, throughout the province. The organization of a system of fifty-five local school boards, as envisaged by the report, was initiated in September 1964. One of the most striking innovations was the introduction of a new two-year level of instruction between the equivalent of grade eleven and university entrance, through "institutes" which would integrate such existing bodies as classical colleges, technical institutes, and normal schools. These would provide a comprehensive range of instruction, both technical and academic. For some students it would represent terminal training prior to entrance into business or administration; for others it would be the sole pathway to university matriculation. The emphasis throughout, particularly in secondary education, was on flexibility through multiple options and on combining technical with general education as essential for an understanding of modern society.

The Lesage government did not survive to implement the full aims of the report, though many of these were pursued under its successor. The Liberals had increased their majority in 1962 at a time when the chief reforms were still germinating, but in June 1966, when the practical consequences were beginning to be felt, they were overthrown in an unexpected upset by a revived Union Nationale under Daniel Johnson. The pace of the quiet revolution may not have been too fast for Quebec's needs, but it was evidently too hurried for the Quebec temperament. Traditional institutions were being upset; secularization, not only in education but in the strengthening of lay elements in the parish councils, perturbed devout supporters of the Church. The increased cost of education was felt by some rural areas to be beyond their resources. Compulsory amalgamation of various small municipalities provoked considerable resentment. Perhaps not least important was the discontent aroused by the effort to curb patronage and political corruption. Licensees, small contractors, and other beneficiaries sorely missed the accustomed fleshpots, and turned back to the heirs of Duplessis and his good old ways.

At the same time, the Johnson government inherited an increased pressure of French-Canadian nationalism for whose support it was ardently competing with its political rivals. The Lesage regime, demanding the fullest concessions to provincial autonomy together with equality of partnership in federal matters, was still committed officially to the maintenance of a Canadian nationality and a federal government acting within its defined sphere on behalf of the whole community. The Johnson government went further in its resistance to Ottawa and in demands for provincial sovereignty and provincial monopoly of direct taxation. And both parties were subjected to the relentless goading of the various nationalist groups whose voluble demands and theories presented such a bewildering kaleidoscope to the rest of the nation.

The most vocal and vituperative were the separatists. The tenacious idea of an independent French-speaking Laurentia had revived with an upsurge of ardor on the part of a small but articulate segment of students and young intellectuals. In their eyes confederation was anathema, the subjection of French Canada to a helot status under Anglo-Saxon tyranny. Their activities ranged from demonstrations against every symbol of Canadian unity, whether the flag or the celebration of national holidays, to raids on arms depots and terrorist bombings that took innocent lives. Repeatedly split into new and rival groups, the active separatists numbered a few thousand at most, but as the spearhead of French-Canadian nationalism they attracted wide sympathy among many who refrained from formal adherence to their program.

A less forthright solution which sought the best of both worlds was the idea of Quebec as an associated state. This would concede almost all the attributes of sovereignty while continuing an Anglo-French partnership on a basis of complete equality between the two races, with a common government entrusted with such limited functions as coinage, customs, and external relations. Even these were subject to attrition. Lesage wanted the provinces to have a voice in tariffs, transportation, and monetary policy. By 1965 he was claiming the right of Quebec to negotiate independently with foreign states on matters within provincial jurisdiction, and the demand was stiffened in 1967 when the Johnson government set up a Department of Intergovernmental Affairs. The growing claims to sovereign status were symbolized by an official release in 1963 which advised that Quebec should be described as a State rather than a Province and the central government referred to as federal rather than national. The dual aspiration was summed up by Daniel Johnson as "master of our destiny in Quebec and equal partners in running the affairs of the country," even though Quebec's contribution to the rest of the country would be reduced to the barest minimum.

To the moderates a more practical path was the one described as cooperative federalism. This, in Lester B. Pearson's words, was a system

in which the two levels of government both fulfil their own responsibilities, and respect each other's, but they do so taking into account their mutual concerns. Where they are responsible for parallel action it should be concerted action and therefore must be built on consultation and cooperation.

Its evolving instrument (which by no means eliminated controversy over lines of jurisdiction) was the federal-provincial conference. This device, unknown to the formal structure of the constitution, was proving increasingly indispensable as a means of harmonizing federal and provincial policies in the national interest, and it was not beyond possibility that it might in due course be formalized as a permanent institution to meet the changing needs of the federal system.

The trouble was that the aims of French-Canadian nationalists went beyond even the widest provincial autonomy attainable by this method. The old dilemma between a Quebec living to itself and a French Canada extending across the whole country would not down. The solution put forward was the two-nation theory, under which the two founding races would have an equal voice in federal affairs irrespective of their disparity in numbers. Quebec would still retain its special status as a province while assuming the role of homeland to the French-speaking population outside its borders. A defect of this proposal was its limited appeal to French groups in the other regions. For the most part they were firmly determined to remain Canadians first, however much they might desire enlarged concessions to their own culture and language. In addition most groups, including particularly the Acadians, felt that they already had a satisfactory stake in their own provinces, and showed little zeal to plunge into the turmoil of Quebec nationalist agitation.

The divergences were exemplified by the proceedings of an unofficial body, which had appropriated to itself the historic title of Estates-General, at its meeting in November 1967. Composed largely of hand-picked members from such corporate bodies as the St. Jean Baptiste Society, municipal councils, school boards and labor unions, it also included a small minority of delegates from French-speaking areas outside Quebec. The latter found themselves consistently ignored and overridden and unable to exercise a moderating influence over the extremist elements that dominated the assembly. Resolutions backed by substantial majorities demanded the elimination of English as an official language in Quebec and restrictions on its use in business, compulsory retention of business profits and reserves within the province, annexation of various areas from Hudson Bay to Labrador, and constitutional changes amounting to virtual sovereignty.

In the background were other events well calculated to add stimulation to confusion. René Lévesque, who had been one of the most dynamic and colorful ministers in the Lesage administration, had embarked on a crusade for a sovereign Quebec in economic association with the rest of Canada, and when this was rejected by the Quebec Liberals, he seceded from the party and founded the Parti Québecois which set out to absorb the other separatist groups. Even more spectacular was the aggressive intervention of President Charles de Gaulle. He seized on the occasion of his visit to Expo 67 in July to assert that Quebec was developing a distinct people and political entity, "a piece of our own people installed, rooted and assembled here"; and on July 24 he climaxed a speech in Montreal by trumpeting the separatist slogan *Vive le Québec libre*. When his action was branded as unacceptable by Prime Minister Pearson, de Gaulle responded by cutting short his stay and canceling his visit to Ottawa. His return to France was followed by continued mischief-making, including assertions that France meant to help Quebec to achieve its liberation aims and that France could not "disinterest herself in the present and future fate of a population descended from her own people and admirably faithful to their country of origin." This was heady stuff for Quebec nationalists, and while their hopes for material support from France proved largely illusory, de Gaulle's moral encouragement had its intended effect of aggravating the political complications within the Canadian structure.

Yet noisy as the agitation was, there remained the question of how deep its practical influence went. In particular, it was hard to judge how far the average citizen of Quebec appreciated the economic implications of separatism or was ready to sacrifice material advantage for the satisfaction of nationalist emotions. Though repeated warnings by analysts, French as well as English, that separation would bring a drastic decline in living standards seemed to make little visible impact, the average Quebecois was far from indifferent to material benefits for himself and his family. A report by a Laval group, lifting a small corner of the veil, remarked uneasily: "Traditionalist French-Canadian culture no longer seems to exercise any influence on the economic behavior of families. . . . We must ask ourselves how this new culture, which is based on mass culture and publicity, can remain French-Canadian." Yet the widening of the gap between the two communities seemed evident and perturbing. A significant aspect was the deterioration of the infrastructure of unity, with Quebec organizations from political parties to student groups, not to mention the already separate Quebec trade unions, severing all but the most tenuous ties with their counterparts in the rest of Canada. The channels of communication were being progressively eroded, with adverse effects on the efforts to conduct a meaningful dialogue.

In the face of this situation the attitude of English Canada was in general one of sympathy tempered by bewilderment. While in some cases a growing impatience tended to harden into resistance to any substantial concessions, the more prevalent desire was to redress any legitimate French-Canadian grievances, so long as the methods adopted would serve to restore and strengthen Canadian national unity. Whether these aims were in fact compatible was the crux of the problem which political leaders, both federal and provincial, were seeking with growing urgency to resolve by the close of the centennial year.

At the end of November the provincial premiers, at a gathering initiated by Premier Robarts of Ontario and christened Confederation of Tomorrow, embarked on a four-day exploration of attitudes and objectives. Their talks showed a genuine desire to find common ground in spite of evident divergences. The western and Atlantic provinces were more concerned with measures to eliminate economic disparities than with constitutional change. Alberta and British Columbia, supported by Newfoundland, were particularly opposed to the drastic constitutional revisions demanded by Quebec. But other provinces recognized that there would have to be substantial adjustments, and all professed a readiness to consider sympathetically whatever realistic proposals gave promise of a workable accommodation.

Hard on the heels of the conference came the publication on December 5 of the first volume of the report by the Royal Commission on Bilingualism and Biculturalism. The appointment of this commission in July 1963 had been one of the early acts of the Pearson administration. The first installment of its findings dealt with the closely linked topics of education and language rights. It recommended that French and English be formally declared official languages for federal purposes with equality of status in government, administration, and the courts. There should be similar equality for legislative and judicial purposes in Ontario and New Brunswick as well as Quebec, and in any other provinces where either language was the mother tongue of 10 percent of the population, or in localities which contained a substantial minority of either linguistic group. Primary and secondary education should be available in either of the two languages where conditions warranted, or in bilingual schools where these seemed appropriate; and the way was left open for the establishment of schools in other minority languages as well.

This document was one of the main items on the agenda of the three-day federal-provincial conference that opened on February 5, 1968. It evoked a broad general consensus, perhaps a trifle shaky at the edges. Ottawa had promised a bill in the next session of Parliament to implement the federal aspect of the report. Premier Daniel Johnson, repudiating extremist demands for a purely French-speaking state, asserted that Quebec would remain bilingual. Ontario and New Brunswick were already committed to carrying out the main recommendations; other provinces recorded their agreement in principle to equality of the two languages and educational concessions to their French-speaking communities. Alberta and British

Columbia, professing a desire to remove legitimate grievances, had some mental reservations about the practicality of bilingualism, and particularly about the desirability of constitutional changes in support of language rights. This was an important aspect of the second main topic, the proposal for a Charter of Human Rights. In contrast to John Diefenbaker's Bill of Rights, the projected measure would be entrenched as a constitutional guarantee. Quebec, however, objected vigorously to any federal intervention in provincial authority over the rights of individuals, and several other provinces expressed serious reservations.

Thus the discussions were at best a hopeful start toward the extensive readjustments that were needed to restore internal harmony. The conference did not attempt a comprehensive review of constitutional change. It agreed that the heads of governments should constitute a continuing committee to undertake this process, assisted by subcommittees of ministers and officials. The process promised to be a protracted one. Premier Johnson was now demanding not merely extensive amendments but a completely new constitution which would drastically alter the distribution of powers and extensively revise the structure of the Senate and the Supreme Court. The rest of Canada, which had already moved a considerable way toward meeting Quebec demands, might have to contemplate even more revolutionary adjustments if the gap was to be bridged.

Yet for all the internal difficulties and their perturbing implications for the future, the operative reality of Canadian nationhood still stood largely unscathed. The economy continued to develop in a national context. Social welfare made striking advances, even though in some matters the provinces were left to decide for themselves how closely they would approximate national standards. Quebec as a province might still be unlike the others, but Quebec at the national level remained a functioning entity in Canadian politics. A promising contingent of younger French-Canadian members emerged under the Pearson government at Ottawa, vigorously championing a strong and united nation with effective Quebec participation in the work of nation-building. Canada's role as a sovereign and united nation remained beyond challenge. Tiny Gabon, with French encouragement, might invite Quebec alone to an education conference over the head of Ottawa, and Paris might give separate and symbolic recognition to Quebec at the conference's second session; but while the long-run implications were disturbing, the episode itself was hardly more than a malicious pinprick which other countries showed no impulse to emulate. Canada had her domestic troubles, but so had other nations both new and old, not excluding France; and none of the internal controversies detracted perceptibly from her role as a free member of the international community.

With Turbulence Surrounded

In international affairs the opportunities for any major influence or independent initiative by Canada diminished after the mid-fifties. Partly this was the result of changing conditions which saw the loosening of the Western alliance, the split in the communist monolith, the multiplication of new sovereignties defiantly pursuing their own individual ends. With international anarchy once more on the increase, a middle power such as Canada, however trusted and respected, lacked the stature to give leadership in a crisis. It might hope to be able to ride out the whirlwind; it was relatively powerless to direct the storm.

In addition, there was lacking during the Diefenbaker regime the sort of personal impact and prestige that sometimes compensates for physical lack of national stature. In that period Canada's foreign policy was sadly in need of both imagination and direction. Yet for twelve weeks after his accession to power, Diefenbaker kept external affairs in his own hands. Sidney Smith, appointed Minister of External Affairs in September 1957, died in March 1959. Diefenbaker resumed control for another twelve weeks before appointing Howard Green in June. These two interludes, if not actually disastrous, were indecisive and confusing, and the situation under the two Ministers of External Affairs was no great improvement. Diefenbaker, distrusting his civil servants as Liberal appointees and disliking to consult with his top officials, was vague and secretive. Smith seemed bewildered by his task and buffeted by his chief. Green, inexperienced and with no first-hand knowledge of other countries, was vague and optimistic. The Liberals brought back expertise in the persons of Lester B. Pearson as Prime Minister and Paul Martin at External Affairs, but their skills were only partly effective in the face of the incoherent world situation. When even the major powers so often found themselves helpless prisoners of uncontrollable events, the role of a middle power was inevitably straitened and confined.

The difficulties were evident in the United Nations, where the rapidly expanding membership of newly formed states increased the problem of giving a lead that would produce a consensus on major issues. Howard

Green, with an enthusiasm as laudable as it was unrealistic, pinned his faith on disarmament, without achieving perceptible success in this or any other field. Pearson and Martin concentrated on the peace-keeping role of the United Nations and met with at least equal frustration. The attempt to solve the payments crisis over existing peace-keeping operations—Sinai, Cyprus, the Congo—through voluntary contributions had limited results. The persistent efforts to establish a system of stand-by forces met with failure. In an attempt to use the alternative of voluntary action, Canada in November 1964 arranged a conference of twenty-two nations who had contributed to United Nations operations; but only a few of these were prepared to earmark forces on a permanent basis, and in December 1966 the General Assembly failed to accept a resolution favoring such a step. There was a still more discouraging setback in 1967 when Egypt, in imminent collision with Israel, successfully demanded that the United Nations Emergency Force, in whose creation in 1956 Canada felt a special pride, leave the country, and particularly insisted that the Canadians withdraw at once. In company with the larger states, Canada was impotent either to avert the Arab-Israeli war or to promote a permanent peace. It was a stark example of how ephemeral the role of peace-keeping forces could be unless their pacifying effect was used to achieve a political settlement—a point which Pearson had vainly emphasized at the time of the Suez crisis. Meanwhile the Congo force, to which Canada had contributed a communications unit, had withdrawn from that still unstable country; and the Cyprus force, with a substantial Canadian component, was maintaining a precarious truce with no pacification in sight. Blessed the peacemakers might be, but the blessings were sometimes hard to discern.

The Commonwealth presented a different set of problems. With the expansion of membership, and particularly the addition of newly freed African states, this anomalous grouping was becoming more incoherent than ever. The shadowy myth of common institutions was stultified by a military coup in Ghana and civil war in Nigeria. Peaceful relations were shattered by an outright though short-lived war between India and Pakistan. Even the tragedy of an armed clash between white Commonwealth communities, hitherto unthinkable, loomed as a possibility with the controversy over Rhodesia.

The advent of Diefenbaker, with his ardent attachment to the British connection, was hailed by imperialist adherents in London as the emergence of a champion against further retreats from empire. It was not long before disillusionment set in, and by 1963 the overthrow of the Conservative government found few in Britain to lament its passing.

A salient issue, growing in emotional intensity as the Commonwealth expanded, was racial equality. South Africa was a special target for the resentment of Asian and African members, and Canadian opinion was strongly sympathetic to their grievances and condemnatory of the inhuman aspects of apartheid. The question came to a focus with South Africa's long-expected decision to proclaim itself a republic and the consequent discussions whether it would be included in the Commonwealth on that basis. At the Prime Ministers' Conference in 1961 the Afro-Asians

strenuous British efforts to paper over the cracks. The conference was confronted with the choice of renouncing South Africa or risking the loss of Asia; and when Diefenbaker threw his support to the Afro-Asians, his stand was decisive. South Africa withdrew its application for membership and departed from the Commonwealth; and while Diefenbaker's attitude aroused resentment in Britain and the other white Dominions, it received almost unanimous support from the Canadian public.

The racial issue, in a somewhat different form, again confronted Pearson in the Conference of 1964. This time it was a question of assuring the progressive widening of the franchise in Rhodesia as a condition for its admission to full Commonwealth membership. The attitude was crystallized by a resolution, put forward by Pearson, calling for all members to aim at a structure of society based on nondiscrimination in respect to race, color, or creed. When Rhodesia in its turn rejected this basis and declared its unilateral independence in 1965, Canada joined with other members in withdrawing recognition, canceling trade preferences, and embargoing arms shipments. On this occasion the measures adopted simply supported the pressures that were applied by the United Kingdom, and Canada felt no need to take further initiatives on its own.

For Canada, in fact, it was the economic aspect of Commonwealth relations that was of most absorbing concern during this period. The dominance of the United States in external trade and investment was increasingly perturbing, and motivated a search for mitigating alternatives. Britain, as Canada's second-best customer, and to a lesser extent the rest of the Commonwealth under a system of trade preferences, seemed the natural resort to redress the balance, even if it meant the adoption of artificial measures to achieve the ends desired.

In the first flush of victory, Diefenbaker trumpeted abroad his intention to divert 15 percent of Canada's imports to the United Kingdom. Since this would mean more than doubling the existing volume of imports from Britain, it was statistically suspect, and it soon became evident that it had no foundation in concrete planning. Its hollowness was exposed when at a conference of Commonwealth Finance Ministers in Canada in September 1957 the British proposed a free-trade arrangement to be achieved by the gradual elimination of tariffs over a period of fifteen years. The Canadian ministers were completely taken aback. The Prime Minister heatedly condemned the proposal. Far from easing the barriers on British goods, the government shortly increased the tariffs on woolens and rubber footwear and upped the valuation formula on British cars. Though the value of British imports later showed some increase, the proportion in Canada's total trade remained virtually unchanged.

A more far-reaching issue in Commonwealth trade relations was raised by the decision of the United Kingdom to seek entry into the European Economic Community. When the common market was first under negotiation, Britain had held aloof, thereby missing her chance to exert a favorable influence on its terms and to forestall the emergence of the Olympian obstacle of de Gaulle. The other Commonwealth members, equally unperceptive of the future, clung tenaciously to the Commonwealth system and failed to explore the possibility of favorable arrangements with the European community. By 1960 Britain at length recognized that the inevitable had also become urgent, but the rest of the Commonwealth was still unreconciled, and Canada was among the most vociferous in opposing Britain's entry.

The most vigorous outburst took place at a meeting of the Commonwealth Economic Consultative Council at Accra in 1961. There were uncompromising demands that Britain renounce her intention of joining the common market. "Britain is launched on a slippery slope," warned Donald Fleming, Minister of Finance; "The Commonwealth can never be the same again." George Hees, Minister of Trade and Commerce, forecast an adverse effect on the standard of living to a point where the Commonwealth would exist in name only. The reaction in Canada to this onslaught was highly critical. "Such emotionalism seems altogether excessive," commented the *Globe and Mail*. "Canada is in the position of screaming before she is hurt." In the end it was not Commonwealth opposition but the obdurate resistance of de Gaulle that frustrated successive British efforts to arrange terms of entry, and the Pearson government was given time to revert to quiet diplomacy and to seek ways of keeping the adverse effects of Britain's reorientation to a minimum.

Trade was also a matter of continuous concern with the United States, as was the continuing growth of control by American capital over the

Canadian economy, but friction over these aspects was minor or episodic. In a few cases there were sharp exchanges over trade policies in their bearing on United States interests abroad. Canadian wheat sales to communist lands, particularly China, were viewed with a rather jaundiced eye. Canada's refusal to join in an embargo against Fidel Castro's Cuba, apart from strategic goods, evoked some recriminations. The chief divergences, however, were still over the political aspects of American world policies, and even these caused little serious trouble at the official level.

For example, while Canadians in general remained unsympathetic toward the refusal of the United States to recognize the Chinese People's Republic, an open clash of policies was still postponed. Repeated hints that Canada was contemplating recognition did not result in action during this period; in fact, Communist China, feuding with almost every other country and torn by internal power struggles, gave little aid or comfort to potential friends. American pressure on Cuba and intervention in the Dominican Republic also aroused considerable criticisms, and may have prompted second thoughts about Canada's still coy flirtation with the Organization of American States.

Above all, there was Vietnam. The deepening American involvement and the progressive escalation of military operations met with considerable opposition in the United States, which was paralleled in Canada by vocal demonstrations and by less noisy but fairly widespread uneasiness throughout the Canadian public. Both Lester B. Pearson and Paul Martin made strenuous and persistent efforts to find a way of ending hostilities, with no perceptible results during this period. Hanoi scornfully rejected all advances; Warsaw and Moscow refused suggestions that they exercise their influence; Washington was cool to proposals for the cessation of bombing without reciprocal concessions. It was one more illustration of how little even the most skillful diplomacy by a smaller power could achieve in the existing state of world affairs.

In the direct relations between the two countries an outstanding event was the treaty providing for joint development of the Columbia River system which crisscrosses the international boundary in the region of the Rockies. The United States, which had almost fully developed its own portion of the system, stood in increasingly urgent need of expanded sources of hydroelectric power as well as more effective measures of flood control. For both purposes it was necessary to build storage dams as well as power installations on the Canadian side of the border. The project, which had long been under study in the International Joint Commission, reached the stage of formal and intensive negotiations in 1960 and led to the signing of the basic treaty in January 1961. The agreement produced heated arguments in Canada, where it was contended that Canada's future needs would be jeopardized by mortgaging the Columbia water resources in perpetuity to the United States. There was strong opposition from British Columbia, which objected to the financial returns and to federal restrictions on the free export of power. The Liberal government was able to overcome the latter obstacle by negotiations with the provincial government, followed in January 1964 by agreement with the United States on a protocol that somewhat modified the original terms. The outcome was that Canada agreed to build three major storage dams and power installations; the United States would pay an initial $274,800,000, plus a further $69,600,000 between 1968 and 1973; Canada retained a right to divert the waters of the Kootenay River under certain conditions, with a more limited right of diversion on the Columbia; and half the additional downstream power would be sold by Canada to the United States, with right of recovery after thirty years. It was a major venture in the joint development of one vital resource—a matter which, with the urgent need of the United States for new sources of fresh water and Canada's ample resources still only partially exploited, showed signs of becoming a crucial issue in the years ahead.

A second important controversy that flared up briefly but heatedly during the Diefenbaker regime was concerned with defense; and while this had wider implications, the fact that it involved the question of nuclear arms made the solution squarely and inescapably dependent on suitable arrangements with the United States.

The problem stemmed from the new equipment that was being acquired by Canada's armed forces. The eight air squadrons now assigned to NATO were provided with modern fighter bombers to replace their obsolescent planes and to fit them for the strike-reconnaissance role which it was agreed they would assume. The ground forces in Europe were being equipped with rocket artillery. Supersonic jet fighters were acquired for Canada's air defense, and with the abandoment of the Arrow, the government agreed to the installation on Canadian soil of two squadrons of Bomarc antiaircraft missiles, in spite of the dubious record of this device in current tests. All these weapons needed nuclear armament for full effectiveness, and some, such as the Bomarc, were useless without it.

Yet the government, which appeared to recognize and accept the implications, hesitated to implement them. Atomic arms could only be acquired from the United States. By American law, such arms must remain in American custody; and though this might mean no more than a sergeant with a key, there were nationalists ready to attack it as an invasion of Canadian sovereignty. In addition, there was a feeling that acceptance of nuclear weapons might hamper disarmament and encourage nuclear proliferation, though it was questionable whether Canada, while renouncing the production of nuclear arms for which she had every capacity, could also dispense with the right to use them in case of a major conflict.

Diefenbaker's solution was to exclude nuclear weapons from Canadian soil yet hold out assurances that they would be available in time of need. Given the lack of any margin of time in case of a nuclear onslaught, his stand was neither satisfactory nor convincing. In the words of one critic, it meant that Canada "had spent $685 millions for the most impressive collection of blank cartridges in the history of military science." And when in January 1963 Diefenbaker tried to convince the Commons that nuclear arms would add nothing to defense, while also revealing that negotiations were going on with the United States for their provision in emergency, he not only added to the confusion but provoked an unusually sharp retort from Washington to correct his misrepresentations. "The Canadian government," the statement flatly asserted, "has not yet proposed any arrangement sufficiently practical to contribute effectively to North American defense." By that time the issue had brought into focus the growing disarray in ministerial ranks and contributed to the trend of events which shortly afterward brought the fall of the government.

Under the Liberals the issue as such subsided. After much heart-searching the party concluded that Canada was committed to acquire nuclear arms and must fulfill its obligations. Arrangements were concluded without fanfare, and the first nuclear warheads for Bomarcs arrived at the end of 1963. But there was no enthusiasm for expanding Canada's nuclear role, and the new government embarked on a searching reassessment of Canada's defense role.

Some existing aspects were clearly open to question. There might be political reasons for keeping Canadian forces in Europe, but there were growing doubts whether they were essential for military purposes and whether they could not be better used elsewhere. Even the value of NORAD in the face of nuclear missiles was becoming dubious, and its operative reliability was shown to be shaky during the crisis over Cuban missile bases in 1962, when Diefenbaker hesitated for most of two days before placing the Canadian air component in a state of alert. The conclusion, expressed in a White Paper in 1964, was that a major war was unlikely while the nuclear deterrent held, and that Canada should emphasize flexibility in conventional operations including peace-keeping under the United Nations. In consequence, Canada decided to integrate the different armed forces in a single organization, with the aim of providing mobile contingents with the most modern equipment for use on call at short notice. There were heated protest from some high-ranking service officers about the resulting loss of identity of individual branches. A number of admirals, abandoning the traditions of the silent (or inarticulate) service, launched their heaviest verbal broadsides against the Minister of Defence, with the support of some of their opposite numbers among the airmen; but the measure was approved by Parliament in 1967, and bade fair to serve as a pilot project from which other nations might draw useful lessons.

In Search of a Government

John Diefenbaker became Prime Minister of Canada at a crucial point in the country's postwar development. Economic expansion showed signs of leveling out as world conditions became more stable. The federal system was confronted by challenges which held potential threats to national unity. New stirrings were jarring old political alignments and demanding new approaches. It was a time for leadership with vigor and imagination, and Diefenbaker showed no doubt that he was the man to provide it.

His self-confidence was hardly justified by the outcome. The strength inherent in an overwhelming parliamentary majority, the largest in Canadian political history, was frittered away by incompetence and indecision. The former consensus on national directions and purposes, which had begun to decline during the last years of Liberal rule, was further dissipated instead of being restored. No new course was charted in any major area, and Canada was left groping for guidance in solving the problems that confronted it.

There were a number of achievements in specific matters. Social welfare was further advanced. A National Energy Board was created to oversee the optimum use of Canada's resources. Western farmers benefited from increased wheat subsidies, and still more from very substantial wheat sales abroad. The controversial South Saskatchewan dam was undertaken to provide power and irrigation, and a vigorous road-building program improved access to certain northern areas. And while efforts to reach agreement on a formula for amending the constitution failed in the end, they represented a sincere and sustained attempt to strengthen the sinews of nationalism.

Yet the constructive side of the record failed to offset the shortcomings. Diefenbaker's authoritarian temperament was not accompanied by a capacity for clear-cut and inspiring decisions. His ministers were frequently left in uncertainty about policy while their chief was making up his mind. On more than one occasion they found their understanding misled, their statements contradicted, their stand repudiated. There was confusion over external policy and a lack of firm direction in economic matters. In the face of mounting unemployment and record peacetime deficits, Diefenbaker devoted his self-laudatory eloquence to the enactment of a Bill of Rights, which did more to confuse than to clarify the legal status of the citizen, and to his glowing vision of national expansion through development of a new northern frontier, which remained almost wholly visionary. The result was a growing popular disillusionment with government by rhetoric as an unsatisfactory substitute for effective leadership.

A particularly damaging episode was the explosive quarrel with the Governor of the Bank of Canada. James E. Coyne, perturbed by the continued economic drift, embarked on a public advocacy of stringent measures to curb inflation and to halt the growing control by American investors over the Canadian economy. The government, resentful of such pressure, demanded his resignation, and on his refusal pushed through the Commons a bill ordering his dismissal. The accompanying exchanges were marked by bitter personal recriminations; the Senate rejected the bill; and it was only after Coyne was given an opportunity for personal vindication before a Senate committee, in spite of government resistance, that he voluntarily retired in July 1961. Even critics of his economic arguments felt that the manner of his ouster reflected no credit on the ministry.

The shadow of this episode still lingered when the currency crisis broke in the early summer of 1962. Although the previous deficits in commodity trade had changed to a modest surplus in 1961, the over-all balance of payments remained unfavorable, partly because of a serious though temporary decline in the inflow of investment funds from the United States. The result was a rapid drain on Canada's reserves and a progressive decline in the exchange value of the dollar, which had been allowed to follow a floating rate. The government continued to deny vigorously that any crisis existed. The Minister of Finance condemned as unsound the proposal that the value of the dollar be pegged. Then on May 2, 1962, it was suddenly announced that the exchange rate would be fixed at $92\frac{1}{2}$ cents American; and when this failed to halt the decline, temporary austerity measures were adopted in the form of surcharges on a substantial range of imports, bolstered by stand-by loans from several sources including the International Monetary Fund. Again it was the manner rather than the substance of the action that was at fault. Devaluation had many advocates; but to take this step in the midst of an election campaign, and in flat contradiction to recent government declarations, savored more of a desperate expediency than of deliberate and reasoned economic policy.

The elections of June 1962 shattered the triumphant Conservative majority of four years earlier. Conservative numbers sank to 116; Liberals rose to 100. The New Democratic party (NDP)—successor to the CCF— elected 19 members; Social Credit reappeared with 30 seats. The shift in pattern was in its way as significant as that in numbers. Under Diefenbaker the Conservative party had renounced its traditional role as the champion of wealth and property. His openly expressed dislike of Eastern business interests was reciprocated in full measure. It was now the Liberals who found their chief strongholds in the growing urban centers. Conservative strength was drawn mainly from rural and small-town areas, and particularly from the once-radical prairies, where subsidies and wheat sales had brought material benefits more potent than old ideologies. And not to be disregarded was the fact that 26 of the 30 Social Credit members came from Quebec, while the previous Conservative representation of 50 had been drastically reduced to 14—a sign that French Canada, discontented with the older federal parties and in search of some new thing, had rallied to a new group with one of the most strikingly negative slogans in political history: "What have you got to lose?"

The Diefenbaker government now rested on a minority in the Commons, and the result was paralysis compounded by confusion. Restiveness in his own party over ineffective leadership was increased by the election results, and was brought to a head by the intensified controversy over nuclear arms. The Minister of Defence, Douglas Harkness, unable to get an unambiguous answer from the Prime Minister on the issue, submitted his resignation on February 4, 1963. A group of his colleagues by this time were planning to force Diefenbaker's own resignation in the hope of restoring unity to a disintegrating ministry. Diefenbaker countered by calling a parliamentary caucus and swaying its members with an emotional appeal to personal loyalty. The plotters went into the meeting dropping dark hints of a coup in prospect; they emerged beaming with assurances that no such move was ever contemplated and that all was sweetness and light. "These men were not telling the truth," burst out the *Globe and Mail*. "This newspaper has had enough of it. We want no more of these treacherous confidences." In fact, disintegration was only partially checked. Both the Minister of Trade (George Hees) and the Associate Defense Minister (Pierre Sevigny) resigned on February 9. Davie Fulton, former Minister of Justice, had already decided to accept the leadership of the provincial party in British Columbia—a career that turned out to be as brief as it was unrewarding. Donald Fleming, recently shifted from Finance to Justice, decided to leave politics and return to his law practice. The ministry was already collapsing when on February 5 the government was overthrown by an adverse vote in the Commons; and Diefenbaker, adopting the role of a martyr battling for the common people against a conspiracy by the big interests, the press, and the United States government, appealed once more to the electorate.

The sympathy of the electorate, it turned out, had been further eroded by these months of indecision and revolt. Conservative seats sank to 95. Minority parties lost a few seats each. The Liberals with 129 members emerged as the largest group, and in April 1963 Lester B. Pearson took over the task of heading a minority government.

The Liberals had given hostages to fortune by a promise that their return to office would be followed by "sixty days of decision." Now, dependent on the uncertain day-to-day support of the minor parties, decision tended to bog down in the struggle to remain in power. The Pearson Cabinet was one of the ablest collections of personal talents in Canadian parliamentary history, but it seemed to have difficulty in providing coherent drive and impact. A number of minor scandals reflecting on the judgment—and in one or two cases the probity—of secondary figures in the government, gave ammunition to attacks by the opposition. The first budget of the new Finance Minister, Walter Gordon— a prominent figure in business circles and a close friend of the Prime Minister—sought to use the tax weapon to check inflation, stimulate employment, and curb the growth of American control, but inept handling and attacks on specific provisions, some of which had to be withdrawn, seriously damaged his reputation and the government's prestige. Pearson's announced determination to adopt a distinctive Canadian flag with a maple leaf motif brought an explosion of outraged patriotism from partisans of the Red Ensign which enshrined the Union Jack, and gave rise to thirty-three days of emotional and exhausting debate which was only ended by the use of closure. In spite of a number of useful measures during the succeeding year—loans to students, machinery for nonpolitical electoral redistribution, provision for railway reorganization—the impression grew that Parliament was fractious and time-wasting and the government weak in leadership when leadership was ardently desired.

This situation convinced Liberal tacticians that vigorous and constructive action would only be possible if a more stable base could be secured, and it was with this aim that Pearson went to the country in November 1965 with a plea for a clear Liberal majority. The gamble was somewhat less than successful. Party standings showed only minor changes. The Liberals, with 131 seats against 97 for the Conservatives, were still numerically at the mercy of a combined opposition. Yet while the government was technically in a minority, the outcome showed that it was now effectively in power. It even managed to survive a week-long crisis in February 1968 as the result of a snap defeat on a finance bill, though not without a considerable loss of prestige. The country wanted a respite from inconclusive elections, and awareness of this fact imposed a sober restraint on the smaller parties against any irresponsible overthrow of the ministry. A cabinet reorganization in which Mitchell Sharp succeeded Walter Gordon at Finance and a number of younger Quebec ministers replaced the somewhat tarnished old guard seemed to provide a greater coherence and sense of drive to the government. The Canada Pension Plan was put into operation, medicare was placed on the statute books, the bill unifying the armed forces was pushed through, and further measures of social and economic advance were forecast for the immediate future.

Yet while leadership seemed at last to be emerging, if still somewhat shakily, a restored national consensus was still to seek. No party had yet shown itself able to recapture the confidence of a decisive majority of the electorate, and all were beset in one degree or another by internal divisions and conflicting views as to the policies demanded by changing circumstances.

The CCF was merged in a new organization as a result of the decision of the Canadian Labor Congress to enter national politics. The two organizations came together in 1961 in a founding convention which produced the New Democratic party under the leadership of T. C. Douglas, whose abandonment of the premiership of Saskatchewan to enter national politics was followed in 1964 by the Liberal capture of that province after twenty years of CCF rule. The new party was not all harmony. Hard-core believers in the CCF attacked a merger which, as one put it, would vest control of the party "in a handful of labor leaders situated outside the House of Commons." There was bitterness over the abandonment of dogmatic socialist principles in favor of a moderate program of social reform. There was a vocal section with strong anti-American overtones which demanded withdrawal from NATO and NORAD and adoption of a neutralist policy; and efforts by the party to woo Quebec by concessions to its autonomist demands were hard to reconcile with the kind of centralism which alone could enable the party to achieve its economic aims.

Social Credit was in even worse plight. The Quebec section, whose views came very close to separatism, had little in common with the group from the far west. Internal friction, to which personal rivalries contributed, brought an open breach by 1963, with the Créditistes splitting off as a separate party, and following this in typical Quebec fashion by further splits among themselves. By 1967 the veteran Premier Ernest Manning, whose party had ruled Alberta for over thirty years, was publicly announcing his conclusion that the party could not hope to be an effective force in federal politics and advocating the regrouping of right-wing opinion in something that he called Social Conservatism.

The official Conservative party on its part was less concerned at the moment with policy than with the obsessive question of leadership. John Diefenbaker, unable to quell dissension and revolt within the ranks, successfully managed to beat off persistent efforts to dislodge him by full use of his talents for political maneuver and heart-rending oratory. It was not until September 1967 that the dissidents succeeded in assembling a party convention in Toronto to review the question of the leadership. (They do these things better in the Kremlin.) In a suspenseful four days the delegates turned from the old chief and all his federal colleagues to choose Robert Stanfield, lured from the premiership of Nova Scotia, as the leader to unify the party and return to it the sweets of power.

Divisions in the Liberal ranks were less open and less disruptive. While one wing, with particular support from the younger elements, favored stronger measures of economic nationalism and more active intervention in the economy by the federal government, the resistance of the more orthodox groups was not so uncompromising as to jeopardize party unity in spite of the accompanying exacerbation of personal rivalries. No leadership crisis afflicted the Liberals as it did the Conservatives under Diefenbaker. Pearson had forecast his voluntary retirement at an early date, and when he publicly announced this on December 14, 1967, the stage was set for the orderly choice of his successor at a party convention early in April 1968.

The victorious contender was Pierre Elliott Trudeau. A relative newcomer to federal politics, he had risen rapidly to ministerial status since his election in 1965. For more than a decade previously he had been a leading voice among a group of young liberal intellectuals in the province of Quebec, and his writings had attracted notice through their incisive criticism of Quebec's lag in adapting to modern conditions and their firm advocacy of effective federal authority. As Minister of Justice he had assumed responsibility for the broadening of Canada's divorce laws and for changes in the penal code which liberalized its provisions with respect to sexual offenses. His strong stand against Premier Johnson's autonomy demands, notably at the constitutional conference in February, gave him added status as the spokesman for federalist sentiment in French Canada. A bachelor in his late forties, he still projected a youthful charisma, and caught the public imagination as a vigorous and decisive personality who promised to bring with him a refreshing wind of change to the Canadian political scene.

With the succession established, Pearson stayed not upon his going. On April 20 Trudeau assumed the mantle as Prime Minister, and on April 23 he announced his decision to seek his own mandate from the people by calling a general election for June 25. This was taking the tide of enthusiasm at its flood, with success as its reward. The Liberals came back with 154 seats. The Conservatives were reduced to 72. The NDP showed little change at 23. The rump of Social Credit was wiped out, though its Créditiste offshoot won 14 seats, entirely from Quebec. After six years of confusion and uncertainty, Canada had once more a government with a parliamentary majority.

Gratifying as this was, the voting pattern showed continuing internal divisions that still gave cause for concern. The recent electoral redistribution, which increased the strength of urban over rural constituencies, perhaps helped to accentuate the political divergence between the cities and the farms. In the chief urban areas the Conservatives were almost wiped out. They won no seats in metropolitan Toronto, only one in Montreal, and a scattered handful in other leading centers. Even the NDP, which had counted hopefully on strong labor support, made few inroads in the face of the Liberal sweep.

The regional divergences, while they overlapped with the urban-rural split, were somewhat less clear-cut. In central Canada the Liberals were overwhelmingly dominant. The Conservatives were strong in the Atlantic provinces, where even traditionally Liberal Newfoundland gave them 6 of its 7 seats. But they sank to 17 out of 88 in Ontario, elected none in British Columbia, and their losses in the recently loyal prairie provinces were enough to assure a Liberal majority and restore that party to a truly national basis. Not least significant were the results in Quebec. There the

Conservatives had wooed the nationalists with a deliberate ambivalence on the "two nations" approach, and had been accorded a substantial measure of support from the Union Nationale, yet all they secured was a meager four seats. The appeal of the Créditistes was to the economically deprived, particularly in the rural areas, rather than to nationalist let alone separatist sentiment. The Quebec voters who gave the Liberals 56 out of 74 seats were clearly no relentless opponents of federalism as represented by Trudeau. It was a heartening augury for the survival of Canada as a nation.

While only an alarmist would envisage disruption as a serious probability, only an optimist would believe that the existing difficulties would be soon or easily overcome. There were still conflicting undercurrents, some of them profound and of long standing, that must be reconciled before a true national consensus could be achieved. Yet the prospects were not without promise. Canada entered its second century with a wealth of natural resources and productive facilities, with a vigorous and progressive population, with an effectively functioning structure of government. Under new leadership and with new directions, it could hope with confidence to realize progressively the great potential for future development that the nation held within its grasp.

Chapter 23

The Trudeau Years

Economic Discomfort

In November 1981 some 80,000 Canadians demonstrated on Parliament Hill. The immediate object of their anger was high interest rates. But the organizers of the demonstration, the Canadian Labor Congress, had other concerns as well. Unemployment exceeded 8 percent of the labor force. Layoffs and plant closings were daily adding to the numbers of the unemployed. The rate of increase in the Consumer Price Index was touching 12 percent annually. Moreover, these were not new phenomena. In the period after the centennial, Canada worried more about its economy than it had at any time since the 1930s. During most of the 1970s, high levels of unemployment and high inflation rates—often accompanied by low rates of economic growth—sharpened conflict between regions, levels of government, and social classes. Canadian unity, under attack even in prosperous times, was strained to the utmost. The country's political and economic future was muddy.

The main target of the protest on that chilly Saturday in November was the prime minister, Pierre Elliott Trudeau. He had taken office on April 20, 1968; thirteen years and four general elections later he still headed the government, joining Sir John A. Macdonald and William Lyon Mackenzie King in the rare achievement of regaining power after losing it. An uncommon and controversial man, he dominated Canadian politics in the 1970s.

They were not easy years, for him or for Canada. His personal life was considered public property; and his marriage to—and subsequent separation from—Margaret Sinclair, a much younger woman, were used against him by his critics and the media. The country had its troubles, too. The economy was a source of constant concern. Discord between the federal government and the provincial governments grew during the 1970s, as did envy and mistrust among the provinces and regions. In 1976 an avowedly separatist government came to power in Quebec. Trudeau, to whom national unity was an overriding goal, governed a deeply divided country. Indeed, the divisions deepened while he was in office.

Some of the rifts between Canadians were of their own making, but many of their economic problems were reflections of the successive shocks and crises that characterized world economic affairs in the 1970s. It was a difficult decade, marked by increasing economic discomfort, and it represented the transition from one definable epoch in the economic history of the world to a new period whose features were in 1981 still unclear.

ECONOMIC INDICATORS: PRODUCTIVITY, INFLATION,
UNEMPLOYMENT, LABOR COMPENSATION

Year	Gross National Product (constant 1971 $) (% increase)	Consumer Price Index (% increase)	Annual rate of unemployment	Labor compensation per unit of output (% increase)[a]
1961–65 (average)	5.6	1.6	5.4	0.8
1966–70 (average)	4.8	3.8	4.4	4.2
1971	6.9	2.9	6.2	3.3
1972	6.1	4.8	6.2	4.2
1973	7.5	7.6	5.5	6.8
1974	3.6	10.9	5.3	13.5
1975	1.2	10.8	6.9	15.3
1976	5.5	7.5	7.1	8.1
1977	2.2	8.0	8.1	6.2
1978	3.4	8.9	8.4	4.3
1979	2.7	9.1	7.5	7.7
1980	0.1	10.5	7.5	10.4
1981	3.0	12.5	7.6	—[b]

Source: Figures for 1961–80: Canada, Department of Finance, *Economic Review*, April 1981; figures for 1981: Statistics Canada.

[a]Commercial non-agricultural sector.
[b]Not available.

The 1970s were very different from the remarkable quarter century that lasted roughly from the Bretton Woods international agreement of 1944 to the late 1960s. Whatever difficulties there were in that post-war period, in retrospect it seems like an economic golden age.

The Bretton Woods system of fixed and infrequently changing exchange rates used the U. S. dollar as the international reserve currency. In transfers between central banks the dollar was convertible to gold at the fixed rate of $35 per ounce. These arrangements provided the basis for a system of international economic cooperation that included the International Monetary Fund (IMF), the World Bank, and the General Agreement on Trade and Tariffs (GATT). The last of these—and the formation of the European Economic Community—significantly reduced barriers to international trade and it grew rapidly. Output, especially of the industrialized countries, expanded and employment was high. Prosperity increased apace.

The structure of international economic cooperation unfortunately proved vulnerable. As early as 1960 one of its chief foundations, the U. S. dollar, began to weaken, partly because of the economic revival of the industrialized countries of Western Europe and Asia. This development might have been accommodated had the administration of President Lyndon Baines Johnson (1963–69) not chosen to lead the United States into a war in Vietnam without raising taxes to pay for it or otherwise dampening the non-military demand for goods and services. Inflation increased accordingly in the United States and elsewhere. As the Canadian-born economist John Kenneth Galbraith has written: "If prices in the United States are rising, there are few other countries that can avoid the resulting impact. They can have more inflation than the United States; they cannot easily have less." (*Money*, p. 356) The outflow of U. S. dollars, as Americans hastened to buy assets abroad and as the American balance of trade fell into deficit, further weakened the U. S. currency until President Richard Nixon (1969–74) ended the Bretton Woods system in 1971. Henceforth the world had a regime of flexible or "floating" exchange rates, as well as a freed—and soon soaring—world price of gold. There was also a persisting inflationary influence in the form of billions of "Eurodollars" that largely escaped the control of any conventional monetary authority.

There were further inflationary shocks to come. Crop failures in several countries in the early 1970s forced food prices upward. An unusually close correspondence in the timing of strong business expansion in all the major industrial countries exerted further pressure on prices. Finally, in late 1973, the Organization of Petroleum Exporting Countries (OPEC) became an effective international cartel, and promptly quadrupled the world price of oil. The impact of this action is still a matter for debate between contending schools of economic thought, in Canada most notably between neo-Keynesians and monetarists. Indeed, the debate itself is part of the history of the 1970s, as economists of different persuasions gave widely varying advice to policymakers.

In the opinion of some economists the effect of the OPEC price increase of 1973—and even more so of the larger increase in 1979—was both strongly depressing and strongly inflationary in the net oil-consuming countries of the world, including Canada. Small wonder that the term "stagflation" (stagnation/inflation) came into common usage in the 1970s. The steep rise in the price of one of the key commodities of an industrialized and motorized society had very much the same impact as a new tax. Less income was available to spend on other goods and services, and producers duly experienced a decline in demand—or at least in the rate of growth of demand—that was only partly offset by higher imports into the OPEC countries and by the investment of some of the oil profits in the consuming countries.

Economists were generally agreed on the depressing effect of the OPEC price increase and on the transfer of income from the oil-consuming to the oil-producing countries. They were also widely agreed that in the long run these effects would be considerably mitigated as consuming countries responded to the OPEC price increases by extracting more of their own oil, substituting other energy sources for oil, or simply using less non-renewable energy in relation to total production and national income. Of course, the depressing effects of higher oil prices on the economies of the consuming countries tended to restrain the growth of energy use, but much more restraint was possible—and desirable—if energy were to be conserved.

Where economists differed was in respect to the inflationary effect of the OPEC price increases. Neo-Keynesian economists, assigning great importance to the role of rising costs in inflation, drew attention to the central position of oil in the world economy and to the spread effects of an increase in its price: not only did the prices of many oil-based and oil-using goods and services rise rapidly as companies passed on increased costs to consumers, but wage and salary demands rose as employees sought to recoup the spending power they had lost. Monetarists, however, believed that inflation was always fundamentally a monetary phenomenon. They held that the OPEC price increases could and should in the short term be accommodated through relative decreases in the prices of commodities other than oil. Governments and central banks should not try to interfere with the international spread of higher oil prices. That would hinder appropriate longer-range responses to higher oil prices, conservation, and substitution. Instead policy-makers should concentrate on steadying—and steadily reducing—the rates of growth in national money supplies. Defining the supply of money proved to be difficult, but that did not reduce the monetarists' concern to limit the supply, however defined.

The monetarist proposition—founded on a relationship between monetary expansion and inflation that few economists would deny—was an appealing one. First, it was simple, and consistent with a philosophy of minimal government intervention in the economy. As memories of effective intervention in the 1940s, 1950s and 1960s faded, and as governments demonstrated uncertainty in dealing with the problems of the 1970s, the demand for government to play a lesser role in the economy grew. Secondly, monetarism removed the responsibility for contributing to inflation from individuals, assigning it entirely to governments and central banks. This relieved any feelings of guilt in those—particularly those with strong market positions—who might otherwise have felt that they were making some appreciable contribution to inflation. Finally, insofar as monetarist doctrine denounced wage and price controls as harmful tinkering with the natural processes of free markets, it suited those who thought they had some power to protect themselves against inflation. They placed more faith in that power—whether it lay in a strong market position in the sale of goods or services, or membership of a strong union, or a relatively secure job in an economically strong organization—than they did in the anti-inflationary intentions of governments.

The first OPEC price increase in 1973 triggered a world-wide recession. Although the decline in Canada was less than in most other countries, we were not exempt. Governments adopted expansionary fiscal and monetary policies to combat the recession, and in due course economic growth resumed. It became disconcertingly apparent, however, that inflation had now become firmly installed at a higher level, with an alarming propensity to jump even higher. It came to be seen as the predominant problem of the 1970s. Governments tried various remedies but never with total success; inflation persisted.

Monetarist ideas gained ground. By the late 1970s they were being officially sanctioned and adopted in Great Britain, the United States, and Canada. Governments committed themselves to cutting back on rates of growth in their expenditures and on their budgetary deficits. In practice this was very difficult, as increased unemployment fed back into deficits in the form of larger unemployment payments and lower tax revenues, and as tighter monetary policies drove up interest rates and public debt charges. Inflation weakened in the late 1970s but surged back stronger than ever in 1979, powerfully reinforced by the second major round of OPEC price increases.

Successive governmental initiatives to "wrestle inflation to the ground"—the phrase was Prime Minister Trudeau's—failed in their purpose. Public expectations of further inflation became more deeply entrenched and self-fulfilling, and the costs of fighting inflation with monetary restriction were becoming clear: high interest rates, recession, unemployment, and bankruptcies. Around the world there was an uneven but fairly general slowing in the growth of output, productivity, and real living standards. In Britain, where a Conservative government administered monetarist medicine with particular vigor from 1979 onward, unemployment exceeded 10 percent of the labor force by 1981. After the middle of that year the United States was in its second economic recession in two years. The immense weight of the American economy meant that the strongly upward trend of American interest rates had spread around the world, just as war-linked inflation in the United

States had in the 1960s. In Canada interest rates exceeded 20 percent in the late summer of 1981, before receding somewhat in the fall; doom was predicted for farmers, small businesses, and homeowners seeking to renew their mortgages.

Rising unemployment revived one of the evils of the 1930s: protectionism. The restraining influence of the "Tokyo round" of scheduled tariff reductions meant that, for the time being, this new protectionism had to take other forms: quotas could be drawn up for clothing imported from Asian producers; Japanese manufacturers could be bullied into imposing "voluntary export restrictions"; and official support could be given to "buy at home" campaigns.

Class consciousness revived, and crudely self-interested attitudes flourished. Generosity, whether domestic or international, became increasingly unfashionable. In the United States, so-called supply-side economists argued for lower income taxes, claiming that the only way to help the poor was to put more money in the hands of the rich.

Given the openness of their economy and society, Canadians were strongly influenced by economic developments abroad. Macro-economic policy-making shifted during the 1970s to inflation-fighting, here as elsewhere. At the outset of the decade the fiscal position of the federal government was

FISCAL AND MONETARY POLICY

Year	Federal government surpluses and deficits (−)		% increase in money supply (currency and demand deposits)
	National accounts ($000,000)	Budgetary accounts[a] ($000,000)	
1961–65 (average)	−63	−496	5.1
1966–70 (average)	287	−268	6.1
1971	−145	−372	12.7
1972	−566	−702	14.3
1973	387	−971	14.5
1974	1,109	−1,405	9.6
1975	−3,805	−1,650	13.6
1976	−3,391	−5,463	8.1
1977	−7,593	−6,210	8.4
1978	−10,955	−10,289	10.1
1979	−9,131	−12,226	7.2
1980	−10,723	−11,480	6.4

Source: Canada, Department of Finance, *Economic Review*, April 1981.

[a]Fiscal year ending 31 March.

BALANCE OF PAYMENTS
(averages for five-year periods in millions of dollars)

Year	Merchandise trade balance	Services balance	Net transfers	Balance on current account	Net capital move- ments	Special Drawing Rights alloca- tions	Net official move- ments[a]
1961–65	336	−1,082	−21	−767	989	—	222
1966–70	1,255	−1,690	121	−314	635	27	348
1971–75	1,679	−3,257	366	−1,213	1,242	47	76
1976–80	3,929	−8,473	579	−3,965	3,164	87	−714

Source: Canada, Department of Finance, *Economic Review*, April 1981.

[a]Net official monetary movements include transactions in official international reserves and official monetary liabilities.

on the whole mildly anti-inflationary, but monetary policy soon became very expansionary. The government tried to combat unemployment and to control a rising trend in the Canadian dollar. Moreover, in the early 1970s the government made some major commitments concerning unemployment insurance and fiscal transfers to the provinces that would lead to greatly swollen federal deficits. The government's decision in 1973 to protect Canadians' income tax bills against inflation—by indexing personal exemptions— would have equally expensive consequences.

By the mid-1970s the government's emphasis shifted perceptibly toward a more singleminded fight against inflation. This shift reflected public alarm not only at the disturbing course of inflation but also at a growing deficit on current account in international trade, a weakening dollar, and the federal government's plunge into budgetary deficit.

From 1975 to 1978 the federal government imposed direct anti-inflationary controls under the supervision of an Anti-Inflation Board. Most provincial governments instituted stiffer restraints on the growth of expenditures, while for some—most notably Alberta—there were large gains in petroleum and other resource revenues. As a result, the provincial governments as a group emerged from budgetary deficit into a substantial surplus. Reducing the federal deficit was much more difficult, not least because of the contractual commitments made some years earlier. Not until the federal government reached an energy-pricing agreement with Alberta in 1981 did the prospect of reducing the federal deficit significantly improve.

The most dramatic anti-inflationary initiative took place in monetary policy. In 1975 the Bank of Canada undertook gradually to reduce the rate of growth in the money supply. One of the results was a steep rise in interest rates. In spite of the actions of governments and the central bank, the inflation rate and unemployment levels remained high, while growth in average real incomes was small or even negative. By the early 1980s almost all Canadians were economically discontented and did not hesitate to show it.

It is impossible to assess how much of their economic discomfort Canadians brought upon themselves through mistaken policies and how much was unavoidably imported from abroad. The Canadian economy was large enough and autonomous enough to give Canadians much latitude in directing—and occasionally misdirecting—their own affairs. Canada did succeed in increasing total employment faster than any other major industrial country. That was just as well, because the labor force was growing even faster as it absorbed the post-war population boom and much greater numbers of working women.

An early assessment is that Canada could not have done well economically in the 1970s, given the troubled state of the world economy. We could, however, have done better. For instance, foreign observers might have expected Canada to accommodate the OPEC price increases better than we did, given our massive tar-sands deposits and long-range energy resources. Oil pricing, however, was one of the most difficult and politically divisive issues of the 1970s. There were three main reasons for this: the high cost of, and lack of ready access to, so much of Canada's reserves of fossil fuels; the location of most of the country's reserves in the West, away from the largest concentrations of population (and voters); and the unfortunate legacy of an earlier period of oil politics that encouraged many Canadians to believe that readily available reserves were much larger than they were.

In the years just before the OPEC coup of 1973, a few Canadians had inquired uneasily about the long-term adequacy of the country's reserves of oil and natural gas. The short-term situation seemed to be one of glut, and the western petroleum industry was busily searching for export markets and export permits. Both industry and government maintained that the future looked bright; the notion of a "900-year supply" gained wide currency. When Canadians learned of higher OPEC prices, the reaction was predictable: Why should we pay OPEC's rigged prices or worry as the Americans did about shortages? We had lots of oil of our own! But new surveys and inquiries revealed that reserves were much smaller than had been thought. Furthermore, the oil industry, politicians, and voters in the West, were united in resisting the notion that petroleum or natural-gas reserves belonged to Canadians as a whole. The resulting confrontation of regional interests dominated much of the politics of the 1970s and demonstrated vividly how a deteriorating economic situation can widen political and social divisions.

People and Their Work

The population of Canada was an estimated 24,106,000 in the middle of 1981. The average age was climbing, a consequence of a decline in both the death rate and the birth rate. The high reproduction rate of the 1940s and 1950s—the "baby boom"—declined throughout the 1960s and continued to drop, though more gradually, in the 1970s. The census of 1971 indicated that Canadian women were having just enough babies to reproduce the population.

Immigration was important as a source of population growth. Net migration (with those who left Canada subtracted from those who entered it) accounted for 33.8 percent of the general increase in population in the 1970s—a higher proportion than in any other decade since the 1920s. Those who came to Canada were mainly people seeking to improve their economic situation. At different times, they also included groups of political refugees, from Czechoslovakia, Chile, Uganda, and Indo-China, and, until the United States withdrew from Vietnam, young Americans escaping the draft.

POST-WAR IMMIGRATION TO CANADA
(selected countries/areas of former residence)

Country/area of former residence	1946–69	1970–79	Total	1970-79 immigration as % of total post-war immigration
All countries	3,267,144	1,444,917	4,712,061	30.7
Caribbean	56,456	134,118	190,574	70.4
China (inc. Hong Kong and Taiwan)	63,419	91,684	155,103	59.1
France	96,610	31,489	128,099	24.6
Germany (West and East)	304,104	25,966	330,070	7.9
Great Britain	897,433	224,751	1,122,184	20.0
Greece	94,892	37,807	132,699	28.5
India	23,772	70,162	93,934	74.7
Italy	439,571	47,616	487,187	9.8
Netherlands	171,026	15,459	186,485	8.3
Poland	104,327	9,794	114,121	8.6
Portugal	72,347	79,891	152,238	52.5
South America	39,635	82,313	121,948	67.5
United States	287,487	193,111	480,598	40.2

Sources: Canada, Department of Employment and Immigration (formerly Department of Manpower and Immigration), *Immigration Statistics* (annually).

By the early 1970s the 150,000 or more immigrants who arrived in Canada annually were much more likely to be from southern than from northern or eastern Europe. A growing proportion was from the West Indies, South America, and Asia. Both the numbers and the origins created concern. Some Canadians feared that too many Roman Catholics were entering; others reacted negatively to the growing number of non-Caucasians. In cities like Toronto and Vancouver, Indian and Pakistani immigrants encountered violence. Some French Canadians were concerned that most of the newcomers joined the English-speaking majority, and that even in Montreal they were more likely to learn English than French.

Early in 1975 the government issued a Green Paper on Immigration that suggested a range of policy options. Each of these options offended one group or another, as a series of meetings held across the country by a Senate-Commons committee made abundantly clear. The report of this committee recommended an annual quota of at least 100,000 immigrants to offset Canada's declining birth rate. It suggested that the country might have trouble absorbing more than 100,000, and it proposed ways in which immigrants might be directed toward less populous areas. The committee's findings had little effect in the form of legislation, in part because the number of immigrants was already declining—to 115,000 in 1977 and 93,000 in 1978. They continued to settle in the large cities, however, and augmented polyglot communities that some Canadians regarded with suspicion but others learned to appreciate.

POPULATION: DISTRIBUTION AND CHANGE

Region	1961	1971	1981 (interim)	% change 1961–71	% change 1971–81
Canada	18,238,247	21,568,311	24,105,163	18.3	11.8
Newfoundland	457,853	522,104	561,996	14.0	7.6
Prince Edward Island	104,629	111,641	121,328	6.7	8.7
Nova Scotia	737,007	788,960	837,789	7.0	6.2
New Brunswick	597,936	634,557	688,926	6.1	8.6
Quebec	5,259,211	6,027,764	6,377,518	14.6	5.8
Ontario	6,236,092	7,703,106	8,551,773	23.5	11.0
Manitoba	921,686	988,247	1,017,323	7.2	2.9
Saskatchewan	925,181	926,242	957,025	0.1	3.3
Alberta	1,331,944	1,627,874	2,207,856	22.2	35.6
British Columbia	1,629,082	2,184,621	2,716,301	34.1	24.3
Yukon	14,628	18,388	22,684	25.7	23.4
Northwest Territories	22,998	34,807	44,684	51.3	28.4

Sources: Statistics Canada, *1971 Census of Canada;* 1981 Interim Census figures, released 15 January 1982.

During the post-war years the Eskimos (Inuit) and native Indians increased rapidly in numbers—the 1971 census listed 18,000 Inuit and almost 300,000 Indians. Compared with Canadians as a whole they were a very young population: their birth rate was much higher than the average, and infant mortality was at last declining. The native peoples constituted a growing, though still small, proportion of the population.

Population growth was uneven across the country. Canadians continued to move from the rural areas into the cities, particularly the cities of the three westernmost provinces. Sustained by an oil and gas boom, the population of Alberta grew by nearly 36 percent from 1971 to 1981. In Saskatchewan— where until the early 1970s there had been concern about a loss of people—the numbers increased again. British Columbia's population was already grow- ing more quickly than that of the other provinces, and this fast growth continued in the 1970s. The mushrooming growth of Calgary and Edmonton was a clear demonstration of the West's prosperity, but the soaring prices of houses and low rental vacancy rates there and in Vancouver and Victoria brought serious social problems.

The two western provinces attracted immigrants from the rest of Can- ada, particularly from Manitoba, Ontario, and the Maritimes. Yet the bulk of Canadians were still living in two provinces: Quebec and Ontario to- gether contained almost 62 percent of the total population in 1981. This regional imbalance complicated political relations between the federal gov- ernment and the resource-rich western provinces; the West suspected that Ottawa's policies were too much influenced by the preponderance of voters at the country's center.

GROWTH OF THE LABOR FORCE AND EMPLOYMENT

Year	Labor force	Employment
	(% increase)	
1967–71 (average)	3.0	2.2
1972–76 (average)	3.4	3.2
1977	2.9	1.8
1978	3.7	3.4
1979	3.0	4.0
1980	2.8	2.8

Sources: Statistics Canada, *The Labour Force* (monthly).

The labor force consisted of almost 11 million Canadians in 1979. Women were a growing proportion of the labor force, as an increasing number pur- sued a career after marriage or returned to work after raising their children.

This phenomenon reflected economic needs as well as the impact of the women's movement.

The political importance of the women's movement was reflected in the Royal Commission on the Status of Women, chaired by Florence Bird. Appointed by the Pearson government in 1967, it reported three years later. The bulk of the commission's 167 recommendations dealt with education, women in the economy, and women in the family. Of the 122 recommendations that were within federal jurisdiction, 42 had been fully (and 37 partially) implemented by 1974. But a decade after the appearance of the commission's report equal pay for equal work of equal value was still a goal, not a fact. Women accounted for more than a third of the labor force, but they were concentrated in white-collar jobs near the lower end of the pay scale. In 1970 men were paid more than women in 96 percent of all similarly described occupations. Indeed, a study published by the new Advisory Council on Women found that in many occupations differences in pay were increasing.

The obvious under-representation of women in professional occupations and at managerial levels lessened somewhat toward the end of the 1970s as women entered law, medicine, accountancy, and business administration in unprecedented numbers. White-collar and public-service unions began to take the interests of women more seriously. In 1981 when the Canadian Union of Postal Workers went on strike, one of the issues was the full compensation of female workers for loss of income during maternity leave. The union successfully negotiated this point, and other unions adopted it as one of their objectives. Daycare facilities, though still inadequate in most places, were becoming more widely available. But in most families women still carried the major responsibility for home and children, whether they were employed outside the home or not. Equality was a long way off.

The spread of employment as a whole continued to change during the 1970s. The growth industries were trade and finance, business, and community and personal service, including public administration. The services sector employed well over half of Canadian workers, and the sector's output exceeded that of manufacturing and construction in the mid-1970s. By 1980 almost two in three Canadians were white-collar workers, while approximately three in ten were employed in factories, construction, and transportation. Only one in twenty now worked in agriculture, and concern grew about rural depopulation and the future of the family farm, especially on the prairies. Only one in fifty workers was employed in forestry, mining, fishing, or trapping.

SHARES OF THE NATIONAL INCOME
(% distribution of net national income by components)

Year	Labor income	Corpo- ration profits before tax	Divi- dends paid to non- residents	Interest and other invest- ment income	Net farm income	Net unin- corpo- rated business	Inventory valuation adjust- ment	Net national income at factor cost
1961–65 (average)	69.6	14.5	−2.0	4.5	3.7	10.2	−0.4	100.0
1966–70 (average)	72.3	13.6	−1.6	4.9	2.7	8.7	−0.7	100.0
1971	74.1	12.3	−1.5	5.5	2.2	8.4	−0.9	100.0
1972	73.5	13.6	−1.3	5.7	2.1	7.7	−1.3	100.0
1973	71.7	16.3	−1.3	5.7	3.2	7.0	−2.5	100.0
1974	71.4	17.6	−1.4	6.7	3.4	−6.1	−3.7	100.0
1975	72.9	15.1	−1.4	6.7	3.0	5.9	−2.3	100.0
1976	73.6	13.5	−1.2	7.5	2.2	5.7	−1.4	100.0
1977	74.9	13.1	−1.3	8.1	1.8	5.6	−2.1	100.0
1978	73.7	14.2	−1.5	8.7	1.9	5.4	−2.5	100.0
1979	71.4	16.8	−1.4	9.2	2.1	5.1	−3.3	100.0
1980	71.4	16.4	−1.4	9.7	2.1	4.9	−3.0	100.0

Source: Canada, Department of Finance, *Economic Review,* April 1981.

PERCENTAGE DISTRIBUTION OF TOTAL INCOME AND UPPER LIMITS OF INCOME OF FAMILIES AND UNATTACHED INDIVIDUALS (selected years)

Quintile	% distribution of total income						
	1951	1961	1967	1971	1975	1979	1980[a]
Lowest	4.4	4.2	4.2	3.6	4.0	4.2	4.0
Second	11.2	11.9	11.4	10.6	10.6	10.6	10.4
Third	18.3	18.3	17.8	17.6	17.6	17.6	17.7
Fourth	23.3	24.5	24.6	24.9	25.1	25.3	25.5
Highest	42.8	41.1	42.0	43.3	42.6	42.3	42.4
Total	100.0	100.0	100.0	100.0	100.0	100.0	100.0
	Upper limits of income (current $)						
Lowest	1,260	1,930	2,592	3,110	5,038	7,331	7,858
Second	2,310	3,586	4,824	6,275	9,793	14,148	15,498
Third	3,180	4,950	6,807	9,295	14,545	21,380	23,583
Fourth	4,320	6,630	9,468	12,941	20,598	30,400	33,192
Highest	—	—	—	—	—	—	—

Sources: Statistics Canada, *Income Distributions by Size in Canada* (annually). The data for 1951 and 1961 are for non-farm units only; the data for 1967 and later years are for farm and non-farm units.

[a]Preliminary figures.

The share of labor income in the net national income rose early in the 1970s, declined in mid-decade, and rose again to a peak in 1977; thereafter it dropped rapidly to the same level as in the mid-1960s. Corporation profits before tax showed the reverse pattern. Interest and investment income rose spectacularly, almost doubling their share of the national income from 1967 to 1979. During those years the share of unincorporated business income fell by 42 percent, while farm income showed an uneven decline from the mid-1960s onward. The distribution of family income, however, was much the same in the late 1970s as it had been in 1951. In 1980 the bottom 20 percent of families received about 4 percent of the national income, the top 20 percent about 42 percent.

Regional inequalities in income persisted. Throughout the 1970s per capita incomes in the Atlantic provinces and Quebec were below the national average, as were those in Manitoba and Saskatchewan. In some provinces—most notably in Quebec and Saskatchewan—the trend was clearly upward. Per capita income in British Columbia stayed well above the national average, and by the late 1970s was higher than in any other province. Per capita income in Ontario declined throughout the decade. Per capita income in Alberta, buoyed by revenues from oil and natural gas, rose after 1973.

PERSONAL INCOME PER CAPITA
(selected years)

Region	1969	1974 (current $)	1979	% increase 1969–79
British Columbia	3,226	5,761	9,821	204
Alberta	2,944	5,238	9,717	230
Ontario	3,470	5,843	9,608	177
Canada	2,943	5,226	8,902	202
Yukon and Northwest Territories	2,596	4,883	8,569	230
Quebec	2,601	4,733	8,341	221
Saskatchewan	2,368	5,021	8,335	252
Manitoba	2,762	4,950	8,198	197
Nova Scotia	2,279	4,156	7,088	211
New Brunswick	2,062	3,882	6,472	214
Prince Edward Island	1,847	3,478	6,057	228
Newfoundland	1,796	3,518	5,862	226

Source: Statistics Canada, System of National Accounts, *National Income and Expenditure Accounts, 1965–1979*, 1980.

Labor union membership continued the expansion that began during the economic recovery of the mid-1960s. By 1976 union membership was 3,042,000—more than double the figure in 1962. In 1964, 29.4 percent

of non-agricultural workers were union members; twelve years later membership was 37.3 percent and rising. Most of the newly organized were white-
collar and service workers, especially those in the public-service sector. There
the newly won right to strike meant that unresolved grievances led to
interruptions of work that were highly unpopular among the general public. (The long postal strike in the summer of 1968 was one such.) Canada as
a whole seemed to become ever more strike-prone as the number of strikes
in a year, the number of workers involved, and the time lost all increased.
The years 1969, 1972, and 1974–76 were particularly troubled. In 1976 more
than 1.5 million workers were out on strike at one time or another—a
staggering 11.6 million person-days of work lost.

STRIKES AND LOCKOUTS IN CANADA

Year	Number of strikes/lockouts	Workers involved	Person-days lost	
			Person-days	% of estimated working time
1961–65 (average)	355	105,625	1,203,998	0.11
1966–70 (average)	572	291,109	5,705,420	0.35
1971	569	239,631	2,866,590	0.16
1972	598	706,474	7,753,530	0.43
1973	724	348,470	5,776,080	0.30
1974	1,218	580,912	9,221,890	0.46
1975	1,171	506,443	10,908,810	0.53
1976	1,039	1,570,940	11,609,890	0.55
1977	803	217,557	3,307,880	0.15
1978	1,058	401,668	7,392,820	0.34
1979	1,050	462,504	7,834,230	0.34
1980	1,028	441,025	8,975,390	0.38

Source: Canada, Department of Labor, *Strikes and Lockouts in Canada* (annually).

The actions of organized labor had as one important purpose the increase
of real income and, with it, more of "the good things of life." "A central
feature of modern economic society," Galbraith writes in *Money*, " . . . is
the rejection by subordinate social classes of . . . prescriptive limits on their
income and consumption." The wage claims of organized workers in the
1970s exceeded gains in productivity. Insofar as the claims were achieved,
and employers passed on the costs of those claims to consumers, they became
one of the causes of inflation. Of course, inflation itself sparked large wage
claims. But many workers, generally in the non-unionized areas of the economy, did not get increases that matched the rise in the Consumer Price
Index. Persistently high unemployment and weakness in various industries
undermined many demands for higher wages. So did the activities of the

Anti-Inflation Board from 1975 to 1978. Real labor income in Canada rose during the early and mid-1970s, though at a decelerating rate. Late in the decade, real labor income began to decline, a process masked by substantial increases in nominal, or dollar, income. After calculating the effects of inflation, many people knew that they were running hard in order to stay in the same place. It was little consolation to Canadian workers to know that some others, such as those dependent on unindexed pensions, were much worse off.

Ottawa Acts

The Pearson government had taken important steps toward creating a comprehensive system of social security. The key pieces of legislation, both passed in 1966, were the Medical Care Insurance Act and the Canada Assistance Plan, but, for different reasons, neither medicare nor income security was in place when Trudeau took office.

Ottawa had committed itself, from July 1, 1968, to pay half of provincially administered medical-care programs. Most provinces were reluctant to establish such programs, fearing that even half the costs would prove too heavy a burden. Only Saskatchewan and British Columbia had programs eligible for cost-sharing when the appointed day came. The remaining provinces could not resist the promise of financial support for as popular a program as medicare would clearly be: Alberta, Manitoba, Newfoundland, Nova Scotia, and Ontario all introduced medicare in 1969, and by the end of the year only Prince Edward Island had not yet promised to introduce a scheme in the near future. The financial costs to governments and taxpayers would be high, but if the programs worked illness would largely cease to be the financial menace it had been for so long.

The Canada Assistance Plan was hailed in a 1965 House of Commons debate as a plan that would achieve "the full utilization of human resources and the elimination of poverty." It failed to achieve either. The Senate Committee on Poverty in 1971 identified the difficulties of the "working poor" (estimated at two million), and argued that the social security system did not help them sufficiently. The poor were often native people, women, and French Canadians. The report of the Royal Commission on the Status of Women emphasized the vulnerability of one-parent families headed by women, and of single, elderly women.

The costs of welfare programs had risen to an estimated $8.5 billion at all three levels of government in 1969–70. Yet the poor were still with us. Wanting to restrain expenditure, convinced that a good part of the money spent on family allowances or old-age assistance was going to people who did not really "need" to be helped, governments began to question the principle of universality in social-security programs; abandoning that principle, some politicians and civil servants believed, would allow funds to be directed where they were most needed.

The attack on universality was evident in a federal White Paper issued in 1970, *Income Security for Canadians*. It strongly favored income-tested programs for assistance to the elderly and to families. The argument was that by identifying those whose incomes were too low and helping only them, you would be able to restrain spending and ensure that the money you did spend was spent effectively. Opponents argued that income-testing would stigmatize the recipients of aid: people could too vividly remember a time when universal programs did not exist, when to receive government aid was an admission of personal failure.

In spite of criticism, the government prepared legislation for an income-tested Family Income Security Plan. It died on the order paper when Parliament was dissolved in 1972, and in the new Parliament the balance of power was held by the NDP, the party that had opposed income testing. When in April 1973 the Minister of National Health and Welfare, Marc Lalonde, presented a new working paper on income security the principle of universality had reappeared.

An increased willingness to spend money found expression not only in Lalonde's working paper but also in a new Family Allowances Act. It almost tripled benefits, though these were now taxable. Eligibility for unemployment insurance benefits—another important income-maintenance program— had been opened up in 1971. Two years later old-age benefits were raised, and a full review of social-security policies and issues by both Ottawa and the provinces was underway. After an election in 1974, however, the Liberals once again controlled the House of Commons. Concerned about the growing federal budget deficit, the government in 1975 cancelled such employment-creating schemes as the Company of Young Canadians and Opportunities for Youth. A desire to cut costs contributed to the decision to withdraw the Social Services Act, introduced in 1976 to provide for federal cost-sharing of a wide range of services; Quebec's opposition to a federal invasion of provincial jurisdiction also played a part. More basically, a mood of restraint was unfavorable to comprehensive wars on poverty. With all its inadequacies, the Canada Assistance Plan was still around.

Like the system of social security, the system of federal taxation had changed less by the late 1970s than the government had anticipated a decade earlier. The Royal Commission on Taxation, headed by Kenneth Carter, reported in 1967. The guiding principle of the report was equity. Different classes of taxpayers should be treated differently and different sources of income should be treated equally: "A buck is a buck is a buck." Two years later the Minister of Finance, Edgar Benson, tabled a White Paper on tax reform. Although it did not include some of the Carter Commission's more rigorously logical but politically unpalatable proposals, the White Paper ran into strong opposition. The business community expressed outrage, not least because of the suggestion that capital gains, which had previously escaped taxation, be taxed at income rates. The two "fundamental goals" of reform were "equity and economic growth," Benson said in a speech in October 1970. "Establishing a fair and just balance between these goals and stopping the abuses that exist in our present system is our real objective." Critics of the White Paper argued that it failed to give due weight to the need for growth.

When the Finance Minister introduced his tax reform legislation in 1971, the criticism of the White Paper had clearly had an impact. Although capital gains were still to be taxed, only half of the amount would be subject to taxation. Largely lost was the notion—central to the Carter report—that taxpayers with different ability to pay should be treated differently, and taxpayers with equal ability to pay should be treated equally. This loss can be ascribed to the effective lobbying of well-financed business interest groups and to the weakening of the economy in 1970–71. The latter emphasized the need for economic growth; the former demonstrated the well-known political principle that small groups of people, each of whom has a large financial stake in the outcome of a government decision, will often "out-lobby" much larger opposing groups whose interests are spread so thinly that each individual's stake is small.

Inflation and unemployment dominated much of government policy-making in the late 1960s and 1970s. Persuaded by the business community that high wage demands were mainly responsible for inflation, the federal government late in 1968 appointed a Prices and Incomes Commission, chaired by Dr. John Young, a University of British Columbia economist. Unable to gain the cooperation of organized labor and lacking powers of enforcement, the Young Commission accomplished little in its three years of life. The rate of inflation did slow in 1970 and early 1971, but that was chiefly the result of an international recession. The government feared that rising unemployment might lose it the next general election and in 1971 duly switched to an expansionary fiscal policy. At the same time the Bank of Canada turned to a policy of "easy money," partly in order to keep the dollar, unpegged in 1970, from appreciating too much against its American counterpart. From the beginning of 1971 to the end of 1973 the money supply grew by almost half. The expansionary fiscal and monetary policies reinforced the effects of an international commodities boom. Economic growth picked up gratifyingly, corporation profits doubled from 1972 to 1974, and unemployment declined. But inflation came storming back, and labor unrest mounted. Most unions were forced to play catch-up, and kept on playing it when the new OPEC-caused recession began in 1974.

In the federal election of 1974 the Liberals ridiculed the wage and price controls proposed by the Conservatives. After winning the election, the Liberal government opted initially for a policy of voluntary restraint on the part of wage earners. Few of them listened. For two years labor compensation per unit of output had lagged behind profits and inflation; now workers wanted large raises. The government, and many economists, believed that such raises would undermine the competitiveness of Canadian products in our major market, the United States. Canadian competitiveness was in any case declining because of the appreciation of our dollar against the American currency since 1970. Exports and jobs were in danger; the deficit in our balance of trade was growing. On Thanksgiving Day in 1975 Prime Minister Trudeau appeared on television to inform Canadians that Parliament would be asked to impose wage controls on several classes of employees, as well as profit and dividend controls on larger firms. The reversal in policy was spectacular, all the more so because the previous year Trudeau had maintained that controls would not work.

Because many workers were, under the constitution, beyond the control of the federal government, Trudeau invited the provinces to adhere to wage and price controls. They did so with varying degrees of enthusiasm. Responsibility for enforcing the guidelines went to an Anti-Inflation Board (AIB), which could order wage or price rollbacks. It was chaired by Jean-Luc Pepin, a former Liberal cabinet minister. The vice-chairperson was Beryl Plumptre, a veteran of the earlier and largely ineffectual Food Prices Review Board.

The AIB's major accomplishment was to limit wage and salary gains markedly and thus to help restore the competitiveness of Canadian goods and services, although the decline of the Canadian dollar after 1976 also contributed. The continuing opposition of labor leaders to controls was understandable: labor's share in the national income was declining and that of capital was growing. But the business community, which had initially been sympathetic, also came to oppose controls. They were irksome and involved a lot of paperwork, and they raised the specter of more comprehensive state planning of the economy. When wage and price controls expired in 1978 few Canadians mourned their passing.

From 1973 onward few federal policies created more conflict than the pricing of oil and gas. As Canada was not a member of OPEC, Canadian oil prices were not bound to go up in 1973. But the oil companies would obviously welcome higher prices, and the government of Alberta—the province in which most Canadian oil and gas were to be found—might wish to take advantage of the situation to raise its royalties. Alberta supplied oil only to the area west of the Ottawa River; to the east, consumers depended on oil from abroad, oil hitherto cheaper than the domestic product. The OPEC increases meant much higher prices for Quebec and the Atlantic provinces. Because the latter was economically the weakest region in Canada, and because Quebec was increasingly disaffected, the federal government wished to shelter them both from the full blast of OPEC price increases.

ENERGY PRICES

Year	Consumer prices					Crude oil prices	
	Gasoline	Natural gas	Electricity	Fuel oil	Total energy	Imported CIF Montreal	Wellhead FOB Edmonton
			(% changes)			($ per barrel)	
1961–65 (average)	1.0	0.2	−0.5	−2.9	n.a.	2.37	2.86
1966–70 (average)	3.0	—	4.7	2.0	n.a.	2.61	2.90
1971	3.5	1.5	3.4	9.6	n.a.	2.95	3.15
1972	0.8	0.6	2.7	6.1	2.8	2.86	3.18
1973	6.8	1.6	8.1	15.7	9.0	3.95	3.79
1974	16.6	10.1	3.8	29.3	15.2	11.29	6.14
1975	13.2	20.8	11.6	13.5	13.5	12.59	7.94
1976	12.4	29.0	16.0	16.1	15.4	12.88	8.88
1977	8.6	13.1	17.0	15.5	12.2	15.16	10.67
1978	5.6	18.8	8.1	14.0	9.3	16.28	12.73
1979	10.2	5.4	8.7	12.4	9.8	22.66	13.76
1980	19.0	11.8	9.3	20.2	16.1	36.99	16.11

Source: Canada, Department of Finance, *Economic Review*, April 1981.

The two-price system was born. As international oil prices rose, the Prime Minister announced that the domestic price would be lower than the export price, and that a tax on exports would help to subsidize the price of oil in the five eastern provinces. The Interprovincial Pipeline would be extended to Montreal in order to reduce Quebec's dependence on oil imported from abroad. Prodded by the NDP, the government announced late in 1973 that it hoped to develop Canadian self-sufficiency in oil by the end of the 1970s. It envisaged a national energy policy based on the exploitation of the huge tar-sands deposits in northern Alberta, the creation of a national oil company, and the construction of a gas pipeline up the Mackenzie Valley in the Northwest Territories.

PetroCanada began operating in 1975. Financial concessions and support from the governments of Canada, Alberta, and Ontario started Syncrude Ltd. on its way to exploiting the tar sands and it began production in 1978. The Mackenzie Valley pipeline had been postponed, pending the outcome of an inquiry into its environmental and social effects, and the government had already discovered that it was easier to announce a national energy policy than to make it succeed.

The central difficulty was that such a policy involved interference with the control over natural resources that the constitution gave to the provinces. The oil- and gas-producing provinces—principally Alberta, but also Saskatchewan and British Columbia—wanted the best possible financial return from their resources. The governments of the consuming provinces looked to Ottawa to maintain the two-price system and to moderate increases in the domestic price. The oil companies wanted to maximize their revenues as the best guarantee, so they argued, of aggressive exploration, new discoveries, and future Canadian self-sufficiency. They urged the removal of Canadian controls over exports to the United States, but the government, acting on advice from the National Energy Board (NEB), was seeking to reduce oil exports. American policy-makers were unhappy about this, and about the two-price policy in oil and large increases in the price of natural gas exports.

To make matters worse, expert estimates of oil and gas reserves varied by hundreds of years. The optimism of some estimates was no preparation for the November 1974 report from the NEB that argued that serious shortages in both oil and gas were imminent unless exports to the United States were cut back further or new supplies were located and tapped.

One of the government's assumptions in late 1973 was that a pipeline in the Mackenzie Valley was necessary to carry Mackenzie Delta gas to southern Canada as well as Alaska North Slope gas for trans-shipment to the United States. But the federal government was worried about the impact of pipelines on the northern Yukon and the Mackenzie Valley; so in early 1974 they appointed Mr. Justice Thomas Berger to undertake a full inquiry. After traveling extensively in the north and giving the native peoples, industry representatives, environmentalists, and others full opportunity to express their views, Berger reported in 1977. *Northern Frontier, Northern Homeland* recommended that no pipeline ever be built across the northern Yukon because of the irreparable damage involved, and that a Mackenzie Valley pipeline be postponed for ten years. This would permit a better assessment of the oil and gas reserves in the delta and the Beaufort Sea, the settlement of native land claims, and the establishment of programs and institutions to help the native peoples during and after construction of the pipeline.

The government accepted the Berger recommendations, and in 1978 Parliament passed enabling legislation for a pipeline routed along the Alcan Highway; this would link up in Alaska with a line carrying gas from Prudhoe Bay. A feeder line would carry gas from the Mackenzie Delta along the Dempster Highway to Dawson, Y. T. In the south the Alcan pipeline would link up with existing or new lines to transmit gas to central and eastern Canada and to the United States. By the fall of 1981 cost estimates for the northern lines had risen to the point that lenders were reluctant to advance funds. Action by the United States Congress would be necessary to provide the loan guarantees needed before northern gas could reach either the Canadian or the American market.

In 1975 Ottawa and the producing provinces reached a pricing agreement that was expected to raise Canadian prices almost to world levels four years later. Canada continued to be a net importer of oil. In 1979 OPEC imposed further huge increases that raised prices to more than ten times their pre-1973 levels. This action not only greatly widened the price gap between Canadian and world prices but also pushed up the cost of the oil subsidy to the eastern provinces to $2.5 billion a year. Victorious in the May 1979 general election, the Progressive Conservatives made self-sufficiency by 1990 a priority. Conservation seemed to be the key, along with new exploration; both were to be achieved through higher prices. The prospect of a series of hikes in the price of oil and an increase in the federal gasoline tax contributed to the Conservatives' election defeat in February 1980.

Back in office, the Liberals returned with renewed vigor to their national energy policy. Late in 1980 the government announced that PetroCanada would expand, that only companies that were at least 75 percent Canadian-owned would qualify for new federal exploration grants, and that foreign participation in the oil and gas industry was to drop over time to less than 50 percent. The new objectives delighted nationalists and enraged many in the oil and gas industry. Some took their drilling rigs south to the United States, where the recent election of a Republican president, Ronald Reagan, promised a less restrictive environment for business.

In September 1981 Ottawa reached a pricing agreement with the government of Alberta. (Saskatchewan and British Columbia soon signed similar agreements.) The bargaining had been difficult and sometimes acrimonious, but the deal promised substantially increased revenues to both Ottawa and Alberta. An early estimate was that the federal government would get $54 billion over the next sixty-six months, and Alberta $64 billion. The oil companies would get $94 billion, but on terms that clearly dissatisfied them. "Old" (already discovered) oil would get only half the price of "new" oil, and natural gas, currently in surplus, would get a separate, lower price. The industry soon complained that they were no better off than before the agreement. But who could sympathize with the oil producers—many of whom had become very wealthy—when Canadian consumers were facing the prospect of paying 80 cents a litre for gasoline in July 1986, 57 cents a litre for heating oil, and $9.95 for 1,000 cubic feet of natural gas—in each case more than double the price in early 1981? Domestic prices would continue to be below world prices. Anyone who traveled abroad was well aware that in 1986 Canadians would still be paying less than most Europeans were paying in 1980, but this was scant consolation to people inhabiting a land of cold winters and long distances. It remained to be seen whether the national energy policy and the new pricing agreement would enable the country to secure self-sufficiency before the end of the century—if ever. Much depended on the extent to which higher prices would induce Canadians to conserve energy.

If there was one federal policy that created more controversy in the 1970s than oil and gas pricing, it was bilingualism. National unity was Trudeau's goal: if the linguistic and cultural equality of French Canadians could be secured, he believed, then Quebec could in constitutional matters be treated simply as another province.

The Official Languages Act became law in 1969. English and French were to be co-equal languages of the federal civil service, the Crown agencies, and the federal courts. An appointed council would set up "bilingual districts" in areas where a minority of either group constituted at least 10 percent of the population; full federal services would be available in both languages there. A federal languages commissioner, who would report directly to Parliament, would monitor the legislation. Speaking to the Press in July 1969, Trudeau explained that:

. . . to build and maintain a strong and united country, it is essential that both French- and English-speaking Canadians should be able to feel at home in all parts of the country, and that their rights as members of our major language groups should be respected by the federal government. That is the objective of the Official Languages Act and of our policy of bilingualism.

There was vocal opposition to the Act, especially in the West, and John Diefenbaker led a small group of Progressive Conservative MPs who voted against it, in defiance of the party's leader, Robert Stanfield.

A professor of political science, Keith Spicer, became the first Commissioner of Official Languages. The Royal Commission on Bilingualism and Biculturalism published *The Work World,* the third volume of its report, in 1969, and the fourth volume, *The Cultural Contributions of the Other Ethnic Groups*, in 1970. Most controversial was the assessment in the third volume that "individual bilingualism" in the civil service was impossible, and the commission's recommendation that, if the service was to cease to be "overwhelmingly an expression of English-speaking Canada," then there must be institutional bilingualism through the creation of French-language work units. The government subsequently spent large amounts of money setting up an elaborate system for teaching French to anglophone public servants. This had the dual purpose of enabling some of them to function in French and of denying to all of them a solid basis for claiming that language was, and could not help but be, an unjust bar to their promotion. The language training program and, indeed, the entire effort to introduce institutional bilingualism earned little support and much criticism in English Canada.

In February 1972 five Progressive Conservative MPs, among them veterans George Hees and Patrick Nowlan, charged that the policy of bilingualism was proof of a "Montreal Mafia" running the country and "destroying the traditions of English Canada." The policy was not a major issue in the federal election later that year, though civil service resentment may have helped the election of the Conservative candidate in Ottawa West. By the fall of 1974 the estimated number of bilingual civil servants was 53,000, approximately 19 percent of the total.

In 1974 the Supreme Court of Canada unanimously rejected a challenge to the constitutionality of the Official Languages Act, but opposition continued. A Gallup Poll in May 1976 revealed that 54 percent of Canadians (73 percent of anglophones, 16 percent of francophones) thought that there was too much emphasis on bilingualism. This was before the June dispute over the use of French in air traffic control over Quebec that brought virtually all air travel in Canada to a halt. It was probably the first popular strike in the country's history. English Canadians overwhelmingly supported the anglophone pilots and air traffic controllers who opposed the Ministry of Transport decision to sanction the use of French. As the historian John Saywell later commented in the *Canadian Annual Review*:

> The question was whether Canadian pilots and air traffic controllers could, in the name of safety in the air (and in reality some combination of real concern over safety,

some concern over job security, and some undoubted anti-francophone prejudices) successfully combat the government's bilingual policy. The answer, seemingly, was that they could and, with the backing of an inflamed opinion in anglophone Canada, did.

Many French Canadians inferred that language, not air safety, was the real issue. The dispute, and the government's almost total capitulation in order to get air traffic moving again, united French Canadian opinion as no other issue had since conscription. Three years later the commission to which the government had handed the problem reported that there were no risks attached to the use of both languages in air traffic control and recommended that bilingual control be introduced over Quebec. Anglophone opinion about the issue had cooled and there was little public reaction when the government of Joe Clark accepted the recommendation. In 1976 the issue significantly assisted the Parti Québécois in the provincial election. A poll taken just before that election showed that 43 percent of Canadians believed that relations between the two main language groups had deteriorated over the previous five years.

Bilingualism fared no better after 1976. The Liberal government in Quebec had promoted the cause of French unilingualism in the province; its PQ successor went even further: it outlawed English or bilingual billboards and business street signs. Nevertheless, anglophones in Quebec were better served in their language than francophones outside Quebec were in theirs, as a report by the *Fédération des francophones hors Québec* demonstrated in 1978. In a study for the C. D. Howe Foundation the sociologist Richard Joy perceived a trend to unilingualism both in Quebec and elsewhere.

When the Task Force on National Unity that was established by the federal government in 1977 reported two years later, it criticized the implementation of "costly and relatively ineffective" institutional bilingualism in the public service. In the western provinces, and particularly in the prairies, the federal government's multicultural program was more popular and had more support from provincial politicians than bilingualism. (This program created a variety of ways for Canadians of all ethnic backgrounds to maintain, strengthen, and celebrate their contribution to Canadian culture.) Given the comparative unpopularity of bilingualism in many parts of Canada, some observers wondered whether the bilingual policy had been worth the trouble and expense it entailed; others asserted that it had done more to divide than to unite the country. Yet a man as critical of the Liberal government as Joe Clark acknowledged that, whatever else might be said about official bilingualism, its success in attracting a larger number of capable francophones into the public service of Canada was a fine, and long overdue, achievement.

Government policy toward aboriginal peoples and their land claims caused growing concern in the 1970s. In June 1969 the government tabled a White Paper on Indian Policy that advocated "the full, free and non-discriminatory participation of the Indian people in Canadian society." Legally and administratively Indians would in time become like other Canadians. Indian reaction was overwhelmingly negative. Harold Cardinal's charge in *The Unjust Society* was typical: the White Paper proposed "cultural genocide," and was "a thinly disguised programme of extermination through assimilation." There was an equally negative Indian reaction to a recommendation strongly urged by the Royal Commission on the Status of Women in 1970: that Indian women should not lose their aboriginal property rights when marrying non-Indians or non-status Indians. Ten years later the recommendation had not been implemented.

In 1971 the government formally retracted the White Paper proposals, and subsequent policy tended to be reactive. After decades of being managed by others, Indians and Inuit were in the 1970s actively seeking to define their own future. The formation of the National Indian Brotherhood in 1968 and the Inuit Tapirisat in 1971 reflected and encouraged this process. The native cause gained strength from a split decision by the Supreme Court of Canada in 1973 on the Nishga land claim in northern British Columbia. Although the Court dismissed the case on a technicality, it led the government to accept the legitimacy of claims to aboriginal rights. Among the results were agreements with the Inuit and Cree in northern Quebec in 1975 in respect of land required by Hydro Québec for its James Bay project, and negotiations with the Inuit in the Northwest Territories and Labrador. The postponement of the Mackenzie Valley pipeline also bore witness to the government's new attitude.

Aboriginal land claims were not simple, particularly where important supplies of natural resources were at stake. The claims to aboriginal nationhood that began to be made in the early 1970s were even more problematic. The Dene Indian nation in 1975 not only laid claim to 1.1 million km² of the Northwest Territories, they also claimed self-determination within Canada. They would achieve this through an all-Indian government, an idea that offended Métis and white opinion in the region. The federal government would not accept the notion, nor a similar proposal from the Inuit Tapirisat. In 1974 the Inuit first broached the idea of dividing the Northwest Territories in two, with the northern half, Nunavut, effectively under Inuit control. In its final form the scheme received the approval of the Tapirisat in 1979.

Trudeau responded to such proposals by announcing in 1977 that, just as there could be no special status for Quebec, there could be none for nations of aboriginal peoples. The government still held to that position in the early 1980s, and it is likely that it accurately reflected opinion in the metropolitan south, and white and Métis opinion in the north.

The government's attitude to aboriginal claims to nationhood complicated the settlement of land claims in the north. In 1978 the Committee on Original People's Entitlement (COPE) succeeded in achieving an agreement in principle with the Department of Indian Affairs and Northern Development that established a basis for the settlement of COPE's claims on behalf of the Inuit of Banks Island in the western Arctic. But three years later the crucial matter of oil and gas exploration and development—and some measure of Inuit control over them—had still not been settled, leading COPE to threaten court action that might tie up exploration in the Beaufort Sea. The pressure on the government to settle land claims was strong, but it was no longer possible to get agreement to the alienation of land, as in the treaties of the nineteenth century or even in the James Bay "cash-for-land" deal of 1975. The question now was whether the federal government would ever accept the notion of special status for native peoples. More basically, would southern Canadians be able to stop thinking of the north as "ours," for "us" to develop, and learn to think of it as a country with its own peoples who could not be shoved aside?

The Federal Government and the Provinces

Relations between the federal government and the provinces have often been difficult, but as a period of particular strain the Trudeau years rank with Sir John A. Macdonald's second term in office (1878–91), the years of the Union government (1917–21), and the Depression of the 1930s. Canada's survival seemed more threatened at the beginning of the 1980s than it had for almost a century.

Much of the squabbling concerned the familiar problem of money, but there were also questions of jurisdiction. The provinces accused the federal government of infringing on areas of provincial jurisdiction; they also, somewhat paradoxically, charged Ottawa with trying to reduce its responsibilities while retaining sources of revenue that, by right or by need, belonged to the provinces.

Speaking in 1968, Pierre Trudeau expressed a certain cynicism about federal–provincial battles: "It's provincial politicians and provincial civil servants wanting more power for themselves . . . and federal politicians and civil servants wanting more power for themselves. . . ." More thoroughly than most Canadian politicians he had developed personal views on federalism. They found expression in his collection of essays, *Federalism and the French Canadians* (1968). He made his operating principle clear in an emergency debate on housing policy in 1969. In response to criticism of federal government inaction, he said he understood the point of view that, once a problem became national in scope, Parliament should act, even though the area was constitutionally within provincial jurisdiction. But he did not share it. It implied that "Parliament ought to be able to amend the constitution unilaterally, without reference to the provinces whose jurisdiction is being changed. . . . The trouble with this view is that it is not really federalism. In many ways it is much more consistent with a unitary state. And a unitary state simply will not work in Canada." The federal government could only assume responsibility for areas within provincial jurisdiction if the provinces agreed.

Although Trudeau was a federalist, he was also a liberal who believed that the state should seek to equalize opportunity for all citizens and mitigate the effects of—or even eliminate—poverty. Liberalism, he said in 1968, stood for "a just distribution of the national wealth." At the federal–provincial conference of December 1969 he stated that "under a new constitution the Parliament of Canada ought to have the power to redistribute income for the purpose of alleviating wide disparities in family income and for the purpose of alleviating poverty generally across Canada." In confronting premiers like Ontario's John Robarts and Quebec's Jean-Jacques Bertrand, Trudeau asserted that "all governments can take money from citizens and all governments should be able to give money to citizens."

He had made his point, though successive premiers of Quebec would continue to quarrel with it. Most of the premiers were more concerned in the 1970s about their ability to finance their own programs than about direct federal payments to individual Canadians. All premiers faced the reality of rapidly rising costs, especially for health care and education. Most of them knew that they could only keep their budgets in balance if they increased taxation or if Ottawa increased its transfer payments to the provinces. Because increased taxation would be widely unpopular, it is not surprising that the premiers showed a marked preference for the second course.

The federal government was prepared to vacate additional tax room for the provinces, provided the latter would assume full responsibility for the increasingly expensive shared-cost programs: hospital insurance, medicare, and post-secondary education. But the federal offer was never sweet enough to tempt most premiers. British Columbia's W. A. C. Bennett more than once proposed that Ottawa vacate the field of direct taxation altogether. Others did not go that far but they did want more tax abatement than the federal government would grant.

The premiers vehemently opposed Finance Minister Edgar Benson's White Paper on tax reform for what they judged would be its negative effect on their revenues. Their objections had the desired effect: they received a guarantee in the 1972 Fiscal Arrangements Act that they would be compensated for any loss in provincial revenues arising from Ottawa's reformed personal and corporate income tax legislation of 1971. The Act did not deal with the shared-cost programs, and the attempt by the federal government in 1973 to end its involvement failed. At a first ministers' conference Saskatchewan's premier, Allan Blakeney, argued strongly for a continued federal presence in financing the programs. Ontario's William Davis and Quebec's Robert Bourassa wanted Ottawa out, but wanted the government to cede 28 tax points as compensation for rising costs of health services and post-secondary education. Trudeau and his cabinet were worried about their own rising costs for programs like unemployment insurance and were unwilling to cede that much. In the absence of a new agreement the two levels of government reluctantly agreed to renew the cost-sharing formula for post-secondary education for three years; health services were to receive further study.

By the end of 1973, conflict over oil and gas had become the main problem in federal–provincial relations. Ottawa's relations with the three westernmost provinces deteriorated rapidly. As head of an NDP government, Premier Blakeney did not reject the federal resolve to ensure that, in his words, "the benefits of our wealth and the burden of our national problems should be shared equitably by all the people, wherever they may live." But why, he asked, apply the rule only to oil? Why not include copper, nickel or other minerals? "It [oil] should be sold at a price, we are told, related to cost. Now Saskatchewan doesn't object to the principle of selling commodities on a cost-plus basis, but why stop at oil?"

Much less sympathetic than Blakeney to government management of the economy, Alberta's Progressive Conservative premier, Peter Lougheed, told the other first ministers early in 1974: "For the rest of Canada to ask Albertans to sell below fair value for any extended period of time is simply an unreasonable request."

Part of Lougheed's problem was that few people outside the oil industry were inclined to regard the OPEC price as fair; Trudeau and his government had the support of most premiers and most Canadians in keeping domestic prices below world levels. Provincial control over natural resources was a high card, but the federal government could trump it by using its powers of direct taxation and control over trade and commerce. It used both in 1973 and 1974, enraging Lougheed and many other Albertans, particularly the inhabitants of Calgary's "Oil Patch." Trudeau only partially mollified Alberta in the 1975 price agreement, which provided for a gradual rise in the domestic price of oil to a point just below the OPEC level. As OPEC increases had slowed down, most premiers supported the agreement. Ominously, Premier Davis opposed it: he feared the effect of rising oil prices on the competitiveness of Ontario's manufacturing industry.

In Saskatchewan, dismay over Ottawa's attitude to two provincial statutes dealing with resources led Premier Blakeney in 1976 to charge the federal government with a "systematic and deliberate attempt to destroy . . . the provincial rights to resource ownership." At issue were two pieces of litigation, *Central Canadian Potash Co. Ltd. et al v. Government of Saskatchewan,* and *Canadian Industrial Gas and Oil Ltd. v. Government of Saskatchewan.* In the former case eleven potash companies challenged the constitutionality of the province's scheme to pro-rate potash production; the scheme had originated with the Liberal government of Ross Thatcher but continued under the NDP. The latter case involved a challenge to the constitutionality of a provincial royalty that limited windfall gains made by petroleum companies as a consequence of rapid price increases. What upset Blakeney was that the federal government became a co-plaintiff in the first case and sought unsuccessfully to become one in the second. It did not help that the Supreme Court of Canada ultimately found for plaintiff in both cases.

Blakeney's annoyance was one instance of an alienation in the West from the policies of the federal government that grew more or less steadily during the 1960s and 1970s. Those who felt seriously disaffected generally directed their anger against the federal Liberals, in office since 1963. Prairie farmers, for example, believed that the Liberal government did not take wheat growing and the family farm seriously enough, and that it failed to appreciate the crucial importance of rail transportation. The Lower Inventories for Tomorrow program (LIFT), prompted by the record grain surpluses of the late 1960s, was well-intended but also deeply disturbing to many farmers—as was the first Grain Income Stabilization Bill of 1970, since the incomes it sought to stabilize had been abnormally low in previous years. Farmers saw both government initiatives as threats to their still-dominant position in prairie society. When prices sky-rocketed after 1971, farmers felt that the government's subsidizing of domestic consumers at the expense of producers was adding insult to injury.

Resentment grew in the West: tax reform in 1971 penalized the mining industry, and Ottawa's bilingual policy seemed irrelevant and even offensive. After suffering losses in all four western provinces in the 1972 general election, the Liberal government recognized the need to improve its image there. In July 1973 it sponsored the Western Economic Opportunities Conference in Calgary. British Columbia, Saskatchewan, and Manitoba had NDP governments; in Alberta the Progressive Conservatives were in office. Representatives of the four provinces found it easy to unite in criticizing federal policies, including tariffs, the transportation policy, the treatment of agriculture, the taxation of mining, and federal energy policy. Liberal fortunes in the West did not improve, and "western alienation" was a reality by the end of the decade. Indeed, by 1980 a separatist movement had emerged in Alberta and British Columbia, and in Saskatchewan a small group led by a former provincial leader of the Progressive Conservative party sought annexation to the United States. Western separatism enjoyed the support of only a small minority, however. It was too early to tell whether that minority would grow.

By 1981, the approaching end of the first five-year term of the Established Programs Financing (EPF) arrangements between Ottawa and the provinces was bringing federal–provincial relations into sharp focus. (The arrangements were to be renegotiated when the first term ended on 31 March 1982.) In 1976 the two levels of government had reached an agreement on the three major shared-cost programs: hospital insurance, medical care, and post-secondary education. Under EPF the federal government withdrew from the shared-cost aspect of these programs. Ottawa would continue to help finance them by yielding personal and corporate tax points to the provinces and by transferring cash to them; the amount of the transfer would escalate annually at the rate of growth in per capita Gross National Product (GNP). The full formula for calculating the amounts of money to be transferred to the provinces was so mind-numbingly complicated that few could assess how EPF might develop. It was all the more complicated because the governments adopted a new equalization formula at the same time. One of its important effects was to shield Ottawa from the dramatic increase in its equalization payments to the "have-not" provinces that rising resource revenues in Alberta, Saskatchewan, and British Columbia would have caused.

The EPF arrangements had come into effect in 1977. They gave both Ottawa and the provinces something they wanted: for the former, control over an important area of expenditure, for it no longer had to match provincial spending on the established programs dollar for dollar; for the latter, the opportunity of saving money on the established programs without having to share the savings with Ottawa. Premier Richard Hatfield of New Brunswick noted at a 1981 conference on university financing:

> These arrangements came into force about the same time that the economy really started slowing down, forcing provincial governments to exercise greater restraint in spending. . . . This was necessary because of slow growth in revenues. And we were not inhibited from doing so because we could do it without losing federal dollars.

Premier Hatfield did not mention it, but slow economic growth also meant that federal revenue grew more slowly than had been expected, more slowly than the increase in per capita GNP. In order to live up to the terms of EPF, the federal government had to make larger-than-anticipated cash transfers; these added to its mounting deficits in the late 1970s. At the same time, the transfers covered a growing share of the cost of the established programs—more than a fair share, the federal government thought, and a share for which it received no political credit. (In the case of post-secondary education Ottawa did not even have the right to be consulted.) The federal government's revenue as a proportion of GNP was declining; provincial revenues as a proportion of GNP were increasing. It was small wonder that by the beginning of 1982 the future of EPF was in doubt. Federal–provincial relations would undergo further strain before new fiscal arrangements were in place.

Quebec and the Constitution

Of many uneasy relationships between the federal government and the provinces in the 1970s the relationship between Ottawa and Quebec was the most difficult. Like other provinces, Quebec wanted to maximize its control over key areas of the economy, but it also wanted something unique: special status as the homeland of francophone Canadians. Its attempt to claim this status led to several confrontations between Ottawa and the Union Nationale and Liberal governments of Quebec in the 1960s and early 1970s; the confrontations intensified after the separatist Parti Québécois took office in 1976.

When the PQ was founded in October 1968 few would have predicted its electoral victory eight years later. The Union Nationale was in office; the Liberals formed the opposition. A Gallup Poll released on 16 October revealed that only 11 percent of the people of Quebec supported separatism, 72 percent opposed it, and the remaining 17 percent were undecided. During the years that followed, a growing number of voters began to believe that the PQ offered the best hope for competent and honest administration. Many voters also came to see a PQ government as the best means of securing the primacy of French in all areas of public life, including business. That primacy was particularly important to intellectuals, for whom language was a key tool in their work. It also mattered to many other people—both middle- and working-class—who believed that establishing the dominance of French would increase their own opportunities to advance, and would enable Quebec to survive and grow. These people were not all separatists; most of them feared that Quebec would gradually be assimilated into an English-speaking continent unless aggressive steps were taken to prevent it.

Education, language, and the place of immigrants in Quebec society were central issues throughout the late 1960s and 1970s. The decision of the school board in the Montreal suburb of St. Léonard in 1968 that all Roman Catholic immigrant children should attend French schools was highly controversial. The provincial government had to take a stand. Bill 63, tabled in the National Assembly in October 1969, made French the prevailing language of instruction but offered parents the freedom to choose whether their children should be taught in French or English. In spite of strong pressure from French-language organizations brought together in the *Front du Québec français,* the government of Jean-Jacques Bertrand refused to abandon the voluntary principle.

The Union Nationale was defeated in the April 1970 election. One reason was the growing weakness of the economy; another was that a large part of the party's *nationaliste* support went to the PQ, which, with 23 percent of the vote, had become the second most popular party, after the victorious Liberals under Robert Bourassa. The PQ's support was diffuse, however, and the party took only seven seats—fewer than either the Union Nationale or the *Ralliement des créditistes,* the provincial Social Credit party.

Montreal life in 1969 and 1970 was notable for its violence. In March 1969 the McGill *français* march that was held to support the demand that McGill University be turned into a francophone institution was accompanied by looting and vandalism. There was rioting on St. Jean Baptiste Day, a major explosion at the federal Manpower Center in August, and the bombing of Montreal mayor Jean Drapeau's house in September. A wildcat strike by Montreal policemen and firemen in October witnessed an outbreak of riot, looting, and arson, and an attack by several hundred taxi drivers on the establishment of Murray Hill, operator of airport limousines and buses, that resulted in one death and several injuries. Bomb explosions continued into 1970, the responsibility mainly of a few members of the *Front de libération québécois* (FLQ). The FLQ's terrorism and radical separatism had little support, and was condemned by the PQ leader, René Lévesque, among others.

On October 5, 1970, a cell of the FLQ abducted the British Trade Commissioner in Montreal, James Cross. Five days later another cell abducted the Quebec Labor Minister, Pierre Laporte. The price of their release was publicity for the FLQ manifesto, free passage to Cuba or Algeria for a number of terrorists ("political prisoners") currently in detention, reinstatement for the drivers of Lapalme, a firm that had lost a Post Office contract, and $500,000 in gold bullion.

Quebec society and, to a large extent, the Bourassa government were in a state of confusion. But neither the Quebec government nor Ottawa would give in to the FLQ demands. The federal government deployed soldiers to protect potential targets of terrorist action. To two reporters an impatient Trudeau said:

> I think the society must take every means at its disposal to defend itself against the emergence of a parallel power which defies the elected power in this country and I think that goes to any distance. . . . It's only : . . weak-kneed bleeding hearts who are afraid to take these measures.

His choice of words was perhaps unfortunate, but his meaning was clear. The overwhelming majority of Canadians applauded it.

In Montreal the tension mounted. Faced with growing university-student unrest, and with a mass rally and street demonstration intended to persuade the government to meet the FLQ's demands, Premier Bourassa concluded that "democratic rule in Quebec is being threatened at this time." Possibly prompted by Trudeau—the evidence is inconclusive—Bourassa and Mayor Drapeau asked Ottawa for emergency assistance. The federal government responded on October 16 by invoking the War Measures Act and proclaiming emergency regulations to deal with "apprehended insurrection." In the House of Commons Trudeau described the action as "an interim and . . . somewhat unsatisfactory measure"; his government would soon introduce more limited emergency legislation that would not need to impose a nation-wide suspension of civil liberties in order to deal with a local problem. (The Public Order Temporary Measures Act became law in December.)

Soldiers patrolled the streets of Montreal and police arrested more than 400 persons on suspicion of being members of the now-outlawed FLQ. But the War Measures Act could not save the life of Pierre Laporte: acting on a tip, police found his corpse in the trunk of a stolen green Chevrolet in the early morning of October 18. There was shock, then grief and rage. Many Canadians illogically attacked those who opposed the use of the War Measures Act. (A poll indicated that 88 percent of all Canadians and 86 percent of the people of Quebec approved the action of the federal government in invoking the Act.)

Some civil liberties groups from the beginning doubted the need for the War Measures Act; others, among them a former dean of law at McGill and a lifelong defender of civil liberties, Frank Scott, gave its use qualified approval. Doubt about the "apprehended insurrection" increased as calm returned to Montreal and the province. There were questions, too, about police efficiency. By the end of 1970, 408 of the 468 persons arrested had been released without being charged, and only 41 remained in custody. Among them were the close friends and alleged accomplices of the Laporte murder suspects. The suspects had at last been apprehended on December 28. By that time James Cross had been free for some weeks and his captors had been given free passage to Cuba in exchange for his life. A growing number of critics argued that the alleged inadequacy of the Montreal police was less important than the overreaction of all three levels of government in October. Others suspected that the federal government had pressured Quebec into asking for emergency measures in order to weaken the separatist cause, presumably by the demonstration of Ottawa's power when constituted authority was under challenge.

Attractive as this interpretation seemed to some, it lacked hard evidence to substantiate it. Whatever the case, the October crisis failed to weaken separatism. Nor did it end violence in Quebec: FLQ-directed bombings continued in 1971. Their ending in 1972 owed much to Pierre Vallières, chief theoretician of the FLQ. Writing in *Le Devoir* late in 1971, Vallières renounced the use of terrorism and urged others to do likewise. The FLQ's strategy and tactics had proved themselves to be counterproductive, he wrote. To the dismay of some of his former comrades, radicals who considered the PQ to be *petit bourgeois* and reactionary, Vallières proposed that, in the interests of Quebec's liberation, "the FLQ should cease to exist and channel its efforts into the Parti Québécois."

The PQ continued to gain steadily in popular support. In the election of October 1973 Bourassa's Liberals swept the province, gaining 55 percent of the vote and 102 of 110 seats. The PQ won only 6, and René Lévesque lost his seat. A scare campaign directed against the PQ and the separatist threat may have had some effect. (It culminated just before the election in an exodus of Brink's trucks carrying securities to Ontario.) Nevertheless the PQ increased its share of the popular vote to 30 percent and was now the official opposition. The Union Nationale was shut out.

Emboldened by its victory, yet apprehensive of the PQ's increasing share of the vote, the Bourassa government in 1974 introduced legislation dealing with language and education. Bill 22 disregarded a recommendation in the report of the Gendron Commission (1973) that nothing be done about language in education for at least three to five years and ended freedom of choice for immigrant parents and their children; they would henceforth attend French-language schools. The Act made French the official language of the province, and required that it normally be used in the civil service, in relations with the government, and between governments. A "francization" policy would advance the role of French as the language of labor.

Those who wanted to make French the sole public language denounced the remaining element of choice—namely, that the children of anglophone parents could be educated in English. Anglophones protested against the downgrading of their language. Most upset were many immigrants who wanted their children to become proficient in English. Some 6,000 to 7,000 children of immigrants went to English schools illegally in the fall of 1974. Bill 22 also made enemies in Ottawa, where politicians and officials recognized it as a challenge to the federal policy of bilingualism.

By 1976 the Bourassa government's hold on office was weakening. Its policy of "cultural sovereignty"—most notably its attempt to control cable television—had so far failed to secure an increase in the province's constitutional powers. A federal challenge of a cable TV license granted by the provincial government was proceeding through the courts. (The Supreme Court of Canada ruled against the province in 1978.) A weakening economy did not help; nor did the findings of the Cliche Commission, which had conducted an inquiry into organized crime that implicated several provincial Liberal politicians. When Bourassa called a snap election he tried once more to make separatism the issue. The economy, his party's organizational disarray, and a resurgent Union Nationale undid him. The PQ ran a low-key campaign that relied heavily on effective constituency organization and promised a referendum on Quebec's constitutional future if the party should win. And win it did. With 41.4 percent of the popular vote the PQ took 71 seats. The Liberals dropped to 26 seats; the Union Nationale came back to win 11. Analysis revealed that the latter had increased its share of the anglophone and immigrant vote—traditionally Liberal—chiefly because of unhappiness with Bill 22.

The PQ victory shocked many Canadians. Commentators had refused to credit the polls that pointed to the outcome. Now a separatist government was in office. The election was not a vote for independence, but Quebec seemed to have taken a giant step in that direction.

The new government moved cautiously. There would be no fundamental rupture with Canada, Premier Lévesque told the Economic Club of New York in January 1977. Instead, a politically sovereign Quebec would join Canada in an economic association. Polls in 1977 suggested that the government's task in preparing for the referendum would not be easy. Even among francophones a majority opposed independence, while province-wide support for sovereignty-association was only 40 percent.

The PQ's language bill—eventually passed as Bill 101 in August 1977—was central to its legislative program. It made French the official language of the province: in the courts and the National Assembly, at work, and in labor relations. It also made it the language of instruction for all but the children of anglophones already living in Quebec. English education would be available to the children of anyone temporarily transferred to the province, with the possibility of a three-year extension; Quebec offered to extend English educational privileges to residents of other provinces that were willing to sign a reciprocal agreement.

The legality of Bill 101 was challenged and in late 1979 the Supreme Court of Canada ruled that the section of the bill dealing with the National Assembly offended against Section 133 of the British North America Act and was therefore *ultra vires*. (At the same time, the court held to be unconstitutional the 1890 statute that ended the official position of French in Manitoba.) All this was small consolation to those in Quebec, particularly immigrants, whose freedom of choice in the matter of education had been permanently curtailed. Anglophones felt that the educators and other intellectuals who dominated the cabinet were determined to undermine further the position of the English language—in education, in the economy, and in society as a whole.

The referendum took place on 20 May 1980. The question that the government asked was both complicated and cautious: would the people of Quebec approve negotiations aimed at securing sovereignty-association, the outcome of such negotiations to be submitted to them for approval in another referendum? The phrasing was meant to make it easier to vote "yes." The federal government and the nine other provinces indicated that they would not negotiate sovereignty-association and stressed the economic benefits of the existing federation, benefits that would be lost to Quebec if it separated. The "no" camp was internally divided. Claude Ryan, the influential newspaper editor who had become provincial Liberal leader in 1978, certainly believed in a more decentralized version of federalism than Pierre Trudeau, but the two men were united in their opposition to the PQ. They and their supporters carried the day.

Eighty-two percent of the electorate voted; almost six in ten said "no" to the question that Lévesque and his Minister of Intergovernmental Affairs, Claude Morin, had phrased so carefully. The non-francophone vote was overwhelmingly negative. The francophone vote was split in two, with older voters and women tending to support the federalist option, and the young and the better educated tending to vote "yes." Only the Saguenay-Lac St. Jean and St. Lawrence North Shore regions gave solid approval to the government's plans.

In speaking to his emotional and forgiving supporters Lévesque promised a "next time." It became clear that there probably would be a next time when in April 1981 the PQ won a second term by a convincing margin: 80 seats to the Liberals' 42. The other parties disappeared from the National Assembly. Defeat in the referendum may have helped rather than hurt Lévesque, for it made the PQ seem less menacing to those voters who appreciated what they believed to be the party's administrative competence or its reformism while opposing its separatism. Its defense of provincial rights did the PQ no harm. In federal elections French-speaking Québécois might vote overwhelmingly for Trudeau's Liberals, but in Quebec City they wanted someone who, like Maurice Duplessis, would stand up for the province. Many members of the PQ, especially on its left wing, still wanted total separation. Whether a majority of the people of Quebec would ever opt for a separate state was doubtful.

Trudeau resisted the idea of a separate Quebec more than most, and this opposition lay at the core of his actions in the 1970s. In 1980 he took a major role in the referendum campaign. The result, he said on the night of May 20, gave Canadians the opportunity to renew confederation "with vision and daring." The following day Trudeau told the House of Commons that he would immediately resume the process of constitutional revision that had been stalled early in 1979.

Constitutional revision was a project that the Trudeau government had inherited from its predecessors. Since 1927 there had been various attempts to get agreement to an amending formula that would permit the bringing home, or "patriation," of the British North America Act. Trudeau was determined not only to find an amending formula acceptable to both the federal and provincial governments but also to include a charter of rights. Such a charter, he hoped, would firmly entrench individual rights—something the Diefenbaker Bill of Rights had failed to do.

A federal–provincial conference in Victoria in 1971 drafted a Canadian Constitutional Charter that for a short time had the support of all eleven first ministers. The amending formula gave a veto to any province that had 25 percent of the Canadian population, to any two Atlantic provinces together, and to any two of the western provinces that together had at least half of the population of the West. A limited number of personal freedoms were to be entrenched, but not the educational and language rights that Trudeau had wanted. More important for the fate of the charter, Quebec did not get the control over social policy that Bourassa had sought. He met with a barrage of criticism at home and soon indicated that his government could not accept the Victoria Charter. The constitutional train was derailed.

In 1975 Trudeau tried to get it back on the tracks. The British North America Act should be patriated with the amending formula agreed on in Victoria, he suggested, leaving the distribution of powers unchanged until the Act was home. But there was less agreement now among first ministers than there had been in 1971. An interprovincial conference in 1976 found that several premiers wanted to expand provincial jurisdiction in various areas as part of the process of patriation; Premiers William Bennett of British Columbia and Lougheed of Alberta also wanted to change the amending formula. Trudeau made matters more difficult when he said in March 1976 that the federal government might have to act unilaterally in bringing home the constitution if the premiers could not agree on a formula. The outlook for patriation deteriorated further when the PQ took office later in the year. Premier Lévesque announced almost immediately that he would not take part in constitutional discussions until after the referendum.

In 1977 Lévesque rejected Trudeau's proposal to entrench language rights in education in a new constitution. Later that year, with Trudeau's trusted associate, Marc Lalonde, now Minister of State for Federal–Provincial Relations, the federal government began to draft a new constitutional proposal. The PQ victory had convinced Trudeau that patriation was necessary as a symbol of national purpose; in order to secure it he was ready to concede more to the provinces than ever before. In June 1978 his government tabled the White Paper on the constitution, *A Time for Action,* as well as the Constitutional Amendment Bill. At a first ministers' meeting in October Trudeau indicated his willingness to concede a measure of the desired decentralization of powers if the premiers could agree on an amending formula and the inclusion of a charter of rights. A further meeting early in 1979 failed to produce a compromise, and the Constitutional Amendment Bill passed into limbo when the Liberals left office.

The constitutional proposal that Trudeau discussed with the premiers in September 1980 was much more centralist than the one they had rejected in February 1979. The conference failed to produce a workable consensus on the division of powers, the amending formula, or the charter of rights. Trudeau and his Minister of Justice, Jean Chrétien, opted for unilateral patriation of the British North America Act. However, the House of Commons and Senate of Canada would ask the British Parliament first to add to the Act an amending formula similar to the Victoria Charter, as well as a Charter of Rights and Freedoms. Led by René Lévesque, six premiers vowed in October 1980 to fight Ottawa in the courts. Two more joined them later, leaving only Ontario's William Davis and New Brunswick's Richard Hatfield in support of the federal position.

Polls indicating that patriation was generally popular steeled Ottawa's resolve. So did indications that the concept of a charter of rights enjoyed strong support even in the West. In the fall and winter of 1980/81 interest centered on Ottawa as a House–Senate Committee heard many groups and individuals; the changes made to the charter as a result of the hearings greatly increased its strength and effectiveness. In the House of Commons a Progressive Conservative filibuster successfully forced the government to abandon its goal of bringing the British North America Act home by July 1, 1981. Instead everyone waited for a Supreme Court ruling: did Ottawa have the right unilaterally to ask the British Parliament for the changes it wanted and to patriate the Act? Appeal courts in Manitoba and Quebec had ruled that Ottawa did; the Newfoundland Court of Appeal had said that it did not. On September 28 the Supreme Court rendered a split judgment that confirmed the legal right of the federal government to do what it wanted to but denied the constitutional propriety of doing so. This put the matter back in the political arena. The NDP—whose federal caucus had so far supported the government—gave notice that it would withdraw its support unless another round of federal–provincial negotiations took place; this may have been decisive. A further conference took place in early November.

On the fourth day a compromise acceptable to all the dissident premiers save Lévesque emerged. The major changes were in the amending formula and in the charter of rights. Dismay greeted the revelation that provincial governments would have the right to override the guarantees of rights to women and native peoples. The effective lobbying of women's groups—and also of Indian and Inuit organizations—forced the premiers to agree to more effective guarantees, although the native peoples were still unhappy that only existing aboriginal rights would be guaranteed. The constitutional proposal passed the House of Commons on December 2 and the Senate on December 8. Justice Minister Chrétien, who had played a major part in shepherding the document to its final passage, accompanied it to London. There it was announced that after the British Parliament had acted on the Canadian request the Queen would come to Canada—the last act in the process of patriating the British North America Act.

"An Act of Pride," was the phrase that *Maclean's* magazine used on its December 14 cover, which showed a seated Trudeau, smilingly accepting a standing ovation by his fellow Liberal MPs. Pride was tinged with apprehension. Quebec was isolated in opposition to patriation, vainly claiming a veto power it had earlier abandoned in order to forge an alliance with the seven disaffected anglophone premiers. Unable to stop patriation, Lévesque spoke of the "betrayal" of Quebec by Ottawa and the other provinces. The annual convention of the PQ responded by voting to eliminate economic association with Canada from the original goal of sovereignty-association. This was dismaying to Lévesque, and disturbing to the country as a whole: more than any other province, Quebec still held the key to Canada's political future.

Canada and the World

In international relations Canada steered an uncertain course. Early in the Trudeau years there was a conscious shift to a less internationalist, more self-preoccupied and self-interested policy. Yet after 1975 the Prime Minister sought to foster a "North–South dialogue" that he hoped would lead to the material improvement of life in the less-developed countries.

In the late 1960s and early 1970s Quebec had to be prevented from assuming too much of a personality of its own in international affairs. It had been encouraged to do so by France's President de Gaulle and there had been a consequent cooling in Canadian relations with France. Quebec eagerly grasped opportunities to participate in francophone conferences dealing with matters that were within provincial jurisdiction, education being the most obvious. Premier Daniel Johnson claimed in June 1968 that "Quebec could not win equality for French Canadians unless and until it had the right to maintain direct links with other countries." The federal government insisted that Quebec's participation in francophone conferences take place only within the context of Canadian participation. Eventually Ottawa won this battle, if only because France lost interest after de Gaulle's retirement.

When he became Prime Minister, Trudeau promised a review of foreign policy. It appeared as a White Paper in June 1970, and consisted of six pamphlets: Europe, Latin America, the Pacific, the United Nations, international development, and "Foreign Policy for Canadians." The pamphlets emphasized six themes: sovereignty and independence, peace and security, social justice, the quality of life, the natural environment, and economic growth. Economic growth came first, ahead of social justice and the quality of life. The White Paper reflected the view—accepted more easily in the Prime Minister's Office than in the Department of External Affairs—that Canada no longer had an important role to play in world affairs. Canadians would still be available for peacekeeping duties, but increasingly our chief concern would be the promotion of international trade, and the Department of Trade and Commerce would gain prestige and influence at the expense of External Affairs.

The House of Commons Standing Committee on External Affairs and National Defense subjected the White Paper to a lengthy review in 1971, concluding that peace and security had been given too low a priority and should rank with economic growth. However, the former diplomat and eminent commentator on external affairs, John Holmes, thought that the White Paper realistically assessed Canada's limitations as a "middle power." The media responded in much the same way.

The year 1970 was notable for at least three other events: by October Canada's recognition of the People's Republic of China was complete; in the same month the International Development Research Center, chaired by Lester Pearson, opened in Ottawa; and in April the government unilaterally introduced pollution guidelines for the Arctic.

This action was one of several developments that strained Canadian–American relations in the early 1970s. The United States did not like the possibility of Canadian interference with oiltanker traffic through the Northwest Passage. Nor did the administration of Richard Nixon and a number of senators and congressmen appreciate Canadian efforts to remove the tax deductibility of advertisements placed in the *Reader's Digest* and the Canadian edition of *Time*. A further bone of contention was that, since the passage of the 1965 Canada–U.S. Automobile Pact, imports of Canadian-made cars into the United States had come to exceed U.S. exports to Canada. Already experiencing serious problems with their international balance of payments, the Americans wanted to eliminate this particular imbalance in trade with Canada.

Most Canadians believed what the White Paper on Foreign Policy claimed: that the need for good relations with the United States was one of the great realities for Canada. Indeed, many Canadians thought that Canada had a "special relationship" with the United States. In August 1971 President Nixon shook Canadian faith in that relationship by announcing a New Economic Policy that contained a number of protectionist measures designed to encourage domestic industry and eliminate the U.S. balance of payments deficit. The new policy made no exception for Canada. As more than two-thirds of Canadian exports went to the United States, there was great apprehension in Ottawa and in Canadian business and labor circles. Little progress was made, in spite of Trudeau's meeting with Nixon in December and other attempts to secure Canadian exclusion from the provisions of the new economic policy. Nixon visited Ottawa in April 1972 and told a joint session of Parliament that the "Nixon doctrine" applied just as much to Canada as it did to other countries. Canadians could now see that, in the economic realm at least, there was no special relationship.

This awareness prompted the appearance in *International Perspectives* in October 1972 of an article signed by External Affairs Minister Mitchell Sharp: "Canada–U.S. relations for the future." It discussed three policy options: *laissez faire* (a continuation of existing policies), closer integration, and greater independence. Sharp opted for the last. The "third option," as it became known, involved a reduction of our economic dependence on the United States and stronger relations with other areas, especially Europe.

In 1973 Canada appointed an ambassador to the European Economic Community (EEC). In the following year the Canadian government made several approaches to the EEC, and Trudeau visited Europe in October and in February–March 1975. Ottawa's desire to formalize a "contractual link" with the EEC was realized in 1976 with the signing of a Framework Agreement for Commercial and Economic Cooperation between Canada and the European Community. The parties agreed that they would give each other "most-favored nation" treatment. Five years later, Canada's exports to Europe represented exactly the same proportion of total exports as they had in 1975: 12.6 percent. The EEC's trade with Canada as a proportion of total trade had actually declined, from 2.7 percent in 1975 to 2.2 percent in 1980. In some instances cooperation and consultation had increased, but there were serious differences over Canadian agricultural exports, fisheries, and the operation of Canada's Foreign Investment Review Act. Canadian trade with countries other than the United States had grown as a proportion of the total by a few percentage points since the mid-1970s, but this could just as easily be ascribed to the weakness of the Canadian dollar after 1976 as to specific policies. By the late 1970s some observers believed that the third option had become such an embarrassment that it was dropped from Ottawa's vocabulary.

Sharing a continent with the United States not only meant that the bulk of Canada's trade was bound to be with that country, in spite of attempts at diversification; it also meant that serious environmental problems had to be shared. They included the possibility of oil spills along the Pacific Coast and in the Strait of Juan de Fuca, the proposed flooding of the Skagit Valley in southern British Columbia, the cleanup of the Great Lakes, and the construction of an oil refinery at Eastport, Maine. For years Canadian politicians and officials opposed the Alaska Pipeline because of the horrendous prospect of a supertanker going aground off the B. C. coast on its way to the oil refinery in the Puget Sound in Washington State. Nevertheless, the pipeline was constructed. Wilderness preservation had seemed relatively unimportant when in 1942 the International Joint Commission had given a Seattle hydro-electric power company the right to flood the Skagit Valley whenever it became necessary to do so as part of a long-range project to provide the city with electricity; nor was conservation an issue when British Columbia and Seattle agreed on compensation in 1967. The NDP government that took office in B. C. in 1972 was unhappy about the agreement, and by 1974 both Victoria and Ottawa were pressing for the deal to be revoked—with little apparent success.

Attempts by both countries to reduce the pollution of the Great Lakes were more successful. The revised Great Lakes Water Quality Agreement, signed in 1978, introduced more comprehensive and stringent regulations and offered some hope of ending—or at least controlling—pollution by chemical plants, mines, and municipal sewage systems. In North Dakota, Canadian pressure led to the modification of the Garrison Diversion Project and its dangerous implications for water quality in Manitoba. In its modified form the project was judged by the late 1970s to be doing no harm to Canadian waters.

The most difficult environmental problem was the destruction by "acid rain" of lakes in the northeastern United States, Ontario, and Quebec. The main cause was the air pollution created by American industry, though Canadian-based enterprises such as the International Nickel Company of Sudbury certainly contributed to the problem. Negotiations on an International Air Pollution Agreement with the United States began in late 1978 in the face of powerful opposition to more stringent controls, not least because of the U.S. government's desire to encourage the use of coal rather than oil. Reducing reliance on oil might be politically and economically sound but it seemed bound to lead to an increase in acid rain. The protesters who greeted President Ronald Reagan when he visited Ottawa in March 1981 made their feelings about the issue abundantly clear.

Americans in the 1970s thought that they had some major reasons for displeasure with Canada. The Canadian cutback on oil exports after 1973, and the adoption of the two-price system for oil and natural gas, annoyed some of them. Annoyance turned to rage in some circles when the Liberal government announced its national energy programme in 1980. Oil producers and some American politicians saw the favoritism shown to Canadian-owned exploration companies, and the planned increase of Canadian ownership in the oil and gas industry to 50 percent, as an unacceptable interference with private enterprise. There were calls for retaliation. Increased Canadian monitoring of foreign investment in Canada seemed further evidence of interference. The Canadian Foreign Investment Review Agency (FIRA) had been established in 1973 to screen and pass judgment on all new direct foreign investment, as well as any move by a foreign-owned company to expand into a new and unrelated area of business. Although most such initiatives were approved, the principle of review—and even more the secretive procedures of FIRA—struck many American (and Canadian) business people as objectionable. Further irritations in the relationship included Canadian agricultural protection, the ending of the tax deductibility of television commercials carried by U.S. channels aimed at the Canadian market, and Saskatchewan's nationalization of the potash industry.

In February 1977 President Jimmy Carter (1977–81) secured for Trudeau an invitation to address a joint session of Congress. In his speech the Prime Minister called Canadian friendship with the United States "so basic, so non-negotiable, that it has long since been regarded by others as the standard for enlightened international relations." That friendship did not prevent either country from seeking her own interests. The difference in the size of the two economies meant, as it had always done, that American policies had a greater impact on Canada than Canadian policies had on the United States. In spite of the mid-decade pursuit of the "third option," however, Canada's economic relations with her neighbor were quite as close at the beginning of the 1980s as they had been ten years earlier.

The same cannot be said of Canada's relations with the Commonwealth. During the 1970s its chief value for the Canadian government lay in providing an entrée into black Africa and the Third World generally. When in 1971 it seemed as though the Commonwealth might be destroyed by continuing British arms sales to South Africa, Canada worked hard and successfully to hold the member countries together. The declining importance that the British government attached to the Commonwealth was illustrated by Britain's entry into the EEC in 1973. The Commonwealth continued to exist, and to prove useful, as a forum in which the leaders of some of the developed and less-developed countries could meet, but by the early 1980s few Canadians took more than a polite interest in it.

The Commonwealth recommended itself to Trudeau precisely because its membership included a number of less-developed countries (LDCs). One of his concerns was the establishing of a new international order in which the relations between the developed countries and the LDCs of Africa, Asia, Latin America, and the Caribbean would be more nearly equal instead of being weighted commercially and economically against the LDCs. In 1968 he warned a convocation audience at the University of Alberta that in the long run "the overwhelming threat to Canada will come from the two-thirds of the world who are steadily falling farther and farther behind in their search for a decent standard of living." The "sweet philanthropy" of foreign aid would not deal with the problem; "preferential trade agreements" were necessary.

Necessary they might be, but in Canada—and the developed countries generally—they were not politically feasible. Among other things, preferential trade agreements would have meant more competition for Canadian manufacturers. The latter objected strenuously to imports from low-wage countries, and argued with considerable effect that such imports would lead to a loss of jobs in Canada. Canada used import quotas rather than preferences in the 1970s.

Trudeau's first major speech abroad in favor of revising the world economic order was in London in March 1975. Among other things, he proposed an expanded role for the LDCs in the World Bank and the International Monetary Fund. The purpose was "nothing less than an acceptable distribution of the world's wealth." In the years that followed he became a firm supporter of an international effort to improve North–South relations. He promoted this cause at the economic summit of the seven leading capitalist countries in Ottawa in July 1981, and at the North–South conference in Cancun, Mexico, in October. These efforts yielded only very modest results. Helping the LDCs would almost certainly require significant sacrifices on the part of the wealthy countries, but Canada and the rest of the developed world were far too concerned with protecting their own interests to be willing to make such sacrifices.

The emphasis on economic growth in Canadian foreign policy in the 1970s led to a certain loss of prestige for the Department of External Affairs and a commensurate gain by the Department of Trade and Commerce.

However, External Affairs acted effectively in the complicated negotiations of the United Nations Law of the Sea (LOS) Conference. Its first substantive session took place in Caracas, Venezuela, in June—August 1974. In the position paper the Canadian delegates claimed for Canada: "exclusive sovereign rights in the management and harvest of all living resources within 200 miles of its coast, as well as preferential rights in respect of such resources in areas adjacent to this zone." Canada also claimed rights to non-living resources "over the whole continental margin comprising not only the physical continental shelf but the continental slope and rise as well." This strongly nationalist position struck many observers as greedy. Nevertheless, the negotiating text that emerged from the 1975 meeting of the LOS Conference in Geneva included most of the Canadian objectives, although not the full claim to the continental shelf and slope. Negotiations continued, with the exploitation of minerals on the ocean floor emerging as the most contentious issue. By 1981, in spite of American misgivings, a treaty was on the horizon. The Canadian negotiators had supported the majority demand for international control of ocean-bed mining, and had won a measure of protection for the Canadian nickel industry.

Fisheries were a major Canadian concern in the negotiations. In 1976 Canada followed several other countries in announcing a 200-mile fishing zone, effective January 1, 1977. (This had a favorable effect on the economies of the Maritimes.) The Northwest Atlantic Fisheries Consultative Organization, founded at a conference in Ottawa in October 1977, created the conditions for the regulation of fishing beyond the 200-mile limit claimed by Canada and the United States. It also provided a forum for the exchange of research findings among scientists, and seemed to offer some hope that overfishing would be ended. Negotiations began in Anchorage, Alaska, to make revisions to the International Convention for the High Seas Fisheries of the North Pacific Ocean.

The control of nuclear proliferation also concerned Canada in this period. When India exploded a nuclear device in 1974 Canada shared the responsibility, for it had given India a great deal of assistance in developing nuclear energy for peaceful uses. Canada promptly withdrew further assistance, but as the political scientist R. B. Byers noted in the *Canadian Annual Review* (1974): "The Indian explosion brought sharply into focus the Canadian dilemma between the desire to control nuclear proliferation and the desire to benefit economically from the export of nuclear technology and equipment." The government was eager to sell CANDU nuclear reactors abroad, and acknowledged an obligation to share nuclear technology and expertise with the LDC's, but, as Trudeau told the Canadian Nuclear

Association in June 1975, it wanted "binding assurance that Canadian-supplied nuclear material, equipment and technology would not be used to produce an explosive nuclear device, whether the development of such a device be stated to be for peaceful purposes or not." Critics in Canada doubted that such assurances, or the safeguards that the Canadian government sought, would be enough to stop any government that was determined to build nuclear weapons. But Ottawa was sufficiently conscious of its responsibilities to halt shipments of uranium at the beginning of 1977 to those countries that had failed to sign safeguard agreements: West Germany, Italy, Switzerland, and Japan; similar action with respect to shipments to France had been taken earlier. After receiving the appropriate assurances, Canada resumed shipments to the countries concerned in 1978. That same year Canada signed a nuclear cooperation agreement with the EEC.

If Canadians paid little attention to foreign policy, they paid even less to defense. Most would consider it not worth spending much money on the defense establishment in peacetime. Trudeau was no exception. Indeed, in 1968, he asked publicly whether it did not make sense to spend more on foreign aid than on defense.

In the half-dozen years that followed, the foreign-aid budget rose more rapidly than the defense budget, although the former was always less than a quarter of the latter. The government's provision for aid was not conspicuously generous but it was less niggardly than it had been in the 1960s. In 1974 Canada ranked third among sixteen donor countries in per capita GNP, fifth in total official and private aid per capita, and seventh in official development assistance. In 1968 the target for aid had been set at 0.7 percent of GNP for official aid, and 1.0 percent of GNP for total official and private aid. By 1976 official aid was $737 million, or 0.58 percent of GNP. Then restraint became necessary, foreign-aid spending declined, and by 1979 it was 0.46 percent of GNP, the same level as five years earlier.

Although defense spending actually increased in the second half of the 1970s, it lagged behind the spending of our allies. Well into the decade all three services suffered from a serious shortage or lack of up-to-date equipment. Morale was also a problem, initially because the unification of the services was not popular, but mainly because of the military's feeling that the government attached insufficient importance to them.

In April 1969 Trudeau issued a paper, "A Defense Policy for Canada," in which he laid out four roles for the forces: (i) the surveillance of Canadian territory and coastlines; (ii) the defense of North America in cooperation with U.S. forces; (iii) the fulfillment of such NATO duties as might be agreed upon; and (iv) the performance of such United Nations peacekeeping roles as Canada might assume. Criticism of our participation in NATO and NORAD as an unhelpful and expensive contribution to the continuation of the cold war had little influence on policy-making. The government did, however, reduce the size of the forces. In September 1969 Defense Minister Léo Cadieux announced the disbanding of a number of units and the reduction of the active forces by 16,000 military and 5,000 civilian positions over a three-year period (to 82,000 military and 30,000 civilian positions). Some bases and supply depots would be closed, and the militia would be reduced in personnel from 23,000 to 19,500. The aircraft carrier HMCS Bonaventure was taken out of service, only two years after a scandalously expensive refit. Finally, Canada's commitment to NATO forces in Europe was halved, to 5,000 men. Bilingualism, one of the government's priorities, was to be fostered in the services: HMCS Ottawa became the first of several "French-speaking" ships, and the three military colleges were made more bilingual.

During the 1970 October crisis close to 10,000 troops were efficiently deployed in or near Montreal while others served in Ottawa. The following year a White Paper on defense reiterated Trudeau's four roles for the forces. The government rejected participation in the two major new systems of interception that the Americans were developing: Over-the-Horizon radar, and the Airborne Warning and Control Sysem (AWACS). However, it renewed membership of NORAD in 1973, not without protest from the NDP.

Canada was an active participant in the thirty-four member Conference on Security and Cooperation in Europe, which had its first meeting in 1973. In that year, too, Canada served briefly on the International Commission of Control and Supervision in Vietnam that was supervising the ceasefire reached in January. Increasingly unhappy about numerous breaches of the ceasefire (in one of which a Canadian officer died), Canada resigned from the commission in July. Later in 1973 Canada contributed a 480-man signals unit to the peacekeeping force established at the end of the Yom Kippur war in the Middle East.

Meanwhile, Canadian forces had to make do with equipment that became older and more ramshackle by the day. Military personnel dropped to 79,000, leading the Progressive Conservative defense critic, Allan McKinnon, to ask in 1974 whether the definition of the "elite force" that the government had promised in its 1971 White Paper was one with ever fewer personnel and less equipment. In June 1975 the maritime commander, Vice-Admiral Douglas Boyle, stated publicly that the limitations on defense spending seriously affected the capacity of the services to carry out their assigned tasks, and that Canada was not meeting its commitments to NATO. Criticism also came from Joseph Luns, Secretary General of NATO, who told reporters that the Canadian forces contributing to NATO were generally ill-equipped.

The government recognized the justice of such criticism and late in 1975 committed itself to a five-year program of capital spending. Major purchases in 1976 included 18 Lockheed CP-140 Aurora long-range patrol aircraft, and 128 German-made Leopard C-1 battle tanks. In 1977 a contract for 350 armored vehicles followed, and the Department of National Defense began a three-year search for a new fighter aircraft. Eventually it signed a $4-billion contract for 137 McDonnell Douglas F18A Hornets. The department in 1980 also announced the acquisition of 6 new frigates, and an increase in the strength of the forces to 83,000. A growing number of these were women—5,285 in 1981. The military colleges finally began to admit female cadets in 1980.

Rearmament did not turn Canada into a military heavyweight. In 1978 per capita expenditure on the military forces was $174 (U.S.), compared with $259 in Denmark, $262 in Great Britain, $304 in the Netherlands, $322 in Belgium and Norway, $350 in France and West Germany, and $499 in the United States. In 1979 Canada spent a smaller proportion of GNP on defense than any other NATO country, with the exception of Luxembourg. It was by no means clear, moreover, that even the increased spending of the later 1970s was sufficient to achieve the objectives expressed in Trudeau's statement of 1969 and the White Paper of 1971. But it is true that the defense budget increased in a time of overall financial restraint, and that to have spent even more money would have been politically difficult, especially if it had entailed increased taxation. Some critics questioned much of whatever spending there was as an ultimately futile contribution to the global arms race. There was still no answer to Trudeau's question of 1968: would not some of the dollars spent on defense be better spent on foreign aid?

Politics in the Trudeau Years

Federal politics in the 1970s revolved around Trudeau. Provincial politics, on the other hand, saw radical changes in its cast of characters—including the total disappearance of Liberal governments: in 1968 there were five; after 1979, none. One interpretation was that many voters reacted against the Liberal presence in Ottawa by voting for any party but the Liberals in provincial elections. Only in the four western provinces, however, did either the Progressive Conservatives or the NDP derive much profit in federal politics from the provincial drift away from the Liberals.

In Alberta the Social Credit hegemony that dated from 1935 ended in 1971; Peter Lougheed became the province's first Progressive Conservative premier. The Conservative hold was strengthened by the huge revenues from oil and gas after 1973. The government established the Alberta Heritage Fund to manage surplus revenue and to help broaden the industrial base of the province. Albertans were conscious that oil and gas were a non-renewable resource, and it seemed advisable to plan for a future when the revenues from that resource would decline. By the beginning of the 1980s the Heritage Fund was almost $10 billion, but paradoxically it was becoming a political liability as debate mounted over the uses to which the fund was being put.

In British Columbia twenty years of Social Credit government ended in 1972 when W. A. C. Bennett lost to the NDP, led by David Barrett. The new government was highly innovative in areas such as social welfare and land-use control. This scared many Liberals and Conservatives into uniting behind the Social Credit party and defeating the NDP in December 1975; Bennett's son William became the new premier. In 1979 the Socreds won narrowly in an election in which the Liberal and Conservative parties all but vanished and the NDP polled almost as many votes as its rival.

In Saskatchewan Ross Thatcher's Liberals gave way to the NDP in 1971. The new premier, Allan Blakeney, emerged as a skilled and knowledgeable contributor to federal–provincial discussions. His government was cautiously reformist, its most dramatic step being the nationalization of the potash industry. During the 1970s, revenues from oil and potash changed Saskatchewan from a "have-not" into a "have" province. Unhappiness with federal Liberal policies helped to undermine the provincial Liberal party, and in the 1978 election it disappeared from the legislature. In the early 1980s a revived Conservative party seemed to have some hope of loosening the NDP's firm grip on power.

The most consistent supporter among provincial premiers of Ottawa's policy of bilingualism was Manitoba's premier from 1969 to 1977, Edward Schreyer. As cautious as its Saskatchewan neighbor, Schreyer's NDP lost office in 1977 amid economic and financial difficulties. In 1978 Schreyer accepted appointment as Governor-General, the first in Canada's history who was of neither British nor French stock. His successor as premier, Sterling Lyon, was as conservative as any Canadian public figure in the late 1970s. He was unable to solve the continuing economic difficulties that were rooted in Manitoba's inadequate resource and manufacturing-industry base; his Progressive Conservative government was defeated late in 1981 by the NDP, led by Howard Pawley. In the election the last remaining Liberal in a western Canadian legislature lost his seat.

In the east, Canada's only living "Father of Confederation," Joey Smallwood, resigned as premier of Newfoundland in 1972. Ten years later the Progressive Conservatives, led first by Frank Moores and then by Brian Peckford, were still in office. Both distinguished themselves by their vigorous assertion of full provincial control of offshore oil and gas resources. Revenue from these resources offered the best hope of ending Newfoundland's position as the poorest province with the highest unemployment. Nova Scotia was also looking to offshore resources for economic salvation. Like all of the Atlantic provinces, Nova Scotia had great economic difficulties in the 1970s; improvement in the fisheries could not compensate for the decline in manufacturing. Economic discontent helped defeat the Liberal government of Gerald Regan in 1978. John Buchanan's Progressive Conservatives were re-elected in 1981. By that time the last surviving Liberal provincial government had also disappeared—Prince Edward Island swung to the Conservatives in 1979. (In the 1970s, PEI had virtually become a ward of the federal government: much of the government's revenue came from Ottawa and economic planning in the province was federally shaped.)

Senior among the Atlantic province premiers was New Brunswick's Richard Hatfield, who replaced the Liberal Louis Robichaud after an election in 1970. An amiable and astute politician, Hatfield gained support from all parts of his economically troubled and ethnically divided province. More than most first ministers he showed a conciliatory attitude toward Ottawa, and played a major part in committing the province to official bilingualism.

Quebec's political fortunes in the 1970s have already been discussed. It remains to marvel over the astonishing persistence of Tory control in Ontario. John Robarts, probably the most widely respected premier of the 1960s, resigned in 1971; he was succeeded by his Minister of Education, the bland and reassuring William Davis. Ontarians needed reassurance, for in the 1970s they lost their status as, per capita, the wealthiest Canadians. The manufacturing sector was increasingly troubled, as plants shut down and jobs disappeared. Nevertheless, in ten years Davis fought and won four elections. In the early 1981 election he won the majority of seats that his party had lost in 1975 and failed to regain in 1977. Ontarians, it seemed, resented hearing from opposition politicians that the province was losing its pre-eminence. They voted against any such change. The "Big Blue Machine," the Tory provincial organization, had sputtered but recovered. In 1983 the Conservatives would celebrate forty years in power.

It is a measure of Pierre Trudeau's own political longevity that not one of the premiers at the first ministers' conference in the fall of 1978 had been in office ten years earlier when he had come to power. He had already served longer than all but three of the prime ministers who preceded him. Yet he had come close to losing office in 1972, and would actually lose it in 1979.

In 1972 the Liberals nearly became the victim of their own fiscal and economic policies. Increasing unemployment in 1971 damaged the government—and Trudeau himself, whom critics saw as an arrogant playboy insulated from the difficulties faced by ordinary Canadians. When he asked for an election on October 30, 1972, Trudeau said that "the challenge is nothing less than the integrity of Canada." Many voters thought otherwise; they saw unemployment, inflation, and taxation as the issues, and considered the Liberal slogan, "the land is strong," highly debatable. The Progressive Conservatives were better organized and financed than at any time since 1958. The NDP had been preoccupied with internal struggle as, from 1969 through 1971, the left-wing "Waffle" movement challenged the party's direction and urged the NDP to become more nationalist and socialist. By 1972 the challenge had been beaten back, and the party under its new leader, David Lewis, launched an effective campaign, including a telling attack on "corporate welfare bums," beneficiaries of the government's policy of granting generous tax concessions to many corporations.

In spite of a Conservative campaign that, reflecting as it did the thoughtful and undemonstrative personality of the Tory leader Robert Stanfield, failed to arouse popular enthusiasm, it seemed on election night as if the Conservatives had one more seat than the Liberals. Recounts changed the standings to 109 Liberals, 107 Tories, 31 NDP and 15 Créditistes. Only the signal failure of the Conservatives to attract support in Quebec kept them from forming the government, for they made important gains in Ontario and the West. As it was, the Liberals decided to stay in office, putting not-so-subtle pressure on the NDP to support them. The NDP wished to consolidate its gains in Ontario and British Columbia and feared that in an early election it might get buried in a rush to majority government. They therefore undertook to support the government, hoping to use the balance of power to secure legislation that would combat unemployment and the high cost of living, limit foreign ownership of the economy, and make the tax system more equitable.

The Progressive Conservatives wanted to bring the government down as soon as possible. The Liberals wanted time. Their policies were influenced by the need to appease the NDP—a strengthened Foreign Investment Review Act and a national energy policy that included a government-owned oil company, PetroCanada, were evidence of this—but the uneasy partnership ended in the spring of 1974. With both the Tories and the NDP opposed to the budget, the government were defeated in the House of Commons.

However, on 8 July the Liberals regained their majority in the country. After a well-organized campaign that had witnessed some of the "Trudeaumania" of 1968, the Liberals gained seats from the Créditistes in Quebec, from the Conservatives in Ontario, and from the NDP in Ontario and the West. In the Toronto constituency of York South, David Lewis lost his seat.

In the aftermath of the election, pundits noted that Trudeau had simply looked and sounded more like a leader than Stanfield. They focused, too, on the Tories' chief proposal, an incomes and prices policy, as a major reason for the Conservative defeat and the halving of the NDP's representation in Parliament. (NDP supporters were said to have voted Liberal because of a dislike of the Conservative policy of wage and price controls.) The real key to Liberal success—aside from improved organization—was the prosperity of the year-and-a-half prior to the election. The slowdown that followed the OPEC price increases of 1973 was only beginning to affect Canada at the time of the campaign. A majority of first-time voters went Liberal, with considerable effect in Ontario and, to a lesser extent, British Columbia. On the prairies, hostility to federal resources, farm credit, and transportation policies kept the Liberals from taking more than five out of forty-five seats.

As the economy weakened in 1975, Liberal popularity declined, dramatically illustrated by a by-election in Hochelaga, in which Pierre Juneau, chairperson since 1968 of the Canadian Radio-Television and Telecommunications Commission (CRTC) and chosen to succeed Gérard Pelletier as Minister of Communications, was defeated by a Conservative. Liberal support dwindled further in 1976, dropping as low as 29 percent in August, the lowest in thirty-three years. The Conservatives won two more by-elections in October, including the "safe" Liberal seat of Ottawa-Carleton by 16,000 votes.

By the end of 1976 Liberal fortunes were improving. The key event was the PQ victory in Quebec in November, but there were also growing doubts about the abilities of the new Progressive Conservative leader, Joe Clark. A young, little-known MP from Alberta, he had gained a narrow victory on the fourth ballot of a leadership convention in February. Although inexperienced and somewhat awkward, Clark was obviously willing to work hard, and got credit for it. But it was increasingly apparent that he simply did not have the leadership qualities of Trudeau or Ed Broadbent, leader of the NDP since 1975. Clark's fundamental decency and his ability to get on well with his colleagues were too easily obscured by his lack of accomplishment outside politics, his pompous platform manner, and his receding chin. To many Canadians he seemed to be a boy trying to do a man's job.

Trudeau's response to the PQ victory was impressive. He made a series of hard-hitting speeches and took steps to prepare his government for the forthcoming referendum in Quebec. "I say to you with all the certainty I can command that Canada's unity will not be fractured," he told the joint Houses of Congress and a television audience in February 1977. That month the Gallup Poll once again put the Liberals ahead of the Tories. In April one of Clark's rivals for the leadership, Jack Horner, crossed the floor to join the Liberals and become Minister without Portfolio. In May the Liberals took a seat from the Conservatives in a by-election in Prince Edward Island. The following month Jacques Lavoie, who had vanquished Pierre Juneau in 1975, joined the Liberal caucus. The Tories were in disarray.

The government may have sounded firm on the PQ issue but in other areas it was faltering. Inflation and unemployment were both on the increase, economic growth was slowing, and the Canadian dollar was steadily losing ground against its American counterpart. Mounting evidence that the RCMP had for years been committing illegal acts in its security operations gave further ammunition to the government's critics. In 1977 and 1978 sensational disclosures of RCMP "dirty tricks" emerged from two official inquiries—a federal Royal Commission chaired by Mr. Justice David C. McDonald and a Quebec commission of inquiry headed by lawyer Jean Keable. (The McDonald Commission reported in 1981 that the government had not authorized or known about specific illegal acts but had, since 1950, ignored more general information about illegalities.)

As one response to the PQ election victory, Ottawa in July 1977 appointed a Task Force on National Unity. Co-chaired by Jean-Luc Pepin and John Robarts, the Task Force set out on an ambitious round of meetings; by the year's end it had gathered a mass of opinion from coast to coast. But concern over national unity and Quebec separatism was waning—and so, in consequence, was Liberal popularity. In 1978 public opinion polls revealed strong disapproval of Trudeau. A series of by-elections in October made the Liberal weakness clear: they retained only two of the seven seats they had formerly held. The Conservatives increased their holding from six to ten, and a Tory victory in the next general election seemed certain.

It came on May 22, 1979. In their campaign the Liberals stressed leadership and put Trudeau front and centre in an attempt to capitalize on the low esteem in which Clark was held. But in this election Trudeau was not an asset to the Liberals in English Canada. Indeed, Ed Broadbent was more respected than either Clark or Trudeau. The Conservative campaign was well financed and well organized; under a different leader the Tories would probably have won a majority. As it was, they took 136 seats, mainly because of increased support in southern Ontario and British Columbia. The Liberals dropped to 114, the NDP took 26, and the Créditistes were reduced to a rump of 6 MPs from rural and small-town Quebec. But if the NDP were all to vote with the Liberals that rump would hold the balance of power. (More than ever Quebec was a Liberal bastion: they had 67 seats there, the Conservatives only 2.)

The new government saw its victory as a mandate for sweeping change, even though polls indicated that this was not the feeling in the country. In any case, the Conservatives wanted to fulfil their promises. Once in office, however, and fully briefed, they encountered major obstacles to the implementation of their policies. These led to an embarrassing retreat from the commitment to shift the Canadian embassy in Israel from Tel Aviv to Jerusalem. The promise to "privatize" PetroCanada was modified once it became evident that most Canadians did not want this to be done. A scheme to allow the deduction from taxable income of mortgage interest and property taxes was altered to the point where it neither satisfied those who had wanted it nor mollified those who had opposed it. The Clark government was losing public esteem.

Finance Minister John Crosbie's budget contained a 4-cents-a-litre increase in the gasoline tax at a time when much higher domestic prices for oil were already in view. This was too much for the six Créditiste MPs. They abstained and the Liberals and NDP voted against the government. Their defeat in the House of Commons took the Conservatives completely by surprise. Trudeau had indicated his intention to resign; surely the Liberals would not try to run an election campaign and a leadership campaign simultaneously? They did not. Trudeau came back to lead his party. On 18 February 1980 the voters confirmed what the polls had predicted since the late autumn: a Liberal return to power.

They won a clear majority of seats: 147 of 282. West of Winnipeg not a single Liberal gained election, but gains in the Atlantic provinces, Quebec, and Ontario were all that was needed. By contrast, it was in Manitoba, Saskatchewan, and British Columbia that the NDP found compensation for losses in Newfoundland, Nova Scotia, and Ontario—when election night ended the party had 32 seats. Social Credit, whose demise had been predicted in every election since the mid-1960s, disappeared from Parliament at last.

Having eagerly accepted the challenge of an election in the hope that, like Diefenbaker's forces in 1958, they would storm to victory, the Progressive Conservatives took only 103 seats. They had one consolation: they were the only party with seats in every province and territory (even though in Quebec they had been reduced to just one seat). Southern Ontario had been vital to their victory in 1979; in 1980 most of the region's seats went Liberal. Support for PetroCanada and dislike of higher oil and gasoline prices were crucial there. In the West the Tories lost ground to the NDP; only Alberta stayed solidly behind Clark.

With the results came the doleful awareness that Clark and his government had defeated themselves. Eager and inexperienced, they had made mistakes and looked less than competent. They had interpreted a vote against Trudeau as a mandate for "real change." Many Canadians did not want the uncertainties of change; they wanted the better times of the past. And they clearly did not want the sort of change with which the Clark government was experimenting in the fall of 1979.

"Welcome to the 1980s," Trudeau began his victory speech. Having already promised to resign as Liberal leader before the next election, he now had a rare opportunity to do some of the things left undone in May 1979. Jostling for priority were the Quebec referendum and the patriation of the British North America Act. Next were a national energy policy and the economy. Sacrifices would be necessary if the country's economic performance were to improve, but few Canadians were in the mood for sacrifice, least of all the wealthy. By 1981 many of the latter were looking enviously at the U.S. president's assaults on social welfare. Meanwhile unemployment exceeded 8 percent, inflation neared 13 percent and interest rates soared over 20 percent.

In an August 1981 by-election the NDP upset one of the safest Liberal seats in English Canada, the Toronto riding of Spadina—a sign that the Liberals were once again in serious trouble. Trudeau's apparent obsession with constitutional change struck many Canadians as peripheral, a diversion of energy from the economic problems that had to be solved. Speculation increased as to when he would resign and who would succeed him. Joe Clark, leading a party many of whose members had little confidence in his leadership, wondered if he, too, would get a second chance or if he would be dumped.

Throughout the 1970s politics was a depressing spectator sport. Canada muddled on, apparently unable to get a grip on the problems of regional disparity and regional conflict, inadequate economic performance, social welfare, and the cost of medical services. Muddling on is not an inspiring activity, and by 1981 more than one opinion poll indicated an unprecedented disenchantment with the performance of governments and politicians. For distraction and inspiration people looked elsewhere.

A declining number of Canadians looked to religion (although some of the evangelical sects grew significantly). For a secularized country the worlds of entertainment and of sport—the line dividing them was blurred—were more attractive. At least two events of the Trudeau years were inspiring symbols of accomplishment. The first was the Canada–Russia hockey series of 1972 and Paul Henderson's winning goal in the closing seconds of the eighth and deciding game. It reassured Canadians that their country was still best in a sport that many regarded as national property. Unhappily, the illusion did not last.

The second event was the courageous trek across Canada made by a young athlete stricken with cancer—Terry Fox's "Marathon of Hope." A recurrence of the disease cut short the marathon near Thunder Bay and aroused a great wave of emotion and moral support, exceeded only by the reaction to Fox's death in 1981. Admiration for his heroism united a country that was sorely divided in other ways. The response showed that many Canadians, faced with a troubled future, wanted to cling to old ideals of endeavor and truths of character. They continued to hope.

Select Bibliography

General Reference

Canada. Department of External Affairs. *Documents on Canadian External Relations.* Vols. 1–. Ottawa: 1967–.

Canadian Annual Review (subsequently *Canadian Annual Review of Politics and Public Affairs*). Toronto: 1901–1937/8, 1960–.

Canadian Historical Documents: Vol. I. *The French Régime*, edited by C. Nish; Vol. II, *Pre-Confederation*, edited by P. B. Waite; Vol. III, *Confederation to 1949*, edited by R. C. Brown and M. E. Prang. Scarborough, Ont.: 1965–66.

Dictionary of Canadian Biography. Vols. 1–4, 9–10. Toronto: 1966–80.

Granatstein, J. L., and Stevens, P., eds. *Canada Since 1867: A Bibliographical Guide.* 2d ed. Toronto: 1977.

Hall, R., and Dodds, G. *Canada: A History in Photographs.* Edmonton: 1981.

Innis, H. A., and Lower, A. R. M., eds. *Documents in Canadian Economic History, 1497–1885.* 2 vols. Toronto: 1929, 1933.

Kerr, D. G. G., ed. *A Historical Atlas of Canada.* 3rd ed. Toronto: 1975.

Light, B., and Strong-Boag, V., eds. *True Daughters of the North: Canadian Women's History—An Annotated Bibliography.* Toronto: 1980.

Reid, J. H. S., McNaught, K., and Crowe, H. S., eds. *A Source-book of Canadian History.* Rev. ed. Toronto: 1964.

Story, N. *The Oxford Companion to Canadian History and Literature.* Toronto: 1967.

Urquhart, M. C., and Buckley, K. A. H., eds. *Historical Statistics of Canada.* Toronto: 1965.

Special Topics

Beck, J. M. *Pendulum of Power: Canada's Federal Elections.* Toronto: 1968.

Berger, C. *The Writing of Canadian History: Aspects of English Canadian Historical Writing: 1900 to 1970.* Toronto: 1976.

Brebner, J. B. *North Atlantic Triangle: The Interplay of Canada, the United States and Great Britain.* Toronto: 1966.

Bryden, K. *Old Age Pensions and Policy-Making in Canada*. Montreal and London: 1974.

Careless, J. M. S., ed. *Colonists and Canadiens, 1760-1867*. Toronto: 1971.

Careless, J. M. S., and Brown, R. C., eds. *The Canadians, 1867-1967*. Toronto: 1967.

Clark, S. D. *The Social Development of Canada: An Introductory Study with Select Documents*. Toronto: 1942.

Cook, R., and Mitchison, W., eds. *The Proper Sphere: Woman's Place in Canadian Society*. Toronto: 1976.

Dales, J. H. *The Protective Tariff in Canadian Development*. Toronto: 1966.

Easterbrook, W. T., and Aitken, H. G. J. *Canadian Economic History*. Toronto: 1956.

Easterbrook, W. T., and Watkins, M. H., eds. *Approaches to Canadian Economic History*. Toronto: 1967.

Eayrs, J. *In Defence of Canada*. 4 vols. Toronto: 1964–80.

Fowke, V. *The National Policy and the Wheat Economy*. Toronto: 1957.

Glazebrook, G. P. de T. *A History of Transportation in Canada*. 2 vols. Toronto: 1964.

————. *A History of Canadian External Relations*. 2 vols. Rev. ed. Toronto: 1966.

Granatstein, J. L., and Hitsman, J. M. *Broken Promises: A History of Conscription in Canada*. Toronto: 1977.

Guest, D. *The Emergence of Social Security in Canada*. Vancouver: 1980.

Hamelin, M. *The Political Ideas of the Prime Ministers of Canada*. Ottawa: 1969.

Harper, J. R. *Painting in Canada: A History*. 2d ed. Toronto: 1977.

Harris, R., *A History of Higher Education in Canada, 1663–1960*. Toronto: 1976.

Harris, R. C., and Warkentin, J. *Canada before Confederation: A Study in Historical Geography*. Toronto: 1974.

Hogg, P. W. *Constitutional Law of Canada*. Toronto: 1977.

Horn, M, and Sabourin, R., eds. *Studies in Canadian Social History*. Toronto: 1974.

Innis, H. A. *Settlement and the Mining Frontier*. Canadian Frontiers of Settlement series. Toronto: 1936.

————. *The Cod Fisheries: The History of an International Economy*. Rev. ed. Toronto: 1954.

————. *Essays in Canadian Economic History*. Edited by M. Q. Innis. Toronto: 1956.

————. *The Fur Trade in Canada: An Introduction to Canadian Economic History*. Rev. ed. Toronto: 1970.

Klinck, C. F., ed. *Literary History of Canada: Canadian Literature in English*. 3 vols. 2d ed. Toronto: 1976.

Levere, T., and Jarrell, R. A., eds. *A Curious Field-book: Science and Society in Canadian History*. Toronto: 1974.

Lower, A. R. M. *Settlement and the Forest Frontier in Eastern Canada*. Canadian Frontiers of Settlement series. Toronto: 1936.

Mackintosh, W. A. *The Economic Background of Dominion–Provincial Relations*. Toronto: 1964.

MacPherson, I. *Each for All: A History of the Co-operative Movement in English Canada, 1900–1945*. Toronto: 1979.

Marr, W. L., and Patterson, D. G. *Canada: An Economic History*. Toronto: 1979.

Martin, C. *"Dominion Lands" Policy*. Canadian Frontiers of Settlement series. Toronto: 1938.

Morton, A. S. *History of Prairie Settlement*. Canadian Frontiers of Settlement series. Toronto: 1938.

Morton, D. *Canada and War: A Military and Political History*. Toronto: 1981.

Panitch, L., ed. *The Canadian State: Political Economy and Political Power*. Toronto: 1977.

Palmer, H., ed. *Immigration and the Rise of Multiculturalism*. Toronto: 1975.

Perry, J. H. *Taxes, Tariffs and Subsidies: A History of Canadian Fiscal Development*. 2 vols. Toronto: 1955.

Porter, J. *The Vertical Mosaic: An Analysis of Social Class and Power in Canada*. Toronto: 1965.

Prentice, A. L., and Houston, S. E., eds. *Family, School and Society in Nineteenth-Century Canada*. Toronto: 1975.

Robin, M., ed. *Canadian Provincial Politics: The Party System of the Ten Provinces*. 2d ed. Scarborough, Ont.: 1978.

Russell, P., ed. *Nationalism in Canada*. Toronto: 1966.

Scott, F. R. *Essays on the Constitution: Aspects of Canadian Law and Politics*. Toronto: 1977.

Sinclair, B., Ball, N. R., and Petersen, J. O., eds. *Let Us Be Honest and Modest: Technology and Society in Canadian History*. Toronto: 1974.

Stacey, C. P. *Canada and the Age of Conflict: A History of Canadian External Policies*. 2 vols. Toronto: 1977, 1981.

Stelter, G. A., and Artibise, A. F. J., eds. *The Canadian City: Essays in Urban History*. Toronto: 1977.

Trofimenkoff, S. M., and Prentice, A., eds. *The Neglected Majority: Essays in Canadian Women's History*. Toronto: 1977.

Underhill, F. H. *In Search of Canadian Liberalism*. Toronto: 1960.

Wade, M. *The French Canadians*. 2 vols. Rev. ed. Toronto: 1975, 1976.

Walsh, H. H. *The Christian Church in Canada*. Toronto: 1956.

Wilson, J. D., Stamp, R. M., and Audet, L.-P. *Canadian Education: A History*. Scarborough, Ont.: 1970.

Winks, R. *The Blacks in Canada*. New Haven, Conn.: 1971.

Wise, S. F., and Fisher, D. *Canada's Sporting Heroes: Their Lives and Times*. Don Mills, Ont.: 1974.

Pre-Confederation

Brebner, J. B. *The Neutral Yankees of Nova Scotia: A Marginal Colony during the Revolutionary Years.* Toronto: 1969.

Burt, A. L. *The Old Province of Quebec.* 2 vols. Toronto: 1968.

Careless, J. M. S. *Brown of the Globe.* 2 vols. Toronto: 1959, 1963.

————. *The Union of the Canadas: The Growth of Canadian Institutions, 1841–1857.* Toronto: 1967.

Careless, J. M. S., ed. *The Pre-Confederation Premiers: Ontario Government Leaders, 1841–1867.* Toronto: 1980.

Cornell, P. G. *The Alignment of Political Groups in Canada, 1841–1867.* Toronto: 1962.

Cowan, H. I. *British Emigration to British North America, 1783–1837.* Rev. ed. Toronto: 1961.

Craig, G. M. *Upper Canada: The Formative Years, 1784–1841.* Toronto: 1963.

Creighton, D. G. *British North America at Confederation.* Ottawa: 1939.

————. *The Empire of the St. Lawrence.* Toronto: 1956.

Eccles, W. J. *Frontenac: The Courtier Governor.* Toronto: 1959.

————. *Canada under Louis XIV, 1663–1701.* Toronto: 1964.

————. *France in America.* Toronto: 1972.

Fregault, G. *Canada: The War of the Conquest.* Toronto: 1969.

Gagan, D. *Hopeful Travellers: Families, Land, and Social Change in Mid-Victorian Peel County, Canada West.* Toronto: 1981.

Griffiths, N. *The Acadians: Creation of a People.* Toronto: 1973.

Harris, R. C. *The Seigneurial System in Early Canada: A Geographical Study.* Quebec City: 1966.

Hitsman, J. M. *Safeguarding Canada, 1763–1871.* Toronto: 1968.

Jaenen, C. J. *The Role of the Church in New France.* Toronto: 1976.

Johnson, J. K., ed. *Historical Essays on Upper Canada.* Toronto: 1975.

Katz, M. *The People of Hamilton, Canada West: Family and Class in a Mid-Nineteenth Century City.* Cambridge, Mass.: 1976.

Kilbourn, W. *The Firebrand: William Lyon Mackenzie and the Rebellion in Upper Canada.* Toronto: 1956.

Lanctot, G. *Canada and the American Revolution, 1774–1783.* Toronto: 1967.

Landon, F. *Western Ontario and the American Frontier.* Toronto: 1967.

LeSueur, W. D. *William Lyon Mackenzie: A Reinterpretation.* Toronto: 1979.

Light, B., and Prentice, A., eds. *Pioneers and Gentlewomen of British North America, 1713–1867.* Toronto: 1980.

Lower, A. R. M. *The North American Assault on the Canadian Forest: A History of the Lumber Trade between Canada and the United States*. Toronto: 1938.

_____. *Great Britain's Woodyard: British America and the Timber Trade, 1763–1867*. Montreal: 1973.

McCallum, J. *Unequal Beginnings: Agriculture and Economic Development in Quebec and Ontario until 1870*. Toronto: 1980.

MacNutt, W. S. *The Atlantic Provinces: The Emergence of Colonial Society, 1712–1857*. Toronto: 1965.

Monet, J. *The Last Cannon Shot: A Study of French-Canadian Nationalism, 1837–1850*. Toronto: 1969.

Morton, W. L. *The Critical Years: The Union of British North America, 1857–1873*. Toronto: 1964.

Neatby, H. *Quebec: The Revolutionary Age, 1760–1791*. Toronto: 1966.

Ouellet, F. *Lower Canada, 1791–1840. Social Change and Nationalism*. Toronto: 1979.

_____. *Economic and Social History of Quebec, 1760–1850: Structures and Conjunctures*. Toronto: 1980.

Pentland, H. C. *Labour and Capital in Canada, 1670–1860*. Toronto: 1981.

Prentice, A. *The School Promoters: Education and Social Class in Mid-Nineteenth Century Upper Canada*. Toronto: 1977.

Rich, E. E. *The Fur Trade and the Northwest to 1857*. Toronto: 1967.

Ryerson, S. B. *Unequal Union: Confederation and the Roots of Conflict in the Canadas, 1815–1873*. Toronto: 1968.

Splane, R. *Social Welfare in Ontario, 1791–1893*. Toronto: 1965.

Stanley, G. F. G. *New France: The Last Phase, 1744–1760*. Toronto: 1968.

Waite, P. B. *The Life and Times of Confederation: Politics, Newspapers, and the Union of British North America*. Toronto: 1962.

Whitelaw, W. M. *The Maritimes and Canada before Confederation*. Toronto: 1966.

Wynn, G. *Timber Colony: A Historical Geography of Early Nineteenth-Century New Brunswick*. Toronto: 1981.

Zaslow, M., ed. *The Defended Border: Upper Canada and the War of 1812*. Toronto: 1964.

1867–1919

Berger, C. *The Sense of Power: Studies in the Idea of Canadian Imperialism, 1867–1914*. Toronto: 1970.

Brown, R. C. *Canada's National Policy, 1883–1900: A Study in Canadian–American Relations*. Princeton, N.J.: 1964.

_____. *Robert Laird Borden: A Biography*. 2 vols. Toronto: 1975, 1980.

Brown, R. C., and Cook, R. *Canada, 1896–1921: A Nation Transformed*. Toronto: 1974.

Cleverdon, C. *The Woman Suffrage Movement in Canada*. Toronto: 1974.

Creighton, D. *John A. Macdonald*. 2 vols. Toronto: 1955.

English, J. *The Decline of Politics: The Conservatives and the Party System, 1901–1920*. Toronto: 1977.

Ferns, H., and Ostry, B. *The Age of Mackenzie King*. Toronto: 1976.

Kealey, L., ed. *A Not Unreasonable Claim: Women and Reform in Canada, 1880–1920*. Toronto: 1979.

Levitt, J. *Henri Bourassa and the Golden Calf: The Social Program of the Nationalists of Quebec, 1900–1914*. Ottawa: 1969.

McKillop, A. B. *A Disciplined Intelligence: Critical Inquiry and Canadian Thought in the Victorian Era*. Montreal: 1979.

Miller, J. R. *Equal Rights: The Jesuits' Estates Act Controversy*. Montreal: 1978.

Neatby, H. B. *Laurier and a Liberal Quebec: A Study in Political Management*. Toronto: 1973.

Parr, J. *Labouring Children: British Immigrant Apprentices to Canada, 1869–1924*. London and Montreal: 1980.

Robin, M. *Radical Politics and Canadian Labour, 1880–1930*. Kingston, Ont.: 1968.

Schull, J. *Laurier: The First Canadian*. Toronto: 1966.

Shortt, S. E. D. *The Search for an Ideal: Six Intellectuals and their Convictions in an Age of Transition, 1890–1930*. Toronto: 1976.

Strong-Boag, V. J. *The Parliament of Women: The National Council of Women of Canada, 1893–1929*. Ottawa: 1976.

Sutherland, N. *Children in English-Canadian Society, 1880–1920*. Toronto: 1976.

Sweeny, A. *George-Etienne Cartier: A Biography*. Toronto: 1976.

Thomson, D. *Alexander Mackenzie: Clear Grit*. Toronto: 1960.

Troper, H. *Only Farmers Need Apply: Official Canadian Government Encouragement of Immigration from the United States, 1896–1911*. Toronto: 1972.

Waite, P. B. *Canada, 1874–1896: Arduous Destiny*. Toronto: 1971.

Weaver, J. C. *Shaping the Canadian City: Essays on Urban Politics and Policy, 1890–1920*. Toronto: 1977.

Young, B. *George-Etienne Cartier: Montreal Bourgeois*. Montreal and London: 1981.

1919–1981

Allen, R. *The Social Passion: Religion and Social Reform in Canada, 1914–1928.* Toronto: 1971.

Avakumovic, I. *The Communist Party in Canada: A History.* Toronto: 1975.

Bissell, C. *The Young Vincent Massey.* Toronto: 1981.

Bothwell, R., Drummond, I., and English, J. *Canada since 1945: Power, Politics, and Provincialism.* Toronto: 1981.

Bothwell, R., and Kilbourn, W. *C. D. Howe: A Biography.* Toronto: 1979.

Clark, S. D., Grayson, J. P., and Grayson, L. M., eds. *Prophecy and Protest: Social Movements in Twentieth-Century Canada.* Toronto: 1975.

Cook, R. *The Political Ideas of John W. Dafoe and the Free Press.* Toronto: 1963.

Diefenbaker, J. *One Canada.* 3 vols. Toronto: 1975–77.

Dirks, G. E. *Canada's Refugee Policy: Indifference or Opportunism?* Montreal and London: 1977.

Douglas, W. A. B., and Greenhous, B. *Out of the Shadows: Canada in the Second World War.* Toronto: 1977.

Finkel, A. *Business and Social Reform in the Thirties.* Toronto: 1979.

Graham, W. R. *Arthur Meighen.* 3 vols. Toronto: 1960–65.

Granatstein, J. L. *The Politics of Survival: The Conservative Party, 1939–1945.* Toronto: 1967.

————. *Canada's War: The Politics of the Mackenzie King Government, 1939–1945.* Toronto: 1975.

————. *A Man of Influence: Norman A. Robertson and Canadian Statecraft, 1929–1968.* Ottawa: 1981.

Granatstein, J. L., and Cuff, R. D. *Ties that Bind: Canadian–American Relations in Wartime from the Great War to the Cold War.* 2d ed. Toronto: 1977.

Gwynn, R. *The Northern Magus: Pierre Trudeau and Canadians.* Toronto: 1980.

Hawkins, F. *Canada and Immigration: Public Policy and Public Concern.* Montreal and London: 1972.

Holmes, J. *The Shaping of Peace: Canada and the Search for World Order, 1943–1957.* Vol. I. Toronto: 1979.

Horn, M., ed. *The Dirty Thirties: Canadians in the Great Depression.* Toronto: 1972.

————. *The League for Social Reconstruction: Intellectual Origins of the Democratic Left in Canada, 1930–1942.* Toronto: 1980.

Kwavnick, D. *Organized Labour and Pressure Politics: The Canadian Labour Congress, 1955–1968.* Montreal: 1972.

Lewis, D. *The Good Fight: Political Memoirs, 1909–1958.* Toronto: 1981.

McNaught, K. W. *A Prophet in Politics: A Biography of J. S. Woodsworth.* Toronto: 1959.

McWhinney, E. *Quebec and the Constitution, 1960–1978.* Toronto: 1979.

Morton, W. L. *The Progressive Party in Canada.* Toronto: 1950.

Neatby, H. B. *William Lyon Mackenzie King.* Vols. II, III. Toronto: 1963, 1976.

Pearson, L. B. *Mike: The Memoirs of the Rt. Hon. Lester B. Pearson.* Vol. I, 1897–1948; Vol. II, 1948–57; Vol. III, 1957–68. Toronto: 1972–75.

Peers, F. W. *The Politics of Canadian Broadcasting, 1920–1951.* Toronto: 1969.

———. *The Public Eye: Television and the Politics of Canadian Broadcasting, 1952–1968.* Toronto: 1979.

Penner, N. *The Canadian Left: A Critical Analysis.* Scarborough, Ont.: 1977.

Pickersgill, J. W. *My Years with Louis St. Laurent.* Toronto: 1975.

Pickersgill, J. W. (and Forster, D., Vols. 2–4), eds. *The Mackenzie King Record.* 4 vols. Toronto: 1960–70.

Richmond, A. H. *Post-War Immigrants in Canada.* Toronto: 1967.

Safarian, A. E. *The Canadian Economy in the Great Depression.* Toronto: 1970.

Simeon, R. *Federal–Provincial Diplomacy: The Making of Recent Policy in Canada.* Toronto: 1972.

Simpson, J. *Discipline of Power: The Conservative Interlude and the Liberal Restoration.* Toronto: 1980.

Smith, D. *Bleeding Hearts, Bleeding Country: Canada and the Quebec Crisis.* Edmonton: 1971.

———. *Gentle Patriot: A Political Biography of Walter Gordon.* Edmonton: 1973.

Stacey, C. P. *Arms, Men and Governments: The War Policies of Canada, 1939–1945.* Ottawa: 1970.

Stairs, D. *The Diplomacy of Constraint: Canada, the Korean War, and the United States.* Toronto: 1974.

Taylor, M. G. *Health Insurance and Canadian Public Policy: The Seven Decisions that Created the Canadian Health Insurance System.* Montreal and London: 1978.

Thomson, D. C. *Louis St. Laurent: Canadian.* Toronto: 1967.

Veatch, R. *Canada and the League of Nations.* Toronto: 1975.

Wearing, J. *The L-Shaped Party: The Liberal Party of Canada, 1958–80.* Toronto: 1981.

Whitaker, R. *The Government Party: Organizing and Financing the Liberal Party of Canada, 1930–1958.* Toronto: 1977.

Wilbur, J. R. H. *H. H. Stevens.* Toronto: 1977.

Young, W. *The Anatomy of a Party: The National CCF, 1932–1961.* Toronto: 1969.

Indians

Bailey, A. G. *The Conflict of European and Eastern Algonkian Cultures, 1504–1700.* Toronto: 1969.

Brown, J. S. H. *Strangers in Blood: Fur Trade Company Families in Indian Country.* Vancouver: 1980.

Fisher, R. *Contact and Conflict: Indian–European Relations in British Columbia, 1774–1890.* Vancouver: 1977.

Heidenreich, C. *Huronia: A History and Geography of the Huron Indians.* Toronto: 1973.

Jaenen, C. J. *Friend and Foe: Aspects of French–Amerindian Cultural Contact in the Sixteenth and Seventeenth Centuries.* Toronto: 1976.

Jenness, D. *The Indians of Canada.* 7th ed. Ottawa: 1967.

LaViolette, F. E. *The Struggle for Survival: Indian Cultures and the Protestant Ethic in British Columbia.* Toronto: 1973.

Patterson, E. P., III. *The Canadian Indian: A History since 1500.* Don Mills, Ont.: 1972.

Ray, A. J. *Indians in the Fur Trade: Their Role as Hunters, Trappers and Middlemen in the Land Southwest of Hudson Bay, 1660–1870.* Toronto: 1974.

Ray, A. J., and Freeman, D. *"Give Us Good Measure": An Economic Analysis of Relations between the Indians and the Hudson's Bay Company before 1763.* Toronto: 1978.

Trigger, B. G. *The Children of Aataentsic: A History of the Huron People to 1660.* 2 vols. Montreal: 1976.

————. *The Indians and the Heroic Age of New France.* Ottawa: 1978.

Upton, L. F. S. *Micmacs and Colonists: Indian–White Relations in the Maritime Provinces, 1713–1867.* Vancouver: 1979.

Van Kirk, S. *"Many Tender Ties": Women in Fur-Trade Society in Western Canada, 1670–1870.* Winnipeg: 1980.

Business

Bliss, M. *A Living Profit: Studies in the Social History of Canadian Business, 1883–1911.* Toronto: 1974.

————. *A Canadian Millionaire: The Life and Business Times of Sir Joseph Flavelle, Bart., 1858–1939.* Toronto: 1978.

Innis, H. A. *History of the Canadian Pacific Railway.* Toronto: 1971.

Levitt, K. *Silent Surrender: The Multinational Corporation in Canada.* Toronto: 1970.

McCalla, D. *The Upper Canada Trade, 1834–1872: A Study in the Buchanans' Business.* Toronto: 1979.

Macmillan, D. S. *Canadian Business History: Selected Studies, 1497–1971.* Toronto: 1971.

Naylor, T. *The History of Canadian Business, 1867–1914.* 2 vols. Toronto: 1975.

Neufeld, E. P. *The Financial System of Canada: Its Growth and Development.* Toronto: 1972.

Porter, G., and Cuff, R. D., eds. *Enterprise and National Development: Essays in Canadian Business and Economic History.* Toronto: 1972.

Regehr, T. D. *The Canadian Northern Railway: Pioneer Road of the Northern Prairies, 1895–1915.* Toronto: 1976.

Safarian, A. E. *Foreign Ownership of Canadian Industry.* 2d ed. Toronto: 1973.

Stevens, G. R. *Canadian National Railways.* 2 vols. Toronto: 1960, 1962.

Traves, T. *The State and Enterprise: Canadian Manufacturing and the Federal Government, 1917–1931,* Toronto: 1979.

Tulchinsky, G. J. J. *The River Barons: Montreal Businessmen and the Growth of Industry and Transportation, 1837–53.* Toronto: 1977.

Labor

Abella, I. M. *Nationalism, Communism and Canadian Labour: The CIO, the Communist Party, and the Canadian Congress of Labour, 1935–56.* Toronto: 1973.

Abella, I., ed. *On Strike: Six Key Labour Struggles in Canada, 1919–1949.* Toronto: 1974.

Abella, I., and Millar, D., eds. *The Canadian Worker in the Twentieth Century.* Toronto: 1978.

Avery, D. *"Dangerous Foreigners": European Immigrant Workers and Labour Radicalism in Canada, 1896–1932.* Toronto: 1979.

Babcock, R. *Gompers in Canada: A Study in American Continentalism before the First World War.* Toronto: 1974.

Bercuson, D. J. *Confrontation at Winnipeg: Labour, Industrial Relations, and the General Strike.* Montreal: 1974.

————. *Fools and Wise Men: The Rise and Fall of the One Big Union.* Toronto: 1978.

Copp, T. *The Anatomy of Poverty: The Condition of the Working Class in Montreal, 1897–1929.* Toronto: 1974.

Craven, P. *"An Impartial Umpire": Industrial Relations and the Canadian State, 1900–1911.* Toronto: 1980.

Cross, M., ed. *The Workingman in the Nineteenth Century.* Toronto: 1974.

Dumas, E. *The Bitter Thirties in Quebec.* Toronto: 1975.

Horowitz, G. *Canadian Labour in Politics.* Toronto: 1968.

Jamieson, S. *Times of Trouble: Labour Unrest and Industrial Conflict in Canada, 1900–1966.* Ottawa: 1971.

Kealey, G. S. *Toronto Workers Respond to Industrial Capitalism, 1867–1892.* Toronto: 1980.

Kealey, G. S., ed. *Canada Investigates Industrialism: The Royal Commission on the Relations of Labour and Capital, 1889.* Toronto: 1973.

Kealey, G. S., and Warrian, P., eds. *Essays in Working Class History.* Toronto: 1976.

Morton, D., and Copp, T. *Working People: An Illustrated History of Canadian Labour.* Ottawa: 1980.

Palmer, B. D. *A Culture in Conflict: Skilled Workers in Hamilton, Ontario, 1860–1914.* Montreal: 1979.

Piva, M. J. *The Condition of the Working Class in Toronto, 1900–1921.* Ottawa: 1979.

Trudeau, P. E., ed. *The Asbestos Strike.* Toronto: 1973.

The Provinces Since 1867

Atlantic Canada

Alexander, D. *The Decay of Trade: An Economic History of the Newfoundland Saltfish Trade, 1935–1965.* St. John's, Nfld.: 1977.

Beck, J. M. *The Government of Nova Scotia.* Toronto: 1957.

Bolger, F. W. P., ed. *Canada's Smallest Province: A History of P.E.I.* Charlottetown, P.E.I.: 1973.

Fischer, L. R., and Sager, E. W., eds. *The Enterprising Canadians: Entrepreneurs and Economic Development in Eastern Canada, 1820–1914.* St. John's, Nfld.: 1978.

Forbes, E. R. *The Maritime Rights Movement, 1919–1927: A Study in Canadian Regionalism.* Montreal: 1978.

Hiller, J., and Neary, P., eds. *Newfoundland in the Nineteenth and Twentieth Centuries.* Toronto: 1980.

Macgillivray, D., and Tennyson, B. *Cape Breton Historical Essays.* Sydney, N.S.: 1980.

Neary, P. *The Political Economy of Newfoundland, 1929–72.* Toronto: 1973.

Pryke, K. G. *Nova Scotia and Confederation, 1864–1874.* Toronto: 1979.

Rawlyk, G. A., ed. *Historical Essays on the Atlantic Provinces.* Toronto: 1967.

————. *The Atlantic Provinces and the Problems of Confederation.* St. John's, Nfld.: 1979.

Thorburn, H. G. *Politics in New Brunswick.* Toronto: 1961.

Quebec

Armstrong, E. *The Crisis of Quebec, 1914–1918*. Toronto: 1974.

Black, C. *Duplessis*. Toronto: 1977.

Cook, R. *Canada and the French-Canadian Question*. Toronto: 1966.

Monière, D. *Ideologies in Quebec: The Historical Development*. Toronto: 1981.

Pinard, M. *The Rise of a Third Party: A Study in Crisis Politics*. Englewood Cliffs, N.J.: 1971.

Posgate, D., and McRoberts, K. *Quebec: Social Change and Political Crisis*. Rev. ed. Toronto: 1980.

Quinn, H. F. *The Union Nationale: Quebec Nationalism from Duplessis to Lévesque*. 2d ed. Toronto: 1979.

Rioux, M., and Martin, Y. *French-Canadian Society*. Toronto: 1964.

Ryan, W. R. *The Clergy and Economic Growth in Quebec, 1896–1914*. Quebec: 1966.

Saywell, J. *The Rise of the Parti Québécois, 1967–1976*. Toronto: 1977.

Stein, M. *The Dynamics of Right Wing Protest: A Political Analysis of Social Credit in Quebec*. Toronto: 1973.

Trofimenkoff, S. M. *Action Française: French–Canadian Nationalism in the Twenties*. Toronto: 1975.

Trudeau, P. E. *Federalism and the French Canadians*. Toronto: 1968.

Young, B. J. *Promoters and Politicians: The North-Shore Railways in the History of Quebec, 1854–1885*. Toronto: 1978.

Ontario

Armstrong, C. *The Politics of Federalism: Ontario's Relations with the Federal Government, 1867–1942*. Toronto: 1981.

Bishop, O. B., Irvine, B. I., and Miller, C. G., eds. *Bibliography of Ontario History 1877–1976: Cultural, Economic, Political, Social*. 2 vols. Toronto: 1980.

Choquette, R. *Language and Religion: A History of English–French Conflict in Ontario*. Ottawa: 1975.

Goheen, P. *Victorian Toronto: Patterns and Process of Growth*. Chicago: 1970.

Jones, A., and Rutman, L. *In the Children's Aid: J. J. Kelso and Child Welfare in Ontario*. Toronto: 1981.

McKenty, N. *Mitch Hepburn*. Toronto: 1967.

Masters, D. C. *The Rise of Toronto, 1850–1900*. Toronto: 1947.

Mattingly, P. H., and Katz, M. B., eds. *Education and Social Change: Themes from Ontario's Past*. New York: 1975.

Nelles, H. V. *The Politics of Development: Forests, Mines and Hydro-Electric Power in Ontario, 1849–1941*. Toronto: 1974.

Oliver, P. *Public and Private Persons: The Ontario Political Culture, 1914–1934*. Toronto: 1975.

————. *G. Howard Ferguson: Ontario Tory*. Toronto: 1977.

Prang, M. *N. W. Rowell: Ontario Nationalist*. Toronto: 1975.

Spelt, J. *Urban Development in South-Central Ontario*. Toronto: 1972.

Swainson, D., ed. *Oliver Mowat's Ontario*. Toronto: 1972.

Tucker, A. *Steam into Wilderness: Ontario Northland Railway, 1902–1962*. Toronto: 1978.

The West and the North

Artibise, A. F. J. *Winnipeg: A Social History of Urban Growth, 1874–1914*. Montreal: 1974.

————. *Western Canada since 1870: A Select Bibliography and Guide*. Vancouver: 1978.

Dosman, E. J. *The National Interest: The Politics of Northern Development, 1968–1975*. Toronto: 1975.

Friesen, J., and Ralston, H. K., eds. *Historical Essays on British Columbia*. Toronto: 1976.

Lipset, S. M. *Agrarian Socialism: The Cooperative Commonwealth Federation in Saskatchewan: A Study in Political Sociology*. 2d ed. New York: 1968.

Lupul, M. R. *The Roman Catholic Church and the North-West School Question: A Study in Church–State Relations in Western Canada, 1875–1905*. Toronto: 1974.

McCormack, A. R. *Reformers, Rebels, and Revolutionaries: The Western Canadian Radical Movement, 1899–1919*. Toronto: 1977.

Macleod, R. C. *The North-West Mounted Police and Law Enforcement, 1873–1905*. Toronto: 1976.

Macpherson, C. B. *Democracy in Alberta: Social Credit and the Party System*. Toronto: 1953.

Morton, W. L. *Manitoba: A History*. 2d ed. Toronto: 1967.

Ormsby, M. *British Columbia: A History*. Toronto: 1968.

Owram, D. *Promise of Eden: The Canadian Expansionist Movement and the Idea of the West, 1856–1900*. Toronto: 1980.

Rea, K. J. *The Political Economy of the Canadian North: An Interpretation of Development in the Northern Territories of Canada to the Early 1960s*. Toronto: 1968.

Robin, M. *The Rush for Spoils: The Company Province, 1871–1933*. Toronto: 1972.

————. *Pillars of Profit: The Company Province, 1934–1972*. Toronto: 1973.

Smith, D. E. *Prairie Liberalism: The Liberal Party in Saskatchewan, 1905–1971*. Toronto: 1975.

_____. *The Regional Decline of a National Party: Liberals on the Prairies*. Toronto: 1981.

Stanley, G. *The Birth of Western Canada: A History of the Riel Rebellions*. Toronto: 1960.

_____. *Louis Riel*. Toronto: 1963.

Swainson, D., ed. *Historical Essays on the Prairie Provinces*. Toronto: 1970.

Thomas, L. G. *The Liberal Party in Alberta: A History of Politics in the Province of Alberta*. Toronto: 1959.

Thomas, L. G., ed. *The Prairie West to 1905: A Canadian Sourcebook:* Toronto: 1975.

Thomas, L. H. *The Struggle for Responsible Government in the North-West Territories, 1870–1897*. Toronto: 1977.

Thompson, J. H. *The Harvests of War: The Prairie West, 1914–1918*. Toronto: 1978.

Ward, P. W. *White Canada Forever: Popular Attitudes and Public Policy toward Orientals in British Columbia*. Montreal: 1978.

Woodcock, G. *Gabriel Dumont: The Metis Chief and His Lost World*. Edmonton: 1975.

Zaslow, M. *The Opening of the Canadian North, 1870–1914*. Toronto: 1971.

INDEX